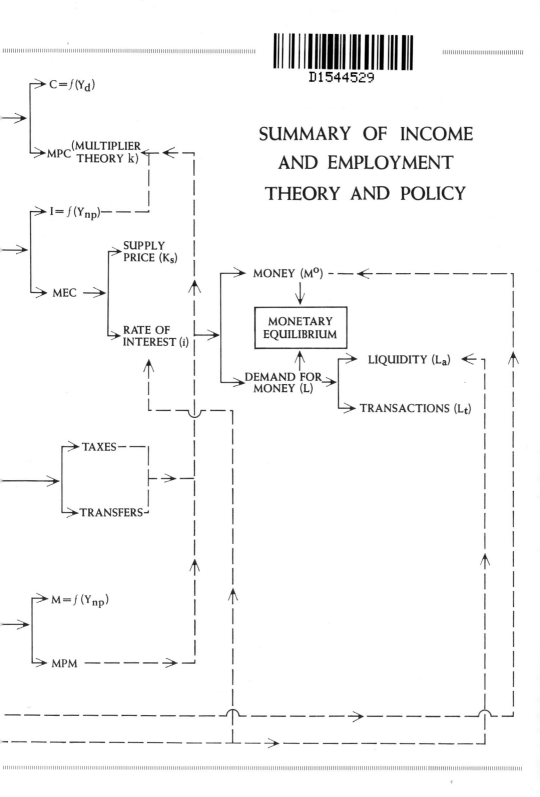

D1544529

SUMMARY OF INCOME
AND EMPLOYMENT
THEORY AND POLICY

Income, Employment, and Economic Growth

REVISED EDITION

Income, Employment, and Economic Growth

REVISED EDITION

By Wallace C. Peterson
UNIVERSITY OF NEBRASKA

W · W · NORTON & COMPANY · INC · New York

To Eunice, Cary, Shelley,
and the memory of my brother Harold

Contents

Preface   xiii

1. The Nature and Scope of Economic Analysis   1

   Implications of the Traditional Definition of Economics · *Science and Economics* · THE NATURE OF SCIENCE · THE VALUE OF SCIENCE · *The Scientific Character of Economics* · *Some Characteristics of Economic Generalizations* · ABSTRACTION · THE CONCEPT OF A FUNCTIONAL RELATIONSHIP · *The Methods of Economic Analysis* · THE DEDUCTIVE METHOD · THE INDUCTIVE METHOD · *Economic Analysis and Economic Policy*

——————————— PART I ———————————

The National Income

2. Basic Concepts of National Income and Social Accounting   25

   The Nature of National Income and Social Accounting · THE USE OF NATIONAL INCOME AND SOCIAL ACCOUNTING · *Income and Wealth* · THE CONCEPT OF INCOME · THE CONCEPT OF WEALTH · PROBLEMS IN THE MEASUREMENT OF WEALTH · THE CONCEPT OF HUMAN WEALTH · INTERACTIONS OF INCOME AND WEALTH · *Basic Components of National Income* · FUNDAMENTAL IDENTITIES AMONG NATIONAL INCOME COMPONENTS · *Appendix: Systems of National Income and Social Accounting* · CURRENT DATA AND IDENTITY EQUATIONS IN AN OPEN ECONOMY

3. The Measurement of National Income and Product   53

   Gross National Product · FINAL AND INTERMEDIATE GOODS AND SERVICES · MONETARY TRANSACTIONS AND PRODUCTIVE ACTIVITY · AN ALTERNATIVE TECHNIQUE FOR MEASURING GROSS NATIONAL PRODUCT · *Other Measures of Product and Income* · NET NATIONAL PRODUCT · NATIONAL INCOME · PERSONAL INCOME · DISPOSABLE INCOME · *Price Indexes and*

Comparisons over Time · Limitations Inherent in Aggregate Measures of Income and Product · NATIONAL INCOME AND PRODUCT ACCOUNT · PERSONAL INCOME AND OUTLAY ACCOUNT · GOVERNMENT RECEIPTS AND EXPENDITURES ACCOUNT · FOREIGN TRANSACTIONS ACCOUNT · GROSS SAVING AND INVESTMENT ACCOUNT · *Summary: Development of National Accounting Systems*

——————————————— PART II ———————————————

The Theory of Income and Employment

4. The Classical Theory of Employment   79

The Meaning of Employment and Unemployment · Employment and Output · The Nature of Classical Economics · THE THREE "BUILDING BLOCKS" OF THE CLASSICAL THEORY OF EMPLOYMENT · THE THEORY OF THE DEMAND FOR AND SUPPLY OF LABOR · THE DEMAND FOR LABOR · THE SUPPLY OF LABOR · THE EQUILIBRIUM LEVEL OF EMPLOYMENT · THE THEORY OF AGGREGATE DEMAND · SAY'S LAW OF MARKETS · SAY'S LAW AND THE CLASSICAL THEORY OF INTEREST · THE THEORY OF THE PRICE LEVEL · A DIAGRAMMATIC SUMMARY · *Policy Implications of the Classical Theory · The Collapse of Classical Employment Theory*

5. The Structure of Modern Income and Employment Theory   110

The Essence of the Income-Employment Problem · The Aggregate Supply Schedule · THE KEYNESIAN AGGREGATE SUPPLY FUNCTION · ALTERNATIVE CONCEPTS OF AGGREGATE SUPPLY · *The Aggregate Demand Schedule* · THE ORIGIN OF SPENDING DECISIONS · *The Equilibrium Level of Income and Employment* · A NUMERICAL EXAMPLE · CHARACTERISTICS OF THE INCOME EQUILIBRIUM · CHANGES IN INCOME AND EMPLOYMENT · *Summary: Modern Employment Theory*

6. The Theory of Consumption, Saving, and the Multiplier   131

The Determinants of Consumption Expenditure · THE CONSUMPTION FUNCTION · TECHNICAL ATTRIBUTES OF THE CONSUMPTION FUNCTION · THE SAVING FUNCTION · *The Process of Income Determination · The Identity of Saving and Investment · The Theory of the Multiplier* · THE FORMAL MULTIPLIER PROCESS · ALGEBRAIC STATEMENT OF THE MULTIPLIER · SUMMARY REMARKS ON THE THEORY OF THE MULTIPLIER · *Other Influences on Consumption* · ATTITUDES TOWARD THRIFT · ASSET HOLDINGS BY THE CONSUMER · STOCKS OF DURABLE GOODS · THE DISTRIBUTION OF INCOME · THE RATE OF INTEREST · PRICE CHANGES AND CONSUMER EXPECTATIONS · CONSUMER CREDIT · *Income, Consumption, and Saving in the Long Run · A Concluding Comment · Appendix*

7. The Theory of Investment 178

Definitions and Concepts · NET AND GROSS INVESTMENT ·
AUTONOMOUS AND INDUCED INVESTMENT · INVESTMENT AND
PROFIT · *The Investment Decision* · INVESTMENT AND EX-
PECTED INCOME · THE COSTS OF INVESTMENT · *The Keynesian
Framework* · THE DISCOUNT FORMULA · THE DEMAND FOR
CAPITAL · THE ROLE OF THE INTEREST RATE · THE INVESTMENT
DEMAND SCHEDULE · THE EPHEMERAL CHARACTER OF THE IN-
VESTMENT DEMAND SCHEDULE · THE SHAPE OF THE INVEST-
MENT DEMAND SCHEDULE · THE INVESTMENT DEMAND SCHED-
ULE AND THE MARGINAL EFFICIENCY OF CAPITAL · *Current
Income and Investment Expenditure* · THE ACCELERATION
PRINCIPLE · *Other Influences on the Investment Decision* ·
THE ROLE OF EXPECTATIONS · THE ROLE OF TECHNOLOGY AND
INNOVATION · THE ROLE OF MARKET STRUCTURES · THE ROLE
OF GOVERNMENT · THE ROLE OF FINANCE · *A Summary
View* · *Appendix*

8. The Theory of the Public Sector: The Resource-Allocation
Problem 227

The Nature of the Public Sector · EXHAUSTIVE EXPENDI-
TURES: THE SATISFACTION OF SOCIAL WANTS · NON-EXHAUS-
TIVE EXPENDITURES: THE REDISTRIBUTION OF INCOME · ECO-
NOMIC STABILIZATION AND GROWTH · *The Growth of the Pub-
lic Sector* · *Causes for the Growth in Public Expenditures* ·
The Allocation of Resources to the Public Sector · THE
CONCEPT OF OPTIMUM ALLOCATION · MECHANISMS FOR THE
ALLOCATION OF RESOURCES · *The Concept of Social Imbal-
ance* · *A Concluding View*

9. The Theory of the Public Sector: The Income-Level Problem 251

*Government Purchases of Goods and Services and the In-
come Level* · GOVERNMENT EXPENDITURES AND THE MULTI-
PLIER · *Transfer Expenditures and the Income Level* ·
TRANSFER EXPENDITURES AND THE MULTIPLIER · *Taxes and
the Income Level* · TRANSFERS, TAXES, AND THE MULTIPLIER ·
BUILT-IN STABILIZERS · *The Balanced Budget Thesis* · *Appendix*

10. The Theory of the Foreign Balance 279

The Nature of the Foreign Balance · THE THREE ACCOUNTS
IN THE BALANCE-OF-PAYMENTS STATEMENT · THE BALANCE OF
PAYMENTS AND EQUILIBRIUM · *Exports, Imports, and the
Structure of Aggregate Demand* · *The Income Equilibrium
in an Open Economy* · *Foreign Trade and the Multiplier* ·
Graphic Illustrations of the Multiplier in an Open System ·
The Foreign-Repercussion Effect · *Income Changes and*

the Balance of Payments · A Summary Comment · Appendix

11. The Theory of Money and Interest   303
The Nature of Money · THE FUNCTIONS OF MONEY · AL-
TERNATIVES TO MONEY: DEBT INSTRUMENTS AND EQUITY IN-
STRUMENTS · The Supply of Money · DEPOSIT MONEY AND
RESERVE MONEY · MONETARY EQUILIBRIUM · The Role of
Money in Classical Theory · The Role of Money in Modern
Theory · MOTIVES FOR HOLDING MONEY · THE TRANSACTIONS
DEMAND FOR MONEY · THE ASSET DEMAND FOR MONEY · BOND
PRICES AND THE RATE OF INTEREST · THE TOTAL DEMAND FOR
MONEY · The Liquidity-Preference Theory of Interest ·
THE BOND MARKET AND THE ASSET DEMAND FOR MONEY · EX-
PECTATIONS AND THE RATE OF INTEREST · AN ALTERNATIVE
EXPLANATION OF THE DEMAND FOR MONEY · CHANGES IN THE
RATE OF INTEREST · THE TOTAL DEMAND FOR MONEY AND THE
RATE OF INTEREST · Appendix · RELATIONSHIPS BETWEEN
MONEY, DEBTS, AND EQUITIES · THE LOANABLE-FUNDS THEORY
OF INTEREST

12. General Equilibrium and Public Policy   340
EQUILIBRIUM IN THE MONETARY SPHERE · THE LM SCHED-
ULE · EQUILIBRIUM IN THE GOODS SPHERE · THE IS SCHED-
ULE · GENERAL EQUILIBRIUM · CHANGES IN THE EQUILIBRIUM
VALUES OF INCOME AND INTEREST · SHIFTS IN THE IS CURVE ·
SHIFTS IN THE LM CURVE · THE PRINCIPLES OF ECONOMIC
POLICY · MONETARY POLICY AND AGGREGATE DEMAND · FISCAL
POLICY AND AGGREGATE DEMAND · MANAGEMENT OF THE PUB-
LIC DEBT · THE APPLICATION OF FISCAL AND MONETARY POL-
ICY · Appendix

13. The Theory of the Price Level   363
The Quantity Theory and the Price Level · THE MODERN
QUANTITY THEORY · Income Theory and the Price Level ·
NON-REVERSIBILITY OF THE PRICE-OUTPUT RELATIONSHIP ·
A General Theoretical Framework · ELASTICITY OF PRICE ·
ELASTICITY OF AGGREGATE DEMAND · ELASTICITY OF OUT-
PUT · ELASTICITY OF RETURNS · ELASTICITY OF THE PRICE
LEVEL · ELASTICITY OF MONEY WAGES · THE PHILLIPS CURVE ·
INTERRELATIONSHIPS OF THE COEFFICIENTS · The Causes of
Inflation · TYPES OF INFLATION · THEORIES OF INFLATION ·
THE DEMAND-PULL HYPOTHESIS · THE COST-PUSH HYPOTHESIS ·
THE STRUCTURAL HYPOTHESIS · The Inflationary Process ·
DEMAND-PULL INFLATION · COST-PUSH INFLATION · STRUC-
TURAL INFLATION · Wage Cuts, Employment, and the Price
Level · THE CLASSICAL VIEW OF WAGES AND EMPLOYMENT ·
THE MODERN VIEW OF WAGES AND EMPLOYMENT

PART III

The Theory of Economic Growth

14. The Nature and Problem of Economic Growth   401

The Nature of Economic Growth · *The Importance of Economic Growth* · MILITARY SECURITY · ECONOMIC AID TO UNDERDEVELOPED NATIONS · PUBLIC RESPONSIBILITIES IN THE DOMESTIC ECONOMY · *The Growth Record of the American Economy* · *Recent Interest in the Problem of Economic Growth* · *The Process of Economic Growth* · *Economic Theory and Economic Growth*

15. Post-Keynesian Theories of Economic Growth   411

Review of the Keynesian Equilibrium · *The Domar Analysis of Economic Growth* · THE CAPACITY-CREATING PROCESS · THE DEMAND REQUIREMENT · THE REQUIRED RATE OF INCOME GROWTH · A NUMERICAL REPRESENTATION OF THE GROWTH PROCESS · A DIAGRAMMATIC REPRESENTATION OF THE GROWTH PROCESS · SIGNIFICANCE AND LIMITATIONS OF THE DOMAR ANALYSIS OF ECONOMIC GROWTH · *The Harrod Analysis of Economic Growth* · THE WARRANTED RATE OF GROWTH · THE ACTUAL RATE OF GROWTH · THE GROWTH PROCESS: THE ACTUAL AND THE WARRANTED RATES COMPARED · THE NATURAL RATE OF GROWTH · *Concluding Observations on the Domar-Harrod Analysis of Economic Growth*

16. Economic Growth and Public Policy   441

The Role of Government in Economic Growth · FISCAL POLICY AND ECONOMIC GROWTH · GOVERNMENT AND PRODUCTIVE CAPACITY · *U.S. Economic Policy in the 1960's* · THE THEORY OF FISCAL STAGNATION · THE REMEDY FOR FISCAL STAGNATION · THE EFFECTIVENESS OF THE 1964 TAX CUT · LOOKING AHEAD

PART IV

The Distribution of Income

17. Theories of Aggregate Income Distribution   461

The Meaning of Income Distribution · *The Classical Theories of Income Distribution* · RICARDO'S THEORY OF INCOME DISTRIBUTION · THE MARXIAN THEORY OF INCOME DISTRIBUTION · A CONCLUDING COMMENT ON MARX AND RICARDO · *Recent Theoretical Developments* · A SIMPLIFIED KEYNESIAN MODEL · KALDOR'S THEORY OF INCOME DISTRIBUTION · WEINTRAUB'S THEORY OF INCOME DISTRIBUTION · *A Concluding Note on Distribution Theory* · *Appendix*

Index   493

Preface

In the preparation of this revision, I have been guided by a desire to incorporate in the text the most recent developments in theory and policy and to improve and sharpen the exposition of fundamental concepts and principles. This task has been made lighter by the many kind and constructive comments received from those who used the first edition. I have sought, however, to preserve largely intact the organization and structure of the first edition. For, as I stated in the Preface to that edition, I approach the subject of income analysis with definite convictions; the further experience I have gained in teaching the course has not changed my views in any fundamental sense.

Before reviewing briefly the more important changes incorporated in this edition, I would like to stress the major objective of the text. My primary concern is to provide the student with an accurate, clear, and thorough explanation of the basic concepts and theories of contemporary income and employment analysis. This is a textbook; thus, its true function should be to enable the student to comprehend essential principles with a minimum of outside help. With this objective in mind, I have striven in this revision for greater precision and clarity in setting forth the basic concepts and theories of macroeconomics. It is hoped that this will provide the instructor with more time to explore in the classroom those facets of modern aggregate economics that cannot be adequately treated in a text.

The most important changes in this revision include the following:

1) The content of each chapter has been carefully reviewed in the light of developments in economic theory and policy since publication of the first edition. This has resulted in a significant amount of rewriting. Further, the statistical material has been brought as nearly up to date as possible.

2) The algebraic material pertaining to determination of the equilibrium income level and the multiplier has been thoroughly reviewed and revised. The result is the development in the text of

a more complete and consistent "model" of income determination. This model is built initially upon quite simple assumptions and then gradually expanded through successive chapters until a complete model in algebraic, arithmetic, and geometric form is presented. This model embodies *all* the key relationships which are crucial to the determination of income and employment levels in the modern economy. In developing this model, the theory of the multiplier is stressed at each stage in its construction, for through development of a single multiplier concept which can be applied against *any* shift in the aggregate demand function, the student is able to see how the multiplier theory blends with key functional relationships to form a unified and logical system of income determination.

3) The material in Chapter 7 pertaining to the Keynesian investment demand schedule has been completely re-organized and re-written. The difficulty with Keynesian investment theory is that it fails to take into account the effect that investment expenditure will have upon the stock of capital. Yet the business firm, which is the point of origin of the investment decision, is primarily concerned with the employment of a specific physical quantity of capital. Thus, aggregate investment theory must effect a reconciliation between total investment spending as a determinant of the equilibrium income level and the optimum stock of capital as a factor in the firm's equilibrium position with respect to the use of capital. In my attempt to derive an investment demand schedule which would take these things into account, I am very much indebted to Professor James G. Witte's stimulating ideas on the *microeconomic* foundations of the investment function.[1]

4) One new chapter has been added to the text. This is Chapter 12, "General Equilibrium and Public Policy." This chapter, which incorporates some material formerly contained in Chapter 11, "The Theory of Money and Interest," has two major parts. First, it draws together all the elements of income determination theory set forth in Chapters 4–11 to develop Professor Hicks' "general equilibrium" model. The student is shown how the forces which determine the income and employment level interact with forces determining the rate of interest to yield a general model of the economic system. Second, the general equilibrium model is employed as a basic theoretical tool for the analysis of contemporary public policy. Specifically, monetary policy, fiscal policy, and debt management are discussed in terms of their

---

[1] James G. Witte, Jr., "The Microfoundations of the Social Investment Function," *Journal of Political Economy*, October, 1963, pp. 441–456.

effectiveness as instruments for economic stabilization. Chapter 12 concludes with a discussion of the application of policy, using the general equilibrium model to explain the possible effects of alternative policies upon income and employment.

5) Chapter 16, now entitled "Economic Growth and Public Policy," is almost wholly a new chapter. The material found in this chapter in the first edition pertaining to economic growth and structural change has been eliminated, for this material seems better suited for treatment in the context of microeconomic analysis. As reconstituted, Chapter 16 now has two main sections. The first, which is retained largely intact from the original edition, is concerned with a discussion of the theoretical role that government has in economic growth. The main thrust of the analysis in this section is to incorporate the public sector into Professor Harrod's growth equations. The second part, which is entirely new, consists of a detailed discussion of the policy measures taken since the early 1960's to stimulate the economy's rate of growth and reduce unemployment. In this section the student is introduced to such recent policy innovations as the concept of the output gap, full employment surplus and the notions of fiscal "drag" and fiscal "dividends." The 1964 tax cut is analyzed, both in terms of its theoretical rationale and its effectiveness. The chapter concludes with a brief discussion of the state of the economy as of late 1966, including a comment upon possible future developments with respect to the effective administration of policy.

6) Professor Harold R. Williams of the Department of Economics of Kent State University has written a workbook especially designed to accompany this revision. It is anticipated that many instructors will find a workbook to be a highly valuable adjunct to the material normally found in the standard macroeconomic text, enabling students to review and apply aspects of the theory which frequently prove to be particularly difficult.

None of the changes alter the original aims of this text; the central concern remains with the forces in the contemporary, developed economy which are crucial to determination of the level of income and employment, the rate of economic growth, and the price level. These areas are the key *aggregate* problems of the modern economy; it is my purpose to draw together in a systematic framework of exposition the best of economic thought bearing upon these areas. The text is Keynesian in the sense that practically all modern analysis relating to the economy as a whole owes an enormous intellectual debt to the thought of John Maynard Keynes. However, the text goes beyond the framework erected in the *General Theory* and aims to bring the intermediate level student abreast of the many refinements in aggregate economic analysis that have taken place in the last thirty years.

A brief review of the organization may be helpful. By way of introduction, there is a separate chapter on the nature of economic analysis. Experience indicates that far too many students have difficulty with economics because they never really grasp what theory is about nor its essential usefulness. I strongly believe that teachers of economics should *not* obscure the fact that their major concern is with economic theory; they should make every possible effort to help the student develop an understanding of the fundamental character of theoretical analysis.

Part I, "The National Income," consists of two chapters devoted to the general task of explaining the meaning of income and the techniques of income measurement. The main emphasis is on understanding the concepts which underlie contemporary systems of national income and social accounting. The major part of the text is found in Part II, "The Theory of Income and Employment." This section sets forth the fundamental theories of macroeconomics which necessarily constitute the heart of any intermediate level course in this branch of economic science. Part III, "The Theory of Economic Growth," is designed to introduce the intermediate level student to some of the recent exciting material pertaining to economic growth which has evolved out of the main body of macroeconomic analysis since the end of World War II. As in the first edition, the Harrod-Domar analysis is deemed to be the most appropriate vehicle for introducing the intermediate level student to contemporary growth economics. Part IV, "The Distribution of Income," has been added by the simple device of shifting the chapter entitled, "Theories of Aggregate Income Distribution" to the position of final chapter in the text. An entire chapter devoted to the theme of the macroeconomic theory of income distribution was one of the important innovations in the first edition; I believe this chapter to be important, but experience has convinced me that its logical position in the development of the subject matter is following and not before the material on economic growth. Placing the chapter on macroeconomic distribution theories at the end of the text does not disturb the basic continuity in development of the main body of macroeconomic analysis.

Among the major innovations of the original edition that have been retained, are Chapter 4 on classical employment theory, Chapter 5 on the basic structure of employment theory, Chapter 8, which treats the problem of allocating resources to the public sector, and Chapter 10 on the international aspects of macroeconomic theory.

As a final comment, I should like to say a word about the use of mathematics in this text. I do not believe that at either the elementary or intermediate level a graph or an equation is wholly self-explanatory; consequently, my concern throughout has been with a complete literary explanation of key ideas and concepts, supplemented, first, with extensive graphic analysis, and, second, with some use of algebra for the presentation of a number of basic propositions. The algebra used in the text rarely gets above the level of a simple equation. In most instances, the algebraic derivations of equations employed in the text are presented in chapter appendices that may be studied or passed over as the instructor chooses.

I am deeply indebted to many persons for their help with both editions of this text, especially to those instructors who used the first edition and were kind enough to pass on to me some of the benefits of their experience. I want to express once again my special appreciation to Professors Robert Lekachman of the State University of New York at Stony Brook and Michael Brennan of Brown University, who read the original manuscript for the text with such exact and painstaking care. Their scholarly criticism was invaluable. Professor Lloyd Orr of Indiana University provided a detailed and constructive review of the original edition which greatly assisted me in preparing this revision. Helpful, too, have been the suggestions of Professor John Blackburn at Duke University. I have profited greatly from a careful critique by Professor Ernst Kuhn, formerly of Roosevelt University and now a colleague at the University of Nebraska. Professor Campbell McConnell, also a colleague at Nebraska, was kind enough to share with me his ideas and suggestions based upon his own experience in using the text over a period of several semesters. Professor Harold Williams, author of the workbook designed to accompany the text, gave me many beneficial comments and suggestions. I also want to thank Mr. E. D. Weldon for the careful work in preparation of the many diagrams in the text. As is traditional, I accept sole responsibility for all errors in the text.

I do not wish to close this preface to the revised edition without mentioning once again my special debt of gratitude to Professor Clarence McNeill, *Emeritus*, who, many years ago, first aroused my serious interest in economic analysis and has always been a source of encouragement. I want to thank, too, my wife, Eunice, for support and patience both in the original writing of the text and during the course of this revision.

January 1967   WALLACE C. PETERSON

Acknowledgment

For kind permission to quote from *The General Theory of Employment, Interest, and Money,* I wish to thank Harcourt, Brace & World, Inc., Macmillan & Co., Ltd., and the Trustees of the Estate of the late Lord Keynes.

Income, Employment, and Economic Growth

REVISED EDITION

1 The Nature and Scope of Economic Analysis

In a brilliant and penetrating address on contemporary economic issues at Yale University on June 11, 1962, the late President John F. Kennedy declared:

> What is at stake in our economic decisions today is not some grand warfare of rival ideologies which will sweep the country with passion but the practical management of a modern economy. What we need is not labels and clichés but more basic discussion of the sophisticated and technical questions involved in keeping a great economic machinery moving ahead.
>
> The national interest lies in high employment and steady expansion of output, in stable prices, and a strong dollar. The declaration of such an objective is easy; their attainment in an intricate and interdependent economy and world is a little more difficult.[1]

This book is about the kind of economics that the President discussed in his historic Yale University commencement speech. Our subject is the economics of the whole society, which is to say we are concerned with understanding the forces that shape and determine the level and rate of growth of national production and employment. As President Kennedy went on to say in his address "the problems of fiscal and monetary policies in the sixties . . . demand subtle challenges for which technical answers, not political answers, must be provided. . . . They are certainly matters that government and business should be discussing in the most sober, dispassionate, and careful way if we are to maintain the kind of vigorous economy upon which our country depends." [2]

[1] John F. Kennedy, "Commencement Address at Yale University, June 11, 1962," *Public Papers of the Presidents of the United States. John F. Kennedy,* 1962 (Washington, United States Government Printing Office, 1963), p. 473.
[2] *Ibid.,* p. 474.

1

This branch of economic analysis is termed macroeconomics, because it centers on the analysis and performance of the economy as a whole. *Macro* is a Greek word meaning "large." The branch of economic study concerned with the behavior of the individual entities of the economy, such as the business firm and the consumer household, is called microeconomics. *Micro*, too, is a Greek word, meaning "small." In contrast to macroeconomic analysis which concerns itself with over-all levels of production and employment, microeconomic analysis focuses on equally valid and important questions relating to the composition of the national output and its distribution among the owners of economic resources.

Before we proceed further with our discussion of the nature of economic analysis, it is useful to consider carefully the fundamental conditions which give rise to the science of economics. These underlying conditions are extremely important for they serve not only as a basis for a broad, formal definition of our subject matter, but also offer an instructive insight into the manner in which the process of defining a subject-matter area exerts a powerful influence upon its scope and content.

Economics is rooted in an age-old human problem, often described as the "wants-means" dilemma. The *wants* of human beings are virtually unlimited in scope; the *means* available for the satisfaction of these wants are scarce. It is out of this situation that the "economic" problem arises, for the scarce resources of a society must be allocated among competing wants in a way that permits the maximum satisfaction of wants. In this sense, economics is the study of scarcity and choice, for if means were not believed to be scarce in relation to wants, the "economic" problem would not exist. Thus, a formal definition of our subject matter might read as follows: *Economics is the organized study of the processes by which scarce resources are allocated among alternative and competing wants with the objective of obtaining a maximum satisfaction of these wants.*

This formal definition of economics may be called traditional because the scarcity theme is nearly always present when the subject matter of economics is defined. It is important that we examine this definition carefully to be aware of some of the assumptions and implications imbedded in it.

Implications of the Traditional Definition of Economics

The traditional definition of economics connotes efficiency; accordingly, economists have made the notion of efficiency the focal point of much of their study. To the economist, efficiency has two major facets. First, there is the problem of efficiency in the allocation of resources among competing wants. In this context, the notion of efficiency implies that the producing and consuming units of the economy should be so organized that the community gets the maximum of the things it wants in the amounts wanted; microeconomic analysis focuses on this problem. Second, and on a different plane, there is the problem of efficiency in the utilization of resources in the economy; resources must be utilized to the fullest extent possible within the existing framework of custom, law, and other institutional practices. Idle resources are evidence *per se* of inefficiency as long as any wants remain unsatisfied. It is from this idea that we derive our concern with the *level* of employment of economic resources, a macroeconomic problem.

Economics thus accepts the concept of efficiency as a part of the social ethic; it is assumed to be a desirable goal. This demonstrates that economics rests upon assumptions which are, in the final analysis, value judgments, for although few people would question the idea that efficiency is a "good" thing, it is nonetheless an assumption that can be neither proved nor disproved.

A second element in the traditional definition of economics concerns the matter of human wants. Most modern textbooks in economics assert, either explicitly or implicitly, that the material or economic wants of human beings are unbounded. Some recognition may be accorded to the idea that wants, in a fundamental sense, are culturally determined, but beyond this it is generally presumed that they are subject to increase without limit. This, too, is an assumption, not an absolute truth, and its effect has been to exclude virtually any analysis of the relative merit of different kinds of wants from the formal body of economic knowledge. Wants are presumed to be "given" data, and the major task of the economist is to gauge the efficiency with which scarce means are applied to the satisfaction of these wants. Since, as a practical matter, it is impossible to separate wants from what people regard as "good," this is, perhaps, tantamount to saying that the economist as an economist has no concern with either the immediate or ultimate values of society.[3] Placing wants outside the domain of the economist may lead to a divorce between economic analysis and economic policy, which may or may not be desirable. We will have more to say about this later in this chapter.

A third implication of the traditional definition of economics is the idea that economic activity is primarily directed toward consumption; consumption of goods and services is the means by which the wants of human beings are satisfied. In this view, goods and services are desired because they possess "utility," that is, they have the capacity to satisfy wants,

[3] It is not difficult to see why economists have traditionally shied away from consideration of the relative merits of the different wants of people in society. Wants are satisfied through the consumption of goods and services and this process is, in the last analysis, a highly subjective matter. Since economics has not yet developed satisfactory techniques for making interpersonal comparisons there seems to be no way in which the economist can "objectively" determine that certain wants ought to be satisfied in preference to others. For an attack upon this traditional viewpoint see J. K. Galbraith, *The Affluent Society* (Boston, Houghton Mifflin, 1958), esp. chaps. 10, 17, and 22.

whereas work, or the process of producing goods and services, represents "disutility" and is by implication distasteful. This idea is derived from a concept of human nature which sees man as a kind of passive creature whose major need is to satisfy the urge to consume—the "economic man" who appeared so frequently in the early literature of economics. At best, though, this is a partial view of human nature, which ignores, among other things, the creative activity that many argue is vital to a purposeful life. This over-simplified view of human nature has caused economists to devote their energies to analysis of the behavior of man as a consumer, to the comparative neglect of man as a producer. Productive activities are viewed as only an adjunct to man's assumed primary goal of maximizing satisfactions. It is not our purpose at this point to discuss the merit or lack of merit in this aspect of economic analysis and its underlying psychology of human behavior, but simply to cite another instance of the influence exercised by an assumption implicit in the traditional definition of economics.

Our discussion so far should warn the reader that assumptions with value implications may be present in such a prosaic matter as the definition of an area of study. And if this is true for a definition, it may also be true for the body of analysis built upon that definition. The significance of this for the study of economics is that a complete separation of analysis and policy (that is, values) *may* not be possible.

Moreover, in economics, as in any discipline, the student should always seek out and make explicit the assumptions upon which any analysis is based. This is particularly necessary in economics because often extremely elaborate analyses are erected upon the foundation of a few, relatively simple assumptions. Failure to be aware of the existence of such underlying assumptions and their implications and limitations will lead to confusion in thought and action.

Science and Economics

We identified economics as a study of the processes by which goods and services are produced, exchanged, and consumed. The data of the economist are variables such as price, production, consumption, wages, interest rates and taxes, but these economic quantities are not primarily significant in themselves. Their significance arises from the fact that they represent the factual evidence of the economic behavior of human beings, which is the economist's real concern. Human behavior in the economic realm manifests itself through measurable quantities like those enumerated above.

This being the case, it follows that economics is a *social science*. E. R. A. Seligman divides sciences into two categories: the natural sciences, which are concerned with the universe, and the mental or cultural sciences, which are concerned with what takes place in man himself—in the realm of his mental life. The latter can be further divided into those dealing with man as a separate individual and those treating man as a member of a group. Thus:

the phenomena . . . related to group activities are commonly called social phenomena, and the sciences which classify and interpret such activities are the social sciences. The social sciences may thus be defined as those mental or cultural sciences which deal with the activities of the individual as a member of a group.[4]

Economics, then, is a social science because it aims at an understanding of the economic aspects of organized or group behavior by human beings.

Having classified economics as a social science, we must take up two additional questions concerning the character of the discipline. The first relates to the nature of science itself, and the second to the authenticity of the claim that economics is truly a scientific discipline. Without answers to these questions it is practically impossible to comprehend either economics as a body of knowledge or what the economist seeks to accomplish.

The Nature of Science

There is no exact, absolute, or final definition for the word "science." In its most general sense, science has to do with the process of knowing; the Latin root *scire* of our modern English word *science* means "to know." But "to know" implies understanding, which means *to be able to explain*. This definition of science, while technically correct, does not go far enough, for we need to know in a more specific way how science seeks to achieve understanding. What do we mean, in other words, by "understanding" and by "being able to explain"?

CLASSIFICATION

Understanding involves, first, the classification of things or phenomena, and second, the discovery or observation of uniformities among the phenomena so classified. Classification, which is the oldest form of scientific activity, attempts to bring order to the universe external to man by seeking out similarities between things and placing them in groups, each group being designated by a name or symbol which is representative of all things brought into it. Classification is a necessary first step toward understanding; it provides the basis for the creative act of finding relationships between phenomena, which lies at the heart of all scientific activity. Professor Jacob Bronowski describes this *creative act* as being the discovery of hidden likenesses in facts or experiences which are separate. In such

[4] E. R. A. Seligman, *Encyclopaedia of the Social Sciences*, Vol. I (New York, Macmillan, 1930), p. 3.

facts or experiences the scientist "finds a likeness which had not been seen before; and he creates a unity by showing the likeness." [5]

GENERALIZATION

The creative act of discovery means the establishment of meaningful generalizations (that is, general statements) pertaining to relationships between phenomena. Such generalizations are meaningful in the sense that they attempt to explain phenomena in the world by linking them together in a cause and effect relationship. The construction of such generalizations, or "laws," is the true essence of scientific activity.

Scientific laws are formulated as "if . . . then . . ." propositions, which is to say that they assert some event or thing will happen if certain conditions are present or satisfied. Formulation of scientific statements as "if . . . then . . ." propositions implies cause and effect relationships. Scientific generalizations, in other words, explain by virtue of the fact that they describe a causal relationship between phenomena. A note of caution is in order here, though, because causation is nearly always complex and difficult to ascertain. Even though an observable relationship may exist between phenomena, the causal significance of such a relationship is not always readily apparent. In the last analysis, attributing a particular cause to a particular effect requires the exercise of the most careful kind of judgment.

To say that scientific laws are essentially "if . . . then . . ." propositions means that all such laws consist of two parts. The "if" part implies that all scientific laws rest upon certain assumptions concerning the data under investigation. The particular function of the assumption is to describe the condition or circumstances under which the generalization possesses validity. For example, it is a well-accepted principle of physics that all bodies fall at a constant rate of acceleration: approximately 32 feet per second per second. But this is true only if the body is falling freely in a vacuum. In this instance the assumption serves to specify the conditions under which the physical law of falling bodies is valid. The conditioning role of the underlying assumptions of a scientific proposition can be illustrated by an example drawn from the economic field. The reader may recall from his earlier study that in equilibrium the business firm will produce at the output level at which marginal cost is equal to marginal revenue. But this general statement as to the behavior of the business firm is true if it can be assumed (1) that the firm is seeking to maximize its profit and (2) that the firm possesses full knowledge of the relevant cost and revenue schedules. Only if these conditions are present does the generalization hold.

The second part of any scientific law consists of the conclusion derived

[5] J. Bronowski, *Science and Human Values* (New York, Julian Messner, 1956), p. 35.

by the process of logic from the basic assumption or postulates. Thus, a scientific law starts with one or more assumptions about the data under investigation and proceeds to derive the logical consequences of these assumptions. The behavior of the business firm described above may be cited again to illustrate this phase of the process of generalization. If the assumed conditions—desire to maximize profit, and knowledge of the relevant cost and revenue curves—are present, logic leads us inevitably to the conclusion that the firm will operate at the level at which marginal costs and marginal revenues are equalized. This is so because the firm can always increase its total profit by expanding output as long as marginal revenue is greater than marginal cost, or by contracting output when marginal cost is greater than marginal revenue. The logical consequence of our assumptions is that the firm will seek to operate at a particular level of output. Taken together, the assumptions and the conclusion derived from them constitute the essence of a scientific law or principle.

VALIDITY

How do we determine whether or not a particular scientific law is valid? Validity depends upon the correct use of logic in deriving conclusions from a given set of assumptions. If the rules of logic are not applied correctly, a generalization will not have validity, irrespective of the merit of its underlying assumptions. More important, a generalization must succeed in explaining that which it sets out to explain. Its conclusions must be compatible with the observed behavior of the data under investigation. Empirical observation is, in other words, the final test of the validity or "truth" of any scientific generalization. This means that a scientific principle should predict what will happen under a stipulated set of circumstances, but it does not mean that such a principle must be an exact and detailed mirror of the real world. Experience can never conclusively "prove" a generalization to be absolutely right, for there will always remain the possibility that a different generalization might better explain the situation under investigation. What empirical observation does show is that the conclusions reached in a scientific principle are (or are not) in accordance with the "facts" of reality.

REALISM IN THE ASSUMPTIONS

Does the validity of the principle require that its assumptions be realistic? This, unfortunately, is a question that cannot be given a categorical yes or no answer. In one sense, the answer is no, for, as we have already seen, the formal validity of the principle is a matter solely of its logical derivation from the underlying assumptions, irrespective of the degree of realism present in the latter. Moreover, the question of exactly what constitutes realism is not easily resolved. To illustrate, let us recall once again the physical principle that governs the acceleration of falling bodies.

Strictly speaking, the underlying assumption of the principle can hardly be termed "realistic," as we rarely find a vacuum existing in the real world. But we know that conditions approximating this assumption do exist often enough in the real world; therefore the principle does serve to explain the behavior of the falling bodies. What we seek is reasonable accuracy in both assumptions and generalizations.

Much the same may be said concerning the assumption frequently employed in economic analysis which asserts that the business firm seeks to maximize its profit. In a strict sense, this assumption is not realistic, for many other considerations besides profit motivate the behavior of the business firm. Nevertheless, generalizations erected on this assumption may be valid because they provide us with an explanation of the behavior of the firm in a particular situation that can be confirmed by an appeal to empirical fact.

If by "realism" in our assumptions we mean something that represents an exact duplication of an extremely complex real world, the validity of a principle cannot be judged in this way simply because such realism cannot possibly be attained. But if by realism we mean some kind of approximation to the real world that serves usefully as a basis for constructing generalizations that can be tested empirically, our assumptions ought to be realistic. This assertion is consistent with our earlier statement that the formal validity of the principle depends strictly upon the correct use of logic in deriving conclusions from a set of assumptions, for unless the latter are in some way rooted in reality, the principle concerned will be without relevance, and thus the question of validity will be meaningless.

The Value of Science

In the foregoing section we said that science is an activity that seeks to discover meaningful relationships in the complex world of reality that lies about us. It is now proper to raise the question of the value of such activity. What, in other words, is the utility of science? To some, given the fact that our age has witnessed a seemingly unending series of scientific accomplishments of obvious usefulness, this question may seem quite unnecessary. Yet, the question is important; unless we understand clearly why we value scientific activity, we will not fully comprehend the essential nature of science. The vague and perhaps intuitive feeling of the average citizen that scientific activity is in some sense desirable is not sufficient for our purposes.

Let us state, first of all, that the creative process of scientific generalization is useful simply because it enables human beings to understand why things happen as they do. Man has an overwhelming sense of curiosity concerning himself, his world, and the universe; the word "why" is perhaps the most important word in the human vocabulary. Scientific generalization is a means—on a high intellectual level, to be sure—whereby human beings satisfy the deeply rooted urge to know the "why" of things.

There is, moreover, another and related sense in which scientific knowledge is essential to mankind. To say that human beings want to know the why of things is tantamount to saying they want to make sense out of the external world. In seeking to do this, man is confronted at every turn with an overwhelming and enormously complex array of "facts." To make sense of the external world requires a broad frame of reference that gives order and meaning to the vast array of facts. This is exactly the task of scientific generalization—or theorizing; generalizations provide the necessary frame of reference through which the facts of reality are related to one another and, thus, rendered intelligible. The practical and absolute necessity of generalization (or theory) as a basis for intelligent comprehension of the complex world of reality cannot be overestimated. The so-called "practical" man who wants "facts" and scorns "theory" is really not practical at all, as facts in themselves are quite meaningless. The "practical man" differs from the "theorist" in that he engages in implicit, haphazard, and often semiconscious theorizing as a means of organizing facts. The vagueness of the theorizing of the practical man often protects fallacies in his theories from discovery and, as a consequence, errant nonsense is put forth as "truth." No one really escapes the burden of theorizing. There are only better or worse theories, simple or more complex theories, implicit or explicit theories.

A second basic reason for the utility of scientific principles is simply that they enable us to predict what will happen or take place under certain circumstances. To be able to anticipate the outcome of a particular situation or action is obviously a matter of some value to human beings. It is important to differentiate between prediction in the scientific sense and forecasting. Prediction means the determination of the outcome of events within a specific "if . . . then . . ." frame of reference, as, for example, the determination of quantity sold in relation to price. Forecasting, on the other hand, is a broader term that has to do with analysis and understanding of basic forces making for future economic change. For example, an economic forecaster may estimate production and employment trends for a new fiscal or calendar year, using not only whatever economic generalizations may be available, but also his personal knowledge and judgment concerning the strength of the various forces that make for economic change.

In the daily routine of living we constantly encounter situations which involve both prediction in the formal "if . . . then . . ." sense and forecasting in a broader vein. These range from the daily forecast of the weather to the expectation of the businessman that by means of a "sale" he can increase the volume of goods sold. All such anticipations of behavior rest upon generalizations. Once again, though, we must proceed cautiously, because the predictive value of the scientific law always pertains to a *general* class or group of things but not to any *specific* or individual entity within the class or group. For example, the economic "law of demand" asserts that, other things being equal, people will purchase more of a given commodity at a lower price than at a higher price. But this "law" or generalization does not tell us whether any particular individual will respond at all times in this way to a change in the price of a commodity; it only tells us that this kind of behavior can be expected of people under certain stipulated conditions. The reader is urged to remember that the predictive value of a generalization will be limited by the character of its underlying assumptions. The "if" portion of the principle necessarily defines one set of conditions under which accurate prediction is possible. In the "law of demand" the assertion that more units of the commodity will be sold at a lower than at a higher price follows only *if* all other things are equal and *if* consumers are rational in the sense that they seek to maximize the satisfaction derived from the expenditure of their incomes.

Finally we can say that scientific generalizations possess great utility because they enable human beings to exercise *control* over their social and physical environment. Prediction implies control, for without a knowledge of what will happen under a particular set of circumstances there is no way either to bring about or to prevent the occurrence of a specific event. The use of the word *control* in this context must be carefully understood. In popular usage the word frequently connotes restraint—particularly physical restraint; here, however, control is meant in a broader sense—the use of the knowledge gained from generalizations to accomplish human purposes. Scientists and engineers, for example, have made use of our knowledge concerning the behavior of gases under various conditions to develop the internal combustion engine and, from it, the automobile. This area of control is, in other words, roughly the area of applied science and technology, wherein use is made of scientific generalizations to achieve a vast variety of practical objectives.

The spectacular achievements of applied science are visible to everyone, and include such diverse accomplishments as the most recently developed antibiotic drugs and the exploration of outer space by manned vehicles. This is the aspect of science most familiar to all of us and which most often captures the public imagination. Yet behind the exciting spectacle of scientific achievement in the modern age lies the much less dramatic task of developing generalizations, without which none of the "miracles" of modern science would be possible. The matter of attempting to discover or develop new generalizations that describe and explain relationships between phenomena in the real world is sometimes characterized as "pure" science, because the persons engaged in this type of activity may not have any immediate concern with any possible practical application of the knowledge they discover. At best, though, there is no sharp dividing line between science that is "pure" and science that is "applied"; both are an essential part of an activity that seeks to enlarge man's ability to understand and control his environment.

The Scientific Character of Economics

What is the basis for the claim that economics is a scientific discipline? The primary objective of economic study is development of generalizations—or principles—that explain relationships between economic phenomena. Like all scientific generalizations, economic principles are basically "if . . . then . . ." statements to which a causal significance is imparted. Thus, if our contention is correct that the key characteristic of scientific activity is the discovery of generalizations that explain the "why" of things, economics is clearly entitled to scientific standing.

Earlier, we pointed out that economics is a *social* science because it deals with human behavior. Since economics concerns itself with human behavior, some may wonder if it is really possible to have a "science of economics." Is it not true that human behavior is, more often than not, wholly capricious? Many persons would argue that man is a free agent and thus uniquely different from all other natural objects, living or inanimate. Under such circumstances how can useful predictions be made about such an uncertain thing as human behavior?

At first it might seem that the obvious answer is that one cannot make such predictions, but a little reflection should convince us that such an answer is too glib and superficial. It is possible to generalize about human behavior because when human beings live together in organized society they behave most of the time in orderly—and predictable—ways. If they did not, chaos would result and civilized living as we know it would be impossible. The reader might reflect for a moment on the extent to which the successful completion of his daily activities depends upon the assumption that the scores of people he has contact with each day will behave in a predictable fashion.

The behavior patterns characteristic of civilized societies manifest themselves in a multitude of ways, ranging from simple customs, or folkways, such as the wearing of particular types of clothing, to highly complex organizational arrangements for achieving the political, economic, or religious ends of a society. Whether the behavior patterns of a society are simple or complex, it is the business of the economist, as well as other social scientists, to develop new and improve existing generalizations that seek to describe and explain these patterns of behavior.

Before leaving this question, it is necessary to say something about the problems posed for economics as a science by the assumption that man is a free agent. We shall not seek to resolve the philosophical problem of whether or not men possess "free will." We need to recognize as a practical matter that man is a thinking being and that this has some vital consequences for economic study. Because man has the power of thought, and because, too, he can learn from experience, he is able to bring about change in society, or, put differently, to establish new behavior patterns. Therefore, a given set of conditions may not produce the same response at one time and place as they do at another time and place.

The foregoing makes prediction in economics and the other social sciences inherently more risky than it is in the natural or physical sciences, but it precludes neither the fact that there are uniformities in human behavior nor the possibility that such uniformities can be discovered. Economics must develop useful generalizations concerning economic behavior and make use of the predictive character of all such generalizations. The student of economics should always remember that man, because he possesses the power to think, can, if he so chooses, take cognizance of the predictive element embodied in a generalization and by so doing modify the outcome. This fact does not in any way change the basic character of economics as a scientific discipline, but it does mean that economics is much less "exact" than such sciences as physics or chemistry.

Some Characteristics of Economic Generalizations

One of the aspects of economics that causes the most concern to students is the abstract character of economic generalizations or economic theory. "Abstraction" is often considered unrealistic; hence economic theory seems to have little or no practical value. But this attitude can only stem from a failure to understand fully and clearly why any economic generalization, principle, or theory must necessarily be abstract.

Abstraction

The object of all scientific inquiry is *to understand* and not simply to reproduce or reconstruct reality. The world of reality is a complex of forces so vast that no one could possibly comprehend all their interrelationships. If progress is to be made toward the understanding of reality, it is essential to simplify the complexities of the real world. We can do this by directing our investigation toward the forces or factors believed to be of strategic importance for an understanding of how things do work in the real world. This is nothing less than the process of abstraction. Thus, economic generalizations and theories are not detailed and photographically faithful reproductions of a portion of the real world, but are, rather, simplified portraits whose purpose is to make the real world intelligible.

It is important for the reader to understand that abstraction is a characteristic of theory in any discipline, including the biological and physical sciences. The major difference between the social sciences and the natural sciences is not in the degree of abstraction, but in the fact that the social sciences are generally unable to resort to a laboratory to determine the validity of their principles. We shall return to a discussion of this point shortly.

The Concept of a Functional Relationship

Another important characteristic of economic generalizations concerns the form in which these generalizations or principles are often presented. Since the economic aspects of human behavior are usually manifested in the form of economic quantities, such as prices, outputs, incomes, and wage rates, economic principles frequently can be stated in mathematical form. The most common practice in this respect is to express the principles of economics in the form of a *functional relationship* between economic variables.

The concept of a functional relationship between variables is essential to an understanding of the nature of economic analysis. In fact, this is perhaps the most important concept the reader can grasp, for if one fully and clearly understands the nature of the functional idea the way to a thorough comprehension of economic analysis is open. *A functional relationship exists between two variables when they are related in such a way that the value of one depends upon the value of the other.* Such a relationship can be expressed in equation form as follows:

$$y = f(x) \tag{1-1}$$

An equation of this form reads "y is a function of x." It means, simply, that the variable represented by the letter y is related in a systematic and dependent way to the value of the variable represented by the letter x.

The concept of a functional relationship enables us to express symbolically (that is, in mathematical form) the essence of a particular economic principle or generalization. For example, the economic "law" of demand can be expressed in equation form as

$$Q_d = f(P) \tag{1-2}$$

which means that the quantity demanded for a particular commodity is a function of its price. The student should note, however, that by itself the above equation does not tell us anything more than that quantity and price are linked together in a systematic and dependable relationship. Knowledge of the exact nature of the relationship between these two variables requires more information than can be obtained from the equation alone, a point to which we shall return subsequently.

Although the functional concept is an important tool for economic analysis, there are limitations inherent in the concept that must be appreciated if it is to be used effectively. In the first place, the fact that two variables are related to one another in a functional sense does not mean that the one is the *cause* of the other. Cause is not easily determined. To determine cause requires keen judgment and a broad knowledge of the situation under study. The "law of demand" provides an excellent example of the need for the careful exercise of judgment. The mathematical expression of this "law" simply tells us that the variables, "quantity demanded" and "price," are functionally related. For a clearer understanding of the nature of this relationship we must be aware of the behavior of buyers in a market situation. More precisely, we must know whether the quantity demanded varies as the price varies, or conversely, whether price varies as quantity demanded varies. If we can answer this, we will be in a position to say something about the causal relationship that may exist between these variables. Since we are discussing the behavior of buyers in a market situation and not the behavior of suppliers of the commodity in question, the more reasonable conclusion be that buyers will vary their purchases in accordance with changes in price. But this is to say that in the equation, quantity demanded (Q_d) is the dependent variable, and price (P) is the independent variable, for quantity demanded varies (inversely) with price and not the other way around. If we say this does it not also mean that we have identified price as the immediate—although not necessarily sole—*cause* of the quantity demanded by buyers? In any common sense meaning of the word "cause" the answer to this question would obviously be yes.

A second important aspect of the functional concept is that a particular variable may be a function of a number of other variables. For example, to say that the quantity demanded of a commodity is a function of its price does not mean that the quantity demanded cannot at the same time be a function of variables besides price. In the case of the law of demand, many things besides price affect a buyer's decision as to the amounts of any specific good he will purchase at any particular time. Thus, we might say that the quantity demanded of a good is a function not only of price, but of the buyer's income, the price of other goods, the buyer's expectations as to future prices, and perhaps a host of other factors.

The fact that an important economic magnitude may be functionally linked to a number of variables presents a difficult problem for economic analysis, particularly when some of the variables cannot be quantified. The usual way in which economists solve this problem is by resort to the device of *ceteris paribus*—"other things are equal." This procedure involves analysis of the relationship between two or more variables on the basis of the assumption that all other variables that might influence the outcome of the situation remain constant. This is a kind of intellectual equivalent to the laboratory procedure that is commonly followed by the physical or biological scientist. The investigator seeks to analyze in isolation the relationship between the variables or factors believed to have the most strategic significance in determining the value of the phenomena under investigation. An extremely clear exposition of the nature of *ceteris paribus* is found in the following statement by Alfred Marshall:

It is sometimes said that the laws of economics are "hypothetical." Of course, like every other science, it undertakes to study the effects which will be produced by certain causes, not absolutely, but subject to the condition that *other things are equal*, and that the causes are able to work out their effects undisturbed. Almost every scientific doctrine, when carefully and formally stated, will be found to contain some proviso to the effect that other things are equal: the action of the causes in question is supposed to be isolated; certain effects are attributed to them, but only on the hypothesis that no cause is permitted to enter except those distinctly allowed for.[6]

Let us add one final word of caution with respect to the use of the functional concept in economic analysis. Reducing economic generalizations to the form of a functional relationship between quantitative magnitudes may suggest much more precision in our knowledge of economic behavior than really is the case. Mathematics is a precise discipline, and its use in conjunction with economic analysis may be misleading. We have already observed that the generalizations of economics and the social sciences are usually less "exact" than those of the physical or biological sciences. This, of course, does not prevent us from using mathematics in economic analysis, but it does require that we guard ourselves against the temptation to view the principles of economics as a set of exact relationships akin to the "laws" of physics or chemistry.

The Methods of Economic Analysis

Economics, as we have seen, is an area of knowledge that can be fitted into our broad definition of science as an activity that explains relationships between phenomena by the process of generalization. Equally important for comprehension of the scientific character of economics is an understanding of the methods employed in economic analysis—that is, its methodology.

Methodology refers to the techniques and procedures used by the economist to acquire knowledge and understanding of economic processes.

---

[6] Alfred Marshall, *Principles of Economics,* 8th ed. (London, Macmillan, 1925), p. 36.

More specifically, it concerns the techniques employed in the construction and verification of economic principles. Unless these techniques are sound, economic generalizations will have little value. In passing, it must be emphasized that there is no single and "best" methodology suitable for all areas of science. The appropriate technique will depend largely upon the kind of data under investigation, for some methods of investigation are wholly applicable in some areas and not at all applicable in others.

The Deductive Method

The most characteristic method of economic analysis has been one usually described as *deductive* or *hypothetical*. In essence, deduction involves the establishment of certain basic premises or assumptions concerning the strategic determinants of economic behavior and then, by reason or logic, inferring their consequences. John Stuart Mill called it the *a priori* method, by which he meant "reasoning from an assumed hypothesis." [7]

The deductive method as applied to economics consists of three major steps. The first is to postulate assumptions about the determinants of economic behavior in a particular situation. The nature of these assumptions deserves careful attention. Critics of the deductive method argue that the assumptions underlying the "laws" of economics are imaginary and unrealistic; consequently, any deductive system erected upon such assumptions is without significance. But in a purely formal sense, as we have already noted, the imaginary or non-imaginary character of the underlying assumptions does not matter, for the validity of a principle *in the abstract* depends solely upon the correct use of logic in deriving the consequences of a given set of assumptions.

However, it is not accurate to say the basic assumptions of economics have no empirical—that is, factual—basis. Professor Lionel Robbins, an eminent British economist, asserts that the underlying postulates of economics are "all assumptions involving in some way simple and indisputable facts of experience relating to the way in which the scarcity of goods, which is the subject matter of our science, actually shows itself in the world of reality." [8] In other words, the assumptions of deductive economics consist of shrewd and imaginative observations about human behavior. To illustrate, we spoke earlier of the assumption that the business firm seeks to maximize profit, and, as a consequence, does or does not do certain things. With respect to any particular business firm the empirical content of this assumption may be relatively low, for the factors that actually motivate a specific firm in a specific real world situation are many and complex. Yet as an insight into the forces that determine the

[7] John Stuart Mill, *Essays on Some Unsettled Questions of Political Economy* (London, Longmans, Green, 1877), p. 143.

[8] Lionel Robbins, *An Essay on the Nature and Significance of Economic Science* (London, Macmillan, 1949), p. 78.

behavior of business firms in general, the assumption of profit maximization is meaningful because it is a realistic description of a major, strategic determinant of economic behavior in a market economy. This is so even though an assumption of this kind can never be fully tested by experience. Ludwig von Mises has said that the "end of science is to know reality" and that "in introducing assumptions into its reasoning, it satisfies itself that the treatment of the assumptions conceived can render useful service for the comprehension of reality." [9] Consequently, an assumption like that of profit maximization, even though it may not be wholly accurate in an empirical sense, can be a tool of great power and usefulness for the comprehension of reality.

The second step consists of determining the consequences that will ensue from the performance of the assumed determinants of economic behavior. This is the purely deductive part of the process, because the essence of deduction, as John Stuart Mill said, consists of reasoning from given premises to their necessary conclusion. Success in this stage of the process depends primarily upon the correct use of logic, although in contemporary economics formal logic is supplemented in many instances by mathematics, a form of logic.

The last step in the deductive method is verification, which consists, in essence, of testing the conclusions reached by the process of logical inference against observed reality. The problem of verification is especially knotty in the social sciences because, as pointed out earlier, it is not possible to conduct "controlled experiments" to determine the validity of a generalization. The merit of the controlled experiment is that by rigidly regulating the conditions under which a particular event takes place, the investigator can isolate the effects of a change in any one of the factors that enter into the situation under study. Verification of a particular hypothesis is achieved through the repetition of the experiment until sufficient "experience" is accumulated to either sustain or disprove the hypothesis.

In all the sciences that concern themselves with the group behavior of human beings the strict application of the controlled experiment as a means of verifying hypotheses is manifestly impossible. This is because the social scientist can never bring a part of society into the laboratory and recreate "experience" over and over again under strictly identical conditions. In the social sciences, consequently, evidence for the validity of a generalization must depend, as Mill said, on "the limited number of experiments which take place (if we may so speak) of their own accord, without any preparation or management of ours; in circumstances, moreover, of great complexity and never perfectly known to us." [10] Mill's

[9] Ludwig von Mises, *Human Action* (New Haven, Yale University Press, 1949), p. 858.
[10] Mill, *op. cit.*, p. 147.

"limited number of experiments" are to be found in recorded facts of human experience, statistical and historical, and it becomes the task of the economist or social scientist to search patiently through the complex fabric of events of the real social world for necessary evidence to verify his generalizations. This task is not as hopeless as it may first appear, for, as Professor Milton Friedman has pointed out, experience does provide us with an abundance of evidence, although the interpretation of this evidence is at once more difficult and less dramatic than that arrived at by the controlled experiment.[11] In spite of the difficulties that economics may present with respect to verification, the final and necessary test of the validity of any economic generalization is observed reality.

The Inductive Method

In contrast to the analytical or deductive technique of analysis, there exists an alternative method that is described as "empirical" or "inductive." The process of induction involves the establishment of generalizations or principles on the basis of a number of specific instances or facts. It is said to be "empirical" because adherents of this method of analysis assert that generalization or the formulation of principles can come only after there has been an extensive compilation of the "raw data of experience." The latter may consist of historical data of an essentially qualitative character, or statistical data. Thus, the "historical" method and "statistical" method are sometimes cited as specific modes of investigation which fit into the broader framework of induction. The major differences between deduction and induction from the point of view of logic are well stated in the following quotation:

> By *deduction* in logic is meant reasoning or inference from the general to the particular, or from the universal to the individual. Still more specifically deductive inference signifies reasoning from given premises to their necessary conclusion. *Induction* is the process of reasoning from a part to the whole, from particulars to generals, or from the individual to the universal.[12]

Some economists have argued that the inductive method is the only truly scientific method of analysis and that if economics wants to achieve and retain standing as a scientific discipline it must become more and more inductive in its analytical techniques. This point of view is summed up in the following statement by Colin Clark:

> Not one in a hundred (of the academic economists)—least of all those who are most anxious to proclaim the scientific nature of Economics—seems to understand what constitutes the scientific approach, namely, the careful

[11] Milton Friedman, *Essays in Positive Economics* (Chicago, University of Chicago Press, 1953), p. 10.
[12] Wilson Gee. *Social Science Research Methods* (New York, Appleton-Century-Crofts, 1950), p. 206.

systematization of all observed facts, the framing of hypotheses from these facts, prediction of fresh conclusions on the basis of these hypotheses, and the testing of these conclusions against further observed facts.[13]

Professor Clark's statement is representative of what some economists today would probably regard as an extreme position with respect to the proper techniques for the acquisition of economic knowledge of a scientific character. Many economists argue that deduction and induction are complementary rather than alternative or opposing techniques of investigation. There can be no such thing as "pure" induction or empirical research without some preconceptions of what is important and the way in which things are related—in short, without some hypothesis to guide the investigation. This is exactly what the deductive process provides, and without it empirical research would degenerate into an incomprehensible accumulation of "facts." On the other hand, "pure" deduction is equally an impossibility if economic analysis is to be something more than an exercise in abstract logic. Deduction without a factual content—that is, without induction—is just as empty and meaningless as induction or empirical research without some preconceptions—that is, without deduction.

The foregoing remarks on the deductive and inductive methods of analysis and their applicability to the science of economics suggest an important conclusion: There is no unique or single method of investigation or analysis that can appropriately be labeled "the scientific method" and which is the only proper or permissible technique to be used for the discovery and elaboration of scientific generalizations. Professor Max Black of Cornell University has defined the "scientific method" as "those procedures which, as a matter of historical fact, have proved most fruitful in the acquisition of systematic and comprehensive knowledge." [14] Such a broad definition is undoubtedly as good as any that can be devised, for even a cursory examination of the history of science will show that the development of scientific generalizations nearly always involves an amalgam of observation, experiment, speculation, and reasoning.

Economic Analysis and Economic Policy

The discussion of the nature of economics would be quite inadequate without consideration of the policy aspects of economics. The word *policy* refers to some course of action that is designed to realize or bring about some specific objective or end. Policy is concerned with what we want and how we get it. Economic policy thus has to do with the means

[13] Colin Clark, *The Conditions of Economic Progress* (London, Macmillan, 1940), pp. vii–viii.
[14] Max Black, "The Definition of the Scientific Method," in Robert C. Stauffer, **ed.,** *Science and Civilization* (Madison, University of Wisconsin Press, 1949), p. 81.

that individuals, groups, or a whole society may utilize to achieve ends or objectives that are primarily of an economic nature. A distinguished economist, Edwin G. Nourse, defines economic policy as:

a sophisticated—that is, an intellectual rather than emotional—way of defining ends to be sought and adopting promising means of pursuing those ends. Perceiving business life as a complex social process about which, in spite of its vagaries, we have some hard-won understanding, policymaking expresses a faith that we can have some measure of control over the outcome.[15]

Since economic policy is concerned with the ends or objectives of society, it involves *value judgments;* it is concerned with questions of what "ought to be" and what "ought not to be." It is important that the significance of value judgments be recognized, for individuals and groups usually have deeply-held convictions about the economy and how things "ought" to be, and such convictions profoundly affect their behavior. Value judgments concerning the proper ends of economic activity are important, too, because they are the source of much that is controversial in economics. Disagreement in economics stems not so much from disagreement over the validity of economic principles, but often from either disagreement over the economic objectives being sought, or over the appropriate means for the realization of these ends.

With this understanding of the nature of economic policy and its significance as a source of controversy in economics, we are prepared to discuss the relation of economic analysis to economic policy. Once again a word of warning is in order, for economists are not in agreement among themselves as to the manner in which these two facets of economics are related to one another. This being the case, we shall begin by describing briefly the major positions that economists hold in respect to the relationship between economic analysis and economic policy.

At one extreme of the spectrum of possible attitudes is the "positivist" view that economic analysis and economic policy are two separate aspects of economics which simply cannot be mixed. This particular point of view asserts that economics is a "positive" science, which means it is an activity that concerns itself only with the discovery of generalizations of the kind we described earlier; it is completely divorced from any consideration of values. John Neville Keynes in his classic work, *The Scope and Method of Political Economy*, defined a *positive* science as "a body of systematized knowledge concerning what is," and contrasted it with a *normative* or *regulative* science, which he defined as "a body of systematized knowledge discussing the citeria of what ought to be, and concerned therefore with the ideal as distinguished from the actual." [16] Pro-

[15] Edwin G. Nourse, *Economics in the Public Service* (New York, Harcourt, Brace, 1953), p. 6.
[16] John Neville Keynes, *The Scope and Method of Political Economy* (London, Macmillan, 1891), p. 34.

fessor Friedman asserts that "positive economics is in principle independent of any particular ethical postition or normative judgments." [17] In sum, the positivist view holds that the economist must, if he is to retain his claim to scientific objectivity, confine his activities to the discovery of significant relationships among economic phenomena and remain scrupulously neutral toward ends or goals of society.

It is doubtful that *most* economists today accept without reservation the positivist view of the nature and scope of economics. For one thing it is argued that values cannot be separated from analysis because economics is a social science and the socal sciences possess significance only to the extent that they contribute to the solution of real social problems. If this is a valid contention, it means that economists and other social scientists can hardly avoid becoming involved in some fashion with the ends or goals of the society of which they are a part. The reader will recognize, of course, that this particular attitude is itself a value judgment, but it is one, nevertheless, that many competent economists share. For example, Professor John H. Williams, a former president of the American Economic Association, states: "Economic theorizing seems to me pointless unless it is aimed at what to do. All the great theorists, I think, have had policy as their central interest, even if their policy were merely laissez faire." [18]

The viewpoint of an economist like Williams does not necessarily refute the positivist position that economic analysis can be neutral in the sense of being completely detached from value judgments, but it suggests that such an economics, if it really could exist, might be a barren discipline.

The phrase "if it really could exist" brings us to the second major reason why some economists assert that economic analysis cannot truly be free of value judgments. The more fundamental objection to the positivist viewpoint is that values are inevitably a part of the analytical techniques employed by the economist. Value judgments are, so to speak, "built into" economic analysis to such an extent that it is vain to expect that economics can be a science completely detached from all value considerations. Several arguments may be advanced in support of this point of view.

The first concerns the definition of a scientific discipline. Definitions are necessary in any science, for without them there would be no way of knowing where one field of inquiry begins and another leaves off. This is true even though definitions must often be quite arbitrary. The determination of content and scope for any area of intellectual inquiry is basically a matter of determining what is important and what is not

[17] Friedman, *op. cit.*, p. 4.
[18] John H. Williams, "An Economist's Confessions," *The American Economic Review*, March, 1952, p. 10.

important, which in turn implies that no scientific discipline can even be defined without the exercise of value judgments.

A second argument concerns the selection of areas to be investigated within the confines specified by the definition of the subject. This, too, involves value judgments, for whenever a selection is made it implies that some things are more important than others. In economics, the choice of the areas for study and analysis is largely influenced by the problems that are of concern to a society at any particular historical epoch. If economic analysis is largely a by-product of the economic problems that beset human societies from time to time, it is difficult to perceive how such analysis can be wholly divorced from values. Since the problems of a society in some sense reflect the values and value conflicts of that society, it logically follows that these will be reflected, too, in the areas selected for investigation and analysis by the economist.

Finally, it can be argued that most, if not all, economic generalizations or principles necessarily contain within themselves specific implications in the matter of economic policy. If economic analysis has its origins in economic problems, then it would seem reasonable—and logical—that such analysis should point the way to a solution of these problems. But if this is the case, then it can hardly be said that the analysis is neutral with respect to values. One or two simple examples will suffice to illustrate this point. Economics has developed an elaborate body of principles that explains how prices are determined and resources allocated through the mechanism of the market. This elegant structure of principles is something more than a scientific explanation of the mechanism of the market, for it implies, among other things, that certain types of market arrangements lead to a more optimum—or "better"—allocation of resources than others. Another case in point is the theory of comparative advantage, which provides a scientific explanation of the basis for trade between nations. It does this, but it also implies that a policy of free trade is desirable if a nation seeks to maximize the material well-being of its citizens. The latter goal, the reader will recall, appears to be one of the value premises implicit in the traditional definition of economics.

The question that we have raised concerning the relationship between economic analysis and economic policy is an especially difficult one for which no final or definitive answer really exists. The viewpoint that is favored in this text, namely that economics cannot remain a "pure" science, detached from important issues of public policy, will be recognized by the careful reader as a value judgment. It arises out of the conviction that economics is worthwhile and a discipline deserving of public support only to the extent that it can contribute something of genuine value toward the solution of real and pressing human problems.

PART I The National Income

2 Basic Concepts of National Income and Social Accounting

The objective of this text is to develop a thorough understanding of the forces that determine income, production, and employment in the modern economy. This is important not only because the well-being of the whole nation depends upon the performance of the economy, but also because the material welfare of each citizen is bound up with the over-all functioning of the economic system. The economy's behavior is not one of steady growth toward higher and higher levels of material production; rather, it typically moves forward in a series of sharp upward thrusts, frequently followed by equally sharp contractions in economic activity. The economy's performance has a distinctive fluctuating character, as witnessed by the output path shown in Figure 2–1. Given the erratic and somewhat cyclical path that the economy follows over time, the serious student of economics must develop an understanding of the basic forces that account for such behavior.

First, it is necessary to understand clearly the meaning and use made of the word *income*, when reference is made not to the income of the individual citizen or business firm, but to the income of the whole economy. Specifically, we seek in this chapter to define and analyze the nature of "national income" and related aggregates that have to do with the over-all performance of the economic system. In Chapter 3 we shall describe in detail the most important measures that economists and statisticians have developed for recording the performance of the economic system.

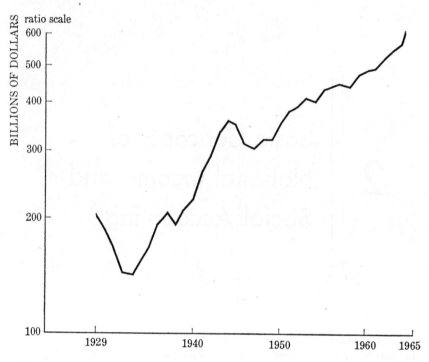

Figure 2–1. Growth of U.S. National Output (billions of current dollars)

The Nature of National Income and Social Accounting

The techniques of national income and social accounting developed in the United States and other nations during the last two to three decades are no different in terms of their fundamental purpose than accounting systems developed for and utilized by the business firm. All accounting systems have as their common purpose the measurement and communication of accurate, numerical information concerning the economic and financial activities during a specified period of time of some entity (such as the household, the business firm, or the nation).

Many readers undoubtedly are familiar with the typical accounts employed by the business firm, like the balance sheet and the profit and loss statement. These accounts provide a numerical record of the activities of the business firm. To conduct the affairs of his firm successfully, the businessman must have at his disposal accurate and current information concerning sales receipts, expenditures, and the profit of his firm. This information is provided by the firm's accounting system, and it is on the basis of such information that the businessman judges the state of economic health of his enterprise. The business entrepreneur could not possibly make intelligent policy decisions respecting future operations of the enterprise without adequate information concerning what has taken place in the firm in the recent past.

National income and social accounting is designed to do for the economy as a whole what more traditional forms of accounting do for the business firm. That is to say, the basic objective of a system of national income and social accounting is to provide a systematic and factual record of the performance of the economy during a specified period of time. The question of precisely what we mean by the economy's performance will be examined shortly; for the moment our purpose is to emphasize that the prime function of such a system is to provide statistical information on what has taken place in the economy during the recent past.

Although accounting itself dates back at least to the fifteenth century, the application of accounting principles and concepts to the measurement of the economic activity of the whole society is of relatively recent origin.[1] In the United States the National Bureau of Economic Research, a private research organization, undertook during the 1920's extensive research into the meaning and measurement of the national income. Earlier, W. I. King pioneered when in 1915 he published a survey of the distribution of wealth and income in the United States. The strongest impetus, though, toward the development of a system of national income accounts came during the Great Depression of the 1930's, when it became painfully evident to policy makers in Washington that accurate and detailed information was needed with respect to the level of economic activity in the country. As a result of a Senate resolution in 1932, the year in which the depression headed to its lowest point, the Department of Commerce in cooperation with the National Bureau of Economic Research began to compile national income statistics for the American economy.[2] The results of this first important foray by the Federal government into national income and social accounting were published in 1934 as a report, *National Income 1929–32*. In the same year the National Income Unit (now the National Income Division) was established in the Department of Commerce and given responsibility for the preparation of annual estimates of the national income. World War II accelerated the development of national income and social accounting in this country, because the full mobilization of the economy's resources for the war effort required more and more exact and up-to-date information concerning the availability and use of these re-

---

[1] For a thoroughgoing review of the development of national income accounting and analysis see: Paul Studenski, *The Income of Nations* (New York, New York University Press, 1958), esp. Part One, pp. 11–160. See also Edgar Z. Palmer, *The Meaning and Measurement of the National Income* (Lincoln, Nebr., The University of Nebraska Press, 1966), Chapters 1–3.

[2] Senate Resolution No. 220, 72nd Congress.

sources. The need for information of this type continued to exist after the war, particularly because the Employment Act of 1946 committed the Federal government to pursue policies to promote "maximum production, employment, and purchasing power." As a result of these various impetuses, the United States possesses an elaborate and comprehensive national income and social accounting system designed to measure the economic activity of the nation.

Responsibility for compilation of the statistical data that go into the accounts of the system still rests with the National Income Division of the United States Department of Commerce. The statistics of national income compiled by the National Income Division are published at periodical intervals in the *Survey of Current Business,* a monthly publication of the Department of Commerce. The Commerce Department has published two important supplements to the *Survey of Current Business* (in 1951 and again in 1954) entitled *National Income,* which describe in detail not only the concepts employed in the United States' system of national income and social accounting, but also the sources and methods utilized in the compilation of the statistics of income for the whole nation. In the August, 1965, issue of the *Survey of Current Business* revised estimates for the national income and product accounts for the United States for 1929–1964 were published. This issue also includes discussion of some definitional changes in the accounts. These publications form the most important sources of information concerning the character of the system of national income and social accounting developed in the United States over the last three decades.

The Use of National Income and Social Accounting

The most important use of national income and social accounting is in the formulation of economic policy, primarily by governments, but also by business firms and labor organizations. Since the great Stock Market crash of 1929 there has been a vast expansion in the role played by government (Federal, state, and local) in the economy; between 1929 and 1964, for example, the purchase of goods and services by all levels of government rose from 8 per cent of the total national output to approximately 20 per cent.[3] As a consequence, public policies relating to taxes and expenditures have become one of the most strategically important determinants of the overall performance of the economic system. Given this amid the growing complexity of the modern economy, detailed statistical information on the performance of the economy as provided by systems of national income and social accounting is indispensable in developing intelligent and workable public policies.

In a recent appraisal of the national income accounting system of the United States, the National Bureau of Economic Research asserted that

[3] U.S. Department of Commerce, *Survey of Current Business,* August, 1965.

national economic accounts are particularly useful in suggesting answers to three types of questions that arise when economic policies of national significance are under discussion.[4] First, national accounts provide information about the availability of resources in the economy, a vital necessity whenever additional resources are needed for the implementation of a particular policy. Second, they measure the impact of specific policies on production, prices, and employment in different parts of the economy. National income accounts are an extremely valuable tool for analysis of the interrelationships existing between different parts of the economy. Intelligent and successful policy formulation must take such interrelationships into account. Finally, the national income accounts provide a basis for predicting how *total* output and employment may change upon implementation of any specific policy. A more detailed discussion of various types of national income and social accounting *systems* is found in the Appendix to this chapter.

Income and Wealth

Having sketched broadly the nature of national income and social accounting, we shall now analyze, first, the concept of income and, second, the meaning of income in reference to the whole society. A similar discussion on wealth will follow; then we shall discuss the relationship between income and wealth.

The Concept of Income

As a concept there are a number of different ways in which income can be defined, but the one thing common to all definitions is the idea that income is a *flow* phenomenon. By a *flow* is meant something that is *measured over time*. For the individual the income flow is usually thought of in terms of money received between two points of time, although one might just as readily—and correctly—conceive of it as a flow of satisfactions during a period of time. The business firm, too, usually thinks of income as money received over time. But no matter how we choose to define income from the point of view of the individual or the firm, the crucial element in our definition is that of flow. Income is a *flow*—whether we are talking about income of the individual or the income of the whole society.

This last statement brings us to the question of what we mean when we talk in terms of the income of the whole society—what, in short, is the meaning of national income. We emphasized that the basic purpose of

[4] National Accounts Review Committee of the National Bureau of Economic Research, *The National Economic Accounts of the United States* (Washington, United States Government Printing Office, 1958), p. 34.

national income and social accounting is to provide a factual record of the performance of the economy. Since the underlying purpose of economic activity is satisfaction of human wants, and since want satisfaction results from consumption of goods and services, the performance of the economy must be measured in terms of the amount of productive activity taking place in a period of time. Productive activity, however, culminates in the output of valuable goods and services, and thus income from the standpoint of the whole society is defined as *a flow of output over a period of time*. Let us inject a word of caution here, because the income of the whole society, even though it is normally measured in money terms, is not the same thing as the aggregate of all money incomes received by persons in the economy. Flows of money income do not always represent or correspond to output flows, and increases in money flows do not always mean that there has been an increase in output flows. We shall develop the reasons for this in greater detail subsequently.

If the basic definition of income in a social sense is that of a flow of output, this presents a difficult problem of measurement. Output consists of a vast and heterogeneous quantity of goods and services that cannot be added together unless they can be reduced to a common unit of measurement. As a practical matter, the only way in which we can add together all the different kinds of goods and services produced by the economy during a period of time is by reducing them to their money value. Money value is the common denominator which enables us to sum up and reduce to a single figure the complex aggregation of goods and services contained in the economy's flow of output during some definite period.

It is possible to reduce the economy's flow of output to its monetary valuation because in a market economy practically all productive activity will be reflected in money transactions. Most activities that are in any sense productive—which lead to the creation of goods and services—are carried on through the mechanism of the market and will thus have a price tag. If a way can be found to summarize all the monetary transactions that reflect productive activity, it becomes possible to measure in money terms the total income or flow of output of the society.

While in principle the summing of money transactions describes the technique by which the output of the whole society is measured, several qualifications to the above statement should be noted. For one thing, all monetary transactions do not necessarily reflect current productive activity; this is the case with sales of second-hand goods or the purchase and sale of various financial instruments, such as stocks and bonds. Second, some productive activity does not pass through the mechanism of the market and thus is not reflected in a monetary transaction. The labor of the housewife is a case in point. Finally, money itself is not a stable unit of measure since the value of money fluctuates as the general level of prices change. These important qualifications to the general principle that the productive activity of the economy is reflected in monetary transactions will be examined in detail in a later section of this chapter.

THE CIRCULAR FLOW OF INCOME AND PRODUCT

Income, as we have seen, is a flow phenomenon. But it is important to note the *circular* character of this flow. This basic concept is illustrated in Figure 2–2. Output originates in the producing units of the economy—

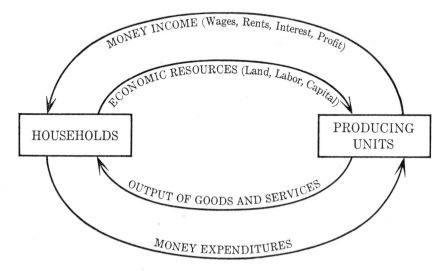

Figure 2–2. The Circular Flow of Economic Activity

including the government as a producing entity—and moves from them to the economy's households, which are not only the ultimate users of the economy's output, but also the owners and suppliers of the economic resources that enter into the creation of output. The existence of a flow of output means there must be a corresponding flow of inputs, for the essence of the productive process is the transformation of the services rendered by the economic resources of land, labor, and capital into economically useful goods and services. Thus, as shown in Figure 2–2, the underlying real economic process consists of a continuous, circular process whereby inputs of resources are transformed by the economy's production units into goods and services. The thoughtful reader will recognize that this is a simplified view of the matter because it lumps all goods and services together and assumes that all of the output is directed toward the households of the economy. This is not actually the case because some of the output consists of capital or investment goods, for which firms rather than households are the ultimate users. This fact, though, should not cloud our thinking with respect to the basically circular character of the economic process.

The input and output flows that constitute the essence of the economic process are matched by two flows of money—one of income and one of expenditure. According to Figure 2–2, which outlines the productive process in a market economy wherein resources are privately owned and most production decisions are privately made, resource owners exchange the services of their resources for money incomes, while the producing entities of the economy exchange their output of goods and services for the flow of expenditures originating in the households of the economy. The flow of income and expenditure matching the real flows of the economy is seen to be circular in the same sense that the underlying flows of product and services of economic resources are circular.

The circular flow diagram, even though oversimplified, illustrates a number of important propositions relating to the economic process and the flow of income. First, the diagram shows that income (or output) creation involves an interaction between the two basic kinds of markets that exist in the economy. Exchanging the services of economic resources for money incomes, depicted in the top half of the diagram, reflects transactions taking place in the resource (factor) market, while the expenditure of money income for the economy's output, depicted in the lower half of the diagram, represents the total of transactions taking place in the economy's market for goods and services. Second, the circular flow diagram aids in understanding why the flow of income, the flow of output, and the flow of expenditures for output are necessarily equal. The reason for this equality is that all of these flows are different measures of the same thing—the volume of productive activity in the economy. Since the circular flow analysis reveals that the total flow of current income is always equal to the value of current output, this means that the productive process will always generate sufficient total money income to purchase the current output of the economy. This point has considerable significance for our later discussions of the process of income determination.

The Concept of Wealth

Another concept of importance to the student of economics is that of *wealth*. Wealth and income are concepts so closely related that it is easy to confuse them and not see that they are distinctly different entities. For sound economic analysis it is vitally important that the differences between wealth and income be clearly understood.

As a starting point, let us define wealth as all material things which possess economic value. Wealth, in other words, consists of goods that can command other goods and services in exchange. Several aspects of this definition should be noted. First, our definition limits wealth to tangible or material things, which is to say that intangibles (for example, services) are excluded. Second, wealth is a *stock* phenomenon in contrast to income, a *flow* phenomenon. Wealth is a concept that relates to the total of material things existing at a moment of time. Contrast this with the income concept which has to do with the flow of output or money over a period of time. This basic difference between wealth and income is reflected in the way in which the two are measured: income can be measured only by reference to some distinct period of time, such as the day, the week, the month, or the year, whereas wealth can be measured only by reference to a specific moment of time, such as the final day of the week, the month, or the year. This difference is reflected in the balance sheet and the profit and loss statements of the business firm. The balance sheet is analogous to the wealth concept; it reveals the existing position of the firm in terms of its assets and liabilities at a given moment of time, usually the close of business on the last day of the year. The profit and loss statement, on the other hand, is analogous to the income concept; it depicts the receipts and expenditures flowing into and out of the firm during the course of a year or some other specific period of time.

Finally, it is important to note that wealth, because it involves stocks of goods, is exhaustible, while income, because it is a flow, is capable of being continuously renewed. Wealth, in other words, can be wholly "used up." Within a specific period income, too, may be used up, but the flow will be renewed in the next period as long as the economic resources that are the basic source of income are not destroyed. It is true that these resources—land, labor, and capital—can be destroyed, worn out, or otherwise depleted, but this would simply have the effect of stopping the income flow until new resources are generated.

Problems in the Measurement of Wealth

In any discussion of wealth, particularly in reference to the economy as a whole, a distinction must be made between *wealth* and *claims to wealth*. Wealth of a nonhuman character consists of material of economic value, while claims to wealth are, in effect, evidence of ownership, such as a share of stock or a deed, or else claims that do not necessarily involve ownership, such as bonds, paper money, and other debt instruments. From the viewpoint of the individual the distinction between wealth and claims to wealth is not critical; the individual, in reckoning his personal wealth position, will usually count both the material items of wealth in his possession, such as a house or land, as well as intangible claims in the form of bonds, shares of stock, and money in the bank. This is a logical position as far as the individual is concerned because for any single individual both the material wealth and claims to wealth that he owns possess exchange value, and can, if necessary, be converted into purchasing power. There exist in the economy many different markets for the purchase and sale of claims to wealth. Organized security markets such as the New York Stock Exchange are a good example of the latter.

For the economy as a whole, however, the distinction betwen wealth and claims to wealth is vitally important. If we are trying to measure or get an inventory of the material wealth of the society, it would be illogical to add up all goods and all claims to goods as well. This would give us a total in which everything has been counted twice. In the economy as a whole the value of all material things would just equal the sum total of all claims possessing exchange value because every material item of wealth must be owned by an individual, a group of individuals, some type of business entity such as the corporation, or by some kind of governmental unit.

In taking inventory of the wealth of a community or the nation, there is an immensely difficult and complex problem of valuation. Wealth can be measured only if valued in some such common denominator as money. Normally items of wealth are valued in money terms as a result of their purchase and sale in a market, but for many items of wealth that ought to be included in a national inventory this method of valuation is simply not possible. What, for instance, is the value of an interstate highway? A national park or forest? Or an ancient building of great historical significance? For items of wealth such as these and, perhaps, for resources which are bought and sold only infrequently, there can only be an arbitrary judgment as to their real value.

Our discussion of the nature of wealth would not be complete without some comment on the basic categories of material wealth existing in any society. The most fundamental classification distinguishes between natural resources and resources that are man-made. In the first category we find all natural wealth, which is to say land and the values inherent in land—fertility, mineral deposits, and climatic characteristics. These things are basically "gifts of nature," even though their economic value over time may be modified by man's actions. Within the category of man-made resources it is necessary to distinguish between wealth possessed by consumers or households, which is often thought of as nonproductive, and wealth possessed by firms, which is regarded as productive (because its services are employed in the production of future output). It is not literally true, of course, that items of personal wealth—for example, automobiles, refrigerators, washing machines, and other household appliances —are nonproductive since they render services to their owners. Granted this, it is still desirable to distinguish items of consumer wealth from the society's stock of productive instruments in the form of buildings and various types of capital equipment. In determining the productive potential of any society, it is wealth in the form of productive instruments that is of critical importance. Wealth in the form of capital goods represents a dynamic and "procreative" element in modern society because the real function of such goods is to produce other goods and services.

The Concept of Human Wealth

Increasingly in recent years economists have begun to apply the wealth concept to the investment by human beings in skills and knowledge. The skills, education, and knowledge that human beings acquire is in a broad sense a form of capital that contributes in a significant way to the process of production. Professor Theodore W. Schultz, one of the foremost advocates of the idea that economic analysis should take into account human as well as material capital, points out that not only does wealth in the form of human skill and knowledge require investment for its creation, but this form of wealth has grown in Western societies at a much faster rate than other, nonhuman types of capital. Further, Professor Schultz says, the growth of human capital may be the most distinctive feature of the modern economy, contributing more to the growth of output over the long run than conventional forms of wealth.[5]

Generally, economists have avoided trying to measure investment in human capital and its contribution to output, partly because the statistical difficulties encountered in any such attempt are truly formidable, and partly, too, because of a reluctance to suggest even remotely that human beings might be looked upon as capital goods. As Professor Schultz points out, to regard human beings as capital that can be augmented by investment runs counter to deeply held values, primarily because of the long struggle of Western man to rid society of any form of slavery or indentured service.[6] In spite of these obstacles important progress is being made both with respect to refinement of the concept of human wealth and to its measurement. There seems little doubt that in the future, investment in human capital will increasingly be incorporated into the formal body of economic analysis.

Interactions of Income and Wealth

We have outlined some of the basic differences between income and wealth; it is important also to have a clear understanding of the way in which they are linked together.

The reader will recall that our fundamental definition of income from the point of view of the whole society is that of a flow of goods and services. Given this definition, a key question is: what use or disposition is made of the economy's income? The simplest answer that we can give is that whatever the economy produces in any particular period of time must either be consumed or not consumed. To consume output means, of course, to use up goods and services in the satisfaction of human wants.

---

[5] Theodore W. Schultz, "Investment in Human Capital," *American Economic Review*, March, 1961.

[6] *Ibid.*

Technically, consumption can be defined as the destruction of utilities in the process of satisfying human wants, whereas production is the creation of utilities necessary to the satisfaction of human wants. Quite obviously the bulk of income is consumed in most societies.

But what happens to the output that is not consumed during the income period in which it is produced? This output becomes an addition to the existing stock of wealth of the economy! This statement reveals the essential relationship between income and wealth; whenever current income exceeds current consumption the stock of wealth automatically is increased, and whenever current consumption is in excess of current income the stock of wealth will automatically be reduced. The relationship between the flow of income and consumption and the stock of wealth may be likened to a reservoir of water, in which the water level (that is, the stock of water) depends upon the rate at which water flows into the reservoir as compared to the rate at which water flows out of the reservoir. If the rate of inflow is greater than the rate of outflow the water level within the reservoir will rise, while if the rate of outflow is greater than the rate of inflow the water level will drop.

The relationship between output and wealth should be viewed in another way. Not only is it true that the stock of wealth is augmented when the economy does not consume all of current output, but it is also true that output is a flow that has its origins in the size, quality, and use made of the economy's stock of both material and human wealth. The act of investment (discussed below) is essential if a society is to maintain intact —or increase—its stock of wealth. Unless the society makes provision for investment, the income flow will be imperiled.

If some part of the current output of an economy is not consumed during the period in which it is produced *saving* has taken place. Two things about saving should be noted. First, saving, like income, is a flow phenomenon. The assets (real and monetary) of both a nation and an individual may increase because of saving, but this should not be confused with the act of saving itself. Second, saving is a negative act, since basically it represents the *nonconsumption* of current output.

There is, however, another facet to the nonconsumption of current output: the addition to the economy's existing stock of wealth that is the inevitable consequence of the act of saving also is defined as *investment*. In a fundamental sense investment means a net addition to the stock of wealth of the economy. As we probe further into national income measurement and analysis we shall see that it is necessary for practical reasons to modify this definition, but this does not change the important underlying idea that the act of investment always involves something *real* in the sense that it has to do with changes in the economy's stock of wealth. Another word of caution is in order here: this overly simple definition will have to be modified when we consider the difference between "net" and "gross" additions to the economy's stock of wealth.

The above comments concerning the nature of saving and investment should help make clear to the reader why in one sense saving and investment are necessarily identical. Whenever we discuss or measure saving and investment in an *ex post* [7] or after-the-fact sense, they are necessarily identical or equal. This follows from the way in which we have defined these phenomena: if some part of the economy's current output is not consumed we say that saving has taken place, but by the same token we say that this represents investment because an act of nonconsumption will add to the economy's stock of wealth. The notion that investment and saving are equal when defined in this manner is highly important in economic analysis and one the student will encounter frequently.

Basic Components of National Income

Our discussion of the relationship of income and wealth provides the conceptual basis for understanding the major categories of output and expenditure actually employed in national income measurement and analysis. Before we examine the major measures of national income and product currently constructed by the Department of Commerce, it is essential to have a clear understanding of the kinds of output that enter into these aggregates. The broad concepts discussed in the previous section must be translated into specific categories that are capable of measurement and practical use in a national income and social accounting system.

CONSUMPTION GOODS AND SERVICES (C)

In most societies the largest proportion of current output will consist of consumer goods and services. These may be defined as goods and services that are designed to satisfy human wants. The usual method for measurement of the economy's output of consumer goods and services is through adding up the expenditures made by all households and private nonprofit institutions. Beyond this it is customary in national income and social accounting to break this category down into three subcategories: expenditures for consumer durables (automobiles, household appliances, household furnishings, etc.); nondurables (mostly food and clothing); and services. (In all subsequent discussion and analysis we shall designate this particular component of the national output by the capital letter C.)

The durable goods component of consumption expenditures presents us with a problem of measurement. A durable good (like an automobile) is essentially a kind of consumer "capital" good. Typically such goods have a life span of a number of years, and their real economic value lies in the fact that they render a service to the consumer during this life span. In the case of an automobile, the service is that of transportation;

[7] For a discussion of the terms *ex post* and *ex ante*, see p. 46.

in the case of a refrigerator, that of food storage and refrigeration. Since the basic purpose of national income accounting is to measure the amount of productive activity taking place in the economy during a specific period, the logical procedure would be to count the services rendered to the consumer during each income period by a durable good, such as an automobile, as a part of the income (or output) of that income period. This logical procedure has not been followed, however, because of the impossibility of measuring statistically the rate at which the economy's enormous stock of consumer durable goods delivers services to consumers. As a result national income accountants and statisticians resort to the more convenient fiction that all consumer goods, including consumer durables, are consumed during the income period in which they are purchased. The only important exception to this procedure is consumer housing, for purchases of new houses are treated as investment rather than consumption expenditures. This point will be discussed in the following paragraph.

INVESTMENT GOODS (I)

In a broad sense the investment goods category of the national output should consist of all additions to the economy's stock of wealth; this was the basic meaning we gave to the term "investment" in our previous discussion. From the standpoint of national income and social accounting, however, it has been necessary to modify this fundamental approach, partly because it is impractical and statistically impossible to include all additions to the economy's stock of wealth in the investment goods category, and partly because it is more desirable from an economic point of view that this category be limited to additions to the economy's stock of productive wealth or capital equipment. (The capital letter I will be used in this and later chapters to designate the investment component of output.)

The usual practice in national income accounting is to measure the economy's output of investment goods by the expenditures made during the income period by the "end-users" (generally business firms) for goods of this type. The Department of Commerce classifies the following as domestic investment expenditure:

1. All purchases by business firms of new construction and durable equipment.
2. All purchases of new houses, that is, all residential construction.
3. All changes in inventories held by business firms.

The rationale for this particular structure of classification warrants explanation. The first category, producer's plant and equipment, obviously consists of additions to the economy's stock of productive instruments. It is less clear, though, why purchases of new houses should be considered as investment goods. Actually the decision to include residential construction in the investment goods category is quite arbitrary, because one could argue with justifiable logic that the purchase of a durable item like a house, which renders a service to its owner over its lifetime, is basically no different from the purchase of other durable consumer goods such as automobiles, stoves, and refrigerators. The logic of such a position would be almost irrefutable if all newly-constructed houses were sold to consumers or households. On the other hand, it would be equally logical to treat houses as a productive instrument if all houses were sold to business firms and then rented to the consumer, for in this case the house would clearly be an instrument for the provision of a service for which the consumer would pay. Actually this is what is assumed in national income accounting and measurement, even though a very large portion of the nation's houses are occupied by their owners. The basic reason for this procedure is that the much longer life of houses as compared to other consumer durables would make the fiction of the consumption of durables in the income period in which they are produced and sold quite absurd if applied to housing. The purchase of new houses, therefore, is treated as an investment expenditure in the income period in which the purchase is made, and a rent is imputed to the owner of the house in the case of owner-occupied housing during subsequent income periods. This imputed rent presumably represents the value of the service provided by the house to its owner over its useful life and thus becomes a part of the economy's output of consumption goods and services.

The inclusion of all changes in the volume of inventories held by business firms in the investment goods category is in accord with our earlier discussion of the fundamental nature of the investment process. Consumer goods, including those in process, and quantities of raw materials produced but not consumed or used up during an income period necessarily represent an addition to the economy's stock of wealth. Such goods and raw materials will, however, represent a net increase in the inventories— or stocks of goods on hand—of the business firms of the economy. Thus changes in inventories properly belong in the investment goods category of the national output.

At this point the reader may wonder what happens if the stock of all types of goods held by business firms is drawn down during an income period. If this takes place there has been *disinvestment* insofar as inventories are concerned. Whenever the net change in inventories is negative, sales are being made from stocks rather than current output. This implies that expenditures reflect not only current output but output from some previous period. Thus if we hope to measure current output by expenditures, it is necessary to deduct expenditures that represent the using up of

past output. Broadly, the process of disinvestment means that the economy has consumed more than it has produced during an income period;
consequently there will be a reduction in the economy's existing stock of
wealth. From an *ex post* viewpoint, disinvestment is conceptually identical with *dissaving,* as the latter takes place whenever current consumption
exceeds current output.

In a discussion of the investment goods category of the economy's output it is critically important to distinguish between investment that is
"gross" and investment that is "net." Once the reader understands the difference between gross and net investment, he will encounter no difficulty
in understanding the difference between gross and net output, a distinction that is of great importance in economic analysis. Basically, the term
"gross investment" refers to the total output of all goods in the investment
goods category during an income period. This total is gross because it
includes capital goods for replacement and for additions to the economy's
stock of physical wealth. Since investment goods output embraces productive wealth in the form of capital equipment, it is logical that some
part of the economy's current total output of these goods should constitute replacement for the portion of the economy's existing stock of productive wealth used up in the course of producing the current output.
The productive process requires use of capital instruments in conjunction
with other resources in order to secure an output, and whenever capital
equipment is used it will experience wear and tear. Thus, in any income
period some part of the total stock of capital equipment or productive
wealth will ultimately be exhausted and have to be replaced. The share
of the total investment goods output that serves to replace worn-out capital instruments is termed *replacement investment.* There are serious statistical problems with respect to measurement of this magnitude, but we
shall defer any discussion of these to a later point.

If we subtract from the total output of investment goods in any income
period the amount representing replacement investment, we are left with
the total, *net investment.* This total is net because, if our figure for replacement purposes is accurate, the difference between this figure and the
total must represent the amount by which the economy's total stock of
productive wealth has increased as a result of the production and disposal
of a given quantity of investment goods during the current income period. Thus, the phrase "net investment" refers to the process by which a
society increases its stock of productive capital instruments. If, during
an income period, net investment is positive, the economy will have experienced an absolute increase in its physical stock of productive wealth,
which will mean that its ability to produce goods and services will have
been enlarged. On the other hand, if net investment is negative, there has
been a reduction in the economy's total stock of productive wealth, a development that normally implies an impairment of productive capacity.

GOVERNMENT PURCHASES OF GOODS AND SERVICES (G)

Up to this point we have discussed two major categories of output: consumption goods and services, and investment goods. In general, it is the practice in national income and social accounting to measure the amount of output in each of these categories by the expenditures made during the income period by the "end-users" of each kind of output, namely households and other nonprofit institutions (if consumption goods and services are involved), and business firms (if investment goods are involved). This is possible because the bulk of the goods and services that fit into these categories are produced and sold on a private basis through the mechanism of the market; consequently, expenditure totals are a good indicator of output.

The above classification, however, is incomplete, as it leaves out a third and increasingly important category—the output of the public or government sector of the economy. The use of the word "output" in connection with the activities of government may at first glance strike the reader as somewhat strange, yet this is a perfectly appropriate and proper use of the term. The public sector of an economy produces a vast array of economically valuable goods and services, ranging from material things like highways, parks, dams, and schools to intangibles like police and fire protection, the services of judicial and postal systems, and the national defense. Output originating in the public sector differs from output originating in the private sector primarily because it has a collective or communal character. In general, the output of the public sector consists of goods and services that normally would not be produced by private firms, or if they were produced, would not be produced in sufficient quantities. Such goods and services are "collective" or "communal" in the sense that they are indivisible, which is to say that their benefits accrue to society as a whole. The individual, to be sure, benefits from their production, but only by virtue of the fact that he is a member of the society in which such goods are being produced. National defense is a case in point, for certainly all members of a nation receive some benefit, intangible though it may be, from the existence of a national defense establishment, yet there is no practical way to measure the amount of this benefit that accrues to each citizen. And if the benefit cannot be measured individually, there is no way in which the good or service can be produced or sold individually.

The basic distinction between collective and private goods and services can be seen through application of the "exclusion principle." If there is no practical way to exclude a person from obtaining the benefits of a good or service—as in the instance of national defense—the good or service is clearly collective in nature. On the other hand, if persons not willing to pay directly for the benefit are *excluded* from the use of the good or service, it is clearly of a private and individual character. The reader should note carefully that this latter point does not mean that such a good or service could not be produced and sold on an individual basis by a government unit.

Of course, not all the goods and services produced by the public sector are so clearly of a collective and indivisible character as national defense. Education, for example, could be produced and sold on an individual basis. In spite of this, the greater portion of education is produced collectively. If our system of public education were entrusted to private enterprise for production at a profit, there would not be an adequate supply of educational services. The well-being of the whole society would be endangered. The same is true with respect to other goods and services produced by the public sector, such as highways, parks and recreational areas, dams, and many different types of services. The private production and sale of such goods and services is clearly not impossible, but in most instances the social benefit would be small as compared to the benefit that results when such goods are produced on a collective basis.

In addition to their social character, goods and services produced in the public sector differ from privately produced goods and services in another important way. In the private sector of the economy output is normally disposed of by sale to the "end-user" of the output, but in the public sector the usual procedure is to distribute this output without charge to the society as a whole. Governments, in other words, do not normally "sell" on an individual basis the collective goods and services which are their responsibility to provide. This means that we cannot measure the value of the output of the public sector in the same way that we measure the value of the output of the private sector, namely by the total of expenditures made by those who purchase the different categories of output. Since the output of the government sector is distributed "free" to all or most members of the community, the only practical measure of the value of this output is in terms of what it costs to supply it to the community at large. In order for the public sector to carry out its function of providing the economy with an array of collective goods and services, it must obtain economic resources; generally, it does this either directly through the hire of labor, or indirectly through purchase of part of the output of the private sector. Therefore, the public sector's purchases of goods and services constitute the *input* of resources necessary to the output of collective goods and services. In national income and social accounting *government purchases of goods and services* is used as a measure of the portion of the total output that originates in the public sector. (It is the usual practice to designate this category of output by the capital letter G.)

Before we conclude this discussion of the public component of the national output, it is necesary to distinguish another and important type of government expenditures that does not enter into the computation of output totals. These expenditures, which occur at all levels of government, are called *transfer payments*, primarily because they involve transfers of income by the government from group to group rather than the acquisition of resources necessary to the production of governmental output. Transfer expenditures, in other words, provide income (real or monetary) to the recipients of such expenditures, but the governmental unit does not receive either goods or services in return. Old-age pensions, unemployment compensation, aid to dependent children, and various forms of aid to war veterans are common forms of transfer payments. Insofar as the national economy is concerned, interest on the public debt, as well as subsidies to business firms, are considered to be transfers. Transfer expenditures may be viewed in another way, too, for they are, in a sense, "negative" taxes. Just as the recipient of a transfer payment does not directly provide the governmental unit making the payment with an equivalent value of either goods or services in exchange, neither does the government, in collecting taxes, provide each citizen individually with an immediate and equivalent value of goods or services in exchange. Transfer expenditures, in other words, are a one-way flow of income from the government to the individual or business firm; taxes, on the other hand, are a one-way flow of income from the individual or the business firm to the government. It is in this sense that we can also speak of taxes as being "negative transfers." (In subsequent discussion in this text we shall designate transfer expenditures by the symbol TR and taxes by the symbol TX.)

NET EXPORTS (I_f)

The category of national income known as net exports is equal to the difference between a nation's exports of goods and services and its imports of goods and services. If there are no *transfers* of income to or from foreign residents, net exports may also be identified as *net foreign investment*, designated as I_f. This latter definition is subject to a number of qualifications (see Chapter 3), but for the moment it will serve as a working definition of net foreign investment. A nation's exports represent expenditures for its output that originate outside the nation's borders, while a nation's imports represent spending by its residents for output that originates in foreign countries. If a nation's exports of goods and services exceed its imports of goods and services, net foreign investment is positive. On the other hand, if imports of goods and services are in excess of exports of goods and services, net foreign investment is negative. Positive net foreign investment increases the claims of the residents of a country against residents of other countries; negative net foreign investment does the reverse.

Since we sought in our discussion up to now to link the various categories of the national output to expenditures made by "end-users" for each of these categories, it is important to understand the sense in which net exports constitutes an expenditure category. If exports of goods and services exceed imports, the difference should be counted as an addition to the other categories of expenditure, the total of which is a measure of the national output. On the other hand, if imports of goods and services exceed exports, the difference should be subtracted from the sum of the other categories of expenditure. Expenditures by the nation and its residents for imported goods and services are normally included in the other categories of expenditure, since there is no practical way to distinguish the exact portion of expenditures for imports in each category. Consequently, total expenditures by residents for imported goods and services should be deducted in order to avoid counting these expenditures twice. This will be done automatically by making the net foreign investment category negative whenever imports of goods and services exceed exports of goods and services.

Net foreign investment is similar in its economic effects to expenditure for investment goods. Expenditure leading to production of capital goods has the effect of creating money income within the economy equal to the amount of the expenditure. But there is not created in the same income period an offsetting volume of consumer goods and services, owing to the durable character of capital goods which produce value equal to their cost in the form of consumer goods only over their entire life—and that usually encompasses several income periods. An excess of exports over imports (positive net foreign investment) will have the same economic effect, because the production of goods and services for export creates money income in the national economy, but no offsetting volume of goods and services for domestic purchase is available. If imports fall short of exports, an excess of money income over the total of goods and services available for purchase during the income period exists. This excess is equal to the difference between exports and imports. On the other hand, an excess of imports over exports means that the physical volume of goods and services available for purchase by the nation and its residents is in excess of the amount of money income created by the process of producing the national output. Expenditures on imported goods and services, it may be noted, are similar in their economic effects to saving, because use of any part of current income to finance the purchase of imported goods means that a part of current income is not being spent on domestically-produced output. This is the same thing that takes place when some part of current income is saved. Thus, in an economic and conceptual sense, imports of goods and services are a counterpart of saving, whereas exports of goods and services are a counterpart of domestic investment.

Fundamental Identities among National Income Components

The manner in which the various component parts of the national output fit together can be expressed symbolically and summarized in a series of *identity equations*. An identity equation defines one variable in terms of other variables; it is an equation asserting an equality which is true by definition. Such equations are normally derived by taking a total (or aggregate) and expressing it as the sum of its parts. Identity equations are to be contrasted with *behavior equations*, which express a relationship between variables. Behavior equations are not necessarily true in the same sense as identity equations. They are a mathematical statement of an hypothesis concerning economic behavior and, consequently, the relationships involved in such equations are causal in nature. If we say, for example, that total consumption expenditures equal expenditures for consumer durables plus expenditures for consumer non-durables plus expenditures for consumer services, we would have an identity equation, because these three forms of consumer expenditure represent the component parts of the total consumer purchases of goods and services. On the other hand, if we assert in equation form that total consumption expenditures are a function of (that is, depend upon) current income, this would be a behavior equation, for it expresses a hypothesis about economic behavior, namely, total expenditures made by consumers.

For our series of identity equations that describe how the component parts of the national output fit together, we will use the following symbols:

$Y =$ the national output and income

$I =$ investment expenditures (output of investment goods)

$I_f =$ net foreign investment (net exports)

$C =$ consumption expenditures (output of consumer goods and services)

$S =$ saving

$G =$ government expenditures for goods and services (output of community or collective goods)

$X =$ export expenditures (domestic output that is exported)

$M =$ import expenditures (foreign output that is imported)

$TR =$ transfer expenditures

$TX =$ taxes

Let us start with an imaginary but highly simplified economic system which has no government and no economic ties with any other nation. In this hypothetical system the origin and disposition of income can be expressed symbolically as follows:

$$Y = C + I \tag{2-1}$$
$$Y = C + S \tag{2-2}$$

Equation (2–1) states that output (and income) has its origin in expenditures for consumption goods and services and investment goods. To put it in a different way, we can say that output consists of consumption goods and services, and investment goods. Equation (2–2), which relates to the disposition of current income, expresses the idea that income created in the productive process must be either consumed or not consumed (that is, saved). The C in Equation (2–2) also represents expenditures for consumption goods and services.

From these equations we can derive a third equation showing the identity between saving and investment. Since income and consumption are common terms in both of the above equations, it follows that investment and saving must be equal to one another. Thus

$$I = S \tag{2-3}$$

This particular identity states in symbolic terms an idea already discussed, namely that saving and investment are identical whenever we are discussing these magnitudes in an *ex post* sense. The above identities are, of course, *ex post* equations because they are descriptive of that which exists or is actual; they do not in any way describe economic behavior in an intended, planned, or *ex ante* sense. This point about the *ex post* identity of saving and investment is stressed because lack of understanding of the exact sense in which saving and investment are always equal has been a cause of serious confusion in economic thinking in the past. The reader should recognize that these two magnitudes must be identical in an *ex post* sense because of the way in which they are defined, but this does not mean that the amounts saved and the amounts invested in the economy in any specific income period always coincide with the amounts that firms or persons intended to save and invest. The latter is an entirely different matter, which we will analyze thoroughly at a later point in the text.

We can proceed closer to reality in the development of our identity equations by dropping the assumption of an economy without a government. We will retain for the moment, however, the assumption that our economy has no relationships with other economies; in other words, it is a "closed" economy. Let us assume, too, that the only function of our government is to provide for collective or communal goods and services; it does not, therefore, engage in transfer expenditures. On the basis of this set of assumptions we would have the following identities:

$$Y = C + I + G \tag{2-4}$$
$$Y = C + S + TX \tag{2-5}$$

$$S + TX = I + G \qquad (2\text{--}6)$$
$$S = I + (G - TX) \qquad (2\text{--}7)$$

Equation (2–4) means that output consists of consumption goods and services, investment goods, and collective goods, or that output has its origin in expenditures by consumers or households, by business firms, and by governmental units. Equation (2–5) relates to the disposition of income, and shows that with the introduction of government a third alternative is now available for the disposition of current income, namely taxes. The economic effect of taxes is similar to saving because taxes also represent a nonexpenditure of current income for consumption goods and services.

Equation (2–6) is a modification of the saving-investment identity. It is made necessary by the introduction of government expenditures and taxes. Saving plus taxes, both of which are "leakages" from the current income stream, are equal to investment plus government expenditures for goods and services. Investment and government expenditures are off-sets to leakages in the form of saving and taxes. Equation (2–7) is a fur-ther modification of the above identity, for if taxes are transferred to the right-hand side of the equation, it means that saving is equal to in-vestment *plus* the government deficit or *minus* the government surplus.

The terms "deficit" and "surplus" as used here do not in any way refer to the budgetary situation of the Federal government. Rather, these terms refer to the current income and product transactions of all governmental units in the economy. For example, if the current expenditures of the public sector for goods and services are in excess of total taxes collected then the public sector has incurred a deficit on its income and product transactions. Insofar as the public sector is concerned, dissaving has taken place because governmental units have spent more than their income, the latter being derived from taxation. If $G - TX$ is placed on the right-hand side of Equation (2–7), it must be positive, because the total saving of the economy must cover investment expenditure plus the amount of the deficit of the public sector.

On the other hand, if the tax collections of the public sector are in excess of the current expenditures of governmental units, then there is a surplus in the income and product transactions of the public sector. This would be a form of governmental saving, for expenditures are less than current receipts. Again if $G - TX$ is placed on the right-hand side of the same equation, it should be negative, as the total saving, S, of the economy is now less than investment expenditure and must be augmented by governmental saving.

We are now able to drop the last of the simplifying assumptions with which we started our discussion, namely the assumptions of a "closed" economy and of no transfer expenditures. When we drop these assumptions, our structure of identity equations becomes realistic, describing accurately how the component parts of the national output fit together. Consequently, we now have the following series of identity equations.

$$Y = C + I + G + X - M \qquad (2\text{-}8)$$
$$I_f = X - M \qquad (2\text{-}9)$$
$$Y = C + I + G + I_f \qquad (2\text{-}10)$$
$$Y = C + S + TX - TR \qquad (2\text{-}11)$$
$$S + TX - TR = I + G + I_f \qquad (2\text{-}12)$$
$$S = I + G + I_f - (TX - TR) \qquad (2\text{-}13)$$

Equation (2–8) is essentially the same as Equation (2–4), except that we have now added expenditures for exports and subtracted expenditures for imports. Since the difference between exports and imports is equal to net foreign investment, as in Equation (2–9), the basic identity equation describing the origin of output and income takes the form shown in Equation (2–10).[8] The existence of transfer expenditures means that we must modify the equation describing the disposition of income to take such transfers into account. This is done in Equation (2–11), in which transfer expenditures are subtracted from taxes. Since transfers are, in effect, "negative taxes," they offset taxes as a leakage from the current income stream. Moreover, once we have introduced transfers into the system, they must be deducted from the components on the right-hand side of the disposition of income equation, or else they would be counted twice. This is the case because transfer expenditures are income to the recipients of such expenditures, and as such can be a source of consumption expenditures, saving, or tax payments just as much as income derived from the process of production. Thus, transfer expenditures will be reflected in consumption, saving, and taxes, in Equation (2–11), showing the disposition of current income.

Finally, the basic saving-investment identity is modified to take into account net foreign investment, which offsets not only saving and taxes in the same manner as investment and government expenditures, but also the effect of transfer expenditures, on the deficit or surplus of the public sector with respect to income and product transactions. Thus, saving plus *net* taxes $(TX - TR)$ is equal to investment plus net foreign investment and government expenditures for goods and services in Equation (2–12). If net taxes are shifted to the right-hand side of this equation, the basic identity equation relating saving and investment takes the form shown in Equation (2–13).[9]

[8] This assumes no *transfers* to or from the rest of the world.
[9] See Appendix for verification of the identities for an "open system" by use of actual national income and product data.

APPENDIX

Systems of National Income and Social Accounting

As pointed out in this chapter, national income and social accounting systems have as their primary function provision of statistical information relating to the performance of the economy. In actuality, most systems of national income and social accounting do not limit themselves to a single format for presenting data on the economy's performance. The term "national income and social accounting" refers to a variety of bodies of systematically arranged statistical data that measure various aspects of the nation's economic activity. In this Appendix we summarize briefly some of the major schemes for presenting statistical data that are included within the broad framework of national income and social accounting.

NATIONAL INCOME AND PRODUCT ACCOUNTS

These accounts are concerned with the flow of income and product through the economy and are designed to show in monetary terms the amount of productive activity that has taken place during a particular period of time. The accounts included in this category are double-entry in their construction, which is the common ingredient in all accounting systems. These accounts seek to show the sources and disposition of income (and product) for the domestic economy's major sectors, namely households, enterprises, and governmental units.

The Department of Commerce system includes five separate accounts in this part of the United States' over-all national income and social accounting system. These are (1) a national income and product account, showing totals of income and output resulting from productive activity during a period; (2) a personal income and outlay account, showing total income and expenditures of households in the economy; (3) a government receipts and expenditures account, showing total receipts and expenditures by all governmental units in the economy; (4) a foreign transactions account, showing purchases by foreign nations from the United States and United States' purchases from foreign nations; and (5) a gross saving and investment account, which shows the saving of the whole economy and the disposition made of that saving. From these accounts we can derive such highly important and widely-used single indicators of economic performance as gross national product, national income, and personal income.

FLOW-OF-FUNDS ACCOUNTS

Flow-of-funds accounting is a relatively recent development; its objective is the systematic presentation of data pertaining to all monetary and credit transactions taking place within the economy during a specified period of time. Flow-of-funds accounting provides a detailed picture of both the origin and use of money and credit in the economy. Flow-of-funds accounts are broader in scope than national income and product accounts because they embrace not only income and product transactions, but also purely financial transactions, such as the purchase and sale of various kinds of securities and the expansion and contraction of bank credit. The procedure in flow-of-funds accounting is to divide the economy into sectors, showing for each sector the source and use of all funds during the accounting period. The first detailed flow-of-funds statement was published by the Board of Governors of the Federal Reserve System in the October, 1955 issue of the *Federal Reserve Bulletin*. The Federal Reserves prepares these data annually for publication in the *Federal Reserve Bulletin*.

INPUT-OUTPUT TABLES

Input-output analysis and construction of input-output tables are an elaboration and refinement of national income and product accounting. Such tables concern themselves with the current productive activities of the economy in much the same manner as national income and product accounts, but they focus attention on inter-industry relationships by measuring the flow of output between the major industrial subdivisions of the economy. Specifically, input-output analysis breaks the economy down into its major producing segments and shows how the output of one industry becomes the input of the other industries. Presentation of the data in input-output analysis is in the form of a matrix, a square-like arrangement in which the same industries are listed across the top and down one side, thus making it possible to see at a glance the disposition of the output of one industry, or how the same industry draws its inputs from the outputs of other segments of the economy.

BALANCE-OF-PAYMENTS ACCOUNTING

Balance-of-payments accounting records the outcome of all transactions —income and product as well as financial—between the residents of one country and the residents of the rest of the world. Balance-of-payments accounting is thus typically broader than the foreign account included in the system of national income and product accounts, for the latter is primarily limited to transactions involving goods and services. Balance-of-payments accounting, however, includes all international transactions, including those that are of a purely financial character. In this respect it is similar to flow-of-funds accounting, except that it is limited to transactions between nations rather than within nations. In the United States, balance-of-payments data are compiled and published by the Balance-of-Payments Division of the Department of Commerce.

NATIONAL BALANCE SHEET ACCOUNTING

This is the direction in which national income and social accounting is presently moving, although as of now a complete and unified system for the presentation of a balance sheet for the whole economy has not been perfected. National balance sheet accounting would attempt to show for various sectors of the economy both the tangible and intangible assets of these sectors, as well as their liabilities and equities. In such a system the breakdown of the economy into sectors would probably parallel the breakdown in the flow-of-funds accounting system because there is an extremely close relationship between the origin and use of money and credit in the economy and changes in the asset and liability position of different segments of the economy. As of now, national balance sheet accounting is an expected development—rather than a functioning component—of the nation's system of national income and social accounting.

The foregoing discussion aims to convey to the reader some idea of the breadth and complexity of the structure of national income and social accounting in a modern economy. This structure, moreover, is by no means completed. It is constantly evolving in the direction of greater comprehensiveness to provide a more complete source of information concerning what is happening in the economy.

Current Data and Identity Equations in an Open Economy

The identity equations that pertain to an "open" economy with transfers may be verified by "fitting" to them actual data from the national income and product accounts for the United States for 1964. First, we have the equation for the origin of gross national product:

$$Y = C + I + G + X - M \qquad \text{(A2-1)}$$
$$\$628.7 = \$398.9 + \$92.9 + \$128.4 + \$37.0 - \$28.5 \qquad \text{(A2-2)}$$

These data are in billions of dollars in 1964 prices and are obtained from the *Survey of Current Business*.

The equation describing the disposition of the gross national product (Equation 2–11) needs to be modified slightly to take into account the fact of transfers to *foreign* residents, both by persons and by governments. Such transfers represent another alternative in addition to taxes and saving for the disposition of income. Thus:

$$Y = C + S + T_n + TR_f \qquad \text{(A2-3)}$$

In the above equation T_n is equal to *net* taxes and is the difference between total taxes TX and domestic transfers TR. Transfers to foreigners are represented by the symbol TR_f.

When the data for 1964 are fitted to this identity showing the disposition of the gross national product, we have:

$$\$628.7 = \$398.9 + \$101.6 + \$126.0 + \$2.8 \qquad (A2-4)$$

There is a statistical discrepancy in the actual data of $0.6, which must be subtracted from the right-hand side of the equation to attain balance. The basic saving investment (Equation 2–13) identity now becomes:

$$S = I + I_f + G - T_n \qquad (A2-5)$$

In the above equation I_f is equal to the difference between exports X and imports M plus transfers to foreign residents TR_f.

With 1964 data fitted to the equation, we now have:

$$\$101.6 = \$92.9 + \$5.7 + \$2.4 \qquad (A2-6)$$

The statistical discrepancy of $0.6 may be subtracted from the left-hand total for saving to attain balance. This equation shows that in 1964 there was a deficit on the income and product transactions of the public sector, which is an offset to saving.

3 | The Measurement of National Income and Product

In the last chapter we analyzed the fundamental concepts that underlie most systems of national income and social accounting. We turn now to discussion of a series of specific measures of national income and product that are used extensively, not only in the American economy, but in most other nations as well. While the techniques of national income and product measurement described in this chapter are those developed and employed by the Department of Commerce in the United States, they are similar to the techniques utilized by other nations. In general, systems for national income and product measurement differ more in detail than in substance.

Our analysis of national income and social accounting in the United States begins with discussion of the national income aggregates that are the best-known of all measures of national income, and which, further, are in wide use as indicators of the economy's performance. Specifically, the five aggregate measures we will discuss are: (1) gross national product; (2) net national product; (3) national income; (4) personal income; and (5) disposable income. The first three of these are measures of both product and money income flows, while the latter two are measures of money income flows only.

Gross National Product

Gross national product, also called gross national income or gross national expenditure, is the best known and most widely used of the various statistical measures developed to gauge the economy's performance. It is defined as *the current market value of all final goods and services produced by the economy during an income period.* The normal income period for most national income and social accounting systems, including that of the United States, is the calendar year. As an expenditure total, gross national product (or GNP as it is usually called) represents the total purchases of goods and services by consumers and governments, gross private domestic investment, and net foreign investment. As an income total, GNP shows both the total income created as a result of current productive activity and the allocation of this income. The output total included in the GNP figure is described as "gross" because it does not take into account capital goods that have been consumed or worn out during the process of production. It is termed "national" because it refers to the productive activities of the nationals of a particular nation, including the contribution to current output of property resources owned by these nationals. Table 3–1 shows GNP data for the United States for the period 1929–1965.[1]

Final and Intermediate Goods and Services

In defining GNP, we stated that it is a measure of the economy's output of final goods and services during an income period. In national income and social accounting, it is necessary to distinguish between *final goods and services*, which are the end products of the economy, and *intermediate goods and services*, which normally are thought of as goods and services purchased for resale. We must make this distinction to avoid double-counting. Intermediate goods and services enter into the production of final goods and services. Therefore, if we added up expenditures for final goods and services as well as expenditures for intermediate goods and services, we would count the same goods and services twice. This would give us an exaggerated total for GNP. For example, the production of bread involves several stages and several transactions. Wheat is produced by the farmer and sold to the miller, who in turn processes the wheat and produces flour, which is sold to the baker, who uses it to produce bread. In this simple example wheat and flour are clearly intermediate products, whose value will be reflected in the value of the final product, bread. This being the case, it would be an error to add separately the value of the wheat produced by the farmer, the value of the flour produced by the miller, and the value of the bread produced by the baker.

There is no exact rule by means of which we can clearly determine whether a good or a service is an intermediate or final product. In our example, flour is an intermediate product because it is sold to the baker for further processing. But if flour were sold directly to a housewife it would be classified as a final product, since the housewife is the ultimate user of the product (as contrasted to the baker, who clearly is not the

---

[1] As an identity equation *GNP* or *Y* equals $C + I + G + X - M$.

ultimate user). In order to distinguish between intermediate and final products in national income measurement, the Department of Commerce has adopted the working definition that a final product is one that is not

TABLE 3–1.

Gross National Product or Expenditure, 1929–1965
(in billions of current dollars)

Year	Personal Consumption Expenditure	Gross Private Domestic Investment	Government Purchases of Goods and Services	Net Exports of Goods and Services	Gross National Product
1929	71.2	16.2	8.5	1.1	103.1
1930	69.9	10.3	9.2	1.0	90.4
1931	60.5	5.6	9.2	0.5	75.8
1932	48.6	1.0	8.1	0.4	58.0
1933	45.8	1.4	8.0	0.4	55.6
1934	51.3	3.3	9.8	0.6	65.0
1935	55.7	6.4	10.0	0.1	72.2
1936	61.9	8.5	12.0	0.1	82.5
1937	66.5	11.8	11.9	0.3	90.4
1938	63.9	6.5	13.0	1.3	84.7
1939	66.8	9.3	13.3	1.1	90.5
1940	70.8	13.1	14.0	1.7	99.7
1941	80.6	17.9	24.8	1.3	124.5
1942	88.5	9.8	59.6	0.0	157.9
1943	99.3	5.7	88.6	−2.0	191.6
1944	108.3	7.1	96.5	−1.8	210.1
1945	119.7	10.6	82.3	−0.6	212.0
1946	143.4	30.6	27.0	7.5	208.5
1947	160.7	34.0	25.1	11.5	231.3
1948	173.6	46.0	31.6	6.4	257.6
1949	176.8	35.7	37.8	6.1	256.5
1950	191.0	54.1	37.9	1.8	284.8
1951	206.3	59.3	59.1	3.7	328.4
1952	216.7	51.9	74.7	2.2	345.5
1953	230.0	52.6	81.6	0.4	364.6
1954	236.5	51.7	74.8	1.8	364.8
1955	254.4	67.4	74.2	2.0	398.0
1956	266.7	70.0	78.6	4.0	419.2
1957	281.4	67.9	86.1	5.7	441.1
1958	290.1	60.9	94.2	2.2	447.3
1959	311.2	75.3	97.0	0.1	483.7
1960	325.2	74.8	99.6	4.1	503.6
1961	335.2	71.7	107.6	5.6	520.1
1962	355.1	83.0	117.1	5.1	560.3
1963	375.0	87.1	122.5	5.9	590.5
1964	401.4	93.0	128.9	8.5	631.7
1965	431.5	106.6	136.2	7.0	681.2

SOURCES: U.S. Department of Commerce, *Survey of Current Business*, August, 1965, July, 1966. *Note:* Details may not add to totals because of rounding.

resold, while an intermediate product is one that is purchased with the normal intention that it be resold.[2] Thus, in the example cited, wheat sold to the miller and flour sold to the baker constitute intermediate products, because in both instances the products will be resold, although in altered form. Bread purchased by the housewife normally will not be resold and therefore can be considered a final product.

Monetary Transactions and Productive Activity

Since GNP is a measure of productive activity, the basic technique for its measurement is through the summation of all monetary transactions that reflect productive activity. There is a problem here, for as pointed out in Chapter 2 some monetary transactions do not represent current productive activity, while certain types of productive activity, on the other hand, will not show up in any monetary transaction. The most common monetary transactions that are not measures of current output are: (1) those involving the purchase and sale of used or second-hand goods, because such goods constitute part of the output of a previous income period (2) those involving purchase and sale of various financial instruments, such as bonds and equities; and (3) transfer payments, both public and private. All of these transactions should be excluded from any monetary measure of current productive activity.

For productive activity not reflected in a monetary transaction, the housewife's activities can again serve as an example. If she bakes her own bread, no monetary transaction reflecting the sale of a final product is involved, although there will be such a transaction if she buys her bread in the bakery or grocery shop. Yet in both instances productive activity has taken place. The same sort of thing takes place if a householder chooses to paint his own house rather than hire a professional painter to do the job. When the householder paints his house, productive activity occurs that is not reflected in the current GNP. But if he hires a painter, the resulting productive activity involves a monetary transaction and hence appears in the current output figures.

Ideally, GNP should be a measure of all current productive activity in the economy, irrespective of whether the activity is reflected in a market transaction. But as a practical matter it is quite impossible to measure with any degree of statistical accuracy the total value of all the "do-it-yourself" type of productive activity and other non-market transactions that occur in the economy. The United States Department of Commerce limits its data to "economic production." The basic criterion used for classifying an activity as "economic production" is whether it is reflected in the sales and purchase transactions of the market economy. The only exception to this is that the Department of Commerce makes estimates of certain income and product flows that are not reflected in trans-

[2] U.S. Department of Commerce, *National Income*, 1954, p. 30.

actions in the market. The most important of these *imputations* (estimates of non-market production) are wages and salaries paid in kind rather than money, fuel and food produced and consumed on the farm, and the rental value of owner-occupied homes.[3] Aside from these imputations, the Department of Commerce does not attempt to measure and record productive activity that is of a non-market character. The decision as to what non-market production ought to be included in national income and product measures is necessarily an arbitrary one, for there is no logical reason, for example, to include the rental value of owner-occupied homes and to exclude the value of the labor of the housewife.

An Alternative Technique for Measuring Gross National Product

An alternative approach to the measurement of GNP is through a summation of "charges" against the output total or, in other words, through the allocation of the gross income created in the process of producing the economy's current output of final goods and services. ("Allocations" and "charges" are different names for what is basically the same technique of measurement.)

Table 3–2 summarizes the two techniques by which GNP can be measured. The right-hand side of the table shows the *expenditure* or *flow-of-product* approach to the measurement of gross output. It is a summation of expenditures for the four major categories of goods and services produced by the economy during the income period. The left-hand side of the table represents the *charges* or *allocations* approach to the measurement of output. It summarizes the total of charges levied against the income total, or shows the allocation of the total income.

Contemporary national income and social accounting practice recognizes three *major* types of charges against the value of GNP. The first of these are *factor costs* or *income charges*, which consists of income received by the owners of economic resources in the form of wages, salaries, and other kinds of employee compensation; rents; interest payments; and profits. The other two are *non-income charges* and consist of capital consumption allowances and indirect business taxes.

FACTOR COSTS

Basically, factor costs consist of necessary payments that have to be made in either money or kind in order to secure the services of the factors of production. The utilization of the services of these factors makes possible the production of goods and services. Items (1) through (7) in Table 3–2 are the factor costs for the gross national product of the American economy in 1965. Each of these is explained as follows:

Compensation of employees consists primarily of all wages and salaries and income in kind paid in return for the services of labor and, in addi-

[3] *Ibid.*

TABLE 3–2.

Sources and Allocations of the Gross National Product, 1965
(in billions of current dollars)

Allocations of Gross National Product		Origins of Gross National Product	
1. Compensation of employees	392.9	1. Personal consumption expenditures	431.5
2. Proprietors' income	55.7	2. Gross private domestic investment	106.6
3. Corporate profits tax liability	31.2		
4. Dividends	19.2		
5. Undistributed profits *	23.8	3. Government purchases of goods and services	136.2
6. Rental income of persons	18.3		
7. Net interest	17.8	4. Net exports of goods and services	7.0
National income	559.0		
8. Indirect business taxes	62.7		
9. Business transfer payments	2.6		
10. *Less:* Subsidies less current surplus of government enterprises	1.0		
11. Statistical discrepancy	−1.6		
Net National Product	**621.6**		
12. Capital consumption allowances	59.6		
Gross National Product	**681.2**	**Gross National Product**	**681.2**

* Includes Inventory Valuation Adjustment

source: U.S. Department of Commerce, *Survey of Current Business*, July, 1966. Details may not add to total because of rounding.

tion, certain supplements to wages and salaries. These latter are contributions made by employers under the social security system (contributions by employees are included in the figure for wages and salaries), employer contributions to private pension plans, and various minor forms of labor income, such as compensation for injuries and pay for individuals in the military reserve.

Proprietors' income is a measure of the monetary earnings and income in kind accruing to all unincorporated business enterprises in the economy. This item is primarily a measure of the profits of sole proprietorships, partnerships, and producer co-operatives.

Corporate profits tax liability consists of the total of federal and state taxes levied against the earnings of all corporations in the economy.

Dividends represent the amount of corporation profits paid out to shareholders during the current income period.

Undistributed profits constitute the part of corporate profits neither paid out to the shareholders as dividends nor collected as taxes by Federal and state governments. The sum of this item and the previous two items gives total corporate profits in the income period.

Rental income of persons equals the money income received by persons from the rental of real property, such as buildings and land.

Net interest is a measure of income in the form of interest payments received by individuals in the economy, with the exception of interest payments by government (Federal, state, and local), and by consumers. The Department of Commerce states that interest on the public debt and interest paid by consumers are not a part of current production; hence they should not be treated as a factor cost.

It may be noted that the sum of Items (1) through (7) in Table 3–2 is labeled national income. This is so because, fundamentally, the term "national income" refers to the factor costs of the goods and services produced by the economy. We shall discuss this particular measure in more detail shortly.

NON-INCOME CHARGES

Indirect business taxes constitute a second major charge against GNP, although they differ from factor costs in that such taxes are a non-income charge. What, specifically, are indirect business taxes? The Department of Commerce regards all taxes levied on business firms with the exception of corporate income taxes as indirect taxes.[4] These taxes are called indirect because it is assumed they are treated by business firms as a part of the cost of doing business; thus they will be included in the sale price of final goods and services produced. If such taxes are shifted forward, as the Department of Commerce assumes, they will be reflected in the expenditure totals for the various component parts of GNP and, consequently, they must appear, too, on the allocations side of current GNP. But the total of indirect taxes cannot appear as a factor cost because they accrue to the government, and it is not the present practice in United States national income and social accounting procedures to treat government as a factor of production. The major types of taxes included in this category of non-income charges are sales taxes, excises, and real property taxes paid by business firms.

Capital consumption allowances, a third type of charge against GNP, ideally should measure the physical wearing-out of capital equipment during the year. Capital goods are a part of the economy's stock of productive resources and their use in the productive process will inevitably entail a gradual wearing-out of such assets. The amount by which the economy's stock of real capital has been used-up (or "consumed") during the current income period is what we try to measure through capital consumption allowances. Like indirect business taxes, these allowances are a non-income charge against the output totals.

It is the practice of the Department of Commerce to measure capital consumption allowances by the sum of depreciation charges by private business firms against their current incomes, plus accidental damage to fixed capital occurring during the income period. The basic difficulty

[4] *Ibid.,* p. 33.

with this procedure is that charges by the business firm for depreciation do not accurately reflect the physical wearing-out of capital goods, for the purpose of depreciation charges from an accounting viewpoint is to allow the individual producer to maintain intact the money value of his equipment. For the most part allowances made by the business firm for depreciation are based on various arbitrary formulas that have little relationship to either the actual physical life of the asset or its use in any particular year. In spite of these deficiencies, the Department of Commerce continues to use business charges for depreciation as the best available measure at the present time of the economy's consumption of real capital during the income period.

Before we discuss the other four national income aggregates that along with GNP make up the five-family series of national income and product measures, two additional and quite minor charges against the output totals must be explained. These appear in Table 3–2 as the items "Business transfer payments," and "Subsidies less current surplus of government enterprises." Business transfer payments are transfers from business to persons; they embody charges against the output total for which no return in the form of factor income is received. Most consist of corporate gifts to nonprofit institutions and consumer bad debts. "Subsidies less current surplus of government enterprises" is really a combined entry. In moving from national income to GNP in Table 3–2, it is necessary to deduct subsidies from the national income total. They are factor costs on the assumption that they constitute a form of payment necessary to secure the services of particular factors, although they are not reflected in the market price of final goods and services. The current surplus— or profit—of government enterprise is not, on the other hand, a factor cost, because government is not regarded as a factor of production; yet the value of goods and services produced by government enterprise and sold through normal market channels will be reflected in the value of final product totals. Electric power produced and sold by a municipal power and light plant is an example of this type of entry. It is the current practice of the Department of Commerce to combine these two relatively minor charges against the output totals into a single item on the allocations side of GNP.

Other Measures of Product and Income

We have devoted a relatively large amount of space to discussion of GNP not only because it is the most widely-used national income aggregate, but also because it is the best point of departure for consideration and understanding of the other aggregates that make up the Department of Commerce's five-family series of national income and product measures.

Net National Product

Net national product is defined by the Department of Commerce as the market value of the *net* output of final goods and services produced by the economy during the relevant income period.[5] In a theoretical sense it is a measure of the nation's output after allowance has been made for the consumption of capital in the current process of production. NNP is derived by subtracting capital consumption allowances from GNP. If business reserves for depreciation and the other items that enter into capital consumption allowances accurately reflected the real depreciation of the nation's stock of physical capital, net national product would accurately measure the amount of output that the nation could use for consumption, for the public sector, or for adding to the existing stock of capital without any impairment of productive capacity because of a failure to provide for the replacement of consumed items of real capital. Unfortunately, though, existing measurement techniques do not permit an accurate measurement of real capital consumption, so the net national product figure is not widely used.

National Income

We have already defined national income as the sum of the factor costs incurred during production of the economy's current output. More specifically, the Department of Commerce defines national income as the aggregate earnings of labor and property which arise from the production of goods and services by the nation's economy.[6] This measure is also described as the *net national product at factor cost* because it is a measure of the factor costs of the net output total. The national income is a concept of fundamental importance; it represents for the economy as a whole the amount of income earned by the owners of economic resources (land, labor, and capital) in return for supplying the services of these resources to the productive units of the economy. As such, it is the major source of money income or spending power for the purchase of the bulk of the national output. The national income figure can be derived either by summing up the total of factor costs incurred in producing the current output, or by deducting indirect business taxes and the other minor charges from the net national product total. It should be noted that the national income is both a measure of product (in the sense that it represents the factor cost of the current output) and a measure of money income earned by the factors of production.

Personal Income

Although the national income aggregate is a measure of income earned by the owners of economic resources through participation in the pro-

[5] *Ibid.*, p. 56.
[6] *Ibid.*

ductive process, it does not measure money income actually received by persons and households during the current income period. The reason is that some parts of earned (or factor) income are not actually received as money income by persons or households, while some households and persons receive money income that is not earned through supplying the services of economic resources to the productive process. The latter consists of transfer payments and interest income from consumers and government. The Department of Commerce defines personal income as the current income received by persons from all sources, including transfer income from government and business.[7] It is normally measured on a before-tax basis, except for individual contributions to social insurance.

The usual procedure for obtaining the personal income measure is to deduct from national income the major categories of earned (or factor) income that are not actually received as money income by persons or households, and then add to this figure the total of transfer incomes received from both government and business. The major deductions are: (1) contributions to social insurance; (2) corporate profits tax liability; and (3) undistributed corporate profit. The chief forms of government transfer payments which must be added in are: (1) interest on the public debt; (2) pensions paid to retired persons; (3) unemployment compensation; (4) various forms of relief payments; and (5) benefits extended to war veterans.

Disposable Income

The final, widely-used measure of income is that of disposable income, which the Department of Commerce defines simply as the income remaining to individuals after deduction of all taxes levied against their income and their property by all governmental entities in the economy.[8] It is obtained by deducting such taxes from the personal income total, and it represents a measure of the after-tax purchasing power at the disposal of persons or households.

Table 3–3 shows the relationships between the above five measures for selected years since 1929. This table should be studied carefully, for one can readily trace from the data some of the vicissitudes of the American economy during the past several decades. These range from the collapse of the depression years, and the vast surge of growth during World War II, to the long postwar expansion.

Price Indexes and Comparisons over Time

The practice of the Department of Commerce is to report the money value of national income and product statistics in terms of the prices pre-

[7] *Ibid.*
[8] *Ibid.*

TABLE 3–3.

National Income and Product Measures: Selected Years, 1929–1965
(billions of current dollars)

	1929	1933	1935	1939	1941	1944	1945	1948	1952	1956	1960	1965
Gross National Product	**103.1**	**55.6**	**72.2**	**90.5**	**124.5**	**210.1**	**212.0**	**257.6**	**345.5**	**419.2**	**503.6**	**681.2**
Less: Capital consumption allowances	7.9	7.0	6.9	7.3	8.2	11.0	11.3	14.5	23.2	34.1	43.4	59.6
Equals: **Net National Product**	**95.2**	**48.6**	**65.4**	**83.3**	**116.3**	**199.1**	**200.7**	**243.0**	**322.2**	**385.2**	**460.3**	**621.6**
Less: Indirect business taxes *	7.4	8.3	8.2	10.7	12.1	16.5	19.2	18.8	30.9	34.4	45.8	62.6
Equals: **National Income**	**86.8**	**40.3**	**57.2**	**72.6**	**104.2**	**182.6**	**181.5**	**224.2**	**291.4**	**350.8**	**414.5**	**559.0**
Less: Social security taxes	0.2	0.3	0.3	2.1	2.8	5.0	6.2	5.3	8.6	12.6	20.7	29.2
Corporate income taxes	1.4	0.5	1.0	1.4	7.6	12.9	10.7	12.5	19.4	21.7	23.0	31.2
Undistributed corporate profits †	3.3	−3.7	−0.4	1.1	3.2	6.2	3.8	13.4	12.0	13.2	13.4	23.8
Plus: Transfer payments	1.5	2.1	2.4	3.0	3.1	3.6	6.1	11.2	13.0	18.5	28.5	39.7
Interest paid by government and consumers	2.5	1.6	1.7	1.9	2.2	3.3	4.2	6.1	8.1	11.2	15.1	20.6
Equals: **Personal Income**	**85.9**	**47.0**	**60.4**	**72.8**	**96.0**	**165.3**	**171.1**	**210.2**	**272.5**	**330.0**	**400.9**	**535.1**
Less: Personal tax payments	2.6	1.5	1.9	2.4	3.3	18.9	20.7	21.1	34.1	39.8	50.9	66.0
Equals: **Disposable Income**	**83.3**	**45.5**	**58.5**	**70.3**	**92.7**	**146.3**	**150.2**	**189.1**	**238.3**	**293.2**	**350.0**	**469.1**

* Includes: Business Transfer Payments, Subsidies Less Current Surplus of Government Enterprises, and Statistical Discrepancy.

† Includes: Inventory Valuation Adjustment.

SOURCES: U.S. Department of Commerce, Survey of Current Business, August, 1965, July, 1966. Details may not add to totals because of rounding.

vailing during the reporting period. Thus, GNP data for 1965 are reported in prices of 1965. If we are only interested in the statistics of income or output for a particular year, this does not create a special problem; but if we want to make comparisons between a number of years, then it is necessary to correct for changes in the general level of prices. This must be done because changes in the monetary value of product totals may result from either a change in the physical quantity of production or a change in the prices at which physical output is valued. The latter type of change is a distortion insofar as comparisons over time are concerned. If such comparisons are to be used meaningfully, it is desirable that we compare *real* changes rather than changes in value due to changes in price. Thus, the effect of price-level changes must be eliminated if income and product data for different years are to reflect real changes.

The procedure for eliminating the effect of price-level changes from income and product data is to divide the data valued in current prices by an appropriate price index. This has the effect of converting the data to a constant-price basis, thus making possible comparisons of real changes over time. While the problem of constructing an appropriate index of prices is complex, the basic principles involved are relatively simple. For our purposes it is only necessary to have an understanding of the underlying rationale of the process for converting data valued in current prices into data valued in constant prices.

An index of prices is a device for comparing the amount by which either one or more prices have changed over a specific period of time. Some specific year is selected as the *base year* (specific point of reference). Prices in all other years are measured as a percentage of the price in this base year. For example, if the price of wheat in 1950—our assumed base year—was $1.00 per bushel, and we found that in 1965 the price of wheat had risen to $1.50 per bushel, it would be correct to say that the price of wheat in 1965 is 150 per cent of the price in the base year, 1950. Thus, the price index for wheat in 1965 is 150 since the price index in the base year must be 100, that is, 100 per cent. The problem is infinitely more complex when a larger number of prices is involved, although again the technique for the construction of the price index is basically the same. If an index of the general level of prices is to be constructed, it is necessary to *weight* the various individual prices that enter into the general price level in accordance with their relative importance. Unless this is done, the resulting price index will not accurately reflect relative or percentage changes in the general level of all prices. For the construction of such a complex index as that of the general price level the two most important problems are, first, selection of the individual items (and their prices) that are to be included in the index and, second, assignment of the proper weights to each of the individual items that make up the index.

Once these steps have been taken the remaining problem is simply that of selecting the proper mathematical technique for computation of the actual index.

The underlying reason for dividing data valued in current prices by a price index in order to get data valued in constant prices can be explained by means of an example. Let us assume that we want to convert GNP data for 1965 to 1958 prices in order that we can compare the actual physical change in GNP between these two dates. Since by definition GNP is a measure of the monetary value of the current output,

$$GNP_{1965} = O_{1965} \times P_{1965} \qquad (3\text{--}1)$$

This equation means that the value of current 1965 output is equal to the actual output (O) times the prices (P) at which the output is sold in that year. From our prior discussion of price indexes, it also follows that the index of prices for 1965, using 1958 as the base year, is equal to the ratio of 1965 prices to 1958 prices. Thus

$$\text{Price index for } 1965 = \frac{P_{1965}}{P_{1958}} \qquad (3\text{--}2)$$

If we divide the GNP data for 1965 by the above price index, the result will be a measure of the physical output of 1965 valued in the prices of 1958. The following equations show algebraically why this is true.

$$\frac{GNP_{1965}}{\dfrac{P_{1965}}{P_{1958}}} = \frac{P_{1965} \times O_{1965}}{\dfrac{P_{1965}}{P_{1958}}} \qquad (3\text{--}3)$$

From Equation (3–3) it follows that

$$\frac{GNP_{1965}}{\dfrac{P_{1965}}{P_{1958}}} = (P_{1965} \times O_{1965}) \times \frac{P_{1958}}{P_{1965}} \qquad (3\text{--}4)$$

In Equation (3–4) the two expressions for 1965 prices, P_{1965}, on the right-hand side cancel out, and thus we have

$$\frac{GNP_{1965}}{\dfrac{P_{1965}}{P_{1958}}} = O_{1965} \times P_{1958} \qquad (3\text{--}5)$$

By dividing GNP measured in current (1965) prices by the current (1965) price index, the GNP data are converted to a figure which values the current output in prices for a selected base year. Table 3–4 shows the United States GNP in both current and constant dollars (or prices) for selected years since 1929. The table also includes in Column (3) the price indexes used to deflate the current dollar amounts.

TABLE 3–4.

Gross National Product in Current and Constant Dollars;
Selected Years 1929–1965
(in billions of dollars)

(1) Year	(2) GNP in Current Dollars	(3) Price Index *1958 = 100*	(4) = (2) ÷ (3) GNP in Constant Dollars
1929	103.1	50.6	203.6
1933	55.6	39.3	141.5
1935	72.2	42.6	169.6
1939	90.5	43.2	209.4
1941	124.5	47.2	263.7
1944	210.1	58.2	361.3
1945	212.0	59.7	355.4
1948	257.6	79.6	323.7
1950	284.8	80.2	355.3
1952	345.5	87.5	395.1
1954	364.8	89.6	407.0
1956	419.2	94.0	446.1
1958	447.3	100.0	447.3
1960	503.6	103.3	487.8
1962	560.3	105.7	530.0
1964	631.7	108.9	580.0
1965	681.2	110.9	614.4

SOURCES: U.S. Department of Commerce, *Survey of Current Business*, August, 1965, July, 1966.

Limitations Inherent in Aggregate Measures of Income and Product

In spite of the fact that GNP and other aggregates discussed are in extensive use as measures of the material performance of the economy, they are subject to a number of limitations, particularly in respect to economic welfare (material performance and welfare are not always identical). The most important of these limitations can be briefly summarized.

ECONOMIC VERSUS SOCIAL VALUES

National income and product figures measure the economic rather than the social value of current productive activity. These data are largely limited to measurement of economic value in terms of the market prices that different types of goods and services may command. But the market price of a good or a service may not accurately reflect the value to the society of the good or service in a more fundamental, philosophical sense. A society, for example, might spend identical sums on education and tobacco, and yet one would hesitate to assert that the *social* as distinct from the economic value of these two types of expenditures is the same. The basic problem here is that the social value of the national output is necessarily a subjective matter, dependent upon individual judgments concerning what "ought to be." It follows that there are no simple, direct, or objective criteria for measurement of the social value of the national output. It is desirable, nevertheless, that the reader be aware of the distinction between economic and social value, and realize that the former is not always representative of the latter.

ECONOMIC VERSUS SOCIAL COSTS

Much of what was said in the foregoing paragraph concerning economic and social values applies equally well to economic and social costs. There is no necessary identity between the economic costs of producing the current national output and the social costs of the output. Economic costs include items such as factor costs, capital consumption allowances, and indirect business taxes—elements identified earlier as charges against GNP, and for which a monetary valuation is available. Social costs, on the other hand, relate to subjective and intangible phenomena such as the general deterioration of the physical and social environment as a result of current productive activity. For example, the beauty of the countryside may be irreparably marred, as has often happened in mining and industrial areas; rivers and the atmosphere may be contaminated through the disposal of industrial wastes; and disease and crime-infested slums may result as a by-product of industrial growth and urbanization. Social costs are as much a part of the real cost of the national output as the more readily measurable economic costs, but because of their subjective nature there are no readily recognizable criteria for judging their magnitude. Their existence, though, should be recognized by the serious student of economics.

THE VALUE OF LEISURE

In any analysis of the economic welfare or well-being of a nation the amount of leisure time at the people's disposal should rank high in importance; yet the national income and product statistics do not in any sense measure the value of leisure to society. Over the last half century the length of the average work-week has fallen from sixty to seventy hours to about forty hours, a development that represents a drastic improvement in welfare. Few would question the proposition that a society that is able to produce a larger output of material goods and services with a smaller expenditure of human effort than heretofore is in some sense better off.

QUALITATIVE CHANGES IN THE NATIONAL OUTPUT

In the discussion of price indexes we pointed out the necessity for eliminating the distortion produced by changes in the prices of goods and services entering into the national income product statistics if comparisons were to be made of the national output at different points in time. Unfortunately, it is not possible to make the same adjustments for changes in the quality of goods and services. It is possible, for example, that the economy might spend (in terms of constant dollars) about the same amount today as it did ten years ago for automobiles, but today's motor car is in a qualitative sense a vastly different product from the automobile produced ten years ago. In some instances, qualitative changes may be so great that for all practical purposes no basis exists for comparing the value of a product now being produced with the value of the same or similar product in an earlier period. In the present stage of development of national income and social accounting no satisfactory technique exists for taking into account qualitative changes in the income and product totals.

THE COMPOSITION OF OUTPUT

The various aggregates that we have been discussing are limited as measures of economic welfare because they do not tell us very much about the composition of the national output, except in the broad terms of consumption, investment, and government expenditure. The welfare implications of an increase in the national output (in constant dollars) cannot be assessed without some knowledge of the composition of that output. For example, real GNP in the United States rose sharply during World War II, yet it would be incorrect to say that the whole of this increase represented an increase in the material standard of living, because the greatest proportion of the increase in output consisted of armaments and other war goods. Moreover, over long periods of time the composition of the national output may change drastically: today, transportation by air is commonplace; fifty years ago, this kind of service did not exist. Thus, to evaluate fully the welfare implications of an increase in a society's real national product, it is necessary to know the composition of the product total and changes that may have taken place in this composition over relatively long periods of time.

THE DISTRIBUTION OF THE NATIONAL OUTPUT

While national income and product data serve as highly useful measures of the economy's over-all productive performance, they do not tell us how the output total is distributed among the members of society. It may be noted that the data indicate how the national income is distributed with respect to various forms of income—that is, wages, rents, profits, and so on—but not how it is distributed to persons. It is impossible, though, to ignore the distribution of output (and income) in any analysis of the welfare implications of a given level of economic activity. There are no wholly objective or purely "scientific" criteria for "proper" distribution of output and income in a society, although many economists and others feel that, other things being equal, more equality in the distribution of income is to be preferred to less equality. In any event, some knowledge of the actual distribution of income in society, and some concept of how income "ought" to be distributed is necessary for an evaluation of the economy's performance in terms of economic welfare.

INCOME AND OUTPUT PER CAPITA

Finally, it is necessary to take into account changes in population as well as changes in real output totals if meaningful comparisons of economic welfare are to be made over time. A rise in real income will not bring an improvement in the material level of well-being if population grows at a faster rate than the output total. For many purposes it is desirable that the aggregate data of national output and income be reduced to a per capita basis before comparisons are made.

The shortcomings described are not the only limitations involved in the use of national income statistics. The careful reader, who understands that such limitations exist, will exercise caution in drawing welfare conclusions from the performance data recorded in national income and product statistics. National income data are of great value for the measurement of the economy's performance, but they must be interpreted correctly.

THE SECTOR ACCOUNTS OF THE UNITED STATES

In Chapter 2 we pointed out that national income and social accounting embraces many different schemes for measurement and presentation of statistical data pertaining to the performance of a national economy. We now discuss the system of *sector* accounts presently utilized in the American economy. Sector accounts differ from the five aggregate measures of performance just discussed. They involve dividing the economy into a number of parts or "sectors," with the objective of showing the flow of income and product through and between the sectors. For each sector an account is established that reveals the sources and disposition of income by all the entities that are a part of the sector. The system is double-entry because all income must originate in one of the sectors and all expenditure must be directed in like fashion toward one of the other sectors. All entries appear in the accounts twice, once as a debit and once as a credit.

The Department of Commerce employs a five-account system embracing the following: (1) national income and product; (2) personal income and outlay; (3) government receipts and expenditures; (4) foreign transactions; and (5) gross saving and investment. Table 3–5 and its subdivisions shows these accounts for the United States for 1965.

TABLE 3–5.

National Income and Product Accounts for the United States, 1965
(in billions of current dollars)

I. National Income and Product Account, 1965

Allocations		Receipts	
1. Compensation of employees	392.9	11. Personal consumption expenditures (*II-1a*)	431.5
1a. Wages and salaries (*II-4*)	358.4	12. Gross private domestic investment (*V-1*)	106.6
1b. Employer contributions for social insurance (*III-9a*)	16.0	13. Government purchases of goods and services (*III-1*)	136.2
1c. Other labor income (*II-5*)	18.5	14. Net exports of goods and services	7.0
2. Proprietors' income (*II-6*)	55.7	14a. Exports (*IV-1*)	39.0
3. Corporate profits	74.2	14b. Imports (*IV-2*)	32.0
3a. Corporate profits tax liability (*III-7*)	31.2		
3b. Dividends (*II-8*)	19.2		
3c. Undistributed profits (*V-4*)	23.8		
4. Rental income (*II-7*)	18.3		
5. Net interest (*II-9a*)	17.8		
National income	**559.0**		
6. Indirect business taxes (*III-8*)	62.7		
7. Business transfer payments (*II-10a*)	2.6		
8. Less: Subsidies less current surplus of gov't enterprises (*III-4*)	1.0		
9. Statistical discrepancy (*V-7*)	−1.6		
Net national product	**621.6**		
10. Capital consumption allowances (*V-5*)	59.6		
Gross national product	**681.2**	**Gross National Product**	**681.2**

National Income and Product Account

This account presents the output of the economy both in terms of final product flows and in terms of the basic types of income generated in its production. In essence, the national income and product account is practically identical with the data presented earlier in Table 3–2, as it shows the origin of GNP and the allocation of this total in terms of the various charges against the value of GNP.

Personal Income and Outlay Account

This account pertains to the transactions of the household sector of the economy. The household sector includes, besides persons, all non-profit

TABLE 3–5 (*continued*)
II. Personal Income and Outlay Account, 1965

Allocations		Receipts	
1. Personal outlays	434.4	4. Wages and salaries (*I-1a*)	358.4
1a. Personal consumption expenditures (*I-11*)	431.5	5. Other labor income (*I-1c*)	18.5
1b. Interest paid by consumers (*II-9c*)	11.3	6. Proprietors' income (*I-2*)	55.7
		7. Rental income (*I-4*)	18.3
1c. Personal transfer payments to foreigners (net) (*IV-4*)	0.6	8. Dividends (*I-3b*)	19.2
		9. Interest income	38.4
2. Personal taxes (*III-6*)	66.0	9a. Net interest from businesses (*I-5*)	17.8
3. Personal saving (*V-3*)	25.7	9b. Net interest from government (*III-3*)	9.3
		9c. Net interest from consumers (*II-1b*)	11.3
		10. Transfer payments	39.7
		10a. From business (*I-7*)	2.6
		10b. From government (*III-2a*)	37.1
		11. *Less:* Personal contributions for social insurance (*III-9b*)	−13.2
Personal outlays, taxes, and saving	**535.1**	**Personal income**	**535.1**

III. Government Receipts and Expenditures Account, 1965

Allocations		Receipts	
1. Purchases of goods and services (*I-13*)	136.2	6. Personal taxes (*II-2*)	66.0
1a. Federal	66.9	7. Corporate profits tax liability (*I-3a*)	31.2
1b. State and local	69.4	8. Indirect business taxes (*I-6*)	62.7
2. Transfer payments	39.3	9. Contributions for social insurance	29.2
2a. To persons (*II-10b*)	37.1	9a. Employer (*I-1b*)	16.0
2b. To foreigners (*IV-3*)	2.2	9b. Personal (*II-11*)	13.2
3. Net interest paid (*III-3*)	9.3		
4. Subsidies less current surplus of gov't enterprises (*I-8*)	1.0		
5. Surplus (+) or deficit (−) on income and product account (*V-6*)	3.2		
Government expenditures and surplus or deficit	**189.0**	**Government receipts**	**189.0**

organizations, private trust funds, and private pension and pension-related funds. This account reveals the transactions of persons and all other entities included in the account with the other sectors of the economy. The right-hand side of the account shows the origin and kinds of income received by persons or households, while the left-hand side shows the disposition made by persons or households of this income. The reader will note that the total income received by entities included in this account is

TABLE 3–5 (*continued*)
IV. Foreign Transactions Account, 1965

Receipts		Allocations	
1. Exports of goods and services (*I-14a*)	39.0	2. Imports of goods & services (*I-14b*)	32.0
		3. Transfer payments from U.S. government (net) (*III-2b*)	2.2
		4. Personal transfer payments to foreigners (net) (*II-1c*)	.6
		5. Net foreign investment (*V-2*)	4.2
Receipts from foreigners	**39.0**	**Payments to foreigners**	**39.0**

V. Gross Saving and Investment Account, 1965

Investment		Saving	
1. Gross private domestic investment (*I-12*)	106.6	3. Personal saving (*II-3*)	25.7
1a. New construction	52.7	4. Undistributed corporate profits (*I-3c*)	23.8
1b. Producers' durable equipment	44.8	5. Capital consumption allowances (*I-10*)	59.6
1c. Change in business inventories	9.1	6. Government surplus (+) or deficit (−) on income and product account (*III-5*)	3.2
2. Net foreign investment (*IV-2*)	4.2	7. Statistical discrepancy (*I-9*)	1.6
Gross investment	**98.7**	**Gross saving**	**98.7**

SOURCE: Department of Commerce, *Survey of Current Business*, July, 1966. Details may not add to totals because of rounding.

the same as the *personal income* aggregate discussed earlier. On the sources side of the account the breakdown is into the major types of income, such as wages, interests, rents, and profits, and transfer payments, while on the allocations side the breakdown is into taxes, personal consumption expenditures, and personal saving.

Government Receipts and Expenditures Account

The account for the government sector of the economy covers the current transactions of all governmental units in the economy, including federal, state, county, and municipal bodies, as well as various social insurance funds administered by these units. This sector does not include the transactions and operations of government enterprises, which consist of agencies of government that cover their costs of operation primarily through the sale of goods and services. The production and sale of electric power by a municipality is an example of government enterprise. The transactions of government enterprises are treated in national income and social accounting in identical fashion with the transactions and activities of private enterprise; thus, they would be reflected in the national income and product account, but not in the government receipts and expenditures account.

The receipts side of this account consists of business and personal taxes and contributions for social security by both employees and employers. Since these accounts are concerned with current income and product transactions, the receipts side of the account for the public sector does not show receipts resulting from financial transactions (chiefly borrowing operations) or from the sale of existing assets (such as the disposal of surplus military material and property). On the expenditures side the major items are the current outlays by the public sector for goods and services, transfer payments to both individuals and foreign sources, government interest (which is considered as a transfer payment in current national income and social accounting practice), and subsidies to business firms after deduction of the current surplus of government enterprises. Transactions that would involve outlays for the repayment of debt or the acquisition of any kind of financial asset are not included as expenditures in the account for the public sector.

The difference between government receipts and expenditures is represented by an entry on the left-hand side of the account entitled *Surplus or deficit* (—) *on income and product account*. A surplus means that the current expenditures of the public sector are less than its current receipts and hence is a measure of the saving originating in the public sector; a deficit represents an excess of current expenditures over current receipts, and thus constitutes dissaving. The reader is cautioned that the deficit or surplus shown in the account for the government sector should not be confused with the deficit or surplus of the Federal government, a fiscal item that excites widespread public interest and curiosity. The account for the public sector does not include expenditures and receipts resulting from purely financial transactions. Also, it embraces all governmental units in the economy. Thus the existence of a surplus or deficit in this particular account does not necessarily indicate whether or not the Federal government has a deficit or surplus on its transactions.

One final point may be noted with respect to this account, and this pertains to the current American practice of treating all purchases of goods by governmental units as a current expenditure, which implies that all assets acquired by governmental bodies in an income period are consumed in the same period. National income accounts in the United States do not recognize the existence of public investment or capital formation in the form of expenditures for public buildings, roads and highways, dams, and various other types of fixed assets that public bodies may acquire. This practice is not universal, however, for both the Organization for European Economic Cooperation [9] and the United Nations recommend that national in-

---

[9] The Organization for European Economic Cooperation (OEEC) was established in 1948 by the sixteen nations of western Europe that were recipients of eco-

come and social accounting recognize public as well as private capital formation. In the United States, the National Accounts Review Committee of the National Bureau of Economic Research recommended development of a capital account for federal, state, and local governmental units.[10] There is no indication at the present time, however, that the National Income Division of the Department of Commerce has any plans to revise its accounting procedures in this respect.

Foreign Transactions Account

In this account the transactions of the various sectors of the economy with foreign nations or the "rest of the world" are summarized. The right-hand side of the account records the receipts accruing to foreign nations as a result of their transactions with the United States. Basically these receipts arise as a result of: imports of goods and services by United States residents, transfer payments in the form of gifts and grants from the United States government and American residents to foreign nations, and net foreign investment (the difference between exports and imports plus transfers to the rest of the world). From the viewpoint of national income and product accounting, the total recorded in the right-hand side of this account represents the portion of money income created as a result of current productive activity that is not being spent for domestically produced goods and services. The money represented by this total is either being spent on imported goods and services, being transferred to foreign nations, or being made available to foreign residents through investment abroad.

The left-hand side of this account records the receipts that accrue to United States residents as a result of expenditures in the United States by foreign residents, business firms, and governments. Viewed from the point of view of the "rest of the world" this side of the foreign transactions account records the amounts spent for the purchase of goods and services from the United States. This, of course, is the same thing as exports by the United States of goods and services, and represents the portion of domestic output that is being diverted from domestic to foreign use. The difference between exports of goods and services and imports of goods and services plus transfers to foreign nations is equal to net foreign investment. This figure appears in the gross saving and investment account as one of the categories of investment and, as such, is an offset to the economy's saving.

---

nomic aid from the United States under the Marshall Plan program. In September, 1961, the OEEC was transformed into the Organization for Economic Cooperation and Development (OECD). The United States is now a member of this body.

[10] National Accounts Review Committee of the National Bureau of Economic Research, *The National Economic Accounts of the United States* (Washington, United States Government Printing Office, 1958), p. 81.

Gross Saving and Investment Account

The gross saving and investment account summarizes for all sectors the origin of the saving total for a particular income period and the kinds of investment which, from the standpoint of the economy as a whole, represent outlets of such savings. Thus, the right-hand side of this account contains data pertaining to the three major sources of saving for the economy as a whole: personal saving (which originates in the household sector), government saving (which originates in the public sector), and saving emanating from business firms. The bulk of the latter is derived from undistributed corporate profits and capital consumption allowances. The various forms of investment representing the "real" or physical counterpart to the foregoing saving flows are shown on the left-hand side of the account. As mentioned, these consist of new construction, producers' durable equipment, net changes in business inventories, and net foreign investment. The total of the first three items is gross private domestic investment.

Summary: Development of National Accounting Systems

The aim of Chapters 2 and 3 has been to outline the structure and main features of the national income and social accounting system of the United States. National income accounting according to the National Accounts Review Committee of the National Bureau of Economic Research is "one of the chief tools for the formulation of Government economic policy and of business policy." Basically, the purpose of national income and social accounting systems is to provide detailed information concerning the performance of the economy; as the economy becomes more complex the necessity for complete and accurate information detailing this performance is increasingly urgent. In the United States the five aggregate measures of income and product discussed earlier are the most widely-used indicators of the economy's over-all performance, but simple aggregates of this kind are increasingly being supplemented by other forms of social accounting, such as the five-account system discussed in this chapter, as well as lesser-known forms of social accounting such as input-output analysis, flow-of-funds accounting, and balance-of-payments accounting. In any event, the development of the various forms of national income and social accounting must be ranked as one of the most important achievements of economic science within the last three or four decades. It does not require much foresight to predict, moreover, that the next decade or so will see an even greater intensification in the pace of development in this area, for as more and more nations resort to various forms of economic planning in order to accelerate their own rate of economic progress, accurate and comprehensive systems of social accounting become practically indispensable.

PART II

The Theory of Income and Employment

4 | The Classical Theory of Employment

In the present chapter we begin formal study of the forces that determine national output, income, and employment in the modern economy. It is the objective of modern *macroeconomic* analysis to understand these forces. To place our study in historical perspective, we will examine the explanation given to the problem of the determinants of the income and employment level by the system of economic analysis known as "classical economics." First let us consider what economists mean by the concept of "full" employment and demonstrate how employment is related to the output level.

The Meaning of Employment and Unemployment

The words "employment" and "unemployment" need to be examined carefully because the idea that full employment is a proper and desirable objective of public policy gained widespread acceptance in the United States and most of the nations of western Europe during and immediately following World War II. In the United States, the Employment Act of 1946 gave legislative sanction to the view that the Federal government has a direct responsibility for the level of employment and income prevailing in the economy. The Act specifically stated:

The Congress hereby declares that it is the continuing policy and responsibility of the Federal Government to use all practicable means consistent with its needs and obligations and other essential considerations of national policy, with the assistance and cooperation of industry, agriculture, labor, and State and local governments, to coordinate and utilize all its plans, functions, and resources for the purpose of creating and maintaining, in a manner calculated to foster and promote free competitive enterprise and the general welfare, conditions under which there will be afforded useful employment opportunities, including self employment, for those able, willing, and seeking work, and to promote maximum employment, production, and purchasing power.[1]

The qualifying phrases found in the Employment Act suggest, on the one hand, that "full employment" is not a social goal to be achieved at all costs and, on the other, that the Federal government has other obligations ranking in importance with that of full employment. Some economists would argue that stability of the general price level is a goal equal in importance to full employment. They believe this because they fear that continuous upward pressure on the price level will not only dissipate the gains resulting from full employment, but jeopardize the economy's ability to maintain conditions of full employment for any lengthy period of time. Economists holding these and similar views may or may not be correct in their assessment of the dangers inherent in inflationary pressure, but the fact that such views exist means that maintenance of full employment is not a policy that can be pursued without careful consideration of other important objectives of public policy.

Although the Employment Act makes maximum or full employment an objective of public policy it does not define exactly what constitutes a fully employed labor force. Yet without some conception of what is meant by "full employment," administration of the Act in any practical sense would be impossible. Thus, it is necessary to define as precisely as possible what we mean by a fully employed labor force. The simplest definition of full employment is a situation in the economy characterized by an absence of *involuntary unemployment*. The latter exists when members of the labor force are willing to work at prevailing wages in their trade or occupation but are unable to obtain employment. If we let N' be representative of the labor force and N stand for the actual level of employment, then full employment exists in the society as $N' - N$ approaches zero.

The reader should note that we used the phrase "approaches zero" rather than "equals zero." The reason for this is that absolute full employment of the labor force, which would prevail if $N' - N$ were equal to zero, is a condition that is seldom, if ever, attained in practice. In almost any society there is likely to be varying amounts of *frictional unemployment*, which results whenever persons in the labor force are temporarily out of work because of imperfections in the labor market. At any given time some workers will be in the process of changing jobs or occupations; others will be experiencing temporary layoffs caused by the seasonal nature of their employment, by shortages of materials in some industries, or

[1] *Employment Act of 1946.*

by shifts in demand that reduce the need for some types of workers and increase the need for others. Many other similar factors cause some proportion of the labor force to be out of work for short periods of time.

In view of these imperfections in the labor market full employment exists when a society minimizes frictional unemployment and there is an absence of involuntary unemployment. Unfortunately, there is no precise or practical way to distinguish unemployment that is frictional from unemployment that is either involuntary or even voluntary. In its 1962 *Annual Report*, the President's Council of Economic Advisors adopted an unemployment rate of 4 per cent as a "reasonable and prudent target for stabilization policy." [2] In the judgment of the council a 4 per cent unemployment rate could be attained without creating substantial upward pressure upon prices.

If we accept the 4 per cent unemployment rate as our measure of the full-employment level, then the American economy has had one long and sustained period of substantially full employment since World War II. From 1947 to 1957 the number of unemployed in the United States averaged 4.2 per cent of the civilian labor force, although in some years during this period the figure rose above the 5 per cent level. In 1949 unemployment climbed to 5.9 per cent of the civilian labor force; in 1954 it reached 5.6 per cent. The rate fell to a little over 4 per cent for the next three years and then rose sharply to 6.8 in 1958, the highest recorded in any of the years since World War II. From 1959 through 1964 unemployment remained above 5 per cent, although the rate began to come down during 1964. In 1965 it fell below 5 per cent for the first time since 1957.

These periods of relatively mild unemployment during an era unprecedented for its widespread and sustained prosperity may be compared to the catastrophic situation during the Great Depression of the 1930's. In 1933, for example, unemployment totaled 24.9 per cent of the civilian labor force, which meant that one out of every four workers was unemployed. Even as late as 1939, ten years after the onset of the depression, unemployment was still at the high figure of 17.2 per cent of the labor force.[3]

Employment and Output

In the foregoing paragraphs we stressed the fact that reasonably full employment for that nation's labor force has become a public policy objective of major significance for contemporary American society. It is equally important to point out that there exists a close link between the employment level and the output level. In other words, we can expect

[2] *Economic Report of the President*, Washington, 1962, p. 46.
[3] Data are from the *Economic Report of the President*, Washington, 1965, p. 214.

the amount of employment to vary more or less directly with the volume of production. Since the latter constitutes the real income of society, it follows that the employment level serves as an indicator of the economy's over-all performance. Conversely, the output level is a good indicator of the prevailing employment situation in the economy.

The link between real income and the employment level is important for economic analysis because it embraces a number of simple but fundamental economic relationships. Basic to an understanding of the determinants of the level of production and employment is the concept of the economy's productive capacity. At any time there exists for the economy as a whole a given productive capacity, that is, a potential for the production of goods and services. Even in the short run the economy's productive capacity is not an exact or unvarying magnitude, for in practically all economies there is some flexibility in the maximum output that can be obtained over short periods of time. Nevertheless, all economies have some upper limit to the amount of goods and services that can be produced, and this upper limit will necessarily constitute an economy's short-run maximum capacity to produce. Over time, of course, this may change, as the process of economic growth brings about expansion in the economy's productive capacity. A *dynamic economy* is characterized by a continuously expanding capacity for production.

What determines the productive capacity of the economy? This is one of the most complex of all economic problems, yet the basic factors in the process can be readily identified. In the simplest sense, productive capacity depends upon, first, the quantity and quality of resources available to the economy; and second, the skill and efficiency with which these resources are brought together for the purpose of production. The latter concerns technology, for in its broadest meaning technology refers to the over-all level of effectiveness attained by an economy in combining resources together in the productive process.

The statements in the foregoing paragraph can be summarized symbolically by the following equation:

$$Q = f(N', R', K'; T) \qquad (4\text{--}1)$$

In the equation the symbols used have the following meanings:

Q = The economy's productive capacity.
N' = The economy's labor force.
R' = The economy's stock of known and economically useful natural resources.
K' = The economy's stock of capital or man-made instruments of production.
T = The level of technology prevailing in the economy.

The meaning of the above equation is that the economy's productive capacity is a function of (the symbol f in the equation) the basic determinants listed above: the quantity of labor, natural resources, capital, and the level of technology. Note that the equation does not in any way specify the exact proportions in which the determinants of capacity are brought together, but merely states that productive capacity depends on these things. Because technology is not a stock, as are labor, capital, and natural resources, it is separated from the other variables by a semicolon. Technically, it is a "shift parameter," whose value determines the output potential associated with specific quantities of the other three determinants.

The productive capacity of the economy can be defined, too, in terms of the labor force, N', and the average productivity of labor, P_r. The productivity of labor, or average output per man-hour (or some other time unit), does not refer to the degree of skill possessed by labor in general, but rather to the efficiency with which labor power is employed in the productive process. Since the latter depends upon the quantity and quality of capital equipment and natural resources used in conjunction with labor, the following is a correct statement of the relevant relationships:

$$P_r = f(R', K'; T) \tag{4-2}$$

The equation states that the productivity of labor is a function of the quantity of natural resources and capital equipment, given the level of technology. This being the case, it follows that the economy's productive capacity is equal to the labor force, N', multiplied by the average productivity of labor, P_r. Symbolically, we have the equation

$$Q = (N' \times P_r) \tag{4-3}$$

Just as the economy's productive capacity depends upon the quantity and quality of available resources, the actual level of output is determined by the extent to which these resources are being used. Output results from the utilization of productive capacity. In economics the physical relationship that exists between the input of resources and the output of goods and services in any given period of time is termed the *production function*. Stated in other terms, the production function embodies a functional relationship between the quantity of input and the quantity of output. In the short run it may take the following form:

$$Y = f(N, R', K'; T) \tag{4-4}$$

This equation means that, given the *stock* of natural resources and capital, as well as the level of technology, output is determined by labor input.

The latter is, of course, the level of employment. It is also true that output can be defined as the product of the employment level and the productivity of labor. Thus:

$$Y = N \times P_r \qquad (4\text{--}5)$$

The concept of the production function is depicted graphically in Figure 4–1, which shows output on the vertical axis and labor input on the horizontal axis. The output curve will eventually level off because of diminishing productivity. On the curve labeled Y_a it may be noted that an increase in the income level from Y_1 to Y_2 results when employment increases from N_1 to N_2. The student should note, too, that the same increase in income may be obtained with *no* change in employment if the entire production function shifts upward to the level depicted by the curve Y_b. This would result from a change in the stock of capital and natural resources, a change in technology, or a combination of the two.

The foregoing discussion provides a basis for an understanding of the close relationship over short periods of time between employment and output. For the purpose of national income analysis we may view the *short run* as a period of time during which it is assumed that the quantity of capital, natural resources, and the level of technology remain relatively fixed. By implication, then, productive capacity is also relatively fixed.

There is no way to define precisely the length of real time involved in the "short run," although a satisfactory working definition is that it is long enough to permit some cyclical fluctuations in income and employment, but not sufficiently long to show a definite trend. The significant factor for our analysis is that the short run is not a long enough period of time to permit any really significant changes in the economy's productive capacity. Consequently, we may assume that the underlying determinants of capacity in Equation (4–1) have relatively fixed magnitudes, although the extent to which they are actually utilized in production is variable. This is particularly true with respect to the labor force, because the level of employment, N, can quite obviously depart rather widely at times from the size of the labor force, N'. For the economy as a whole the output level, Y, in the short run will tend to vary directly with the employment level, N. Thus a good workable hypotheses is as follows:

$$Y = f(N) \qquad (4\text{--}6)$$

In this formulation the level of employment, N, has meaning not only in relation to the over-all supply of labor, N', but also as a barometer of the extent to which the economy's productive capacity is actually being utilized. In the analysis to follow we will make frequent use of this simple but important notion that over relatively short periods of time employment and real income move together.

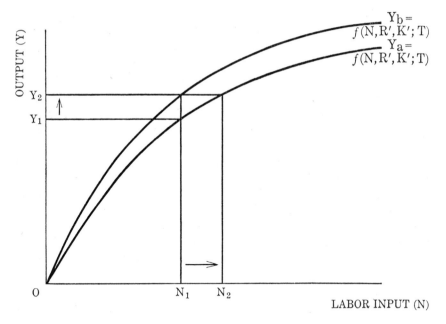

Figure 4–1. The Production Function

The Nature of Classical Economics

Classical economics is the system of economic analysis developed in England in the late eighteenth and early nineteenth centuries, which stood largely intact until the 1930's as the main body of economic principles accepted by economists. In his famous treatise, *The General Theory of Employment, Interest and Money*, John Maynard Keynes employed the term to characterize the followers of the early nineteenth century British economist David Ricardo and included John Stuart Mill, Alfred Marshall, and A. C. Pigou. These British economists were deemed by Keynes to be most representative of the classical system of economic analysis.[4]

The chief objective of classical economic analysis was to explain the working of a capitalistic economic system founded upon the institution of private property. Essentially this involved construction of a set of principles that would explain how a market structure of competitive prices

[4] John Maynard Keynes, *The General Theory of Employment, Interest and Money* (New York, Harcourt, Brace, 1936), p. 3. (Keynes' use of the word "classical" is not strictly correct, for actually the phrase "the classical economists" was originally used by Karl Marx and referred to Ricardo and his predecessors, including Adam Smith.)

functioned to determine what goods and services were to be produced, how resources were to be allocated for the production of goods and services, and how the final output was distributed to the owners of economic resources. In this scheme the motivating force was the self-interest of entrepreneurs, resource owners, and consumers seeking, respectively, to maximize profits, income, and satisfactions. Implicit within the theoretical structure of the classical economists is a set of propositions that purport to explain how the employment level is determined; it is this facet of classical thinking that will occupy our attention throughout the remainder of this chapter.

As a body of economic principles, classical economics rested upon two major assumptions. The first was that the economic order is dominated by the kind of rigorous competition which denies *any* control over prices to either the sellers of goods and services, or the sellers of the services of economic resources. This is what modern textbooks usually describe as "pure competition." The social function of competition is to play a regulatory role and insure that the free play of self-interest in the commodity and resource markets will lead to results that are desirable for the whole economy. Adam Smith, the father of modern economic analysis, was the first economist to express the concept of a self-adjusting market economy. In the *Wealth of Nations* he made his famous statement to the effect that every producer, in seeking to promote his own gain, is led by "an invisible hand to promote an end that was no part of his intention." [5] This end is, of course, the general well-being or the public interest.

The second underlying assumption of the classical system was that man is a rational being. Rationality to the classical economists meant essentially the "pleasure-pain" calculus. Man, in other words, was a creature who sought to avoid "pain" and achieve "pleasure." In all his activities, including those pertaining to economics, he would rationally attempt to order his affairs so as to maximize pleasure and minimize pain. The balancing of pleasure against pain—or gain against cost—is, according to the classical view, the strategic, motivating force in the economic system. As a consumer, man attempted to maximize the satisfaction derived from the expenditure of income; whereas as a resource owner or entrepreneur, he sought to maximize the return obtained from the sale of the goods and resources at his disposition. On the basis of this sweeping assumption concerning human nature, the classical economists constructed through deductive logic an elegant and complex structure of economic analysis, much of which remains valid and in use.

The Three "Building Blocks" of the Classical Theory of Employment

The phrase "the classical theory of employment" is to some extent a misnomer because none of the writings of the leading classical economists

[5] Adam Smith, *An Inquiry into the Nature and Causes of the Wealth of Nations*, Cannan edition (New York, Modern Library, 1937), p. 423.

contains an explicit account of what were thought to be the chief determinants of the level of income and employment. Nevertheless, there exists in the literature of classical economics basic ideas relating to employment, which, when brought together, constitute a logical and coherent explanation of how the employment level is determined. Awareness of the existence of these ideas has largely come about since the publication of Keynes' *General Theory*. Since Keynes asserted that a major objective of his own treatise was to refute the classical theory, it was inevitable that the publication of the *General Theory* would stimulate thought and discussion among professional economists concerning the nature of the classical system. As a result we now have a reasonably clear conception of classical employment theory.

In essence, the classical theory of employment consists of three propositions. The first of these is a theory of the demand for and the supply of labor, which was derived from the economics of the individual firm and generalized to apply to the economy as a whole. The second pertains to the level of effective demand for the economy as a whole. The third involves a theory of the general level of prices. Our discussion of classical employment theory will consist of a detailed analysis of each of these three "building blocks" of the classical system.

The Theory of the Demand for and Supply of Labor

The starting point for the classical theory of employment is the production function, which expresses the idea that output will vary directly with the employment level. Classical employment theory takes as given the other major determinants of capacity and output, namely the quantity and quality of capital equipment and natural resources, and the level of technology. Thus, in classical economics the level of output depends only upon the employment level.

The Demand for Labor

In the classical system the level of employment both in the individual firm and in the whole economy rests upon the demand for and the supply of labor. The classical concept of the demand for labor can be summed up in the proposition: the demand for labor is a function of the *real wage*. The latter is the purchasing power of the money wage. In equation form this idea is expressed as follows:

$$N = f(W) \qquad (4\text{--}7)$$

Keynes expressed this same notion when he asserted in connection with his discussion of the postulates of the classical theory that "the wage is equal to the marginal product of labor." [6] The fundamental idea involved here is that, other things being equal, the firm will hire more labor only as the real wage declines. Thus, the demand for labor is an inverse function of the real wage, or the demand curve for labor has a negative slope, which is to say that it slopes downward to the right. This relationship is shown in Figure 4–2. It follows from this relationship that in order to raise the level of employment it is necessary to reduce the real wage. We may note is passing that Keynes did not question the view that the demand for labor is an inverse function of the real wage.

The reason for the existence of an inverse functional relationship be-

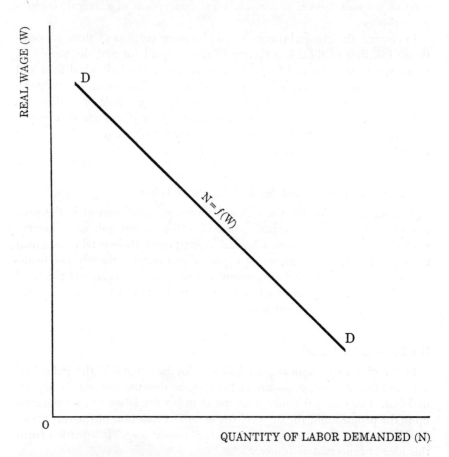

Figure 4–2. The Classical Demand Schedule for Labor

tween the real wage and the level of employment can be understood if we look at the situation as it appears at the level of the individual firm.

[6] Keynes, *op. cit.*, p. 5.

Classical economics assumes that the entrepreneur attempts to maximize his profits; consequently, he will be guided by the profit-maximization principle in the use of labor just as he is in determining the appropriate level of output for his firm's operations. Essential to the most profitable use of labor is the principle of diminishing returns (or productivity).

According to the principle of diminishing productivity, the additional product resulting from the employment by the firm of additional units of labor will become smaller and smaller as the total volume of employment rises. In more technical language this principle means that in response to increased employment the *marginal physical product* of additional units of labor will decline. What interests the firm in this situation is the yield which results from the employment of additional amounts of labor. This depends not only upon the additional output it gets from additional labor—that is, the marginal physical product—but also on the price at which the additional units of output are sold. For the sake of simplicity, let us assume the firm operates in a purely competitive market. Insofar as the firm is concerned, this means that all output can be sold at a constant price. Because of diminishing marginal productivity, though, the *value* of the firm's marginal physical product will inevitably decline as more labor is employed.

Profit-maximization requires that the firm adjust its level of operations to the point at which the value of additional output to it is just equal to the cost of that output. When this principle is applied to employment, it means that the firm should adjust its employment to that point at which the cost for the last units of labor hired is just equal to the value of the marginal physical product of that labor. If this is done the firm will be in a position of equilibrium in respect to its employment of labor. The cost to the firm of the additional (or marginal) amounts of employment depends upon the number of additional workers hired and the prevailing money wage. Thus, the firm's equilibrium position with respect to the employment it is willing to offer in a purely competitive situation is one in which the marginal physical product of the last workers hired multiplied by the price at which the product sells is equal to the number of workers in the last group hired multiplied by the money wage at which they are hired.

The question may now be raised as to how the foregoing concerns the real wage and its relationship to the level of employment. The *real wage* is the purchasing power of a given money wage, which depends upon the relationship between the money wage and the general price level. Symbolically, the real wage, W, can be defined as the money wage, w, divided by the general price level, p.

$$W = \frac{w}{p} \qquad (4\text{--}8)$$

The real wage will fall if the general price level rises while money wages remain constant, because in such a situation the purchasing power of any given money wage would decline. The reverse will be true if the money wage increases while the general price level remains constant.

Let us now return to our discussion of the firm and examine how its equilibrium position will be affected by a change in either the general price level or in money wage rates. If we assume that our firm has an equilibrium position, then a fall in the money wage rate will upset this equilibrium by reducing the cost to the firm of the marginal physical product of the last group of wokers hired, assuming no change in the product price. If this happens, the firm can employ additional labor. In fact, the profit-maximization principle requires that it do just that, but as additional workers are employed their marginal physical product will decline. Eventually, the firm will reach a new equilibrium position at which once again the value to the firm of the marginal physical product of the last group of workers hired will be just equal to their cost to the firm. *But it will be an equilibrium at a higher level of employment.* Note that this is tantamount to saying the employment level is an inverse function of the real wage, for if the money wage declines while the general price level remains unchanged, real wages will have declined. The reader can readily see that the same result will be obtained if the general price level rose while the money wage remained fixed. This would disturb the firm's equilibrium by increasing the value of the marginal physical product of the last group of workers hired and thus necessitate the same sort of upward adjustment in the employment level.

The equilibrium we have just described pertains to the employment decision of the individual firm, but the same reasoning may be applied to the economy as a whole. For short periods of time for the economy as a whole, as well as for the individual firm, labor is the variable input. Thus, employment for the whole economy can be increased up to the point at which the marginal product of the last increment of employed workers is just equal to the real wage. For the economy as a whole this is a condition of employment equilibrium. If ΔY stands for the change in real output and ΔN for the change in employment level, then $\Delta Y / \Delta N$ is the marginal product of labor for the whole economy. The equilibrium condition, that is, the employment level at which the marginal product equals the real wage, is thus

$$\frac{\Delta Y}{\Delta N} = \frac{w}{p} \qquad (4\text{--}9)$$

By clearing fractions we arrive at the necessary condition for profit maximization:

$$\Delta Y p = \Delta N w \qquad (4\text{--}10)$$

In this equation the monetary value of the last increment of output equals the monetary cost producing this last increment of output.

The importance of the above is that the *aggregate* demand curve for labor is conceptually identical with the individual firm's demand schedule for labor. The aggregate demand schedule slopes downward to the right and, other things being equal, the volume of employment for the whole economy must vary inversely with the level of real wages. Such, in essence, is the classical concept of the economy's demand schedule for labor.

The Supply of Labor

Classical ideas concerning the supply of labor may be expressed algebraically in the equation:

$$N' = f(W) \qquad (4\text{--}11)$$

In this equation N' represents the number of workers in the labor force and actively seeking employment. Supply, however, is interpreted to mean not only the number of workers but the hours of labor supplied by both old and new workers. The equation itself states that the supply of labor is a direct function of the real wage; hence, the supply curve of labor in the classical system has a positive slope. This is shown in Figure 4–3.

The view that the number of workers seeking employment is a function of the real wage rests partly on the classical assumption that the worker, in offering his services in the labor market, seeks to maximize his income in the same way that the entrepreneur seeks to maximize his profit. Keynes, in speaking of this postulate of the classical analysis, said it means that the utility of the wage associated with a given volume of employment will be just equal to the disutility of that amount of employment. Stated differently, the real wage represents that which is necessary to overcome the irksomeness (or disutility) of work and thus induce people to become employed.[7] The real wage is the purchasing power in goods and services of the money wage. Since utility consists of the ability of something to satisfy wants, the utility of the money wage will necessarily depend upon what it can actually command in the way of goods and services.

The functional relationship between the supply of labor and the real wage is also based upon the classical assumption that workers and other resource owners do not suffer from the *money illusion*. The term money illusion was coined by the American economist Irving Fisher and refers

[7] *Ibid.*

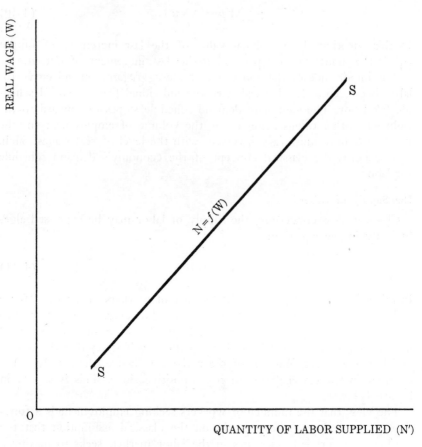

Figure 4–3. The Classical Supply Schedule of Labor

to "a failure to perceive that the dollar or any other unit of money expands and shrinks in value." [8] In other words, the monetary unit is believed to be stable in value, and thus a rise in money income is considered, *ipso facto*, a rise in real income. Under these circumstances— that is, an economy "suffering" from the money illusion—the supply of labor could just as easily be a function of the money wage as the real wage. But this is not the classical view of the matter. Money, to the classical economist, is fundamentally a medium of exchange, a means to an end; the use of money in modern societies should not obscure the fact that basically the economic process is concerned with an exchange of goods for goods. Money is significant only because it is more convenient to have a generally accepted medium of exchange than it is to

[8] Irving Fisher, *The Money Illusion* (New York, Adelphi, 1928), p. 4.

resort to barter. The implication of such a view is that resource owners, including workers, will value the services of their resources in terms of the real returns they can command.

The Equilibrium Level of Employment

The significance in the classical system of the two schedules discussed —the demand for labor and the supply of labor—is that when brought together they uniquely determine both the employment level and the real wage. Moreover, the classical demand and supply schedules for labor necessarily intersect at the level of full employment. The process by which employment and real wage are mutually determined in the classical analysis is depicted in Figure 4–4.

In the figure, *DD* represents the demand schedule for labor, while *SS* is the supply schedule for labor. Given these two schedules, competition

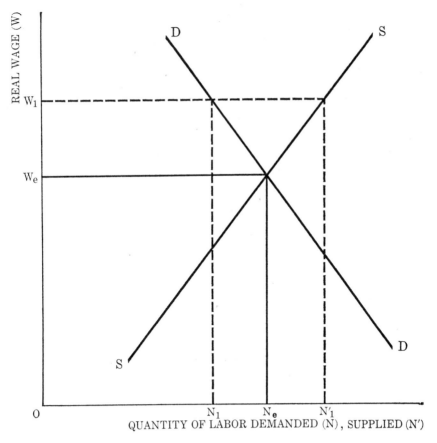

Figure 4–4. The Equilibrium Level of Employment

in the market among employers for workers and among workers for employment will drive the real wage and the employment level to the values represented at the point of intersection of the two schedules. As long as the two schedules do not shift, no other level of either employment or real wages can prevail. If, momentarily, real wages were at the level represented by W_1, the number of workers actually seeking employment would be equal to the distance ON'_1. But at the W_1 level of real wages the demand for labor would be equal only to the distance ON_1. The distance $N_1N'_1$, consequently, represents the surplus of workers seeking employment at the momentarily prevailing level of real wages. Competition for employment among these workers would lead some of them to offer their services to prospective employers at reduced money wages. As this happens, the real wage will decline, assuming other things remain constant, and employment will increase. Equilibrium in the labor market will prevail at the level of real wages W_e and the level of employment N_e. This is the essence of the classical explanation of how the economy's level of employment is determined. The criticisms set forth by Keynes against this portion of classical employment theory will be examined at a later point in this chapter.

The equilibrium employment level determined by the intersection of the classical demand and supply schedules for labor has to be one of full employment. If any unemployment (aside from frictional unemployment) exists after equilibrium is obtained, it must be voluntary unemployment. This is true for essentially two reasons. First, the classical postulates imply that if nonfrictional unemployment persists after the equilibrium situation, it must be because some workers are demanding wages too high in relation to the marginal productivity of labor. If these workers are unemployed because of their refusal to accept lower money wages, their unemployment must be regarded as voluntary. If they would accept a reduction in money wages, the real wage would decline, other things being equal, and more employment would be forthcoming.

The second reason why the employment level is one of full employment is simply that the traditional theory maintains that *money* wage bargains between workers and entrepreneurs determine the *real* wage; consequently, the workers in general are in a position to determine their real wage (through money wage bargains), and, therefore, the level of employment. If this is true, it necessarily follows that any unemployment that actually exists at a given level of real wages has to be voluntary unemployment.

These classical conclusions, according to Keynes, are intended to apply to the whole body of labor in the economy, not just to the amount of labor utilized by a firm or by an industry. They are based, moreover, on the belief that a reduction in the general level of money wages in the economy will, in the short run, be accompanied by a similar, though not necessarily proportionate, reduction in real wages.

The Theory of Aggregate Demand

We observed that classical economic analysis purports to show how the volume of employment is determined in the economy, and why there cannot be any involuntary unemployment in the system resulting from a deficiency of the demand for labor. The level of employment determined in this matter is significant, too, because it also determines the level of production in the economy. Real income, according to our earlier discussion of the classical production function, is dependent on the level of employment; consequently, once we have determined the employment level, we have simultaneously determined output of the economy.

But these facts, true as they may be, raise another question pertaining to the possibility of involuntary unemployment for the economy. For the economy as a whole output is the same thing as real income, but real income is necessarily the basis of any economy's demand. The monetary value of current output is the same thing as the economy's gross money income. This means, as Keynes phrased it, that "the income derived in the aggregate by all the elements in the community concerned in a productive activity necessarily has a value exactly equal to the *value* of the output." [9] This being the case, it raises the interesting possibility that there might be involuntary unemployment in the economy because of a deficiency of total or aggregate demand. If income (money or real) is, in fact, the basis for demand, is it not possible that the economy as a whole may fail to generate sufficient demand to consume all the goods and services produced in a particular income period? If this happened, there could be involuntary unemployment, not because of any error in the classical analysis of the nature of the demand for and supply of labor, but because the economy as a whole failed to spend income at a rate sufficient to justify production at the level associated with a given volume of employment. In short, unemployment might result from "overproduction."

Say's Law of Markets

The possibility of this kind of involuntary unemployment is denied by classical economic theory. It is denied because of the general acceptance by classical economists of a curious doctrine known as Say's Law of Markets. Jean Baptiste Say was a French economist of the early nineteenth century who disseminated and popularized the ideas of Adam Smith in France and on the European continent. His Law of Markets,

[9] Keynes, *op. cit.*, p. 20.

which Galbraith described as having had the status of an article of faith with classical economists for over a hundred years,[10] is the formal expression of the idea that widespread and involuntary unemployment because of general overproduction is impossible. To put the matter slightly differently, there cannot be any involuntary unemployment because of a deficiency of total demand.

The simplest possible statement of this doctrine is that "supply creates its own demand." The meaning of this statement, as pointed out by Keynes in his *General Theory*, is that in some sense the whole of the costs of production must necessarily be spent in the aggregate, directly or indirectly, on purchasing the product. Every producer who brings goods to the market (that is, creates supply) does so in order to exchange them for other goods (that is, creates demand). Classical economics assumed that the end purpose of all economic activity is consumption, but consumption depends upon income, which in turn is derived from production. In consequence of this, every act of production must necessarily represent the demand for something.

The conclusion that follows from the assertion that all supply is potentially the demand for something is that there cannot be any general "overproduction" or deficiency of total demand for the economy as a whole. True, there may be some misdirection of production and consequently an oversupply of some commodities, but the pricing mechanism will correct this and cause some entrepreneurs to shift their output to other and more profitable lines. But such oversupply cannot be the case for the whole economy because the act of production *always* creates sufficient value or purchasing power to take off the market all goods and services produced. If there cannot be deficiency of total demand in the economy, it also follows that any involuntary unemployment because of the phenomenon of overproduction is impossible.

The most explicit statement in English of Say's Law of Markets is to be found in John Stuart Mill's *Principles of Political Economy*, a famed treatise that represents one of the best and most comprehensive statements of the classical viewpoint. In a chapter devoted to a discussion of the impossibility of overproduction, Mill poses the following question and then proceeds to answer it with an express statement of the principle embodied in Say's Law.

Is it . . . possible that there should be a deficiency of demand for all commodities, for want of means of payment? Those who think so cannot have considered what it is which constitutes the means of payment for commodities. *It is simply commodities.* Each person's means of paying for the productions of other people consists of those which he himself possesses. All sellers are inevitably and *ex vi termini* buyers. Could we suddenly double the

[10] John Kenneth Galbraith, *American Capitalism: The Concept of Countervailing Power* (Boston, Houghton Mifflin, 1952), p. 22.

productive powers of the country we should double the supply of commodities in every market, but we should by the same stroke double the purchasing power. Every one would bring a double demand as well as supply: everybody would be able to buy twice as much because everybody would have twice as much to offer in exchange. It is a sheer absurdity that all things should fall in value and that all producers should, in consequence, be insufficiently remunerated.[11]

As stated by Mill, Say's Law is expressed in barter terms. But the classical economists believed that the principle was equally valid if money were introduced into the analysis. In a monetary economy Say's Law is interpreted to mean that money income will automatically and continuously be spent at the same rate at which it is being generated through the act of production. If this is true, then money makes no difference and supply will continue to create demand.

Say's Law and the Classical Theory of Interest

One possible trouble spot in this otherwise harmonious picture is saving. Saving, as defined earlier, is the nonexpenditure of current income for currently produced goods and services. Thus, if some persons or groups in the economy save a portion of their money income there may be a deficiency of aggregate demand equal to the amounts being saved. This possibility, too, was denied by the classical economists, because in their view saving is nothing more than another form of spending. Specifically, it represents spending for capital goods. All saving, in other words, is automatically transformed into investment spending. Thus the act of saving cannot give rise to a deficiency of total demand or an interruption in the flow of income and expenditure. This belief of the classical economists is illustrated in the following statement by Alfred Marshall:

The whole of a man's income is expended in the purchase of services and commodities. It is indeed commonly said that a man spends some portion of his income and saves another. But it is a familiar economic axiom that a man purchases labour and commodities with that portion of his income which he saves just as much as he does with that he is said to spend. He is said to spend when he seeks to obtain present enjoyment from the services and commodities which he purchases. He is said to save when he causes the labour and the commodities which he purchases to be devoted to the production of wealth from which he expects to derive the means of enjoyment in the future.[12]

The mechanism in classical thought that transforms saving (nonspending) into investment (spending for capital goods) is the rate of interest. The classical theory of interest is a necessary part of the classical theory

[11] John Stuart Mill, *Principles of Political Economy* (London, Longmans, Green, 1936), Book III, Ch. XIV, Sec. 1, p. 551. (*Ex vi termini* in Mill's quotation means: "By the meaning of the word.")
[12] Alfred Marshall, *The Pure Theory of Domestic Values* (London, The London School of Economics and Political Science, 1949), p. 34.

of employment because it is the means whereby Say's Law remains valid in a monetary economy. Interest in the classical system brings the demand for investment into equilibrium with the willingness to save. Since investment represents the demand for investible resources, and saving represents their supply, interest is the "price" at which the two are equated.

Figure 4–5 presents geometrically the essence of classical thinking with respect to the rate of interest. In the figure, DD is the demand for investible resources, while SS is saving, or the supply of investible resources. Since saving is non-consumption, the act of saving releases resources from the production of consumer goods and services. The demand for these resources is similar to the demand for any economic resource, which is to say that it depends basically upon the productivity of the resource. Thus, the DD schedule in Figure 4–5 has its origins in the productivity of capital.

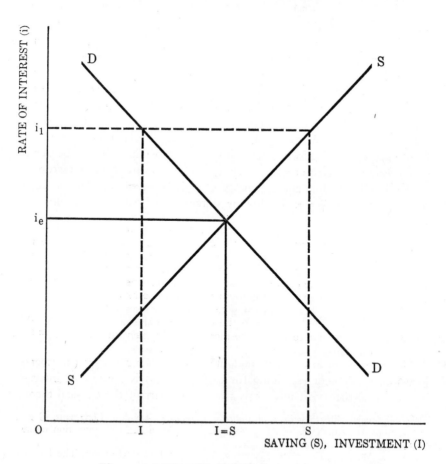

Figure 4–5. The Classical Theory of Interest

If, in the economy as a whole, individuals, households, and business firms attempt to save more out of current income than business firms want to spend for new capital equipment at the prevailing market rate of interest, forces will be set in motion that will reduce saving and increase investment until they are brought into equality with one another. For example, if the market rate of interest is at i_1 in the figure, this means that saving groups in the economy are attempting to save more than is wanted for the purchase of new capital equipment. But this disequilibrium will cause the rate of interest to fall, and as it falls the incentive to save will be lessened, while the incentive to invest (i.e., to purchase capital goods) will increase. Market adjustment will continue until the market rate of interest has reached the level at which the demand for and the supply of savings are equated. In Figure 4–5 this condition prevails at the indicated interest rate of i_e. As Keynes stated, the rate of interest in classical theory is the nexus that unites decisions to abstain from present consumption—that is, saving—with decisions to provide for future consumption—that is, investment. As long as this is the case, Say's Law remains intact.

The classical theory of interest may be summarized in two equations that express the investment and saving functions. These equations are

$$I = f(i) \qquad\qquad (4\text{–}12)$$
$$S = f(i) \qquad\qquad (4\text{–}13)$$

The above equations assert that both investment, I, and saving, S, are functions of the rate of interest. Since I and S in the equations (and the schedules of Figure 4–5) are *ex ante* concepts, equilibrium exists only when I and S are equal. This prevails at the point of intersection of the investment and saving schedules shown in Figure 4–5. If $S > I$, the rate of interest will fall, and if $I > S$, the rate of interest will rise. Algebraically, the necessary condition for equilibrium is that $I - S = 0$.

One final point concerning the classical theory of interest should be mentioned. This has to do with the *interest-elasticity* of both the demand schedule for and supply schedule of savings. This is a technical point but one of some significance from a policy point of view, since, in general, it is the classical contention that both schedules are highly interest-elastic. What this means is that both the demand for savings for investment and the supply of savings are highly sensitive to small changes in the market rate of interest. As a consequence, only minor changes are needed in the market rate of interest to bring about equilibrium between investment and savings. Through changes in the money supply and the rate of interest, monetary policy can bring about new levels of investment expenditure and thereby regulate the income and employment level. For most of the classical economists, however, questions of this sort were academic, because the whole structure of classical employment theory was designed to show that full employment is the normal state of affairs in the economy. Nevertheless, the reader should recognize that the classical assumptions concerning the interest-elasticity of savings and investment schedules do carry with them certain specific policy implications.

The Theory of the Price Level

The final building block in the classical structure is the theory of how the general level of prices in the economy is determined. This theory also explains the role that money occupies in the classical scheme. Classical thinking about the price level is contained in what is known as the *quantity theory of money*. In actuality there is no single quantity theory of money with which all the classical economists were in agreement. But the various versions of the quantity theory all focus attention on the relationship between the quantity of money in circulation and the general level of prices.

A good starting point for discussion of the quantity theory of money is the *equation of exchange*, which may be expressed algebraically in the following form:

$$M^o v = p \cdot Y \tag{4-14}$$

In the equation M^o is the money supply; v the income velocity of circulation (that is, the number of times each unit of money turns over in income and product transactions during a given time period); p the general price level; and Y real income. Expressed in this form, the equation of exchange is simply a truism, for it must follow that the quantity of money multiplied by the number of times each unit of money is used in a period equals the goods and services produced during the period times the average price level for the goods and services. Each side of the equation represents a different way of describing the same thing.

However, if we begin to make assumptions about some of the variables contained in the truistic equation of exchange, as was done by the classical economists, it is possible to work out some causal relationships with respect to the role of money in the economic system. For instance, the classical economists assumed that the velocity of circulation v was relatively stable. The velocity of circulation was believed to be deeply rooted in the habit patterns of the community and hence slow to change. Since *full* employment was the presumed outcome in the classical scheme, output also had to be a constant. Thus the only magnitudes that varied in the short run were the money supply, M^o, and the general price level, p.

To understand fully the classical relationship between the money supply and the general price level, it is first necessary to recall the classical attitude toward money. To the classical economists money was simply a medium of exchange. Its only important function was to facilitate the real process of exchange, which was one of exchanging goods for goods. As a consequence, the classical economists saw no reason why people would want to hold money as such. If an individual came into possession of additional amounts of money this simply meant that he had additional purchasing power at his disposal and, given the medium-of-exchange function of money, he would choose to spend it. In the classical view, therefore, more money in circulation in the economy could only mean more spending.

Let us see what this means in view of the above-mentioned classical assumptions concerning the stability of both N and Y. What will happen, in other words, if there is an increase in the supply of money in the economy? An increase in the money supply means more spending; if output cannot change because the economy is always at full employment, and if the velocity of circulation remains stable, then the only thing that can change is the general price level. In effect, then, the classical quantity theory of money asserts that the general price level, p, is a function of the supply of money M^o.

$$p = f(M^o) \qquad (4\text{--}15)$$

It should be noted that this general statement does not tell us exactly how p varies with changes in M^o. A rigid version of the quantity theory holds that prices always vary in exact proportion to changes in the money supply, a view that also implies that v and Y do not vary at all. Less rigid versions maintain that the price level tends to vary directly with changes in the money supply, although not necessarily in the same proportion. The latter is the more meaningful interpretation.

The classical theory of the price level can be depicted geometrically, as is done in Figure 4–6. Real income is shown on the vertical axis, while the general price level is charted on the horizontal axis. The $M^o v$ curve provides the necessary link between real income (output) and the price level. The amount of money in circulation times its income velocity will be a constant; thus, with a fixed amount of money in circulation as represented by M^o_1, real income can rise only if the price level falls. As long as the money supply is fixed, real income and the general price level must move inversely to one another.

The way in which an increase in the money supply will affect the general price level can be shown in the figure. Assume that Y_1 is the full employment level of output, and that M^o_1 represents the initial supply of money in the economy. Under these circumstances the general price level will be p_1. What will happen if the curve representing a constant volume of expenditure shifts upward to $M^o_2 v$? Since we have assumed

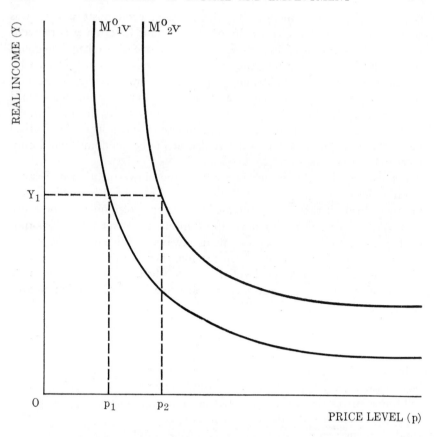

Figure 4–6. The Classical Quantity Theory of Money

that the economy is already at the full employment level, real income Y cannot change. The only thing that can change is the general price level; it will rise to the level indicated by p_2 in the figure.

A Diagrammatic Summary

We have discussed the major propositions that make up the classical theory of employment. It is appropriate at this point to draw these propositions together and briefly summarize the essential features of the classical theory. Figure 4–7 portrays geometrically the key elements in the classical theory of employment. We may summarize these as follows:

(1) The supply of and the demand for labor determine both the *real wage* and the level of employment. This proposition is represented by diagram A in the upper left-hand corner of Figure 4–7.

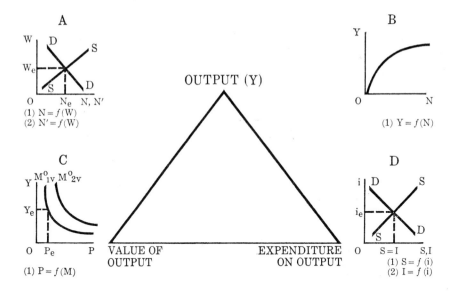

Figure 4–7. The Classical System

(2) With a given technology and a fixed quantity of resources other than labor, real income is uniquely determined by the level of employment. This is the classical production function, and it is depicted by diagram B in the upper right-hand corner of Figure 4–7.

(3) The monetary value—or value in current prices—of real income determined in the manner described depends, in the classical analysis, on the general level of prices. The latter, in turn, depends upon the money supply. These relationships are depicted in diagram C in the lower left-hand corner of Figure 4–7.

(4) Finally, the rate of interest is determined by the supply of savings and the demand for real capital assets, that is, the demand for saving. The rate of interest has the unique function of insuring that money income saved will always be spent for capital goods and thus not leak out of the income stream. This aspect of the classical theory is shown in diagram D in the lower right-hand corner of Figure 4–7. (The triangle shows how output, the value of output, and expenditure on output are linked together by the functional relationships that enter into the classical analysis.)

Before we turn to a discussion of the broad policy implications of the classical analysis, two things need to be said about the "model" we have been discussing. In the first place, the system is so constructed that it tends automatically toward a level of full employment. The demand for and the supply of labor curves have the role of determining the actual employment level, but they are so conceived that this employment level is by definition one of full employment. Moreover, Say's Law of Markets, in conjunction with the classical theory of interest, makes certain that there is no possibility of involuntary unemployment in the system because of any deficiency of aggregate demand. Second, if there is within the system any temporary deviation away from the full employment equilibrium, the appropriate remedy is clearly indicated. This is a reduction in the real wage, which can be brought about either by an increase in the money supply, with its consequent effects on the general price level, or by a cut in money wages.

Policy Implications of the Classical Theory

The classical ideas just discussed consist of a structure of abstract ideas and relationships that purport to explain how the economy works in the determination of the income and employment level. These ideas form a body of economic theory. But like most other sets of theoretical ideas in economics, this particular set contains within itself significant implications for public policy.

The classical theory of employment implies a predilection for *laissez faire*, the "hands-off" (or noninterference) policy that minimizes the extent to which government intervenes in the operation of the economy. In a broad sense there are two major reasons why the state—that is, the government of a nation—might intervene in the nations' economy.[13] The first is that imperfections in the market economy may lead to an undue concentration of economic power in private hands. The second is that the private or market sector of the economy may not function sufficiently well to provide jobs for all members of the labor force actively seeking employment.

Actually both of the above possibilities are denied by the classical system. As we saw earlier classical economists assumed that competition is a normal characteristic of the economy. The kind of competition they envisaged as being dominant in the economy was the *atomistic* variety, in which the number of firms in every industry is so great in relation to the demand for the output of the industry that no single firm can exercise any control over the price at which its product is sold. If no firm is in a position to exercise any control whatsoever over price, no firm (or person) can possess any real economic power over other firms (or

---

[13] This is aside from the fact that there are certain activities necessary to the functioning of a complex society that can only be done by the state; for example, maintenance of law and order and provision for national defense.

persons). All firms and persons are at the mercy of the impersonal market forces of supply and demand. If this is a correct evaluation of the situation in the economy, then there is no basis for intervention by the state for the sake of redressing any abuse of private economic power. The latter does not exist in the classical scheme.

The second reason for state intervention is the continued existence of a significant amount of *involuntary* unemployment. As we have seen, classical employment theory leads to the conclusion that involuntary unemployment on a large scale for anything more than brief periods is an impossibility. If the economy has an inherent and automatic tendency toward equilibrium at full employment, then there is no real need for public intervention on the ground that employment is inadequate. Under such circumstances *laissez faire* is the appropriate policy.

Competition plays a vital role in this respect because its presence within the economic system insures the flexibility of wages and prices, including the rate of interest. The system will move toward an equilibrium at full employment only if wages respond instantly to the least discrepancy between the demand for and supply of labor in the market. The same holds true for the rate of interest, for unless interest responds to any discrepancy between the demand for and supply of saving, the system will not attain the equality between saving and investment necessary to insure the working of Say's Law in a monetary economy. Price and wage flexibility stems from competition, and the more highly competitive the system, the more responsive wages and prices will be to market forces.

The Collapse of Classical Employment Theory

The classical theory of employment is no longer widely accepted, either by the general public or by academic and business economists. Few people today really believe that there is any automatic tendency for the economic system to reach equilibrium at the level of full employment. In addition, there are very few economists who still support the classical analysis as a good theoretical explanation of how the employment level is actually determined.

The collapse of the classical theory of employment ushered in a new phase of economic thought, for this theory had enjoyed the support of practically all economists of any importance for nearly a century. This collapse can be attributed to two major factors: the experience of the Great Depression, and the appearance of an alternative—and more feasible —explanation of how the employment level is determined.

Until the 1930's, as Galbraith has pointed out, the American economy had never experienced a deep and prolonged depression.[14] In the past there had been periods of unemployment and falling prices, but these

[14] Galbraith, *op. cit.*, p. 67.

were rarely of long duration, and were generally followed by a prompt recovery of the economic system to high employment levels. Until the 1930's, in other words, the experience of the American economy tended to confirm the classical theory and its conclusion that full employment was a *normal* condition. The fluctuations in income and employment that actually did take place could be "explained" as resulting from frictions and imperfections in the market, or else as the consequence of war and its aftermath.

All of this changed with the depression that began with the cataclysmic collapse of stock market values in the autumn of 1929 and continued until the wartime mobilization of the 1940's once again brought full employment to the American economy. For ten long years serious and prolonged unemployment became the *normal* condition of the economy. Under these circumstances not even the staunchest defender of the classical analysis could seriously maintain that there existed within the economy forces that would automatically generate continuous full employment. The Great Depression was a social catastrophe without previous parallel in American economic life; classical employment theory simply proved to be incapable of coping with such a phenomenon. We pointed out earlier that experience is the ultimate test of the validity of any theory, and on this basis the classical analysis was found wanting.

The second reason for the collapse of the classical employment theory was the appearance of an alternative theory during the decade of the 1930's. While it is true that the facts of experience in the 1930's were clearly not in accord with the classical analysis, it is equally true that facts alone will not destroy a theory. As James B. Conant, former president of Harvard University, has said, "It takes a new conceptual scheme to cause the abandonment of an old one." [15] This took place in 1936 when Keynes published his *General Theory*, which has become the intellectual foundation of all modern employment theory.

Keynes' purpose in the *General Theory* was twofold. In the first place, he sought to demonstrate the basic failings of the classical theory of employment not so much by appealing to the facts of experience, but rather by demonstrating that the theory itself was internally inconsistent and logically untenable at a number of points. Second, Keynes sought to construct an alternative theory or explanation of how the employment level is determined in a complex industrial society. He called his treatise *The General Theory of Employment, Interest and Money* because he believed that the techniques and analytical tools characteristic of classical thinking were applicable only in the special case of full employment, while his own analysis was applicable at all levels of employment.

Keynes' theory of employment determination is basically the concern

[15] James B. Conant, *On Understanding Science* (New Haven, Yale University Press, 1947), p. 89.

of the remaining chapters of this book, but we may at this point allude briefly to his major criticisms of the classical theory, even though each of these will be examined later in more detail.

Keynes' criticism of the classical analysis is directed, first, at the classical view that the employment level and the real wage were determined by the intersection of the demand and supply schedules for labor; and second, at the idea that saving is, after all, nothing more than spending for capital goods. He refutes, in other words, the validity of Say's Law of Markets for a monetary economy.

In attacking the classical doctrine that the supply of and demand for labor determine both the real wage and the employment level, Keynes makes two points. He denies, in the first instance, that the supply of labor is a function of the *real* wage by pointing out that workers do not normally withdraw from the labor market if there has been a fall in real wages as a result of a rise in prices with money wages unchanged.

A fall in real wages due to a rise in prices with money wages unaltered, does not, as a rule, cause the supply of labor on offer at the current wage to fall below the amount actually employed prior to the rise of prices. To suppose that it does is to suppose that all those who are now unemployed though willing to work at the current wage will withdraw the offer of their labour in the event of a small rise in the cost of living.[16]

Keynes' second point concerns the relationship between money wages and prices. He refutes the notion that workers are in a position to determine the real wage and with it the volume of employment by the money-wage bargains they make with the employers. Workers cannot do this, he asserts, because money wages cannot move independently of the general level of prices. To prove his point Keynes utilizes analytical concepts developed by the classical economists in the area of price and value theory. Under conditions of pure competition and with a given demand schedule, prices will be governed by marginal costs expressed in money. This follows from the profit-maximization principle which asserts that the firm will adjust output to the level at which marginal cost and marginal revenue are equal. Money wages will necessarily make up the major part of marginal costs. Consequently, any change in money-wage rates would cause prices to change in about the same proportion. If this analysis is correct, it means that changes in the money wage will not necessarily bring about any change in the real wage and with it a change in the employment level. Keynes thought that the classical economists were so preoccupied with the idea that prices depend on the quantity of money that they failed to see the implications inherent in their own analysis of the behavior of the business firm.

The second major argument of Keynes strikes at the heart of Say's

[16] Keynes, *op. cit.*, p. 12.

Law. In a monetary economy Say's Law reduces itself to the proposition that money income will automatically be spent at the same rate at which it is being created by the process of production. Keynes contends in the *General Theory* that the classical economists reached this erroneous conclusion because they confused the proposition that all income must be spent at the same rate at which it is created with another proposition which is quite true, namely that the "income derived in the aggregate by all the elements in the community concerned in a productive activity necessarily has a value exactly equal to the *value* of that output." [17] In other words, there is a basic truth in Say's Law in the sense that output or productive activity is the source of income for the whole community, but it does not logically follow that income will necessarily be spent at a rate which will clear the market of all that is produced. Much of the *General Theory*, in fact, is devoted to showing why decisions to produce, i.e., to create income, will not necessarily always coincide with decisions to spend that income.

The classical theory of interest is a necessary part of Say's Law in a monetary economy, for the rate of interest joins the decision to save with the decision to invest. But this too is challenged by Keynes, who takes the common-sense view that decisions to save and decisions to invest are two different kinds of decisions that cannot be automatically linked together in any simple way. More importantly, he attempts to show through the development of an alternative theory that the rate of interest is *not* necessarily a nexus that unites the decision to save and the decision to invest. Once this link is severed between saving and investment, Say's Law breaks down and the way is open for the existence of involuntary unemployment due to a deficiency of total or aggregate demand.

Before concluding our summary of the Keynesian criticism of classical employment theory one final point needs to be underscored. Although Keynes was a vigorous critic of the classical theory of employment, the reader should not conclude that Keynes—and modern economists in general—rejected the whole of the classical tradition and body of economic analysis. Keynes explicitly accepted the validity of classical analysis in the area of price and distribution theory, as the following quote from the *General Theory* well illustrates:

If we suppose the volume of output to be given, i.e., to be determined by forces outside the classical scheme of thought, then there is no objection to be raised against the classical analysis of the manner in which private self-interest will determine what in particular is produced, in what proportion the factors of production will be combined to produce it, and how the value of the final product will be distributed between them.[18]

[17] *Ibid.*, p. 20.
[18] *Ibid.*, p. 378.

In one other respect, Keynes was very much in harmony with the classical tradition, even though he rejected the employment theory of the classical economists. As we saw in our earlier discussion, the deductive approach was the typical methodology of classical analysis. In this sense Keynes remains close to the classical tradition because the methodology of the *General Theory* is basically deductive. This will become increasingly apparent to the reader in subsequent chapters.

5 | The Structure of Modern Income and Employment Theory

In this chapter we turn to a discussion of the structure, or framework, of modern employment theory, which has largely developed from the thought and writing of John Maynard Keynes. Specifically, the task of this chapter is to outline the essential characteristics of the modern theory, leaving to the chapters that follow a more detailed analysis of the component parts of the theoretical structure.

The Essence of the Income-Employment Problem

A logical point of departure for our study of income and employment determination is the concept of capacity. It will be recalled from the discussion in the previous chapter that capacity is defined as the economy's potential for the production of goods and services. For purposes of economic policy, the President's Council of Economic Advisors defines potential GNP as the volume of goods and services that the economy would ordinarily produce at the interim target unemployment rate of 4 per cent.[1] For 1965 the council's estimate of potential GNP was in excess of $600 billion in 1958 prices. The actual GNP was $614.4 billion.

If we begin with the concept of productive capacity, certain consequences follow logically. First, output will depend upon the extent to which this capacity is being utilized. This will be true up to the limits of capacity. Second, output will depend upon the level of employment as long as all resources other than labor are fixed. This brings us to the key question of modern employment theory: *What is it that determines*

[1] *Economic Report of the President*, Washington, 1966, p. 40.

110

the extent to which the economy's productive capacity is being utilized?

In a sense the answer to this question is deceptively simple, for it is the *expectation* of the businessman that he will be able to sell what he produces which leads him to make use of the productive capacity at his disposal. The presumption here is that the output will be sold at prices that cover costs of production. Stated in more formal terms, productive capacity will be brought into use (or production will take place) whenever there exists the expectation that demand for the output will be sufficient to clear the market of what is being produced. Note carefully two points. First, this statement describes the conditions under which productive capacity will be utilized in a market economy, that is to say, an economy in which the basic decisions about what is to be produced and in what quantities are made by private individuals rather than public authorities. Second, the key word in the statement is expectation, which is a way of stressing the fact that production in a market economy is carried on, for the most part, in anticipation of demand.

If it is true that the expectation of demand is the essential condition required to bring productive capacity into use, it follows that *the theory of income determination in the modern economy is basically a theory of aggregate demand.* In other words, if we are to understand how the level of output and employment is actually determined, it is necessary that we understand how demand for the output of the whole economy is determined. In sum, aggregate demand is the crucial determinant of the level of income and employment during short periods when productive capacity is assumed to be relatively fixed. This is the central theme of the *General Theory.*

In the long run the income-employment problem is more complex. Over the long run productive capacity is subject to change. Thus, a long-run theory of income and employment determination must explain, first, changes in the economy's productive capacity over time; and, second, how aggregate demand adjusts over time to such changes. This is the essence of post-Keynesian growth theory with which we will be concerned in Part III.

The Aggregate Supply Schedule

The idea that there exists for the economy a given productive capacity which will be utilized in greater or lesser degree according to the aggregate of expectations held by entrepreneurs is represented in the aggregate supply schedule or function. As a concept, the aggregate supply schedule for the whole economy is very much like the supply schedule for any individual commodity. A typical supply curve for a commodity has a positive slope—that is, it slopes upward to the right—and shows the prices at which various amounts of the commodity will be forthcoming.

It is an *ex ante* concept in the sense that it depicts the intended response of the suppliers of the commodity to varying circumstances. The schedule is, in effect, a series of "supply prices" for varying amounts of the commodity. The "supply price" for any particular quantity of a commodity is that price which will just induce the producer or supplier to continue to offer that quantity of the commodity on the market; thus the supply *schedule* shows the amounts of the commodity that will be forthcoming at any and all possible prices. The aggregate supply schedule represents not the response of a single producer supplying the market with a particular commodity, but the summation, in effect, of the responses of all producers supplying the whole of the output of the economy. It seeks to show, in other words, the conditions under which varying amounts of total output will be supplied or produced. It is in this sense that the aggregate supply schedule is conceptually similar to the ordinary supply schedule for a single commodity.

The Keynesian Aggregate Supply Function

In the *General Theory* Keynes defined the aggregate supply price of the output of a given amount of employment as "the expectation of proceeds which will just make it worth the while of the entrepreneur to give that employment." [2] What Keynes had in mind was a schedule which would show for any and all possible levels of employment the volume of receipts from the sale of output that would justify the varying quantities of employment. Such a schedule shows the amount of employment that entrepreneurs in the aggregate can be expected to offer on the basis of any and all possible volumes of proceeds from the sale of the output resulting from the different amounts of employment. In the *General Theory* Keynes linked employment, rather than output or real income, to expected proceeds because at the time he was writing (1936) statistical techniques for the accurate measurement of important aggregates such as GNP were not highly developed. He thought that employment constituted the best single measure of total or aggregate economic activity.

A highly simplified version of the Keynesian aggregate supply function is illustrated by the hypothetical data in Table 5–1, which relate employment and expected proceeds. For the sake of simplicity we assume that labor is the *only* resource, and thus the only costs of production that must be covered in the aggregate by the sales proceeds are labor costs. It is further assumed in Table 5–1 that the normal work-week is 40 hours, and that workers are employed for 50 weeks each year. In the table there are two schedules: Schedule *A* and Schedule *B*. Schedule

---

[2] John Maynard Keynes, *The General Theory of Employment, Interest and Money* (New York, Harcourt, Brace, 1936), p. 24.

TABLE 5-1.

The Aggregate Supply Function

Employment (N) (in millions of workers)	Schedule A		Schedule B	
	Money Wages (per hour)	Aggregate Supply Price (Z) (in billions of dollars)	Money Wages (per hour)	Aggregate Supply Price (Z') (in billions of dollars)
68	$2.00	$272	$2.00	$272
70	2.00	280	2.10	294
72	2.00	288	2.20	317
74	2.00	296	2.30	340
76	2.00	304	2.40	365
78	2.00	312	2.50	390
80	2.00	320	2.60	416

Note: 40-hour work-week and 50-week work-year assumed. Data rounded to nearest whole number.

A is based upon the assumption that the money wages of workers remain constant at $2.00 per hour, regardless of the actual level of employment or demand for labor. Schedule *B* is based upon the assumption that the money wage will rise as more employment is offered. This implies that, as the demand for labor increases, its price, i.e., the money wage, will rise.

Let us examine each of these schedules in a little more detail. Schedule *A* shows what the minimum expected sales proceeds must be for entrepreneurs to offer employment to specified numbers of workers. For example, if employers in the aggregate are to offer employment to 78 million workers, the expected proceeds from the sale of the output produced by these 78 million workers must, *as a minimum*, be equal to $372 billion. Why is this? The $312 billion represents the total money costs of this amount of product which must be covered by sales proceeds if entrepreneurs in the aggregate are to continue to offer this amount of employment. Thus, the $312 billion is the aggregate supply price of this amount of employment. In Schedule *B* the aggregate supply price for each level of employment subsequent to 68 million is higher because of the assumption that the money wage will rise from $2.00 per hour to $2.60 per hour as the total volume of employment climbs from 68 to 80 million workers.

Figure 5-1 illustrates graphically the Keynesian aggregate supply function.[3] In the figure, employment is plotted on the horizontal axis, and expected sales proceeds on the vertical axis. If we then plot the data of

---

[3] The student should not confuse the above curves with the production function, which normally shows the relationship between employment and output.

Table 5–1 we get the two curves shown in the figure. The one labeled Z is the aggregate supply schedule based upon a fixed money wage of $2.00 per hour, whereas the schedule labeled Z' reflects the fact that the money wage may rise as the level of employment rises. The more rapidly the money wage rises with actual changes in the level of employment, the less responsive is the employment level to any given change in expected proceeds. Technically, this means that, as the elasticity of the

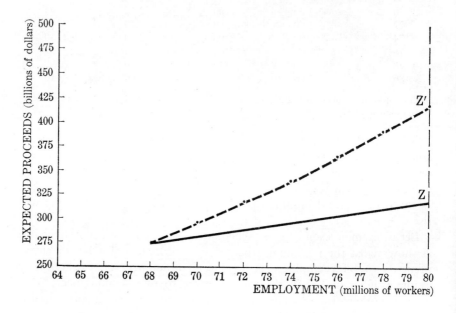

Figure 5–1. The Keynesian Aggregate Supply Function:
Employment and Proceeds

employment level decreases, the money wage becomes more sensitive to any increase in the demand for labor. The aggregate supply schedule will become perfectly inelastic with respect to expected proceeds at the level of employment which represents full employment of the existing labor force. If, for example, the employment level of 80 million workers is the upper limit to the labor supply in our hypothetical economy, then the two curves, Z and Z', will terminate at this point. Since no more workers are available once employment has reached the 80-million level, actual employment cannot exceed this amount, irrespective of what happens to expected proceeds. This is shown in Figure 5–1 by the dotted line extending vertically upward at the 80-million mark on the horizontal axis.

Alternative Concepts of Aggregate Supply

The Keynesian aggregate supply function just examined linked employment to expected proceeds primarily because Keynes thought employment to be the most satisfactory measure of changes in the current output of the economy. In the more than three decades since publication of the *General Theory*, various alternative measures for determining total output have been developed. The extensive and rapid development of national income accounting during this period has provided the economist with excellent techniques by means of which the heterogeneous complex of goods and services produced by the economy can be reduced to a single aggregate. Procedures for measurement of real changes in this aggregate over time are similarly well developed. Consequently, the aggregate supply function can be formulated in terms of total output (or real income) rather than the level of employment, and this has become the standard practice in modern employment theory.

The more recent formulation of the aggregate supply schedule is shown in Figure 5–2. The aggregate supply schedule is represented by the line *OZ*, which, it should be noted, bisects the origin at an angle of 45°. (Generally in modern income theory the aggregate supply function is depicted by a 45° line.) To understand the significance of the 45° line, the reader should recall that the aggregate supply schedule consists of a series of points, each one of which represents "supply price" for the output associated with different amounts of employment. The aggregate supply schedule must show the conditions under which entrepreneurs in the aggregate will produce a particular volume of goods and services and, more important, continue to produce that volume. This is what the 45° line in the Figure 5–2 attempts to do.

Real income is measured on both the vertical and horizontal axes of the figure, but the sense in which we are measuring real income differs for each of the two axes. The horizontal axis measures the money value in *constant* prices of the economy's current output of goods and services, but this is also equivalent to the total costs—including a normal profit—incurred by entrepreneurs in the aggregate in producing any given output. Statistically and in the aggregate, the value of any given quantity of physical output must be equal to the costs of producing that output. Thus, we can interpret the horizontal axis of the figure as a measure of current output seen from the viewpoint of the costs that entrepreneurs incur when they decide to produce a particular volume of goods and services. Specifically, the costs involved are those listed earlier (Chapter 2) in the discussion of the allocations side of the gross national product: wages, rents, interest, profits, capital consumption allowances, and indirect business taxes.

Since the aggregate supply schedule or function must show the condi-

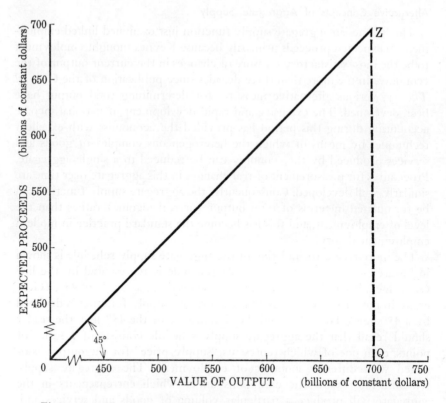

Figure 5-2. The Aggregate Supply Schedule: Expected Proceeds and
Value of Output in Constant Prices

tions under which any particular level of production will continue, it
follows that entrepreneurs in the aggregate must receive a return flow
of expenditures equal to the costs they incur if they produce any given
aggregate of goods and services. Since Figure 5-2 measures real income
(output valued in constant prices) on both the horizontal and vertical
axes, the only possible line that will conform to the conditions described
above is the 45° line that bisects the point of origin. In other words, if
the vertical axis is viewed as measuring the flow of expenditures or expected proceeds in constant prices, then the 45° line must of necessity
be the aggregate supply schedule, for each point on such a schedule represents the amounts that entrepreneurs must receive back as receipts (as
measured on the vertical axis) if they are to continue to produce varying
amounts of output (as measured on the horizontal axis).

As was the case with the Keynesian aggregate supply function, there
will be some level of output which represents full employment for the

45° aggregate supply schedule. This may be represented by a point upon the horizontal axis, for once the economy has achieved full-employment (capacity production) no further increases in output are possible. In Figure 5–2 this point is represented by the vertical line ZQ. It is possible though not customary in modern income analysis, to combine the Keynesian aggregate supply schedule with the 45° aggregate supply schedule by measuring employment as well as output or real income on the horizontal axis. This can be done because each possible level of output will correlate with a specific amount of employment. Because of the law of diminishing returns, however, employment will not necessarily vary in the same proportion as output, a fact which makes it difficult to compute the exact amount of employment which might be associated with each and every possible level of real output. (See footnote 2.) As a consequence, most modern income theorists have been content to measure real income only on the horizontal axis and simply assume—correctly—that employment will vary more or less directly with changes in the level of real income.

A third type of aggregate supply schedule which explicitly allows for changes in the general level of prices can be constructed if we change the vertical axis in our diagram from a measure of output in *constant* prices to a measure of output in *current* prices. This is done in Figure 5–3. In the figure we still measure real income on the horizontal axis. But the vertical axis now measures the current market value of output, which is its value in present prices. The aggregate supply function now takes on the shape of the curve OZ'. This curve shows that the general level of prices will rise with successive rises in real income.[4] As a consequence, the flow of expected proceeds that entrepreneurs must receive to induce them to continue to produce at varying levels must increase proportionally more than the increase in output. The closer the economy gets to the full-employment and full-capacity output, the sharper will be the increase in the general price level; hence the steeper the rise in the aggregate supply curve OZ'. When the full-employment output level is attained, the curve becomes completely inelastic. Output will no longer respond to changes in the flow of expenditures. All that can happen from this point is a further upward shift in the general level of prices. The curve OZ' in Figure 5–3 was constructed from actual GNP data for the period 1958 through 1965. Values of GNP in both constant (1958) and current prices for each year are given by the dots next to each year shown. It may be observed that the "fit" of the OZ' curve, while not perfect, clearly reflects the concepts just discussed.

[4] This increase in the price level may be accounted for by an increase in unit costs of production as output expands because of diminishing returns, as well as an increase in wage rates and other money costs that ensue when production increases.

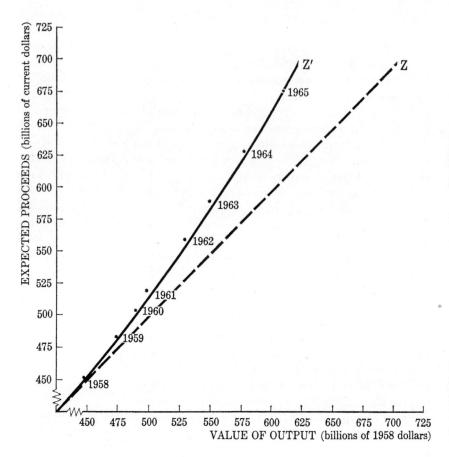

SOURCE: *Economic Indicators*

Figure 5–3. The Aggregate Supply Schedule: Expected Proceeds in
Current Prices and Value of Output in Constant Prices

Thus far we have considered three different formulations of the aggregate supply function. No single one can be regarded as "best," as each
formulation has its uses in connection with different aspects of modern
income and employment analysis. Nevertheless, the concept that is most
widely employed in contemporary income analysis is the 45° aggregate
supply schedule, and it is the one that we shall generally use in ensuing
discussions. The 45° aggregate supply schedule forces us to formulate
the entire analysis in real, i.e., constant-price, terms, which is the most
meaningful procedure from the standpoint of the employment level.
Modern employment theory maintains that employment can be expected

to change primarily when there is a change in output, not necessarily when there is a change in the monetary value of that output.

The Aggregate Demand Schedule

The second major analytical tool in modern income and employment theory is aggregate demand. Just as aggregate supply is conceived of as a schedule showing the expected proceeds necessary to induce a given quantity of employment or amount of output in the economy, aggregate demand is also conceived of as a schedule showing the amounts the major spending units in the economy are prepared to spend at each and every possible level of real income. It is a schedule that links real income and spending decisions for the economy as a whole. The idea that the aggregate demand schedule involves a relationship between decisions to purchase the different categories of output and the level of output itself is a gross oversimplification of a concept that is quite complex. But such a definition of the aggregate demand schedule is, nevertheless, a good point of departure for our analysis.

Figure 5–4 depicts the relationship described above. The line DD is the aggregate demand schedule. As in Figure 5–2, the vertical axis measures income as a flow of expenditure, while the horizontal axis depicts income as a flow of output. Thus, the curve DD can be said to represent the spending decisions associated with any and all possible levels of output or real income.

Since the aggregate demand schedule seeks to show how much the economy is disposed to spend for the various categories of output at different levels of real income, it is therefore an *ex ante* phenomenon. The aggregate demand schedule does not represent any particular level of statistical demand, but rather the demand that will prevail if certain conditions are satisfied. The notion of an aggregate demand schedule is important for our analysis because it underscores the fact that those who make the decisions to spend are not necessarily the same individuals or groups who make the decisions for production and employment. This will become fully apparent when we examine the process by which the income and the employment level is actually determined.

The Origin of Spending Decisions

Where do the spending decisions of the economy originate? Or, stated in different terms, who or what are the spending units in the economy? This is a question that concerns the component parts of the aggregate

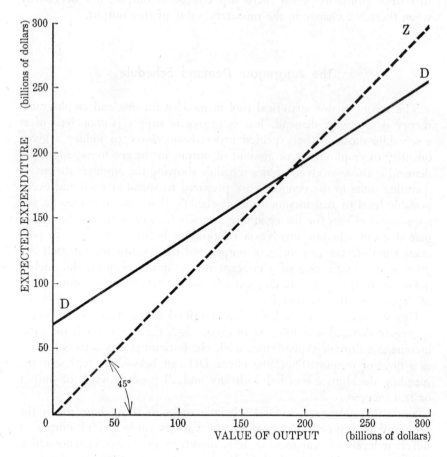

Figure 5-4. The Aggregate Demand Schedule

demand schedule, and a complete answer depends upon the discussion to follow in the next several chapters. But a brief answer can be given here that will serve to outline the basic problem involved in the analysis of demand for the output of the whole economy.

If we ignore for the moment any economic ties the economy may have with other nations, decisions to purchase a portion of the current output of the economy must originate in one of three major economic sectors: (1) the household or consumer sector, which is the purchaser of consumer goods and services; (2) the business or firm sector, which is the purchaser of capital or investment goods; and, (3) the public or government sector, which is the point of origin for decisions relating to the economy's output of government or "collective" goods and services. In a symbolic sense, then, the schedule of aggregate demand will be equal to the sum of consumption, C, investment, I, and government expenditure, G, for goods and services. In other words,

$$DD = C + I + G \qquad (5\text{--}1)$$

Since the aggregate demand schedule represents the spending intentions of the major spending units in the economy, a corollary question concerns the source of spending power at the disposal of these major spending units. In a monetary economy spending power requires access to a quantity of money, and thus the question pertains to the source of supply of money for the economy's spending units. Fundamentally, there are three possible sources of spending power for an individual spending unit in the economy. In the first place, a spending unit may finance its current expenditures by drawing upon assets accumulated during past income periods. These may be in the form of holdings of money or in the form of other assets which can be converted to money. A household, for example, might finance some of its current expenditures by drawing down a savings account, or perhaps by the sale of some of its holdings of stocks or bonds. Second, current expenditures may be financed out of current income. For the household or consumer sector of the economy and for the bulk of government purchases of goods and services this is the typical pattern. Most of us as individuals have to depend upon our current money income to finance the major portion of our current expenditures.

In the past the more usual practice in the business sector of the economy was to finance capital expenditures by borrowing rather than out of current and internal resources. Increasingly, however, business firms are resorting to internal financing for major items of capital expenditure, and thus the firm can, like the consumer, draw upon assets accumulated in past income periods to finance current outlays. For the business firm, depreciation reserves represent a prime internal source of finance for capital expenditures. But borrowing remains important as the third and final source of spending power for current expenditures. Consumers frequently resort to loans for financing large items of expenditures, such as houses, automobiles, and other durable goods, while it is quite commonplace for governmental units in the economy to borrow to meet a portion of their current expenditures. National governments, we may note in passing, possess the unique distinction of having the power to create money.

These remarks about the source of the money that provides the basis for spending power in a monetary economy apply to the whole economy much in the same way as they apply to individual spending units within the economy. For the aggregate of all spending units, in other words, spending or purchasing power can be derived from current income, borrowing, or the drawing-down of previously accumulated cash balances. If all spending units resort to the latter two sources for some portion of their purchasing power, new or additional quantities of funds are injected into the economic system. How this comes about will be examined in greater detail later.

These various sources of purchasing power rule out the possibility of any simple and direct relationship between the spending decisions embodied in the aggregate demand schedule and the income level. One major component of aggregate demand, consumption, can be related functionally to the real income level, but this is not necessarily the case with the other two components. To repeat, the kind of schedule shown in Figure 5–4 is an oversimplification. Such a schedule, though, is an extremely valuable analytical tool, for what counts from the standpoint of the income and employment level is the willingness of the entrepreneur in the economy to make use of the economy's productive capacity. And this is directly tied to his expectations concerning demand, which, in turn, depend upon the decisions made by the major spending entities in the economy.

The Equilibrium Level of Income and Employment

The schedules of aggregate supply and aggregate demand take us directly to the heart of modern income and employment theory. The basic —and in many respects simple—idea that Keynes put forth in the *General Theory* is that the aggregate supply and demand schedules of the economy between them determine the level of income and employment. According to Keynes, "the volume of employment is given by the point of intersection between the aggregate demand function and the aggregate supply function . . . this is the substance of the General Theory of Employment." [5]

The way in which aggregate supply and aggregate demand, considered together, determine the income and employment level is shown in Figure 5–5. As in Figure 5–2 and 5–4 real income is shown on both the vertical and horizontal axes. Again the 45° line OZ is the aggregate supply function, while the schedule DD represents the aggregate demand function. Given these two schedules, the volume of income and employment will inevitably adjust to the level found at the point of intersection of these two schedules. This is represented by the income level Y_e, which is both the equilibrium income level and the equilibrium employment level.

The reason why income and employment must of necessity adjust to the level represented by Y_e and why this particular level represents income and employment equilibrium can best be understood if we analyze what will happen assuming for the moment that some other income level exists

[5] Keynes, *op. cit.*, p. 25.

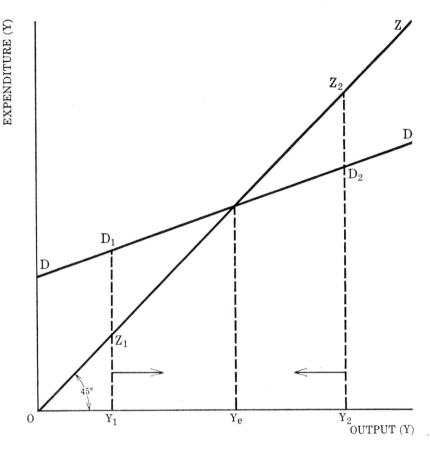

Figure 5–5. Aggregate Supply, Aggregate Demand, and the
Equilibrium Level of Income

in the economy. The actual income level, as we have seen, can always be depicted by some point on the 45° aggregate supply schedule, as well as by points on the horizontal or vertical axes. (Since our analysis is framed in real terms, prices remain constant.) Let us assume that the actual or realized income of the current income period is represented by point Y_1 on the horizontal axis. Geometrically, this income level is also represented by the vertical distance from Y_1 to point Z_1 on the aggregate supply schedule OZ. This distance represents the amount of production entrepreneurs in the aggregate decided to undertake in the expectation that sales proceeds would cover all costs incurred in producing this output. This distance also represents the amount of current money income being generated by current production.

What is the situation with respect to aggregate demand? The current income level, Y_1, is not an equilibrium income level, because at this particular level aggregate demand, DD, exceeds aggregate supply, OZ. At the point Y_1 the DD schedule lies above the OZ schedule. Specifically, this means that at the income level Y_1, the spending intentions of all spending units in economy are such that these add up to an amount equal to the distance Y_1D_1, which is in excess of the current output or income level Y_1Z_1. In short, the demand for current output exceeds the supply of output. This is an unstable or *disequilibrium* condition that cannot be sustained; instead it will drive the economy toward higher levels of income and employment.

Let us look more closely at what is taking place in the current income period. In the first place, additional purchasing power over and above the amounts generated by current income is being injected into the economy's income stream. Diagrammatically, this is represented by the distance Z_1D_1, since the excess of aggregate demand over aggregate supply is a measure of the amount of purchasing power required beyond that being generated by the process of production. For our immediate purposes the exact source of this purchasing power does not matter; what does matter is that new spending power is being injected into the income system. If the distance Z_1D_1 is a measure of the excess of current spending intentions over current (actual) output, how will the spending plans of the economy's spending units be satisfied? Since our analysis is in real terms, we have precluded any increase in the general level of prices as a result of the excess of aggregate demand. But if we rule out price changes, and if current supply falls short of demand, there remains only one other alternative: the excess of aggregate demand must be satisfied by sales out of existing *stocks* (*inventories*) of goods. The distance Z_1D_1 represents not only the excess of aggregate demand over aggregate supply in the current income period, but also the amount by which current inventories of goods must be drawn down to satisfy this demand. From the standpoint of the whole economy the distance represents *unintended* (*unplanned*) *disinvestment* in stocks. Such disinvestment is unintended because it results solely from the failure of production or output plans to coincide with spending plans in the current income period.

How does the situation that we have been describing appear from the point of view of the business firms of the economy? Typically, in this situation business firms will find their sales running ahead of current production, and they will revise their production plans upward for the next income period in the belief that the existing demand is a reliable indicator of demand in subsequent income periods. If most firms in the economy act accordingly, then output and employment will rise throughout the whole economy. This process of adjustment will necessarily continue until a situation is achieved in which output and spending decisions coincide. In Figure 5–5 this is the situation depicted by the intersection of the aggregate supply and aggregate demand schedules.

The foregoing analysis serves not only to show the essentials of the process by which income and employment adjust toward equilibrium values, but also should underscore the fact that disequilibrium—which always implies change—occurs whenever expected, or *ex ante*, values diverge from actual, or *ex post*, values. In the analysis we have been pursuing, the expected aggregate demand of entrepreneurs would be at the level Y_1Z_1, which originally led them to produce output at the rate Y_1. But actual or *ex post* aggregate demand turned out to be at the level Y_1D_1. Changes in the income and employment levels in subsequent income periods stem from this initial divergence between expected and actual values. There is no inherent reason why expected and actual values should always coincide. Modern income and employment theory stresses that spending and output decisions are made by different groups or persons, so there is no reason to expect the two values to be always equal. The reader should note this carefully for it is basic to the explanation of the "why" of changes in income and employment levels in the modern economy.

To round out our present discussion of the equilibrium income level, let us postulate a situation just the opposite of the one we have considered. Let us assume that in the current income period the supply of output is in excess of the demand for that output. In Figure 5–5 this is depicted at the income level Y_2, as measured on the horizontal axis. At this income level the aggregate supply schedule, OZ, lies above the aggregate demand schedule, DD. Output in the current income period equals Y_2Z_2, but spending decisions on current demand for that output only add up to the distance Y_2D_2. The result is a deficiency of aggregate demand equal in amount to the distance D_2Z_2, with the consequence that, for the income period in question, there is *unintended (unplanned) investment* in stocks or inventories. More money income or purchasing power is being generated by current output than is being spent on that output; once more, a disequilibrium situation exists.

The typical business firm sees this as an unhappy situation in which sales fall short of current production and the firm suffers losses. Unless an immediate change to a better sales position is anticipated, the firm will have no choice but to revise downward its production plans for subsequent income periods. As most firms in the economy do this, output and employment levels for the whole economy will decline. Such a downward adjustment of income and employment must continue until a point is reached at which the supply of output is no longer in excess of current demand for the output. This, again, is the situation shown in Figure 5–5 by the intersection of the aggregate supply and aggregate demand schedules.

A Numerical Example

The process of adjustment of income and employment to an equilibrium level can be illustrated by means of a simple arithmetical example that employs a set of hypothetical data pertaining to employment, aggregate demand, and aggregate supply. Table 5–2 provides these data. In Column (1) are shown the varying amounts of employment associated with different levels of aggregate output or national income for our imaginary economy. The various possible levels of national output are given in Column (2), which is the aggregate supply schedule. For each of these various output levels, producers will incur costs exactly equal to the value of the output produced. Column (3) is the aggregate demand schedule and shows the amounts that spending units are prepared to spend at each possible income or output level shown in Column (2). Column (4) tells us which direction income and employment can be expected to change in response to the various levels of aggregate supply and aggregate demand.

TABLE 5–2.

The Equilibrium of Income and Employment

(1) Employment (N) (in millions of workers)	(2) National Income Aggregate Supply (OZ) (in billions of dollars)	(3) Aggregate Demand (DD) (in billions of dollars)	(4) Direction of Change in Income and Employment
68	560	600	Rise
70	590	620	Rise
72	620	640	Rise
74	650	660	Rise
76	**680**	**680**	**Equilibrium**
78	710	690	Fall
80	740	700	Fall

In Table 5–2 there is only one possible income level at which total spending in the economy is just equal to the value of current output. This condition occurs at an output level of $680 billion and an employment level of 76 million. At all other possible values for income and output disequilibrium is present. Suppose, for example, that current output is equal to $590 billion. At this level the aggregate demand schedule, Column (3), shows that spending units in the aggregate intend to spend at a rate of $620 billion. Total spending, in other words, will run ahead of total output by an amount equal to $30 billion. Under these circumstances, and in view of our explicit assumption that prices remain constant, there can be only one possible outcome—employment and production must rise. In these circumstances, the $30 billion of excess demand represents the amount by which stocks of goods will be drawn down during the income period so that the spending intentions of the spending units can be satisfied.

Just the reverse will hold true if output in any income period rises above the equilibrium level of $680 billion. If production proceeds, say, at an annual rate of $740 billion, producers are doomed to disappointment because at this particular income level the total of spending decisions in the economy amount to only $700 billion. Producers will find that inventories of unsold goods are accumulating at an unwanted rate of $40 billion per year. The reader should note carefully that the economy has not failed through its current productive activity to generate enough purchasing power to clear the market of all goods and services produced, but rather it has failed to spend this purchasing power at the same rate at which it is being created. This is the point at which Say's Law goes awry, because it assumes that income will always be spent at the same rate at which it is created. In this connection Keynes asserted that "the conclusion that the *costs* of output are always covered in the aggregate by the sale-proceeds resulting from demand, has great plausibility, because it is difficult to distinguish it from another, similar-looking proposition which is indubitable, namely that the income derived in the aggregate by all the elements in the community concerned in a productive activity necessarily has a value exactly equal to the *value* of the output." [6]

Characteristics of the Income Equilibrium

The analysis we have pursued up to this point attempts to explain how, in a most fundamental sense, aggregate demand and aggregate supply are the key determinants of income and employment levels. This is the crux of modern employment theory, for if the schedules of aggregate supply and aggregate demand are known, it is possible to determine both the income and employment level for the economy.

But—and this is a point of critical importance—the equilibrium level of income and employment brought about by the interaction of aggregate demand and aggregate supply will not automatically be one of *full employment*. Since decisions to produce and decisions to spend are made independently, it is largely a matter of chance whether or not they happen to coincide at a level of output that represents full employment of the economy's labor force. The economic forces embodied in the analytical concepts of aggregate supply and aggregate demand must of necessity drive the economy toward an equilibrium position, but there is nothing special in these forces that will in any way make full employment the "normal" state of affairs for the economy.

[6] *Ibid.*, p. 20.

In fact, the basic lesson of modern income and employment analysis, in contrast to the classical theory, is that any level of employment may be "normal" in the sense that it may be sustained over a considerable period of time. For example, during the whole decade of the 1930's large-scale unemployment was the "normal" situation in the American economy. If there is a deficiency of aggregate demand, the economy will experience a "deflationary gap" and may reach equilibrium at less than full employment. On the other hand, if aggregate demand persistently runs ahead of aggregate supply, there will be an "inflationary gap." The latter situation will be characterized by strong upward pressure on the price level and the per cent of the labor force unemployed will fall below the level normally thought of as "full" (Chapter 4). Sometimes the imprecise term "overly-full" employment is used to describe the conditions associated with an "inflationary gap." Something like this took place during 1966. The essential point to remember is that in the short run the economy can achieve equilibrium of income and employment at levels that represent full employment, less than full employment, or overly-full employment. No one level is in any sense inherently more "normal" than any other level. It all depends upon the relationship existing at any given time interval between aggregate supply and aggregate demand.

Changes in Income and Employment

Besides explaining how the level of employment is determined, the foregoing analytical framework serves to illuminate clearly the how and the why of change within the economic system. The vital principle running through our analysis is that change is the inevitable outcome of a situation in which expected and actual events do not agree. As pointed out earlier, change will occur whenever *ex ante* and *ex post* values do not coincide. Insofar as income and employment are concerned, this means that these magnitudes will be changing whenever aggregate supply and aggregate demand are not equal.

It is necessary to note, however, that within this rather broad analytical framework two distinct kinds of change can be envisaged. In the first instance, change may come about because, with given schedules of aggregate supply and aggregate demand, actual output or income fails to correspond to the demand for that output. This is the kind of situation depicted in Figure 5–5. The resultant change is the adjustment of the income and employment level toward equilibrium values that are based upon a given position for the schedules of aggregate supply and aggregate demand. Changes of this type originate with the producing units of the economy because they come about as a result of the failure of entrepreneurs to judge accurately the level of demand for the output of the whole economy.

Change is also involved in the movement of the economic system from one equilibrium level to another. In the short run such change results from a shift in the position of the aggregate demand schedule that occurs when the spending units of the economy are predisposed to spend more (or less) on current output at any and all levels of income. This shift in the position of the aggregate demand schedule will disturb a previously existing equilibrium between spending and output decisions, and thereby set in motion all of the forces involved in the adjustment of the economy toward equilibrium values for income and employment.

The latter type of change is illustrated in Figure 5–6. Schedule DD represents the original position of aggregate demand; output will adjust to the level Y_e, which is the intersection of the aggregate supply schedule, OZ, and the aggregate demand schedule, DD. If, however, aggregate demand shifts to the level represented by schedule $D'D'$, then the existing

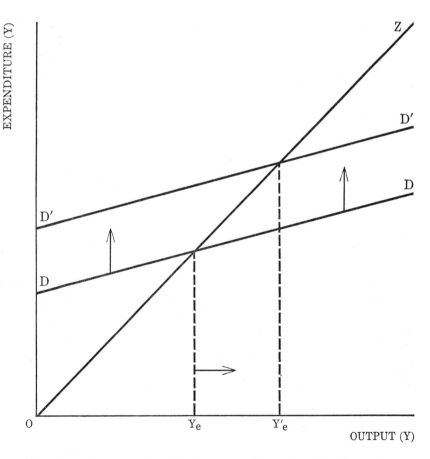

Figure 5–6. Aggregate Supply, Aggregate Demand, and Shifts in the Equilibrium Level of Income

equilibrium income level, Y_e, is disturbed. The immediate consequence of this shift is to create a new situation in which aggregate demand at Y_e exceeds aggregate supply or output. This will set in motion forces making for change; income and employment will rise until a new equilibrium obtains at the level Y'_e. The important thing to note is that the original impetus for this type of change came from the spending rather than the producing units in the economy.

Summary: Modern Employment Theory

The essential elements of the modern theory of income and employment may be summarized as follows:

1. In the short run, defined as a period of time in which productive capacity is fixed, the employment level will vary directly with the extent to which productive capacity is being utilized.

2. In the private sector of the economy the extent to which productive capacity is actually utilized depends upon the entrepreneur's expectation that his sales proceeds will be sufficient to cover the costs incurred in the production of any given volume of output. The aggregate supply schedule represents the formal, analytical expression of this idea, for it is a schedule showing the expected proceeds necessary to induce entrepreneurs in the aggregate to offer on a continuing basis a given amount of employment or produce a given output of goods and services.

3. The aggregate demand schedule associates spending decisions with differing levels of real income. It shows, in other words, the amounts that will be spent for output at each and every possible income level.

4. Given the aggregate supply and aggregate demand schedule for the economy, the equilibrium level of income and employment will be determined by the intersection of these two schedules. There is nothing inherent in these forces of aggregate supply and aggregate demand to assure that this equilibrium will be one of full employment.

5. Change in the economy's level of income and employment results from the failure of the output and spending plans embodied in the schedules of aggregate supply and demand to coincide. In the short run such changes may take the form of a movement toward an equilibrium position, given an initial imbalance between output and spending, or a movement from one equilibrium position to another. This latter type of change is contingent upon a shift in the schedule of aggregate demand.

The Theory of Consumption, Saving, and the Multiplier

6

In the preceding chapter, the point was made that in the short run aggregate demand is the key determinant of the level of income and employment. The reason is that aggregate demand determines the extent to which the economy's productive capacity will be utilized. The aggregate demand schedule is a summation of decisions to use the economy's output. But since the output of the economy consists of several different categories of goods and services, the demand for the output of the whole economy is a demand for the various categories of goods and services that enter into the national output. Structurally, aggregate demand (in a closed economy) consists of the sum of expenditures for consumer goods and services, C, investment or capital goods, I, and government or "collective" goods and services, G. In an open economy it is necessary to take into account net foreign investment, I_f.

Given the underlying assumption that output and employment in the short run depend primarily upon the level of aggregate demand our basic task is to understand the forces that enter into the determination of the demand for the output of the whole economy. Since we have already identified the component parts of the economy's structure of total demand, the logical procedure is to understand the determinants of each of these component parts, following this with an analysis of how these parts are linked together to form a schedule of demand for the economy's whole output.

The Determinants of Consumption Expenditure

Keynes' basic hypothesis with respect to the volume of consumption expenditure in the economy is that *income is the prime determinant of*

131

consumption expenditure. This is the case for the individual and for the economy as a whole. Keynes stated, "aggregate income . . . is, as a rule, the principal variable upon which the consumption constituent of the aggregate demand function will depend." [1] To say that income is the prime determinant of consumption expenditure is not to say that there may not be other determinants. For the moment, however, we shall put aside any other possible determinants and concentrate on the variable of income.

Before we turn to a detailed analysis of the income-consumption relationship, it is desirable to consider which particular measure of income is appropriate for the analysis. Should we regard consumption as a function of GNP, national income, personal income, or some other income measure? Since we are concerned primarily with an aspect of consumer behavior, it would seem logical that the income concept most appropriate to our analysis is one that most nearly approximates the idea of take-home pay. If there is validity to the hypothesis that income is a prime determinant of the consumer's consumption expenditure, income in this context must mean the income which is wholly at the disposal of the consumer for consumption expenditure (or nonexpenditure). Within the framework of national income aggregates, the particular measure that meets this requirement is *disposable income*, which, the reader will recall, is defined as the income remaining to individuals after deduction of all personal taxes. It is the closest approximation to take-home pay at the national level. Accordingly, contemporary income and employment theory has generally formulated the consumption function in terms of the relationship between disposable income and consumption expenditure. Consumption is thus held to be a function of disposable income. (In this connection the reader should note that for analytical purposes and abstract "model-building" the national income and social accounting distinction between disposable and other forms of income is often ignored.)

If we assume that all saving other than capital consumption allowances originates in the household sector, disposable income will be equal to the net national product minus taxes and plus transfer payments. In equation form we have:

$$Y_d = Y_{np} - TX + TR \qquad (6\text{--}1)$$

In the discussion which follows in this and ensuing chapters *net* national product (Y_{np}) will be used as our basic income measure rather than gross national product, primarily because use of the latter in the algebraic models requires making the extreme assumption that saving even in the form of capital consumption allowances originates in the household sector. Use

[1] John Maynard Keynes, *The General Theory of Employment Interest and Money* (New York, Harcourt, Bruce, 1936), p. 96.

of *net* national product does not in any way change the basic analysis or principles.

In the *General Theory* Keynes postulated two basic ideas concerning the relationship between consumption and income. These ideas are the underpinning of the modern theory of consumption and saving. In the first place, Keynes asserted that consumption expenditure is related to income in a systematic and dependable way. Symbolically, we have the equation

$$C = f(Y_d) \qquad\qquad (6\text{--}2)$$

Keynes defined the functional relationship between a given level of income and the consumption expenditure out of the level of income as *the propensity to consume*.[2] It may be noted, parenthetically, that the functional relationship posited by Keynes is one that concerns real consumption and real income.

The second key idea Keynes advanced in connection with the relationship between income and consumption is known as his "fundamental psychological law."

The fundamental psychological law, upon which we are entitled to depend with great confidence both *a priori* from our knowledge of human nature and from the detailed facts of experience, is that men are disposed, as a rule and on the average, to increase their consumption as their income increases, but not by as much as the increase in their income." [3]

Basically what Keynes meant is that when an individual's income increases he will spend more for consumption because of the increase, but he will not spend the whole of the increase. Some portion of the increase, in other words, will be saved. Keynes believed that this was especially true in the short run, for our consumption standards tend to become habitual, and are not quickly adjusted either upward or downward. If income rises, spending, and our standard of consumption, may not immediately adjust upward to a new and higher level. The reverse, it may be noted, will be the case when income falls.

The Consumption Function

In modern income and employment theory these two Keynesian ideas with respect to income and consumption are brought together in the concept of the *consumption function*, which may be defined as a *schedule showing the amounts that will be spent for consumer goods and services at different income levels*. The nature of the consumption function is

[2] *Ibid.,* p. 90.
[3] *Ibid.,* p. 96.

shown in the upper portion of Figure 6–1. Aggregate real income is measured on the horizontal axis and real consumption expenditure on the vertical axis. The curve $C = f(Y_d)$ is the representation of the consumption function; this curve shows the amount of consumption expenditure forthcoming at any and all income levels.

The notion of the consumption function as a schedule follows logically from Keynes' definition of the *propensity to consume* as the functional relationship between income and consumption. This functional relationship can be represented by a schedule which shows the range of values over which the dependent variable (consumption) moves as a result of changes in the independent variable (income).

It should be noted that, as a concept, the consumption function is quite similar to the ordinary demand curve, which is the graphic representation of a schedule showing the amounts of a commodity or service that buyers are willing to purchase at any and all possible prices within a specified period of time. The ordinary demand schedule is the embodiment of the idea that quantity demanded is a function of price. Thus, it is correct to state the "law of demand" in the form of an equation, such as $q = f(p)$, in which q represents quantity demanded and p represents the price of a good or service.

The income-consumption schedule, like all similar schedules in economic analysis, is an *ex ante* phenomenon. The schedule shows intended values, that is, the levels to which consumers plan to adjust their consumption expenditures on the assumption that any particular income level is achieved and maintained for a reasonable period of time. The consumption function is presumed to define the normal relationship of consumption to income.

Technical Attributes of the Consumption Function

Although Keynes used the term *propensity to consume* to refer to the schedule relating consumption and income, modern employment theory usually uses the term *consumption function* to describe the schedule relationship between income and consumption. This will be the usage in this text. The *average propensity to consume* is the ratio of consumption to income, C/Y_d, at a specific level of income. It is the proportion of a given income that is spent for consumption purposes. This is the first significant attribute of the function. The average propensity to consume may vary as the income level varies. In Figure 6–1, for example, the average propensity to consume is 100 per cent at the point at which the consumption function $C = f(Y_d)$ crosses the aggregate supply function, OZ. At this point, consumption is exactly equal to income. To the left of this point, the average propensity to consume will be more than 100 per cent because at *every* possible income level *intended* consumption is greater than income. Thus the ratio C/Y_d will be greater than 100 per cent. To

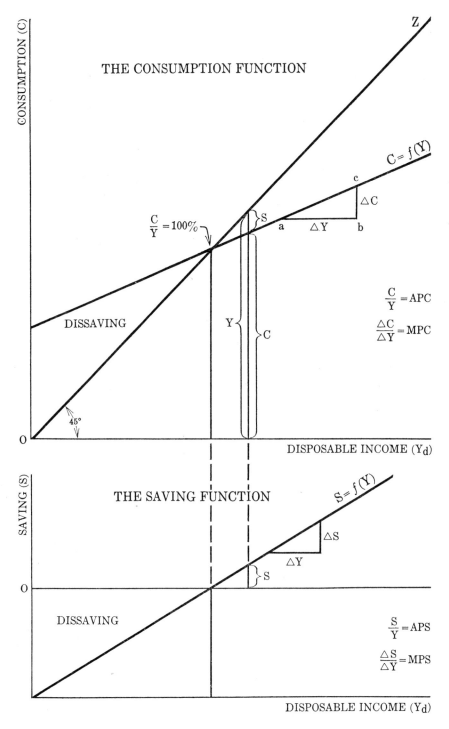

Figure 6-1. The Consumption Function and the Saving Function

the right of the point of intersection, on the other hand, the average propensity to consume will be less than 100 per cent, because at every income level above that at which consumption and income are equal, intended consumption is less than income.

The second important attribute of the consumption function is the *marginal propensity to consume*. This concept is the formal expression of Keynes' "fundamental psychological law," which, the reader will recall, states that men are disposed to increase or decrease their consumption by less as their income increases or decreases. We may define the marginal propensity to consume as the ratio of a change in consumption, ΔC, to a change in income, ΔY_d. With an increase in income, the marginal propensity to consume defines in per cent the amount by which consumption will increase. If income declines, the marginal propensity to consume will define—again in per cent—the amount by which consumption expenditure will decline. If we assume, for example, that the marginal propensity to consume of the economy is 0.75 (i.e., 75 per cent), consumption expenditure will increase by $0.75 with every increase of $1.00 in the income level, and fall by the same amount with every $1.00 decline in the income level.

In Figure 6–1 the marginal propensity to consume is measured by the slope of the consumption function, because, in mathematical terms, the slope of a line is determined by the ratio of the vertical distance to the horizontal distance (when movement takes place horizontally). Since consumption, C, is measured on the vertical axis and income, Y_d, on the horizontal axis, the marginal propensity to consume must necessarily be the same thing as the slope of the curve. In Figure 6–1 the marginal propensity to consume can be depicted by reference to the triangle *abc*. The vertical side of the triangle is the change in consumption expenditure ΔC, while the horizontal side is equal to the change in income, ΔY_d. The reader should note carefully that as long as the consumption function is assumed to be linear—that is, drawn as a straight line—the marginal propensity to consume will have a constant value. The basic reason for this is that all triangles formed by ΔY_d and ΔC will be similar (in a geometric sense) to the triangle *abc*, and consequently the ratio of their vertical sides to their horizontal sides will always be the same. The marginal propensity to consume and its constant value is to be contrasted to the changing value of the average propensity to consume.[4]

In an analytical sense the role of Keynes' "fundamental psychological law" is to establish limiting values for the slope of the consumption func-

---

[4] The above remarks do not necessarily imply that the income-consumption relationship must be linear. The consumption function may have a shape such that the *marginal* as well as the *average* propensity to consume declines as the income level rises. For reasons of simplicity in analysis, however, most economists operate on the assumption that the consumption function is linear.

tion. In the *General Theory* Keynes held that normally the marginal propensity to consume is positive, but its value is less than unity. This means that the slope of the consumption function will normally be less than 1. Since we are not told anything further about either its shape or slope, there is nothing in the Keynesian law that precludes us from drawing a consumption function whose slope is such that the average and marginal propensities to consume are equal. Keynes' basic—and only—stipulation was that as income increases consumption will increase but not by so much as the increase in income, and when income falls consumption will fall, but again not by so much as the decrease in income. Keynes did not specify that consumption had to change either in proportion to or less than in proportion to the change in income. As a matter of fact, a change in consumption expenditure that is proportional to the change in income is just as compatible with the fundamental law as is a change in consumption expenditure that is less than proportional to the change in income.

By the marginal propensity to consume we mean consumption expenditure that is *induced* by a change in income. The marginal propensity to consume can be viewed geometrically as a movement along a known consumption function. This kind of induced change in a variable should not be confused with the change that may come about as a result of a shift in the consumption function itself. Keynes assumed that normally the consumption function is stable, so that most changes in consumption are induced by income changes. This means that fluctuations in the income and employment level are not likely to have their origins in the consumption component of the aggregate demand schedule. Whether or not this particular conclusion is warranted remains to be seen; for the moment, though, our chief concern is with the marginal propensity to consume as a phenomenon having to do with induced changes in consumption expenditure. The analytical significance of the idea of induced consumption expenditures is that we find in such phenomena the basis of the theory of the multiplier, an aspect of modern income and employment theory that we shall develop in full detail later in this chapter.

Our discussion of the consumption function would not be complete without the algebraic expression of this relationship. If we assume the function is linear, as we did in Figure 6–1, the consumption function can be stated as

$$C = C_o + aY_d \qquad\qquad (6\text{--}3)$$

In the above expression, C is the level of consumption; C_o is the amount of consumption when income is zero; a is the marginal propensity to consume. Geometrically, C_o is the point at which the consumption function cuts the vertical axis, and a is the slope of the consumption function. Students of algebra will recognize this equation for the consumption function as the formula for a graph of a straight line of the type depicted in Figure 6–1.

The Saving Function

The counterpart to the consumption function is the *saving function*, which we may define as a *schedule showing the amounts that income recipients intend to save at different levels of income*. Saving basically is the non-consumption of current income, and because we are not at the moment concerned with any disposition of income other than consumption or saving, it logically follows that saving, too, is a function of income. In algebraic terms

$$S = f(Y_d) \qquad\qquad (6\text{–}4)$$

Since we are assuming for the moment that consumption and saving are the only alternative uses of income, the saving schedule can be derived directly from the consumption function. At each income level intended saving will equal the difference between the aggregate supply function and the consumption function, and these are the amounts that should be plotted to derive such a schedule as shown in the lower portion of Figure 6–1.

Since the saving function is conceptually similar to the consumption function, it is characterized by similar technical attributes. Thus the *average propensity to save* may be defined as the ratio of saving to income, S/Y_d, at a given level of income. It is the proportion of any given income that is saved. Like the propensity to consume, the ratio of saving to income may vary as the income level changes. At the intersection of the saving function and the horizontal axis (point *s* in Figure 6–1), the volume of saving is zero; hence the average propensity to save is zero. To the left of this point, the saving function drops below the horizontal axis, which means that saving is negative, or that dissaving is taking place. If this is the case, the saving-income ratio, S/Y_d, will be negative, which is as it should be, since the consumption-income ratio, C/Y_d, is greater than 1 under these circumstances. As long as we assume that consumption and saving are the only alternative uses of income, C/Y_d and S/Y_d must add up to unity. To the right of point *s*, the average propensity to save is not only greater than zero, but increases in value as the income level rises. The proportion of income saved increases as the income level increases.

The counterpart of the marginal propensity to consume is the marginal propensity to save. It is defined as the ratio of a change in saving, ΔS, to a change in income, ΔY_d. Analogous to the representation of the consumption function, the marginal propensity to save is depicted graphically by the slope of the saving schedule. If this schedule is assumed to be linear, the marginal propensity to save will have a constant value. Numerically, the marginal propensity to save is equal to 1 *minus* the marginal propensity to consume. This is true only so long as we adhere to our assumption that all income must be either consumed or saved. A marginal propensity to consume of 0.75 would mean a value of 0.25 for the marginal propensity to save, for if $0.75 is spent for consumption purposes out of an additional $1.00 of income, the balance of $0.25 is by definition saving. The ratio $\Delta S / \Delta Y$ must equal 0.25.

Up to this point in our analysis we have advanced two general propositions. The first of these is that consumption (and saving) is primarily a function of income, and the second is that the functional relationship between consumption (and saving) tends (in the short run) to assume the shape and character depicted by the schedules shown in Figure 6–1. But how well do these propositions accord with the facts of experience? In other words, do the statistical data pertaining to income and consumption expenditures tend to confirm the existence of the kind of behavior pattern embodied in the notion of the consumption function? Table 6–1 contains data on disposable income and personal consumption expenditures for the American economy for the period 1929–1965. The table also shows the percentage of disposable income spent for consumption goods and services in each of these years. The data are computed in 1958 prices; thus we are dealing with real income and real consumption expenditures. A careful inspection of the data reveals a rather general tendency of consumption expenditure to conform to the pattern suggested by the Keynesian hypothesis. For example, from 1929 to 1933 disposable income declined, but the *average* propensity to consume rose. This is the type of behavior pattern for consumption expenditure suggested by the consumption function in Figure 6–1. From 1933 to 1937, a period in which disposable income was rising, the *average* propensity to consume underwent a decline. The same is true for the period 1938 through 1941. Between 1941 and 1945 the figures lose much of their value, since these were war years, and consumption expenditures as a per cent of disposable income fell sharply because of wartime rationing, cutbacks in the production of consumer durables, pressures on the consumer to save and purchase war bonds, and general shortages of consumer goods and services. For the postwar period, beginning in 1946, disposable income has risen in relatively steady fashion. Consumption expenditure too has increased, but the average propensity to consume has shown, particularly in recent years, a somewhat greater tendency toward a constant value than was true of the prewar years. Nevertheless, the postwar data appear to be roughly in line with the consumption function hypothesis.

A better view of the extent to which actual data conform to the Keyne-

TABLE 6–1.

Disposable Income and Personal Consumption Expenditure
1929–1965
(in billions of 1958 dollars)

	(1)	(2)	(3)	(4) = (3) ÷ (2)
	Year	Disposable Income	Personal Consumption Expenditures	Propensity to Consume (in per cent)
	1929	150.6	139.6	92.7
	1930	139.0	130.4	93.8
	1931	133.7	126.1	94.3
	1932	115.1	114.8	99.7
	1933	112.2	112.8	100.5
	1934	120.4	118.1	98.1
	1935	131.8	125.5	95.2
	1936	148.4	138.4	93.3
	1937	153.1	143.1	93.5
	1938	143.6	140.2	97.6
	1939	155.9	148.2	95.1
	1940	166.3	155.7	93.6
War Years	1941	190.3	165.4	86.9
	1942	213.4	161.4	75.6
	1943	222.8	165.8	74.4
	1944	231.6	171.4	74.0
	1945	229.7	183.0	79.7
	1946	227.0	203.5	89.6
	1947	218.0	206.3	94.6
	1948	229.8	210.8	91.7
	1949	230.8	216.5	93.8
	1950	249.6	230.5	92.3
	1951	255.7	232.8	91.0
	1952	263.3	239.4	90.9
	1953	275.4	250.8	91.1
	1954	278.3	255.7	91.9
	1955	296.7	274.2	92.4
	1956	309.3	281.4	91.0
	1957	315.8	288.2	91.3
	1958	318.8	290.1	91.0
	1959	333.0	307.3	92.2
	1960	340.2	316.2	92.9
	1961	350.7	322.6	91.9
	1962	367.3	338.4	92.1
	1963	381.3	353.3	92.3
	1964	406.5	373.8	91.9
	1965	430.8	396.2	91.9

SOURCE: U.S. Department of Commerce, *U.S. Income and Output*, 1958; *Survey of Current Business*, August, 1965, July, 1966.

sian hypothesis can be obtained if we plot the data of Table 6–1 on a graph. This is done in Figure 6–2, wherein disposable income is measured on the horizontal axis and personal consumption expenditures on the vertical axis. When all the points representing consumption expenditure associated with disposable income for specific years are plotted, we have what statisticians term a *scatter diagram.* Such a diagram is highly useful for it helps us to determine whether or not values for two variables are related. As Professor R. G. D. Allen points out, if two variables are independent, then the value of one of the variables will be associated equally with large and small values for the other variable. In such a case the points will spread over the scatter diagram as if they were thrown there at random. On the other hand, if the value of one of the variables is uniquely determined by the value of the other variable, the points will lie on a line or curve that represents the *perfect* relationship between the variables.[5] Such a line or curve is said to describe a perfect relationship in the sense that this would be the way in which the two variables are related if the value of one of the variables was determined solely by the value of the other variable. This, of course, is rarely the case with any two variables in the real world.

The plotted data in Figure 6–2 fall into three distinct periods: 1929 to 1940, 1941 to 1945, and 1946 to 1965. In view of the fact that World War II wrought many profound changes in the American economy, it is reasonable to consider the prewar and postwar data separately. We shall not consider the war years, which formed an abnormal period. Keynes argued that the stability of the consumption function depended upon the existence of normal conditions, by which he meant the absence of wars, revolutions, or any form of social upheaval that might seriously distort the income-consumption relationship.

If we fit a curve to the plotted data of Figure 6–2 we obtain two distinct schedules, one appropriate to the period 1929–1940, and the other appropriate for the postwar years 1946–1965[6] Inspection of these curves shows, first, that the "fit" is not perfect, as all the points do not lie on the curves but, second, that there does appear a tendency for the actual data to be in accord with the consumption function hypothesis. The general shape and slope of the curves is similar to the hypothetical consumption function of Figure 6–1. The fact that the fit of the curves is not perfect suggests that other factors besides income play a role in the determination of the level of consumption expenditure in the economy. Actually, there

[5] R. G. D. Allen, *Statistics for Economists* (London, Hutchinson House, 1953), p. 120.
[6] In Figure 6–2 the schedules are "fitted" to the plotted data by simply drawing them in in such a manner that they pass as closely as possible to all the dots. There are, of course, more exact and specialized statistical techniques for fitting a curve to data, such as that plotted in Figure 6–4, but the approximation method employed here is adequate for our purposes.

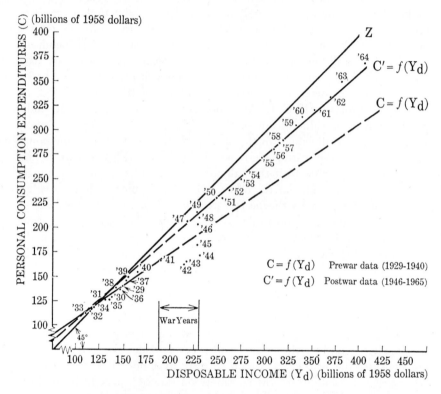

Figure 6–2. Consumption Expenditure and Disposable Income, 1929–1965

is nothing surprising in this for neither Keynes nor any other modern economic theorist seriously maintains that income is the *sole* determinant of consumption expenditure. When we posit the notion of a functional relationship between income and consumption we are saying in effect that of the many factors that probably influence the level of consumption expenditure, income is of the most strategic significance. Later on we shall analyze some of the other factors.

Before we conclude our discussion of the empirical validity of the consumption function hypothesis, let us consider an additional fact revealed by the plotted data in Figure 6–2. It is apparent that the postwar curve differs from the prewar curve in both level and slope. In order to compare these two curves, we have extended the straight-line curves that best seems to fit the prewar data alongside the postwar years. This extension is shown as a dotted line, which, the reader should observe, lies below the curve fitted to the postwar data and has a slope that is not so steep. What is the significance of this? The answer we can give at this point is that simply the empirical data suggest that over time the consumption function tends to shift upwards. There are strong logical as well as empirical reasons to suspect this is the case, but we shall defer any further consideration of this point until we discuss later in this chapter recent theoretical attempts to deal with this apparent phenomenon of the shifting consumption function.

The Process of Income Determination

Now that we have defined the consumption function, it is appropriate that we examine its usefulness as an analytical tool. In Chapter 5 we constructed a basic analytical framework designed to show how, in the short run, the level of income and employment depends primarily on the aggregate demand function. It is desirable that we re-examine this framework with the objective of showing how the consumption function fits into the structure of aggregate demand.

We shall assume a hypothetical economy in which there are only two categories of output or expenditure, consumption and investment. Table 6–2 contains data pertaining to this hypothetical economy. Column (1)

TABLE 6–2.

The Process of Income Determination
(in billions of constant dollars)

(1)	(2)	(3)	(4)	(5)
				Aggregate
Income	Consumption	Saving	Investment	Demand
Y_{np}	C	S	I	$C + I$
0	100.0	−100.0	75	175.0
350	362.5	− 12.5	75	437.5
400	400.0	—	75	475.0
450	437.5	12.5	75	512.5
500	475.0	25.0	75	550.0
550	512.5	37.5	75	587.5
600	550.0	50.0	75	625.0
650	587.5	62.5	75	662.5
700	**625.0**	**75.0**	**75**	**700.0**
750	662.0	87.5	75	737.5
800	700.0	100.0	75	775.0
850	737.5	112.5	75	812.5

in this table lists possible income levels for the economy (from 0 to $850 billion), while Column (2) represents the economy's consumption function, in that it reveals the intended consumption associated with these income levels.[7] This consumption function is also shown graphically in

[7] Since the hypothetical economy has only the two categories of output, consumption and investment, there are neither taxes nor transfer expenditures. Consequently, net national product and disposable income are identical. Thus: $(Y_{np} = Y_d)$. The consumption function is constructed such that the marginal propensity to consume has a value of 0.75.

Figure 6–3. The 45° aggregate supply function (*OZ* in the figure) implies that the analysis is in real terms because output in constant prices is measured on both the horizontal and the vertical axes.

We shall assume that investment expenditure is autonomous with respect to the income level, that is, that the amount of investment expenditure is independently given—not determined by any of the other variables that enter into our hypothetical economic system, or "model." We are not implying that economic analysis has nothing to say about the determinants of investment spending. Rather, for the sake of convenience and analytical simplicity, we assume its value as "given" in the same sense that the schedule for the consumption function is "given." Furthermore, we assume that the amount of investment expenditure will not change as the income level changes. Column (4) of Table 6–2 is this autonomous investment schedule. The term schedule is used deliberately here because the values shown are *ex ante*.

Since the schedule of aggregate demand consists of the sum of *ex ante* consumption and *ex ante* investment expenditure, we can construct this schedule for our hypothetical economy by adding an amount equal to autonomous investment to the consumption function. In Table 6–2 the results of this procedure are shown in Column (5). In Figure 6–3 we derive the aggregate demand function diagrammatically by drawing $C + I$ parallel to the consumption function and at a distance equal to the assumed value for autonomous investment expenditure. Thus aggregate demand is equal to the consumption function plus autonomous investment. We can express this idea algebraically in the form of an equation,

$$DD = (C_o + aY_d) + I \tag{6-5}$$

Given the fact that we have established an aggregate demand schedule, $C + I$, for this hypothetical economy, the process by which an equilibrium income level is attained is as described in Chapter 5. The equilibrium income (and employment) level is to be found at the point of intersection of the aggregate demand and aggregate supply schedules. On the basis of the data contained in Table 6–2 the income equilibrium is $700 billion. It is at this income level that the aggregate demand schedule of Figure 6–3 intersects the aggregate supply schedule. If actual income (i.e., output) is below the $700-billion level in any income period, a disequilibrium situation in which aggregate demand is in excess of aggregate supply will result. This will set in motion forces that tend to drive the income level higher. As long as aggregate demand is in excess of aggregate supply, income and employment will continue to rise toward the equilibrium position. Contrariwise, an income level above $700 billion cannot be sustained because aggregate supply then runs ahead of aggregate demand, a condi-

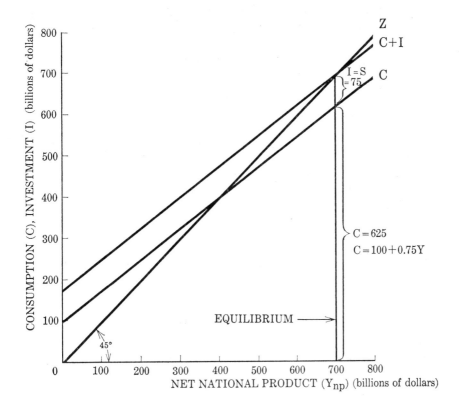

Figure 6-3. The Process of Income Determination

tion that will lead to unwanted inventory accumulation and eventual cutbacks in output. A downward adjustment in income and employment levels would continue until output is once again in balance with total demand. Equilibrium is a situation in which producing and spending intentions coincide and, given the assumed schedules of consumption and investment for this hypothetical economy, the only income level at which such coincidence is possible is $700 billion.

The Identity of Saving and Investment

In the discussion of the relationship between income and wealth in Chapter 2, the statement was made that saving and investment are necessarily identical when conceived of in an *ex post* sense. This *ex post* equality (or accounting identity of saving and investment as it is sometimes called) logically follows from the way in which we defined saving and investment. The basic identity equations for a simple economy in which consumption and investment are the only categories of output permit us to demonstrate that saving and investment must be equal. This equality holds good all the time.

There is, however, a condition in which saving and investment are not necessarily always equal. This is when saving and investment are conceived of in an *ex ante* sense, which means intended or planned saving and investment. The claim that in one sense saving and investment are always equal, and that in another sense they are not necessarily equal, may at first glance seem to be logically impossible. For a number of years after the publication of Keynes' *General Theory* lively controversy raged among professional economists over the exact meaning of these concepts and the sense in which they were equal or not equal. Actually, however, it is not difficult to reconcile the seemingly contradictory claims.

Let us assume that the economy in Table 6–2 and Figure 6–3 has not yet attained an equilibrium income level. Income in the current period, let us say, is at the level of $600 billion. We know that this particular level cannot be maintained, but for the moment that is not of primary concern to us. We want to understand what is taking place during the current income period, irrespective of how income may change in subsequent periods. The consumption function indicates that if the income level is $600 billion, consumption will be $550 billion. This is planned consumption expenditure, since the consumption function is an *ex ante* phenomenon. If planned consumption is $550 billion, then it follows logically that *ex ante* saving must equal $50 billion, because the saving function is the counterpart of the consumption function and is derived (in this hypothetical economy) by subtracting the consumption function from the aggregate supply schedule. But since the actual income level must always lie on the aggregate supply schedule, this is tantamount to saying the *ex ante* saving is equal to the distance between actual income and *ex ante* consumption.

But what of investment? Column (4) of Table 6–2 has already been described as the autonomous investment schedule. This means that the unchanging level of *ex ante* or intended investment expenditure is $75 billion. But if investment *ex ante* is equal to $75 billion, while saving *ex ante* is equal to $50 billion, we have a situation in which these two entities are not equal. The failure of *ex ante* saving and investment to be in balance is a prime indicator of the existence of a disequilibrium condition with respect to the income and employment level; the income equilibrium must be defined in terms of equality between *ex ante* saving and *ex ante* investment.

There is nothing mysterious about the notion that saving and investment *ex ante* are not always equal, because there is no inherent reason why the intentions or plans of savers in the economy should always coincide with the intentions or plans of those undertaking investment expenditure. They may coincide, of course, although it is more likely that they will not.

Returning now to the idea that saving and investment *ex post* must always be equal, let us see how this concept of the identity between saving and investment can be explained through reference to the data of Table 6–2. By definition, saving is the nonconsumption of current income, so in this hypothetical economy saving *ex post* (or actual) must be equal to $50 billion at the income level of $600 billion. Investment has been defined as the net addition to the economy's stock of wealth that results when the whole of current income (i.e., output) is not consumed. Thus actual investment in an income period is the difference between income and consumption. In the income period which we have under consideration, actual or *ex post* investment equals current income ($600 billion) minus current consumption ($550 billion), or $50 billion. This is the same as *ex post* saving during the income period.

At this point the reader may wonder how to reconcile *ex post* investment of $50 billion with *ex ante* investment of $75 billion. Since our analysis is constructed to rule out any change in the general level of prices, if planned or intended investment runs ahead of actual investment, the difference between intended (*ex ante*) and actual (*ex post*) investment represents the portion of total demand that is satisfied through sales from *existing* stocks of goods. In Figure 6–3 it can be seen that at the $600-billion level of income this difference of $25 billion between investment *ex ante* and investment *ex post* is the identical amount by which the aggregate demand schedule exceeds the aggregate supply schedule. This $25 billion represents the amount of inventory *disinvestment* that has taken place in the income period because aggregate demand is in excess of aggregate supply. This inventory disinvestment is unintended or unanticipated and comes about primarily because producers (in the aggregate) have underestimated the level of aggregate demand. It is *unintended* disinvestment or investment in stocks that is the balancing item between planned and actual investment.[8]

Before leaving this subject, let us examine one more situation in which *ex post* and *ex ante* values fail to coincide. Again using the data of Table 6–2, let us assume that the current income level is $800 billion, a disequilibrium level. The consumption function indicates that at this income level *ex ante* consumption will be $700 billion. Thus saving *ex ante* equals $100 billion. Our schedule of *ex ante* investment expenditure remains the same, so planned investment expenditure at the $800-billion income level is

---

[8] It is possible that there can be unplanned saving as well as unplanned investment. Unplanned saving may come about if consumption expenditure lags behind changes in income. In our analysis, however, we are assuming that consumption expenditure adjusts immediately to any change in income. This is not necessarily the case in reality.

equal to $75 billion. At this income level, in other words, *ex ante* investment falls short of *ex ante* saving, a fact that also tells us that aggregate demand falls short of aggregate supply.

The *ex post* values for both saving and investment at the income level of $800 billion are obtained in the same manner as previously. By definition, both saving and investment *ex post* equal the difference between income ($800 billion) and consumption ($700 billion), and therefore they both are equal to $100 billion. Again the reader will see that there is a $25-billion difference between investment *ex ante* and investment *ex post*.

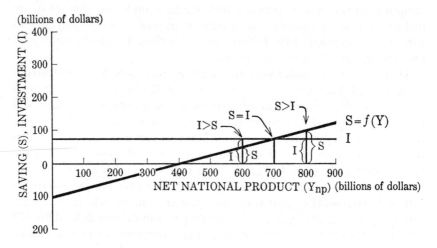

Figure 6–4. Equilibrium of Saving and Investment

What this means is that in the income period there has been unplanned inventory investment in the amount of $25 billion. The stock of goods of all kinds on hand has simply accumulated by this amount because total sales fell short of output. Once again it should be noted that in Figure 6–3 the amount by which aggregate demand falls short of aggregate supply at the $800-billion level is just equal to the difference between investment *ex post* and investment *ex ante*.

From the foregoing discussion we emerge with the important conclusion that equilibrium insofar as the short-run income and employment level is concerned requires that saving and investment *ex ante* be equal. Equilibrium also means that *ex ante* and *ex post* values coincide. Disequilibrium exists if saving and investment are not equal in an *ex ante* sense, and whenever this is the case, forces are set in motion that make for a change either upward or downward in the income and employment level.

This process and the nature of the relationship between saving and investment *ex ante* can also be demonstrated through the use of saving and investment schedules alone. In Figure 6–4 we have plotted the saving and investment schedules derived from the data of Table 6–2. These plotted schedules tell us exactly the same story as Figure 6–3. At the $600 billion income level the saving schedule lies below the investment schedule; hence saving *ex ante* is less than investment *ex ante*. At the $800-billion level the reverse is the case. Only at the $700-billion income level are the two equal, and hence only at this level does equilibrium prevail.

The Theory of the Multiplier

In Chapter 5 we pointed out that changes in the income and employment level can be of two distinct types. In the one instance, we have the kind of change just discussed that involves adjustment toward a specific equilibrium level, given known positions for the schedules that enter into the structure of aggregate demand. There is also the kind of change that takes place when an existing equilibrium situation is disturbed as a result of a shift in the position of the aggregate demand schedule. A change of this type can be brought about by a shift in any of the schedules that constitute the aggregate demand schedule. This includes the consumption function, which Keynes believed to be highly stable under normal conditions. The implications of shifts in the aggregate demand schedule lead us into consideration of one of the most significant facets of modern income and employment theory, the *multiplier* process.

Let us assume, using data for the consumption function from Table 6–2 and Figure 6–3, that the autonomous investment schedule shifts upward by $25 billion. This means simply that at *all* the relevant income levels businessmen are prepared to spend for investment goods at *an annual rate* of $100 billion rather than $75 billion. Table 6–3 contains data for this new situation. Inspection of this table reveals that the effect of this increase in autonomous investment expenditure has been to shift the aggregate demand schedule upward by a like amount, namely, $25 billion. These new data for our hypothetical economy are plotted in Figure 6–5.

What has been the consequence for the income equilibrium of this upward shift in the schedule of autonomous investment expenditure and the upward shift in the aggregate demand schedule? If we look at the numerical data of Table 6–3 and the graphic presentation of these data in Figure 6–5, we are struck by the fact that the equilibrium income level has risen not by $25 billion, but by $100 billion. Here is a clear illustration of the multiplier process: an autonomous change in one of the variables that enters into the structure of aggregate demand has brought about a change in the income level several times greater than the amount of the initiating

Table 6-3.

Increased Investment and the Income Equilibrium
(in billions of dollars)

(1)	(2)	(3)	(4)	(5)
Income Y_{np}	Consumption C	Saving S	Investment I	Aggregate Demand $C + I$
0	100.0	−25.0	100	175.0
350	362.5	−12.5	100	462.5
400	400.0	—	100	500.0
450	437.5	12.5	100	537.5
500	475.0	25.0	100	575.0
550	512.5	37.5	100	612.5
600	550.0	50.0	100	650.0
650	587.5	62.5	100	687.5
700	625.0	75.0	100	725.0
750	662.5	87.5	100	762.5
800	**700.0**	**100.0**	**100**	**800.0**
850	737.5	112.5	100	837.5

change. Technically, the multiplier can be defined as the coefficient which relates an increment of expenditure to an increment of income.[9] Keynes discussed the multiplier process entirely in terms of an *investment multiplier*, which he designated by the symbol k. The investment multiplier "tells us that, when there is an increment of aggregate investment, income will increase by an amount which is k times the increment of investment." [10] In algebraic form this idea is expressed as

$$\Delta Y_{np} = k\Delta I \qquad (6\text{--}6)$$

From this equation it follows that we can define the multiplier as a ratio of a change in income ΔY_{np}, to a change in investment, ΔI. Thus

$$k = \frac{\Delta Y_{np}}{\Delta I} \qquad (6\text{--}7)$$

[9] Basically the multiplier process is concerned with *real* changes. We are assuming that any change in expenditure for either consumption or investment goods leads to a corresponding increase in the output of these goods. This does not mean that a multiplier effect in purely monetary terms cannot take place in the economy. If, for example, there would be an increase in expenditure when the economy is at a level of full employment, the multiplier would still come into play, but the ensuing income changes would be wholly the result of changes in the general level of prices.

[10] Keynes, *op. cit.*, p. 115. The net national product, Y_{np}, equals disposable income, Y_d, for in the simple system under discussion, which has neither taxes nor transfers the two measures of income are identical.

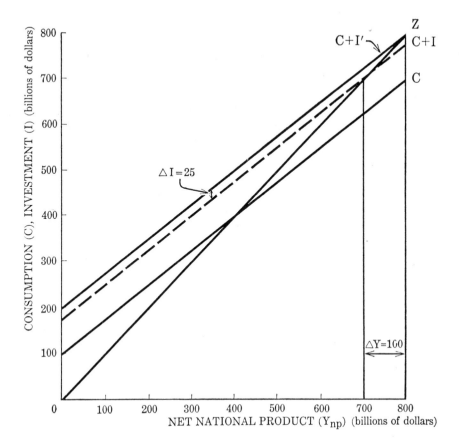

Figure 6–5. Multiplier Effect of a Shift in the Investment Function

Although Keynes analyzed the multiplier process almost entirely in terms of the relationship between changes in investment and changes in income, the reader should not be misled into thinking that the multiplier effect is limited to changes in investment expenditure. Actually it is a coefficient that links *any autonomous* shift in aggregate demand to the consequent change in income. This point is emphasized because it is usually most convenient to introduce and discuss the theory of the multiplier through analysis of changes in the investment component of the aggregate demand structure.

What lies behind the fundamental idea of the multiplier that any change in the expenditure rate for any of the component parts of the aggregate demand schedule will have magnified effects upon the overall income level? To answer this, let us go back and trace what happens in the economy when, as is assumed in Table 6–3, there is an increase in the rate of investment expenditure equal to $25 billion. For the moment we need not be concerned with the means by which this extra $25 billion of investment expenditure is financed; all that interests us is that businessmen have increased their spending for investment goods by $25 billion.

When this happens, the first discernible result is that the producers or suppliers of investment or capital goods will find their incomes have risen by $25 billion, because increased spending for investment goods will lead to an increase in their production and, as more output is generated, incomes will rise. Thus, the primary effect of the increased spending for investment goods will be to create an equal amount of new income (in the form of wages, rents, interest, and profits) which will accrue to resource owners in the capital-goods producing sector of the economy. What will happen after this? For the answer to this question we return to Keynes' assertion that whenever income increases there will be a strong tendency for the beneficiaries of such increases to step up their expenditures for consumption goods and services. In the case of our hypothetical economy, the beneficiaries of the initial increase in spending are those engaged in the production of investment goods. Since the members of this group have experienced a rise in their incomes, it is to be expected that they will spend some part of this additional income for consumption goods and services. There will be, in other words, *induced* changes in consumption expenditure. These induced changes can be described as a *secondary* effect flowing from the increased spending for investment goods.

We have been able to isolate and describe two major effects associated with an increase in expenditure of the kind that leads to an increase in output and increased incomes for the producers of the output. These effects are a *primary* (or initial) effect, which is associated with the initial change in income, and a *secondary* (or induced) effect, which arises out of the fact that the original recipients of the increased income will in turn spend some portion of this increase for consumer goods and services. It is in this secondary effect that we have the real key to the multiplier process, for in the absence of any induced or secondary changes in spending, the impact of increased investment expenditure (or any other form of spending) on the income level could be no greater than the amount of the initial change in income. The multiplier effect results from the sum of the initial and induced changes in expenditure (and output) that ensue from a change in the rate of expenditure for any of the component parts of the aggregate demand structure.

What, however, determines the amount of induced spending? The answer is quite simple: the *marginal propensity to consume*. Once we know what proportion of an increment of income will be spent for consumption goods and services, we are in a position to determine how great will be the secondary or induced effects resulting from autonomous increases in expenditure. The marginal propensity to consume thus provides the analytical key to the increases in secondary spending and, consequently, to the numerical value of the multiplier.

The Formal Multiplier Process

To understand the multiplier process clearly the first step is to trace in detail the effects of the increase in investment expenditure of $25 billion. The hypothetical consumption function presented in Tables 6–2 and 6–3 is constructed in such a way that it has a slope of 75 per cent. This means that the marginal propensity to consume for this function is 0.75; out of every $1.00 increment of income $0.75 will be spent for consumption. On the basis of this and given our assumed increase in investment outlays of $25 billion, we have constructed Table 6–4 to show how this initial increment in investment expenditure will generate a whole chain of respendings. The first column, which contains only the figure of $25 billion, represents the *initiating* increase in expenditure. The second column represents groups of income recipients, designated by letters of the alphabet; while the third column records the increments of income that accrue to each of these groups as a result of successive rounds of spending. The fourth column shows the *induced* consumption spending that results from the income increases experienced by each successive group.

The initial increase in investment expenditure accrues as income to group A, which then increases its consumption expenditures by $18.75 billion (75 per cent of $25 billion). Group A's spending will accrue as income to the suppliers of these consumption goods and services, namely, group B. This group also increases its consumption expenditures by 75 per cent of the rise in its income, providing additional income for yet a third group. And so forth. We can thus see that the initial increase in expenditure will generate a series of spendings and respendings, which, if carried far enough, will raise income by some multiple of the original increment. The data in Table 6–4 show that ultimately the sum of induced consumption expenditure will total $75 billion, which, with the original increase in investment expenditure of $25 billion, will add up to a total increase of income of $100 billion or four times the initiating increase. The value of the multiplier in this case is 4.

Two further aspects of Table 6–4 should be noted. First, the multiplier has a time dimension, since it would be quite impossible in reality for the whole series of spending and respending to occur simultaneously. This point is stressed because in theoretical analysis we often ignore, for reasons of simplicity, the time element in the multiplier process. Second, the data of Table 6–4 show only what happens with a single, non-recurring increment of investment expenditure. If we extended our example over a greater time span, income, which at first rose, would gradually fall back to its original level. The total increase in income spread over the whole time period in which the multiplier process was at work would, of course, equal the $100 billion shown in Table 6-4, but this

Table 6-4.

The Multiplier: With a Single Initiating Increase
in Investment Expenditure
(in billions of dollars)

| (1) | (2) | (3) | (4) |
Initiating Increase in Expenditure	Income Recipients	Income Changes	Induced Consumption Spending
$25.00	A	$25.00	$18.75
	B	18.75	14.06
	C	14.00	10.55
	D	10.50	7.91
	E	7.88	5.93
	F	5.91	4.45
	G	4.43	3.32
	H	3.32	2.49
	I	2.49	1.87
	J	1.87	1.40
	K	1.40	1.05
	L	1.05	0.79
	M	0.79	0.59
	N	0.59	0.44
$\Sigma = \overline{25.00}$ *		$\Sigma = \overline{100.0}$ *	$\Sigma = \overline{75.0}$ *

* After an infinite number of spendings and respendings.

would not be a permanent change. In order for the equilibrium income level to rise permanently to a new and higher level—which is the situation depicted in Table 6-3 and Figure 6-5—the increase in expenditure that initially triggers the expansion must be a *sustained* increase. Investment expenditure would have to expand from $75 billion to $100 billion and remain at that level if an enduring increase in the income level from $700 to $800 billion were to be brought about.

The nature of the multiplier process, given the assumption of a sustained increase of $25 billion in investment expenditure, is shown in Table 6-5. The data shown for Period 0 pertain to the equilibrium existing prior to the increase in investment expenditure by $25 billion. In Period 1 investment expenditure increases by $25 billion, a development which amounts to a shift upward in the aggregate demand schedule from $700 billion to $725 billion. In this table we are operating on the assump-

Table 6-5.

The Multiplier: With a Sustained Increase in Investment Expenditure
(in billions of dollars)

(1) Period	(2) Aggregate Demand (DD)	(3) Aggregate Supply (OZ)	(4) Actual Increase in Output (ΔZ)	(5) Planned Consumption Expenditure (C)	(6) Additional Consumption Expenditure (ΔC)	(7) Ex Ante Investment (I)	(8) = (3) − (5) Ex Post Investment (I')
0	$700.00	$700.00	—	$625.00	—	$ 75.00	$ 75.00
1	725.00	700.00	—	625.00	—	100.00	75.00
2	743.75	725.00	$25.00	643.75	$18.75	100.00	81.25
3	757.18	743.75	18.75	657.81	14.06	100.00	85.94
4	768.36	757.81	14.06	668.36	10.55	100.00	89.45
5	776.27	768.36	10.55	676.27	7.91	100.00	92.05
6	782.20	776.27	7.91	682.20	5.93	100.00	94.07
7	786.65	782.20	5.93	686.65	4.45	100.00	95.55
8	789.99	786.65	4.45	689.99	3.34	100.00	96.66
∞	800.00	800.00	—	700.00	—	100.00	100.00

tion that output cannot respond instantaneously to an increase in expenditure; consequently, output does not rise to the level of aggregate demand of Period 1 until Period 2. In Period 2 the actual increase in output of $25 billion—Column (4) in the Table—induces additional consumption expenditure in the amount of $18.75 billion as shown in Column (6). This is because the assumed value for the marginal propensity to consume is 0.75. Aggregate demand in Period 2, therefore, is equal to the total of planned consumption expenditure ($625 billion plus $18.75 billion) and planned investment expenditure ($100 billion). Output in this period has risen in response to the level of aggregate demand of the previous period, but aggregate demand has risen even higher because of the phenomenon of induced consumption expenditure. Gradually, though, the increments of induced consumption become smaller and smaller as the new equilibrium level of $800 billion is approached. In theory, this level will be reached only at the expiration of an infinite number of income periods, but, as a practical matter, the increments of both income and consumption expenditure will become insignificantly small after a finite number of periods. Once the new equilibrium income level has been attained, consumption expenditure will total $750 billion and investment expenditure will be $100 billion. There has been a multiplier effect of 4, because the initial increase of $25 billion in investment expenditure has brought about a total increase in income of $100 billion.

Algebraic Statement of the Multiplier

Now that we have examined by means of a numerical example the multiplier process, let us formalize the concept by stating it in terms of some relatively simple algebraic formulas. From our investigation of the multiplier process we have discovered that the magnitude of the multiplier effect depends upon the sum of initial and secondary effects. We saw that the key to the magnitude of the secondary effect is the marginal propensity to consume. Let us begin our algebraic analysis with the basic identity

$$Y_{np} = I + C = Y_d \qquad (6\text{--}8)$$

The above equality is true because we are assuming neither taxes nor transfer payments (see footnote 10). In the following algebraic discussion, the multiplier is defined in relation to net national product, which is the same as disposable income, given the foregoing assumption.

From the above identity it follows

$$\Delta Y_{np} = \Delta I + \Delta C \qquad (6\text{--}9)$$

In the preceding analysis it was concluded that induced consumption expenditures depend upon the value of the marginal propensity to consume. In Equation (6–3) the marginal propensity to consume out of disposable income ($\Delta C / \Delta Y_d$) was designated as a. Since Y_d and Y_{np} are assumed to be equal, we can substitute $a \Delta Y_{np}$ for ΔC in Equation (6–9). We now have

$$\Delta Y_{np} = \Delta I + a \Delta Y_{np} \qquad (6\text{–}10)$$

We can manipulate this equation algebraically as follows:

$$\Delta Y_{np} - a \Delta Y_{np} = \Delta I \qquad (6\text{–}11)$$
$$\Delta Y_{np}(1 - a) = \Delta I \qquad (6\text{–}12)$$
$$\Delta Y_{np} = \Delta I \times \frac{1}{1 - a} \qquad (6\text{–}13)$$
$$\frac{\Delta Y_{np}}{\Delta I} = \frac{1}{1 - a} \qquad (6\text{–}14)$$

The left-hand side of Equation (6–14) is essentially the same as that which was defined in Equation (6–7) as the multiplier, the ratio of a change in income to a change in investment. From this we may conclude that in a formal, mathematical sense the multiplier is equal to *the reciprocal of 1 minus the marginal propensity to consume.*[11] In our simple and hypothetical economy the multiplier would also be equal to the reciprocal of the marginal propensity to save, for as long as saving and consumption are viewed as the only alternatives for the disposition of income, it is a simple matter of arithmetical truth that one minus the marginal propensity to consume, $1 - \Delta C / \Delta Y_d$, equals the marginal propensity to save, $\Delta S / \Delta Y_d$. But one must be careful here not to generalize that the value of the multiplier is always equal to the reciprocal of the marginal propensity to save. It is equal to this only in the absence of taxes and foreign trade.

Now that we have defined the multiplier algebraically, we shall review the process and apply the formula to the data of our hypothetical economy. Originally, the income equilibrium level was $700 billion, given the consumption function and a level of investment expenditure of $75 billion (Table 6–2). The marginal propensity to consume is 0.75, which yields a numerical value for the multiplier of 4. All that is necessary is to

---

[11] The theoretical limits to the value of the multiplier are 1 and infinity (∞). If the value of the marginal propensity to consume is zero (0), then the multiplier will have a value of 1; if, on the other hand, the value of the marginal propensity to consume is 1.00 (100 per cent), the multiplier will have a value of infinity (∞). The reader should work out the simple arithmetic to convince himself that it is true.

apply this coefficient to the change in investment expenditure, $25 billion. A change of investment expenditure of this amount will cause income to rise by $100 billion ($k \times \Delta I = 4 \times \$25$ billion $= \$100$ billion). As a result of this $100-billion increase in income, consumption expenditure will rise by $75 billion.

Summary Remarks on the Theory of the Multiplier

Before we discuss other important aspects of consumption theory, it is desirable to summarize the salient features of the multiplier concept.

First, the multiplier is a device for explaining why a change in spending may have exaggerated or cumulative effects upon the income level. The multiplier may be associated with any autonomous change in expenditure in the economic system; it is not limited, as in our example, to changes in investment expenditure.

Second, the multiplier is properly regarded as an aspect of consumption theory, since its value depends upon induced consumption spending.[12] The amount of induced or secondary consumption spending that will ensue is a function of the marginal propensity to consume, the slope of the consumption function.

Third, the magnitude of the multiplier effect is inversely related to the total of *leakages* from the current income stream. Income that is not spent for currently-produced consumption goods and services may be regarded as having *leaked out* of the income stream. Keynes and most other economists regard the marginal propensity to consume as normally having a value of less than 1, because it is felt that some leakages are bound to be present. In our hypothetical economy saving represented the only form of leakage from the income stream. In reality, though, there are other forms of leakages. Tax collections and expenditures for imported goods and services can be considered as leakages. A leakage is anything that reduces the tendency toward the spending or respending of income on currently-produced domestic goods and services; the greater such leakages, the smaller will be the multiplier effect. It is for this reason that we cannot claim that the multiplier is always equal to the reciprocal of the marginal propensity to save. If we could determine and measure *all* leakages as marginal propensities, then we could state comprehensively that the multiplier has a value equal to the reciprocal of the sum of all leakages.

Finally, we must be very careful to note that the computation of a numerical value for the multiplier depends upon accurate knowledge of the economy's consumption function and marginal propensity to con-

---

[12] It should be noted that consumption expenditure is not the only type of expenditure that may be induced through a change in income. It is possible for investment expenditure, too, to be induced. This is a matter that we shall discuss in the following chapter.

sume. The empirical data examined earlier suggests that consumers *tend* to behave in the fashion indicated by the consumption function hypothesis, but this does not mean that we can successfully construct a statistical consumption function that can be used to determine with great exactness the value of the multiplier for the economy. In actuality, such a possibility seems rather remote, for there are too many unpredictable variables that may enter into and alter a situation before the effects of any single change have worked themselves out. In essence, we are cautioning here against an overly simple interpretation of the multiplier phenomenon, and against any tendency to assume that we can measure the multiplier with a high degree of precision. If we recognize and understand these limitations, we are still left with a concept of great value for analysis of the process of change in the income and employment level.

Other Influences on Consumption

In our earlier discussion of the degree to which empirical data concerning income and consumption bears out the consumption function hypothesis, we pointed out that few economists believe that income is the *only* determinant of consumption spending. Let us now examine some of the other variables that may exert an influence on consumer expenditures. The general practice in analysis of consumer spending is to treat variables other than income as *parameters*, whose values determine the level and slope of the consumption function.[13] If the income-consumption relationship is described by the equation $C = C_o + aY_d$, the level of the function is given by C_o, which represents consumption expenditure when income is zero; and the slope of the function by a, the marginal propensity to consume. Analytically, this means that changes in the value of any of these parametric factors will result in a *shift* in the position of the entire schedule, rather than a movement along it. While parametric factors are generally recognized to influence the level of consumption expenditure, many of them are not subject to quantification and precise measurement. This being the case, we have to depend in part upon deduction to arrive at dependable conclusions concerning the way in which such variables influence consumer expenditures.

Attitudes Toward Thrift

In a general way, we can group together in this category the psychological attributes of human nature which lead people to save rather than spend some part of current income, as well as various business practices and institutional arrangements of a society that make for saving. In con-

[13] Parameters are values assumed to be constant and, as such, determine the position of the function. The parameters of the C function are C_o and a; changes in all other factors influencing the consumption decision act to change the value of these "constants."

nection with the former, Keynes suggested that there are at least eight motives of a subjective nature that lead individuals to refrain from spending out of their incomes.[14] These include the following desires: (1) to build a reserve for unseen contingencies (Precaution); (2) to provide for anticipated future needs, such as old age, education of children, or the maintenance of dependents (Foresight); (3) to obtain a larger future income through investment at interest of funds saved from current income (Calculation); (4) to enjoy a gradually increasing expenditure and standard of life as a result of saving some of current income (Improvement); (5) to enjoy the sense of independence and power that comes from sustained saving (Independence); (6) to secure a *masse de manœuvre* to carry out speculative or business projects (Enterprise); (7) to bequeath a fortune (Pride); and (8) to satisfy pure miserliness (Avarice). The reader will readily recognize the highly subjective character of these motives; yet their existence is real enough. The most we can say is that if these motives are strong in a society, then the society will be favorably predisposed toward thrift, which, other things being equal, will lower the consumption function or raise the saving function.

Cultural factors that condition a society's attitudes toward thrift and spending are probably deeply rooted in its past and not readily subject to change. In the United States the Puritan tradition with its stress on the intrinsic virtues of work and frugality operated in times past to create a social climate more favorable to saving than to spending. On the other hand, recent developments such as the growth of consumer credit and time-payment plans may have had a counter effect, although the impact of such phenomena on the position of the consumption function is by no means a simple or one-way affair.

Installment purchasing and other forms of borrowing that raise the propensity to consume are to some extent offset by developments of modern life which tend to raise the propensity to save. The twentieth century, in fact, has witnessed a powerful tendency toward the "institutionalization of saving" through commitments of income to life insurance, private pension plans, and long-term mortgages on private homes. Since saving is the nonexpenditure of current income for currently produced goods and services, these institutional arrangements create a continuous flow of quasi-compulsory saving that does not change simply because the income level has changed. The average person does not usually think of premiums on life insurance, payroll deductions for a pension plan, or monthly amortization of home loans as forms of saving, yet they represent saving from the viewpoint of the whole economy. Moreover, most saving of this type is contractual in nature, and thus cannot readily be changed.

[14] Keynes, *op. cit.*, p. 107.

Asset Holdings by the Consumer

Another factor believed by many economists to exercise a powerful influence on consumer spending patterns has to do with assets held by the consumer. The term *asset* is used to refer to both financial assets in the form of cash on hand, bank accounts, bonds, stocks, and other financial claims, and physical assets in the form of stocks of durable goods in possession of the consumer.

FINANCIAL ASSETS

The most plausible hypothesis that we can advance regarding the influence of financial assets on expenditures is simply that spending will vary *directly* with the value of private holdings of financial assets. Such holdings, particularly if they are easily converted into purchasing power, constitute a reserve of spending power which the consumer can draw on in emergencies. As a consequence there is less need to save out of current income in order to build such a reserve. This means that an increase in holdings of liquid assets by consumers would, other things being equal, shift the consumption function upward. The experience of the period immediately following World War II lends some support to our hypothesis, for the statistics of income show a decided rise in the average propensity to consume, a development attributed by many economists to the sharp increase during the war in consumer holdings of liquid assets. We might note parenthetically that the volume of liquid assets at the disposal of the consumer may work in an indirect manner to affect the level of consumer spending because households possessing stocks of liquid assets are more willing and more able to finance consumption spending by borrowing.

The hypothesis of a direct relationship between consumer spending and holdings of financial or liquid assets is subject to important reservations. For one thing, the distribution of ownership of liquid assets will have an obvious bearing upon their over-all impact on consumer spending. If, for example, ownership is concentrated in the upper-income groups, it is doubtful that the size or value of such holdings will have much influence upon the level of consumption for the whole economy, since high-income earners as a group tend to save a large proportion of their income at all times. In fact, it has been suggested that large holdings of liquid assets result from past saving and the people who have been able to save and accumulate are most likely to be the people who will save in the future.[15] If this point of view is valid, then it follows that holdings of liquid assets will not necessarily tend to raise the consumption function. But Professor Lawrence Klein has suggested that existing

[15] George Katona, *Psychological Analysis of Economic Behavior* (New York, McGraw-Hill, 1951), p. 168.

empirical evidence does not show conclusively that holdings of liquid assets exert an influence on consumer spending in one direction or another.[16]

In addition to the distribution of ownership, it has been pointed out that changes in the *real* value of liquid assets may exercise an influence on the consumer's spending-saving decisions. For example, if the general level of prices rise, the real value of financial assets in the form of bank deposits, bonds, and other types of debt instruments will decline. This is not necessarily the case with equities, as they may appreciate in value along with the rise in the general level of prices. However, if there is a decline in the real value of the consumer's stock of liquid assets, this may induce him to save more out of his current income in order to recoup a desired position with respect to his holdings. The possibility of a unique relationship between the real value of the stock of liquid assets, the general level of prices, and the position of the consumption function has lead to another view known as the *Pigou effect*, after A. C. Pigou, a British economist and staunch defender of the classical analysis.[17] Pigou argued that a fall in the general level of prices would stimulate the economy by tending to shift the consumption function upward. The price drop would *increase* the real value of the consumer's financial assets and thereby lessen his need to save. We shall encounter the Pigou effect again in our later discussion of the general price level, but it is doubtful if many economists today take it very seriously. It is more in the nature of an exercise in abstract logic than an attempt to deal with forces that operate in the real-world economy.

Stocks of Durable Goods

The second type of asset that may affect the spending-saving pattern of the consumer consists of the stock of durable goods in his possession. As a general proposition, a large stock of durable goods in the hands of consumers may, other things being equal, have a tendency to depress consumption spending. For the consumer such goods represent a kind of capital investment which will provide him with a stream of services as long as the good is in existence. The man who owns an automobile, for example, need not spend much of his income for other forms of transportation. Similar results flow from the ownership of other types of durable goods, such as television sets and radios, home laundry equip-

---

[16] Lawrence R. Klein, "The Empirical Foundations of Keynesian Economics," in Kenneth K. Kurihara, ed., *Post Keynesian Economics* (New Brunswick, N.J., Rutgers University Press, 1954), p. 293. See also Robert Ferber, "Research on Household Behavior," *American Economic Review*, March, 1962, p. 37.

[17] A. C. Pigou, "The Classical Stationary State," *Economic Journal*, December, 1943; and "Economic Progress in a Stable Environment," *Economica*, August, 1947. The latter is reprinted in *Readings in Monetary Theory* (Philadelphia, Blakiston, 1951), pp. 241–251.

ment, and various other household appliances. It should be recognized, though, that ownership of durables may stimulate other expenditures. The owner of an automobile, for example, must purchase large quantities of gasoline, new tires, and spare parts. He is, moreover, a purchaser of insurance and other services that stem directly from his ownership of an automobile. On balance, it is difficult to say which of these influences is the strongest, and the objective evidence pertaining to this point is inconclusive.

In another way, too, the stock of durable goods may affect consumption spending. One might expect that a large stock of durables in the hands of consumers would depress consumption spending, because once the consumer has acquired a new car, refrigerator, stove, washing machine, and other items of household equipment, he will not again become a potential purchaser of these goods for a relatively long period of time. But when their stock of durables is depleted, consumers seek to replenish the worn-out or discarded equipment, and a higher level of consumption spending may be ushered in.

The one conclusion we can draw concerning influence of stock of consumer durables on consumer spending is that such goods by their very durability introduce strong elements of uncertainty into consumer spending. Beyond this it is difficult to say more with certainty because economists have yet to accumulate sufficient empirical data to indicate any precise relationship between the stock of consumer durables and consumption expenditure.

ASSET HOLDINGS AND LIVING STANDARDS

One fruitful line of analysis with respect to the influence that asset holdings may have upon consumer expenditures has been suggested by Professor J. P. Lewis,[18] who contends that consumption expenditure must be related to the *standard of living*. According to Lewis, the standard of living includes the consumer's assets, both financial and durable, as well as in his current purchases of goods and services. In order to achieve a desired standard, the consumer at times may be primarily interested in increasing his stock of consumer durables, which leads temporarily to more consumption spending and less saving; at other times, his primary objective may be to enlarge his stock of liquid assets, which will have the contrary effect. In support of this hypothesis, Lewis reviews the postwar behavior of the consumption-income ratio. He finds that between the end of World War II and the outbreak of the Korean War the propensity to consume was, on the average, much higher than in prewar periods. The upward shift in the consumption function in this period he attributes not, as other economists have done, to the depletion

[18] John P. Lewis, "The Lull that Came to Stay," *The Journal of Political Economy*, February, 1955.

of the stock of consumer durables during World War II, but rather to the fact that real incomes rose sharply during the war, which led consumers to aspire to higher living standards as mirrored in the possession of durable goods. By about 1950, however, the urge to raise living standards in terms of ownership of durable goods was fairly well satisfied. Consumer interest then shifted to improving living standards through acquisition of financial assets, a development which brought about a downward trend in the consumption function after 1950. The saving-income ratio, in other words, rose from the abnormally low level it reached during the period when the prime interest of consumers was in building up their stock of assets in the form of durable goods.

The hypothesis advanced by Lewis seems to introduce a further element of instability into the consumption-income relationship. Shifts in the consumption function may come about as a result of changes in the desires of consumers to build up one type of asset at the expense of the other. Such shifts may be either upward or downward, depending upon the relative strength of the consumer's desire to increase his holdings of durable goods or liquid assets. Whether it is possible to determine the direction of future shifts in the consumption function by following the interplay of these two forces is highly problematical.

The Distribution of Income

Economists have long regarded distribution of the money income of a society as one of the important parametric determinants of the consumption-income relationship. This particular influence on consumption is thought to be stable, as the pattern of income distribution in any society is determined by a complex of institutional factors, including the structure of property rights, the distribution of ownership of productive assets, the tax system, and the social security system, all of which appear to change with relative slowness. Insofar as the pattern of income distribution has an influence upon the level and slope of the consumption function, the view is held among some economists that, other things being equal, a movement toward more equality in the distribution of income will raise the level—and possibly, too, the slope—of the consumption function, whereas any movement toward greater inequality in the distribution of income will have the opposite effect. This deduction is based on the fact that studies of income and its disposition at the level of the household show that families in the lower-income brackets have a higher average propensity to consume than families in the upper-income brackets. Such studies are less conclusive with respect to the *marginal* propensity to consume of the two income groups, although economists have tended to assume on *a priori* grounds that the marginal propensity to consume would be low for the upper-income groups and high for the lower-income groups.

Setting aside for the moment the question of the marginal propensity to consume, let us consider the relationship between differences in the average propensity to consume for families in different income brackets, the over-all distribution of income, and the level of the consumption function. If the distribution of income in a society is relatively unequal, it means that families or spending units in the upper-income brackets receive a large proportion of the total income. If this is the case, the average propensity to consume for the whole society will be low, irrespective of the level of total income of the society, since the upper-income groups tend, on the average, to consume a comparatively low percentage of their income. On the other hand, if the distribution of income is relatively equal, families or spending units in the lower-income brackets will receive the largest proportionate share of the income total. Since the average propensity to consume for these groups is high, the ratio for the society as a whole will also be high, regardless of the level of total income. Thus runs the supporting argument for the view that equality in the distribution of income tends to raise the level of the consumption function, while inequality has the opposite effect.

This argument, buttressed by the assumption that the *marginal* as well as the average propensity to consume is higher for spending units in the lower income brackets, led some economists to suggest during the depression years that the level of the consumption function could be boosted if steps were taken to bring about a greater degree of equality in the distribution of money income. Taxation and transfer expenditures were viewed as the means by which the Federal government could achieve this goal. For example, if group A with an assumed marginal propensity to consume of .50 had its disposable income reduced by $100 through taxation, and this sum was transferred to group B, which has a marginal propensity to consume of .75, the result would be a net increase in consumption spending of $25. How would this increase come about? As a consequence of the $100 drop in its disposable income, group A reduces its current consumption expenditure by $50. Group B, with its $100 gain in disposable income, increases its consumption expenditure by $75. The net increase in spending is thus $25.

This scheme for bringing about an upward shift in the consumption function has been challenged on two scores. In the first place, statistical evidence exists to suggest that the differences in the marginal propensity to consume between the upper- and lower-income groups are much smaller than differences in the average propensity to consume.[19] If this is the case, a redistribution of income from the upper- to the lower-income groups would not appreciably affect consumption spending. The decline in consumption spending resulting from a reduction in the dis-

---

[19] Harold Lubell, "Effects of Redistribution of Income on Consumers," *American Economic Review*, March, 1947; and "Correction," *ibid.*, December, 1947.

posable income of households in the upper brackets would approximately equal the increase in spending that would occur as households in the lower-income brackets experienced an increase in their disposable income. This is a perfectly sound position as long as the marginal propensity to consume is the same for all groups. There is, however, a flaw in the argument. The governing influence of the marginal propensity to consume is limited to the initial change in the disposable incomes of both the upper- and lower-income groups. If redistributional measures are continued, a permanent alteration will occur in the pattern of income distribution in the direction of greater equality. Once this has taken place, *average* rather than marginal propensities to consume will govern.

The notion that the consumption function can be raised by fiscal and other measures that bring about a redistribution of personal or disposable income has faced a second and different type of challenge. Critics have argued that income redistribution theory is valid only upon the assumption of an "absolute-income" hypothesis, which asserts that a consumer's preferences for goods and services are formed independently of the preferences of other consumers. Income, according to this hypothesis, is the *sole* determinant of consumption, and if families or households move into a different income bracket—as a result, say, of measures designed to redistribute income—they will assume the income-consumption pattern of prior occupants of the bracket.

In place of the "absolute-income" hypothesis, critics of the income redistribution theory advance a "relative-income" hypothesis, which states that consumer preferences are *interdependent* rather than independent. According to this hypothesis, the level of consumption of any family or spending unit depends upon its income *relative* to other families or spending units.[20] This means that consumption standards are "emulative," in that the amount an individual spends upon consumption does not depend simply on his own income, but also on the consumption patterns of families or spending groups on a higher rung of the income-distribution ladder. If consumer preferences are interdependent and consumption standards emulative, this leads to the conclusion that a redistribution of income in the direction of greater equality may not increase consumption expenditure; on the contrary such a redistribution may lower consumption. If, in an interdependent or emulative society, income and consumption of groups in the upper-income brackets are reduced, the pressure toward consumption spending for groups situated at lower levels on the income-distribution scale will lessen. The standards of consumption that such groups emulate have been lowered, and thus their own consumption standards will follow suit.

In the face of such arguments, our conclusion about the probable effects

---

[20] James S. Duesenberry, *Income, Saving, and the Theory of Consumer Behavior* (Cambridge, Harvard University Press, 1949), pp. 17–46.

of income redistribution measures on the level of the consumption function cannot be anything but nebulous. Most economists would agree that the prevailing pattern of income distribution is an important determining factor of the level and slope of the consumption function in any society. But economists do not agree upon either the extent to which income distribution can be changed in the short run or the immediate effects, if any, of such changes on the level of the consumption function. Recent theoretical developments of the kind that we have just discussed underscore the fact that to raise the level of aggregate consumption by a redistribution of income is not so simple a matter as economists once believed.

The Rate of Interest

At one time many economists would have been inclined to list the rate of interest as probably the most important determinant of consumption and saving. According to classical thought, to save is to exchange present satisfactions (gained from consumption) for future satisfactions, but a price must be paid to persuade people to make such an exchange. This price is interest. The higher the price, the greater the willingness of people to postpone consumption; the lower the price, the smaller their willingness. As a consequence, in classical thought, interest came to be regarded as a prime determinant of the amount that families and spending units would save out of their income.

Today many economists do not believe that the rate of interest exercises any appreciable effect one way or the other on the level of consumption or saving. No statistical or empirical evidence of significance exists to lend support to the classical view,[21] while from a deductive point of view it is possible to show that increases in the level of interest rates may actually reduce saving. For one thing, a rise in interest rates means that if people save in order to amass a sum designed to yield them some specific annual income, a smaller absolute sum would yield an identical annual income at higher interest rates as a larger sum at lower rates. If, for example, the rate of interest rose from 3 to 6 per cent, a saver would have to amass only $33,333 rather than $66,666 in order to obtain an annual income of approximately $2,000 through interest payments. A rise in the rate of interest also may tend to reduce some types of contractual saving, such as life insurance. At higher interest rates a *fixed* amount of life insurance requires smaller premiums.

In defense of the classical position, it is only fair to point out that a rise in interest rates will reduce the current market value of financial assets such as bonds and other fixed-income obligations. This might lead to a higher level of saving, although again no empirical evidence exists to substantiate this conclusion. It is also possible that higher interest rates

[21] Klein, *op. cit.*, p. 292.

will reduce consumer spending by raising the cost of consumer credit. Again there is no evidence on this point, and many economists would be inclined to argue that what matters to the consumer in time-payment purchasing is not the interest charge, which the consumer rarely knows, but the amount of the down payment required plus the size of the monthly payments relative to the consumer's income.

Price Changes and Consumer Expectations

Changes in the general level of prices and shifts in consumer expectations for the future are two additional and related factors that economists recognize as potential influences on spending and saving levels. Our knowledge of the impact of these particular variables is still more speculative than empirical. There is a presumption that a rise in the level of all prices will raise the *average* propensity to consume, assuming (somewhat tenuously) that money income does not change in the same degree. If this did happen, real income would decline, causing a higher consumption-income ratio. The reader should note, however, that a change in the average propensity to consume resulting from a change in real income would not necessarily imply a shift in the function; it might take place as a movement along the consumption function. It is also possible, in the face of a fall-off in real income, that consumers will attempt to maintain the same absolute level of real consumption. This would result in a shift upward of the consumption function, for consumption spending would absorb a higher proportion of an absolutely lower real-income level.

We touched briefly a few pages back on another way in which a general change in prices might affect the consumption function. If the "Pigou effect," which, it will be recalled, concerns a shift in the consumption function brought about by a change in the real value of the consumer's liquid assets, were operative, a rise in the general level of prices would tend to shift the consumption function downward rather than upward. This is exactly the opposite outcome from that discussed in the preceding paragraph.

Consumer expectations concerning future prices may also influence the position and slope of the consumption function. It is possible, for instance, that widely-held expectations that prices will continue to rise—that the economy may experience a continuous "creeping inflation"—will lead consumers to devote a higher proportion of their current income to consumption purchases than would otherwise be the case. Statistical support for this proposition is not very conclusive, although some economists cite as evidence the sharp increase in consumer spending following the outbreak of the Korean War in the summer of 1950. In this instance it is alleged that the brief but marked buying spree was a reaction by consumers who remembered the upward pressure on prices as well as the shortages of goods that were characteristic of the economy in World War II.[22]

Consumer expectations concerning future income may also be of significance, affecting not so much the level as the slope of the consumption function. The slope of the function is the marginal propensity to consume, which specifies the way in which consumers react to a change in their incomes. Logically, one would expect that an individual (or spending unit) would react differently to an increase (or decrease) in income, depending upon whether or not the change was expected to be permanent. Although Keynes did not deny this, he thought such expectations would probably average out for the economy as a whole and thus not exert much influence on consumer behavior. More recent research, particularly by the Survey Research Center at the University of Michigan, suggests that Keynes' view is not necessarily the correct view and that expectations do strongly condition spending and saving behavior.[23] Although research into consumer attitudes of the type carried on at the Survey Research Center holds much promise for enlarging our understanding of consumer behavior, it has not yet developed any new, powerful, and widely-accepted hypotheses concerning this behavior.

Consumer Credit

The significance of consumer credit on consumption is readily apparent; the availability of credit permits more spending for consumption purposes than would be possible if current income were the only source of purchasing power. The practical importance of consumer credit as a factor in consumer expenditure in the United States is enormous. In 1965 the volume of outstanding consumer credit of all types was nearly $86 billion, an amount more than double the total of ten years earlier.[24] Moreover, the volume of credit extended to consumers has increased in every postwar year, irrespective of the recessions of 1949, 1954, 1958, and 1960–1961.

The obvious fact concerning consumer credit is that borrowed funds represent additional financial resources that can be used for current consumption expenditures. If consumers borrow sufficiently so that the total of their indebtedness increases—i.e., new borrowings exceed repayments —the consumption function would tend to shift upward. Total consumption spending would rise relative to income, since borrowing has given the consumer control over financial resources greater than the amount represented by current income. It is interesting to note that through the postwar period consumers have added to their borrowings at a greater rate than they have repaid their obligations. Consumer credit in this pe-

[22] Paul J. Strayer, *Fiscal Policy and Politics* (New York, Harper, 1958), p. 66.
[23] Katona, *op. cit.*, pp. 140 ff.
[24] Joint Economic Committee, *Economic Indicators*, February, 1966.

riod thus created upward pressure on the consumption component of aggregate demand.

While it is true that an initial extension of credit to the consumer tends to raise the propensity to consume, it is equally true that the subsequent effects of such credit extension may depress consumption expenditure. Such loans must be repaid. If Mr. Jones, for example, borrows $1,500 to help finance the purchase of a new automobile, his expenditure of the proceeds of the loan will take an item of *current* output off the market. Subsequently, though, a portion of Mr. Jones' current income will no longer be available to spend for currently produced goods and services, since he must repay the loan. If he arranges to repay the $1,500 at the rate of $50 a month, then for a period of 30 months (ignoring interest and other charges connected with the loan) the amount of current income that he can spend for currently produced goods and services will be $50 less than usual.

What lesson does this hypothetical example hold for the economy as a whole? Unless there are new borrowings sufficient to offset the repayment of old borrowings, any stimulus to consumption expenditure that came from an extension of credit to the consumer will be short lived. If borrowing by the consumer tends to raise the level of the consumption function, repayment of loans has the opposite effect. Economists interested in the influence of consumer credit on consumption expenditure are more concerned with the relationship between the rate of new borrowing and the rate of repayment than with the absolute amount of consumer credit outstanding at any particular time.

The rate at which consumers increase their indebtedness is no doubt in some way tied in with expectations. Again there is scant empirical evidence to help us determine the precise nature of this relationship. It does not require any great feat of the imagination to see how disastrous it could be for the economy if consumers decided all of a sudden to reduce drastically their rate of new borrowing. The result would be a precipitate fall in the level of the consumption function.

Income, Consumption, and Saving in the Long Run

Before we conclude our discussion and analysis of income and consumption in the modern economy, let us consider a problem that has intrigued economists for a number of years. The consumption-income relationship, as depicted in Figure 6–1, is one in which the average propensity to consume falls as the income level rises. The slope of a function of this type is such that it intersects both the aggregate supply function and the vertical axis. Since this consumption function pertains to the behavior of consumption expenditure over relatively short periods of time, it is usually described as a short-run or "cyclical" function. The statistical data shown in Table 6–1 and plotted in Figure 6–2 tend to confirm the existence of this type of relationship.

A dilemma is created by the fact, however, that statistics on income, consumption, and saving for very long periods of time show that the consumption-income ratio, C/Y, is a *constant*.[25] In other words, consumers spend about the same proportion of their incomes, irrespective of the fact that over the long run there has been a relatively steady rise in the level of real income. In an arithmetical sense this means that the average and marginal propensities to consume are not only constant, but are equal. The long-term consumption function thus appears diagrammatically as a straight line from the point of origin whose slope is such that the marginal and average propensities to consume are the same. Such a consumption function is shown in Figure 6–6. The consumption-income relationship shown in the diagram is usually described as the "secular" consumption function, as it represents the behavior of consumption expenditure in the long run.

The dilemma faced by economists is how to reconcile statistical evidence on the long-run constancy of the average propensity to consume with equally worthy statistical evidence which shows that in the short run the consumption-income ratio is not a constant. Actually, we have already suggested the proper solution to this dilemma, for in our earlier discussion of the empirical validity of the consumption-function hypothesis we pointed out that the short-run data on income and consumption indicate that over time the consumption function is actually shifting upward. This "secular upward drift of the consumption function," as it has been called, is clearly seen in Figure 6–2 when we extrapolate the prewar data into the postwar period and note that the curve lies below the curve most appropriate to the postwar data. Logic too supports our empirical findings. For if we assumed that the type of short-run function shown in Figure 6–1 is characteristic of behavior patterns in the long run, we would be forced to the absurd conclusion that eventually the economy would save a greater portion of its income than it would consume. There is no evidence, statistical or otherwise, to indicate that this has happened or is likely to happen. The only way in which we can reconcile empirical findings with respect to the short- and long-run average propensities to consume is to postulate the hypothesis of an upward shift over time of the consumption function.

A number of economists have sought to advance a theory in explanation of this phenomenon. One theory that is widely known is that of Professor James S. Duesenberry of Harvard University.[26] His hypothesis

[25] Simon Kuznets, *Uses of National Income in Peace and War* (New York, National Bureau of Economic Research, 1942), p. 31, Table 2; and p. 35, Table 6.

[26] Duesenberry, *op. cit.*, p. 45. Professor Duesenberry became a member of the Council of Economic Advisors in January, 1966.

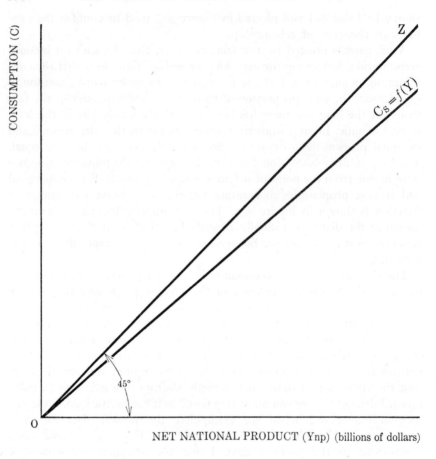

Figure 6–6. The Secular Consumption Function

is based upon two key ideas. First, consumption (or saving) is not a function of current income alone, as the purely Keynesian view would have
it, but rather a function of a relationship between current income and the
highest income that consumers have ever previously experienced. Second,
consumer preferences are interdependent, which means, as we have seen,
that the average propensity to consume will not change as long as the
relative distribution of income among spending units is unaltered. Let us
examine by means of a diagram the workings of Professor Duesenberry's
hypothesis.

In Figure 6–7 the curve labeled C_s is the secular, or long-term consumption function, whereas the curves labeled C_1, C_2, and C_3 represent
a series of cyclical, or short-term, consumption functions. Let us assume
that initially the income level is given by Y_1, and that this represents the
highest level of income yet achieved in the economy. We are at the peak

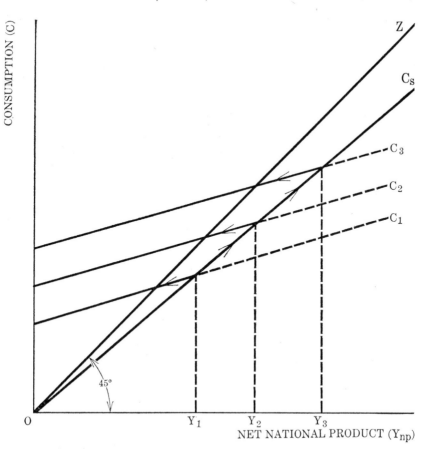

Figure 6–7. The Upward Drift of the Cyclical Consumption Function

of a cycle. What will happen now if income falls from the level of Y_1?
On the diagram this is, of course, a movement to the left. According to
Duesenberry's theory, consumption will move along the short-run path
represented by the function C_1, because the most immediate and strongest influence on consumption will be the recent experience of achieving
an income level equal to Y_1. Consumers, having become accustomed to
this level during the boom will strongly resist any reduction in their
standard of consumption. Consumption will decline, of course, but more
slowly than income. This is exactly the kind of behavior pattern envisaged
by Keynes, since the most important influence at work is the consumer's
habitual standard of life. The movement of consumption spending along
the C_1 curve also means that the average propensity to consume will rise
and the average propensity to save will fall. As the income level moves
back to its original position, which will come about as the economy moves

out of a recession, consumption will rise again along the path of C_1, at least until restoration of the previous high peak of income is achieved. As the income level moves back toward its prior peak, consumers will want to restore the earlier relationship between consumption and saving, and consequently the saving-income ratio, S/Y, will rise and the consumption-income ratio, C/Y, will fall.

What will happen once the economy regains the level Y_1 and, in a surge of growth, moves on toward Y_2, a new and higher income level? In this instance, according to Duesenberry's theory, consumption will rise along the path of the secular function, C_s, until the new peak level Y_2 is achieved. The movement of consumption increases proportionally to income. Why? For one thing, the prior income peak, Y_1, no longer exercises its influence over consumer behavior, since the economy is moving toward a new peak. In such a situation increments to income will be allocated between spending and saving in a constant ratio, the latter being the ratio regarded as normal at the prior highest income level. Also, the "relative-income" hypothesis tells us that the average propensity to consume for the economy as a whole will not change as long as the distribution of income does not change. During the period when the economy is moving toward a new peak income level, there is no reason why the pattern of income distribution should change. All spending units will enjoy a higher absolute level of income because the income level of the whole economy has risen, but the *relative* position of each group will not necessarily change. Therefore, the average propensity to consume for the whole economy will not change.

Much the same conclusion concerning the relationship between the cyclical and secular consumption functions was independently reached by another economist, Professor Franco Modigliani.[27] He also suggests that the ratio between income and saving (or consumption) has to be linked not merely to current income but to a ratio or index that embodies both current income and the highest income level previously reached. In this respect his analysis is quite similar to Duesenberry's. In the Modigliani analysis consumption will also follow a Keynesian path when the income level goes below the highest level yet achieved. He attributes this not only to consumer resistance to a reduction in acquired consumption habits, but to the growth in unemployment in the downward phase of the cycle and to the redistribution of income that occurs when the income level falls. With respect to the growth of unemployment, Modigliani's thesis asserts that even if there is a long-run tendency for employed persons to consume a constant proportion of their income, the ratio of consumption to income will rise when there is growing unemployment because unem-

---

[27] Franco Modigliani, "Fluctuations in the Saving-Income Ratio: A Problem in Economic Forecasting," in *Studies in Income and Wealth*, Vol. 11 (New York, National Bureau of Economic Research, 1949), pp. 379 ff.

ployed persons consume even though they have no incomes. The redistribution of income that occurs in the downward phase of the cycle is likely to be in favor of groups having the highest propensity to consume. This is because the greatest income squeeze in a recession or depression is on profits. All these factors taken together account for the rise in the average propensity to consume when the income level falls, and the reverse when the income level is rising. With respect to the long-run picture, Modigliani agrees with Duesenberry that a constant proportion of income will be consumed once the economy moves beyond the highest income level previously achieved. But he explains this by the continuous appearance of new products and the improvement of old commodities. Portions of the income increments that accrue to all groups as a result of the long-term rise in the real income of the whole economy are absorbed by new goods and services that gradually become available. This is the basic reason offered by Modigliani for the long-term constancy in the consumption-income or saving-income ratio.

Before completing our discussion of the long-term relationship between income, consumption, and saving it is appropriate to say a word about a theory recently advanced by Professor Milton Friedman of the University of Chicago.[28] In attempting to arrive at the fundamental character of the relationship between income and consumption, Professor Friedman developed what has come to be called the "permanent-income" hypothesis. His theory is one of proportionality, and constitutes an explanation for the long-term equality between the marginal and average propensities to consume. Friedman's theory assumes that the income of an individual can be divided into a *permanent* and a *transitory* component. The individual's permanent income is the income which he reasonably expects to receive over a period of at least several years, while the transitory component consists of unexpected or unforeseen additions or subtractions to his income. Over the long run such additions and subtractions ought to cancel out. Given these components, Friedman's basic hypothesis is that permanent consumption is proportional to permanent income. Saving may increase (or decrease) whenever there is an increase (or decrease) in the *transitory* component of income. This will account for such short-run fluctuations in the saving-income (or consumption-income) ratio as are found in the short-term or "cyclical" function. Over the long run, however, consumption will rise in proportion to changes in the permanent component of the individual income.

A Concluding Comment

We have examined in this chapter in detail the findings of modern economic analysis with respect to the determinants of consumption ex-

[28] Milton Friedman, *A Theory of the Consumption Function* (Princeton, N.J., Princeton University Press, 1957).

penditure. The impetus for study and analysis of this key component in the structure of aggregate demand comes from Keynes' *General Theory*. Keynes' belief in the existence of a functional relationship between real income and real consumption has been formalized in the concept of the consumption function. This has become one of the key analytical tools of modern income and employment theory. In retrospect, we can say that while economists are no longer as sure as they once were of either the stability or simplicity of the consumption-income relationship, they do regard its embodiment into the formal body of economic analysis as one of the major achievements of economic science within the last several decades.

APPENDIX

Formal algebraic proof that the value of the multiplier k is equal to $1/1{-}a$

The value of the multiplier depends upon the sum of the *initial* injection of funds into the system plus the ensuing induced expenditures. The multiplier effect of an additional \$1 of investment expenditure can be expressed in equation form as shown below. In the equations, a is the marginal propensity to consume and n represents the number of income periods.

(1) $k = 1 + a + a^2 + a^3 + a^4 + \ldots + a^n$

(2) $ak = a + a^2 + a^3 + a^4 + a^5 + \ldots + a^{n+1}$

(3) $(k - ak) = (1 - a^{n+1})$ [Equation (2) subtracted from Equation (1).]

(4) $k(1 - a) = 1 - a^{n+1}$

(5) $k = \dfrac{1 - a^{n+1}}{1 - a}$

(6) When the number of income periods, n, is very large, the value of a^{n+1} will be so small as to be negligible, if $0 < a < 1$. Therefore, we conclude that

$$k = \frac{1}{1 - a}$$

Algebraic proof that a equals the marginal propensity to consume

(1) $C = C_o + aY_d$

(2) $C + \Delta C = C_o + a(Y_d + \Delta Y_d)$

(3) $C + \Delta C = C_o + aY_d + \Delta Y_d$

(4) $\Delta C = a\Delta Y_d$ [Equation (1) subtracted from Equation (3).]

$$(5) \quad a = \frac{\Delta C}{\Delta Y_d}$$

Algebraic determination of the equilibrium income level

(1) $Y_{np} = C + I$ The basic identity

(2) $C = C_o + aY_d$ The consumption function

(3) $C = C_o + aY_{np}$ This follows because $Y_d = Y_{np}$ when taxes and transfers are zero

(4) $I = I_o$ Autonomous investment

(5) $Y_{np} = C_o + aY_{np} + I_o$ Substitution of Equations (3) and (4) into (1).

(6) $Y_{np} - aY_{np} = C_o + I_o$

(7) $Y_{np}(1 - a) = C_o + I_o$

(8) $Y_{np} = \dfrac{1}{(1-a)}(C_o + I_o)$

(9) $Y_{np} = k(C_o + I_o)$

7 | The Theory of Investment

In this chapter we turn to the second major category of expenditure entering into aggregate demand: investment expenditure. There are three basic reasons why investment expenditure occupies a highly significant role in the functioning of the economy. In the first place, the demand for investment goods is a large and important part of the total demand picture. In 1965, for example, gross private domestic investment was $105.7 billion, an amount equal to 15.6 per cent of GNP. Investment expenditures play an especially strategic role in the economy, because changes in both income and employment are more likely to result from fluctuations in spending for capital goods than from fluctuations in spending for consumer goods. Changes in spending for consumer goods generally come about as a result of changes in the income level, rather than the other way around.

Second, investment expenditures are highly volatile. Students of change and growth have long been aware that fluctuations in capital goods production are more violent than fluctuations in the production of consumer goods and services. This is true both in a relative sense and in an absolute sense. Investment expenditures not only initiate change in income and employment levels, but also act to exaggerate the effects.

Finally, investment expenditures are significant because of their impact on the economy's productive capacity. Investment expenditures involve the acquisition of capital goods, the "procreative" element in an industrial society. Their function is to produce other goods and services. This means that even though investment expenditures play a key role in determining current levels of income and employment, their influence reaches beyond the present by means of their impact upon capacity. Investment expenditures thus are vital factors in economic growth, which depends to a great extent upon how rapidly productive capacity is being enlarged.

Definitions and Concepts

Before we plunge into an analysis of the determinants of investment expenditure, a review of some of the definitions and concepts important to this aspect of income and employment theory may be helpful. As we saw in Chapter 2, investment includes expenditures for producer's durable equipment, new construction (residential and business), and the net change in inventories. This classification is arbitrary, as neither inventory change nor new home construction fits easily into the idea that the process of capital formation involves additions to the economy's stock of *productive* instruments. Mention is made of this because the theory of investment developed in this chapter is most appropriate to the purchase by business of new plant and new equipment. The theoretical framework for investment expenditure applies primarily to investment expenditure carried out by the private business firm in the setting of a competitive market. Its usefulness for analysis and appraisal of public investment (public buildings, highways, and dams, for example) is relatively limited because capital of this kind is not produced in the expectation of a monetary profit.

Net and Gross Investment

A useful distinction from an analytical point of view is between net investment and gross investment. Net investment, it will be recalled from our discussion in Chapter 2, is investment that enlarges the economy's stock of real capital assets, thereby adding to productive capacity. Gross investment, on the other hand, includes both new capital and replacement capital. Replacement investment would seem to do no more than maintain intact a given stock of capital with respect to size, quality, and value. Such investment would also seem to be financed automatically from depreciation allowances. In reality, however, the distinction between new and replacement investment is not so clear-cut. Because of constantly shifting factors such as technology, prices, and costs, investment expenditure financed from depreciation reserves rarely represents a simple replacement of capital assets that have become worn out or obsolete. In most instances a new machine or structure will likely be a better machine or structure than the one it replaces, and, as a consequence, an element of expansion of productive capacity is often concealed in what purports to be merely replacement investment. Although the real-world distinction between replacement and new (or net) investment is a blurred one, it is still useful to make this a theoretical distinction.

Autonomous and Induced Investment

Another distinction quite useful in theoretical analysis is between autonomous and induced investment. In our discussion of the consumption function and the process of income determination, we utilized the concept of autonomous investment. In a technical sense, investment expenditure that is autonomous results from forces that are not a part of the system of variables under analysis. In Chapter 6, for example, the simplified "model" of the economy involved only three major variables, consumption, investment, and income. Investment expenditure was autonomous because we assumed that the level was determined independently of the value of either of the other variables in the system. In economic analysis investment expenditure believed to be independent of current income is often regarded as autonomous. Professor Alvin Hansen maintains that autonomous investment is generally associated with such factors as the introduction of new production techniques or products, the development of new resources, or the growth of population and the labor force.[1]

Induced investment, on the other hand, is investment expenditure that can be linked in some way with current output or demand; it is defined as investment expenditure that is related functionally to output levels. It is usually interpreted as investment that is undertaken specifically to furnish a larger output.[2] The concept of induced investment underlies the theory of the accelerator, which we shall consider at a later point in this chapter.

Investment and Profit

In reality it is not easy to distinguish autonomous investment from induced investment. *All* investment expenditure is basically undertaken in the expectation of profit, and it is difficult, if not impossible, to separate expectations of profitability from actual profitability, which is dependent upon current levels of output, sales, and costs. This does not mean that investment is undertaken only when current profits are satisfactory, because in many instances firms with low profit margins will invest in money-saving equipment in an effort to reduce costs.[3]

Generally speaking, there are two ways in which investment in capital will improve the profitability of the firm's operations. First, investment in new and improved equipment is a means of reducing production costs. Capital equipment is productive partly because it can supplement or take the place of other resources, particularly labor. Capital goods are tools. Through their use the effectiveness in production of both labor and natural resources may be enormously enhanced. It is estimated, for ex-

---

[1] Alvin H. Hansen, *Business Cycles and National Income* (New York, Norton, 1951), p. 190.

[2] D. Hamberg, *Economic Growth and Instability* (New York, Norton, 1956), p. 42.

[3] Walter W. Heller, "The Anatomy of Investment Decisions," *Harvard Business Review*, March, 1951.

ample, that machines in a modern factory supply from thirty to seventy times as much energy as could be provided by human muscle.[4] Capital is also productive because it frequently represents the means by which new methods or techniques of production are introduced into the economic process.

The second way in which investment in capital equipment may improve the profitability of the firm's operations centers on market conditions. Frequently, the firm will be confronted with an opportunity to increase its profits either by introducing a new product or by expanding the output and sales of existing products. In either case, added capacity may be required if the firm is to exploit fully the profit potential of a favorable market situation; investment in new equipment and plant is necessary to provide this added capacity. In the quest for greater profitability, many firms engage extensively in product research and sales promotions. Both these activities almost force a firm to invest in more plant and equipment.

The Investment Decision

Now that we have examined briefly the reasons why investment expenditure cannot be separated from profitability in the operation of the firm, let us examine the nature of the investment decision. How does the entrepreneur look upon an item of capital equipment? What factors does he have to take into account when he is contemplating the purchase of additional capital equipment? These questions lie at the heart of the investment decision, and investment theory, if it is to be meaningful, must provide at least tentative answers to them.

Investment and Expected Income

Since the entrepreneur undertakes investment expenditure in the expectation that it will be profitable, he sees an item of capital equipment essentially as a stream of expected income, or, as Keynes described it, "a series of prospective returns." [5] To the businessman, the value of a capital good lies in the stream of income that the asset is expected to yield over its life. The stream of income is an *expected* stream primarily because capital is durable and thus yields value to its user only over a relatively long period of time. The size of the expected income stream depends upon, first, the physical productivity of the capital instrument; second, the price at which the output produced with the aid of the capital equipment can be sold (which is primarily a matter of future demand and mar-

[4] A. J. Brown, *Introduction to the World Economy* (New York, Rinehart, 1959), p. 51.
[5] John Maynard Keynes, *The General Theory of Employment, Interest and Money* (New York, Harcourt, Brace, 1936), p. 135.

ket conditions); and finally, the nature and amount of other expenses in the form of wages and material costs that may be incurred from the use of additional amounts of equipment. These expenses, too, depend upon future market conditions. In analysis of the investment decision the usual practice is to think of the stream of expected income associated with the use of additional amounts of capital as being *net* of all other expenses that the firm may incur as a result of using more capital. Added expenditures for labor and materials, as well as any other additional operating expenses, are deducted from the contemplated income stream or prospective returns on the capital good. This is done because the entrepreneur is primarily interested in what the equipment will yield him in the way of income over and above any additional expenses that may be involved in its operation.

Having stripped the stream of expected income of all costs incidental to the process of producing additional output, the entrepreneur is faced with the question of whether the investment is worthwhile. Will it, in other words, be profitable? The businessman in modern industrial society obtains a profit by converting money, which is the most liquid of all assets and which can always be loaned out at interest, into a less liquid form, that of a capital asset. Through the sale of its output, the capital asset is converted back to monetary form. This operation—a movement from money to goods and back to money—is spread over the life of the asset. It will be profitable to the entrepreneur only if the asset yields him more than the cost of its acquisition. Here is the nub of the investment decision. The entrepreneur will find an investment worthwhile if it yields him a stream of income greater than what he must pay to acquire the asset. The investment decision involves balancing expected gain against the costs of acquiring the gain.

The Costs of Investment

What are the costs that the entrepreneur has to take into account in estimating the profitability of an investment expenditure? If we ignore momentarily the element of risk present in the acquisition of *any* capital asset, we can distinguish two fundamental types of costs that enter into the investment decision: the cost under current market conditions of the capital asset itself and the cost involved in the use of money or funds to acquire the asset.

The cost of the capital good under current market conditions is what Keynes called the *supply price* of the asset. This he defined as the price which would induce the manufacturer of any particular type of capital asset to produce one additional unit of the capital asset in question.[6] The

---

[6] *Ibid.*

supply price for a particular capital asset is not the current market price of existing assets of that kind, but, basically, the cost of producing a new unit. It is the price that lies somewhere on a supply curve for the kind of capital equipment under discussion. From a monetary standpoint this represents what the entrepreneur must spend in order to acquire the asset. It also represents the absolute, irreducible minimum that the entrepreneur expects to get back from the purchase and utilization of a capital good. In a world dominated by the profit motive no entrepreneur would contemplate the purchase of a new capital asset unless he believed that the asset would yield a stream of income which, in the very least, would be equal to the supply price of the asset. In actuality, he would expect more, but this notion of a kind of irreducible minimum gives us a point of departure.

The above statements would be wholly correct if the use of money did not involve any costs. Then we could say that it would be profitable to acquire a capital asset whenever the value of the stream of expected income was greater than the current supply price. This, though, is not the case, for in a monetary society there is always a cost involved in the use of money. The entrepreneur contemplating the acquisition of a capital asset has two choices open to him. Since he cannot obtain the asset without money, he must either borrow the necessary funds to finance its purchase or else draw upon his own accumulated reserves. If he borrows, he must pay the current market rate of interest appropriate to a loan of the type and duration necessary. The interest rate is the *financial cost* that enters into the investment decision. Even if the entrepreneur uses his own funds to finance his purchase of capital equipment, the interest rate measures the financial cost. In this event the financial cost is implicit, since by using his own funds for the purchase of a capital instrument, the return on which is uncertain, the entrepreneur forgoes the possibility of securing a return on these funds equal to the current market rate of interest, which he could get by lending his funds. It is only proper for the entrepreneur to treat such foregone interest income as a cost element in the acquisition of a capital asset. The market rate of interest is a measure of the "opportunity cost" involved in the use of funds to purchase an item of capital in preference to lending such funds to someone who is willing to pay the going rate to secure their use.

We have said that the investment decision ultimately rests upon the expectation of profit. How large the excess of expected income over costs has to be before the entrepreneur will actually go ahead with an investment project depends chiefly upon the element of risk involved in the acquisition of a particular kind of capital equipment. This, of course, is a very important matter, but we will defer its consideration to a later point in this chapter.

The Keynesian Framework

Now that we have examined the essential character of the investment decision, we shall turn our attention to the formal framework of investment theory that Keynes postulates in the *General Theory*. In the foregoing discussion the point was emphasized that an excess of expected revenues from the use of a capital good over its supply price means that the good yields a prospective profit. This is true, irrespective of the financial costs of the investment, as long as the expected income stream is greater than the supply price. The excess of the expected yield over the cost of the capital can be expressed as a rate; more specifically, a *rate of return over cost*, in which the net return *per unit of time* is shown as a per cent of the original cost. For example, a machine might cost an entrepreneur $10,000 and yield him a net annual return of $1,000. Without at this moment considering the question of the useful life of the machine, we can say that such a machine yields *a rate of return over cost* of 10 per cent.

The rate of return over cost relates the expected yield of a capital good to its supply price. It is this relationship that Keynes calls the *marginal efficiency of capital*.

The relation between the prospective yield of a capital asset and its supply price or replacement cost, i.e., the relation between the prospective yield of one more unit of that type of capital and the cost of producing that unit, furnishes us with the *marginal efficiency of capital* of that type. More precisely, I define the marginal efficiency of capital as being equal to that *rate of discount* [italics added] which would make the present value of . . . the returns expected from the capital asset during its life just equal to its supply price.[7]

The above definition emphasizes the word "marginal." We are here interested in the expected rate of return on *additional* units of capital, not the rate of return now being earned on existing capital. Keynes defines the marginal efficiency of capital as a rate of discount; specifically, as the rate of discount which will make the present value of the income stream derived from the capital good just equal to its supply price. The marginal efficiency of capital is a rate of discount because the *present value* of either a specific sum or a series of sums expected in the future must be less than its absolute amount. This is so because of the phenomenon of interest. Money now available can earn for its owner an income in the form of interest. This is not possible for money that represents only potential ownership because it is due at some future date. A dollar held today is worth more than a dollar due.

[7] *Ibid.*

The Discount Formula

There exists a mathematical formula for finding the present value of an expected future income. It involves *discounting* the sum expected at some future data. The process of discounting is just the opposite of compounding. It means shrinkage at a constant rate, just as compounding means growth at a constant rate. The discount formula applies a factor to some expected future sum that will cause it, as it were, to shrink in value. The usual procedure for determining the present value of some expected income stream is to discount it at the current rate of interest. To see how this works, let us assume that we have an asset that will yield an income of $3,000 per year for a three-year period ($9,000 over its total life span). We want to know the present value of this asset. The discount formula for finding the present value of a future income is

$$V_p = \frac{R_1}{(1+i)} + \frac{R_2}{(1+i)^2} + \cdots + \frac{R_n}{(1+i)^n} \qquad (7\text{-}1)$$

In the equation, V_p is present value; $R_1, R_2 \ldots R_n$ is the expected income stream in absolute amount; and i is the current rate of interest. The numerical subscript appended to each R represents the year in which each of the specific sums that are a part of the total is due. If we assume that the current rate of interest is 5 per cent, we can apply the above formula to find the present value of our asset.

$$V_p = \frac{\$3,000}{(1.05)} + \frac{\$3,000}{(1.05)^2} + \frac{\$3,000}{(1.05)^3}$$

And clearing fractions,

$$V_p = \$2,857 + \$2,721 + \$2,597 = \$8,175$$

The present value of the series is thus $8,175, an amount less than the sum of the absolute amounts to be received in the three years.

This example shows that the more remote the date in the future at which the income is expected, the less its present value; $3,000 due in three years, for example, has a lower present value than $3,000 due in one year. Again leaving aside any question of uncertainty, simple arithmetic tells us that if we lend the sum of $2,857 for a period of one year at a rate of interest of 5 per cent, we will get back $3,000, which includes the original sum and interest. This being the case, no one would be willing to pay more than $2,857 for an asset that would yield a total return of $3,000 one year hence. By the same reasoning, if we lend $2,721 for a period of two years at a rate of interest of 5 per cent we will get back

$3,000, for $2,721 compounded at a rate of 5 per cent for two years equals $3,000. Thus no one would be willing to pay more than $2,721 for an asset that yields a total return of $3,000 two years hence. The same reasoning applies to the third sum in our series, namely $2,597, if it is made available as a loan for a three-year period at the rate of 5 per cent.

We have examined the process of discounting in some detail to show that there is some rate of discount which will make the present value of prospective returns from a capital good equal to its supply price. This is the rate that Keynes calls the marginal efficiency of capital, which we shall designate by r.

Let us now modify the discount formula by substituting the current supply price of the capital instrument for present value, V_p, and also by substituting the marginal efficiency of capital, r, for the current rate of interest, i. The formula now appears as

$$K_s = \frac{R_1}{(1+r)} + \frac{R_2}{(1+r)^2} + \cdots + \frac{R_n}{(1+r)^n} \qquad (7\text{--}2)$$

The expected income stream (or series of R's) is the same as in Equation (7–1). The current supply price, K_s, is a known value in contrast to the unknown present value, V_p, in the earlier equation. In the above formulation the unknown is the marginal efficiency of capital, r, or discount rate, which will make the present value of the expected income stream $R_1, R_2 \ldots R_n$ equal to the supply price, K_s. The equation must be solved for the unknown r.

As long as the computed value of the marginal efficiency of capital is positive, we know that the capital asset in question will yield some rate of return. This means the income stream expected from the use of the capital asset is at least large enough to cover the supply price. But, the current supply price of the asset represents only a part of the cost of acquiring an added unit of capital. In addition to the supply price, there is the financial cost that arises from the use of money funds in the acquisition of the asset. Since this cost element is measured by the current rate of interest, we can compare it directly with the marginal efficiency of capital; both are rate phenomena.

If such a comparison is made and we find that the marginal efficiency of capital is greater than the current rate of interest, the situation is favorable to investment. The income stream expected from the use of an additional unit of capital exceeds the costs of acquiring the capital. Consequently, the capital instrument will be purchased. Of course, an entrepreneur may use his resources to purchase a financial asset rather than an item of capital equipment, and presumably he will do so whenever the marginal efficiency of capital falls below the current rate of interest.

The idea that, other things being equal, investment expenditure will take place whenever the marginal efficiency of capital is greater than the current rate of interest is the key element in Keynes' theory of investment. It is the formal, theoretical expression of the view that profitability is the dominant factor in the investment decision. Unless the prospects are such that the expected yield of a new item of capital exceeds its supply price plus financial cost, it will not be purchased by the business firm. When we say that the marginal efficiency of capital, r, is greater than the rate of interest, i, we are also saying that the present value, V_p, of the capital asset (which is obtained by discounting its expected income at the current rate of interest) is greater than its supply price K_s.

The Demand for Capital

At the level of the firm and industry the demand for capital must be formulated in relationship to the *stock* of capital goods. When a firm undertakes investment expenditures because the marginal efficiency of capital is greater than the current rate of interest, it has decided to add units of capital to its current stock. Thus, the first step in developing a theory of investment expenditure applicable to the economy as a whole is to examine the character of the demand for capital at the firm in order to see how this can be translated into investment spending. There is a paradox to be resolved, for what is of interest to the firm is its *stock* of capital, including additions and subtractions from that stock, but what is of paramount concern with respect to income and employment levels for the economy as a whole is the over-all *flow* of investment spending.

Figure 7–1 depicts the demand for capital as seen by the firm. The vertical-axis measures present value, V_p, and the horizontal axis the quantity of capital, K. For *each* possible level of the rate of interest there exists a single down-sloping demand curve for capital. In Figure 7–1 three curves are shown. It should be noted that other things being equal, the lower the rate of interest, the higher will be the level of the demand curve. The reason for this can be seen by reference to Equation (7–1) for any given income stream (R_1, R_2 . . . R_n), its present value must be larger the lower is the rate of interest. This is a matter of the mathematics.

The fundamental explanation for the negative slope of any single demand curve for capital lies in the principle of diminishing productivity. Given the rate of interest, and with all else held constant, including demand for the final product, the expected profitability of each successive increment to the capital stock must decline. In the terms of the variables of Equation (7–1), the expected income stream will decline as the capital stock is enlarged. In this context it is crucial to note and understand that

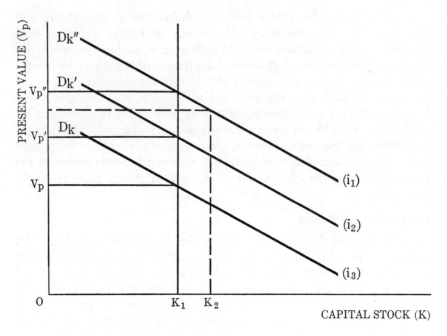

Figure 7–1. The Demand for Capital

net investment takes place in the economy whenever firms are in the process of adding to their capital stock; net disinvestment results whenever the reverse process takes place, which is to say whenever firms reduce their stock of capital instruments.

The Role of the Interest Rate

The effect of a change in the rate of interest is to shift the position of the demand curve for capital. If the rate of interest is lowered the curve will be shifted upward. The economic reason for this is that a fall in the rate of interest will increase the present value of the firm's marginal unit of capital, making it more profitable for the firm to utilize additional capital. From the viewpoint of the firm, the consequence of a fall in the rate of interest is to increase the capital intensity of production, i.e., to cause firms to use more capital per unit of labor and other resources. If all firms in the economy are affected in similar fashion by a decline in interest rates, what will be the over-all result? This is the question to which we must now turn.

Let us begin the analysis with the assumption that prior to the reduction in the interest rate firms *in the aggregate* were in an equilibrium position with respect to their use of capital. This means that present value and the supply price are equal. This is also to say that, on balance, they were neither increasing nor decreasing the amount of capital used in the production process. This assumption means, too, that the total stock of capital of the economy is fixed. All investment expenditure at this point is replacement investment. The existing stock of capital is depicted by the schedule K_1 in Figure 7-1. In technical terms capital is momentarily in completely inelastic supply.

Let us assume further that the rate of interest declines from i_3 to i_2. Under these circumstances the demand curve for capital will move to the level D_k'. The *immediate* consequence of this is to raise the present value of existing capital stock from V_p to V_p'; this is because we have had an increase in demand for a resource whose supply is temporarily fixed. This will also lead to an increase in the current price of capital goods which will evoke a supply response. Capital goods production increases, because the suppliers of capital goods respond to an increase in the price of their product in the same manner as any other supplier, namely by increasing output. Because it was assumed prior to this change that the economy was in equilibrium with respect to the quantity of capital employed in production, additional output of capital results in *net investment*. Our analysis thus leads us to associate a fall in the rate of interest with an increase in the rate of investment, assuming initially an equilibrium position in the use of capital. A rise in the rate of interest would lead to opposite results.

If we start from an equilibrium position, the actual volume of net investment that we can associate with a specific rate of interest is determined by the output response of capital goods production to a change in the rate of interest. This is a matter, first, of the extent to which the demand curve for capital shifts as the interest rate changes, and, second, the reaction of the industries supplying capital goods to the change in the price of capital goods which results from the shifts in the demand curve for capital. This latter point means, in effect, that supply conditions in the capital goods sector are a prime determinant of the level of net investment for the economy as a whole.

The Investment Demand Schedule

The foregoing discussion brings together the key elements involved in decisions at the firm level to increase the use of capital relative to other resources. The problem now confronting us is to derive a schedule which will relate the rate of investment expenditure to the rate of interest. If this can be done, we shall have the rudiments of a theory of investment which can be incorporated into our broader frame of reference, the theory of aggregate demand.

Figure 7-2 shows the relationships involved in the derivation of this schedule. In Part A of the figure the 45° line represents equality conditions between present value and the supply price of newly produced units of capital, K_s. The latter are represented on the horizontal and vertical axes respectively. Part B contains a supply schedule for capital

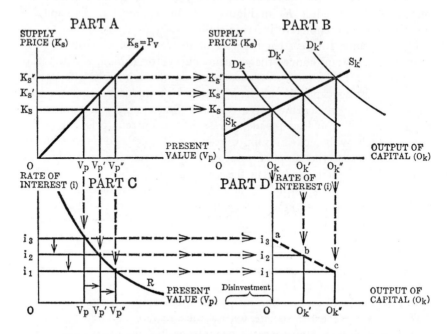

Figure 7–2. The Rate of Interest and the Output of Capital

goods output, showing the latter on the horizontal axis and the supply price on the vertical axis. This curve has the usual positive slope characteristic of a supply curve, indicating that more output will be supplied only as the price increases. Part C of the figure contains a curve which relates present value to the rate of interest. This curve, which is based upon expected proceeds, depicts graphically the relationship inherent in Equation (7–1), namely present value, V_p, will vary inversely with the rate of interest. Part D contains the schedule which relates the *net* output of capital goods to the rate of interest. This schedule is the one in which we are most interested and it is derived from the relationships depicted in the other three parts of this diagram.

Let us begin our analysis by assuming the economy is initially in equilibrium with respect to the use of capital. The stock of capital equals K_1 (Figure 7–1), and the rate of interest is i_3. In equilibrium present value and the supply price must be equal. This equilibrium is shown in Part A of Figure 7–2 at the point on the 45° line at which $V_p = K_s$. By project-

ing the equilibrium supply price to the right (Part B), we can determine
from the supply schedule $S_k S_k'$ the output of capital goods associated with
this price. This is O_k in Part B. By projecting the equilibrium present
value downward (Part C), we can show that V_p is associated with the
interest rate i_3. If we now project the output of capital goods O_k (Part B)
downward, and the rate of i_3 (Part C) to the right, we find they will
intersect at point a in Part D of the figure. Thus, we have established
a point which relates the *net* output of capital to the rate of interest. Net
output of capital goods at the interest rate i_3 is zero because our beginning assumption was that the economy had attained equilibrium with
respect to its use of capital.

We shall now examine what will transpire with a fall in the rate of
interest. The student should note carefully at this point that the diagrams
contained in Figure 7–2 are of such a nature that they can only depict
effectively the end result of a disturbance to equilibrium; they cannot
show the process through which change takes place. This is a consequence of their static nature. We begin by assuming a fall in the rate of
interest from i_3 to i_2. The fall in the rate of interest increases the present
value of the existing stock of capital, assuming no change in the series
of expected proceeds. This change is shown in Part C, wherein present
value rises to V_p' as the rate of interest falls to i_2. Momentarily we find
that present value exceeds the current supply price (Part B) and, as a
consequence, it will be profitable for firms to increase their use of capital.
Because the capital goods sector cannot respond instantly to the increased
demand for capital, the current market price for existing capital goods
will rise. This leads, in turn, to an increase in the output of capital goods.
For the economy this results in net investment, because additional capital
goods output will, under the circumstances assumed in our analysis,
increase the stock of capital. Output of capital expands until it reaches
the level given by O_k' in Part B of Figure 7–2, for at this level of production present value and the current supply price of capital are once
more in balance.

It is now necessary to repeat our previous process and project the
output of capital O_k' (Part B) downward and the rate of interest i_2
(Part C) to the right to get an additional point of intersection. This is
point b in Part D of the figure. We now have a second point relating
the net output of capital goods to the rate of interest. If the rate of
interest falls still further to the level i_1 the process just described will
ensue once again, and we shall get still a third point c in Part D of the
figure relating capital goods output to interest.

If we connect these three points (the dotted line in Part D) we have,
in effect, constructed a schedule which shows how the *rate* of capital
goods production (net) is linked to the rate of interest. What is of significance concerning this schedule is that it postulates, *ceteris paribus*,

an inverse relationship between the rate of interest and the demand for units of newly produced capital goods, which will be added to the capital stock. The relationship shown in Part D of Figure 7–2 is the theoretical basis for construction of an aggregate investment demand schedule which makes total investment expenditure an inverse function of the rate of interest. In the *General Theory* Keynes stated it was possible to construct such a schedule directly upon the basis of relationships embodied in Equation (7–2) because increased investment in any type of capital would lead to a decline in the marginal efficiency for capital of that type.[8] The difficulty with this approach is that it overlooks the fact that the demand of the firm is for a fixed quantity of capital to be employed in conjunction with other resources in the production process. Thus, it is really not possible to construct a schedule relating investment expenditure to the rate of interest without at the same time bringing the stock of capital into the analysis. This is what is done in Figure 7–2.

To construct an investment demand schedule for the economy as a whole on the basis of the relationship shown in Part D of Figure 7–2 it is necessary to translate the rate of output shown on the horizontal axis of the diagram into a rate of investment expenditure. Conceptually this can be done by multiplying the output data shown by the current supply price of the newly produced capital goods to get an expenditure total for capital appropriate to each level of the interest rate. The results should then be deflated by an appropriate price index so as to reduce investment expenditures to "real" terms. A schedule derived in this manner is depicted in Figure 7–3, in which the rate of investment expenditure is shown on the horizontal axis and the rate of interest measured on the vertical axis. This is an investment demand schedule of the type that Keynes envisaged in the *General Theory*.

In algebraic terms the relationship embodied in the investment demand schedule is given by the equation:

$$I = I_o - ci \qquad (7\text{–}3)$$

In this equation I_o is investment expenditure which will take place at zero rate of interest and c is the coefficient relating investment expenditure to the rate of interest. The fact that c has a negative value reflects the *inverse* correlation between investment and the rate of interest, which is to say that the greater the value of i, the smaller will be the value of I.

At this point the student should note carefully the similarity of our treatment of investment expenditure with our earlier analysis of consumption expenditure. Compare, for example, Equation (7–3) with Equation (6–3). What this means, essentially, is at this point investment

[8] *Ibid.*, p. 136.

is made a function of a single variable, namely the rate of interest. This does not mean, however, that other variables are not also important as determinants of the aggregate level of investment expenditures. Rather, it means we are treating the other variables as parametric factors whose values determine the level and shape of the investment demand function.

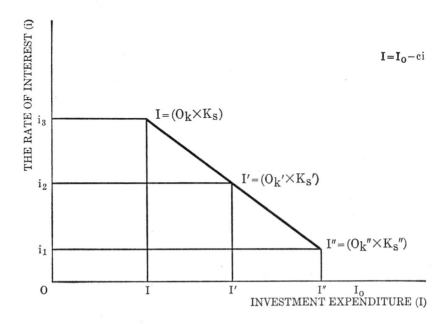

Figure 7-3. The Investment Demand Schedule

This procedure is identical to what we followed in the analysis of the consumption function and is a standard analytical technique in economics.

As is true of any demand schedule, the investment demand curve depicted in Figure 7-3 is subject to either upward or downward shifts. Shifts in the schedule are to be explained in terms of underlying determinants discussed in conjunction with Figure 7-2. Essentially, we can identify two major sources of a shift in the investment demand schedule. These are, first, a change in the expected yield of capital [the R series of Equations (7-1) and (7-2)] and, second, a shift in the supply curve for capital goods. The first result may come about either because there have been advances which increase the physical productivity of capital or else other events have created a more favorable set of expectations on the part of the business community.

The manner in which either an increase in expected yields or a shift in the supply schedule could lead to a rightward shift in the investment demand schedule is depicted in Figure 7–4. The curve in Part D relating the output of capital to the level of interest rates shifts to the right. The basis for such a shift may be either an increase in expected yields, which is depicted by a rightward shift of the R curve in Part C, or developments in the capital goods producing sector which leads to a shift downward in the supply schedule for capital goods, Part B. The positions of the

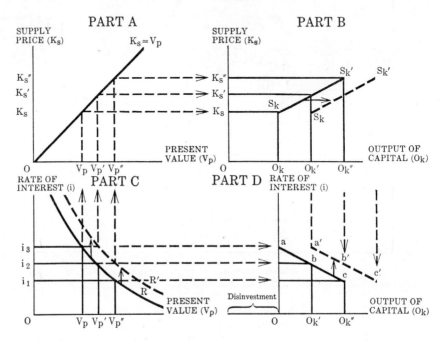

Figure 7–4. Shift in the Schedule of Capital Output and Interest

relevant curves *following* the foregoing shifts are shown by the dotted lines in Figure 7–4.

The Ephemeral Character of the Investment Demand Schedule

The investment demand schedule developed in the foregoing section has a limited life. Essentially, what it tells us is the volume of investment expenditure associated with various levels of the interest rate *only* until such time as the firms in the economy have reached a new level of equilibrium with respect to the capital stock. Once the latter is achieved net investment will necessarily cease. When this happens a schedule constructed on the basis of events which ensue whenever a change in the rate of interest disturbs a pre-existing equilibrium no longer has any meaning. Let us examine why this is so by referring once again to Figure 7–2.

As the output of capital goods continues at the rate O_k'' (Part B of Figure 7–2), the effect will be to increase the total capital stock. The stock of capital schedule K_1 in Figure 7–1 shifts to the right as *net* investment takes place. As a consequence, the present value of additional units of capital declines, partly because any increase in the capital stock under *ceteris paribus* conditions brings into play the principle of diminishing productivity, and partly, too, because the increase in price necessary to induce capital goods producers to increase their output raises the supply price, K_s, for each newly produced unit of capital [See Equations (7–1) and (7–2)]. With the demand curve for capital at the level D_k'' and with, too, a shift to the right of the total stock of capital curve, K, eventually the economy will, *ceteris paribus*, reach a new equilibrium at which the present value of the last unit of capital added to the over-all stock will be just equal to its supply price. This new equilibrium position is depicted in Figure 7–1 by the intersection of D_k'' and the dotted line representing a larger capital stock K_2. When this point is reached the output of capital goods adjusts to a level that represents replacement demand only; *net* investment must cease. Once the new equilibrium is reached, the schedule shown in Part D of Figure 7–2 (as well as the investment demand schedule of Figure 7–3) no longer has validity in the sense of showing the net output of capital (and net investment expenditure) associated with interest rates in the range i_1 to i_3. What Part D of Figure 7–2 told us was that starting from an *initial* equilibrium with a capital stock equal to K_1 and a rate of interest equal to i_3, *net* output of capital goods would vary from zero to a rate equal to O_k'' as the rate of interest declined from i_3 to i_1. But this is *all* we can conclude from the schedule shown in Part D and the investment demand schedule derived from it depicted in Figure 7–3. If subsequent changes in the rate of interest disturb the *new* equilibrium position, represented by the intersection of D_k'' and K_2 in Figure 7–1, it is necessary to start afresh in the construction of an investment demand curve. *Any* investment demand schedule relating the rate of interest and aggregate investment expenditure is meaningful only during the time in which the capital stock is adjusting from one equilibrium position to another. Unfortunately, there is nothing in the analysis pursued to this point that reveals the amount of time required for such an adjustment.

The Shape of the Investment Demand Schedule

A question of concern to economists with significant implications in the area of public policy has to do with the shape of the investment demand schedule postulated in Figure 7–3. Technically, this is a matter of the *interest-elasticity* of investment expenditure, by which we mean the responsiveness of aggregate investment expenditure to a change in the rate of interest. If the latter variable is subject to change by policy makers, and if, too, investment is a variable of strategic significance in the determination of the income level, then the question of the degree to which investment outlays respond to changes in the interest rates is of paramount importance.

Specifically, the interest elasticity of the investment demand schedule, which we shall designate as e_i, is equal to the ratio of a percentage change in investment expenditure to a percentage change in the rate of interest. In algebraic terms the interest elasticity of the investment demand schedule is given by the following formula:

$$e_i = \frac{\Delta I/I}{\Delta i/i} = \frac{\Delta I}{i} \times \frac{i}{\Delta i} \qquad (7\text{--}4)$$

An investment demand schedule that is relatively *elastic* will have a coefficient of elasticity whose absolute value is greater than 1, whereas an investment demand schedule that is relatively *inelastic* will have a coefficient of elasticity whose absolute value is less than 1. For policy purposes an elastic schedule is obviously of most significance; unless the schedule is relatively elastic, total investment expenditures and hence aggregate demand cannot be significantly influenced by changes in the rate of interest. Interest rate changes belong to the sphere of monetary policy; thus we shall advance the hypothesis that for monetary policy to be an effective instrument of control, the investment demand schedule must be relatively interest elastic.

This last comment brings us to the crucial question of the determinants of the elasticity of the investment demand schedule. Basically, there are two major determinants. The first has to do with the extent to which the demand curve for capital shifts upward or downward in response to a change in the rate of interest; the greater this shift, the greater will be the change in present value, and, hence, the more responsive investment expenditure becomes to a change in the rate of interest. Two factors govern the magnitude of the shift in the demand schedule for capital. The one is the *relative* price of the factors—land, labor, capital—which enter into production. A fall in the rate of interest, *ceteris paribus*, makes capital less expensive relative to other resources and may induce, therefore, a substitution of capital for other resources. This is a matter of increasing the capital intensity of production and its probability depends not only on relative prices for the factors, but also on the technical feasibility of substituting capital for other resources. If the latter is not possible, then a change in relative factor prices cannot affect investment. The second factor governing the shift in the schedule is the physical life of the capital asset. The effect of physical life can be readily seen by examination of the variables in Equation (7–1). The longer the physical life of a unit of capital, the smaller will be the net expected return on the asset in any one year [R_1 in Equation (7–1), for example]. But the smaller the net return in any single year, the more pronounced is the impact on present value of a given change in the rate of interest. It follows that the greater the change in present value, the greater will be the increase in investment expenditure resulting from a change in the rate of interest.

The other determinant of the elasticity of the investment demand schedule is the supply schedule for capital goods (Part B of Figure 7–2). The more elastic this supply schedule, the greater will be the output response in the capital goods sector for a given shift in the position of the demand curve for capital. If the production of capital goods can be significantly increased without a sharp rise in their prices, aggregate investment spending will respond favorably to a decline in the rate of interest. On the other hand, an inelastic supply schedule for capital goods means that the supply price for newly produced capital rises sharply, which will have the effect of causing the marginal efficiency of each newly produced unit to drop, thus offsetting the favorable effects upon investment spending of a decline in interest rates. Inelasticity in the supply schedule for capital goods makes for inelasticity in the investment demand schedule.

The Investment Demand Schedule and the Marginal Efficiency of Capital

At this point the perceptive student may be concerned about the relationship of the investment demand schedule to the marginal efficiency of capital. In our discussion of the concept of the marginal efficiency of capital, it was pointed out that investment expenditure occurs whenever the marginal efficiency exceeds the rate of interest. This, of course, is the same as saying that investment will take place whenever present value exceeds the supply price for a newly produced unit of capital. We also pointed out that in the *General Theory*, Keynes argued that it was possible to construct a schedule that would relate the marginal efficiency of capital to the rate of investment; such a schedule would be, in his view, an investment demand schedule, showing for the economy as a whole that investment expenditure would be "pushed" to the point at which ". . . there is no longer any class of capital-asset of which the marginal efficiency exceeds the rate of interest." [9]

Actually, as our discussion in the preceding sections indicates, this is not a proper interpretation. The appropriate context for discussion of the marginal efficiency of capital is in terms of a schedule relating it to the *stock* of capital—not the *flow* of investment spending. This kind of a schedule is shown in Figure 7–5. The rationale for this is best under-

[9] *Ibid*, p. 136.

stood by referring again to the nature of the marginal efficiency of capital concept. It is the *expected* rate of return over cost associated with an *additional* unit of capital.

The relationship between the marginal efficiency of capital and investment demand can be seen by reference to both Figure 7–2 and Figure 7–5. In Figure 7–5, the stock of capital K_1 corresponds to the initial equilibrium position depicted in Part A of Figure 7–2. At this point the

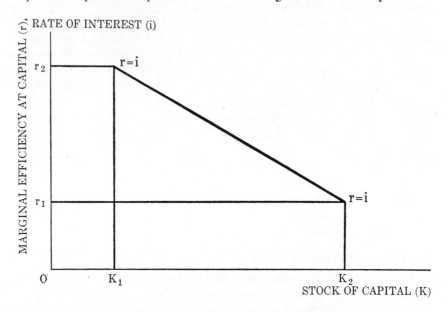

Figure 7–5. The Schedule of the Marginal Efficiency of Capital

rate of interest and the marginal efficiency necessarily must be equal. When the rate of interest declines (Vertical axis of Figure 7–5), net investment will ensue, which, as we have seen, leads to an increase in the capital stock. The latter shifts toward the level K_2 as shown in Figure 7–5. As the capital stock is increased, the marginal efficiency of capital will decline. The student should note carefully that when the marginal efficiency of capital has fallen to the level of r_1, which happens as soon as the capital stock reaches K_2, *net* investment must cease. Equilibrium will be re-established in terms of lowered values for both the marginal efficiency of capital and the rate of interest and a larger stock of capital instruments.

Current Income and Investment Expenditure

The central idea in Keynes' theory of investment is the inverse relationship between investment expenditure and the rate of interest. Since publication of the *General Theory*, many economists have concluded that income, too, is a major determinant of investment expenditure. This approach involves the phenomenon of *induced* investment, which we shall designate as I_i. In algebraic terms $I_i = f(Y)$. This equation should be interpreted to mean that investment outlays will increase as income increases. The income measure appropriate to this relationship is the net national product.[10]

In Equation (7–3), it was stated that $I = I_o - ci$. Let us designate the latter expression as I_o' and define it as all investment expenditure which is autonomous with respect to the income level. We can then postulate the following identity:

$$I = I_o' + I_i \tag{7-6}$$

This equation simply states that total investment consists of the two major categories of autonomous and induced investment. Since the latter is a direct function of income, we can transform the Equation (7–6) into the following form:

$$I = I_o' + bY_{np} \tag{7-7}$$

In the above expression b is the *marginal propensity to invest*, which algebraically we may define as:

$$b = \frac{\Delta I_i}{\Delta Y_{np}} \tag{7-8}$$

The student will note that we defined the marginal propensity to invest in a fashion analogous to the marginal propensity to consume and the marginal propensity to save, namely at the ratio of a change in investment to a change in income (net national product). The marginal propensity to invest concept implies that some portion of any increase income will be directed toward investment expenditure, a logical outcome of the assumption that current investment expenditure is linked functionally to the current income level. The marginal propensity to invest also measures the slope of the schedule which relates induced investment to income. A schedule of this type is displayed in Figure 7–6. Net national product is measured on the horizontal axis and investment on the vertical axis. Because investment is an increasing function of income the schedule slopes upward to the right. The level at which the schedule intersects the vertical axis equals I_o', investment which is independent of the income level.

The assumptions embodied in this relationship are, first, that investment depends upon profitability, and second, that profitability is directly linked

---

[10] Net national product Y_{np} and disposable income Y_d remain equal because we are still assuming neither taxes nor transfer payments are present in the system.

to the current income level. If these are correct assumptions, then a rising level of income will be accompanied by rising profit margins. As business-men project current profit experiences into the future, expectations will be favorable and, consequently, investment expenditure will rise in re-sponse to the rising income level. This, of course, is an oversimplification

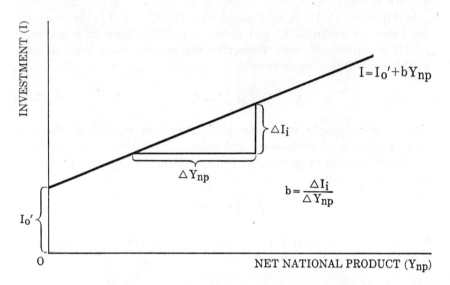

Figure 7–6. Investment and the Income Level

of a complex relationship. But the proposition that investment is a direct function of income enables us not only to deal with the phenomenon of induced investment in a direct way, but also to incorporate investment expenditure into the equilibrium income determination process and the theory of the multiplier far more readily than when we consider invest-ment expenditure as a function of the rate of interest.

THE MARGINAL PROPENSITY TO INVEST AND EQUILIBRIUM INCOME

Let us examine how the concept of the marginal propensity to invest may be incorporated into our formal equilibrium analysis by means of an income equilibrium diagram. In Figure 7–7 the 45° line OZ again repre-sents the aggregate supply function; the schedule labeled C is the con-sumption function. The basic difference between this figure and Figure 6–3 of Chapter 6 is that the aggregate demand schedule does not lie par-allel to the consumption function; investment expenditure is not autono-mous with respect to the income level, but increases as the income level increases. We construct the aggregate demand schedule by adding an in-vestment schedule of the kind shown in Figure 7–6 to the consumption function. Equilibrium is attained at the point of intersection of the schedules of aggregate demand and aggregate supply. However, because we have included induced investment, the equilibrium level is higher than otherwise would be the case.

This can be clearly seen by contrasting an aggregate demand schedule constructed with an autonomous investment function with the aggregate demand schedule constructed with a function involving induced investment. In Figure 7–7 the dotted line $C + I_o$ is an aggregate demand schedule of the former type, while schedule $C + I_o + I_i$, on the other hand, incorporates the phenomenon of induced investment. $C + I + I_i$ intersects the aggregate supply schedule at a higher income level than $C + I_o$, and it should be noted that the slope of $C + I_o + I_i$ is greater than the slope of $C + I_o$. The slope of $C + I_o + I_i$ is equal to the sum of the marginal propensity to consume and the marginal propensity to invest; the sum of these two marginal propensities can be defined as the *mar-*

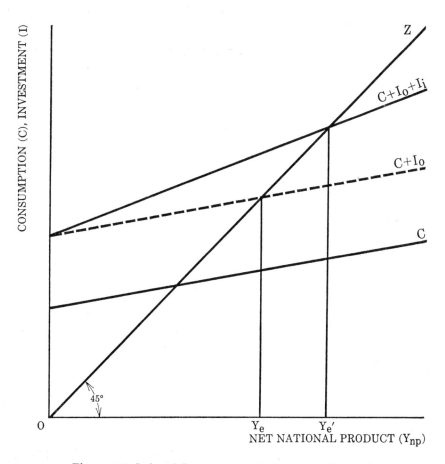

Figure 7–7. Induced Investment and Aggregate Demand

ginal propensity to spend, a concept particularly relevant to multiplier analysis because, as was shown earlier, the value of the multiplier depends upon the amount of additional spending that is *induced* by an exogenous change in spending.

INDUCED INVESTMENT EXPENDITURE AND THE MULTIPLIER

Let us explore briefly the manner in which induced investment expenditure may be incorporated into multiplier theory. In order to facilitate the exposition, we shall break the investment component of the aggregate demand schedule into two sub-categories: autonomous investment, which we have already designated as I_0 in Figure 7-7, and induced investment, represented symbolically by I_i. We assume that investment and consumption are the only expenditure categories, and that changes in the income level are initiated as the result of shifts in the autonomous investment function. Given these basic assumptions, we can postulate the following two definitional equations:

$$Y_{np} = I_o + I_i + C \qquad (7\text{--}9)$$

$$k' = \frac{\Delta Y_{np}}{\Delta I_o} \qquad (7\text{--}10)$$

Equation (7–9) is the basic identity equation which states that income (net national product) is equal to the sum of consumption and investment, except that investment is broken down into its two sub-categories. Equation (7–10) is the basic definition of the multiplier, k, except that in this instance we are using the symbol k' to indicate the multiplier because we incorporate into it the phenomenon of induced investment.

From Equation (7–9) we get the following identity pertaining to a change in the income level:

$$\Delta Y_{np} = \Delta I_o + \Delta I_i + \Delta C \qquad (7\text{--}11)$$

Since the change in induced investment expenditure, ΔI_i, depends upon the value of the marginal propensity to invest, b, and since the change in consumption expenditure depends upon the value of the marginal propensity to consume, a, we have

$$\Delta I_i = b \times \Delta Y_{np} \qquad (7\text{--}12)$$

and

$$\Delta C = a \times \Delta Y_{np}[11] \qquad (7\text{--}13)$$

[11] $\Delta Y_{np} = \Delta Y_d$ when taxes and transfers are zero.

If we substitute the above values for ΔI_i and ΔC in Equation (7–11) we have

$$\Delta Y_{np} = \Delta I_o + b\Delta Y_{np} + a\Delta Y_{np} \qquad (7\text{–}12)$$

This equation can be manipulated algebraically as follows:

$$\Delta Y_{np} - a\Delta Y_{np} - b\Delta Y_{np} = \Delta I_o \qquad (7\text{–}13)$$
$$\Delta Y_{np}\,(1 - a - b) = \Delta I_o \qquad (7\text{–}14)$$

$$\Delta Y_{np} = \Delta I_o \times \frac{1}{1 - a - b} \qquad (7\text{–}15)$$

$$\frac{\Delta Y_{np}}{\Delta I_o} = \frac{1}{1 - a - b} \qquad (7\text{–}16)$$

Thus, we can define k', the effective multiplier, as the reciprocal of 1 minus the marginal propensity to consume and the marginal propensity to invest. A quick examination of the algebra shows that by introducing an additional kind of induced spending into our analysis—namely, induced investment spending—we will obviously get a larger, ultimate increase in spending for any initial exogenous increase in spending.

In the foregoing discussion we assumed a constant value for the marginal propensity to invest, b, which in turn enables us to compute an exact value for the multiplier k'. Reality, of course, is not so accommodating, and it is most unlikely that the marginal propensity to invest will have a constant value for any significant length of time. This particular approach to induced investment rests on the assumption that current profits are sufficient to engender favorable expectations with respect to the profitability of additional capital equipment. If the current profit picture is not satisfactory, however, there is no reason to believe that any amount of investment expenditure will be induced by the current income level. Thus, there is no real assurance that the value of the marginal propensity to invest will remain stable, and, for that matter, there is no positive assurance that it will remain above zero.

The Acceleration Principle

A much more complex and dynamic analysis of the phenomenon of induced investment is based on the *acceleration principle*. This principle asserts that *net* investment is a function of the *rate* of change in final output rather than of the *absolute* level of output. This is an important distinction. The earliest complete formulation of the acceleration principle was made in 1917 by Professor John Maurice Clark in a renowned article, "Business Acceleration and the Law of Demand: A Technical Factor in Economic Cycles." [12] Clark set out to show, first, that a special and

[12] Reprinted in *Readings in Business Cycle Theory* (Philadelphia, Blakiston, 1944).

technical relationship exists between the demand for a final product and the demand for the capital equipment necessary to produce the final product, and second, that this technical relationship is of such a character that it can be employed to explain not only the nature of the demand for new capital instruments, but also why the demand for capital fluctuates much more violently than the demand for final goods. Since the publication of Clark's historic article, many economists have analyzed and refined this principle, using it to explain the apparent cyclical nature of much economic activity.

In our discussion of the acceleration principle we shall use the income symbol Y to designate *output of final goods and services*, and the symbol K to designate capital stock. The technical relationship existing between a given level of output and the quantity of capital necessary to produce that output is defined as the *capital-output ratio*. We shall designate this ratio by the capital letter A. Thus we have

$$A = \frac{K}{Y} \qquad (7\text{--}17)$$

If we assume no change in the technical condition under which resources are combined in order to obtain a given output, it is reasonable to assume that an increase in output once full capacity has been achieved will require additional capital equipment in the proportion indicated by the capital-output ratio. For example, if we find that, on the average, it requires capital equipment in the amount of $3.00 for each $1.00 of output, then as long as there is no change in the technical conditions under which capital is combined with other resources in the productive process, every $1.00 increase in output above the level of existing capacity will require $3.00 worth of additional capital equipment. We can draw the formal generalization that, given constant technical conditions of production, the *marginal* capital-output ratio will equal the capital-output ratio proper. The latter is generally designated as the *average* capital-output ratio when we are discussing the technical relationship between capital and output for the whole economy. In any event, when the average and the marginal capital-output ratios are equal

$$A = \frac{K}{Y} = \frac{\Delta K}{\Delta Y} \qquad (7\text{--}18)$$

By definition, though, the change in the capital stock, ΔK, is the same thing as net investment in the economy, I_n. Substituting I_n for ΔK in the algebraic formula and transposing ΔY to the left-hand side of the expression, we have the following:

$$A = \frac{I_n}{\Delta Y} \qquad (7\text{-}19)$$

$$A \times \Delta Y = I_n \qquad (7\text{-}20)$$

Equation (7-20) is the formal algebraic expression of the acceleration principle, as it tells us there exists some coefficient A, which, when multiplied by the change in output will give us net investment expenditure. To put the matter the other way around, we can say that the formula tells us that if output is to increase by an amount equal to ΔY, then additional capital equipment in the amount I_n is required. This is necessary because, as it can readily be seen from the formula, the larger the *absolute* change in output, the larger the amount of induced investment.

If we set this analysis within a time sequence, it is relatively easy to see why the acceleration principle makes induced investment expenditure a function of the *rate* at which output is increasing (or decreasing). Net investment in the current income period (designated by the symbol t) is equal to the difference between the capital stock of the current period, K_t, and the capital stock of the previous period, K_{t-1}. Thus

$$I_t = K_t - K_{t-1} \qquad (7\text{-}21)$$

The change in income in the current period, ΔY_t, is equal to the difference between current income, Y_t, and the income of the previous period, Y_{t-1}. Therefore, we have

$$\Delta Y_t = Y_t - Y_{t-1} \qquad (7\text{-}22)$$

The rate at which income (or output) changes between one period and the next is measured by the ratio of ΔY_t to Y_{t-1}. For example, if income rose by \$45 billion between the present and the past income period, and if Y_{t-1} was \$450 billion, then the rate of income increase, $\Delta Y_t/Y_{t-1}$, will be 10 per cent. The importance of this is that the rate of change in income depends upon the absolute change in income in a period relative to the income level of the previous period. The larger the absolute change relative to income of the previous period, the larger will be the rate of change. But the acceleration formula, Equation (7-20), shows that, given a fixed technical relationship between capital and output, the amount of induced investment will vary directly with the size of the absolute change in output. Consequently, the acceleration principle means *induced net investment is a function of the rate of change of final output.*

PRACTICAL IMPLICATIONS OF THE ACCELERATION PRINCIPLE

There are two important implications flowing from the acceleration principle. In the first place, as suggested earlier, we can employ the principle to explain a phenomenon long observed by economists, namely that the output of capital instruments fluctuates much more violently than the output of goods in general. The exaggerated impact of an increase (or decrease) in demand for final output on the demand for capital goods can be illustrated by means of a simple arithmetical example. Let us imagine a hypothetical industry whose output of final goods is 100 units per income period (see Table 7–1). The capital-output ratio for this in-dustry is assumed to be 3, which means 300 units of capital are required to produce this output. These units of capital have an average economic life of 10 income periods, so the normal replacement demand for capital equipment is 30 units per income period. Let us now see what will hap-pen if there is a 10 per cent increase in demand for the final product. A 10 per cent increase in demand will mean the production of 10 additional units of final product per income period. But if the industry is operating at its capacity level prior to this increase in demand, then the production of 10 additional units of final product per income period will require 30 additional units of capital. Now if this increase in demand of 10 per cent for the final product is presumed to take place within the confines of a single income period, the demand for capital goods will increase by 100 per cent in this same income period. The reason for this is that the 30 units of capital needed to provide an additional 10 units of output are added to the normal replacement demand of 30 units, thus making a 100 per cent increase in demand for capital goods. In the subsequent income period, however, the demand for capital goods will fall back to the level dictated by normal replacement needs,[13] because, according to the accel-eration principle, only during the time that the demand for final output is actually changing will there be additional induced investment. The reader should also note that the more durable the capital instrument, the greater will be the fluctuation in the demand for capital instruments rela-tive to the demand for final output. If, in our hypothetical example, the capital units had an average economic life of 20 rather than 10 income periods, a 10 per cent increase in demand for final output would have brought about a 200 per cent increase in demand for capital instruments (15 replacement units plus 30 additional units of capital). This would be true as long as the capital-output ratio remained equal to 3.

Our hypothetical example demonstrates the most important single fact about the acceleration principle: There will be induced investment expenditure only so long as final demand is increasing. Once the latter stabilizes at a new and higher level, induced investment expenditure will cease. Expressed in formal terms, the *absolute* level of induced net invest-ment will enlarge as long as final demand is increasing at an increasing

---

[13] The normal replacement demand will be 30 units of capital per income period, until the new units added have to be replaced. Eventually, replacement demand will rise to 33 units.

rate; once the rate of increase of final demand begins to slow down, the *absolute* level of induced net investment will decline. To illustrate, let us refer once again to our hypothetical industry with its 100 units of output and 300 units of capital. In the first income period a 10 per cent increase in final demand, because of the prevailing capital-output ratio, caused a 100 per cent increase in the demand for capital goods. In absolute amount this was equal to 30 units. Now let us assume that in the subsequent income period the demand for final output advances by 5 per cent, which

TABLE 7-1.

The Acceleration Effect and the Demand for Capital

Income Period	Capital Stock	Output	Replacement Demand	Demand for New Capital	Total Demand
1	300.0	100.0	30.0	0.0	30.0
2	330.0	110.0 *	30.0	30.0	60.0
3	346.5	115.5 †	30.0	16.5	46.5
n ‡	346.5	115.5	34.6	0.0	34.6

* 10 per cent increase in final demand.
† 5 per cent increase in final demand.
‡ when capital added in period, 2 and 3 begins to be replaced.

still is an increase, but at a decreasing rate. This 5 per cent increase in demand over the level of the previous period will require production of 5.5 additional units,[14] which, in turn, will require 16.5 additional units of capital. The *absolute* level of induced investment has fallen from 30 to 16.5 units as the rate of increase in demand for final output fell from 10 to 5 per cent (see Table 7-1).

These observations about final demand and the level of investment expenditure lead us to a second practical implication of the acceleration principle. In combination with the Keynesian investment multiplier, the acceleration principle can be used to explain why fluctuations of a cyclical character tend to be an inherent characteristic of a market economy. Professor Paul Samuelson demonstrated, by assuming various values for both the investment multiplier and the acceleration coefficient, that an initial exogenous change such as an increase in autonomous investment expenditure can not only have an explosive, cumulative effect on the income level, but can also set in motion a self-generating cyclical movement of income.[15] According to Samuelson, an exogenous increase in aggregate demand, such as results from an upward shift in the autonomous investment function, will induce additional consumption spending

[14] Five (5) per cent of 110 units is 5.5.
[15] Paul A. Samuelson, "Interactions Between the Multiplier Analysis and the Principle of Acceleration," *The Review of Economics and Statistics*, May, 1939. Reprinted in *Readings in Business Cycle Theory, op. cit.*

by means of the multiplier process. The rising level of output which results from the combination of the original increment in investment spending and the induced consumption spending may induce additional investment spending by means of the accelerator. It is the combined effect of the induced consumption spending (via the multiplier) and the induced investment spending (via the accelerator) that can bring about a powerful, cumulative upward movement of income. The multiplier and the accelerator can act together to produce a kind of self-generating cyclical movement of the income level, because the acceleration principle makes induced investment a function of the rate of change in output. When the multiplier process gets under way, induced consumption expenditure will occur, but the increments of added consumption expenditure in each successive round of spending and respending will become smaller and smaller. Since the amount of induced investment varies directly with the absolute change in income (or output), net induced investment will at first rise and then decline. But the multiplier process, it will be recalled, comes into play whenever there is a *net* change in the rate of spending. Consequently, if the rate of net induced investment begins to decline, a multiplier process in reverse is set in motion. This tends to create the self-generating cyclical movement of the income level.

A simplified example of this process is shown in Table 7–2, in which an initial equilibrium income level of 100 units is disturbed by the injection of 10 units of autonomous investment expenditure into the economy. To work this out in terms of the combined action of the multiplier and the accelerator, we have assumed a value of 0.5 for the marginal propensity to consume, giving us a multiplier of 2. A value of 2 for the accelerator is assumed, and, to avoid complication, the acceleration effect is limited to investment expenditure induced solely by a change in consumption expenditure. A close study of these hypothetical data will reveal how the multiplier and acceleration effects may combine to produce a continuous series of fluctuations in the income level.

LIMITATIONS OF THE ACCELERATION PRINCIPLE

In spite of the usefulness of the acceleration principle as a device for explaining the cyclical movement of income and sharp fluctuations in the output of capital goods, there are some rather severe limitations inherent in the concept. For one thing, most economists recognize that the acceleration principle is too mechanical to serve as an explanation of such a complex phenomenon as the investment process in a modern economy. One criticism is that the acceleration principle has little or no motivational content. The entrepreneur is presumed to act like a thermostat, noting when capacity is overtaxed and then taking the necessary steps to

TABLE 7–2.

Interaction of the Multiplier and Accelerator

(1) Period	(2) = (4) + (7) Current Income (Y)	(3) Autonomous Investment (I_o)	(4) Current Consumption (C)	(5) Changes in Consumption (ΔC)	(6) Induced Investment (I_i)	(7) Total Investment $(I_o + I_i)$
0	100	0	100	—	—	0
1	110	10	100	—	—	10
2	125	10	105	5	10	20
3	139	10	113	8	16	26
4	144	10	120	7	14	24
5	139	10	123	3	6	16
6	124	10	120	−3	−6	4
7	106	10	112	−8	−16	−6
8	95	10	103	−9	−18	−8
9	98	10	98	−5	−10	0
10	114	10	100	2	4	14
11	134	10	108	8	16	26
12	148	10	118	10	20	30
13	149	10	125	7	14	24
14	138	10	126	1	2	12
15	118	10	120	−6	−12	−2
16	100	10	110	−10	−20	−10
17	92	10	101	−9	−18	−8
18	87	10	93	−8	−16	−6
19	94	10	90	−3	−6	4

Note: The multiplier and accelerator each have a value of 2. Figures in the table have been rounded to the nearest whole numbers. The change in consumption lags behind the change in income by one period.

overcome this deficiency.[16]

A more serious criticism and limitation of the principle concerns the matter of productive capacity. In a strict sense, the acceleration principle is effective only when an industry or the economy as a whole is operating at a level of full utilization of existing capacity. Since the principle is based upon a technical relationship between capital and output, it logically follows that additional capital will not be required to make possible additional output unless existing productive capacity is being fully utilized. If surplus capacity exists in the economy, the principle breaks down because added output can be supplied from the untapped capacity. This has led some economists to conclude that insofar as business cycle analysis is concerned the principle may have validity during the upswing (when rising demand eventually presses hard against existing ca-

[16] John R. Meyer and Edwin Kuh, *The Investment Decision* (Cambridge, Mass., Harvard University Press, 1957), p. 14.

pacity), but not in the downswing or depression phase of the cycle (when excess and idle capacity is one of the most common features of the economy).

Another and related objection concerns the sticky matter of the definition of capacity. As one economist has pointed out, there is little, if anything, in the voluminous literature that has grown up around the acceleration principle that attempts to define precisely the meaning of such terms as "capacity" and "surplus capacity." [17] In a literal sense, the acceleration principle asserts that net investment is induced, or more capital is created, because output has risen. Because of the technical relationship between capital and output fundamental to the acceleration principle, additional output can be forthcoming only if the stock of capital has already been increased. This is the dilemma that faces us if we interpret both the acceleration principle and its underlying assumption of full-capacity production quite literally. The only way out of this dilemma is to interpret the notion of capacity somewhat freely and suggest that at some point the entrepreneur will reach the conclusion that his existing facilities will be overtaxed if he attempts to provide for an expected demand without expansion. This, of course, does not destroy the notion of the acceleration principle, but it does make the whole matter much more subjective—and hence less precise—than do mechanical models of the principle based upon a constant technical relationship between capital and output. As has been said, there is "an element of truth in the acceleration principle; but it is an element that is so heavily overlaid by other factors that the acceleration principle by itself is inadequate as a theory of investment." [18]

Other Influences on the Investment Decision

Within the basic analytical framework of the investment demand schedule, other determinants of investment are treated as parametric factors whose basic role is to determine the position of the schedule. Changes in the value of any of these factors cause a shift in the position or slope of the schedule. As was true with the consumption function, many of the "shift parameters" of the investment demand schedule [19] are extremely subjective and hence not capable of exact quantitative measurement. But there is a growing amount of empirical investigation in the area of the investment decision, and many of the conclusions economists have reached concerning determinants of investment expenditure have a sound basis

[17] A. D. Knox, "The Acceleration Principle and the Theory of Investment: A Survey," *Economica*, August, 1952.

[18] *Ibid.*, p. 296.

[19] The phrase "shift parameters" is one used by Professor Kenneth K. Kurihara. See his *Introduction to Keynesian Dynamics* (New York, Columbia University Press, 1956), p. 60.

in fact, even though the way in which such determinants are linked to investment expenditure cannot be reduced to a precise mathematical formula. The investment determinants that we shall discuss at this point in no sense represent all the factors other than interest and income that bear on the level of investment; we have selected those that we believe to have the most telling effects.

The Role of Expectations

Expectations are probably the dominant and at the same time the most nebulous of the many factors that enter into the investment decision. They are dominant because *all* the elements that influence the investment decision must operate through expectations. The marginal efficiency of capital is based upon the *expected* income to be derived from the employment of an additional unit of capital; it is something that looks to the future, and hence it has no existence apart from some set of expectations concerning future economic developments. As Keynes pointed out, expectations are the means by which the changing future influences the present.[20]

Expectations are of a nebulous nature partly because they cannot be fitted easily and precisely into the framework of investment theory. That expectations are subjective is readily apparent, since they consist of beliefs held by businessmen concerning future economic events, and the future is an unknown quantity. Professor B. S. Keirstead has defined expectations as "beliefs held at the present moment about the probable magnitude of economic quantities or variables at some future moment of time." [21] This does not mean that there are no objective and ascertainable factors underlying any particular set of expectations, as all expectations have to rest upon something, but rather that the evaluation and interpretation of any set of "objective" facts is a subjective undertaking. It is often possible in economic analysis to identify the underlying and objective factors that may form the basis for any given set of expectations, but economists do not yet know a great deal about the process by which expectations are formed. Expectations are nebulous, too, because they are not easily measured. The attitudes that people hold with respect to future developments may be determined in a general way through surveys. But it is difficult, if not impossible, to place a quantitative tag on such attitudes, or to show in a precise way how attitudes affect action. In spite of these limitations, however, expectations must be dealt with in economic analysis because of their strategic influence on the investment decision.

Before we consider the means by which the businessman or entre-

[20] Keynes, *op. cit.*, p. 145.
[21] B. S. Keirstead, *An Essay in the Theory of Profits and Income Distribution* (Oxford, Basil Blackwell, 1953), p. 17.

preneur formulates expectations concerning future economic developments, two points should be clarified. The first pertains to the difference
between risk and uncertainty, both of which are involved in the notion
of expectations. Keirstead asserts that *uncertainty* is the relevant concept
with respect to expectations and the investment decision. *Risk,* he points
out, is the term used to define a calculable chance, the computation of
the probability distribution of future consequences of present acts.[22] Risk
is something that can be insured against. Since this is the case, risk is not
relevant to the investment decision. Uncertainty, on the other hand, involves future events that cannot be insured against. It is uncertainty,
more than anything else, that gives a subjective character to the investment decision.

The second point to be noted is that despite the subjective nature of
expectations, the business community as a whole tends to accept a given
set of expectations. Keirstead offers this explanation:

> Businessmen tend to be recruited from the same social groups, have similar
> education and experience, and live in a common intellectual environment.
> They tend to belong to the same clubs, read the same newspapers, journals,
> and private, so-called "intelligence" reports, and they listen to, and fre-
> quently deliver, the same speeches.[23]

In consequence, expectations become a causal factor of great significance in the economic process. For example, if businessmen expect a
downturn (or upturn) in economic activity, they will tend to behave
in such a manner as to bring about that which they expect. But a word
of caution is in order. We should not push this notion of the causal significance of expectations too far, or else we are led into accepting the
naive theory that by varying our frame of mind, we can literally talk
ourselves into or out of a recession or depression. This is simply not sub-
stantiated by historical experience.

SHORT-TERM AND LONG-TERM EXPECTATIONS

In the *General Theory* Keynes draws a distinction between short-term
and long-term expectations. Short-term expectations are concerned with
the price that a producer or manufacturer expects to obtain for a finished
output, such expectations being formed at the time the producer begins
the process that will produce the good.[24] Short-term expectations concern production plans made and carried out within the confines of *existing* plant and equipment. Long-term expectations, on the other hand,
have to do with what the entrepreneur hopes to earn through the acquisition of additional capital equipment. It is these expectations then,

[22] *Ibid.,* p. 18.
[23] *Ibid.,* p. 22.
[24] Keynes, *op. cit.,* p. 47.

that are most relevant to the problem of investment expenditure.

The short-term expectations of the entrepreneur, according to Keynes, are largely determined by the results of the most recent past; entrepreneurs presume that recently-realized prices, outputs, and employment levels will continue, unless there are very definite reasons for expecting a change. Short-term expectations, in other words, are formed by projecting recent experience a short distance into the future. Keynes stressed that such expectations continuously undergo gradual revision on the basis of realized results, with the consequence that "expected and realised results run into and overlap one another in their influence." [25]

Long-term expectations in the Keynesian view are based in part on "existing facts which we can assume to be known more or less for certain" and in part on "future events which can only be forecasted with more or less confidence." [26] Among the former Keynes listed such factors as the size of the existing stock of capital and the strength of the consumer demand for goods and services which require a large amount of capital in their production. The latter considerations include future changes in the type and quantity of the stock of capital assets, future changes in consumer tastes, and finally the strength of effective demand for the goods produced as a result of new investment in capital equipment. Knowledge of these things is not certain; in fact, Keynes asserts that long-term expectations are psychological expectations, formed partly by projecting the facts of the existing situation into the future. But the businessman has to make forecasts about what is likely to happen in the future. In this connection, Keynes believes that the key element is the degree of *confidence* that entrepreneurs have in their own forecasts. To the extent that entrepreneurs have confidence in their own forecasts, expectations will be stable; if the state of confidence is weak, this will make for instability in the state of expectations.

EXPECTATIONS IN A MARKET ECONOMY

The key point in this discussion of expectations is the fact that the marginal efficiency of capital is based upon highly uncertain knowledge of the future. Keynes states this idea as follows:

The outstanding fact is the extreme precariousness of the basis of knowledge upon which our estimates of prospective yield have to be made. Our knowledge of the factors which will govern the yield of an investment some years hence is usually very slight and often negligible. If we speak frankly, we have to admit that our basis of knowledge for estimating the yield ten years hence of a railway, a copper mine, a textile factory, the goodwill of a patent medicine, an Atlantic liner, a building in the City of London amounts to little and sometimes nothing; or even five years hence. In fact, those who

[25] *Ibid.*, p. 50.
[26] *Ibid.*, p. 147.

seriously attempt to make any such estimate are often so much in the minority that their behaviour does not govern the market.[27]

Thus the investment demand schedule should be interpreted as a highly unstable function, subject to sudden and unexpected shifts as the state of confidence and the long-term expectations of the business community undergo change. A situation like this is, perhaps, to be expected in a market economy, for in such an economy the level of investment expenditure is not determined by any centralized, decision-making authority, but rather is the cumulative outcome of thousands of independent decisions by individual entrepreneurs and businessmen, each seeking to interpret the trend or direction of future developments. This and the fact that any given set of expectations tends to be held in common by the business community largely account for the highly volatile character of the investment demand schedule.

THE EFFECT OF ECONOMIC STABILITY ON EXPECTATIONS

The view given above of the role of expectations in shaping the investment function has been held by most economists since Keynes. Hansen has said, for example, that "the volatile investment demand schedule may shift violently up and down, swayed by the waves of optimism and pessimism." [28] He recognizes, of course, that there may be important underlying factors, such as population growth and technical change, continuously at work that make for a steady volume of investment expenditures, although the expectations founded upon such factors remain subjective and highly sensitive. More recently, though, this view has been challenged. Dexter Keezer argues that there are a number of forces at work in the contemporary American economy that make not only for a high level of investment expenditure, but for much more stability in such expenditures than has been true in the past.[29] Keezer asserts that the major factors now leading to a high level of investment expenditures are a shortage of available labor relative to population, a formidable backlog of overage and antiquated facilities that need replacement, and finally increasing difficulty in obtaining key industrial raw materials (crude oil and iron ore, for example). Greater stability in investment spending results, he contends, from the growth in long-range investment planning by business firms and also the growth of more assured sources of funds to carry out a steadily increasing investment program. The latter resulted principally from the expansion in depreciation allowances as a source of investment financing, which in turn reflects the enormous investment in new plant and equipment carried out in the economy since the end of World War II.

[27] *Ibid.*, p. 149.
[28] Hansen, *op. cit.*, p. 141.
[29] Dexter M. Keezer, *New Forces in American Business* (New York, McGraw-Hill, 1959).

Long-term investment planning by private business firms has become feasible primarily because of the Employment Act of 1946 which implies that the national government will take whatever action is necessary to maintain reasonable conditions of stability and growth in the economy. Prior to the acceptance of such responsibility by the national government, investment expenditure was unquestionably the most unstable element in the entire structure of aggregate demand. Now, however, the implied promise of the national government to prevent the recurrence of a serious depression makes possible long-term investment planning, and eliminates an element of instability that has been a major cause in the past of severe downturns in economic activity.

The Role of Technology and Innovation

Among all the possible factors that enter into the investment process, probably a majority of economists would rate changing technology and innovation near the top in terms of influence and importance. This is true even though technology and innovation are concepts that cannot be defined with precision or clearly distinguished from one another. Moreover, there is much obscurity in economic analysis with respect to the *specific* manner in which the investment decision is affected by these forces.

The concept of innovation as a significant force in economic life is most closely associated with the work of the late Professor Joseph A. Schumpeter of Harvard University. As a result of his analysis, innovation has come to be connected with the idea of change and the introduction of new commodities and resource combinations into the economic process. In his classic work, *The Theory of Economic Development*, Schumpeter defined innovation in terms of a change falling into one or more of the following categories:

1. The introduction of a new good, or of a new quality of an existing good.
2. The introduction of a new method of production.
3. The opening of a new market.
4. The conquest of a new source of supply.
5. The establishment of a new organization of industry.[30]

It has been suggested elsewhere that there are two classes of innovations: those having to do with new goods and those having to do with new ways to produce old goods.[31] Within these broad classifications, changes in the first and third categories in Schumpeter's list would clearly fall into the class of new goods; changes in Schumpeter's second and fourth

---

[30] Joseph A. Schumpeter, *The Theory of Economic Development* (Cambridge, Mass., Harvard University Press, 1951), p. 66.

[31] Charles P. Kindleberger, *Economic Development* (New York, McGraw-Hill Second Edition, 1965), p. 140.

categories would belong to the class of new ways to produce old goods. A change in the fifth category could fall into either class.

Technology as a concept is generally construed as dealing more with the productive process than with the introduction of new goods or substantial changes in the quality and style of an existing good. The usual definition of *technological change* is a change involving a shift in the production function.[32] The production function, it will be recalled from Chapter 4, concerns the technical relationship between inputs of economic resources in the form of land, labor, and capital, and the output of product. Any particular combination of economic resources will embody a particular level of technology, and a change in technology means either more product from the same quantity and combination of resources, or else the same amount of product with a smaller quantity of resources. If a change in technology involves a shift in the production function, it follows that innovations which lead to a reduction in costs and new ways of producing old goods cannot, in practice, be distinguished from changes in technology. On the other hand, innovations that have to do with the introduction of new goods may not involve new or different production techniques, and thus need not necessarily be construed as a change in technology. In any event, the reader is reminded that any real distinction between innovation and technological change is a subtle thing. In reality it is difficult to imagine a change in techniques of production that will not, sooner or later, affect at least the equality of existing goods, and thus ultimately become innovational in character. In our discussion of the impact of these two phenomena on the investment decision, we shall try to keep them separate; but the student should keep in mind that this is an arbitrary procedure, done primarily for analytical purposes.

INNOVATION AND INVESTMENT

Introduction of a new product or development of a new market may or may not require new investment; there is no inherent reason why these kinds of innovation should require a drastic change in the physical quantity of any particular resource, such as capital. As Schumpeter points out, economic development results primarily from the employment of existing resources in a different way, or in doing new things with them rather than in increasing their quantity.[33] Thus, innovation may simply lead to a re-adjustment in existing capital equipment rather than an increase in the physical quantity utilized by the firm. If this happens, it is necessary to look to conditions affecting the demand for the product in question before we can say anything about the probable effect of the innovation on investment expenditure. One possibility, of course, is that

---

[32] Yale Brozen, "Determinants of the Direction of Technological Change," *The American Economic Review*, May, 1953.

[33] Schumpeter, *op. cit.*, p. 68.

the introduction of a new product will be followed by such a rapid rise in demand for the product that the original introducer of the product, as well as his imitators, will have to expand capacity. In this case more investment will be forthcoming. In general, we can say that the manner in which the introduction of a new product or development of a new market will affect investment demand, assuming there are no special technological reasons that necessitate new equipment in order to produce the new good, will depend largely upon the competitive character of the industry or market involved. Other things being equal, we might expect that the firm which introduces a new product in a highly competitive industry would gain a momentary advantage over its rival that could lead to more investment.

TECHNOLOGICAL CHANGE AND INVESTMENT

How does technological change affect the demand for capital instruments? The traditional view is that technological change is highly favorable to investment spending. Hansen, for example, has argued that capital goods are the physical embodiment of new production techniques, consequently, the latter cannot be introduced without at the same time creating more capital.[34] It has also been argued that the adoption of techniques that shift the production function requires that the ratio of capital to other resources be increased, and that technological change renders other and existing capital goods obsolete. Both of these tendencies, if present in the economy, would link the demand for capital very closely to the rate of technological change.

While many economists would agree that technological change is an important factor in the investment decision, there are reasons to doubt that the relationship between technological change and the investment decision is as simple and as direct as suggested by the traditional view. Howard R. Bowen, for example, questions the view that technological change will require more capital relative to other resources and that technologically-induced obsolescence will increase the demand for capital.[35] Does technological change raise the capital-output ratio? If it does, then clearly technological change will increase the demand for capital. But, as Bowen points out, many innovations of a technological character are capital-saving in the sense that they reduce the capital-output ratio. If technological change tends to be capital-saving rather than capital-using, its effects on the demand for capital may be reduced.[36] Bowen also

[34] Alvin H. Hansen, "Toward a Dynamic Theory of the Cycle," *The American Economic Review*, May, 1952.

[35] Howard R. Bowen, "Technological Change and Aggregate Demand," *The American Economic Review*, December, 1954.

[36] If the amount of capital required per unit of output is reduced, it does not necessarily follow that the demand for capital has been reduced. A reduction in the capital output ratio means that the productivity of capital has been increased, and

argues that a rapid rate of technological change may be inimical to a high level of investment expenditure because it increases the risk of obsolescence. If technological change makes existing capital obsolete, it may create a demand for new capital. But because obsolescence raises the element of risk in all investments, the entrepreneur may demand higher rates of return from prospective capital investments than otherwise would be the case. Thus, it is entirely possible that technological change can inhibit as well as spur investment expenditure.

Several studies cast doubt upon the assumption that technological change must necessarily be embodied in new capital instruments. These studies sought to determine the relative importance of different types of resource inputs—labor, capital, etc.—and of technological change in determining the nation's economic growth over the long run. In recent research, Benton F. Massell found that 90 per cent of the increase in output per man-hour between 1915 and 1955 in the United States can be attributed to technological change and only 10 per cent to an increase in the physical quantity of capital employed per man-hour.[37] Studies like Massell's should not be interpreted to mean that technology and technological change have no impact on investment expenditure, but rather that a distinction can be made between changes in technology and changes in the capital stock. They suggest that economists ought to pay more attention than heretofore to the factors that govern the rate at which new technological developments take place within the economic system.

The Role of Market Structures

The term *market structures* is used in reference to the kind and degree of competition characteristic of the industrial environment within which the firm functions. Traditionally, economists have argued that a competitive economic environment is highly conducive to both economic progress and a high rate of investment expenditure. This view rests upon the assumption that since business firms seek to maximize profits, a major way of achieving this objective is to reduce production costs. In an environment of rigorous competition firms will be forced, if they are to survive, to seize every opportunity for the introduction and exploitation of cost-reducing innovations. Since innovation may lead to investment

---

this may lead to an increase in the demand for capital. On this point see especially the article by Robert Eisner, "Technological Change and Aggregate Demand," *The American Economic Review*, March, 1956. See also John LaTourette, "Sources of Variations in The Capital-Output Ratio in The United States Private Business Sector, 1909–1959, *Kyklos*, Fasc. 4, 1965.

[37] Benton F. Massell, "Capital Formation and Technological Change in United States Manufacturing," *The Review of Economics and Statistics*, May, 1960. See also Robert M. Solow, "Technical Change and the Aggregate Production Function," *The Review of Economics and Statistics*, August, 1957; and Edmund S. Phelps, "Tangible Investment as an Instrument of Growth," In *The Goal of Economic Growth* (New York, Norton, 1962), pp. 94–105.

expenditure, it follows that a competitive market structure may be favorable to a high level of investment activity.

The classic reasons for the belief that monopoly is inimical to both investment expenditure and economic progress are summarized in an important article by Professor Evsey Domar.[38] When the business firm is confronted with a technological or innovation change that requires additional investment in capital equipment, it must reach a decision with respect to two different and possible developments. In the first place, investment in new equipment often leads to the scrapping of older equipment which has become obsolete; the firm must balance the gain from the introduction of new equipment against the capital losses involved in scrapping older equipment. It is Domar's contention that if the industry is competitive, the individual firm really has no choice. Inevitably, other firms in the industry would introduce the new equipment, and the individual firm would face capital losses because its equipment was outmoded. A monopoly, on the other hand, can avoid the capital losses involved in the acquisition of new equipment by introducing new production techniques at a more leisurely pace and financing the necessary investment out of depreciation reserves. The capital losses that result from the scrapping of obsolete equipment are a part of the price that a competitive economy must pay for both a rapid rate of technological change and a high rate of capital formation.

The second possibility confronting the firm concerns its market position. Domar argues that a technological or innovational development that leads to a reduction in costs or the introduction of a new product may present the firm with the opportunity to enlarge its share of the total market. This is most likely in oligopolistic industries. In the purely competitive type of industry, such as exemplified by agricultural production, no single firm can ever command more than a negligible portion of the total market. But in markets which are dominated by a relative handful of firms (the automobile industry is perhaps the classic example), the share of each particular firm in the over-all market is a subject of concentrated and continual interest on the part of management.[39] Under these circumstances, innovation and investment may be a particularly attractive means for enlarging the firm's share of the total market. Monopoly would not lead to this result, for the monopolist does not have to worry about his firm's relative position in the market.

Some economists maintain that with respect to certain conditions monopoly in an industry may be just as conductive as competitive oligopoly to innovation, technological change, and a high rate of investment expenditure. A Dutch economist points out, for example, that the ability

[38] Evsey D. Domar, "Investment, Losses, and Monopolies," in *Income, Employment, and Public Policy* (New York, Norton, 1948), pp. 33–53.
[39] Meyer and Kuh, *op. cit.*, p. 20.

of a firm to innovate and invest depends to a large degree on its entrepreneurial and managerial capacity and its financial power.[40] To the extent that this is true, the monopolistic firm will be in a better position than the typical small firm in a highly competitive industry which has neither the ability to attract the best entrepreneurial talent nor the financial power to undertake the investment that is often necessary for the introduction of new techniques. It is argued that only the financially powerful firm, characteristic of monopoly and oligopoly, can afford to underwrite the extensive, formalized research that is the necessary prelude to new developments in production and products in a world of rapid technological change.

We can best sum up this discussion of market structures and investment by pointing out that the traditional and classic view that an economy dominated by the competition of many small units is most conducive to economic progress is not particularly appropriate in a world in which research and technological change have become dominant factors in the competitive position of the firm. Competition remains necessary and desirable, but it is a different type of competition than that envisaged in the model of a "purely" competitive market economy. It is, rather, the competition of a relatively few large economic units with the ability and power to bring together the human talent and other resources necessary for performing the increasingly specialized functions of research and introduction of the fruits of research into the economic process.

The Role of Government

There has been an enormous expansion in the role and influence of the public sector in this century, a development which could not help but have far-reaching repercussions on the investment decision and the level of investment expenditure. Governmental units purchase an important part of the final output of goods and services in the economy and, as we have seen, demand for final output has a direct effect on investment outlays. To some extent public expenditures may introduce an element of stability into the investment process because such expenditures are often on a contractual basis.

The public sector may exert a less obvious influence on investment activity through transfer payments. Transfer expenditures and the taxes that finance such expenditures affect both the distribution of personal income in the economy and the pattern of consumption expenditures. Changes in the latter will affect the demand for final goods and services and thus, indirectly, the demand for investment goods.

Probably the most important influence that public activity has on in-

---

[40] P. Hennipman, "Monopoly: Impediment or Stimulus to Economic Progress?" in Edward H. Chamberlin, ed., *Monopoly and Competition and Their Regulation,* (London, Macmillan, 1954), p. 427.

vestment expenditure operates through taxes and the tax laws. The marginal efficiency of capital is concerned with the profitability of additional amounts of capital to the business enterprise, so it is to be expected that the businessman or entrepreneur would be acutely aware of the influence of anything as direct as taxation on the expected rate of return on capital assets. Investment expenditure depends upon the expected rate of return over cost, and it can thus be presumed that taxes, because they lower the expected returns, will lower investment expenditures. High taxes, to put it differently, impinge on incentives, and therefore adversely affect the investment decision. Unfortunately, it is difficult to show by appeal to empirical evidence the existence of any meaningful relationship between tax rates and investment incentives, because there is no objective way of measuring incentives to invest.

Any consideration of the impact of taxation on investment should take account of certain indirect effects. Although statistical data are scanty and inconclusive, it may be argued that high personal and corporation income taxes will reduce saving and thereby dry up important sources of finance for investment expenditure. On the other hand, a reduction in taxes that impinge directly on the marginal efficiency of capital —such as the corporation income tax—will not necessarily react favorably on investment outlays if the cuts in these taxes are offset by an increase in, say, excise taxes which may adversely affect consumption spending. Lower levels of consumption spending might, in turn, prompt lower levels of investment expenditure because of the derived character of the demand for investment goods.

Postwar studies at the Harvard Business School on the effects of Federal taxation on growing enterprises concluded that the relatively heavy tax burdens imposed on the American economy since World War II did not seriously impair or destroy either incentives or the willingness of individuals to work, save, or invest.[41] Three general observations emerge from these studies. First, non-tax considerations seemed to have much greater significance than tax considerations in the basic decisions of the business enterprise. With respect to incentives, tax considerations tended to determine *how* a thing was to be done rather than *whether* it was to be done. Second, the weight of the existing tax structure was much less severe than popularly believed because of the existence of numerous opportunities for business firms and individuals in the upper-income ranges to avoid the full impact of the ordinary income tax rates. One such opportunity was to treat the receipt of income as a capital gain rather than ordinary income. Third, it was found that the impact of the relatively high tax burden of the postwar years was not particularly adverse to in-

[41] J. Keith Butters, "Taxation, Incentives, and Financial Capacity," *The American Economic Review*, May, 1954.

vestment and other economic incentives because the tax burden was imposed on an expansionary economy.

The foregoing relatively optimistic view with respect to the lack of an adverse impact of postwar levels of taxation upon investment was not shared by the Council of Economic Advisors appointed to office by President Kennedy. In testimony before the Joint Economic Committee of the Congress, Walter Heller, Chairman of the Council, made it clear that the council believed investment spending was lagging because taxes on corporate income were too high.[42] The President's 1963 proposals for tax cuts, which were passed by the Congress in 1964 with minor modifications, sought to stimulate investment incentives by reducing the basic corporate rate from 52 per cent to 47 per cent.

The Role of Finance

In our examination of factors other than the rate of interest that enter into the investment decision it remains to inquire into the possible influences of various sources of funds that finance investment expenditure. Traditionally, economists have tended to assume, as we did in our analysis of the marginal efficiency of capital concept, that the financial cost to the firm of any given capital investment is measured by the current rate of interest for loans of a duration comparable to the expected life of the asset. For the individual firm this implies a perfectly elastic (horizontal) supply of funds schedule, the level of which is determined by prevailing rates of interest. For the economy as a whole, though, the supply of funds schedule would have a positive slope because even though it is possible for one firm to obtain more funds without forcing up the price —i.e., rate of interest—at which additional amounts of funds are obtained, it is not possible for *all* firms to do so.

This concept of the supply schedule of finance may have been adequate for classical analysis, in which it was presumed that saving was the major source of funds and that the rate of saving was positively correlated with the rate of interest. Recent studies, however, cast doubt on its validity. For one thing, a curve of this kind assumes that there exists some sort of homogenous source of funds which the business firm draws upon to finance its investment activity. A finding of empirical studies of the investment process, however, shows that firms are as much concerned with the *source* of funds as with their cost. Evidence exists to suggest that the source and availability of funds may exert as much or more influence on the investment decision as either the explicit or implicit monetary cost of obtaining funds.

For the business firm there are, typically, three major sources of funds. Two of these, depreciation reserves and retained earnings, are internal.

---

[42] *Hearings on the January 1963 Economic Report of the President* (Washington, D.C., U.S. Government Printing Office, 1963), pp. 3, 4.

The third is external, consisting of funds obtained either by borrowing or by the sale of new equities. Empirical studies show that business firms have very strong preferences for internal sources for financing investment expenditure. The preference for internal financing grows out of a desire to *avoid* one or more of the following:

1. The costs, delays, and inconveniences involved in getting outside money.
2. The necessity of revealing to bankers or the SEC some of the most carefully guarded operations of the business.
3. In the case of financing through the sale of stock, the dilution of control and per-share earnings.
4. In the case of financing through borrowing, the fixed commitments and possibility of banker-veto of future management proposals.[43]

The preference for internal financing, coupled with acute business awareness of presumed advantages and disadvantages of various sources of funds, has led to the suggestion of a supply schedule of funds for the firm which has the appearance of a series of steps.[44] Such a supply schedule is shown in Figure 7–8. Each section of the schedule has reference to a different source of funds; for each of the two internal sources of funds the schedule is deemed to be perfectly elastic up to the limit of the particular source. The first segment refers to the availability of depreciation allowances as a source of investment financing, and lies at a low level. Technically, this ought not to be below the current rate of return on government bonds, which represents the minimum opportunity cost of using such funds internally. Depreciation reserves are viewed as the least costly form of finance for the firm because of the assumption that managements take for granted the fact that in both good times and bad such funds will automatically be reinvested. The next segment of the curve pertains to funds retained by the firm after payment of taxes and dividends. Retained earnings are, of course, a major and important source of investment finance, but this segment of the curve lies at a higher level than the previous segment because the opportunity cost involved in the use of retained earnings is somewhat higher than that involved in the use of depreciation reserves. Since investment of retained earnings in new capital equipment is less automatic than reinvestment of depreciation reserves, there is a presumption that the prospective marginal efficiency of capital must be somewhat higher to induce the firm to retain and invest these earnings. Finally, the third segment of the schedule represents the recourse to outside funds, and here it is assumed that external funds, whether obtained through borrowing or by new equity issues, become more costly as the amount of funds obtained increases.

[43] Heller, *op. cit.*

[44] Edgar M. Hoover, "Some Institutional Factors in Business Investment Decisions," *The American Economic Review*, May, 1954.

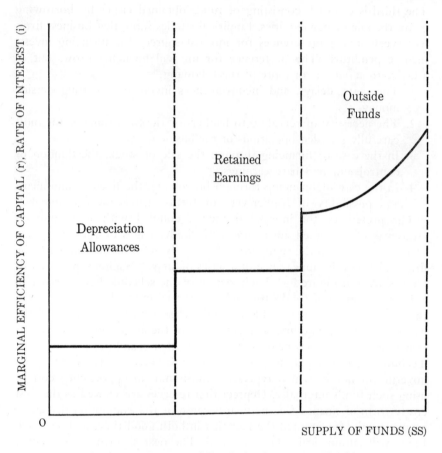

Figure 7–8. Sources of Funds for Investment Outlay

What are the implications for the investment decision of the kind of theory of the source of funds represented by the schedule in Figure 7–8? Aside from the fact already mentioned that firms as a rule prefer to finance investment from internal sources, the major implication of the theory is that the availability of funds from particular sources is a chief determinant of investment expenditure. In a way, this amounts to a transposition in the usual order of things, for it is tantamount to saying that if the funds are available, the firm will seek an outlet for them internally through investment expenditure. This implies that most firms have a backlog of desirable investment projects on the shelf, so to speak, that would be undertaken if the necessary finance could be obtained without going outside the firm. There is some empirical evidence to support this view.

The stress placed by firms on internal sources of finance has led to the formulation of the "residual-funds" theory of investment which holds that in the short run, at least, investment by the firm in both fixed and working capital—i.e., stocks or inventories—is a residual phenomenon, that is, it depends upon the total inflow of funds from current operations less established or conventional dividend payments.[45] The proponents of this theory also assert that in the longer run something like the acceleration principle comes into play because most entrepreneurs seek some sort of a fixed relationship between capital and output over time. Studies of this sort show that the role of finance in the investment process is considerably more complex than the traditional supply of funds schedule suggests, and that the availability of finance can become, under certain circumstances, a major determinant of investment expenditure in its own right.

A Summary View

We have sought in this chapter to examine and analyze the most important things that contemporary economic theory has to say about the determinants of investment expenditure. The investment decision remains one of the most involved problems relating to the operations of the modern economy, for the factors that enter into it are more varied and less predictable than, say, those that enter into the consumption-saving decision. In the area of consumption theory the economist has at least the solid fact of income upon which to build his analysis; no matter what other influences may be involved, it is impossible to ignore or overlook the dominant role that income plays as a determinant of consumption expenditure. In investment theory, however, there is no such prime determinant to provide a foundation for analysis. In the early days of Keynesian analysis, economists believed that the rate of interest could occupy the same role in investment theory that income occupies in consumption theory, but research into the mechanics of the investment decision has tended to undermine faith in this view. Modern investment theory remains cast in the framework of the investment demand schedule. But, at best, this approach is a device to organize our thinking, a means of getting started, not a complete theory that adequately explains the fluctuating phenomenon of investment. Many of the more important determinants are to be found in the area that we have labeled "other influences," and the major difficulty here is not that their existence and importance go unrecognized, but that they are essentially subjective in character. Most of the time these other determinants cannot be measured quantitatively, and there is no ready way to assess their relative impacts on the level of investment expenditure.

[45] Meyer and Kuh, *op. cit.*, p. 204.

APPENDIX

Algebraic determination of the income level with the inclusion of induced investment

$(1)\ Y_{np} = C + I_o' + I_i$ The basic identity

$(2)\ C = C_o + aY_d$ The consumption function

$(3)\ C = C_o + aY_{np}$ This is correct when taxes and transfers are zero

$(4)\ I_o' = (I_o - ci)$ Investment expenditure which is independent of the income level

$(5)\ I_i = bY_{np}$ Induced investment

$(6)\ Y_{np} = C_o + aY_{np} + I_o' + bY_n$ Substitution of Equations (3) and (5) into Equation (1)

$(7)\ Y_{np} - aY_{np} - bY_{np} = C_o + I_o'$

$(8)\ Y_{np}(1 - a - b) = C_o + I_o'$

$(9)\ Y_{np} = \dfrac{1}{1 - a - b}(C_o + I_o')$

$(10)\ Y_{np} = k'(C_o + I_o')$

8 | The Theory of the Public Sector: The Resource-Allocation Problem

In this chapter and the next we shall embark on an analysis of the relationship between governmental (or public) activity and the economy's performance. We shall consider, first, the nature of the public sector, with some comment on factors that account for the growing significance of the government's role in the economy; then we shall analyze the increasingly important problem of the proper allocation of economic resources between public and private use. Discussion of the impact of taxes and public expenditures on levels of income and employment is reserved for Chapter 9.

The Nature of the Public Sector

The term *the public sector* refers to the activities of government. Governments are the major element in the political structure of a society, and in a democratic nation may be thought of as the instruments which give the individual citizen a voice in decisions relating to collective activity.[1] These decisions often involve the diversion of economic resources to public use, and it is this aspect of the governmental process that is of particular interest to the economist.

Professor Richard A. Musgrave suggests that the complex activities and objectives of modern governments can be grouped into three headings which reflect the major economic functions of the modern state. These are:

[1] James M. Buchanan, *The Public Finances* (Homewood, Ill., Irwin, Revised Edition, 1965), p. 15.

227

1. *Satisfaction of social wants:* This requires the government to impose taxes and purchase goods and services from the private sector. In this way resources are allocated to the public sector, and social or collective goods to satisfy social wants are created.

2. *Redistribution of income:* This requires the government to use its power to alter the distribution of money income that results from the play of market forces. To do this the government adds to the income of some through transfers and reduces the income of others by taxation.

3. *Economic stabilization:* This requires the government to perform functions (1) and (2) in a manner calculated to maintain high levels of income and employment as well as stability in the value of money.[2] Many economists today would add to this maintaining an adequate rate of economic growth. The Council of Economic Advisors to the President has since 1961 made a satisfactory growth rate a major objective of public policy.

Taxes and expenditures are the major means by which the state carries out these functions. Taxes, of course, provide the state with control over economic resources, and expenditures are usually the chief means of providing for social wants. Income redistribution can—and is—affected by both taxation and expenditures. For an understanding of the economic role of the public sector, it is useful to make a distinction between government expenditures which are *exhaustive* (or resource-using) and those which are *non-exhaustive* (or transfers). Let us examine this distinction carefully.

Exhaustive Expenditures: The Satisfaction of Social Wants

The term *exhaustive expenditures* refers to goods and services purchased by governmental units. Such expenditures are "exhaustive" because they use up resources in the same manner as do private purchases of either consumption goods and services or investment goods. The goods and services purchased by the government sector constitute the *input* of resources necessary for the *output* of social goods and services.[3] Exhaustive expenditures measure the economic value of social goods since they are not normally sold on an individual basis via the mechanism of market processes.

It will be worthwhile at this point to restate that, generally speaking, social goods and services constitute that portion of the total output which, if left to market forces, would either not be produced at all or produced in insufficient quantity for the needs of society. The most important single characteristic of social goods and services is the *indivisibility* of

[2] Richard A. Musgrave, "Principles of Budget Determination," in *Federal Expenditure Policy for Economic Growth and Stability* (Washington D.C., Joint Economic Committee, 1957), p. 108.

[3] See Chapter 2, p. 42.

their benefits. In a technical sense indivisibility means that governmental output cannot be divided into units of which an individual can be given exclusive possession.[4] The benefits of social goods and services accrue to all individuals alike, irrespective of any particular individual's contribution to their cost of production.

Not all goods and services originating in the public sector are completely indivisible and thus not suitable for private production and sale on an individual basis.[5] We cited education as a case in point. Housing, medical care, recreation, transportation, and communications are other activities that are often provided for in part by the market system and in part by the public economy. In general, we find these activities treated to a degree as social goods or services whenever the public, acting through the normal political processes of a democratic society, judges that insufficient production and consumption of such goods and services will take place if their supply is determined by market considerations alone.

In addition to the key fact of indivisibility, there are other important characteristics of social goods and services that should be remembered. First, social goods are normally distributed without charge to all members of the community. Second, the production costs of social goods are normally covered by the process of taxation. In view of this, the distribution of the tax burden determines who ultimately pays their cost, and in what degree. Finally, the production of social goods and services means that resources must be allocated from private to public use. The significant question of what is a "proper" allocation of resources between public and private use is one to which we shall turn later.

Non-exhaustive Expenditures: The Redistribution of Income

Non-exhaustive expenditures, which we also call *transfers*, are mainly concerned with the redistributive function of government. Transfer expenditures (or payments) are "non-exhaustive" because they do not absorb resources; rather their chief effect is that of redistributing income between individuals, social and economic groups, or geographical regions. Transfer payments are distinguished, too, by the fact that the government receives no equivalent value in either goods or services from the recipient of the outlay.

Increasingly, the modern state has become an instrument for effecting changes in the distribution of income. Taxes and transfer payments are the major means for accomplishing this objective. Income redistribution results from the fact that individuals and groups do not always benefit directly from public expenditures and transfers in an amount equal to what they pay in taxes. It is practically impossible to impute benefits on

---

[4] Howard R. Bowen, *Toward Social Economy* (New York, Rinehart, 1948), p. 173.
[5] See Chapter 2, p. 42.

an individual basis for *all* government outlays, but we can usually identify the recipients of transfer payments. If the taxes employed to finance transfers can be also identified and their incidence determined, it becomes possible to show how the existence of a tax-financed system of transfer payments will alter a market-determined pattern of income distribution.

Transfer payments normally can be classified in one of three major categories. First, there are transfers of money income that go to persons. Most transfer expenditures in this category can be linked to welfare concepts and programs. These are the kind of transfers that have the most direct effect upon the distribution of money income in a society. Relief payments, unemployment compensation, old age retirement benefits, and aid to dependent children are examples.

Second, there are transfer payments in the form of subsidies to business firms or resource owners. These subsidies frequently are designed to bring about a greater production of a particular commodity than would be forthcoming if the regulation of production was left exclusively to market forces. Sometimes, too, such subsidies are designed to supply goods or services to particular groups at a cost below the market price; for example, low-cost school lunch programs financed by Federal grants to the states. Subsidies can also be used to aid entire sectors, as in the case of price supports for various agricultural commodities. Subsidies to business firms and resource owners may alter the distribution of income in much the same manner as transfer payments going to persons, although usually they are not so clearly rooted in equalitarian welfare concepts.

Finally, there are transfer expenditures in the form of interest on the public debt. Interest on the public debt is not regarded as a payment for the services of economic resources currently employed in productive activity. Logically, interest incurred from debt financing of public buildings, highways, or dams ought to be regarded as a payment for the services of economic resources, but this is not the current practice. *All* interest on government debt is regarded as a transfer payment.

Economic Stabilization and Growth

The third major function of government that we have listed is economic stabilization and growth. Exhaustive expenditures are the chief means through which government provides for the satisfaction of social wants, and transfer expenditures (and taxes) are the means by which the redistributional function is performed. The performance of the government as an effective force for stabilization and growth requires not only that it use exhaustive as well as non-exhaustive expenditures and taxes, but also that it utilize its powers to regulate the supply of money and credit. Policy measures that involve government expenditures and taxation as instruments for economic stabilization and growth belong to the realm of *fiscal policy*. Policy measures, on the other hand, that center on government control and regulation of the supply of money and credit as a means to these ends belong in the sphere of *monetary policy*. The effectiveness of both fiscal and monetary policy as instruments for stabilization and growth in the modern economy is a subject that we shall reserve for discussion in Chapter 12.

The Growth of the Public Sector

The public sector has become a vital concern of macroeconomic analysis ever since governmental activities expanded sufficiently to exert a decisive influence on both income and employment levels. The economic influence of government has intensified steadily throughout this century, becoming particularly pervasive during the last thirty years.[6]

What are the appropriate techniques for measuring the growth in economic importance of the public sector? First, expenditures are probably the best single measure because the performance of government's two basic functions, satisfying social wants and redistributing income, requires that governmental units undertake expenditures of both an exhaustive and transfer nature.

Second, in any discussion of the economic significance of public activity, it is not the absolute level of public expenditures that is important, but their level *relative* to the other major expenditure components (i.e., consumption or investment). Thus we should examine public expenditures as a per cent of an appropriate national income aggregate if we want to understand the changing economic significance of government activity.

Finally, we should not lump both government purchases of goods and services (exhaustive expenditures) and transfers (non-exhaustive expenditures) indiscriminately together in making such a comparison. These two expenditure categories reflect performance of distinctly different economic functions, and they should be compared to different national income aggregates. The economic significance of the public sector as a supplier of social goods can be determined by computing government expenditures for goods and services as a per cent of GNP. This will show what proportion of total output is being absorbed by public bodies and presumably being utilized for the satisfaction of social rather than private wants. The degree to which the government has become an instrument for the redistribution of income can be measured by computing transfer expenditures as a per cent of national income. Recall that national income is a measure of income earned by resource owners by supplying the services of economic resources to the productive process. If transfers are computed as a per cent of this total it will show the proportion of earned income that has been redistributed by action of the public sector.

[6] Buchanan, *op. cit.*, pp. 29–45.

With these criteria for measurement of the economic significance of the public sector in mind, let us examine three tables that reveal important changes that have taken place in the economic role of government since 1929. Table 8–1 contains data linking government expenditures in the form of the purchase of goods and services to GNP. Table 8–2 contains similar data on a per capita basis, and Table 8–3 contains data on transfer expenditures and the relationship of such expenditures to both the national income and the total of government expenditures.

The second column of Table 8–1 shows that exhaustive expenditures in constant prices increased more than fivefold since 1929. Compared with the threefold increase in real GNP, in the same period, this signifies a pronounced change in the share of the total output being absorbed by the public sector. The percentage data contained in the fifth column show this clearly; between 1929 and 1965 total government purchases as a per cent of the gross national product rose from 10.8 to 18.6. Thus, the relative importance of social goods in the output total nearly doubled in the past thirty-six years.

The breakdown of the data in the seventh and eighth columns between purchases of goods and services by the Federal government and similar purchases at the level of state and local governments shows clearly that the expansion in the relative importance of exhaustive expenditures by governmental units in the economy has been entirely at the Federal level. State and local expenditures for goods and services as a per cent of GNP have actually been below the 1929 level in most postwar years. State and local government outlays for goods and services as a per cent of the GNP did rise above the 1929 level during the depression years of 1930 through 1940. Federal government expenditures for goods and services have shown, on the other hand, a sharp rise in relative importance. In 1929 these expenditures in real terms amounted to only 1.7 per cent of GNP; in 1965 this figure had become 9.4, nearly a sixfold increase. The percentage went to considerably higher levels in the intervening years.

The per capita data of Table 8–2 also bear out the conclusion that the expansion in the economic role of the Federal government has been much greater over the last three decades than similar expansion at the level of state and local governments. For example, the data show that total government purchases of goods and services per capita rose from $180 (in constant prices) in 1929 to $589 in 1965, more than a threefold increase. State and local government expenditures per capita did not quite double in the same interval ($151 to $291), but Federal outlays per capita jumped drastically from $28 in 1929 to $298 in 1965, over a tenfold increase.

Although Tables 8–1 and 8–2 show that there has been a decided increase in the relative importance of the share of the output total (GNP) absorbed by the economy's public sector, these tables do not provide us with an entirely accurate picture of the government's changing economic role. The greatest share of increased expenditures by the Federal government has been caused by war and defense needs in the years following World War II. What, we might ask, would our analysis show with respect to changes in the economic position of the public sector if the influence of expenditures for national security purposes were eliminated from the data? In a recent study, Professor Francis M. Bator of the Massachusetts Institute of Technology attempted to answer this question.[7] His study shows that real exhaustive expenditures at all levels of government and for non-defense purposes only slightly more than doubled between 1929 and 1957. The over-all total of public outlays for non-defense purposes expanded at just about the same rate as real GNP less defense outlays. With defense and war-related expenditures eliminated from both GNP and exhaustive-expenditures totals, the change in the relative economic position of the public sector appears quite meager. In 1929, according to Bator's analysis, non-defense purchases of goods and services absorbed 7.5 per cent of the non-defense GNP; by 1957 this figure had risen to just 10.3 per cent. If we examine Bator's data on the role and relative position of the Federal government, the results are even more interesting. In 1929 non-defense purchases of goods and services by the Federal government amounted to only 0.6 per cent of the non-defense GNP; yet in 1957 the ratio of Federal non-defense purchases of goods and services to the non-defense gross national product had risen to only 1.3 per cent. Moreover, Bator's data show that at no time during the postwar years from 1945 to 1957 did this percentage exceed the 4.3 per cent figure recorded in 1939.[8] These data do not lend statistical support to the view that the era beginning in 1929 brought an enormous expansion in the economic role of the public sector *relative* to the private sector.

Data pertaining to transfer expenditures to persons by public bodies are shown in Tabe 8–3. As was true of the data on government expenditures of an exhaustive character, the data on transfers reflect an increase in the economic importance of public activity. For example, the first column shows that transfers to persons as a per cent of the national income rose from 1.1 per cent in 1929 to 6.6 per cent in 1965. The data of Table 8–3 show, moreover, that there has been a fairly persistent growth since 1929 in the proportion of national income subject to redistribution through the mechanism of transfer expenditures. The growing importance of the redistributional function of government is also demonstrated by the fact that transfer expenditures computed as a per cent of total government expenditures have exhibited the same rather steady growth since 1929. In 1929 transfers to persons accounted for 8.8 per cent

[7] Francis M. Bator, *The Question of Government Spending* (New York, Harper, 1960).

[8] *Ibid.*, p. 143. Since 1957 the ratio of non-defense Federal purchases of goods and services to non-defense GNP has risen to slightly more than 2 per cent.

Table 8-1. Government Purchases of Goods and Services, 1929–1960

| Year | Gross National Product | Total Government Purchases of Goods and Services | Federal Government Purchases of Goods and Services | State and Local Government Purchases of Goods and Services | Total Government Purchases of Goods and Services | Federal Government Purchases of Goods and Services | State and Local Government Purchases of Goods and Services |
| | | | (in billions of 1958 dollars) | | | (as a per cent of GNP) | |
(1)	(2)	(3)	(4)	(5)	(6)	(7)	(8)
1929	$203.6	$ 22.0	$ 3.5	$18.5	10.8%	1.7%	9.1%
1930	183.3	24.3	4.0	20.2	13.2	2.2	11.0
1931	169.2	25.4	4.3	21.1	15.0	2.5	12.5
1932	144.1	24.2	4.6	19.6	16.8	3.2	13.6
1933	144.5	23.3	6.0	17.3	16.5	4.2	12.2
1934	154.3	26.6	8.0	18.6	17.2	5.2	12.1
1935	169.6	27.0	7.9	19.2	15.9	4.7	11.3
1936	193.0	31.8	12.2	19.6	16.5	6.3	10.2
1937	203.3	30.8	11.5	19.4	15.2	5.7	9.5
1938	193.0	33.9	13.3	20.6	17.6	6.9	10.7
1939	209.4	35.2	12.5	22.7	16.9	6.0	10.8
1940	227.2	36.4	15.0	21.4	16.0	6.6	9.4
1941	263.7	56.3	36.2	20.1	21.4	13.7	7.6
1942	297.8	117.1	98.9	18.3	39.3	33.2	6.1
1943	337.2	164.4	147.8	16.6	48.8	43.8	4.9
1944	361.3	181.7	165.4	16.3	50.3	45.8	4.5

1945	355.4	156.4	139.7	16.7	44.0	39.3	4.7
1946	312.6	48.4	30.1	18.4	15.5	9.6	5.9
1947	309.9	39.9	19.1	20.8	12.9	6.2	6.7
1948	323.7	46.3	23.7	22.7	14.3	7.3	7.0
1949	324.1	53.3	27.6	25.7	16.4	8.5	7.9
1950	355.3	52.8	25.3	27.5	14.9	7.1	7.7
1951	383.4	75.4	47.4	27.9	19.6	12.4	7.3
1952	395.1	92.1	63.8	28.4	23.3	16.1	7.2
1953	412.8	99.8	70.0	29.7	24.2	17.0	7.2
1954	407.0	88.9	56.8	32.1	21.8	14.0	7.9
1955	438.0	85.2	50.7	34.4	19.5	11.6	7.9
1956	446.1	85.3	49.7	35.6	19.1	10.9	8.0
1957	452.5	89.3	51.7	37.6	19.7	11.4	8.3
1958	447.3	94.2	53.6	40.6	21.1	12.0	9.1
1959	475.4	94.7	52.5	42.2	19.9	11.0	8.9
1960	487.8	94.9	51.4	43.5	19.5	10.5	8.9
1961	497.3	100.5	54.6	45.9	20.2	11.0	9.2
1962	529.8	107.5	60.0	47.5	20.3	11.3	9.0
1963	551.0	109.6	59.5	50.1	19.9	10.8	9.1
1964	580.1	111.3	57.8	53.4	19.2	10.0	9.2
1965	614.4	114.1	57.8	56.3	18.6	9.4	9.2

SOURCES OF TABLE 8–1: U.S. Department of Commerce, *Survey of Current Business*, August, 1965, July 1966.

TABLE 8–2.

Per Capita Government Expenditures for Goods and Services, 1929–1960
(in 1958 dollars)

Year	Gross National Product Per Capital (GNP/P)	Total Government Purchases of Goods and Services Per Capita (G/P)	Federal Government Purchases of Goods and Services Per Capita (FG/P)	State and Local Government Purchase of Goods and Services Per Capita (SG/P)
1929	$1,672	$ 180	$ 28	$151
1930	1,489	197	32	164
1931	1,364	205	35	170
1932	1,154	144	37	157
1933	1,127	186	48	138
1934	1,221	210	63	147
1935	1,333	212	62	151
1936	1,507	248	95	153
1937	1,578	239	89	151
1938	1,487	261	102	159
1939	1,599	269	96	173
1940	1,715	275	113	162
1941	1,973	421	270	150
1942	2,212	870	735	136
1943	2,496	1,216	1,094	123
1944	2,698	1,357	1,235	122
1945	2,663	1,172	1,047	125
1946	2,222	344	214	131
1947	2,151	277	132	144
1948	2,206	348	162	155
1949	2,171	357	185	172
1950	2,340	348	167	181
1951	2,490	490	308	181
1952	2,526	589	408	182
1953	2,597	628	440	187
1954	2,514	549	351	198
1955	2,653	516	307	208
1956	2,654	507	296	212
1957	2,643	522	302	220
1958	2,568	541	308	233
1959	2,687	535	297	238
1960	2,710	527	286	242
1961	2,717	549	298	251
1962	2,850	578	323	256
1963	2,921	581	319	266
1964	3,031	582	302	279
1965	3,170	589	298	291

Note: P represents "total U.S. population."
SOURCES: U.S. Department of Commerce, *Survey of Current Business*, August, 1965,
July, 1966. *Statistical Abstract of the United States*, 1965. Totals have been rounded
to the nearest dollar.

TABLE 8–3.

Transfer Expenditures to Persons, 1929–1965
(in per cent)

Year	Total Transfers to Persons as a Per Cent of National Income (TR/NI)	Total Transfers to Persons as a Per Cent of Total Government Expenditures (TR/E)
1929	1.1%	8.8%
1930	1.3	9.0
1931	3.5	16.7
1932	3.5	13.5
1933	3.3	13.6
1934	3.1	12.1
1935	3.2	13.5
1936	4.5	18.2
1937	2.7	12.1
1938	3.6	14.3
1939	3.5	14.3
1940	3.3	14.6
1941	2.5	9.1
1942	1.9	4.1
1943	1.4	2.6
1944	1.7	3.0
1945	3.1	6.1
1946	6.0	23.9
1947	5.6	26.1
1948	4.7	21.9
1949	5.3	19.7
1950	5.9	23.5
1951	4.2	14.6
1952	4.1	12.8
1953	4.2	12.6
1954	4.9	15.5
1955	4.9	16.5
1956	4.9	16.4
1957	5.4	17.3
1958	6.6	18.9
1959	6.2	19.0
1960	6.4	19.5
1961	7.1	20.4
1962	6.8	19.5
1963	6.9	19.8
1964	6.6	19.5
1965	6.6	20.0

SOURCES: U.S. Department of Commerce, *Survey of Current Business*, August, 1965, July, 1966.

of total expenditures by public bodies, but by 1965 this proportion had climbed to 20 per cent.

Causes for the Growth in Public Expenditures

Our brief presentation of statistical data on government expenditures supports the contention that there has been a major increase over the past thirty years in the scope and economic significance of public activity. We have already seen that government expenditures for war and defense needs far outstrip government expenditures for nonmilitary affairs; they form the most important single factor in the growth of public expenditures during the last three decades. Federal spending for national defense has increased from less than $1 billion in 1929 to a total of $49.9 billion (in current prices) in 1965 and accounted for more than one-third of the total purchases of goods and services ($134.8 billion) by all governmental units in the economy in 1965.[9] In addition, a significant portion of government transfer expenditures are the result of war and defense activities. Bator suggests, for example, that about four-fifths of the interest charges on the public debt can be attributed to the financing of World War II. Also, he has estimated that as recently as 1957 cash payments to war veterans accounted for about one-fourth of all transfer payments made to individuals.[10]

A second major cause of the expanded role of the economy's public sector has been the emergence and increasing public acceptance of the concept of the welfare state. There is no precise and universally accepted definition of modern welfare state but, as the distinguished Swedish economist, Gunnar Myrdal, points out, the essence of this concept lies in the explicit commitments of most democratic governments in the Western world to the "broad goals of economic development, full employment, equality of opportunity for the young, social security, and protected minimum standards as regards not ony income, but nutrition, health, and education for people of all regions and all social groups." [11] The most immediate and striking consequence of the welfare-state concept is an expansion in the volume of transfer or non-exhaustive expenditures. The reason for this is clear because transfer expenditures (and taxes) are the chief means by which a government can provide not only for a minimum standard of material well-being for all its citizens, but for the greater degree of equality in the distribution of income that the welfare-state doctrine implies. In the United States transfer payments to individuals, the bulk of which are related to various welfare programs, have

[9] Joint Economic Committee, *Economic Indicators*, May, 1966.
[10] Bator, *op. cit.*, p. 143.
[11] Gunnar Myrdal, *Beyond the Welfare State* (New Haven, Yale University Press, 1960), p. 62.

grown steadily over the last three decades. In 1965, for example, transfer payments to individuals by the Federal government, not including interest on the Federal debt, amounted to $30.3 billion; state and local transfer payments to individuals added another $6.9 billion to this total.[12]

Although war, national defense, and the emergence of the modern welfare state are by far the most important sources of the growth in economic power and influence of the economy's public sector in the present century, they are not the only factors accounting for this trend. The continued expansion of the economy itself, is in part responsible for the enlargement of public activity relative to private activity. Economic growth over the long term has not only brought higher standards of material well-being for the population, but also an increasing number of complex problems that can generally be resolved only through some form of public action. Economic growth, for example, means industrialization which brings increases in the size, power, and complexity of the business enterprise. As the competition of many small units of a simpler era gives way to a more complex and less clearly competitive situation involving a few gigantic firms in the economy's major industries, the regulatory operations of the government must be stepped up. The growth in the size and complexity of the modern business firm and the increasingly important role of science and technology in industry demand higher levels of skill and training on the part of workers and employees. And this leads to a constantly growing demand for more and better educational facilities, most of which must be supplied by public action.

Economic growth has also spurred a trend toward urban living. As a larger proportion of the nation's population becomes concentrated in urban areas, the inevitable result is an increase in demand for a vast variety of services that must be provided through the public sector. Police and fire protection, streets, sewage systems, and recreational facilities must all be expanded in a spreading metropolis.

There is also considerable evidence to suggest that economic growth is accompanied by a demand for better standards of performance in the public sector. As real incomes rise in our society, the demand increases not only for better quality in privately-produced goods and services, but for better quality in social goods as well. As a consequence, virtually every government function has been expanded since 1900.[13]

Statistical and other empirical evidence on the growth in both absolute and relative importance of the public sector—as reflected in its expenditures—has lead some students of fiscal economics to search for a general principle or economic "law" to explain this development. Perhaps the most celebrated of such attempts is Wagner's Law of the Increase in

[12] U.S. Department of Commerce, *Survey of Current Business*, July, 1966.
[13] Solomon Fabricant, *The Trend of Government Activity in the United States since 1900* (New York, National Bureau of Economic Research, 1952), pp. 82, 83, 123.

State Activities. Adolph Wagner was a German fiscal theorist of the nineteenth century and one of the first economists to state explicitly that economic progress would bring a *relative* increase in the economic importance of government activity. More specifically Wagner's Law states:

Comprehensive comparison of different countries and different times shows that, among progressive people, with which we alone are concerned, an increase regularly takes place in the activity of both the central and local governments. This increase is both extensive and intensive; the central and local governments constantly undertake new functions, while they perform both old and new functions more efficiently and completely. In this way the economic needs of the people, to an increasing extent and in a more satisfactory fashion, are satisfied by the central and local governments. The clear proof of this is found in the statistics which show the increased needs of central and local political units.[14]

Not all modern economists and fiscal theorists would accept the apparent implication of Wagner's Law that there is an inevitable tendency at work in the economy toward the enlargement of the economic role of the public sector. Wagner's principle has been criticized, for example, on the grounds that the proportion of the nation's economic resources devoted to public rather than private uses depends, in a democratic society at least, upon the concepts people hold as to the proper functions of government.[15] One economist has gone so far as to suggest that there is an absolute upper limit to the relative expansion of the public sector. Colin Clark argues that a level of taxation in excess of 25 per cent of the national income must result in inflation of a particularly disastrous sort, and it is this "fact" which serves sooner or later to put the brake on an expansion of public activity.[16]

More recently, two British economists, Alan T. Peacock and Jack Wiseman, have suggested a new and alternative hypothesis to explain the growth in public expenditures.[17] They contend that public outlays fail to return to earlier levels following a war or other major economic disturbance because of what they describe as a *displacement effect*. In "normal" times—which presumably are marked by the absence of war, revolution, or serious depression—the public soon regards the prevailing level of government expenditures and taxes as normal. As long as no extraordinary political or economic upheaval occurs, there will be strong resistance to expansion in the scale of public activity, rooted in the belief that the prevailing level of expenditures and taxes also represents the tolerable upper limit with respect to the size of the public sector. But

[14] Adolph Wagner, as quoted in Charles J. Bullock, ed., *Selected Readings in Public Finance*, second ed. (New York, Ginn, 1920), p. 32.

[15] Buchanan, *op. cit.*, p. 50.

[16] Colin Clark, "Public Finance and Changes in the Value of Money," *The Economic Journal*, December, 1945, p. 376.

[17] Buchanan, *op. cit.*, p. 53.

during a war or serious depression, the public discovers that much higher levels of both taxes and expenditures are possible without disastrous results. This has the effect of displacing upward the public view of what constitutes a normal or safe level of governmental activity. Consequently, the scale of activity in the public sector is not likely to return to prior levels following the end of an emergency.

The displacement thesis and Wagner's Law attempt to explain in a general way why there has been such a pronounced growth in the scale and economic influence of the public sector, but they fall short as economic principles because they do not provide a firm basis for prediction of the probable scope of public activity in the future.

The Allocation of Resources to the Public Sector

The hypotheses of economists like Wagner who have sought a general explanation for the growth of public expenditures do not provide us with an answer to the increasingly important problem of determining the "rightful" share of the public sector in national output and expeditures totals. How does an economy secure an *optimum* allocation of economic resources between the public and private sectors? This is the question to which we shall now direct our attention.

The Concept of Optimum Allocation

Optimum allocation of economic resources is a problem with which economic theory has been long concerned, for the central problem in price economics, or value theory, is to determine how a society allocates its economic resources (land, labor, and capital) among alternative uses through the mechanism of markets. Out of this type of economic analysis has developed the concept of an optimum allocation of economic resources among alternative uses.

To begin, let us consider what is meant by the idea of an optimum with respect to resource allocation. For one thing, the word optimum implies that resources are being utilized with maximum efficiency. But what is the meaning of efficiency in resource use? If we go back to the assumption that underlies most economic analysis, namely that the objective of productive activity is the satisfaction of human wants, it follows that the greatest efficiency in the use of economic resources prevails when consumer satisfaction is maximized. More specifically, economic efficiency prevails when the allocation of economic resources among alternative uses is such that no increases in consumer satisfaction could be obtained by further shift in resources from one use to another—that is, by a reallocation of resources.

How do we determine when such a condition exists? An optimum allocation of economic resources will exist when the marginal unit of any resource yields the same economic value in all possible uses for this resource.[18] This means, in other words, that the satisfaction consumers obtain from the goods and services produced by the marginal unit of the resource is the same in all the alternative uses to which the resource can be put. Since there is no objective measure of consumer satisfaction other than the prices that consumers are willing to pay for the goods and services they acquire, an optimum allocation of economic resources exists when the economic value (which depends upon price) of the marginal product of a resource is the same in all possible uses, that is, when no increase in value can be obtained by a shift in resource use.

On the assumption of a constant technology, an optimum allocation of resources will result if the economy is characterized by pure competition in both product and factor markets. As we have observed, pure competition is a market situation in which each firm is so small in relation to the total market that the individual firm cannot influence the price of either the commodities it sells or the resources it buys. In addition, the product is presumed to be homogeneous so that buyers are indifferent as to their source of supply, and there are no restrictions on the entry either of firms or resources into any industry or on their movement out of any industry. This implies a perfect mobility of resources.

The theory of a purely competitive economy holds that in the long run the force of competition will push output in all industries to the point at which prices for all the goods and services produced are equal to average costs of production. This is the nature of the long-run equilibrium position of the firm and the industry under conditions of pure competition. In equilibrium the firm also has adjusted output to the point at which marginal cost and marginal revenue are equalized. Since marginal revenue is the same as price in a purely competitive industry, this means that price and marginal costs are equal. If this is true for all firms and all industries, then the value of the marginal contribution of an economic resource is the same for all industries in which the resource is being used. The equilibrium condition in which average cost, marginal cost, and marginal revenue are equal in all industries means that no alternative uses exist in which any resource would yield a greater amount of economic value (or satisfaction). If this condition is realized, then there must be an optimum allocation of economic resources among alternative uses.

The foregoing analysis pertains primarily to the theory of an optimum resource allocation in a market economy, an economy, involving the interplay of free and individual choices by both consumers and producers. Our principal interest, though, is in the more specific problem of determining whether the contributions of traditional value theory to the concept of an optimum allocation of economic resources can serve as a

---

[18] Abba P. Lerner, *The Economics of Control* (New York, Macmillan, 1949), p. 61.

guidepost for attaining an optimum allocation of resources between the private and public sectors of the economy.

In a general sense, application of the marginal concept to the public sector requires that government expand the production of social goods up to the point at which the *marginal social benefit* for all social goods is just equal to their *marginal social costs*. Such a condition would mean not only that the final or marginal dollar of expenditure on all social goods would yield the same satisfaction, but also that the marginal dollar of expenditure on social goods yields the same satisfaction as the marginal dollar of expenditure for privately-produced goods.

Marginal social benefit may be defined as the benefit that society derives from the production of an additional unit of output of a good or service; marginal social cost may be defined as the sacrifice to society that results from having the marginal unit of a resource used to produce the good in question rather than an alternative good. It is the alternative marginal social benefit that would have resulted if the resource had been used elsewhere.[19] Since marginal social benefit and marginal social cost are concepts that apply to the production of private as well as social goods, an optimum allocation of economic resources between public and private use must exist when marginal social benefit and marginal social cost are equal for *all* kinds of output, including the output of the public sector. In sum, the output of both social and private goods should be extended to the point at which the marginal unit of the resources employed in the production of both types of goods results in the same amount of economic value (or satisfaction).

Mechanisms for the Allocation of Resources

Up to this point, our discussion of the optimum allocation of resources has been based on theoretical concepts, not on the actual processes at work. We now must relate our analysis to the mechanisms that exist in the economy for the allocation of resources among alternative uses, and determine whether these mechanisms operate in such a way as to bring about an optimum allocation of resources.

In the private sector of the economy the problem of resource allocation is largely "solved" through the mechanism of the market. In a social sense, the market is a device for the organization of economic activity, and it functions by transmitting consumer preferences, as revealed through the expenditure of income, to producers, who, in the process of adjusting output to correspond with these preferences, direct economic resources into various and alternative uses. The result of this interplay between consumer preferences and the response of producers is a vast and complex structure of prices and costs. This structure reflects the relative values that consumers place on the goods and services that the

[19] *Ibid.,* p. 75.

economy is capable of producing, and, in so doing, indicates how resources ought to be allocated. As a mechanism for the allocation of economic resources, the market operates on the basis of individual choice,
and the culmination of the whole process is the act of exchange whereby
the consumer pays directly and individually for any good or service he
wishes to acquire. The presumption is that the price he is willing to pay
in the market for a good or a service reflects the value or benefit he
expects to derive from its use. This is the essence of the *theory* of the
competitive market as a mechanism for resource allocation. In reality,
few market situations approach the ideal of the purely competitive solution to the allocation of resources among alternative uses. Nevertheless,
the market does exist and does function, although imperfectly, as the
primary mechanism through which resources are allocated in the private
sector of the economy.

The market is not, however, the primary mechanism by which resources are allocated between private and public use in the economy.
The collective and indivisible character of most social goods makes it
manifestly impossible to utilize a mechanism which is firmly rooted in
the act of individual exchange. Social goods are indivisible for the most
part, and thus their production and disposition on a voluntary and individual basis is not feasible. As a consequence, economic resources in our
society are allocated to public use by means of a *political* process rather
than through the mechanism of the market. Governments ordinarily
acquire the necessary resources for the output of social goods through
taxation, which involves coercion, rather than through voluntary payments by individuals and business firms. In a democratic society citizens
determine collectively (through voting and legislative representatives) the
amount of their incomes that they will surrender in the form of taxes,
but this does not alter the fact that tax payments to cover the production
costs of social goods are compulsory.

How effective are the mechanisms we have described as instruments
for attaining an optimum allocation of economic resources? We shall not
weigh the effectiveness of the market mechanism other than to note in
passing that contemporary economic theory implies that something less
than an optimum resource allocation will prevail if actual market conditions depart significantly from the purely competitive model. Our
main concern is with the effectiveness of the political process as an instrument for achieving a "proper" or optimum allocation of economic
resources between private and public use.

One approach to this problem is to assert that the political process by
which resources are allocated between public and private use is fundamentally no different from the market process through which resources
are allocated among alternative uses in the economy's private sector. This
point of view has been called "the voluntary-exchange theory of public

economy."[20] In essence, the voluntary-exchange theory argues that the revenues and expenditures of the public sector are phenomena of value and price and thus governed by the same economic principles that determine price in the market sector of the economy. Taxes are therefore seen as voluntary payments made to the state by the individual in exchange for the services provided by the state. Taxes, moreover, reflect the individual's estimate of the value he receives from these services. If this were true, it would follow logically that the marginal social benefits would equal marginal social costs for all social goods and services, and consequently an optimum allocation of resources between private and public use would exist.

Unfortunately, though, this thesis will not withstand critical examination. The voluntary-exchange theory is faulty, in the first place, because it assumes that the individual can compare the satisfaction derived from the consumption of an *indivisible* social good "purchased" through his taxes with the satisfaction he gets from his purchase and consumption of privately-produced goods and services on an individual basis. This assumption has doubtful validity. The act of exchange in the market sector presumably involves an equivalence between price and benefit, but in the public sector such equivalence is clearly impossible because the benefits derived from the consumption of social goods cannot be parceled out on an individual basis that is in any sense measurable.

The voluntary-exchange theory also breaks down because of its underlying assumption that taxes are really voluntary payments made in exchange for social goods. As we have already stated, taxes always involve compulsion; the individual must contribute to the support of government in accordance with some legally-defined set of rules, irrespective of his willingness or unwillingness to share in the cost of social goods. Professor Musgrave attributes this in part to the special nature of social wants and social goods.[21] All individuals must consume *in equal amount* the social goods and services that are the means for the satisfaction of social wants. Conversely, no one can be excluded from the consumption and enjoyment of these social goods and services. This being the case, Musgrave argues, individuals are not compelled to reveal their true preferences with respect to the value they place on social goods and services, and therefore cannot be expected to pay for such goods and services on a voluntary basis.

In rejecting the idea that the political process is simply the market process in a different guise, we also reject the implication that the political process in a democratic society will bring about an optimum allo-

[20] Richard A. Musgrave, "The Voluntary Exchange Theory of Public Economy," *Quarterly Journal of Economics*, February, 1939, pp. 213–237.
[21] Richard A. Musgrave, "Principles of Budget Determination," in *Federal Expenditure Policy for Economic Growth and Stability, op. cit.*, p. 109.

cation of resources between public and private use in the same manner that the market process may, under certain conditions, lead to optimum resource allocation in the private sector. The allocation of economic resources through a political process is not only fundamentally different from allocation by market forces; it may in some instances produce far less than optimum results, as we shall see.

Although we have found the voluntary-exchange concept of the public economy wanting, we need not abandon the general principle that an optimum allocation of resources requires an equality between marginal social cost and marginal social benefit. On the contrary, it is a good and sound principle; the real difficulty in applying it stems from the fact that both marginal social benefit and marginal social cost are subjective concepts that defy any precise measurement. Money costs and prices in the market sector result from the interplay between consumer choices and the response of producers. There is at least a presumption that the over-all structure of prices and costs bears some relationship to the relative values that consumers put on alternative uses of economic resources. In the public sector, however, we do not get the kind of relatively precise reflection through price of the preferences of consumers that, presumably, the price system provides in the private sector; consequently, there are no objective data comparable to price which might be said to even approximate marginal social benefit and marginal social cost in the public sector.

It might be argued in rebuttal that the amount of public expenditures of an exhaustive character provides an objective measure of both marginal social benefit and marginal social cost because the total of such expenditure must reflect the valuation citizens place upon social goods in comparison with private goods. But this is nothing more than an assertion that the political process in a democratic society will always work to bring about an optimum allocation of resources between public and private use. The contention that administrative and legislative bodies in a democratic society achieve a kind of rough or approximate balance between marginal social costs and marginal social benefits need not rest upon any elaborate theoretical foundation; rather, it rests upon the assumption that the citizens of a democratic state are basically rational in their behavior. The division of resources between the public and private sectors therefore reflects a considered weighing on the part of these citizens of the relative benefits of both private and social goods. This point of view, however, has been subject to challenge, and it is to these challenges that we shall now turn.

The Concept of Social Imbalance

Critics of the point of view that the political process cannot be depended upon to bring about an optimum allocation of resources between public and private use assert that modern democratic political processes may lead to an actual misallocation of resources in the sense that too large a share of the national output is used for private purposes and too small a share for public purposes.

Probably the best-known proponent of the thesis that our society is characterized by a misallocation of resources between public and private use is Professor John Kenneth Galbraith. In his book *The Affluent Society*, Galbraith develops a "theory of social balance," which asserts that there exists a tendency in our society for the output of social goods and services to lag seriously behind the output of privately produced goods and services.[22] In any advanced society a fundamental relationship exists between the production of private goods and services and the provision of additional goods or services by the state. Increased production and sale of private automobiles, for example, requires that the public sector provide, sooner or later, more roads and other facilities for the motorist. Galbraith uses the term *social balance* to describe the existence of a satisfactory relationship between the supply of privately-produced goods and services and the supply of social goods.[23] If a society fails to achieve a satisfactory relationship of this kind, it will suffer from social imbalance —a misallocation of resources between public and private use.

Although Galbraith would no doubt deny the existence of any scientifically objective criteria for attainment of social balance, he argues that the question of a disparity between the flow of private and social goods is not simply a matter of subjective judgment. Serious consequences will ensue for the society that allows this disparity to become too great. In a vivid passage, Galbraith describes some of these consequences:

In the years following World War II, the papers of any major city . . . told daily of the shortages and shortcomings in the elementary municipal and metropolitan services. The schools were old and overcrowded. The police force was understrength and underpaid. The parks and playgrounds were insufficient. Streets and empty lots were filthy, and the sanitation staff was underequipped and in need of men. Access to the city by those who work there was uncertain and painful and becoming more so. Internal transportation was overcrowded, unhealthful, and dirty. So was the air. Parking on the streets had to be prohibited, and there was no space elsewhere. These deficiences were not in new and novel services, but in old established ones. Cities have long swept their streets, helped move their people around, educated them, kept order, and provided horse rails for vehicles which sought to pause. That their residents should have a nontoxic supply of air suggests no revolutionary dalliance with socialism.[24]

[22] John Kenneth Galbraith, *The Affluent Society* (Boston, Houghton Mifflin, 1958), pp. 251–269.

[23] *Ibid.*, p. 255.

[24] *Ibid.*, p. 252. See also the recent interview with Professor Galbraith in *Challenge*, January–February, 1967, pp. 18–21.

Social imbalance, according to Galbraith, involves not only the failure to provide the necessary complementary output of social goods when private output increases, but also the loss of opportunities for a society to maximize its satisfactions. Maximum satisfaction is just as dependent upon an adequate supply of schools and other public services as it is on an abundance of privately-produced goods.

Galbraith bolsters his case for social imbalance in the economy by pointing to three powerful forces which are in the main responsible for the inherent tendency for the output of social goods to lag behind the output of private goods. First, there is the force of advertising. In our economy the vast array of powerful techniques for influencing consumer behavior are placed almost entirely at the disposal of private rather than public purposes. It is simply not possible for the individual citizen to make a calm and rational evaluation of the relative merits of private and social wants. Second, there is the matter of cost. Typically, social goods are evaluated in terms of what it costs to supply them as measured by taxes rather than in terms of the benefits or satisfactions they might yield the community. Since there is often bitter failure to come to agreement over taxes, the output of some social goods and services is often either prevented or curtailed at an inadequate level. Finally, Galbraith sees persistent inflation as a major factor accounting for the phenomenon of social imbalance, because the wages and salaries of public employees rise less rapidly during inflationary periods than wages, salaries, and other forms of income that originate in the private sector. Many of the better civil servants then find private employment more attractive, and the result is a further deterioration in the quality, if not the quantity, of public services.

A view on social imbalance similar to Galbraith's has been advanced by a political scientist, Professor Anthony Downs. Like Galbraith, he holds there is a strong tendency in a democratic society for a lag to develop in the output of public or social goods relative to private goods. More specifically, Downs asserts that this misallocation is a consequence of a chronic state of ignorance on the part of the electorate with respect to both the costs and benefits of many existing and potential government policies.[25] Downs finds this ignorance to result primarily from the fact that the costs and benefits of social goods are not linked directly and individually as are the costs and benefits of private goods. The electorate tends to underestimate the benefits of government action for two reasons. First, many of the benefits of public action are extremely remote from the electorate, although their costs are real and immediate. Economic aid to foreign nations is an example. Many government expenditures which are preventive in nature produce benefits that are not always fully

[25] Anthony Downs, "Why the Government Budget is Too Small in a Democracy," *World Politics*, July, 1960, pp. 541–563.

comprehended by the electorate. Second, the benefits from many public activities are often highly uncertain. This is particularly true, Downs finds, in such areas as international relations and national defense. There are so many unknowns involved in these areas that the benefits stemming from any particular governmental policy are hard to pin down.

Somewhat offsetting the low estimates of social benefits is a similar tendency for voters to underestimate the costs of social goods as compared to private goods, If, for example, government expenditures that benefit particular groups are largely financed by taxes whose incidence is obscure, as often is true of sales or excise taxes, there will be a tendency to underestimate the actual cost of such benefits. Since expenditures that benefit particular groups rather than the whole society often represent legislative efforts to placate special-interest groups, the over-all cost of governmental programs is likely to go up more than the individual tax-payer anticipated. This is especially true when the tax structure does not reveal the true cost of these "log-rolling" programs. Generally, Downs argues, the forces that lead the electorate to underestimate the benefits of public activity are stronger than those leading it to under-estimate their costs. The consequence is social imbalance, misallocation of economic resources between public and private use.[26]

A Concluding View

The problem of social balance is not easily resolved; yet it is a problem that will assume increasing importance in the decades ahead. As a society gets more and more affluent, to use Galbraith's descriptive term, the range and complexity of both its private and social wants grow accordingly. A rich and productive society can quite easily eliminate most forms of poverty and assure satisfaction of basic or minimal human needs, but it is still faced with the difficult and complex problem of deciding to what other ends it should utilize its productive resources.

In most Western nations the market remains the major instrument for the allocation of resources among alternative uses in the private sector. Economists have developed some important theoretical concepts relating to the conditions under which optimum—or maximum—efficiency in resource use could be obtained. But we should be careful not to confuse the reality of the market economy with the necessary conditions for such an optimum as demonstrated by the economic theorist. The latter requires, as we have seen, a market situation characterized by pure competition, but in the real world this is a condition which is rarely, if ever, realized. Reality in the market and in the price mechanism is that of oligopoly, monopolistic competition, and sometimes monopoly, all of which repre-

[26] See also Campbell R. McConnell, "Social Imbalance. Where Do We Stand," *The Quarterly Review of Economics and Business,* May, 1961, p. 7–23.

sent market forms in which sellers and producers exercise economic influence and power. It is extremely unlikely, given the character of most markets in the actual economy, that this mechanism will yield a "solution" to the resource-allocation problem in the optimum or ideal sense postulated by economic theory.

We have seen that the allocation of resources between public and private use, in practically all societies is accomplished by a political rather than a market process. Although economic analysis and its concepts of marginal social benefit and marginal social cost provide us with some broad guidelines to the proper allocation of resources in this sphere, we have found no real assurance that the political process, even in a democratic society, will actually function so as to achieve an optimum with respect to the division of resources between public and private use. Critics like Galbraith argue persuasively that existing political processes are most unlikely to achieve such an optimum.

Economic theory, given its current state of development, can provide us with nothing more than very broad and general principles to serve as guidelines in dealing with the problem of attaining maximum efficiency in resource use. The notions of marginal benefit and marginal cost that the economist uses as analytical tools cannot be reduced to objective or measurable content. Thus it becomes impossible to determine with a kind of detached scientific objectivity whether the market process in the private sector and the political process in the public sector function "efficiently" as mechanisms for attainment of an optimum allocation of resources. This is not to say, of course, that the economist should not concern himself with this problem, for resource allocation is a matter of overriding importance to all economics. It is to stress, though, that, on the one hand, this is an area where economic analysis and theory cannot very readily separate itself from the values or goals of a society; and, on the other, it is an area in which economic theory and analysis offers us only a very rough sort of guide to action and policy.

9 The Theory of The Public Sector: The Income-Level Problem

In this chapter we return to the analysis of the determinants of the income and employment level. Since our objective is to understand the impact of government expenditures and taxation on these aggregates, we shall approach this problem through the structure of the economy's aggregate demand function. Government purchases of goods and services exert a direct influence on the level of the aggregate demand schedule because they represent a direct demand for a part of the final output; government transfer expenditures and taxes exert an indirect influence as their impact is on the non-governmental components of the schedule, consumption and investment.

Government Purchases of Goods and Services and the Income Level

To show how the purchase of goods and services by governmental units enter into the structure of aggregate demand, we shall make use again of data pertaining to a hypothetical economy, as was done in Chapter 6.[1] These data for our hypothetical economy are shown in Table 9–1. Our economy is still "closed," which is to say it has no economic ties with any other nation, but now we have assumed that there are three rather than merely two categories of output (or expenditure): consumption, C, investment, I, and government, G. The consumption function is given in Column (2) and shows the intended consumption expenditures at income levels ranging from 0 to $800 billion. The mar-

[1] Chapter 6, pp. 143.

ginal propensity to consume of this schedule is 0.5 or $\frac{1}{2}$. Investment expenditure, shown in Column (3), includes both autonomous and induced investment outlays. The marginal propensity to invest is 0.1 or $\frac{1}{10}$. Government purchases of goods and services are shown in Column (4). For the sake of analytical simplicity we assume that government expenditures are autonomous with respect to the income level. Although

TABLE 9–1.

A Closed Economy with Three Categories of Output
(in billions of dollars)

(1)	(2)	(3)	(4)	(5)
Net National Product Y_{np}	Consumption C	Investment I	Government Expenditures G	Aggregate Demand $(C+I+G)$
0	100	40	60	200
350	275	75	60	410
400	300	80	60	440
450	325	85	60	470
500	**350**	**90**	**60**	**500**
550	375	95	60	530
600	400	100	60	560
650	425	105	60	590
700	450	110	60	620
750	475	115	60	650
800	500	120	60	680

it is likely that government expenditures increase as income increases, the exact nature of any such relationship is not clearly known.

Once we have assumed values for the investment function and autonomous government expenditures, the aggregate demand schedule is obtained by adding these to the consumption function, the position and slope of which is given by the parameters C_o, consumption at zero income, and a, the marginal propensity to consume. The parameters for the investment function are I_o', investment expenditure which is autonomous with respect to the income level, and b, the marginal propensity to invest.[2] The results of this addition are given in Column (5), which now shows the aggregate demand schedule, $C+I+G$.

We have done this graphically in Figure 9–1. The aggregate demand schedule, $C+I+G$ or (DD), is derived by adding to the consumption function the appropriate values for investment and government expenditures. The process of income determination that results from the construction of an aggregate demand schedule which includes government expenditures is identical to the process discussed in earlier chapters.

[2] Chapter 6, p. 137, and Chapter 7, p. 199.

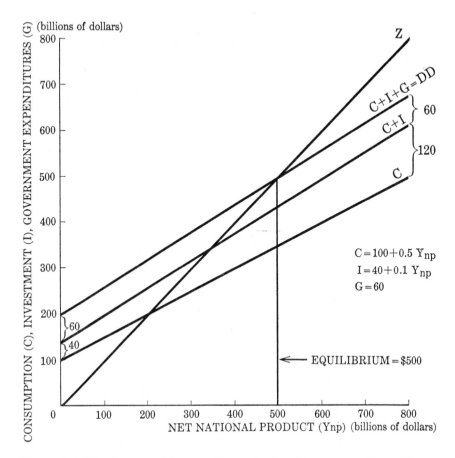

Figure 9–1. The Process of Income Determination; Government Expenditures and Aggregate Demand

Equilibrium income is at the point of intersection of $C + I + G$, the aggregate demand schedule and OZ, the aggregate supply schedule. In this instance, equilibrium is at $500 billion. This is the only output level at which the *three* major expenditure categories will add up to an amount identical with aggregate supply. At any output level greater than $500 billion $C + I + G$ would fall short of output, and we would have a disequilibrium situation in which aggregate supply, OZ, would be greater than aggregate demand, DD. Consequently, the income level would fall. At any income level below $500 billion the reverse would be the case. Aggregate demand, DD, would run ahead of aggregate supply, OZ, and the income level would rise.

The reader will recall that income equilibrium was defined not only in terms of an equality between the aggregate demand and aggregate supply schedules, but also as a situation in which saving and investment *ex ante* were equal.[3] It was possible, on the basis of the data assumed in Chapter 6 for the hypothetical economy, to construct saving and investment schedules and show why the point at which they intersect must necessarily be the equilibrium income level.[4] Now that we have included

TABLE 9–2.

Equilibrium of S and $I + G$
(in billions of dollars)

(1)	(2)	(3)
		Investment plus
Net National Product	Saving	Government Expenditures
Y_{np}	S	$I + G$
0	−100	100
350	75	135
400	100	140
450	125	145
500	**150**	**150**
550	175	155
600	200	160
650	225	165
700	250	170
750	275	175
800	300	180

government purchases of goods and services in the analysis we can do essentially the same thing, except that we must modify the definition of an equilibrium in terms of equality between saving and investment to take into account these purchases. This is done in Table 9–2.

In Table 9–2, Column (3) is the sum of investment and government expenditure totals of Table 9–1. Column (2) is obtained by subtracting intended consumption as shown in Table 9–1 from each income level. The difference between income and consumption we shall still define as saving, simply because at the moment we are not concerned with the matter of taxes. They will be brought into our analysis shortly. It may be noted, however, that taxes are similar to saving in their economic effects because they also represent a leakage from the current income stream.[5] In a closed economic system income not consumed must be disposed of either as saving or as taxes. Consumption, saving, and

[3] Chapter 6, p. 147.
[4] See Figure 6–4, p. 148.
[5] Chapter 6, p. 158.

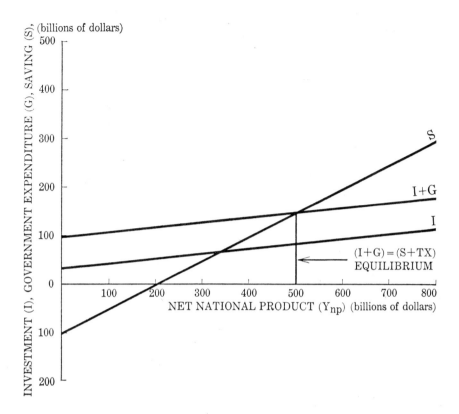

Figure 9-2. Equilibrium of $I + G$ and S

taxes are the only three alternatives for the disposition of income in a closed economy. In an open economy the purchase of imported goods and services is a fourth alternative. Returning to Table 9-2, we find the sum of investment and government purchases of goods and services in Column (3). Equality between S and $I + G$ exists when income is $500 billion.

The data of Table 9-2 are plotted graphically in Figure 9-2. The equilibrium level of income is determined by the intersection of the two schedules. At the equilibrium income level of $500 billion, $I + G$ *ex ante* is equal to S *ex ante*. Leakages out of the the current income stream through saving are just being offset by expenditures for investment goods and government purchases of goods and services. This being the case, income must be in equilibrium.[6]

---

[6] The manner in which G is being financed is discussed later.

Government Expenditures and the Multiplier

Since the public sector buys a part of the national output in the same manner as consumers and business firms, the economic impact of government expenditures of the exhaustive type is essentially the same as that associated with either consumption or investment expenditure. Consequently, a change in government purchases of goods and services will shift the level of the aggregate demand function in exactly the same manner as either an autonomous change in investment spending or an autonomous shift in the consumption function. It follows logically that there will be a multiplier effect associated with a change in government expenditures that is identical in concept with the general multiplier effects discussed earlier.

TABLE 9–3.

Results of an Expansion in Government Expenditures
(In billions of dollars)

(1) Net National Product Y_{np}	(2) Consumption C	(3) Investment I	(4) Government Expenditures G	(5) Aggregate Demand $(C + I + G)$
0	100	40	100	200
350	275	75	100	450
400	300	80	100	480
450	325	85	100	510
500	350	90	100	540
550	375	95	100	570
600	**400**	**100**	**100**	**600**
650	425	105	100	630
700	450	110	100	660
750	475	115	100	690
800	500	120	100	720

In Table 9–3 we have assembled another set of data pertaining to our hypothetical economy. The only difference between these data and those of Table 9–1 is that the level of autonomous government expenditures, G, has risen from $60 billion to $100 billion. We leave aside temporarily the question of how these increased government expenditures are being financed; for the moment it suffices to point out that if prior to this change, saving was equal to the sum of investment and government expenditures, the expansion of government expenditures by the amount of $40 billion means that new funds are being injected into the income stream. The data of Table 9–3 show that the increase in government expenditure by this amount has, *ceteris paribus*, brought about a rise in

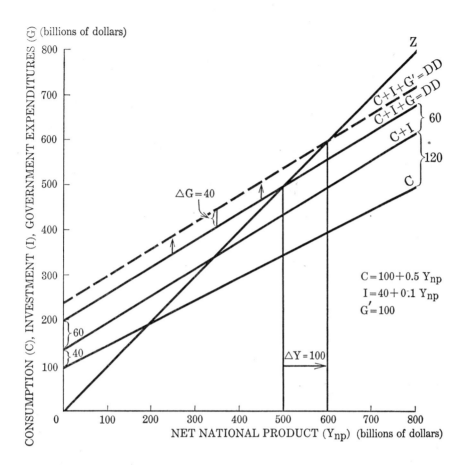

Figure 9–3. Increase in Government Expenditure

the equilibrium level of income to $600 billion. There is an increase of
$100 billion in the income total as a result of an autonomous change in
government expenditures of $40 billion. Thus we have a multipler of 2.5.
Figure 9–3 shows these results graphically.

The underlying logic of the multiplier effect associated with changes
in government expenditures is the same as that of the multiplier effect in
conjunction with changes in investment expenditure or autonomous shifts
in consumption.[7] The multiplier effect results from the combined impact
of the initial (or primary) change in spending (which in this instance is
the amount by which government purchases of goods and services have

---

[7] Chapter 6, especially p. 152.

increased) and the induced (or secondary) spending that is a consequence of the increased income resulting from the original increase in expenditures. Induced spending is in the form of purchases of consumer goods and services and additional investment outlays.

The multiplier effect associated with the change in government expenditures can be explained through a series of simple algebraic formulas. In a formal sense and as was the case with investment changes, we define the multiplier as the ratio of a change in income, ΔY_{np}, to a change in government expenditures for goods and services, ΔG. As the income variable relevant to our analysis is *net national product*, we have

$$k' = \frac{\Delta Y_{np}}{\Delta G} \qquad (9\text{--}1)$$

In a closed economy output consists of three categories: consumption, C, investment, I, and government purchases of goods and services, G. Consequently, we postulate the following identity:

$$Y_{np} = C + I + G \qquad (9\text{--}2)$$

From the above it follows that a change in income must be composed of either a change in government expenditures, ΔG, a change in consumption expenditures, ΔC, a change in investment expenditures, ΔI, or some combination of all three. This gives us the following identity:

$$\Delta Y_{np} = \Delta C + \Delta I + \Delta G \qquad (9\text{--}3)$$

Since the change in government expenditures is the autonomous change, it follows that any change in either consumption expenditures or investment expenditures will be of an induced nature. Induced consumption depends upon the value of the marginal propensity to consume while induced investment depends upon the value of the marginal propensity to invest. The former, it will be recalled, is designated by a and the latter by b.[8] Induced consumption, ΔC, will be equal to $a \times \Delta Y_{np}$, on the assumption that taxes and transfers are still zero, and induced investment, ΔI_i, will be equal to $b \times \Delta Y_{np}$. If we substitute these values for ΔC and ΔI_i in Equation (9–3) we have

$$\Delta Y_{np} = \Delta G + a\Delta Y_{np} + b\Delta Y_{np} \qquad (9\text{--}4)$$

This expression may now be manipulated algebraically as follows:

[8] See footnote 2, p. 252.

$$\Delta Y_{np} - a\Delta Y_{np} - b\Delta Y_{np} = \Delta G \qquad (9\text{-}5)$$

$$\Delta Y_{np} (1 - a - b) = \Delta G \qquad (9\text{-}6)$$

$$\Delta Y_{np} = \Delta G \times \frac{1}{1 - a - b} \qquad (9\text{-}7)$$

$$\frac{\Delta Y_{np}}{\Delta G} = \frac{1}{1 - a - b} = k' \qquad (9\text{-}8)$$

Equation (9-8) tells us that the value of the multiplier in a closed system with investment and government purchase of goods and services is equal to the reciprocal of 1 *minus* the marginal propensity to consume and the marginal propensity to invest. It should be noted at this point that the mathematical expression $(1 - a - b)$ is a measure of *leakages* expressed as marginal propensities. The formal mathematical statement of the multiplier relationship just developed serves to underscore the fundamental idea that the over-all magnitude of the multiplier effect associated with *any* shift in the aggregate demand function depends upon the total of secondary spending that is induced by such a shift.

Transfer Expenditures and the Income Level

Unlike government purchases of goods and services which are a part of the aggregate demand function, transfer expenditures exert only an indirect influence on aggregate demand. It is primarily by their impact on the volume of consumption expenditures that transfer payments influence the level of aggregate demand. To a lesser degree they may affect investment expenditures as well, but our analysis will be directed basically toward the manner in which they affect expenditures for consumer goods and services.

To understand the influence of transfer expenditures on aggregate demand, it is necessary, first, to recall that the crux of the income-consumption relationship is that the amount of spending for consumption purposes is determined by the income level. In the discussion of the empirical validity of the consumption function hypothesis, we concluded that the most meaningful income measure appropriate to this relationship is that of *disposable income.*[9] Since we have assumed a linear relationship between income and consumption, the consumption function in equation form is as follows:

$$C = C_o + a(Y_d) \qquad (9\text{-}9)$$

The reader will recall that disposable income was defined in Chapter 6 as the net national product *less* taxes (direct and indirect) paid by the

[9] Chapter 6, p. 132.

owners of economic resources *plus* transfer payments received by individuals and households. Since we assumed that all saving (other than capital consumption allowances) originates with individuals or households and that government is the only source of transfer payments, disposable income was defined as follows:

$$Y_d = Y_{np} - TX + TR \qquad (9\text{--}10)$$

In Equation (9–10), Y_{np} is the net national product; TX, the total of all taxes, including indirect taxes; and TR, the total of all transfer expenditures. The consumption function can now be written as

$$C = C_o + a\,(Y_{np} - TX + TR) \qquad (9\text{--}11)$$

It is apparent from Equation (9–11) that transfer expenditures influence consumption expenditure and thus indirectly the level of aggregate demand by affecting the amount of disposable income in the hands of individuals and households. A change in transfer expenditures will bring about a change in disposable income which in turn will induce a change in consumer spending, since the amount of disposable income constitutes the point of origin of spending for consumer goods and services. Schematically, the chain of causation appears as follows:

$$\Delta TR \longrightarrow \Delta Y_d \longrightarrow \Delta C$$

Let us refer once again to the data of the hypothetical economy for a demonstration of how this chain of causation may work out in actuality. To show the relationships involved, we shall turn to Table 9–4 and Figure 9–4, confining the analysis initially to the impact of transfer expenditures on the consumption function. In Column (2) of Table 9–4 the consumption function for the hypothetical economy is as set forth in Table 9–1. This schedule appears as the solid line C in Figure 9–4. We may note that Table 9–1 contained no transfer expenditures, and consequently net national product and disposable income were the same. In Table 9–4 net national product and disposable income are equal prior to the introduction of transfer expenditures. They appear in Column (1).

What impact does the introduction of transfer expenditures into the analysis have on the level of consumption? Let us assume that the government of our hypothetical economy undertakes transfer expenditures of $40 billion. (We shall not concern ourselves at this point with the manner in which this new expenditure is financed.) The immediate effect of this new expenditure is to increase disposable income at all possible income levels, as shown in Column (4) of the table. This is the same at all

income levels because the assumed increase in transfer expenditures of
$40 billion must have the same effect on disposable income irrespective
of the actual income level. The impact of this increase in disposable income on consumption expenditure depends upon the value of the marginal
propensity to consume. Our original consumption function was drawn
with a slope such that the marginal propensity to consume has a value of
0.5. If we assume that the introduction of transfer expenditures into the
analysis in no way affects the slope of the schedule, it follows that con-

TABLE 9–4.

Results of an Increase in Transfer Expenditures
(in billions of dollars)

(1) Net National Product * Y_{np}	(2) Consumption C	(3) Change in Disposable Income † ΔY_d	(4) Disposable Income Y_d	(5) Change in Consumption ‡ C	(6) New Level of Consumption C'
0	100	40	40	20	120
350	275	40	390	20	295
400	300	40	440	20	320
450	325	40	490	20	345
500	350	40	540	20	370
550	375	40	590	20	395
600	400	40	640	20	420
650	425	40	690	20	445
700	450	40	740	20	470
750	475	40	790	20	495
800	500	40	840	20	520

* Net National Product = Disposable Income when taxes and transfers are zero.
† This is equal to the increase in transfer expenditures.
‡ The marginal propensity to consume is 0.5.

sumption expenditures *at each and every possible level of income* will increase by $20 billion, one half of the increase in disposable income. This
change is shown in Column (5) of Table 9–4. The over-all impact of the
introduction of transfer expenditures may be described *as a shift in the
position of the consumption function.* The consumption function has
shifted upward because of the added factor of transfer expenditures. As
a consequence, consumption expenditures are higher at all levels of the
net national income. This shift is shown graphically in Figure 9–4. The
new and higher consumption function is labeled C'. Thus, transfer expenditures constitute one of the key factors that influence the level of
the consumption function. In a technical sense transfers exercise their influence through the parameter C_o, which determines the level of the function. A change in transfer expenditures will, therefore, bring about a

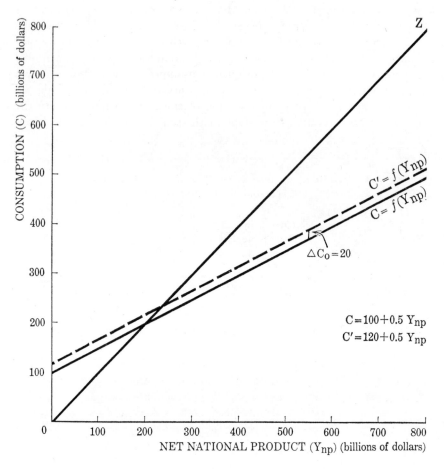

Figure 9–4. Shift in the Consumption Function

shift in the position of the schedule, and in this way affect consumption spending and the level of aggregate demand.[10]

Let us refer once again to the data of Table 9–1 and the income equilibrium level associated with these data. On the assumption that government expenditures for goods and services totaled a constant $60 billion, the equilibrium income is $500 billion, given the original position of the consumption function as shown in Column (2) and the investment function shown in Column (3) of Table 9–1. What will happen to the equilibrium income if an additional $40 billion in government transfer expenditures are injected into the picture? The immediate result is to shift the con-

[10] It is possible, too, that a change in transfers may affect the *slope* of the function, but this is precluded in our example.

TABLE 9–5.

Transfer Expenditures and Aggregate Demand
(in billions of dollars)

Before Transfers				After Transfers *			
(1) Net National Product Y_{np}	(2) Dis- posable Income Y_d	(3) Consump- tion C	(4) Aggregate Demand $C+I+G$†	(5) Net National Product Y_{np}	(6) Dis- posable Income Y_d	(7) Consump- tion C'	(8) Aggregate Demand $C'+I+G$†
0	0	100	200	0	40	120	220
350	350	275	410	350	390	295	430
400	400	300	440	400	440	320	460
450	450	325	470	450	490	345	490
500	500	350	500	500	540	370	520
550	550	375	530	550	590	395	550
600	600	400	560	600	640	420	580
650	650	425	590	650	690	445	610
700	700	450	620	700	740	470	640
750	750	475	650	750	790	495	670
800	800	500	680	800	840	520	700

* Transfers = $40
† $I + G$ are the same as in Table 9–1.

sumption function upward as we have done in Table 9–4. This means, in turn, an equal upward shift of the aggregate demand schedule. The immediate (or initial) increase in spending that this change entails is equal to the amount by which both the consumption function and the aggregate demand schedule have shifted upward. This is $20 billion, and if we multiply this change by the general multiplier of 2.5, we find that the new equilibrium level will be $50 billion higher than previously. This value of 2.5 for the general multiplier is based upon our assumed value of 0.5 for the marginal propensity to consume and 0.1 for the marginal propensity to invest. The effect on the income level of a change in transfer expenditures is shown numerically in Table 9–5 and graphically in Figure 9–5. In the table the original position of the consumption function is given by Column (3); its position after the introduction of transfer expenditures by Column (7). The aggregate demand function, $C + I + G$, at the new and higher level of the consumption function is shown in Column (8). The new equilibrium income level is $550 billion.

Transfer Expenditures and the Multiplier

There is a multiplier effect associated with a change in the level of transfer expenditures similar in a fundamental conceptual sense to all the multiplier effects previously discussed. An increase (or decrease) in transfer expenditures will lead to an increase (or decrease) in the income level

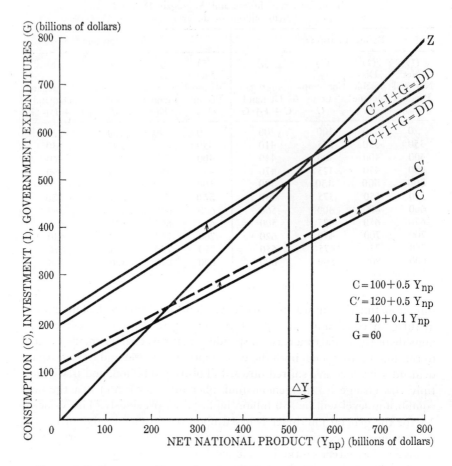

Figure 9–5. Aggregate Demand and a Shift in the Consumption Function

that is some *multiple* of the original change in transfers. This is identical to what takes place when there is an autonomous change in investment outlays or government purchases of goods and services. But there is an important difference between the multiplier effect associated with transfers and that associated with the G or I components of the aggregate demand schedule. Normally, the multiplier effect associated with transfer expenditures will be smaller than the multiplier effect of a change in either investment or government expenditures. Let us see why this is true.

The multiplier phenomenon results from the combination of initial and induced changes in spending. But a change in transfer expenditures does not operate directly on the aggregate demand function in the same way as does a change in either investment expenditures or government purchases of goods and services. Additional transfer expenditures trigger, *first*, a change in disposable income, *then*, via the marginal propensity to consume, a new level of consumption spending. But so long as Keynes' "fundamental psychological law" holds true—that is, that normally the marginal propensity to consume is less than 100 per cent—consumption cannot rise (or fall) by the full amount of the change in transfer expenditures. Consequently, *the shift in the aggregate demand function*, which is the initial or primary change in spending that gives rise to the multiplier process, *must always be smaller than the change in transfer expenditures.* It follows that, if the initial effect of any given change is smaller, then the induced effect will also be smaller. Thus, the multiplier effect will be smaller for transfers than for investment or government expenditures.

Taxes and the Income Level

Our extensive analysis of the way in which transfer expenditures affect the income level by their influence on disposable income and consumption spending makes it relatively easy for us to consider the impact of taxes on the income level. Once we realize that taxes are, in a sense, nothing more negative transfers, it can be seen that they will affect the income level in a manner exactly the reverse of transfers. Taxes, *ceteris paribus*, have the effect of reducing disposable income, as we saw in Equation (9–10). Thus an increase in taxes would tend to reduce consumption spending because it would reduce disposable income. On the other hand, a decrease in taxes would have the opposite effect of increasing consumption spending because it would increase disposable income. The foregoing remarks apply primarily to a situation in which taxes increase (or decrease) by a specific amount. Changes in taxation that may accompany changes in the income level present a more complex problem, as we shall see shortly.

In view of the above similarities between the impact of transfers and taxes on the income level, let us assert as a general principle that the absolute level of taxes is a factor which, like the absolute level of transfer expenditures, influences the level of the consumption function. This statement applies to that part of the tax total that is independent of the income level. Given this general principle, it follows that any increase in taxes that is autonomous with respect to the income level will, *ceteris paribus*, shift the consumption function downward. On the other hand, an autonomous reduction in the level of taxation will, *ceteris paribus*, shift the consumption function upward. As is the case with transfer expenditures, the amount by which the consumption function shifts as a result of a change in taxation depends upon the value of the marginal propensity to consume. Taxes change disposable income, and consumption spending will change in accordance with whether the value of the marginal propensity to consume is high or low.

Let us refer once again to the data of our hypothetical economy to analyze the impact of an introduction of taxes into the system. We shall

TABLE 9–6.

Results of the Introduction of Taxes
(in billions of dollars)

(1) Net National Product Y_{np}	(2) Consumption * C'	(3) Change in Disposable Income † ΔY_d	(4) Disposable Income Y_d	(5) Change in Consumption C	(6) New Level of Consumption C''
0	120	−80	− 40	−40	80
350	295	−80	310	−40	255
400	320	−80	360	−40	280
450	345	−80	410	−40	305
500	370	−80	460	−40	330
550	395	−80	510	−40	355
600	420	−80	560	−40	380
650	445	−80	610	−40	405
700	470	−80	660	−40	430
750	495	−80	710	−40	455
800	520	−80	760	−40	480

* Same as Column (6) of Table 9–4.
† This is equal to the increase in taxes ($80 billion).

assume a flat total of taxes in the amount of $80 billion is imposed. The effect of this change on disposable income and the consumption function is shown in Table 9–6. Essentially, the effect of new taxes in the amount of $80 billion is to reduce, first, disposable income by a like amount at *all* levels of the net national product, and, second, to reduce consumption spending in accordance with the value of the marginal propensity to consume. This value is 0.5, which means, in effect, that at all levels of the net national product consumption spending will decline by $0.5 \times \Delta TX$. This is $40 billion; thus, we have an autonomous downward shift in the consumption function in the amount of $40 billion. The new position of the consumption function is shown in Column (6) of Table 9–6.

The data contained in Table 9–7 indicate the effect of the introduction of taxes into the system upon aggregate demand and the equilibrium income level. Prior to this change, the equilibrium income was $550 billion and the position of the consumption function was given by Column (7) of Table 9–5. The initial impact of the added taxes is to reduce autonomously the consumption function by $40 billion—as we have just seen—

and if it assumed that no change in either government purchases of goods or services nor the investment function follows, this means, too, that the aggregate demand function shifts downward by $40 billion. When the general multiplier of 2.5 is applied against this shift, the ultimate decline in the net national product is $100 billion. Thus, the new equilibrium position is depicted in Table 9–7 as being at the $450 billion level. These changes are depicted graphically in Figure 9–6.

In Table 9–7 the concept of net taxes is introduced. The reader should

TABLE 9–7.

Taxes and Aggregate Demand
(in billions of dollars)

(1) Net National Product Y_{np}	(2) Net Taxes T *	(3) Disposable Income Y_d †	(4) Consumption C''	(5) Aggregate Demand $C'' + I + G$ ‡
0	40	−40	80	180
350	40	310	255	390
400	40	360	280	420
450	**40**	**410**	**305**	**450**
500	40	460	330	480
550	40	510	355	510
600	40	560	380	540
650	40	610	405	570
700	40	660	430	600
750	40	710	455	630
800	40	760	480	660

* $T = $ Net Taxes $= (TX - TR)$.
† $Y_d = Y_{np} - T$.
‡ $I + G$ is the same as in Table 9–1.

carefully note this concept, as it is crucial to a clear understanding of the algebraic derivation of the multiplier in a system which incorporates *changes* in both taxes and transfer expenditures as the net national product changes. Net taxes are defined as total taxes less transfer payments; they represent the *net* withdrawal of income from the income stream as a result of the combined effect of both taxes and transfer payments. In symbolic terms we have:

$$T = (TX - TR) \qquad (9-12)$$

From this it follows that the consumption function can be written:

$$C = C_o + a(Y_{np} - T) \qquad (9-13)$$

Earlier in this chapter we pointed out that taxes are a leakage from the income stream in the same sense as saving. This being true, equilibrium requires that leakages in the form of *net* taxes plus saving must be offset

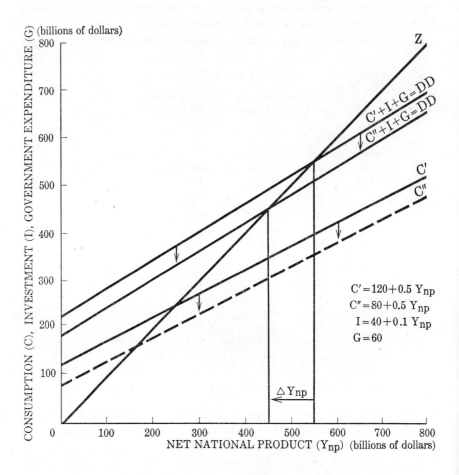

Figure 9–6. Effect of Taxes on the Aggregate Demand Schedule

by investment expenditure and government purchases of goods and services. Now that net taxes have been introduced into our analysis, we can plot schedule—or *ex ante*—values for $I + G$ and $S + T$ and show that equilibrium obtains at the intersection of these schedules. This is done in Figure 9–7.

Transfers, Taxes, and the Multiplier

In the prior section the effect of transfers and taxes on the income level was examined. It was seen that there is a multiplier effect associated with either a change in transfer expenditures or taxes, although normally the effect is smaller than the multiplier effect resulting from changes in either government purchases of goods and services or investment outlays. The reason for this is that transfers and taxes directly affect disposable income, but only indirectly affect the level of aggregate demand.

We shall now proceed to derive algebraically the multiplier in a system which includes both transfers and taxes, as well as induced investment. In Equation (9–12) we defined net taxes T as the difference between total taxes and transfer payments. We may also define net taxes as follows:

$$T = T_o + tY_{np} \qquad (9\text{–}14)$$

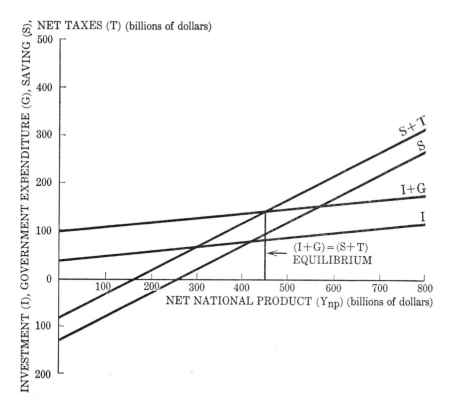

Figure 9–7. Equilibrium of $I + G$ and $S + T$

In this equation T_o represents net taxes which are independent of the income level, while t may be defined as the net marginal propensity to tax out of net national product. It is equal to $\Delta T / \Delta Y_{np}$. If the tax system is so constructed that taxes in absolute amount increase as the income level increases, t will be positive. A tax system based upon income and with either a proportional or progressive rate structure will yield a positive value for t. Equation (9–14) is the net tax function.

The consumption function shown in Equation (9–13) can be further modified by the substitution of the net tax function given above for T in the equation. This gives the following:

$$C = C_o + a[Y_{np} - (T_o + tY_{np})] \qquad (9\text{--}15)$$
$$C = C_o + aY_{np} - aT_o - atY_{np} \qquad (9\text{--}16)$$
$$C = C_o - aT_o + (a - at)Y_{np} \qquad (9\text{--}17)$$

We shall designate $(C_o - aT_o)$ as C_o'. This represents consumption that is independent of the level of the net national product. The expression $(a - at)$ is the marginal propensity to consume out of the net national product.[11] We shall designate this as a'. We now have the equation:

$$C = C_o' + a'Y_{np} \qquad (9\text{--}18)$$

Since both transfer payments and taxes have been introduced into our analysis, there no longer is equality between disposable income and the net national product. The multiplier formula must take this into account. We shall designate the multiplier which reflects the effect of both transfers and taxes as the "effective" multiplier, letting k' now be the symbol for the multiplier. Algebraically, the effective multiplier is

$$k' = \frac{\Delta Y_{np}}{\Delta D} \qquad (9\text{--}19)$$

In the foregoing, ΔD refers to any autonomous shift in the aggregate demand function. To complete our analysis, let us assume that it is an increase in government purchases of goods and services which is the source of an autonomous shift in the aggregate demand function. Then $\Delta G = \Delta D$. If this happens, it follows that

$$\Delta Y_{np} = \Delta G + \Delta C + \Delta I \qquad (9\text{--}20)$$

[11] See the Appendix for algebraic proof that $a' = (a - at)$.

By substitution we have

$$\Delta Y_{np} = \Delta G + a'\Delta Y_{np} + b\Delta Y_{np} \qquad (9\text{--}21)$$
$$\Delta G = \Delta Y_{np} - a'\Delta Y_{np} - b\Delta Y_{np} \qquad (9\text{--}22)$$
$$\Delta G = \Delta Y_{np}(1 - a' - b) \qquad (9\text{--}23)$$

If we substitute the right-hand portion of Equation (9–23) for ΔD in Equation (9–19) we get

$$k' = \frac{\Delta Y_{np}}{\Delta Y_{np}(1 - a' - b)} = \frac{1}{(1 - a' - b)} \qquad (9\text{--}24)$$

When a' is replaced with $(a - at)$ in the above expression, the equation defining the effective multiplier becomes

$$k' = \frac{1}{1 - (a - at) - b} = \frac{1}{1 - a + at - b} \qquad (9\text{--}25)$$

By careful examination of the above equation the student can see clearly the effect of both transfer payments and taxes on the value of the multiplier and hence on income changes as a result of an autonomous shift in aggregate demand. Any development which increases the value of the net marginal propensity to tax, t, will have the effect of reducing the size of the effective multiplier; any development that reduces t will have the opposite effect.

Built-in Stabilizers

The fact that both taxes and transfer payments may vary with changes in the income level is the basis for "built-in stabilizers," which have come to play an important role in the functioning of the economy. The term "stabilizers" is used because these features of the economic system operate in a manner that counteracts fluctuations in economic activity. They are described as "built-in" because they come into play automatically as the income level changes. These built-in stabilizers do not depend, in other words, upon discretionary action by the monetary and fiscal authorities.

To illustrate, taxes may act as a stabilizing influence upon the economic system if the tax structure is designed so that the *amount* of taxes collected by the government rises with an increase in the net national product. If this is the case the effect will be to lessen the expansion in disposable income that accompanies any autonomous shift in the aggregate demand function. From a stabilizing point of view the consequence of this will be a less rapid rise in induced consumption spending than would be the case in the absence of a tax system possessing this character. If the tax system is constructed so that not only the absolute amount of taxes but also the percentage of income going to taxes increases with an increase in *net* national product the stabilizing impact will be even greater. This situation will prevail if the rate structure for the tax system is progressive, with the effective rate at which income is taxed increasing as the level of income increases. In terms of the analysis in the preceding section such a system is one in which the net marginal propensity to tax is not only positive, but its value is an increasing function of the income level. Stabilizing effects of a reverse character come into play when the income level declines. The fiscal system, in short, operates in a countercyclical or stabilizing fashion if its over-all effect is to insulate to a degree disposable income from changes in the net national product.

The effect of different tax structures on net taxes, disposable income, and consumption spending is indicated by the hypothetical data contained in Tables 9–8 and 9–10. In these examples transfer expenditures are assumed to be constant, but net taxes are determined on the basis of three different types of tax systems. In a "regressive" tax system, total taxes TX are constant at all levels of net national product. This type of system is labeled "regressive," because it means the rate of taxation (TX/Y_{np}) declines as the tax base—the net national product—increases. A second system is "proportional" taxation, in which taxes are a constant per cent or proportion of the net national product. The rate in this example is 20 per cent. Finally, we have "progressive" taxation, which is a system in which the rate increases as the tax base increases.

Table 9–8 shows what the amount of net taxes T will be at each possible level of the net national product, given a constant volume of transfer expenditures of $40 billion and the different tax structures described above. "Regressive" taxation will obviously not have any stabilizing effect, as net taxes remain constant irrespective of the level of net national product. "Proportional" taxation will lead to an absolute increase in the amount of net taxes as net national product increases (Column [6]), but the absolute increase is not nearly so large as it is with the "progressive" taxation (Column [9]). Table 9–9 shows how both disposable income and consumption expenditures will be affected by the different tax systems. The important point to note is that consumption increases (or decreases) much less rapidly with the progressive tax structure than is the case with either the proportional or regressive system.

TABLE 9–8.

Alternative Tax Structures
(in billions of dollars)

(1) Net National Product Y_{np}	(2) Transfer Payments TR	Regressive		Proportional		Progressive		
		(3) Taxes TX	(4) Net Taxes T	(5) Taxes TX'	(6) Net Taxes T'	(7) Taxes TX''	(8) Tax Rate TX/Y_{np}	(9) Net Taxes T''
0	40	80	40	0	− 40	0	0%	− 40
350	40	80	40	70	30	42	12	2
400	40	80	40	80	40	56	14	16
450	40	80	40	90	50	72	16	32
500	40	80	40	100	60	90	18	50
550	40	80	40	110	70	110	20	70
600	40	80	40	120	80	132	22	92
650	40	80	40	130	90	156	24	116
700	40	80	40	140	100	182	26	142
750	40	80	40	150	110	210	28	170
800	40	80	40	160	120	240	30	210

The consumption function shown in Column (10) not only yields a higher volume of consumption expenditures at the lower income levels, but its slope is such that the marginal propensity to consume out of net national product *declines* as the income level rises. The latter has the effect of exerting a greater dampening effect for either an autonomous shift upward or downward in the aggregate demand function than is possible with either of the other schedules shown in the table (Columns [4] and [7]).

TABLE 9–9.

Alternative Consumption Schedules
(in billions of dollars)

(1) Net National Product Y_{np}	(2) Net Taxes T	Regressive		Proportional			Progressive		
		(3) Dis-posable Income Y_d	(4) Consump-tion C	(5) Net Taxes T'	(6) Dis-posable Income Y_d'	(7) Consump-tion C'	(8) Net Taxes T''	(9) Dis-posable Income Y_d''	(10) Consump-tion C''
0	40	− 40	80	− 40	40	120	− 40	40	120
350	40	310	255	30	320	260	2	348	274
400	40	360	280	40	360	280	16	384	292
450	40	410	305	50	400	300	32	418	309
500	40	460	330	60	440	320	50	450	325
550	40	510	355	70	480	340	70	480	340
600	40	560	380	80	520	360	92	508	354
650	40	610	405	90	560	380	116	534	367
700	40	660	430	100	600	400	142	558	379
750	40	710	455	110	640	420	170	580	390
800	40	760	480	120	680	440	210	590	400

This brief discussion of built-in stabilizers has concentrated on taxes, but the reader should be aware that various forms of transfer expenditures affect the economy in a similar countercyclical fashion. If transfer payments are to have a stabilizing effect, they must *decrease* in absolute amount when the net national product (or national income) increases and increase when the reverse happens. Transfers in the form of unemployment compensation payments provide a good example of this kind of behavior. When output and employment are falling, payments to the unemployed automatically increase, thus insulating disposable income to a degree from a decline in earned income—i.e., net national product and the national income. When unemployment declines with a recovery from a recession or depression, transfer payments fall off and, thus, disposable income does not rise as rapidly as would be the case otherwise.

An important question which will occur to the thoughtful student is: how effective are the built-in stabilizers? One study which analyzed the behavior of the stabilizers over two periods of contraction and three periods of expansion for the period 1948 through mid-1957 concluded the following:

On the average a fall in national income has led to a rise in transfer payments and a fall in tax collections, totaling a swing of approximtely 50 percent of the decline in national income. During upswings the automatic stabilizers have exhibited a swing to increases in national income of slightly less than 30 percent on the average. Thus, assuming a $10 billion increase in national income, disposable income will rise by $2.8 billion less than it would have had automatic stabilization been inoperative. Had national income fallen by $10 billion, the induced drop in disposable income would have been $5.1 billion less as a consequence of the presence of automatic stabilizers.[12]

Another and more recent study estimated the extent to which the stabilizers reduced the potential change in income during three recessions and three expansions between 1948 and 1960. In this instance it found that the stabilizers are capable of reducing declines in the national income by about 50 per cent, if the values for the marginal propensity to consume out of disposable income and the marginal propensity to invest *out of retained corporate earnings* are close to 0.9 and 0.5 respectively. (The student should note that the higher the value of the marginal propensity to consume out of disposable income, the greater is the impact of transfer expenditures in maintaining disposable income in the face of a decline in the national income.) It was also found that during expansions the stabilizers would prevent over 40 per cent of the potential increase in income if the values for the marginal propensity to consume out of disposable income and the marginal propensity to invest out of

[12] M. O. Clement, "The Quantitative Impact of Automatic Stabilizers," *The Review of Economics and Statistics*, February, 1960, p. 60.

retained corporate earnings were as above, and if, further, government spending upon goods and services remained unchanged.[13]

Few economists today would argue that the stabilizers by themselves can smooth out fluctuations in income and employment in the complex economy characteristic of a modern nation, but most would probably agree that they are a vital and effective complement to discretionary action.

The Balanced Budget Thesis

The analysis showing how the multiplier effect associated with changes in both taxes and transfers is normally smaller than the multiplier effect associated with a change in government exhaustive expenditures is useful in demonstrating that an increase in the latter type of expenditures may, under rigidly assumed conditions, have an expansionary effect, even though these expenditures are matched by an equal increase in taxes. This possibility has come to be known as the *balanced budget thesis*.

To illustrate the nature of this thesis, let us refer once again to the data of Table 9–3. We made the assumption there that government exhaustive expenditures had increased by $40 billion. Let us now assume further that taxes are simultaneously increased by an equal amount so that the new and higher level of government expenditures can be financed. Our problem is to determine how the combined impact of the increase in both government expenditures and taxes will affect the income level. Contrary to what might be assumed at first glance, a change of this type is not neutral in its effects on the income level.

The effect of simultaneous change in both government expenditures and taxes depends upon the combined impact of the increase in government expenditures and the increase in taxes upon the aggregate demand function. In our example let us assume, as earlier, that the marginal propensity to consume out of disposable income, a, is 0.5; the marginal propensity to invest, b, is 0.1; and the marginal propensity to tax, t, is 0.2. The value of the effective multiplier, according to Equation (9–25), is thus 2. The shift in the aggregate demand function will equal the increase in government expenditure, ΔG, less the autonomous shift downward in the consumption function which results from the tax increase. This latter shift is designated as ΔC_o. In algebraic terms we have

$$\Delta D = \Delta G - \Delta C_o \qquad (9\text{--}27)$$

[13] Peter Eilbott, "The Effectiveness of Automatic Stabilizers," *The American Economic Review*, June, 1966, p. 463. See also George E. Rejda, "Unemployment Insurance as an Automatic Stabilizer," *The Journal of Risk and Insurance*, June, 1966, pp. 195–208.

But ΔC_o depends upon the value of the marginal propensity to consume (out of disposable income) and the change in disposable income. The latter is the same as the increase in taxes. Thus we have

$$\Delta C_o = a\Delta Y_d = a\Delta TX \qquad (9\text{--}28)$$

Given a value of 0.5 for a, we find that ΔC_o is equal to $20 billion. The combined effect of the increase in government purchases of goods and services and the increase in taxes will be to shift the aggregate demand function upwards by $20 billion. When the effective multiplier of 2 is applied against this increment in aggregate demand, the final change in the net national product is $40 billion, which is just equal to the amount by which government expenditures for goods and services increased. The significant point to note is that the expansion of exhaustive expenditures, even though accompanied by an equal increase in taxes—the balanced budget thesis—*was not* neutral with respect to its impact upon the output level. In other words, an expansion of government purchases of goods and services under balanced budget conditions may cause a rise in the output level; if the expansion were to occur with full employment conditions, the result would be a significant increase in pressure on the price level.

In the foregoing example the student will note that the net national product increased by an amount just equal to the increase in government expenditures, namely $40 billion. If the marginal propensity to tax, t, were zero rather than 0.2, the increase in the net national product would have been $50 billion rather than $40 billion. On the other hand, if the value of the marginal propensity to tax is greater than 0.2, the increase in the net national product will be less than $40 billion, but will still be greater than zero. It would be a useful exercise for the reader to compute, assuming different values for the marginal propensity to consume out of a disposable income, a, how large a tax increase would have to be to prevent *any* increase in the net national product, given a $40 billion increase in government outlays. The student should note carefully, too, that the shift in the aggregate demand function, given the amount of the tax increase, is governed by the value of the marginal propensity to consume out of disposable income while the size of the ultimate change in the net national product, given both the increase in taxes and the value of a, depends upon the value of the marginal propensity to tax, t.

APPENDIX

Transfers, Taxes, and the Multiplier: An Alternative Treatment

Some writers prefer to treat the multiplier effects associated with both transfer payments and taxes in a different fashion. Rather than develop, as done in the text of this chapter, a general multiplier which can be applied against a shift in the aggregate demand function, and which, too, embodies the effect of both transfers and taxes, they prefer to speak of a transfer or tax multiplier as such. This multiplier coefficient, when multiplied by the change in either transfer payments or taxes, yields the resulting change in income (net national product). The student should understand clearly that in no sense does this approach involve a "different" type of multiplier than discussed to this point; rather, it is simply a different way of approaching the multiplier effects associated with either transfers or taxes. To illustrate this we shall derive algebraically a "transfer expenditures multiplier." A tax multiplier could be derived in identical fashion, except that its value would be negative.

(1) $k_{tr} = \dfrac{\Delta Y_{np}}{\Delta TR} = $ a formal definition of the "transfer multiplier"

(2) $\Delta Y_{np} = \Delta C_o + \Delta C_i + \Delta I$ [The increase in the net national product will be equal to the increase in autonomous consumption, ΔC_o, plus the induced changes in consumption and investment. This equation is an identity.]

(3) $\Delta C_o = a\Delta TR$ [The increase in autonomous consumption—i.e., the shift in the consumption function—depends upon the increase in transfers and the value of the marginal propensity to consume out of disposable income, a.]

(4) $\Delta Y_{np} = a\Delta TR + \Delta C_i + \Delta I$ [By substitution.]

(5) $a\Delta TR = \Delta Y_{np} - \Delta C_i - \Delta I$ [From (4) above.]

(6) $\Delta TR = \dfrac{\Delta Y_{np} - \Delta C_i - \Delta I}{a}$ [From (5) above.]

(7) $k_{tr} = \dfrac{\Delta Y_{np}}{(\Delta Y_{np} - \Delta C_i - \Delta I)/a} = \dfrac{a\Delta Y_{np}}{\Delta Y_{np} - \Delta C_i - \Delta I}$

(8) $k_{tr} = \dfrac{a}{1 - \dfrac{\Delta C_i}{\Delta Y_{np}} - \dfrac{\Delta I}{\Delta Y_{np}}} = \dfrac{a}{1 - a' - b}$

$\dfrac{\Delta C_i}{\Delta Y_{np}} = a' = $ the marginal propensity to consume out of net national product

(9) $k_{tr} = \dfrac{a}{1 - a + at - b}$ \qquad $a' = (a - at)$

Since a (the marginal propensity to consume out of disposable income) is normally less than unity, this formula for the transfer multiplier means that its numerical value will be smaller than the "effective" multiplier developed in the text. The "tax" multiplier can be derived in the same fashion, but its value will be negative.

Formal proof that $(a - at) = a'$, the marginal propensity to consume out of net national product

(1) $a = \dfrac{\Delta C}{\Delta Y_d} =$ the marginal propensity to consume out of disposable income

(2) $a' = \dfrac{\Delta C}{\Delta Y_{np}} =$ the marginal propensity to consume out of net national product

(3) $t = \dfrac{\Delta T}{\Delta Y_{np}} =$ the net marginal propensity to tax out of net national product

(4) $(1 - t)\dfrac{\Delta Y_d}{\Delta Y_{np}} =$ the net marginal rate of retention of income / This is derived as follows:

    (a) $Y_{np} = Y_d + T$

    (b) $\Delta Y_{np} = \Delta Y_d + \Delta T$

    (c) $1 = \dfrac{\Delta Y_d}{\Delta Y_{np}} + \dfrac{\Delta T}{\Delta Y_{np}}$ / Divide both sides of (b) by ΔY_{np}

    (d) $\dfrac{\Delta Y_d}{\Delta Y_{np}} = 1 - \dfrac{\Delta T}{\Delta Y_{np}} = (1 - t)$

(5) $(1 - t) \times a = \dfrac{\Delta C}{\Delta Y_{np}} = a'$ / This is derived as follows:

    (a) $\dfrac{\Delta Y_d}{\Delta Y_{np}} \times \dfrac{\Delta C}{\Delta Y_d} = \dfrac{\Delta C}{\Delta Y_{np}} = a'$ [By substitution.]

    (b) Therefore: $a' = a(1 - t) = (a - at)$

Algebraic determination of the equilibrium income level using the effective multiplier

    (1) $Y_{np} = C + I + G =$ the basic identity

    (2) $C = C_o' + a' Y_{np} =$ the consumption function

    (3) $I = I_o' + b Y_{np} =$ the investment function

    (4) $Y_{np} = (C_o' + I_o' + a' Y_{np} + b Y_{np} + G)$ [Substitution of (2) and (3) into (1).]

    (5) $Y_{np} - a' Y_{np} - b Y_{np} = (C_o' + I_o' + G)$

    (6) $Y_{np} (1 - a' - b) = (C_o' + I_o' + G)$

    (7) $Y_{np} = \dfrac{1}{(1 - a' - b)} \times (C_o' + I_o' + G)$

    (8) $Y_{np} = \dfrac{1}{1 - a + at - b} \times (C_o' + I_o' + G)$

    (9) $Y_{np} = k' (C_o' + I_o' + G)$

10 | The Theory of the Foreign Balance

Up to this point in our analysis we have assumed a "closed" economy, an economy that does not have any economic transactions with other nations. In this chapter we shall drop this assumption and undertake an analysis of the manner in which the international economic transactions of a nation interact with income and employment levels in the domestic economy. Specifically, we shall examine, first, how changes in the international economic position of a nation affect its internal economy, and, second, how internal economic changes may affect the nation's international economic position. Our approach will be primarily in terms of relationships existing between international economic transactions and the aggregate demand function.

The Nature of the Foreign Balance

A nation's international economic balance involves all of the economic transactions that residents of one nation enter into with residents of all other nations during some specific period of time.[1] The most important tool for analysis of the international economic position of a nation is the balance-of-payments statement. This accounting statement records (in principle) all the economic transactions that residents of one country make with residents of foreign countries during a given period of time, normally the calendar year. Since an economic transaction generally con-

[1] For the purpose of balance-of-payments accounting the word "residents" is interpreted to mean not only physical persons, but also business firms, governments, and international agencies. Persons are considered residents of the country in which they normally reside. Residents are not necessarily or always citizens.

279

sists of a payment or a receipt in exchange for a good, service, or some type of financial asset, the balance-of-payments statement constitutes a record of payments made by residents of a country to foreigners and payments made by foreigners to residents of the country in question.

In balance-of-payments accounting practice, transactions that require foreigners to make payments to residents of the domestic economy or, alternatively, provide residents of the domestic economy with the means to make payments to foreigners are treated as *credit* entries in the balance-of-payments statement. Thus an export of merchandise by an American firm to the United Kingdom and a loan extended by a British bank to American residents would be credit entries in the American balance-of-payments statement. On the other hand, transactions that require residents of the domestic economy to make payments to foreigners or, alternatively, provide foreigners with the means to make payments to residents of the domestic economy are treated as *debit* entries in the balance-of-payments statement. Imports and loans extended to foreigners would fall into the category of debit transactions in the balance-of-payments statement of the domestic economy.[2]

The Three Accounts in the Balance-of-Payments Statement

It is the usual practice in balance-of-payments accounting to break the statement down into three sub-categories or "accounts," as they are usually called. These are the *current* account, the *gold* account, and the *capital* account.

THE CURRENT ACCOUNT

The current account section of the balance of payments records all *current* transactions, which are transactions that involve either the export or import of goods (i.e., merchandise) and services. Under "services" are grouped income from transportation, banking, and insurance; income in the form of interest and dividends from various financial assets; and expenditures by tourists. Transactions involving services are described as *invisible* items, whereas transactions in goods or merchandise are classified as *visible* items. In general, goods and services exported by the domestic economy are a part of the national output, but goods and services imported constitute a form of disposition of the national income. There are exceptions to this principle, but they are for the most part of minor significance.[3]

The difference between the export (or credit) items and the import (or debit) items in the current account represents its net balance. If the credit transactions exceed the debit transactions, it is customary to de-

---

[2] For a more extended discussion of the mechanics of balance-of-payments accounting see Charles P. Kindleberger, *International Economics,* third ed. (Homewood, Ill., Irwin, 1963), Chapter 2.

[3] *Ibid.,* p. 29.

scribe the current account balance as *active*. On the other hand, an excess of debit over credit transactions is usually spoken of as a *passive* balance on the current account. In Chapter 2 we pointed out that the net foreign investment component of the national output (GNP) can be *approximately* defined as the net difference between a nation's exports of goods and services and its imports of goods and services,[4] because any excess of receipts from exports over payments for imports—or vice versa—reflects a net change in the international asset position of the nation concerned. The word "approximately" is emphasized because the Department of Commerce defines net foreign investment as the difference between exports and imports *plus* transfer payments to foreign residents.

THE GOLD ACCOUNT

The gold account in the balance-of-payments statement records transactions involving monetary gold. The term *monetary gold* refers to gold that is being used internationally as a medium of exchange. A nation, for example, that has a deficit in its current account transactions must obtain the necessary amount of foreign exchange (i.e., foreign money) to finance the deficit, and may do this through the sale (or export) of gold. Since gold is almost universally accepted by nations in the settlement of international balances, any country can obtain nearly any type of foreign exchange via gold exports. The export of gold for monetary purposes is recorded as a credit entry in the nation's balance-of-payments statement. Conversely, the import of monetary gold is a debit item.

THE CAPITAL ACCOUNT

The capital account represents, in a sense, the financial counterpart of transactions involving currently-produced goods and services that are recorded in the current acccount. If we ignore for a moment the role of monetary gold in the settlement of international balances, we can discern the nature of the capital account more clearly. Let us assume, for example, that a nation has in the current income period an excess of exports (of goods and services) over imports. Since exports generate payment claims against foreign residents and imports generate payment claims by foreigners against domestic residents, it can readily be seen that the export surplus increases the claims of the domestic economy against the rest of the world. An import surplus would, of course, have just the opposite effect. Within the context of the current income period, settlement of the net export surplus can be effected in a number of ways. Foreigners, for example, may borrow the needed funds from residents of the domestic economy. If this is done, there will be a net increase in the foreign claims or internationally-held assets of residents of the domestic economy. A transaction of this type is called a *capital export*, and in the

[4] Chapter 2, p. 43.

balance-of-payments statement of the domestic economy it is recorded as a debit item since it provides foreign residents with the means to make payments to residents of the domestic economy. Alternatively, it is possible that foreign residents may finance the aforementioned export surplus of the domestic economy by drawing down bank balances they may hold in the banks of the domestic economy. If this is done, it means there has been a *net decrease* in the liabilities owed by domestic residents to foreign residents because a bank deposit is a liability of the bank.

The capital account section of the balance-of-payments statement basically reflects the net change during the accounting period in the claims and liabilities (real and financial) of the domestic economy *vis-à-vis* the rest of the world. But this net change can take the form of a capital export, an increase in claims (or decrease in the liabilities) of domestic residents relative to foreign residents; conversely, it can take the form of a capital import, a decrease in the claims (or increase in the liabilities) of domestic residents relative to foreign residents.

The Balance of Payments and Equilibrium

As an accounting instrument, the balance-of-payments statement must necessarily be in balance; for every credit entry there has to be an offsetting debit entry. But this does not mean that an *equilibrium* exists with respect to a nation's international economic position. While there is no clear-cut method of determining economic equilibrium with respect to a nation's international payments position, Professor Charles P. Kindleberger defines equilibrium as "that state of the balance of payments over the relevant time period which makes it possible to sustain an open economy without severe unemployment on a continuing basis." [5] International finance specialists interpret this definition to mean that a nation is "paying its way" internationally, which is to say that it is obtaining sufficient foreign exchange on a sustainable basis to meet its needs to make payments abroad. Normally a nation obtains foreign exchange through its exports or by borrowing abroad on a long-term basis. But increasingly since World War II, grants by governments and international agencies have become important as sources for certain currencies, particularly the dollar. Disequilibrium in a nation's balance of payments implies a condition that is not sustainable; one or more items in either the current account or capital account must undergo change if an equilibrium condition is to be restored, and this can affect income and employment levels in the domestic economy.

The current account is the most significant section of the balance-of-payments statement for determining how international economic transactions affect income and employment levels within the domestic economy. A nation's exports and imports of goods and services are linked

[5] Kindleberger, *op. cit.*, p. 501.

directly to its national output and income, and thus become the means by which changes in the nation's international economic position are transmitted to the domestic economy. Transactions that are reflected in either the gold or the capital account may, of course, affect the domestic economy just as do current account transactions, but their impact is mirrored in the current account.

Changes in any of the three basic accounts that make up the balance-of-payments statement may be described as either autonomous or induced. An *autonomous* change in the current account is one that is not the consequence of a change in either the gold or capital account; an *induced* change in the current account is one that does follow from a change in either the gold or capital account. For example, a nation may find as a result of events abroad that its exports increase, and an export surplus develops in the current account. If imports remain unchanged, then this development requires an offsetting transaction in either the gold or the capital account. This offsetting transaction, which will take the form of an import of gold or an outflow of capital, is properly described as *induced* because it is a consequence of a change that has already taken place in the current account. On the other hand, a nation may undertake lending operations abroad (i. e., a capital export) quite independently of any current account developments. If such *autonomous* capital transactions take place, they must be followed by offsetting transactions in either the current or the gold account. In this event, changes in the current account would be of an induced nature. From an examination of the statistical data contained in a balance-of-payments statement it is not always possible to determine whether the recorded changes are autonomous or induced, but these concepts are nonetheless useful for economic analysis.

Exports, Imports, and the Structure of Aggregate Demand

To analyze the manner in which exports and imports of goods and services fit into the structure of aggregate demand, let us begin by a review of the basic identity equations appropriate to an "open" economy. In an open economy exports of goods and services enter directly into the aggregate demand function because they represent the portion of the demand for the national output that originates abroad. The demand for a nation's exports, X, is as much a part of the demand for its output as is the demand for consumption goods and services, C, investment goods, I, or social goods, G. Thus, in an open economic system the origin and component parts of the net national output can be summed up in the following identity equation: [6]

$$Y_{np} = C + I + G + X - M \qquad (10\text{-}1)$$

[6] See the earlier discussion on identities in Chapter 2, p. 45.

What determines the level of exports for a nation? We shall not try to answer this question wholly at this point, but only make the assumption that expenditures for exports are autonomous with respect to output and employment levels in the domestic economy. This is not an unrealistic assumption, although we shall need to modify it later in the analysis. Since export expenditures constitute demand for domestic output that originates outside the nation, their level will not be significantly affected by changes in the domestic income and employment levels. Thus the export function may be shown as a horizontal line, as in Figure 10–1.

A nation's imports of goods and services do not represent expenditure for any part of the domestic or national output, but they do repre-

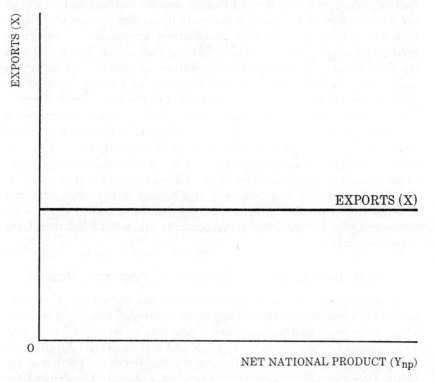

Figure 10–1. The Export Function

sent a form of disposition of the money income created as a consequence of current productive activity—specifically, the part of the domestic income that is directed toward the purchase of the output of other nations. In this sense, imports are a form of leakage from the domestic income stream and analogous in their economic effects to saving and taxes.

With respect to the level of imports, M, we are on somewhat surer ground than with exports. Since imports are a form of disposition of domestic income, the most reasonable hypothesis that we can advance at this point is that the level of imports of a nation is basically a function of the general level of economic activity within the nation. More specifically, this means that imports are presumed to be a function of the income level, as in the following equation:

$$M = f(Y_{np}) \qquad (10\text{--}2)$$

In most societies an important share of the import total will consist of consumer goods and services. Given this, we would expect a society's expenditures on imported consumption goods to rise as its income level rises. Equation 10–3 is therefore nothing more than an extension of consumption theory to the situation of an open economy. Beyond this it is not unreasonable to expect that expenditures for imported goods which enter into the investment and government expenditures components of aggregate demand will rise along with rising levels of income and employment.

Since imports are analogous in their economic effects to saving and taxes, it follows that the import-income relationship can be expressed as a schedule. This is done in Figure 10–2. Income is shown on the horizontal axis; and imports on the vertical axis. For the sake of simplicity the import function, $M = f(Y)$, is presented as a straight line, although in reality the relationship between imports and the national income is not necessarily linear. The point at which the import function crosses the vertical axis indicates the amount of expenditures on imports at a zero income level. This, of course, is primarily a theoretical rather than a practical proposition. Algebraically the import function may be defined as:

$$M = M_o + mY_{np} \qquad (10\text{--}3)$$

The technical attributes of this function are conceptually similar to those associated with both the consumption and the saving function. M_o represents import expenditures at zero income. The ratio between the level of imports, M, and the level of income, Y, at any and all possible income levels is the *average propensity to import*. This ratio shows the proportion of any given income level that is being spent for imported goods and services. Like the average propensity to consume and its counterpart, the average propensity to save, the ratio M/Y will vary as the income level varies. The ratio of a change in imports, ΔM, to a change in the income level, ΔY, is the *marginal propensity to import*. This ratio measures the slope of the import function (as shown in Figure 10–2) and

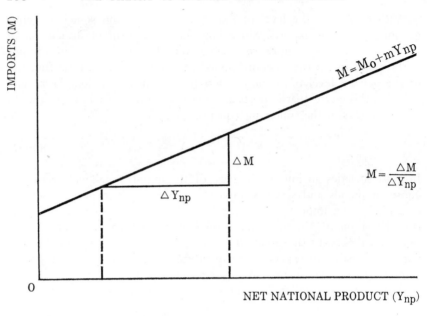

Figure 10–2. The Import Function

indicates how (in percentage terms) imports will vary as the income level shifts. From the standpoint of the impact of changes in the export-import balance on the level of income and employment in the domestic economy, the marginal propensity to import, m, is a vital concept.

The Income Equilibrium in an Open Economy

The determination of the equilibrium income level in an open economy is essentially a matter of fitting both exports and imports into the kind of analytical structure that we have developed in earlier chapters. In Table 10–1 are found data pertaining to a hypothetical economy. These data are similar to those in Chapter 9, except that now included is a column representing the value of the economy's exports. For the moment we shall assume that imports are zero. The export figures shown in Column (6) are the same for all income levels because of the autonomous nature of exports relative to the net national product. Investment and government purchases of goods and services are the same as in Table 9–3, while the consumption function is drawn from Table 9–6. The aggregate demand function for this hypothetical—and open—economy is obtained by adding the stated values for investment, government expenditures, and exports to consumption at each indicated level of the net national product. This result is shown in Column (7). Given this aggregate demand schedule, we find that the equilibrium income level for this open system is $600 billion. The reader should observe that Table 10–1 also contains an aggregate demand schedule for a closed economic system—that is, no exports or imports. This is shown in Column (5). In the absence of exports the equilibrium level of the net national product is $550 billion. The upward shift of the aggregate demand function by $20 billions—the amount of the exports—has the effect of increasing the equilibrium value of the net national product by $50 billion. Thus, a change in the foreign balance can exercise a multiplier effect upon the domestic economy. We shall discuss shortly the operation and value of the multiplier in an open system.

TABLE 10–1.

Exports, Aggregate Demand, and Equilibrium Income
(in billions of dollars)

(1) Net National Product Y_{np}	(2) Consumption * C''	(3) Investment I	(4) Government Expenditures G	(5) Aggregate Demand $(C'' + I + G)$	(6) Exports X	(7) Aggregate Demand $(C'' + I + G + X)$
0	80	40	100	220	20	240
350	255	75	100	430	20	450
400	280	80	100	460	20	480
450	305	85	100	490	20	510
500	330	90	100	520	20	540
550	355	95	100	550	20	570
600	380	100	100	580	20	600
650	405	105	100	610	20	630
700	430	110	100	640	20	660
750	455	115	100	670	20	690
800	480	120	100	700	20	720

* From Table 9–6, Chapter 9.

The process of income determination is shown graphically in Figure 10–3. The aggregate demand schedule, DD, now includes exports, X, as well as the other components of output included heretofore. As in our previous analysis, the income equilibrium is determined at the point of intersection of the aggregate demand, DD, and aggregate supply, OZ, functions. This, according to the figure, is an income level of $600 billion. Given the position of the aggregate demand schedule, it is the only possible income level at which our *four* major expenditure categories will add up to an amount equal to aggregate supply.

For simplicity's sake we assumed in the foregoing example that imports were zero. We can now make our hypothetical model more realistic by introducing an import function into the analysis. This is done in Table 10–2, in which the import function is shown in Column (5). In our ex-

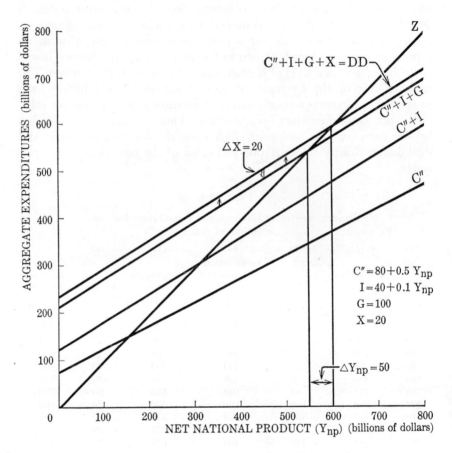

Figure 10-3. Exports and Aggregate Demand

ample imports, M, are equal to $3 billion plus $0.02\ Y_{np}$. M_o, in other words, is equal to $3 billion and the marginal propensity to import, m, equals two per cent (0.02). The aggregate demand function now becomes the sum of the four expenditure categories contained in Table 10–2 *less* imports $(C'' + I + G + X - M)$. This new aggregate demand schedule is shown in Column (6) of Table 10–2. Since imports constitute, in effect, a "leakage" of income from the domestic income stream, the effect of the introduction of an import function is to lower over-all the level of the aggregate demand function. A comparison of the data in Tables 10–1 and 10–2 will show that at each possible value for aggregate supply—Column (1) in each table—aggregate demand is less in Table 10–2 than it is in Table 10–1.

The data of Table 10–2 are plotted in Figure 10–4. A comparison of

TABLE 10–2.

Exports, Imports, Aggregate Demand, and Equilibrium Income
(in billions of dollars)

(1)	(2)	(3)	(4)	(5)	(6)
Net National Product Y_{np}	Consump-tion * C''	Investment and Government Expenditure $I + G$	Exports X	Imports † M	Aggregate Demand $(C'' + I + G + X - M)$
0	80	140	20	3	237
350	255	175	20	10	440
400	280	180	20	11	469
450	305	185	20	12	498
500	330	190	20	13	527
550	355	195	20	14	556
600	380	200	20	15	585
650	405	205	20	16	614
700	430	210	20	17	643
750	455	215	20	18	672
800	480	220	20	19	701

* Same as Table 10–1.
† $M = 3 + 0.02 \, Y_{np}$.

this diagram with Figure 10–3 shows clearly that the introduction of the import function shifts the level of aggregate demand function below the position given by the data of Table 10–1. The equilibrium level of net national product is now $564 billion rather than $600 billion. (See the Appendix to this chapter for the algebraic formula for determination of the income level in an open economy.)

The equilibrium level of the net national product in our open system can also be explained in terms of schedules which represent *ex ante* values for expenditures other than consumption (investment, government purchases of goods and services, and exports), and "leakages" out of the domestic income stream (saving, net taxes, and imports). Equilibrium exists at the point at which these expenditures $(I + G + X)$ just offset the leakages from the current income stream $(S + T + M)$. The sum of the expenditures items $(I + G + X)$ is shown in Column (2) of Table 10–3 and the sum of leakages $(S + T + M)$ is given in Column (3) of the same table. Equality between the two exists at the $564 billion level of the net national product. Individual schedules for each of these variables are plotted and summed in Figure 10–5, which depicts graphically the determination of the equilibrium level of the net national product in terms of the schedule values for $(I + G + X)$ and $(S + T + M)$. Income equilibrium requires that *ex ante* values for all leakages be offset by *ex ante* expenditures. At any level of the net national product at

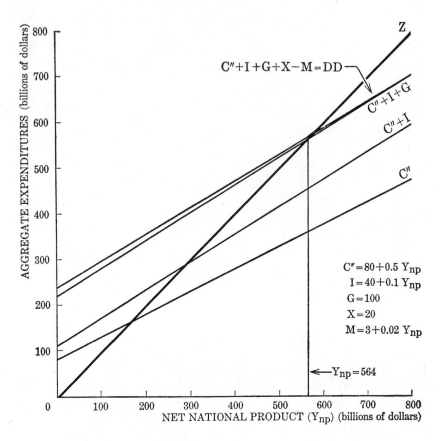

Figure 10–4. Exports, Imports, and Aggregate Demand

which $(S + T + M)$ is greater than $(I + G + X)$, aggregate supply will be in excess of aggregate demand, and output will fall. If the reverse situation prevails, output and employment will rise.

Foreign Trade and the Multiplier

An important implication of the preceding analysis is that income equilibrium in an open economy also means that equilibrium exists in the nation's balance-of-payments situation. Equilibrium in the nation's international economic position does not require that exports and imports be exactly in balance, but it does require that any surplus or deficit in the current account balance be offset by appropriate and sustainable capital transactions. In equilibrium, in other words, the nation's international economic position *will not be undergoing change*. A change in a nation's international payments position will affect the export-import balance directly or indirectly. When this happens the position of the aggregate demand function will be altered. As we know from our previous study, a change in the position of the aggregate demand schedule will have a multiplier effect upon the income and employment levels

TABLE 10-3.

Equilibrium of $(I + G + X)$ and $(S + T + M)$
(in billions of dollars)

(1) Net National Product Y_{np}	(2) Investment, Government Expenditures, and Exports $(I + G + X)$	(3) Saving, Net Taxes, and Imports $(S + T + M)$
0	160	− 77
350	195	105
400	200	131
450	205	157
500	210	183
556	215	209
564	**217**	**217**
600	220	235
650	225	261
700	230	287
750	235	303
800	240	339

within the domestic economy. Since a change in the current account balance will affect the position of the aggregate demand function, there will be a multiplier effect associated with such a change. Some writers prefer to talk of the *foreign trade* multiplier when discussing this phenomenon, but actually what is involved is nothing more than the application of the general theory of the multiplier to shifts in the aggregate demand function which have their origin in a change in the nation's international economic position. We saw in Table 10–1 that an autonomous increase in exports in the amount of $20 billion led to an ultimate increase in the net national product of $50 billion.

To derive algebraically the multiplier in an open system, let us begin, as in Chapter 9, with our basic definition of the effective multiplier, k'. This is

$$k' = \frac{\Delta Y_{np}}{\Delta D} \qquad (10\text{--}4)$$

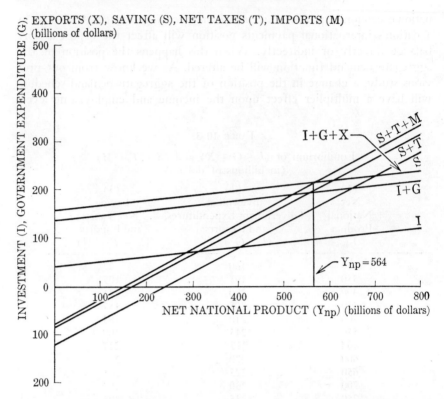

Figure 10-5. Equilibrium of $(I + G + X)$ and $(S + T + M)$

In an open economy it follows from Equation (10–1) that

$$\Delta Y_{np} = \Delta C + \Delta I + \Delta G + \Delta X - \Delta M \qquad (10\text{–}5)$$

By substitution we then have

$$\Delta Y_{np} = a'\Delta Y_{np} + b\Delta Y_{np} + \Delta G + \Delta X - m\Delta Y_{np} \qquad (10\text{–}6)$$

If we assume that $\Delta G = O$, we then have

$$\Delta X = \Delta Y_{np} - a'\Delta Y_{np} - b\Delta Y_{np} + m\Delta Y_{np} \qquad (10\text{–}7)$$
$$\Delta X = \Delta Y_{np}(1 - a' - b + m) \qquad (10\text{–}8)$$

Since the change in aggregate demand ΔD is the same as the change in exports ΔX, we can substitute the right-hand portion of Equation (10–8) for ΔD in Equation (10–4). We thus get

$$k' = \frac{\Delta Y_{np}}{\Delta Y_{np}(1 - a' - b + m)} = \frac{1}{(1 - a' - b + m)} \qquad (10\text{–}9)$$

Equation (10–9) gives us the value of the multiplier in an open system. It includes, the reader should note, not only the marginal propensity to import, but also the marginal propensity to tax. The latter is the case because $a' = (a - at)$. By further substitution we can define the multiplier in an open system as

$$k' = \frac{1}{(1 - a + at - b + m)} \qquad (10\text{–}10)$$

Graphic Illustrations of the Multiplier in an Open System

Figure 10–6 depicts the effects on the net national product and imports that result from an autonomous change in exports. We assume a simplified economy which has neither investment and saving, nor government expenditures and taxes. In such a system the necessary condition for equilibrium is that exports *ex ante* and imports *ex ante* be equal, because only when they are equal will leakages represented by imports, M, be just offset by expenditures originating outside the economy, i.e., exports, X. In Figure 10–6 the equilibrium income level is determined by the intersection of the schedule of *ex ante* exports (depicted by the lower horizontal line) and the import function, $M = M_o + mY_{np}$. At this income level exports and imports are in balance.

A shift upward in the export function from X to the new level X' causes a movement of the equilibrium net national product from Y_{np} to Y_{np}'. The magnitude of this change depends upon the value of the multiplier, which in this instance is determined solely by the value of the marginal propensity to import, m. The important point to note is that as the multiplier process works itself out and the income level rises, the volume of imports will also continue to rise. This is true because we have assumed a positive value for the marginal propensity to import. In our hypothetical system, in which there are no leakages other than expenditures for imports, the import level will have to continue to rise until once again it is equal to the volume of exports. The autonomous increase in exports disturbed a pre-existing balance in the current account of our hypothetical economy, but the increase in income that was generated by the change in exports induced a sufficient rise in imports to

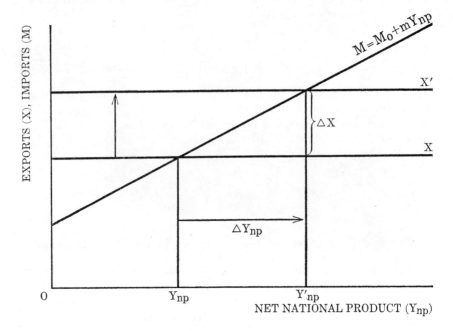

Figure 10–6. Foreign Trade and the Multiplier
(I, G, S, and T omitted)

restore the export-import balance. At the new equilibrium income level, exports and imports are once again in balance. Changes in the opposite direction would, of course, take place if the economy experienced a decline in exports.

A more realistic picture results if we reintroduce both investment and saving as well as government expenditures and taxes into the analysis. This is done in Figure 10–7. The initial income equilibrium Y_{np} is at the point of intersection of the $I + G + X$ schedule and the $S + T + M$ schedule. The diagram is so drawn that at the initial equilibrium income level exports X and imports M are in balance, although the reader should note that this does not necessarily have to be the case. From the stand-point of the income equilibrium all that is required is that $I + G + X$ ex ante be just equal to $S + T + M$ ex ante, not that I be exactly offset by S, G be exactly offset by T, or X be exactly offset by M.

Let us examine the impact on the economy of an increase in exports. This change will shift the entire $I + G + X$ schedule upward. The new position of the schedule is given in Figure 10–7 by the line labeled $I + G + X'$. The increase in exports, ΔX, will, via the multiplier process, drive income to the new and higher equilibrium level of Y_{np}'. The rise

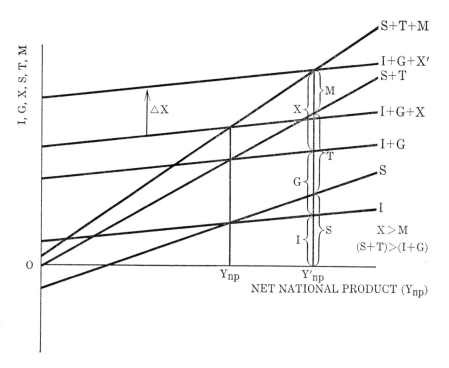

Figure 10–7. Foreign Trade and the Multiplier
(I, G, S, and T included)

in the income level brought about by the increase in exports also induces in this instance not only an increase in imports, but additional saving and taxes as well. At the new and higher income equilibrium Y_{np}', the sum of $I + G + X$ is again in balance with the sum of $S + T + M$. Imports have not risen sufficiently to restore balance in the nation's international accounts because leakages in the form of both taxes and saving also rise as the income level rises. The amount by which exports and imports differ at the new and higher income level will be just offset by the difference between domestic investment and saving or government expenditures and taxes, or both. Since $X > M$, then $S + T$ must be greater than $I + G$ by a like amount.

The Foreign-Repercussion Effect

Up to this point we have not been concerned with the impact of a change in the international balance of the domestic economy upon foreign economies. This is a possibility that must be considered because the imports of one nation are the exports of another. Consequently, the levels of income and employment in different economies may be linked together through their international economic transactions. The possibility that a change in the international economic position of the domestic economy can have repercussions abroad which in turn reverberate back to the domestic economy is described as the *foreign-repercussion effect*. Such an effect exists only when the economy of one nation is relatively large as compared to the economy of other nations. Changes in the balance-of-payments position of a very small nation are not likely to affect significantly the income and employment levels of other nations. However, a change in the imports of the United States, for example, could significantly affect the national income of one or more countries because of the sheer size of the American economy.

The nature of the foreign-repercussion effect can readily be described. For the sake of simplicity in the analysis we shall assume only two countries. We shall call the domestic economy A, the foreign economy B. Let us assume, first, that there is an autonomous shift upward in the investment demand schedule in A. This will start the usual multiplier sequence in motion and bring with it not only an increase in income, but also induce additional imports as well as saving and taxes. For our present purposes the important point is that the rise in income in the domestic economy, A, will cause imports to rise as well. The sequence of events is as follows:

$$\Delta I_A \longrightarrow \Delta Y_A \longrightarrow \Delta M_A$$

The foreign repercussion is concerned primarily with the effect that this change has on income and employment levels in the domestic economy. The increase in imports in A consequent to the increase in A's income is, given our assumption of only two countries, the same thing as an increase in the exports of B. But if B experiences an increase in its exports, its domestic income and employment level will be affected by the foreign-trade multiplier. Further, the increase in income in B can be expected to increase its imports as well. Thus, for country B the sequence of events will be

$$\Delta X_B \longrightarrow \Delta Y_B \longrightarrow \Delta M_B$$

The above increase in B's imports will reverberate back to the economy of A and cause its income to rise *more* than would be the case if domestic investment alone had changed. More exports by A will further stimulate its economy. The economy of A is linked to the economy of B through its exports; in identical fashion the economy of B is linked to the economy of A.

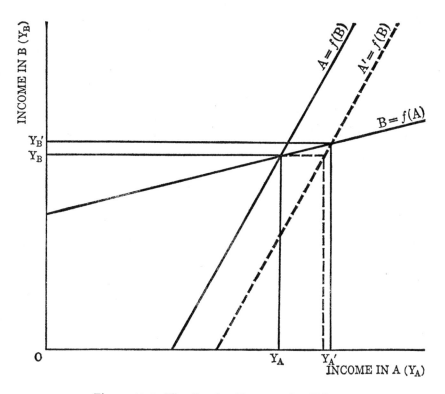

Figure 10–8. The Foreign-Repercussion Effect

The essential character of the foreign-repercussion effect can be demonstrated by a relatively simple geometric diagram such as Figure 10–8.[7] The income of the domestic economy, A, is shown on the horizontal axis; the income of the foreign economy, B, on the vertical axis. The curve $A = f(B)$, which slopes upward to the right, shows how the income level of A will vary directly with changes in the income level in B. The position of the curve depends on the strength of the other determinants of income within the domestic economy, such as domestic investment, government expenditures, and the consumption function. The curve $B = f(A)$ shows the same thing for the foreign economy, that is, the manner in which the income level in B will vary with changes in the income level in A.

The point of intersection of the two schedules represents a condition of equilibrium with respect to the income levels of the two nations and their trade and payments relationships with each other. At this point

[7] Romney Robinson, "A Graphical Analysis of the Foreign Trade Multiplier," *Economic Journal*, September, 1952, pp. 546–64.

neither the international payment position nor the income level of A or B shows any disposition to change. There is equilibrium in both nations. The foreign repercussion is demonstrated in the diagram through a shift to the right in the schedule representing the income level in A. The new position of the schedule for A is: $A' = f(B)$. The shift is the result of a change in any of the internal determinants of the income level in A, such as a shift upward in either the investment or government expenditures component of the aggregate demand function. The effect of this is to move the equilibrium income level upward in both A and B, from Y_A to Y_A' in A, and from Y_B to Y_B' in B. The nature of the foreign-repercussion effect is indicated by the fact that in the domestic economy the change in income from Y_A to Y_A' is greater than the difference between old schedule $A = f(B)$ and new schedule $A' = f(B)$. The amount of the change in income in the economy of A that is due solely to *internal* factors is indicated in the figure by the distance from Y_A to the dotted line.

What determines the size or significance of the foreign-repercussion effect? Since it involves the relationship between exports and the national income of the countries involved, the size of the foreign-repercussion effect is determined largely by those factors that influence the size of the foreign-trade multiplier. For example, the smaller the marginal propensities to save, tax (net), and import in the domestic economy, the larger will be the foreign-repercussion effect. When these marginal propensities are small, the multiplier is large; thus the effect on the domestic income level of any given change in exports will be considerable. In the foreign economy a high marginal propensity to import will, *ceteris paribus*, make for a greater foreign-repercussion effect in the domestic economy, although this lowers the value of the multiplier effect abroad. On the other hand, if the marginal propensities to save, tax, and import are low abroad, this will raise the value of the multiplier in the foreign nation and thus cause income to rise quite rapidly as a result of an increase in its exports. But for this increase in income abroad to reverberate back to the domestic economy to any significant degree requires a high value for the marginal propensity to import in the foreign economy. Thus, from the standpoint of the foreign nation no simple generalization concerning the factors making for a strong foreign-repercussion effect in the domestic economy is possible.

Income Changes and the Balance of Payments

Our analysis has been largely directed toward the effect of a change in the balance-of-payments position on income and employment levels in the domestic economy. Before we conclude this chapter, however, it is appropriate that we look at the other side of the coin and analyze briefly how internal changes in the income level may affect a nation's international payments position.

Income equilibrium in an open economy may be defined in terms of an equality between $I + G + X$ *ex ante* and $S + T + M$ *ex ante*. For the sake of simplicity let us assume that government expenditure, G, and net taxes, T, are equal (and therefore eliminate them from the foregoing equality). Thus, in our equilibrium condition, $I + X = S + M$. Transposing the terms in this equation, we get the following:

$$X - M = S - I \qquad (10\text{--}11)$$

The meaning of the above equation is that *ex ante* the current account balance must be equal to the difference between saving and investment if an income equilibrium is to exist. Since the values that we have been discussing in this context are *ex ante* in nature, we can express $X - M$ and $S - I$ in the form of schedules that link both of these to the income level. This is done in Figure 10–9.[8] Net national product is measured on the horizontal axis; the *net* differences between exports and imports, $X - M$, and between saving and investment, $S - I$, are measured on the

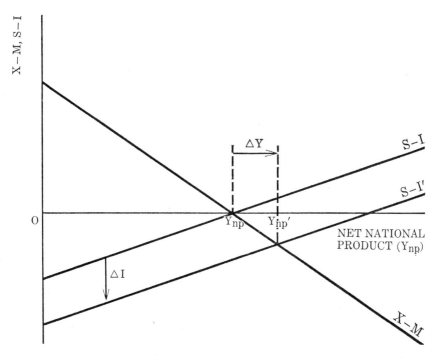

Figure 10–9. Income Changes and the Foreign Balance

[8] Kindleberger, *op cit.*, p. 190.

vertical axis. The $X - M$ schedule slopes downward to the right because even though the level of exports is presumed to be autonomous with respect to the domestic income level, the level of imports will rise as the domestic income level rises. Thus, as the economy moves from a lower to a higher income level, the export-import balance will shift from a positive to a negative value. The $S - I$ schedule slopes upward to the right because saving increases as the income level rises at a rate greater than investment.

To illustrate the impact of a change in domestic income on the balance of payments, let us start the analysis with a balanced position in the nation's international accounts. This is shown in Figure 10–9 at the income level Y_{np}. The $X - M$ curve and the $S - I$ curve intersect so that the net difference between exports and imports, $X - M$, and saving and investment, $S - I$, is zero. Thus the current account is in balance. The effect on the domestic income level as well as the balance of trade of an increase in the level of autonomous investment is depicted by a shift downward in the $S - I$ schedule.[9] The new and higher equilibrium income level occurs at Y_{np}', a point determined by the intersection of schedule $X - M$ and the new and lower schedule $S - I'$. The point of intersection of these two schedules now lies below zero on the vertical axis, which means that $X - M$ is now negative, or that imports exceed exports. We can therefore conclude that a change in the domestic income level—in this instance an increase—has induced an increase in imports sufficient to cause an adverse balance to develop in the nation's balance of payments. Our analysis ignores the foreign-repercussion effect which would shift the $X - M$ schedule upward, thus raising the income level even more, but reducing the balance-of-payments deficit.

The preceding discussion of the impact of a change in the domestic income level on the balance-of-payments position has been worked out on the assumption of an increase in the income level, leading to a worsening of the export-import balance. This, of course, is not the only possibility, as study of Figure 10–9 will reveal. The income level may fall, for example, as a result of a shift upward in the saving function. This will raise the $S - I$ curve, and cause it to intersect with the $X - M$ curve at a lower income level. This change, on the assumption that the foreign-repercussion effect can be ignored, will lead to an export surplus in the current account. In reality, though, it is unlikely that such a surplus could be maintained for long because the decline in imports will have repercussions abroad which are likely to be felt in the domestic economy. In this instance, the foreign repercussion would take the form of a shift downward in the $X - M$ schedule that would further lower the domestic income

---

[9] The reason for this is that at every income level, $(S - I)$ will be less than it was prior to the increase in autonomous investment. This presumes, of course, that the saving function is unchanged.

level.

Starting from a balanced international position, an increase in the domestic income level will, *ceteris paribus*, lead to a current account deficit and weaken the nation's international payments position. If the current account deficit can be financed on a sustaining basis, no serious problem results. If not, the disequilibrium in the nation's international accounts may sooner or later force a downward adjustment in the domestic income level. What will happen if, starting from a balanced international position, the domestic income level falls? Precisely the opposite of what we have just described.

A Summary Comment

In this and the four preceding chapters our concern has been with analysis of the component parts of the economy's structure of aggregate demand. As was stressed in Chapter 5, the central thesis of modern employment theory is that in the short run, when the economy's capacity to produce is relatively fixed, the key to both the income and employment level is demand for the economy's whole output or, more simply, aggregate demand. Expectation of demand leads to the creation of output —and income. Thus, if we can analyze what determines the level of demand for the output of the whole economy, we learn something about the determination of income and employment.

As a result of theoretical developments stemming from the work of Keynes and of advances in the field of national income accounting, it is possible to identify the four major components of the economy's aggregate demand structure: consumption, investment, government purchases of goods and services, and the export-import balance. Our purpose has been not only to tie these four forms of demand together into a single integrated structure representing the demand for the economy's total output, but to analyze, too, the determinants of the level of each of these individual parts of the aggregate demand function. Moreover, we have sought to show how changes in the income (and employment) level are linked to changes in the economy's aggregate demand function, and how changes in this function are the result of shifts in any or all of its component parts.

APPENDIX

Algebraic determination of the income level in an open economy

(1) $Y_{np} = C + I + G + X - M$ = the basic identity
(2) $C = C_o' + a'Y_{np}$ = the consumption function
(3) $I = I_o' + bY_{np}$ = the investment function

(4) $M = M_o + mY_{np} =$ the import function

(5) $Y_{np} = C_o' + a'Y_{np} + I_o' + bY_{np} + G + X - M_o - mY_{np}$

(6) $Y_{np} - a'Y_{np} - bY_{np} + mY_{np} = (C_o' + I_o' + G + X - M_o)$

(7) $Y_{np} (1 - a' - b + m) = (C_o' + I_o' + G + X - M_o)$

(8) $Y_{np} = \dfrac{1}{(1 - a' - b + m)} (C_o' + I_o' + G + X - M_o)$

11 | The Theory of Money and Interest

Our objective in this chapter is to examine the vital role money plays in the determination of income and employment levels in modern society. In earlier chapters we did not accord money any special significance because its chief function in the analysis was to serve as a unit for measurement of economic activity. In this chapter, however, we shall view money as an economic force in its own right, which under certain circumstances may powerfully affect economic activity.

The view that money possesses certain peculiar attributes which may be distinguished from its role as a medium of exchange can largely be traced back to the thinking of John Maynard Keynes. In an essay prior to the *General Theory*, Keynes developed the outline of the "theory of a monetary economy." This is the theory of an economy in which money is more than simply a device for facilitating the real economic process of production and exchange. In a "monetary economy," according to Keynes, "money plays a part of its own and affects motives and decisions and is, in short, one of the operative factors in the situation, so that the course of events cannot be predicted, either in the long period or in the short, without a knowledge of the behavior of money between the first state and the last." [1] In such a world money is not a neutral phenomenon, as Keynes argued was true of the classical theory, but rather a phenomenon governed by principles very different from those that hold sway over the process of production and exchange.

[1] Quoted in Kenneth K. Kurihara, ed., *Post-Keynesian Economics* (New Brunswick, N.J., Rutgers University Press, 1954), p. 6. This essay is reprinted in the *Nebraska Journal of Economics and Business*, Autumn, 1963.

In modern income and employment analysis there are two "spheres" of economic activity. There is, on the one hand, the "real" or "goods" sphere of activity, which has to do with the forces of aggregate demand and supply and the conditions under which an equilibrium of output and employment is achieved. On the other hand, there is the "monetary" sphere in which the economic forces at work are those centering around the demand for money. These forces are subject to principles of behavior quite different from those that govern activity in the economy's "goods" sector. According to the contemporary view, the existence of a separate "monetary" sphere of activity is a fact of profound significance; what takes place in the monetary sphere may suddenly and dramatically influence the level of both output and employment.

The method by which Keynes introduces money into the operation of the economy is through development of a theory of interest in which the demand for money is dominant. The rate of interest [2] is the link between the real sphere and the monetary sphere. It is the factor around which the theory of investment is constructed, and investment outlays comprise one of the strategic determinants of the level of income and employment. In the opinion of Keynes, interest is a monetary phenomenon which must be related to the demand for and the supply of money. It is not, as the classical economists believed, a "price" which equates the demand for and supply of saving.[3]

Our main purpose in this chapter is to develop the basically Keynesian theory of the interest rate as a means of showing how money enters into determination of income and employment levels. It is appropriate to stress at this point that there is by no means universal agreement among economists that Keynesian analysis is the only acceptable approach to an explanation of the phenomenon of interest. In the appendix to this chapter we shall consider the most important alternative theory of interest rate determination and show how it is related to the Keynesian analysis.[4]

Before we take up interest theory proper, it will be useful to consider some of the essential characteristics of money, following this with a brief review of classical ideas on the role money plays in the operation of the economy.

---

[2] It is an oversimplification to talk of "the rate of interest," for in actuality there is not a single interest rate in the economy, but a whole series of different rates. It is meaningful to speak in generalized terms about "the rate of interest." The reader should remember, though, that such a term really refers to the entire structure of interest rates characteristic of the modern economy.

[3] Chapter 4, p. 98.

[4] Keynes' approach to the theory of interest is usually identified as the liquidity-preference theory; the most important alternative approach is described as the loanable-funds theory.

The Nature of Money

The fundamental characteristic of money is that it is a generalized *claim* that can be exercised against all other goods, services, and claims of whatever kind and irrespective of their origin. Thus the essential nature of money does not lie in the physical properties of whatever material substance may happen to fulfill the role of monetary exchange in a society at any particular time; it springs from the fact that the material substance in question is universally accepted as a generalized claim against all other things that possess economic value. The modern demand deposit, a major form of money in many highly-developed economic systems, can hardly be said to possess physical properties of value. It consists of nothing more than notations in the ledger of the bank, yet it is something that is almost universally accepted in payment for goods and services, or in the settlement of claims.

Given the nature of money as a generalized claim against all things or entities that possess economic value, it follows that money is the most *liquid* of all assets. *Liquidity* relates to the ease or convenience with which an asset can be converted from one form to another *without loss of value*. Money meets this requirement better than any other type of good or claim. Further, the costs of money are negligible as compared to the carrying costs that may be involved if one's assets are held in some other form.

Although money is the asset with the highest degree of liquidity, it suffers from the disadvantage that it does not yield its holder any return —as normally is the case with other kinds of assets. This is a matter of key importance in modern interest theory, as will become apparent in our analysis of interest-rate determination.

The Functions of Money

Economic analysis traditionally states that money performs four major functions. First, money serves as a *standard for the measurement of value*. Without some such standard it would be impossible to reduce the vast and heterogeneous activity of the modern economy to anything meaningful and comprehensible. Unfortunately, money is not a perfect measuring rod because its value will fluctuate as the general price level changes, although this defect can be compensated for (to some extent) by statistical techniques for eliminating the effect of price changes on our measurements.[5] Second, money acts as a *medium of exchange*. In this sense, money is extremely important to the efficient functioning of the economy, for without some medium which everyone is willing to accept in exchange for any good, service, or asset the economy would have to operate on a

[5] Chapter 3, pp. 62–66.

barter basis—and a barter system would be clumsy and inefficient. Third, money serves as a *store of value*. Since money is essentially a generalized claim to all forms of economic value, this means that economic value can be kept intact in the form of money over time. Of course, any claim or form of wealth that is not highly perishable can serve to store value over time, but money is best suited for performing this function. Finally, money can function as a *standard of deferred payments*. It is customary to measure a debt or promise for future payment in terms of money rather than some commodity or service.

Of the four functions of money we have outlined, the second and third —money as the medium of exchange and as a store of value—are most germane to the analysis in this chapter.

Alternatives to Money: Debt Instruments and Equity Instruments

In a broad sense, each form of wealth represents a claim against every other form of wealth for it is usually possible to convert items of wealth into money (through sale) and then reconvert the money into a different form of wealth (through purchase). The ease with which this can be accomplished without a loss of economic value varies widely, depending on the nature of the specific item of wealth in question. Of immediate significance to our analysis are certain financial instruments which are in the nature of claims, although of a less generalized character than money. One of the most important of these is the *debt instrument*. A debt instrument is any kind of a note that legally obligates an individual, a business firm, or a governmental unit to make repayment at some date of a sum borrowed. Normally most debt instruments are interest-bearing; the borrower agrees to pay to the lender a sum over and above the specific sum borrowed.

Two types of debt instruments are important to economic analysis. First, there is the *bill*, basically a short-term document (usually three months) which promises to pay a specific sum at a future date. The bill normally does not contain an explicit statement about interest; instead, interest is paid through the procedure of promising to pay a larger sum at the bill's maturity than the amount borrowed. This is called discounting. The lender, in effect, deducts the interest in advance. Treasury bills, which are short-term obligations of the U.S. Treasury, often are used by business firms as a form of wealth-holding for very short periods. Such bills are almost as liquid as money, and they have the advantage of yielding the holder a return in the form of interest.

The second form of debt instrument of special interest to us is the *bond*. Basically, the bond is a document that promises to pay to the holder (that is, the lender) a fixed sum of money as interest at stated intervals and repay the sum initially borrowed at a specific future date.[6] Bonds

---

[6] This is not true with the Savings Bonds issued by the U.S. Treasury. Bonds of this type, which are the kind most people are familiar with, do not entitle the holder

are considered as long-term debt instruments, because they normally have a life of more than one year. In actuality, most bonds are drawn for periods of from ten to twenty or more years.

In most developed economies active markets exist for the purchase and sale of debt instruments in the form of both bills and bonds. Through these markets the original holder may sell his debt instrument long before its date of maturity. Markets for the purchase and sale of debt instruments provide a supply of interest-bearing claims of various types for individuals and others seeking to hold wealth in relatively liquid form for short or long periods of time. These markets, in other words, make debt instruments relatively liquid alternatives to money as means for storing wealth. There is, of course, a risk involved in storing wealth in the form of debt instruments rather than money because the current market value of any debt instrument is subject to sudden and unpredictable changes. This fact has a vitally important bearing on contemporary interest theory.

A second financial claim that is important in economic analysis is the *equity instrument*. In contrast to a debt instrument, which involves a promise to pay, an equity instrument is a claim involving ownership of wealth. The most important type of equity instrument for our purposes is the *share*, or certificate of ownership in a joint-stock company. As most readers are aware, the *stock market* is the place in which equity instruments in the form of shares are bought and sold. In the modern economy, shares are easily acquired or disposed of because a ready market exists for them. But since the current market value of equities is probably even more volatile than that of debts, there is a definite risk element involved in holding equities in preference to money.

The Supply of Money

There must be an adequate supply of money in an economy to perform the four functions we have discussed. By the *supply of money* we mean essentially *the existing stock of all claims that are both acceptable in payment of debt and for goods and services and are used as a medium of exchange.*[7] Since we are dealing with a stock phenomenon, the existing supply of money must be held at all times by someone or something in the economy. This is a point of some significance in our analysis because it is necessary to make a distinction between the amount of money that is actually being held at a point in time and the amount that people and institutions may, for various reasons, *want* to hold. The amount held and the amount wanted do not necessarily coincide.

---

to receive interest at periodic intervals; rather interest is accumulated over the life of the bond and at the time it is cashed the holder receives back his orginal sum plus the accumulated interest.

[7] Lester V. Chandler, *The Economics of Money and Banking,* fourth ed. (New York, Harper, 1964), p. 14.

Deposit Money and Reserve Money

What types of exchange media constitute the economy's stock or supply of money? In modern societies the money supply consists of: (1) metallic coins, (2) paper money issued by governments, and (3) checking deposits or checkbook money.[8] Professor Alvin H. Hansen has suggested that the money supply can be classified into the two major categories of *deposit* (or commercial-bank) money, and *reserve* (or central-bank) money.[9] Deposit money consists primarily of demand deposits, although sometimes and for some purposes it may be desirable to include time deposits as a part of the money supply. Demand deposits are transferred by check and are thus "checkbook" money. Normally, this portion of the money supply grows when the assets of the commercial banks increase and shrinks when these assets decrease. Commercial-bank assets consist of cash, loans, and investments.[10] This portion of the money supply is in active circulation because it is held by the public or the Federal government. Reserve or central-bank money consists, in the United States, of Federal Reserve notes and the reserve balances of member banks. Federal Reserve notes are, of course, a part of the money supply in active circulation, but the reserve balances of member banks on deposit in the Federal Reserve Banks are not in circulation. While the money supply is generally interpreted to mean money actually in circulation, Hansen's idea of including the reserve balances of member banks in the concept of the money supply is useful for analysis of the impact of changes in the money supply on economic activity. Reserve money will fluctuate in accordance with changes in the assets of the central bank—primarily gold, government securities, and private securities in the form of discounts and advances to the commercial banks.

In income and employment analysis the money supply is considered an autonomous variable because the size of the economy's monetary stock is primarily determined by action taken by the central bank, and thus cannot be *related* functionally to the other variables in the income system. The key to the economy's money supply is the size of the reserves of the member banks. These reserves form the basis for demand deposit money, which, in the contemporary American economy, constitutes by far the largest portion of money in active circulation. Government influence on the money supply is largely achieved through the exercise of control over the reserves of the member banks. In the modern economy the central bank can control most of its own assets, and thereby the reserves of the commercial banks, through the "open" market purchase or sale of secur-

[8] *Ibid.,* pp. 50–61, for an explanation in greater detail of the different forms of money.

[9] Alvin H. Hansen, *Monetary Theory and Fiscal Policy* (New York, McGraw-Hill, 1949), pp. 28–32.

[10] *Ibid.,* p. 28.

ities or by variations in its discount policy. For this reason, Hansen finds it analytically useful to include the reserves of the commercial banks in his concept of the money supply, even though such reserves are not in active circulation. Governmental policies that aim at influencing the size of the money supply work largely through the reserve position of the commercial banks.

Monetary Equilibrium

Before we review the classical analysis of money and the economy, it is desirable to introduce the concept of monetary equilibrium. By now the reader is well aware that equilibrium as used in economic analysis refers to a situation that shows no disposition to change. We therefore define monetary equilibrium as a situation in which the amount of money in existence—the money currently being held by individuals, firms, or governments—is just equal to the amount that these entities *want* to hold. In short, monetary equilibrium exists when the demand for money is just equal to the current supply. Such a condition may or may not exist at any particular moment of time. When actual holdings and desired holdings are not in balance, we have *monetary disequilibrium*. The concept of monetary equilibrium or disequilibrium is essential to understand how money as a phenomenon in its own right may significantly influence the level of income and employment.

The Role of Money in Classical Theory

Classical thinking about money and its role is largely summed up in the quantity theory, which the reader will recall, is essentially a theory of price level determination.[11] Reduced to its simplest form, the quantity theory asserts that the general level of prices varies directly in proportion to the quantity of money.

Classical analysis focuses primarily on the medium-of-exchange function of money. People want money only as a means of facilitating the *real* process of exchanging goods for goods; they do not in any sense want to hold money as such. But if the only important function of money is that of a medium of exchange, and if too, money possesses no intrinsic characteristic which lead people to desire it for its own sake, then the only thing that can really be done with money is to pass it on as soon as possible through purchase of goods and services. The normal thing to do with money is to spend it.[12]

This view of money as something essentially neutral insofar as the

---

[11] Chapter 4, pp. 100–102.

[12] In the classical view, even if money is saved, it is spent in the sense that it is used to purchase some kind of an income-bearing asset such as a bond or share of stock. Money is simply not held as money.

economic process is concerned, together with the classical view of the economy's tendency toward full employment, provides the real explanation of the quantity theory. If money exists only to be spent, and if resources are normally fully employed, then any change in the quantity of money in circulation can only have an impact upon the general level of prices. In this simplified version of the quantity theory it is assumed that the velocity of circulation of the money supply is a constant. Only if this assumption is made does the more rigid version, in which the price level varies directly and *proportionally* to the money supply, hold good. It is not essential to the quantity theory that the velocity of money be assumed constant, but it is essential that the general price level vary *directly* with the quantity of money, even though the relationship between money and prices may not be one of strict proportionality.

A more elaborate and sophisticated version of the quantity theory was developed by Alfred Marshall. In this approach, known as the "Cambridge" version of the quantity theory, emphasis is shifted to the desire of individuals to hold a definite quantity of cash balances.[13] While the Marshallians recognized that individuals may want to hold money as such, exploration of the motives for holding money had to wait on the appearance of the *General Theory*. Nevertheless, the Cambridge version of the quantity theory represents an important advance over the earlier and more rigidly orthodox concept primarily because it is a step away from the overly-simplified classical assumption that money is of real importance only as a medium of exchange.

The essential nature of the Marshallian or Cambridge theory is summarized in the following equation:

$$M^o = \phi(Y) \qquad (11\text{--}1)$$

In this equation M^o represents the quantity of money, Y the national income, and ϕ the coefficient that brings the two sides of the equation into balance. But ϕ is more than just a numerical coefficient; it represents the *proportion* of the national income that residents of a nation wish to hold as cash balances. As such it is basically a psychological propensity that may change. Over the long run the value of ϕ was thought to remain reasonably stable, but in the short run it might shift in a sudden and unpredictable manner as a result of changes in the public's state of confidence. It is this possibility that brings the Cambridge version of the quantity theory much closer to modern thinking on the subject of money.

The distinction between these two approaches to the quantity theory is demonstrated diagrammatically in Figure 11–1. For this analysis we

[13] Alfred Marshall, *Money, Credit, and Commerce* (New York, Macmillan, 1923), pp. 44–45.

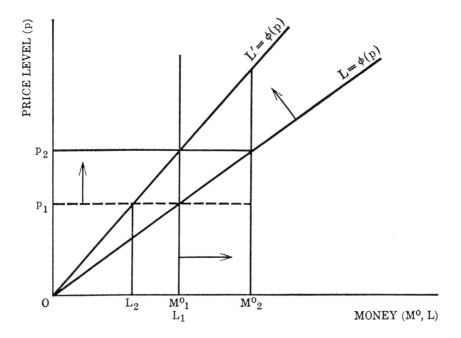

Figure 11-1. The Quantity Theory of Money

shall introduce a new symbol L to represent the demand for cash balances. The Cambridge version of the quantity theory now is stated as $L = \phi(Y)$, which is to say that demand for money to hold is equal to some proportion of the national income. If we accept for the sake of analysis the classical view that full employment is normal, which means that real output is constant, it follows that the quantity of money people will want to hold will vary in proportion to the general price level, p. Thus we can say:

$$L = \phi(p) \qquad (11\text{-}2)$$

In Figure 11-1 both the money supply M^o and the quantity of money that people want to hold, L, are shown on the horizontal axis, while the general price level, p, is shown on the vertical axis. The curve sloping upward to the right and labeled $L = \phi(p)$ is the geometrical expression of the notion of a functional relationship between L and p. The value of the coefficient ϕ is equal to the reciprocal of the slope of this curve. Line $M^o{}_1$ depicts the money supply. $M^o{}_1$ is shown as a vertical line because the amount of money in circulation (the distance from the origin to the point where $M^o{}_1$ meets the horizontal axis) is autonomously determined by the monetary authorities. Monetary equilibrium exists at the point of intersection of the money supply schedule and the $L = \phi(p)$ schedule. The price level at this point is p_1.

In the earlier and more rigid version of the quantity theory a change in the general price level could come about only as a result of a change in the money supply. Such a change would disrupt a pre-existing monetary equilibrium and result in either more (or less) spending with a consequent rise (or fall) in the general price level. To illustrate, let us assume that the money supply curve in Figure 11–1 shifts to the right. Its new position is given by the schedule labeled $M^o{}_2$. This injection of additional money into the economy upsets the prior equilibrium between L and M^o. As a result the amount of money actually in existence is now greater than the amount the people want to hold, L_1, at the existing price level p_1. Since the rigid version of the quantity theory views money as only a medium of exchange, the new money injected into the economy will be spent. As this happens, prices will rise because of the assumption that real output is a constant. Prices will continue to rise until the normal relationship between the price level, p, and the demand for money to hold, L, is once again restored. This is at a higher level of prices, p_2, and is depicted at the point of intersection of the new and larger money supply curve, $M^o{}_2$, and the $L = \phi(p)$ schedule. Opposite effects would ensue if the money supply schedule were shifted to the left. This analysis is properly described as the more traditional version of the quantity theory because the initiative for a change in the price level comes from a change in M^o. There is no question of any *change* in the value of ϕ.

In the Cambridge version of the quantity theory the general price level may rise from p_1 to p_2, but the manner in which this rise is brought about is altogether different. This is demonstrated in Figure 11–1 by a shift *upward* in the $L = \phi(p)$ schedule to the level indicated by $L' = \phi(p)$. What is the significance of this shift? Essentially it means a change in the value of ϕ, which is to say a change in the psychological propensity of the public to hold some portion of national income in the form of money. If the $L = \phi(p)$ schedule shifts upward the value of ϕ has declined. Given the new position of $L' = \phi(p)$, the amount of money people want to hold at the price level p_1 is equal to L_2. This is a lesser amount than L_1. This disturbs the equilibrium because now the money supply, $M^o{}_1$, is again greater than the cash balances people want to hold, L_2. At this point the Cambridge version falls back upon the notion that money is basically wanted as a medium of exchange, and as a consequence the surplus of money, $M^o{}_1 - L_2$, will be spent as people seek to rid themselves of excess balances. Again this will only serve to drive up the general level of prices because of our assumption that real output is a constant. Thus equilibrium between the money supply and the amount of money people want to hold will be restored when prices climb to the level p_2.

In the Cambridge analysis, a shift downward in the $L = \phi(p)$ function would mean that the public had decided to hold a *larger* proportion of national income in the form of money balances. In view of this and on the continuing assumption that real output is a constant, the restoration of equilibrium between M^o and L requires a fall in the general price level. In the rigid version of the quantity theory, this same result requires a reduction in the supply of money.

The Role of Money in Modern Theory

The Cambridge version of the quantity theory represented an important advance in our understanding of the economic significance of money because it shifted analytical emphasis from the supply of money *per se* to the idea that people desire and need to hold money as such. But the Cambridge theorists did not push the analysis deeply into the reasons why people may want to hold money. The Cambridge ϕ implies a desire to *hold* cash balances, but it does not offer any clear explanation of the reasons for this desire. Keynes, however, fashions an explanation in the *General Theory* through development of the concept of *liquidity-preference*. His approach to the role of money in the economy is accepted by many contemporary economists. It differs from the classical analysis primarily because it focuses attention on the demand for money rather than on the supply of money. From this approach a theory of interest is developed that provides the crucial link between money, income, and the employment level.

Motives for Holding Money

The liquidity-preference concept forms the core of the modern analysis of money and its role in the economy. Keynes used the term "liquidity preference" to mean the demand for money *to hold*.[14] The demand for a commodity or a service is conceived in terms of the amount of money that a person is willing to give up in order to obtain the commodity or service. But this notion of demand cannot apply to money, since money is obviously not exchanged for money. The demand for money to hold is a demand for objectives which are one step removed from the act of holding money itself. As a consequence of Keynes' pioneering analysis, modern income and employment theory postulates three major reasons why individuals and business firms want to hold money balances: the transactions motive, the precautionary motive, and the speculative motive.

THE TRANSACTIONS MOTIVE

The transactions motive relates to the need to hold some quantity of money balances to carry on day-to-day economic dealings. Practically all transactions in a money-using economy involve an exchange of money,

[14] John Maynard Keynes, *The General Theory of Employment, Interest and Money* (New York, Harcourt, Brace, 1936), p. 166.

and since the receipt of income is not synchronized exactly with all transactions involving money outlays, it is necessary that some money be held in order to meet this need.

Money held to satisfy the transactions motive is related primarily to the medium-of-exchange function. Money balances held idle in response to this motive provide a means of payment for transactions which will take place in the future. The amount of money in relation to income that people and business firms find it necessary to hold to satisfy the transactions motive depends on the time interval within which income is received relative to the income. To illustrate with a simple example, let us assume an individual has an annual income of $9600. If this individual is paid only once a year and, further, if he spends his whole income during the year, his money balance will be $9600 at the beginning of the year and zero (0) at the end of the year. His *average* holding of money during the year will be $4800, or 50 per cent of his income. Thus a person paid in this fashion would have to hold, on the average, 50 per cent of his annual income in the form of money balances to satisfy the transactions motive. This assumes that income is spent at a uniform rate. Now let us consider what happens if this individual's employer decides to pay him twice a year. Every six months he will receive $4800 and he will spend the whole of this before the beginning of the next pay period. His money balances will total $4800 at the beginning of the six-month pay period and zero at the end. Thus his average money balance will total $2400 in each pay period during the year. This means that a person paid twice a year must, on the average, hold but 25 per cent of his annual income as money balances in order to satisfy the transactions motive. The more frequent the pay period, the smaller is the proportion of an individual's annual income that must be held to carry on day-to-day transactions.

THE PRECAUTIONARY MOTIVE

The precautionary motive is the desire to hold some quantity of money balances to meet unforeseen emergencies or contingencies. It is, in other words, a desire to set aside some money balances to provide for a "rainy day." The need to hold money to satisfy this particular motive arises out of the fact that we do not have certain knowledge concerning future transactions; a situation may arise in which the need for money balances is much greater than the amount required to carry on normal day-to-day transactions. For the individual this may be the result of unemployment, illness, or some other form of economic misfortune, although it should be stressed that all unforeseen developments that require extraordinary expenditures on the part of either individuals or business firms are not necessarily of an adverse character.

The speculative motive is the most complex and the most important of the three major sources of demand for cash balances, which modern income and employment theory postulates. It is the key to an understanding of contemporary interest theory and the manner in which money may powerfully affect the operation of the economy.

Fundamentally, the speculative motive relates to the desire to hold a part of one's assets in the form of cash in order to take advantage of future market movements. It involves, according to Keynes, holding money balances with the objective of "securing profit from knowing better than the market what the future will bring forth." [15] The speculative motive shifts emphasis from the medium-of-exchange function of money, which dominated classical thinking, and which underlies the transactions and precautionary motives, to the store-of-value function. Under the speculative motive, money is wanted as an asset rather than as a medium of exchange that can be drawn upon as needed at some future date. Money is being held in preference to holding assets in some other form.

Since idle money balances do not, like debt or equity instruments, yield income, why would an individual or a business firm wish to hold on to them? The answer is *uncertainty*—and fear—with respect to the future, particularly future values of other asset forms. As Keynes stated, the "desire to hold money as a store of wealth is a barometer of the degree of our distrust of our calculations and conventions concerning the future." [16] Individuals and firms choose to retain some portion of their assets in the most liquid form possible so as to be in the most favorable position possible to take advantage of future movements in the market for other types of assets.

The Transactions Demand for Money

Now that we have defined the three major forms of demand for money to hold, let us direct the analysis to the problem of the determination of the actual amounts of money held to satisfy each of these motives. For this purpose it is logical to lump the transactions and precautionary demands together since both are related primarily to the medium-of-exchange function of money. Let us call the combined demand for money to satisfy the transaction and precautionary motives the *transactions demand* and designate it by the symbol L_t.

Given the existence of some kind of a normal ratio with respect to the *proportion* of income that the public wants to hold as money balances in

[15] *Ibid.*, p. 170.

[16] John Maynard Keynes, "The General Theory" in Seymour E. Harris, ed., *The New Economics* (New York, Knopf, 1947), p. 187.

response to L_t, the actual *amount* of money held to satisfy this motive will vary directly with income. Thus L_t is, *ceteris paribus*, a function of income. Algebraically we have

$$L_t = f(Y) \qquad (11\text{-}3)$$

The fundamental reason for this is not difficult to see. In a complex society the volume of economic transactions of all kinds varies directly with the income level. Consequently, the absolute quantity of money balances needed to carry on these transactions also varies directly with the income level. The amount of money that can be held strictly in response to the precautionary component of the transactions demand schedule is for most people a residual sum which will vary with income. The higher the income level, the easier it will be for individuals and firms to hold idle balances to meet unforeseen contingencies.[17]

The functional relationship between the transactions demand for money L_t and the income level is depicted in Figure 11–2. The transac-

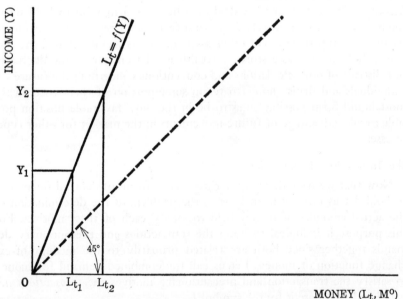

Figure 11–2. The Transactions Demand for Money: As a Function of the Income Level

---

[17] This should not be confused with saving. Funds held idle to satisfy the precautionary motive may represent one way in which savings are disposed of, but they are not to be mistaken for the act of saving itself.

tions demand, L_t, and the money supply, M^o, are shown on the horizontal axis; the income level, Y, on the vertical axis. The transactions function is the curve labeled $L_t = f(Y)$. The function is a straight line, drawn so that its slope is greater than $45°$. This indicates first, that the *ratio* of money balances held for transactions purposes to income, L_t/Y, is normally less than unity (100 per cent), and second, that this ratio is assumed constant. Given these assumptions, the figure shows that the amount of money demanded for transactions purposes, L_t, varies *directly* with the income level, Y. For example, at the income level Y_1 the transactions demand is L_{t1}, and at the income level Y_2, the transactions demand is L_{t2}.

Since idle money balances do not yield any income, should not the amount of money people are willing to hold as balances be related to interest rates? As a matter of fact this is the crucial relationship insofar as the demand for money to satisfy the speculative motive is concerned, but most economists believe the transactions demand is unresponsive to the rate of interest, except at very high interest levels.

Hansen has suggested a diagram to show the relationship between the transaction demand, the rate of interest, and income.[18] This diagram is reproduced here as Figure 11–3. The transactions demand, L_t, and the money supply, M^o, are depicted on the horizontal axis, but now we

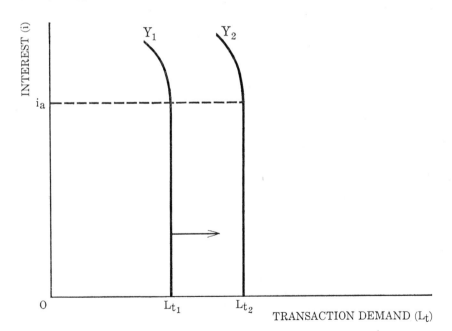

Figure 11–3. The Transactions Demand for Money

[18] Hansen, *op. cit.*, p. 67.

measure the rate of interest, i, on the vertical axis. The demand for money balances for transactions purposes at a given income level is represented by a straight line parallel to the vertical axis *up to* the interest rate i_a. This is the crucial level at which the transaction demand for money balances becomes responsive to an *increase* in the rate of interest; thus the curve begins to bend backwards at this point. At high interest rates individuals and business firms will "economize" in the use of money. They seek to make each unit do more work, thus freeing some of their balances for lending under the high-interest conditions prevailing in the economy. This is tantamount to an increase in the velocity of circulation of the money supply.

The distance between the vertical axis and the vertical portion of the transactions demand curve is determined by the income level. Thus in Figure 11–3, the distance OL_{t1}, as measured on the horizontal axis, is equivalent to the distance OL_{t1} in Figure 11–2. This being the case, it is appropriate to designate this transactions demand curve of Figure 11–3 as Y_1. If there is an increase in the income level, the transactions demand for money will increase. In Figure 11–2 this is depicted by the change from L_{t1} to L_{t2} on the horizontal axis. In Figure 11–3 this same change must be shown by a *shift to the right of the curve* representing the transactions demand for money. At the higher income level the position of the curve is given by Y_2 and the demand for money balances corresponding to this income level is given by the distance OL_{t2}.

The Asset Demand for Money

The third type of demand for money balances stems from the speculative motive. The essential feature which distinguishes this demand from the two categories considered previously is that it represents demand for money to hold *as an asset*. In our analysis we will call this demand the *asset demand* and designate it by the symbol L_a.

The essence of the asset demand for money is that money is regarded as a way of holding economic value over time which is preferable to debt instruments and equity instruments.[19] Debt instruments normally yield the holder a *fixed* income in the form of interest, while equity instruments yield the holder an *uncertain* income in the form of a profit. Although profit can be expressed as a rate of return and thus compared directly with the income derived from a debt instrument, we will simplify our analysis at this stage by assuming that the person who wants to hold economic value over time has only two alternatives, holding money or holding debt instruments. We shall use the bond to represent debt instruments. In the appendix to this chapter we shall reintroduce equity

[19] A person holding either a debt or equity instruments may experience either a "capital gain" or "capital loss" because of unforseen changes in the current market value of the asset. The possiblity of a capital loss is a risk a debt or equity instrument holder assumes.

instruments into the analysis as a third alternative for holding economic value.

Why would an individual hold money, which yields no return, in preference to a fixed-income debt instrument? The answer, as Keynes pointed out, lies in the fact of uncertainty—uncertainty with respect to the future market value of the debt instruments. The corollary of this is that the income foregone by holding money in preference to a fixed-income obligation such as a bond becomes the *cost* of holding money. If we limit the alternative forms in which economic value may be held to money and bonds, then the rate of interest is the cost of holding money as an asset in satisfaction of the speculative motive, since interest is the income foregone when one chooses to hold money in preference to bonds. This implies that the amount of money held as an asset is a function of the rate of interest, although an *inverse* one. Thus we have algebraically

$$L_a = f(i) \qquad\qquad (11\text{-}4)$$

The higher the rate of interest, the more costly it becomes to hold money rather than bonds and, consequently, the smaller will be the amount of money held as an asset.[20]

The functional relationship between the asset demand for money and the rate of interest is shown as a schedule in Figure 11-4. The asset demand, L_a, and the money supply, M^o, appear on the horizontal axis, while the rate of interest, i, is on the vertical axis. The curve $L_a = f(i)$ shows the quantity of money that persons and firms *want* to hold as an asset at different rates of interest. The reader should note that the asset demand schedule becomes perfectly elastic—that is, horizontal—at very low levels of the interest rate. This is an important characteristic which will be explained when we introduce expectations into our analysis.

The asset demand function is also termed the liquidity-preference schedule because, given the fact that money is the most liquid of all assets, the demand for money as an asset is necessarily a demand for liquidity. Keynes used *liquidity preference* to mean the total demand for money in response to all three motives discussed, not just the demand for money to satisfy the speculative motive. In the economic literature that has appeared since Keynes first offered his own ideas on the subject of money, the term "liquidity preference" is generally used in the more restrictive sense to mean simply the asset demand for money. This matter of terminology is stressed because the interest theory based upon the asset demand for money is usually described as the liquidity-preference theory of interest.

[20] In reality the asset demand for money involves more than the simple fact that interest foregone is the opportunity cost of holding money. We shall analyze this relationship more fully after we establish the basic framework for Keynesian interest theory.

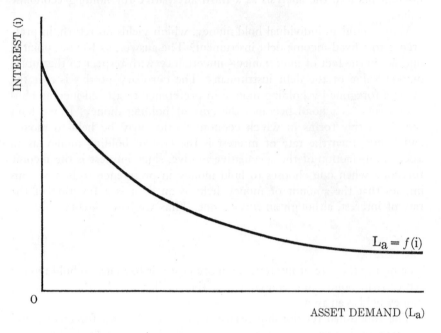

Figure 11-4. The Asset Demand for Money

Bond Prices and the Rate of Interest

In the preceding section reference was made to holding bonds as an alternative to holding money. To comprehend fully the rationale for such an alternative the student must understand the relationship between the current market price of bonds and the rate of interest. A bond is a promise to repay at some future date a sum of money which represents the amount borrowed initially by the issuer of the bond. In addition, a bond normally embodies a contractual obligation to pay interest on the amount borrowed. The amount of contractual interest is determined by prevailing market conditions at the time the loan is first made. To illustrate, let us assume that a business corporation issues a series of $100 bonds at a time when the market rate for similar long-term bonds is 5 per cent. Every individual who purchases one of these bonds—that is, lends the corporation $100—is entitled to receive $5.00 per year until such time as the bonds mature and as long as he retains ownership of the bonds. (Most bonds, both private and public, can be sold prior to the maturity date.) Let us assume that one of the original purchasers wishes to recover the funds he invested in the bonds before they mature. To do so the bondholder can dispose of his holdings in the bond market. If there is a brisk demand for these particular bonds, he may be able to sell his holdings at a unit price of more than $100. If the market is not particularly active, he may be forced to accept less than $100. Consider now what takes place if he sells at a price above $100, let us say $102. The purchaser of the bond is buying a promise on the part of the business corporation to pay $100 at some future date; he also stands to receive $5.00 per year as interest on the bond. But the new holder of the bond has paid $102—the current market price of the bond—for an asset which will yield him the same interest, $5.00 per year, as the original owner received on an investment of $100. Thus the current rate of interest has fallen below 5 per cent. On the other hand, if the new owner of the bond had been able to purchase it in the market for a price less than $100, say, $98, this would mean that the current rate had risen, because for $98 he obtains an asset which will yield him an annual income of $5.00, which as a rate is better than 5 per cent.

The Total Demand for Money

Up to this point we have considered the transactions demand for money, L_t, and the asset demand for money, L_a, as separate functions. This is logical because the determinants of the amount of money held are, in the first instance, income, and in the second, interest. It is possible, though, to combine these two demand functions and obtain a total demand for money. First, we posit the following identity:

$$L = L_t + L_a \qquad\qquad (11\text{--}5)$$

This equation states that the total demand for money is equal to the sum of the transactions demand and asset demand. This being true, we can posit the following functional relationship:

$$L = f(Y,i) \qquad\qquad (11\text{--}6)$$

In this equation the *total* demand for money, L, is a function of *both* the income level, Y, and the rate of interest, i.

The combined transactions and asset demand for money is illustrated in Figure 11–5. The rate of interest is measured on the vertical axis; the total demand for money on the horizontal axis. Income as a variable influencing the level of the over-all demand for money is introduced by adding the transactions demand L_t *appropriate to each income level* (see Figure 11–3) to the asset demand function $L_a = f(i)$. The result is a total demand function for money, $L = f(i, Y)$, which shows that the *total* demand for money balances will increase if the income level is rising. Thus, we have a series of demand curves for money balances, each one of which is associated with a different level of income. The student should note that the L curves shown in Figure 11–5 are drawn

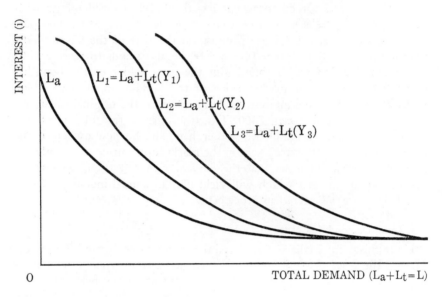

Figure 11-5. The Combined Asset and Transactions Demand for Money

so that they begin to "bend backwards" at the upper ranges of the interest rate. This is because even the transactions demand for money becomes sensitive to the rate of interest at high interest levels.

The Liquidity-Preference Theory of Interest

Keynesian interest theory is derived from the idea that money may be wanted as a store of value just as much as it may be wanted as a medium of exchange. The liquidity-preference theory of interest is based primarily upon the asset demand function, although, as we shall see later, a complete theory of interest is not possible without consideration of the transactions demand function.

Fundamental to an understanding of the liquidity-preference approach is the concept of interest that is embodied in the analysis. In the classical theory interest is regarded as the price which equates the supply of and demand for saving; it is considered a phenomenon related to *flows* rather than *stocks*. Moreover, in the classical analysis interest is thought of primarily as the price that is paid for abstinence—the necessary price that must be paid to persuade people not to consume some portion of their current income. The essence of the classical view is that interest is a reward for waiting.

But it is precisely this concept of interest as a reward for saving that

Keynes challenges in the *General Theory*. Interest, he argues, cannot be a reward for saving as such because if a person *hoards* his savings in cash, he will receive no interest, although he has, nevertheless, refrained from consuming all of his current income. Rather than being a reward for saving as such, interest is regarded by Keynes and other proponents of the liquidity-preference approach as a reward for parting with liquidity.[21] Interest is the price that must be paid to persuade those who hold idle money balances in response to the speculative motive to part with the liquidity inherent in such balances. This particular view of the nature of interest takes us back to the question we broached earlier: Why should anyone wish to hold money as an asset in preference to some other form of asset which will yield an income? The answer is *fear and uncertainty* with respect to the future value of assets held in forms other than cash. It is necessary to pay people a premium in the form of interest to compensate for the insecurity and diminished liquidity involved in holding assets in other than monetary form at a time of uncertainty. The greater the degree of uncertainty with respect to future economic values, the higher will be the rate of interest.

As stated in the *General Theory*, the rate of interest is "the 'price' which equilibrates the desire to hold wealth in the form of cash with the available quantity of cash." [22] Since we defined the desire to hold wealth in the form of cash in terms of the asset demand function, we can say that the rate of interest is determined by the intersection of the schedule representing the demand for money as an asset—the L_a function—and a schedule representing that portion of the total money supply which is available to hold as an asset. The latter we shall designate with the symbol $M^o{}_a$. This approach to the determination of interest embodies demand and supply concepts, but it is oriented toward *stocks* rather than *flows*.

The mechanism through which the rate of interest is determined in the liquidity-preference theory is demonstrated in Figure 11–6. Interest is on the vertical axis, while the demand for money for asset purposes, L_a, and the supply of money for asset purposes, $M^o{}_a$, are shown on the horizontal axis. The asset demand function, $L_a = f(i)$, slopes downward to the right, as suggested previously, and the money supply function, $M^o{}_a$, is shown as a straight line drawn parallel to the vertical axis. This signifies that the supply of money for asset purposes is autonomous with respect to the rate of interest. The reason for this is that the liquidity-preference analysis assumes that the supply of asset money $M^o{}_a$ is, given the total supply of money, M^o, a *residual* which is determined by subtracting the quantity of money required to satisfy the transactions demand, L_t, from the total money supply. Given this assumption, the rate of interest is determined by the intersection of the $M^o{}_a$ and L_a schedules for only at this point will

[21] Keynes, *The General Theory of Employment, Interest and Money*, p. 167.
[22] *Ibid.*

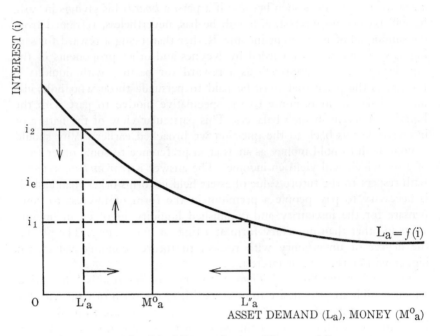

Figure 11–6. The Liquidity-preference Theory of Interest-rate
Determination

the demand for money as an asset be in balance with the quantity of
money available to satisfy the speculative motive. This rate is the equilibrium rate and it is designated in the figure as i_e.

In order to understand more fully why the demand for L_a and the
supply of $M^o{}_a$ must be equilibrated at this particular level of interest rates,
let us analyze what will transpire if, momentarily, some other level of
the interest rate prevails. For example, what will happen if the interest
rate is at the level of i_2, which is higher than the equilibrium rate i_e. At
this particular level the asset demand for money L_a' is smaller than the
available supply, $M^o{}_a$, and, consequently, the rate of interest must fall.
Why must it fall? Because at the rate i_2 there exists a situation in which
the current price for the surrender of liquidity is so high that people do
not want to hold all the asset money that is available. There is, in other
words, a surplus of money to hold as an asset, and under such circumstances it is to be expected that the price necessary to persuade people
to part with liquidity will come down. This price will continue to fall
until a level is reached at which the surplus of asset money is no longer
available. This is the equilibrium rate i_e.

The reverse will be true if the rate of interest is below the equilibrium level. Thus at the rate i_1, the demand for money for asset purposes, L_a'', is in excess of the available supply, $M^o{}_a$. The rate of interest i_1 is therefore a disequilibrium rate and must rise, because as long as people want to hold more money as an asset than is currently available for this purpose, they will bid up the price for the surrender of liquidity in an effort to persuade some holders to part with their asset money. This process will continue until once again the demand for and supply of money balances are again in equilibrium.

The Bond Market and the Asset Demand for Money

The liquidity preference theory of interest rate determination cannot be fully understood until we see how the asset demand function, or schedule of liquidity preference, is linked to the market for the purchase and sale of bonds.

The essential character of the bond market is shown in Figure 11–7. This is an ordinary demand and supply diagram in which the price of bonds is measured on the vertical axis, and the quantity demanded and supplied is measured on the horizontal axis. *DD* depicts the demand for bonds, and it has the typical negative slope of a demand curve which shows, *ceteris paribus*, that the quantity demanded varies inversely with the price. This curve tells us that buyers are willing to purchase more bonds at a lower price than at a higher price. *SS* represents the supply schedule. This curve ultimately becomes *inelastic* with respect to price because if the price goes high enough *all* bondholders will want to dispose of their holdings. It is the existing supply of fixed-income assets in the form of bonds that is crucial to the determination of both bond prices and interest rates. Newly issued bonds may have some influence in this connection, but by and large their influence is small in comparison to that exercised by the existing supply.

In Figure 11–7, equilibrium in the bond market exists at the point of intersection of the *DD* and *SS* schedules. The price P_e is the equilibrium price which equates the demand for and supply of bonds. Let us assume that, momentarily, the actual market price is at the level of P_2. This is clearly a disequilibrium situation because at P_2 the quantity of bonds offered (the distance *OM* in the figure) is in excess of the quantity of bonds demanded (the distance *ON*). Why is this so? Since we assumed that bonds and money are the only means to hold economic value over time, and since, too, the existing supply of bonds must be held by someone, the situation shown at the price level P_2 is one in which *some* bondholders want to exchange their bonds for an alternative asset form—money. These bondholders fear that if they continue to hold bonds they may suffer capital losses. The current price level, P_2, is, in their opinion, too high; prudence dictates that they shift to holding cash in anticipation of a decline in bond prices. But if some bondholders want to shift from bonds to cash, this is the same as saying that the demand for money as an asset is in excess of the available supply. Why? First, the existing supply of asset money is fixed, and second, if some bondholders prefer to shift to money as an asset, the demand for money inevitably becomes greater than the existing supply. The counterpart of the situation shown in Figure 11–7, in which the quantity of bonds supplied, OM, is in excess of the

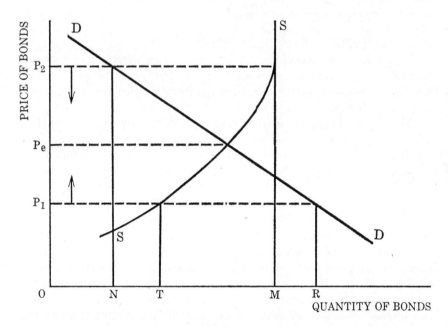

Figure 11–7. The Bond Market

quantity demanded, ON, is to be found in Figure 11–6 at the rate of interest i_1, for at this rate (which is below the equilibrium rate) the demand for money for asset purposes, L_a'', is in excess of the available supply $M^o{}_a$.

Once it is understood that Figures 11–6 and 11–7 refer to the same basic phenomenon, it is easy to see why the rate of interest must rise whenever the asset demand for money is in excess of the current supply. Since the situation shown in Figure 11–6 at i_1 is merely a different way of describing a disequilibrium situation in the bond market wherein the current supply of bonds exceeds the current demand at an existing price, then it is inevitable that the rate of interest will rise. As some bondholders try to shift from bonds to money, current prices for bonds will decline. But a decline in the current market prices of bonds leads to a rise in current interest rates. This process of adjustment will continue until a level of bond prices is reached at which no further attempts are made by *present* bondholders to shift from bonds to money. This is the price P_e in Figure 11-7, and it corresponds to the equilibrium rate i_e in Figure 11-6. If no further attempts are made on the part of bondholders to shift to money, the demand for money as an asset has been brought into balance with the available supply.

A situation exactly the opposite is shown in Figure 11-7 by assuming bond prices to be at the level P_1. At this price the quantity of bonds demanded (the distance OR in the figure) is in excess of the quantity currently available (the distance OT). If the demand for bonds is in excess of supply, this situation is the equivalent of one in which the demand for asset money, L_a, falls short of the current supply, M^o_a. Consequently, this kind of disequilibrium situation in the bond market is identical to the situation shown in Figure 11-6 at the level of the rate of interest represented by i_2. At this level, the asset demand for money, L_a', is smaller than the available supply, M^o_a. Thus the rate of interest will fall; the excess of demand for bonds over the existing supply drives up the current price of bonds, and the rate of interest comes down.

Expectations and the Rate of Interest

Our understanding of the liquidity-preference theory of interest is not complete without consideration of the role of *expectations*, specifically the expectations held by both individuals and business firms concerning future economic values. Certain peculiarities of the asset demand function which are of critical economic significance can only be understood through reference to expectations. We saw earlier that uncertainty with respect to the future is the basic reason why some persons prefer to hold money rather than an income-earning asset. This is perfectly sound and logical, but it is not enough. Expectations as to future economic values provide the basic explanation of why individuals and firms shift from money to debt or equity instruments, and vice versa.

Let us return to our model of the bond market in Figure 11-7. At the price level P_2 the available supply of bonds in the market OM is in excess of the quantity currently in demand ON. This leads to a fall in the price of bonds. But the disequilibrium situation existing at the price level P_2 means that market conditions are such that there is a general shift from holding bonds to holding money because of *fear and uncertainty* with respect to future economic values. In the context of this particular market situation, there are more bondholders who expect future bond prices to fall (interest rates to rise) than there are who expect future bond prices to rise (interest rates to fall). At the level of prices represented by P_2 the preponderance of opinion in the market is "bearish." A pronounced movement from bonds to cash gets under way, and will continue until bond prices in the market have fallen to a level at which the expectations of those who anticipate further declines in bond prices are exactly offset by the expectations of those who anticipate price increases.

Expectations concerning future prices and the kind of behavior that is the consequence of such expectations has meaning only in relation to notions about what constitutes a "normal" level of bond prices (or interest rates). The balance of opinion in the market is "bearish" at the price level P_2 only if the majority of traders in the market believe that there does exist some "normal" level for bond prices, which in this instance must lie below the current price, and to which level current prices will return. As the current price level declines opinion in the market concerning future prices will become less and less "bearish." Equilibrium will be reached when "bearish" opinion in the market is counterbalanced by opinion that is "bullish."

The foregoing analysis of the shift from bonds to cash can be formulated just as readily in terms of the liquidity-preference theory of interest. The situation represented by a price level P_2 for bonds is one in which the rate of interest is at a level such that the demand for money for asset purposes, L_a, is larger than the quantity of money currently available to meet this need, M^o_a. In Figure 11–6 this is the rate of interest represented by i_1. Within the framework of interest-rate theory, this situation is one in which the weight of opinion in the market is bullish with respect to future interest rates. The majority of traders currently active in the market expect future interest rates to be higher, which is another way of saying that the market anticipates lower prices for bonds. From this situation there arises the excess demand for cash over the available supply. Again it must be underscored that both current and future interest rates can be interpreted meaningful only in relation to some concept of normality. The current rate i_1 must be thought of as being below what the market has come to regard as "normal." Consequently, expectations that future rates will be higher outweigh expectations that they will be lower. As the *current* market rises, however, the preponderance of favorable sentiment in the market with respect to future interest rates will subside until eventually an equilibrium rate is reached, at which favorable and unfavorable opinion is again in balance. In Figure 11–6 this gradual shift in the climate of opinion of the market is reflected in a movement upward along the asset demand schedule from the point representing the asset demand for money at the rate of interest i_1 to the point of equilibrium given by the rate of interest i_e.

The introduction of both the bond market and expectations with respect to future value into our analysis provides us with a much fuller explanation of the shape of the asset demand function than is embodied in the idea that interest is the cost of holding money in preference to some other asset form. Once we understand the relationship between the asset function, the bond market, and expectations, it is possible to see that more is involved in the demand for money than simply the cost of holding money. To illustrate, if the current rate of interest is high relative to what is generally regarded as a "normal" level, not only will the current cost of holding money be high, but expectations with respect to future prices of bonds will be such that the majority of participants in the market believe that these prices will be higher rather than lower. Thus there is little incentive to hold money in order to take advantage of future market movements. At very high levels of the interest rate, the weight of market opinion will be so overwhelmingly bullish with respect to bond prices that the demand for speculative balances or asset money will be zero. In Figure 11–6 this is, of course, the point at which the asset demand function intersects the vertical axis.

Precisely opposite conditions will prevail at interest rates which are low relative to what the market regards as "normal." Not only does the cost of holding money become more and more negligible as the rate of interest declines, but, more important, the lower the rate of interest, the greater will be the number of participants in the market who expect future bond prices to be lower rather than higher. As long as some notion of normality exists with respect to both bond prices and interest rates, low levels of the interest rate mean high bond prices and a bond market that is increasingly bearish with respect to future values for bonds. Thus the demand for money for speculative or asset purposes will inevitably grow as the interest rate sinks more and more below levels believed to be normal.

This relationship provides the basis for an explanation of an interesting phenomenon described as the *liquidity trap*. In Figure 11–6 this is the point at which the asset demand function becomes perfectly elastic with respect to the rate of interest. Keynes described this as a situation in which liquidity preference may "become virtually absolute in the sense that almost everywhere one prefers cash to holding a debt." [23]

The basic explanation for the existence of such a liquidity trap is that at extremely low rates of interest (or high levels of bond prices) the risk of a capital loss in holding bonds rather than money becomes so overwhelmingly great that virtually no one desires to hold bonds. The demand for money as an asset becomes infinitely elastic. At these low interest levels the monetary authority of a country may no longer be able to exercise effective control over interest rates.

An Alternative Explanation of the Demand for Money

One basic difficulty inherent in the Keynesian explanation of interest in terms of the schedule of liquidity preference and the available supply of money for asset purposes is that it presupposes that persons in the money market will either hold bonds if their expectations are "bullish"

[23] *Ibid.*, p. 207. The *liquidity trap* is more of a theoretical curiosity than a real possibility for the contemporary economy. In the Great Depression of the 1930's and during World War II, however, interest rates fell to very low levels at the same time that cash balances increased. See James Tobin, "Liquidity Preference and Monetary Policy," *Review of Economics and Statistics*, May, 1947, pp. 124–131, and Lawrence R. Klein, "The Empirical Foundations of Keynesian Economics," in Kurihara, ed., *Post-Keynesian Economics*, *op. cit.*, pp. 277–319.

with respect to future bond prices, or cash if their expectations are "bear-ish." In reality, though, matters are not this simple because an individual's portfolio of personal assets may include at a particular time *both* bonds and money.[24] Some explanation must be found for this fact, as well as for the phenomenon of shifts from holding one form of asset to another, if we are to arrive at a full understanding of the nature of interest.

Professor James Tobin, former member of President Kennedy's Council of Economic Advisors, utilizes the concept of risk to explain, first, how it is possible that an individual's asset portfolio may be divided between bonds and cash, and second, why the liquidity-preference function (the asset demand) is negatively sloped.[25] Tobin reaches virtually the same conclusion as Keynes with respect to the shape of this function, but his explanation is formulated primarily in terms of attitudes toward risk rather than expectations with respect to future bond prices.

In Tobin's view the world of wealth-holders consists of two kinds of people: *risk-lovers* and *risk-averters*. These terms come from the fact that whenever a person holds bonds in preference to cash, he incurs the risk of a capital loss or gain because of uncertain knowledge concerning future bond prices. The larger the proportion of assets held as bonds in preference to money, the greater the risk. The risk-lovers do not have to be induced by higher interest rates to hold bonds instead of cash; they will maximize both risk and interest income by holding all their assets in bonds. If all participants in the money market were risk-lovers an asset demand schedule of the kind shown in Figure 11–4 could not exist.

It would appear, however, that more people in the market are risk-averters than risk-lovers. The risk-averter will, first of all, diversify his asset holdings. More important, he will assume more risk—i.e., hold a greater proportion of his portfolio in bonds—only as the rate of interest increases. Higher interest rates are necessary, in other words, to compen-sate for the additional risk assumed when more bonds and less cash are held. Since this is the case, the asset demand function assumes the shape shown in Figure 11–4. In reality both attitudes toward risk and expecta-tions with respect to future movements of bond prices—or interest rates—constitute forces at work which determine the nature of the asset de-mand for money.

Changes in the Rate of Interest

Within the framework of the liquidity-preference theory, two types of changes in the level of interest rates may be envisaged.[26] One kind of

---

[24] Equities, too, may be included in the portfolio. The relationship between money, debts, and equities is discussed in the appendix to this chapter.

[25] James Tobin, "Liquidity Preference as Behavior towards Risk," *Review of Economic Studies*, February, 1958, pp. 65–86.

[26] The analysis here is analogous to that discussed in connection with changes in the equilibrium income level in Chapter 5, p. 128.

change involves movement of the interest rate toward an equilibrium position, given the L_a function and the quantity of money available for asset purposes. The mechanics of a change of this type were fully described in the sections which dealt with the liquidity-preference of interest and the relationship of the bond market to the asset demand for money.

The other type of change involves movement of the rate of interest from one equilibrium level to another. This kind of change will result from either a shift in the position of the liquidity-preference function, $L_a = f(i)$, or a change in the quantity of money available for asset purposes. The latter can be brought about either by autonomous action on the part of the monetary authorities,[27] or as a result of changes in either the income level or the velocity of circulation. Such changes increase or decrease $M^o{}_a$. Changes in the income level affect significantly the *total* demand for money (see Figure 11–5) and consequently the rate of interest, but we shall delay consideration of this until after discussion of the effect upon interest rate of shifts in the liquidity-preference schedule.

Figure 11–8 shows a change in the equilibrium interest rate as a result of a once-over change in the position of the asset demand schedule. The shift is from $L_a = f(i)$ to $L_a' = f(i)$. A change of this type will drive the equilibrium rate from the level i_e to the level i_e'. It is best described as a

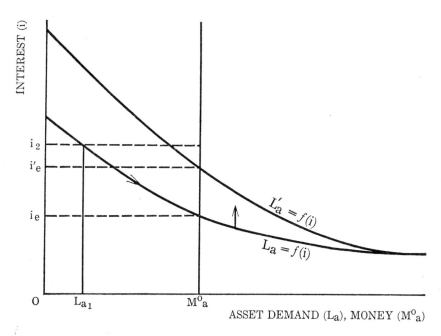

Figure 11–8. Shift in the Asset Demand Function

[27] For a discussion of the mechanism of expansion and contraction in the money supply see Chandler, *op. cit.*, Chapters 5 and 8, and Hansen, *op. cit.*, Chapter 2.

shift in the over-all "climate of opinion" which affects all participants in the market in the same way. In our earlier discussion of a downward movement of the interest rate from level i_2 to the level i_e, everyone in the market did not change their expectations about future movements of the rate of interest; only enough had to switch from a "bearish" position (with respect to interest rates) to a "bullish position" to make an equilibrium possible at the rate i_e. But the upward shift of the asset demand function is interpreted to mean that the market *as a whole* expects interest rates to be higher (or bond prices to be lower). Hence there is engendered a general and widespread increase in the demand to hold money as an asset that will lead to a new and higher equilibrium level of the interest rate, i_e', as long as the supply of money available as an asset is unchanged. A pronounced shift in the over-all position of the asset demand function means, too, that there has been a change with respect to what is regarded as the "normal" level of interest rates (or bond prices).

It is difficult to explain precisely what factors cause sudden shifts in the general climate of opinion of the market, although it appears that changes of this type are most likely to be associated with sudden and sharp movements of the economic system from prosperity and expansion into crisis and recession. The demand for money as an asset is likely to be unusually high in such circumstances, thus bringing about a sharp upward movement in the entire schedule of liquidity preference. Downward shifts of the liquidity function, on the other hand, are more likely to be associated with a recovery from recession or depression lows and the return of confidence in future economic values.

The Total Demand for Money and the Rate of Interest

Keynes' liquidity-preference theory of interest would be a relatively simple and acceptable theory of interest rate determination, as well as a practical alternative to the classical supply and demand for saving theory,[28] if we did not have to take into account the impact of income upon the total demand for money and the relationship of the latter to the rate of interest. Introduction of income into the analysis not only complicates the theory, but makes it impossible to derive a determinate theory of the interest rate apart from a general theory involving the simultaneous determination of the income level *and* the rate of interest.[29] Let us see why this is true.

The reader will recall that we constructed the *total* demand for money by adding the transactions demand prevailing at a given income level to the asset demand. This is shown in Figure 11–5. The significance of this is that we do *not* have a single curve which relates the demand for money

---

[28] The essential features of the "loanable funds" theory of interest, which is in many respects similar to the classical theory, are discussed in the appendix to this chapter.

[29] This general theory of the economic system is developed fully in Chapter 12.

to the rate of interest and which is *independent* of the income level. The asset demand part of the total money demand curve may be independent of income, but the transactions demand part is not. Thus, we have a series of demand schedules, the position of any one of which is determined by the level of income. What this means for the theory of interest can best be seen by adding a total money supply schedule to our analysis; this is done in Figure 11–9.

Monetary equilibrium, as explained earlier, requires that the *total* demand for money be just equal to the supply. If we have a series of demand schedules as depicted in Figure 11–9, then there is no single equilibrium rate of interest, but several such rates, each one of which will be associated with a different level of income. Thus, an equilibrium value for the interest rate cannot be determined unless the position of the *total* demand curve is known. The latter depends, however, upon the income level, and the income level, in turn, depends upon the level of investment, given the consumption function. Investment outlays cannot be determined without knowledge of the interest rate. We are therefore confronted by a chain of interlocking variables, and, our system of income determination cannot be complete until we can construct on the basis of the relationships developed this far in our text a general theory showing not only the simultaneous determination of both income and the rate of interest, but the manner in which all the key variables are related to one another. This task is undertaken in Chapter 12.

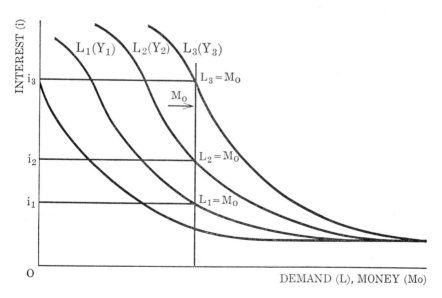

Figure 11–9. The Demand for Money, the Supply of Money, and the Rate of Interest

The Significance of Keynesian Interest Thought

The true significance of Keynes' liquidity-preference theory of interest does not lie in the fact that it is simply an alternative to the classical theory in which the analysis is cast in terms of stocks rather than flows.[30] The Keynesian theory of interest is important, first, because it spells out precisely the nature of the "monetary sphere" of the economic system. Keynesian interest theory makes it clear that monetary equilibrium is the product of different forces than those which produce equilibrium in income and employment. The demand for money as an asset is a major economic force in its own right, but the principles which govern this demand are significantly different from those which govern the demand for goods and services.

The second major reason for attaching significance to Keynes' interest theory is that it provides the necessary theoretical framework to demonstrate that money is not "neutral." In the classical theory, money is unimportant precisely because it is "neutral," which is to say that money has *no* role to play in the determination of output and employment. It functions simply as a medium of exchange, in no way affecting the underlying "real" process of production, exchange, and consumption. Keynes called an economy which uses money merely as "a neutral link between transactions in real things and real assets and does not allow it to enter into motives or decisions . . . a *Real-Exchange Economy*." [31] But in the Keynesian analysis this is not the case. Money, operating through the liquidity-preference function, is capable under the right set of circumstances of exerting a powerful influence upon the level of both output and employment. Keynes went on to suggest that the non-neutrality of money was the major source of the failure of a market economy to attain continuous full employment without the intervention of government. Most economists today would not go this far in attributing significance to the non-neutrality of money, but there are few who would deny that money does make a difference and that the principles which govern the behavior of an economy in which money is not neutral are significantly different from those which govern the real-exchange economy of the classical analysis.

APPENDIX

Relationships between money, debts, and equities

In the text of this chapter we listed equity instruments as a third form —in addition to money and bonds—in which economic values might be

---

[30] See the appendix to this chapter.

[31] John Maynard Keynes, "On The Theory of a Monetary Economy," reprinted in the *Nebraska Journal of Economics and Business*, Autumn, 1963, pp. 7–9. For a comprehensive discussion of Keynes' views on the significance of money, see Dudley Dillard, "The Theory of a Monetary Economy," in Kurihara, ed., *Post-Keynesian Economics, op. cit.*, pp. 3–30.

held over time. Equity instruments involve consideration of future values for the marginal efficiency of capital as well as for the rate of interest. If persons and firms have available this third alternative of equities as a means of holding economic value over time, they will have to make judgments about the future yields of capital assets and compare these expected yields with anticipated returns from bonds. Holding equities means that economic value is stored in the form of real capital assets; wealth-holders must therefore consider future values of such assets as well as their prospective yields as reflected in the marginal efficiency of capital. But the value of a capital asset—both present and expected—depends in part on current and expected interest rates. Because of this the three basic forms in which economic values can be held over time are linked together in an intimate and complex fashion. Let us examine briefly the possible relationships that may exist between money, debts, and equities as a result of changing levels of income and expectations.[1]

In the development of this analysis there are certain things that the reader should keep in mind. We are dealing with events taking place in the monetary sphere of the economy. The key problem centers on the form in which value will be held over time rather than on the production of economic value. The desire of people to hold economic value as either money, debts, or equities depends on expectations held with respect to future economic values, and these can be expected to change as the income level changes. We shall assume a simplified, *cyclical* movement of income over time and distinguish four major phases of this movement.

Let us begin with the *crisis* phase of the cycle, the brief and dramatic end to a period of boom and prosperity. For our purposes the most important characteristics of the crisis are, first, a general collapse of all economic values, and second, a spreading demand for liquidity. These are but different aspects of the same phenomenon because it is the widespread scramble for liquidity in the panic atmosphere of the true economic crisis that leads to the general collapse of prices and economic values. In a vain effort to become perfectly liquid—i.e., hold all economic value in the form of money—asset holders hastily dump all their assets on the market. In terms of the theoretical framework developed in this chapter, the liquidity-preference function shifts sharply upward, while the demand schedule for bonds and the investment demand schedule collapse—i.e., they shift drastically to the left. The crisis phase is thus characterized by a decided and often dramatic movement from bonds and equities to cash. A sharp rise in interest rates is the inevitable consequence. The demand for liquidity is excessively strong, and a very high premium in the form of interest has to be paid to persuade people to part with the liquidity inherent in money.

The crisis phase is followed by a period of *contraction*, the length of

[1] This analysis was originally worked out by Professor Alvin H. Hansen. See his *A Guide to Keynes* (New York, McGraw-Hill, 153), pp. 135–139.

which will depend not only upon the character and duration of the preceding boom and the severity of the crisis, but also upon the vigor and
speed with which public action is taken to counteract the downward
tendencies now at work in the economy. Our concern, though, is not
with the length of the contraction period, but with what happens to the
liquidity-preference function and the demand for assets in other forms
during this period. In Hansen's view, the contraction phase is still dominated by pessimism with respect to future yields and values of real capital
assets; hence the movement away from equities that began in the crisis
phase is continued.[2] Interest rates will subside from the extraordinarily
high levels they reached during the preceding liquidity panic. This decline in interest rates during the contraction phase is the result of both a
downward movement in the asset demand function and a growing willingness on the part of wealth-holders to hold some of their assets in the
form of bonds. Prices of bonds begin to recover from the lows to which
they plunged during the crisis, and this, too, will lower the rate of interest. The contraction is thus characterized by a continued shift away from
equities as a form of wealth-holding, a decline in the over-all intensity of
the asset demand for money, and some shift back to debt instruments,
particularly high-grade bonds. Within the framework of the liquidity-
preference analysis, the contraction phase can be seen as a period of falling real income accompanied by a downward movement of the asset demand function. The basic reason for this is that during this phase more
favorable expectations with respect to future bond prices permeate the
market and shift the position of the L_a schedule.

Economic contraction must sooner or later give way to economic *recovery*. This will bring further changes in income, expectations, and the
forms in which economic value is held. This chief characteristic of the
recovery phase is the gradual re-establishment of confidence in future
economic values. The shift into bonds will continue, but as the recovery
gains momentum the movement into equities begins to become increasingly more significant. Potential purchasers of equities are encouraged by
the fact that interest rates fall as long as bond prices continue to rise,
while the increasingly favorable economic outlook tends to boost the expected rate of return on real capital assets. As long as the outlook for expected future prices of both debts and equities remain favorable, the
growing gap between the falling rate of return on debt (i.e., interest) and
the rising rate of return on equities (i.e., the marginal efficiency of capital) will spur wealth-holders to convert cash into equities. This trend will
become more and more pronounced as the recovery phase moves along.

Once the economy has regained the levels of economic activity that
prevailed prior to the onset of the crisis and depression, the recovery
phase merges gradually into what Hansen terms the *expansion* phase. Real

[2] *Ibid.*, p. 138.

income (and employment) moves to new levels, higher than heretofore. This is a period characterized by a strong upward surge of activity, particularly in the market for equities. Confidence in the continued growth of the economy is high and widespread, especially in the early stages of the expansion phase. Confidence and optimism with respect to future values generate an increase demand for equities, because the continued appreciation of current market values for existing equities and the favorable outlook for new capital assets increasingly make equities appear to be the most favorable form for holding economic value. A shift from bonds into equities begins to develop. Such a shift will tend to force interest rates higher as bond prices move downward, but the upward movement of interest rates will not begin to exert a "squeeze" on anticipated returns and values for real capital assets until the expansion phase has moved into truly boom conditions. Then, however, the asset demand function will begin to shift upward as more and more uncertainties develop with respect to a continuation of boom conditions and rising prices for equities. As the end of the boom approaches, the demand for liquidity will increase, and as the boom comes to an end and is succeeded by the crisis phase, there will again be a drastic movement away from both debts and equities. The cycle is complete.

In reality, of course, the economy does not advance in this precise cyclical way; its performance is more likely to be characterized by a series of sporadic advances and retrogressions of varying intensities. Yet the analysis serves to stress the important point that as the income level shifts upward and downward over the short run, expectations with respect to future economic values also shift, and thereby directly influence the form in which persons and firms are willing to hold economic value. Within the context of the liquidity-preference theory of interest, this means that the position of the *asset demand function* cannot be determined apart from a knowledge of the income level. Different income levels lead to different expectations of future values. As a result, the function that combines both the transactions and the asset demand for money into a single schedule relating the total demand for money to the rate of interest must be conceived of as a series of schedules, each associated with a different income level. The total demand for money increases as the income level rises, not only because of a rising transactions demand, but also because the asset demand function also tends to shift upward as the income level rises.

The Loanable-funds Theory of Interest

An alternative to the liquidity-preference theory of interest rate determination is the loanable-funds theory. The loanable-funds approach to determination of the interest rate is, in the last analysis, not so much an alternative theory as a different way of looking at the forces which enter into determination of the level of interest rates.

According to the loanable-funds theory, interest is the price which equates the demand for and the supply of loanable funds. In concept the theory is essentially similar to the classical theory, except that the schedules represent more than the supply of saving and the demand for saving. In the usual formulation of this theory the supply schedule of loanable funds consists not only of saving out of current income as in the classical analysis, but also of *net* dishoarding and hoarding of money balances and newly-created money. The demand schedule for loanable funds is usually thought to consist of the demand for funds for investment as in the classical analysis, although there is no reason why demand originating with consumers and government units cannot be incorporated into the analytical apparatus.

The nature of the loanable-funds theory is shown in Figure 11–10. The quantity of loanable funds, Q, represented on the horizontal axis; the rate of interest, i, on the vertical axis. The supply schedule SS slopes upward to the right, indicating that the quantity of loanable funds supplied to the market is a *direct* function of the rate of interest. The demand schedule DD has a negative slope, indicating that the demand for loanable funds is an *inverse* function of the rate of interest. Since this is a typical supply and demand situation, the equilibrium rate of interest, i_e, is that rate

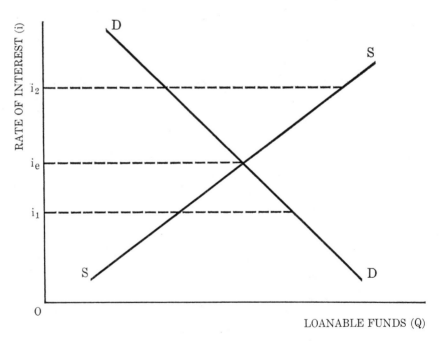

Figure 11–10. The Loanable-funds Theory of Interest

which equates the demand for and supply of loanable funds.

What is of key significance with respect to the loanable-funds theory is that it represents an analysis of the phenomenon of interest in terms of *flows*, whereas the liquidity-preference theory represents an analysis of the same phenomenon in terms of *stocks*. Once these two different modes of presentation are understood, it is relatively easy to see how the two theories are related, and how they are essentially different ways of looking at the same thing. In the loanable-funds analysis the supply schedule depicts the rate at which funds are flowing into the market during some interval of time. In this analysis, as in all analyses involving schedules of demand and supply, there is implicit a time dimension. The schedule tells us that the rate of inflow is a function of the rate of interest. The demand schedule represents the rate at which loanable funds are flowing out of the market. Equilibrium will prevail when the rates of inflow and outflow are equalized at a particular level of the interest rate.

How can this theory be reconciled with the liquidity-preference theory of interest? If equilibrium exists in the market for loanable funds as depicted in Figure 11-10, it means that there is neither a building up or a drawing down of money balance in the economy. This is identical with the necessary condition for equilibrium in the liquidity-preference analysis, in which equilibrium is a condition marked by equality in the demand for and the supply of money balances. If the latter are equal, then *net* hoarding or dishoarding is zero. Suppose in contrast, though, that the supply of loanable funds is in excess of the demand for loanable funds at the prevailing interest rate (rate i_2 in Figure 11-10). In this instance the rate of inflow is greater than the rate of outflow, and thus the interest rate will fall. Again, though, this is analogous to a situation in which the supply of money balances is in excess of the demand for money balances, $M^o_a > L_a$, and the holders of money balances will attempt to convert their excess holdings into a different asset form, interest-bearing securities. But as they do this, they will in effect draw down their money balances (or dishoard) and increase the inflow of loanable funds into the market. The opposite conditions would prevail if the demand for loanable funds is in excess of the current supply (rate i_1 in Figure 11-10). In this instance, the demand for money balances is greater than the supply, $L_a > M^o_a$. As persons seek to build up their money balances (hoard), the rate of interest will rise. A situation in which the inflow of loanable funds is smaller than the outflow means that holders are seeking to convert their interest-bearing securities into cash, which is what takes place whenever the asset demand for money, L_a, is greater than the current supply, M^o_a.

12

General Equilibrium and Public Policy

There is a dual objective in this chapter. The first aim is to develop a general equilibrium model of the aggregate economy which draws together the major strands of the analysis pursued in Chapters 4 through 11.[1] The second is to discuss the chief policy instruments at the disposal of modern governments and, with the aid of our general equilibrium model, to illustrate their applicability to problems relating to fluctuations in income and employment.[2]

Aside from its usefulness as an integrating device for all the important elements entering into the theory of income determination, this general model of the economic system can be employed to demonstrate several important features of the economic system. Keynes' liquidity preference theory of interest, examined in the previous chapter, analyzes the forces at work in the monetary sphere of the economy. Through the general model which we shall develop in this chapter, it is possible to show fully and clearly both the basic nature and the essential differences between the monetary and the goods sphere of activity in the economic system. The stress on the distinction between these two segments of the economy is one of the most fundamental differences between Keynesian and classical economics. The general equilibrium model also provides a simple and effective means to illustrate the idea advanced in the final section of the preceding chapter that money is not neutral, that the forces having to do with

[1] This model of the economic system was originally developed by professor J. R. Hicks. See his article, "Mr. Keynes and the Classics: A Suggested Interpretation," reprinted in *Readings in the Theory of Income Distribution* (Philadelphia, Blakiston, 1946), pp. 461–76.

[2] Economic policies oriented toward economic growth are discussed and analyzed in Chapter 16.

the demand for money are capable under certain circumstances of exercising an independent influence on income and employment levels.

Another important use of the model is to demonstrate through the concept of general equilibrium the manner in which the two spheres of the economy are linked together. The rate of interest provides a bridge between forces affecting the demand for money as such and those which revolve around the demand for goods and services.

The interdependence of the rate of interest and the level of income makes the model truly general; the underlying system of functional relationships which constitute the fundamentals of contemporary income theory operates in such a manner that it is not possible to determine the equilibrium income level without simultaneously determining the rate of interest. The model illustrates this clearly.

The approach that we will use in the development of the general model is to show the necessary conditions under which equilibrium may obtain in each of these two spheres of activity taken separately, and then, the conditions under which equilibrium may exist in both spheres simultaneously. The latter analysis will provide us with the model which demonstrates the nature of equilibrium in the economic system as a whole.

Equilibrium in the Monetary Sphere

The *monetary sphere* refers to the economic activities that center around the demand for and the supply of money to hold. These activities are also lumped under the phrase *the money market* because they include the different forms in which wealth-holders seek to hold economic value over time.

Monetary equilibrium exists when the demand for money to hold, L, is equal to the current supply, M^o. The demand for money, as we have seen, breaks down into two major components, the transactions demand, L_t, and the asset demand, L_a. Thus, $L = L_t + L_a$. The money supply, which is autonomously determined, can also be broken down into the quantity needed for transactions purposes, M^o_t, and a residual amount available for holding as an asset, M^o_a. Consequently, $M^o = M^o_t + M^o_a$. Therefore the following equation gives us a symbolic statement of the essential condition for monetary equilibrium:

$$L_t + L_a = M^o_t + M^o_a \qquad (12\text{--}1)$$

The total demand for money, L, is a function of both income and the rate of interest because one of its components, the transactions demand, is a function of income, while its other component, the asset demand, is a function of the rate of interest. This means that equilibrium with respect to the transactions demand is linked to income, and equilibrium with respect to the asset demand is linked to the rate of interest. Consequently, general equilibrium in the monetary sphere must be defined in terms of both the income level and the rate of interest.

Part A of Figure 12–1 is a series of L functions, each representing a combined transactions and asset demand function. Each function is associated with a different level of income. The vertical line M^o is an autonomous schedule representing the money supply. The figure yields a series of monetary equilibria; each equilibrium is associated with a particular income

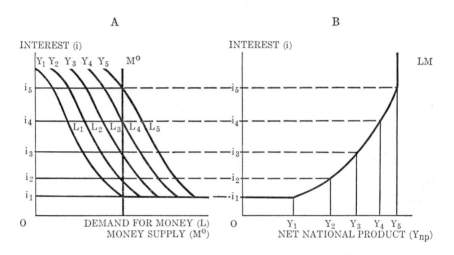

Figure 12–1. Equilibrium in the Monetary Sphere

level and a particular rate of interest. To illustrate, if the economy's income level is equal to Y_1, the money demand function, L, will be at the level of the curve labeled L_1. Given this particular function, and given the fixed money supply, M^o, monetary equilibrium exists at the point of intersection of the L_1 and the M^o schedules. This is at the rate of interest i_1. Now if the income level rises to Y_2, the money demand function will necessarily shift upward. Its new position is given by the curve L_2. With the money demand function at this level, monetary equilibrium again prevails at the point of intersection of the money demand and money supply curves, but it will be at the higher rate of interest i_2. As long as the income level is rising, this process continues and monetary equilibrium exists only at higher and higher rates of interest.

The explanation for the series of L functions in Figure 12–1 was given in Chapter 11. If the money supply is fixed, additional amounts of money needed to sustain more transactions can only be obtained by drawing them out of idle balances. But interest is the price that must be paid to persuade people to surrender the liquidity inherent in holding money balances; therefore, the only way to draw more and more funds out of inactive holdings is through higher and higher interest rates. The general lesson of our analysis should be quite clear: A rising level of real income will almost inevitably lead to higher interest rates unless the money supply is increased sufficiently to offset the continuous upward shift of the money demand function.

The LM Schedule

The essential nature of equilibrium in the monetary sphere and the manner in which it is linked to both the income level and the rate of interest are shown graphically in part B of Figure 12–1, which is derived directly from part A. The income level, Y, is measured on the horizontal axis; the rate of interest, i, on the vertical axis. Using the data from part A we can plot a series of points, each point representing a particular rate of interest and income level at which monetary equilibrium, $L = M$, prevails. Thus, at the income level Y_1 monetary equilibrium exists at a rate of interest equal to i_1; at the income level Y_2, at the rate of interest i_2; and so on. When we connect all these points together, we obtain a smooth curve known as the LM schedule, since it describes a series of equilibria between the demand for money, L, and the supply of money, M^o, in terms of a relationship between the income level and the rate of interest.

In Figure 12–1 it will be noted that at relatively low income levels the LM schedule lies flat or, in technical terms, is perfectly elastic with respect to the rate of interest. On the other hand, at relatively high income levels the LM schedule becomes vertical or perfectly inelastic with respect to the rate of interest. What are the reasons for this? The LM curve is constructed, it will be recalled, on the assumption that the total supply of money is fixed. This being the case, at low levels of income, the transactions demand for money, L_t, will also be relatively low. Therefore a large portion of the total money supply will be available for holding as idle balances. But any increase in the quantity of money available to hold as an asset, M^o_a, drives the rate of interest down. There is a limit to the extent that the rate of interest can fall, for as we saw in the analysis in the last chapter the asset demand function becomes perfectly elastic at relatively low rates of interest. This is the "liquidity trap." Once we reach the critical level at which interest rates do not respond to any further increases in the quantity of money available for holding as idle balances, then the LM curve must become perfectly elastic with respect to the rate of interest. A further decline in income will not, in other words, cause any further decline in interest rates through the impact of money balances released by a declining transactions demand.

The vertical character of the upper reaches of the LM curve is also explained by the assumption that the money supply is fixed. The essential point is that there is some maximum to the level of income that can be financed with a fixed quantity of money.[3] Money, in other words, can become a bottleneck that will choke off an expansion of income beyond some given level. As the income level rises, the transactions demand for money will obviously increase. A higher level of income means more transactions, and more money will be needed to sustain the larger volume. But the assumption of a fixed money supply means that additional quantities of money can be obtained for transactions purposes only by drawing them out of idle balances. The cost of doing this is a higher rate of interest, and thus as the income level rises, interest rates must rise higher and higher. Eventually the economy will reach a critical level at which any further expansion in the income level becomes impossible because the entire money supply is now held in transactions balances. In Figure 12–1 (part B) Y_5 is assumed to be the maximum income that an amount of money M^o can sustain, assuming *no* change in velocity.

The effect of an increase in the money supply on the position of the *LM* curve is shown in Figure 12–2. The initial position of the *LM* curve is shown by the solid line LM_1. The dotted line LM_2 shows the position of the curve following an increase in the money supply. The reason why such an increase will shift the curve to the right can be easily understood by referring once again to Figure 12–1 (part A). The existence of a fixed

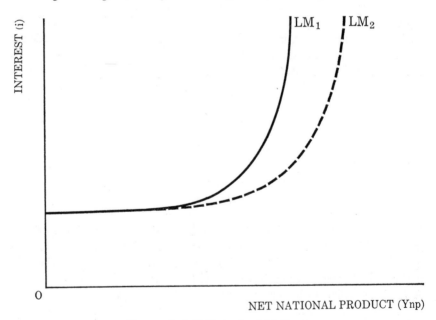

Figure 12–2. Shift in the LM Curve

[3] J. R. Hicks, *op. cit.*, p. 470.

money supply as given by the M^o schedule meant that monetary equilibrium at each and every possible income level was uniquely associated with a particular rate of interest. An increase in the money supply shifts this curve to the right, thus making possible monetary equilibrium at any particular income level at a *lower* rate of interest than heretofore. To show this situation in terms of the *LM* curve, it is necessary to shift this curve to the right as is done in Figure 12–2. Each point on the LM_2 curve represents a particular income level that is uniquely correlated with a rate of interest that is lower than the rate correlated with the point representing the same income level on curve LM_1.

Equilibrium in the Goods Sphere

The *goods sphere* refers essentially to those economic activities involving the production and use of goods and services. Our concern here is with the forces that center in aggregate demand and supply and with the conditions under which an equilibrium exists with respect to the demand for and the supply of goods and services for the economy as a whole.

The major portion of the analysis pursued prior to this chapter has aimed at defining the various conditions under which income equilibrium exists in the economy. Thus if we postulate a simple economy without government and without foreign transactions, the necessary condition for equilibrium is that investment and saving *ex ante* be equal. (*See* Figure 6–4.) If we introduce government into the analysis, but retain the assumption that there are no international transactions, the necessary condition for equilibrium becomes one in which *ex ante* investment plus government purchases of goods and services, $I + G$, is equal to *ex ante* saving plus net taxes, $S + T$. (*See* Figure 9–2.) Finally, the introduction of international transactions into the analysis means that the necessary condition for income (and output) equilibrium is one in which the sum of *ex ante* investment plus government purchases of goods and services plus exports, $I + G + X$, equals the sum of *ex ante* saving plus net taxes plus imports, $S + T + M$. (*See* Figure 10–7.)

In constructing our general equilibrium model, we shall assume for the sake of simplicity a closed economy, although the inclusion of foreign transactions changes in no way the basic principles involved. In a closed economy, the basic condition for equilibrium is the *ex ante* equality of saving and net taxes $(S + T)$ and investment plus government purchases of goods and services $(I + G)$. Saving and net taxes are a function of income in the model, whereas investment expenditures are an inverse function of the rate of interest, and government purchases of goods and services are assumed to be autonomous with respect to both income and the rate of interest.[4]

[4] To simplify the construction of the graphic model, we shall not explicitly take into account investment expenditures induced by a change in the income level, although the phenomenon of induced investment is built into the model in its

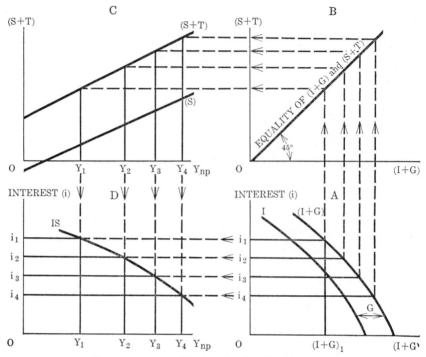

Figure 12–3. Equilibrium in the Goods Sphere

The *IS* Schedule

The interaction of schedule values for $(I + G)$ and $(S + T)$ in the determination of an equilibrium value for income is shown in Figure 12–3. In part A of the figure, an investment demand schedule relating investment outlays inversely to the rate of interest is shown. To this schedule at all possible levels of the interest rate is added a fixed amount representing autonomous government expenditures for goods and services. The result is the schedule $(I + G)$, showing an inverse relationship to the rate of interest for the combined total of I and G. In part C of the figure, the combined saving plus net taxes function is shown, both of which vary directly with income. By means of the schedules shown in part A and part C, we can link income and the rate of interest in the goods sphere.

To illustrate, let us assume that initially the rate of interest is at the level i_1. This rate will yield a combined total of I plus G expenditure equal to $(I + G)_1$. The latter is measured on the horizontal axis of the diagram in part A. Part B in Figure 12–3 shows $(I + G)$ on the horizontal axis and $(S + T)$ on the vertical axis; the 45° line bisecting the figure in part B thus represents equality between $(I + G)$ and $(S + T)$. By projecting

---

graphic form (Figure 12–3) and the equation system which underlies the model. (See the appendix to this chapter).

vertically from $(I + G)_1$ in part A until we intercept the 45° line in part B and projecting horizontally from this point until we intercept the $(S + T)$ function in part C, it is possible to determine graphically the *specific* equilibrium value for the net national product that will result from an interest rate equal to i_1. This equilibrium value is Y_1 on the horizontal axis of the figure in part C. Essentially, our analysis to this point shows that, given the $(S + T)$ function, a high value for the rate of interest will mean a low level of combined $(I + G)$ expenditures, and, hence, a low income level. If we lower the rate of interest, this will increase $(I + G)$ and push the income level higher. Each successively higher equilibrium value for the net national product which results from successive cuts in the rate of interest is one which will prevail *after* the multiplier effects have worked themselves out.

The main point is that, given both the $(S + T)$ function and the $(I + G)$ function, equilibrium in the goods sphere of the economy is achieved at higher and higher income levels only as the rate of interest declines. This relationship between the rate of interest, the level of income, and successive equilibrium positions in the goods sphere can be expressed in schedule form in a manner analogous to the construction of the *LM* curve. In part D of Figure 12–3 net national product, Y_{np}, is measured on the horizontal axis and the rate of interest, i, on the vertical axis. Since an equality between $(S + T)$ and $(I + G)$ at successively higher income levels results only as the rate of interest declines, the curve that links income and the rate of interest in terms of the $(S + T) = (I + G)$ equilibrium will slope downward to the right. This curve is labeled the *IS* schedule because each point on it relates equilibrium in the goods sphere to income and the rate of interest.

The shape of the *IS* schedule depends upon the essential character of the $(S + T)$ function and the investment demand function. If, for example, the investment demand function is assumed to be relatively *interest-inelastic*, then it logically follows that the *IS* curve, too, will be relatively interest-inelastic because any given change in the rate of interest will have only a modest effect on the volume of investment spending. As a consequence, the income level will also be little affected by changes in the rate of interest. A change in the position of either the $(S + T)$ function or the $(I + G)$ schedule shifts the over-all position of the *IS* curve. For example, an upward movement in the investment demand schedule will shift the *IS* curve to the right, and make possible an equilibrium between $(S + T)$ and $(I + G)$ at a higher level of income than heretofore. A shift of this type is depicted by the dotted IS_2 curve in Figure 12–4.

Including exports and imports in our analysis does not materially change the nature of the curve describing the relationship between income and the rate of interest in terms of the necessary conditions for equilibrium in the goods sphere. The curve would simply lie further to the right, and our conception of it would have to be enlarged to see each point on it as rep-

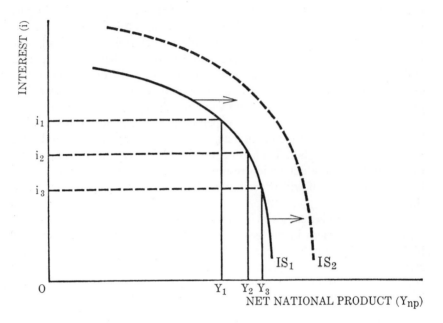

Figure 12-4. The IS Curve

resenting a condition in which $I + G + X$ was equal to $S + T + M$ at specific levels of both income and the rate of interest. Since it can be assumed that G and X are autonomous with respect to both income and the rate of interest, the $I + G + X$ curve would still slope downward to the right; including G and X in the aggregate demand function does not change the inverse functional relationship between investment and the rate of interest.

General Equilibrium

By combining the *LM* and *IS* curves in a single diagram we are able to construct in graphic form a general model of the economic system which shows, particularly, the manner in which the monetary sphere and the goods sphere are linked together through the rate of interest. Such a graphic model is shown in Figure 12–5. This model can be employed to demonstrate how the rate of interest and the income level are mutually determined, and to show a number of different and important situations that may be characteristic of the economic system.

In Figure 12–5 the *IS* and *LM* curves intersect at a point where net national product is at Y_e and the rate of interest is at i_e. These are equilibrium levels with respect to income and the rate of interest, both of which are mutually determined by the intersection of the *IS* and *LM* schedules. At the point of intersection of these curves, the output level, Y_{np}, and the rate

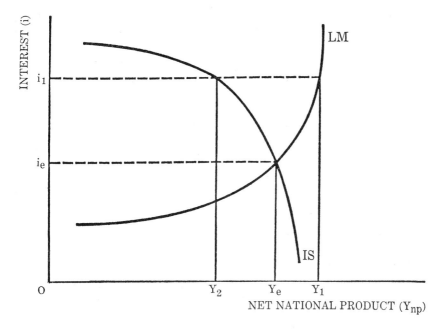

Figure 12–5. The General Equilibrium Model of the Economic System

of interest, i, are such that $(S + T)$ and $(I + G)$ are in equilibrium, and the demand for money, L, and the supply of money, M^o, are also in equilibrium. There are any number of levels of both the rate of interest and income that are compatible with equilibrium of either $(S + T)$ and $(I + G)$ alone, or the demand for and supply of money also considered alone, but there is only *one* rate of interest and *one* level of income that is consistent with equilibrium in both the monetary and the goods sphere. The actual level of both income and interest that is consistent with equilibrium in the two spheres depends upon the shape and level assumed for the *LM* and *IS* curves, and this, in turn, is dependent upon the characteristics of the functions which lie back of these schedules.

The reasons why the point of intersection of the *IS* and *LM* schedules depict a condition of general equilibrium for the whole economy can best be seen if we imagine that income and the rate of interest are, momentarily, at a level different from Y_e and i_e.

Let us assume for a moment that the rate of interest and income are *actually* at levels represented by i_1 and Y_1, as shown in Figure 12–5. This represents a disequilibrium condition in the system as a whole, for while these values for both income and the rate of interest are compatible with equilibrium in the monetary sphere, they are not compatible with income in the goods sphere. At the interest rate i_1, for instance, income would have to be at the level of Y_2 to bring equilibrium in the goods sphere, as determined by the *IS* curve. The system will of necessity move toward an equilibrium point; at the interest rate i_1 investment expenditure will not be sufficient to maintain an income level of Y_1, and hence the latter will decline. But as the income level declines, a portion of the money supply is released from use in response to the transactions motive, and as this happens the rate of interest declines, thereby making possible equilibrium in the monetary sphere at successively lower rates of both interest and income. This adjustment process will continue until a level of interest rates and income is reached that is compatible with equilibrium in both spheres of economic activity. Then, and only then, will a general equilibrium condition for the whole economy prevail.

Changes in the Equilibrium Values of Income and Interest

A change in the equilibrium level of the net national product and the rate of interest comes about within the framework of our graphic model of the economic system as the consequence of a shift in the position of either the *IS* or *LM* curve. It should be noted carefully that all shifts in equilibrium values for income embody the multiplier process; which is to say, every equilibrium value for income shown in the model is arrived at *after* the multiplier process has worked itself out.

For convenience in our analysis, we can describe changes which affect the equilibrium values for both income and the rate of interest as being either *real* or *monetary* in origin. By *real* changes we mean those that originate in the goods sector, and that thus come about because the *IS* curve has shifted. *Monetary* changes, on the other hand, refer to developments emanating from the monetary sphere and, consequently, manifest themselves through a change in the position of the *LM* schedule. Examination of the major sources of shifts in both the *IS* and *LM* schedules will provide us with the necessary background for a discussion of contemporary economic policy and its application to fluctuations in income and employment.[5]

Shifts in the *IS* Curve

The fundamental explanation for a rightward shift in the *IS* curve is an increase in the aggregate demand function. Four major explanations for an upward movement of the aggregate demand function can be distinguished. First, there may be an autonomous increase in the investment demand function. In this instance, schedule *I* in part A of Figure 12–2 shifts to the right, indicating a higher level of investment spending at all ranges

---

[5] In the discussion that follows we shall focus our attention on shifts to the right in both the *IS* and *LM* schedules. The same reasoning and explanations apply with respect to shifts in the opposite direction.

of the interest rate. Second, there may be an autonomous increase in government spending for goods and services. If such an increase takes place with *no* increase in taxes, the maximum shift in the aggregate demand schedule will be obtained. However, even if taxes are increased in an amount equal to an increase in government spending for goods and services, the balanced budget theorem examined in Chapter 9 indicates that the aggregate demand function will still be displaced upward. Third, there may be an autonomous upward shift in the consumption function. This could come about because of an increase in transfer payments, a reduction in personal income taxes, or a general tax reduction with no change in the level of either government expenditures or investment outlays. It might also result from changing attitudes toward thrift, which would have the effect of reducing the propensity to save at all income levels. Finally, the aggregate demand function may shift because of an increase in exports rela-

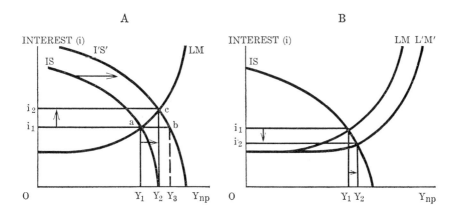

Figure 12–6. Shifts in the IS and LM Curves

tive to imports. This may result from an absolute increase in exports or a downward shift in the import function.

Within the framework of our general equilibrium model the effect upon income of an upward shift in the aggregate demand schedule depends upon (1) the extent to which the *IS* curve is displaced to the right (the distance *ab* in part A of Figure 12–6), and (2) the impact that a rising rate of interest will have upon forces which determine equilibrium in the goods sphere (the distance *bc* in the same figure). The factors which govern the magnitude of the shift in the *IS* curve are those which influence the size of the multiplier effect, given an increase (or decrease) in aggregate demand. These latter are the array of factors which determine the extent of "leakages" from the income stream. If there is no change in the position of the *LM* schedule with a given shift to the right in the *IS* curve, the result will be a rise in the rate of interest. This is due to the fact that the increase in the transactions demand which accompanies the rightward shift in the *IS* schedule can be met only by drawing money out of the asset sphere, a development which necessarily entails higher interest rates. The over-all impact of the rise in the interest rate is to dampen down the income-increasing effect of the rightward shift in the *IS* curve. The magnitude of this dampening effect depends upon both the steepness of the *LM* curve at the point of shift in the *IS* schedule, and the interest elasticity of the investment component of the aggregate demand function. In our discussion of policy, we shall return to this point.

Shifts in the LM Curve

The effect of a rightward shift in the *LM* curve upon both the equilibrium income level and the equilibrium value for the rate of interest is depicted in part B of Figure 12–6. Essentially, there are three major explanations for a shift to the right in the *LM* function. First, such a shift may take place because of an autonomous increase in the money supply. The reasons why an increase in the money supply shifts the *LM* curve were touched upon in the discussion in conjunction with Figure 12–2. A change in the money supply is most likely to be the source of a shift in the *LM* schedule. Second, the *LM* curve may shift to the right because of a downward shift in the asset demand component, L_a, of the total demand for money. This would be the result of a general decline in the demand for liquidity throughout the economy. The effect of a downward shift in the liquidity preference function is to release funds from idle balances, which spill over into the bond market, pushing up the prices of the latter and, thereby, reducing interest rates. It follows from this that monetary equilibrium in relation to any given income level will be achieved at a lower rate of interest. Finally, the *LM* curve may shift because of a fall in the general price level, assuming no change in the money supply. When prices fall, the transactions demand for money will be less at any and all levels of real income; hence, the series of schedules representing the total demand for money, *L*, will shift to the left (part A, Figure 12–1). The results in this case are identical with an increase in the supply of money; which is to say, monetary equilibrium at any given income level is possible at a lower rate of interest.[6]

[6] This has sometimes been called the "Keynes effect," primarily because Keynes argued that a general decline in prices and money costs would leave *real* values un-

In general, the effect upon the equilibrium income level of a shift to the right in the *LM* curve depends upon (1) the extent to which the rate of interest declines as a result of the shift in the *LM* schedule, and (2) the responsiveness of forces in the goods sphere to a decline in the rate of interest. The latter is *primarily* a matter of the interest elasticity of the investment demand schedule, although other components of aggregate demand may be affected by a change in the rate of interest. We shall elaborate further upon this in our subsequent discussion of policy and its application.

In connection with shifts in the *LM* curve, one additional point should be noted: with the exception of changes taking place in the range of interest rates equal or below the horizontal portion of the *LM* schedule, a shift to the right in the *LM* schedule will *always* reduce the rate of interest. The significance of this is that the full multiplier effect will follow; there will be, in other words, no offsetting changes in the rate of interest as is the situation confronting the economy when the *IS* curve shifts.

The Principles of Economic Policy

The formulation of economic policy is a difficult and subtle art, and involves, as Edwin G. Nourse, first chairman of the President's Council of Economic Advisors, has said, choice among conflicting values and judgment as to what is "best" in a total situation.[7] But economic policy must be soundly grounded in economic theory if it is to be effective, and it is thus desirable that we give some thought and attention to the possible policy implications that flow out of the theoretical analysis in this and earlier chapters.

Professor Musgrave, the reader will recall, listed economic stabilization as one of the three major functions of government in modern society. The growth of the economic role of the public sector is the basic reason why modern governments possess such great potential to act as the major stabilizing force in the economy. The power potential inherent in the expanded role of the public sector puts government in a position to promote stability along with full employment and maximum production, and, in the United States, the Employment Act of 1946 gave congressional sanction to the idea that the national government has a responsibility for income and employment levels in the economy.[8]

---

affected; hence, there would be no shift in the aggregate demand function. In contrast to this, there is the "Pigou effect" (see Chapter 6), which argues that the increase in the real value of assets resulting from a fall in the general price level will induce an upward shift in the consumption function and the aggregate demand schedule. The Pigou effect would lead to a rightward shift in the *IS* curve as a consequence of a fall in the general price level, whereas the Keynes effect leaves the *IS* curve unchanged, but shifts the *LM* schedule.

[7] Edwin G. Nourse, *Economics in the Public Service* (New York, Harcourt, Brace, 1953), p. 18.

[8] Some persons, economists and others, would argue that price stability as a goal of public policy should be given the same type of legislative sanction as full employment.

Monetary policy and fiscal policy are the two chief instruments at the disposal of the central government for attainment of economic stabilization. Our major interest is, first, in the manner in which both monetary and fiscal policy can be expected to work, and second, in their effectiveness as instruments for the control of aggregate economic activity.

As a general proposition stabilization policy involves the exercise of influence on the economy's over-all expenditure level because the essential lesson of modern theory is that fluctuations in income and employment are primarily matters of too much or too little spending in relation to existing supply or capacity. Both monetary and fiscal policy measures must be evaluated in terms of their impact on expenditure levels, which is to say, in terms of their impact on aggregate demand.

Monetary Policy and Aggregate Demand

Monetary policy works primarily through controls exercised over the supply of money. In an advanced economy this basically means control over the volume of bank lending. In the United States the Federal Reserve System is the chief agency through which such control is exercised. The objective in controlling the money supply, including bank lending, is indirectly to control spending. More specifically, control over the money supply will be reflected in changes in interest rates, which, in turn, will have an impact on spending. The brunt of this impact will be borne by investment expenditure, as neither the consumption nor the government expenditures component of aggregate demand is readily linked to the rate of interest. Thus, the question of the efficacy of monetary policy as an instrument of economic stabilization largely turns on the issue of the shape of the investment demand schedule, about which economists are not in full agreement.

There are two broad sets of controls through which monetary policy is implemented. First, there are general or indirect controls, which include changes in the reserve requirements of the commercial banks, changes in the rediscount rate, and open market operations by the central bank—that is, the Federal Reserve System. Second, there are selective or direct controls aimed at controlling specific types of credit, such as installment credit, mortgage credit, or credit extended for the financing of stock market transactions. Indirect controls are used to alter the over-all volume of credit available to the economy; they do not seek to influence the allocation of credit (that is, money funds) among alternative uses. General credit controls have been by far the most important activities of the Federal Reserve System. Hence any general discussion of monetary policy must be directed primarily toward the use and effectiveness of indirect controls.

Critics of monetary policy usually argue that it discriminates in favor of

---

For a discussion of this, see Donald Stevenson Watson, *Economic Policy* (Boston, Houghton Mifflin, 1960), pp. 539–551.

the large firm primarily because the investment plans of large firms are not nearly so dependent upon access to borrowed funds as are those of smaller firms. More serious perhaps is the criticism that monetary policy is ineffective because if it is applied with sufficient vigor in a period of inflation to bring about a contraction in investment spending, it will push the economy into a recession. On the other hand, monetary policy cannot be relied upon to bring the economy out of a serious depression, because even a drastic change in the interest rate is not enough of an incentive to stimulate investment spending when aggregate demand is at a low level. Proponents of monetary policy are likely to point in reply to the indirect character of monetary policy as one of its chief virtues because the government is not involved directly in the regulation of economic activity. Monetary policy can be said to possess the virtues of speed and flexibility since normally it is administered by central banks and thus does not require legislative action.

Economists are by no means in complete agreement with respect to either the effectiveness or desirability of monetary policy, although the experience gained in both monetary and fiscal policy in the last thirty years has probably convinced most economists that fiscal policy is the more powerful instrument for the control of economic activity. This does not mean that monetary policy has no role to play, but rather that its role is, by and large, subordinate to fiscal policy.[9]

Fiscal Policy and Aggregate Demand

Fiscal policy embraces deliberate changes in government expenditures and taxes as a means of controlling economic activity. The budget of the national government is the key instrument through which fiscal policy is effected. Government expenditures for goods and services directly affect the level of economic activity because such expenditures are a component part of the aggregate demand function; transfer expenditures and taxes, on the other hand, affect disposable income and thus indirectly influence the other two major components of aggregate demand, consumption and investment spending. Fiscal policy therefore works through changes in the government's budget which, in turn, increase or decrease the level of spending in the economy.

Economists are not fully in agreement as to the form and scope of fiscal policy. At one extreme is the concept of *functional finance* which asserts that the primary consideration of the government in all its operations ought to be the effects of its actions on income and employment levels.[10] The

---

[9] Henry C. Wallich, "Postwar United States Monetary Policy Appraised," in *United States Monetary Policy* (New York, The American Assembly, Columbia University Press, 1958), p. 117. For a contrary view on the effectiveness of monetary policy, especially in stimulating the growth of the economy, see Allan H. Meltzer, "The Money Managers and the Boom," *Challenge*, March/April, 1966, pp. 5–7.

[10] Abba P. Lerner, *The Economics of Control* (New York, Macmillan, 1949), pp. 302 ff.

staunchest advocates of functional finance argue, for example, that government should raise (or lower) taxes not because it needs more (or less) money, but because it wants to decrease (or increase) consumption spending. Also, the major consideration with respect to the level of government spending should be its impact on the level of aggregate demand rather than the economy's need for, say, social goods. Proposals like those embodied in the notion of functional finance rest upon the assumption that economic stabilization is the one really important function of the modern government, a point of view that will be disputed by those who are keenly interested in the problem of an adequate supply of social goods and services in an expanding and affluent society. We may note parenthetically that here is a point of potential conflict and contradiction because a growing need and demand for social goods may make it difficult, if not impossible, at times to adjust the tax and expenditure budgets of the public sector to the requirements of stabilization policy.

At the other extreme are proposals which suggest that the budget of the Federal government ought to be so constructed that taxes and expenditures would be automatically in balance at an income level somewhat below that of full employment. If this were done, and if, further, tax *rates* and government expenditures remained constant, then a budgetary surplus would automatically be generated as the economy approached the full-employment level. But if income fell below the level at which taxes and expenditures are in balance, an automatic deficit would ensue.[11] A budgetary policy which leads to a surplus in prosperity and a deficit in recession or depression is generally recognized as counter-cyclical because the surplus draws funds out of the current income stream and the deficit adds funds to the income flow. The proposal described here is counter-cyclical in this sense (something which is true generally of modern fiscal policy), but it is unique in being wholly dependent upon the built-in characteristics of the tax structure that cause taxes automatically to rise in periods of income expansion and to fall in periods of income contraction. In such a proposal there is no room for discretionary fiscal action by either the executive or legislative branch of the government.

The views of most economists as to the manner in which fiscal policy should be applied lie somewhere between these two extremes. Economists today are in almost universal agreement that there is no sound economic reason why the budget of the national government should be balanced on an annual basis. It is only necessary, according to the rules of modern fiscal policy, that deficits incurred during a depression or recession be offset by surpluses acquired in subsequent periods of prosperity. Beyond this, though, there is no general consensus on the proper mix of automatic stabilizers (as

[11] This is the position that has been taken in the past by the Committee for Economic Development. For further details see the studies issued by the C.E.D.: *Taxes and the Budget*, November, 1947; and *Monetary and Fiscal Policy for Greater Economic Stability*, December, 1948.

envisaged in the program just described) and discretionary action by appropriate authorities.

More recently, and under the influence of the Council of Economic Advisors, the focus of fiscal policy has shifted away from minimizing the ups and downs of cyclical fluctuations in both income and employment. Beginning with President Kennedy's Council of 1962, whose chairman was Professor Walter W. Heller of the University of Minnesota, the emphasis has been upon the use of discretionary fiscal policy to maintain economic growth at a rate equal to the growth in the economy's potential.[12] We shall discuss these policies in detail in Chapter 16.

Fiscal policy is undoubtedly a more powerful instrument for economic stabilization than monetary policy, but it is subject to difficulties and limitations. First, fiscal policy measures that involve changes in public expenditures may conflict with the long-term character of many governmental expenditure programs. It is not possible continually to adjust expenditures for basic social goods and services to meet the shifting exigencies of economic stabilization. Second, the political process through which changes in expenditures and taxes are effected is so long drawn out and fraught with so many uncertainties that it is nearly impossible in a democratic society to obtain the necessary speed and flexibility that fiscal policy requires if it is to be successful as an instrument for economic stabilization. Finally, it is averred that the key concept of modern fiscal policy, the cyclically balanced budget at the national level, does not work. There is no serious objection politically to a governmental deficit in a recession or depression because nearly everyone will benefit from the stimulus this brings to the economy. But opposition to the kind of tax policy necessary to generate a surplus may be so strong that the required budgetary surplus will fail to appear in periods of prosperity.[13]

Which of the two policy approaches to economic stabilization is more effective cannot be definitively answered. Actually, this is not the really important question. Monetary and fiscal policy should be complementary rather than competitive. Perhaps a majority of economists today would be in sympathy with Professor Alvin Hansen's view that our primary hope for attainment of economic stabilization must rest with fiscal policy, but this must be supported by monetary policy of a moderate character.[14] Be-

[12] See especially the paper by Walter W. Heller, "Adjusting the 'New Economics' to High Pressure Prosperity," in *Managing a Full Employment Economy*, The Committee for Economic Development (New York, 1966), pp. 8–21.

[13] This difficulty is dramatically illustrated by the obvious reluctance of the administration to request a tax increase at any time during the first three quarters of 1966, even though the rising level of defense expenditures for the war in Viet Nam put the economy under strong inflationary pressures. The consumer price index rose from 110.1 in January, 1966 (1957–1959 = 100) to 113.3 as of July, 1966, a sharper increase than experienced in any comparable period in the 1960's.

[14] Alvin H. Hansen, *The American Economy* (New York, McGraw-Hill, 1957), p. 56.

yond this, policy-makers ought to strive particularly to improve the timing and flexibility of both types of policy.

Management of the Public Debt

One other policy area requires a brief mention before we turn to the application of policy to our general equilibrium model. This is the area of public debt management, by which is meant actions of both the Federal Reserve System and the Treasury which affect the *composition* of the public debt of the central government.

The size of the debt is determined by the fiscal policies of the government. Composition of the debt has to do with the differences in the securities which make up the debt on the basis of their maturities. The Federal Reserve System can affect the composition of the debt held by the public through its open market operations, while the Treasury affects the debt's composition whenever it goes into the market to get funds. The latter is done when either the size of the debt is being increased, or the Treasury is engaged in refunding operations for outstanding debt.

Basically, the public debt consists of two types of securities, namely, short-term issues (Treasury bills) and long-term issues (bonds). Short-term securities are highly liquid, carry a low rate of interest, and often are a close substitute for money. Long-term securities, on the other hand, are less liquid, generally carry a higher rate of interest, and are not so universally regarded as money substitutes. It is these differences between short and long-term securities which are the basis for analysis of the possible effects of debt management policies upon the stability of the economic system. In general, a policy of "shortening" the structure of the public debt tends to raise the level of aggregate demand, partly because such a move puts more liquidity and near money into the system, and partly, too, because the government would not then be competing in the market for long-term funds, which then could go, presumably, to finance investment spending. Management which aims at "lengthening" the debt's structure would have the opposite effect. Orthodox debt management policies call for issuing long-term securities (for new issues or refunding operations) during inflationary periods and short-term securities during a recession or depression. Actually, the Treasury has had only limited success in pursuing such policies; furthermore, there is little knowledge available concerning the quantitative effects of alternative policies.[15]

The Application of Fiscal and Monetary Policy

Some of the problems and situations which may be encountered in the application of monetary and fiscal policy may be illustrated by means of our general equilibrium model. This can be done by combining shifts in

[15] See W. Carl Biven, *Economics and Public Policy* (Columbus, Ohio, Charles E. Merrill Books, Inc.), pp. 118, 119.

either the *IS* or *LM* schedule with situations in which the *IS* curve intersects the *LM* curve at various points along the latter. The different conditions which might be present in the economy and which will confront the
policy-maker are illustrated in Figure 12–7.

In this figure the original position of the *LM* curve is shown as a solid

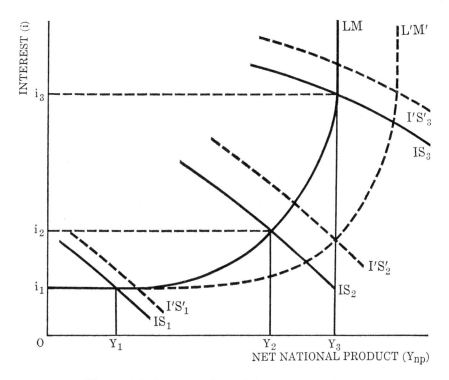

Figure 12–7. Interpretations of the Economy via the
General Equilibrium Model

line. Three different *IS* curves in solid lines are shown, and they intersect
the *LM* curve at three different points. IS_1 intersects the *LM* curve in the
range at which the latter is perfectly elastic with respect to the rate of interest; IS_3 intersects the *LM* curve at a point at which the curve is perfectly
inelastic with respect to the rate of interest; and IS_2 intersects the *LM* curve
at a point in between these two extremes. The dotted lines in the diagram
depict shifts in both the *IS* and *LM* curves. Shifts in these curves are
brought about by the application of either fiscal or monetary policy measures.

If the *IS* curve intersects the *LM* schedule in the range at which the latter
is perfectly elastic with respect to the rate of interest, certain significant
policy implications follow. Such a situation may arise because the econ-

omy is in a depression, with both income and the rate of interest declining to relatively low levels. In this situation monetary policy involving an increase in the money supply will be completely ineffective. An increase in the money supply will shift the *LM* curve to the right, and this will, *ceteris paribus*, tend to raise the income level, but only if the rate of interest lies *above* the critical level at which the *LM* schedule is perfectly elastic. The point of intersection of *IS*₁ and the *LM* curve typifies a situation in which the demand for liquidity is so great that any increase in the money supply simply is added to existing idle balances. The increase, in other words, drops into the *liquidity trap*, and no change in either the rate of interest, investment expenditure, or the income level will ensue. A rise in the income level must wait upon a higher position of the *IS* curve which would require an upward shift in the aggregate demand function. If we are dealing with a depression situation, the obvious implication of our analysis is that fiscal rather than monetary policy measures are needed. This is particularly true if it is assumed that the investment demand schedule becomes increasingly interest-inelastic in a depression.

An interesting corollary of the foregoing analysis is that in the early stages of recovery from a depression the income level can rise—at least up to a point—without any corresponding pressure on the interest rate, even if the money supply is fixed. At extremely low levels of income the relative excess of money available as an asset because of the low volume of transactions is so great that no additional premium—that is, interest—is needed to induce some holders of liquidity to part with it once the income level begins to rise.

A situation quite the opposite of that just described prevails if the *IS* curve intersects the *LM* curve at a point at which the latter is perfectly inelastic with respect to the rate of interest. This is shown in Figure 12–7 by the intersection of *IS*₃ and the *LM* schedule at the income level Y_3 and the rate of interest i_3. This is a classic case of a situation in which the *only* effective means to increase income is through monetary policy. If the money supply is increased, the interest rate will fall, and the income level will rise as investment expenditure responds to a lower rate of interest. The consequence of the increase in the money supply is shown by the shift to the right—to the dotted line *L'M'*—of the *LM* schedule. At *L'M'* and with the same *IS*₃ curve, the equilibrium income level will be higher and the equilibrium rate of interest lower. If the intersection of the *IS* and *LM* curves in the range in which the latter is perfectly interest-inelastic implies the desirability of monetary policy, it is equally true that intersection in this range implies the complete unworkability of fiscal policy. A fiscal policy embodying measures that induce an upward shift in the aggregate demand function without any corresponding change in the money supply is bound to be self-defeating. This is readily shown in Figure 12–7, for if the aggregate demand function shifts upward, the *IS* curve also shifts upward. But, as the reader can see, a shift upward of IS_3 to $I'S'_3$ has no effect whatsoever on the income level. The only consequence of this change is an increase in the rate of interest. An upward shift in the aggregate demand function, assuming no change in the money supply, merely drives interest rates higher because of the rising transactions demand induced by the original shift in the aggregate demand function. The net result ultimately is *no* change in the income level, but equilibrium of saving and investment at a higher rate of interest.

The points of intersection of the IS and LM curves which lie between the two extreme situations discussed above represent situations in which both monetary and fiscal policy may be effective in varying degrees. For example, if the economy's IS curve lies at the position shown by the schedule labeled IS_2, the equilibrium income level is then Y_2 and the equilibrium rate of interest is i_2. Under these circumstances, either an increase in the money supply (monetary policy) or a shift upward in the aggregate demand function (fiscal policy), or a judicious combination of both will have the effect of raising the income level. As a general principle, the nearer the point of intersection lies to the i_3 rate of interest, the more effective is monetary policy, and conversely, the nearer the point of intersection lies to the rate of interest i_1, the more effective is fiscal policy.

One final word of warning: the reader should not forget that our discussion and analysis pertain to what takes place within the confines of a graphic "model" of the economy, and thus the conclusions offered with respect to the effectiveness of both monetary and fiscal policies should not be thought of as providing definitive answers to the complex problems of policy that exist in the real economic world. At best they represent insights into the workings of the economy and suggest only the broadest sort of guidelines to actual policy formulation.

APPENDIX

Algebraic presentation of the general equilibrium model

Equilibrium in the goods sphere in an "open economy."
(1) $Y_{np} = C + I + G + X - M$ = the basic identity
(2) $C = C_o' + a'Y_{np}$ = the consumption function
$\qquad a' = (a - at)$ = the MPC out of net national product
$\qquad C_o' = (Co - aT_o)$ = consumption that is independent of the income level. Taxes are reflected in both a' and C_o'
(3) $I = I_o' + bY_{np}$ = the investment function
$\qquad I_o' = (I_o - ci)$ = investment as an inverse function of the rate of interest. I_o' equals investment which is independent of the income level
(4) $M = M_o + mY_{np}$ = the import function
(5) G = autonomous government expenditures for goods and services
(6) X = autonomous exports

(7) $Y_{np} = C_o' + a'Y_{np} + I_o' + bY_{np} + G + X - M_o - mY_{np}$ [Equilibrium in the goods sphere.]

Equilibrium in the monetary sphere

(1) $M^o =$ the autonomous money supply

(2) $L_t = pl_tY_{np} =$ the transactions demand function

$p =$ the price level

(3) $L_a = pl_a / i =$ the asset demand function. This function shows that the asset demand for money is an inverse function of the rate of interest up to a minimum level for i

(4) $L = L_a + L_t = p (l_tY_{np} + l_a / i) =$ the total demand for money

(5) $M^o = p (l_tY_{np} + l_a/i)$ [Defines equilibrium in the monetary sphere.]

General equilibrium thus depends upon the solution of two equations— Equation (7) in the goods sphere and Equation (5) in the monetary sphere —in two unknowns, namely Y_{np} and i.

13 | The Theory of the Price Level

In this chapter we consider the forces that determine the *general* level of prices in the economy. Up to this point we have developed our analysis in *real* terms—that is, a stable price level has been assumed. It is now appropriate to drop this assumption and analyze the important problem of changes in the price level. We seek to understand how changes in income, employment, and the money supply are related to changes in the general price level, and how changes in the latter may affect income and employment. We encounter a particularly challenging problem because most Western nations, including the United States, have had high levels of employment since the end of World War II, but they have also experienced a persistent —and, in some cases, a pronounced—rise in prices during the same interval.[1]

There are two fundamental approaches to the problem of the price level. The Keynesian, or income-expenditure approach, focuses attention upon income and its rate of expenditure in attempting to explain price level phenomena, while the classical approach directs attention to the quantity of money as the key variable in any explanation of the general price level. The modern restatement of the classical position continues to emphasize the quantity of money, but relates it not only to the price level as did the classical economists, but to the income level as well.

Both approaches raise some basic issues with respect to determination of the price level. In the first place, we want to know how both the money supply—the classical approach—and aggregate demand—the Keynesian approach—affect the price level. Second, we need to know how money

---

[1] In the United States the general price level as measured by the index used to deflate GNP rose at an annual average rate of 2.25 per cent for 1947–1965. GNP in constant prices rose at an annual average rate of 3.92 per cent during the same period.

and aggregate demand are related; in other words, do increases in the quantity of money raise the level of spending, as the classical analysis maintains, or are increases in the quantity of money the outcome of spending decisions previously taken? A general theory of price level determination must provide answers.

Statistical data available on output, the money supply, and the price level do not solve the problem, for they show that price level movements are correlated closely with *both* changes in output, which presumably responds to changes in aggregate demand, and to changes in the money supply. Figure 13–1 is a scatter diagram of the index of real GNP, using 1947 as the base year, against an index of the general price level with the same base.[2] The period covered is 1947 through 1965. The pattern revealed by the scatter indicates quite clearly that, over time, increases in real GNP are accompanied by significant increases in the price level.

Figure 13–2 is another scatter diagram, although in this case the price level index is plotted against an index of the money supply, using 1947 again as the base period for both indices. This diagram shows, too, an apparently significant relationship between increases in the money supply, which consists of currency plus demand deposits, and increases in the general price level.

In this chapter a basic analytical framework will be developed to fit the kind of relationships just described. Within this framework, we shall also discuss some of the specific causes economists have stressed in recent years

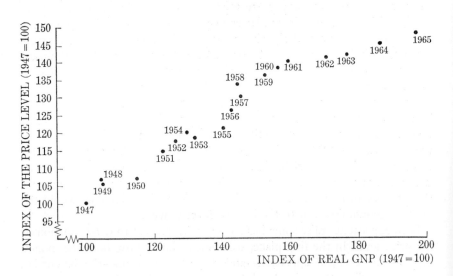

Figure 13–1. Real GNP and the Price Level

[2] The price index used is the U.S. Department of Commerce GNP deflator.

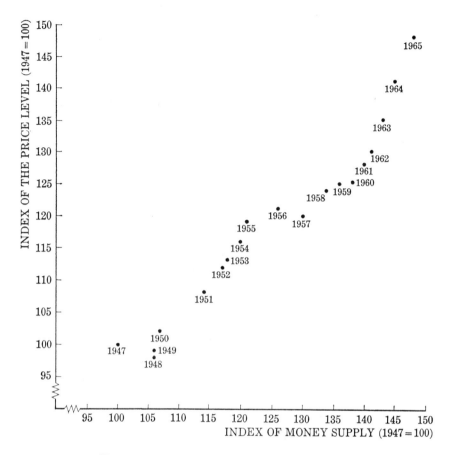

Figure 13–2. Money Supply and the Price Level

to explain changes in the general price level. To begin, we shall first review classical thinking on the price level, including a brief comment on
the modern restatement of the classical position. We shall follow with an
explanation of the analytical apparatus which Keynes developed in the
General Theory and which is designed to integrate the classical approach
with its emphasis upon the quantity of money with Keynes' own analytical
system built around the concept of aggregate demand. This analysis provides the most satisfactory mechanism for showing how the money supply
can be related to aggregate demand, and how both aggregate demand and
the money supply are related to the price level. What is particularly significant about Keynes' approach is that he seeks to explain the general price
level through reference to the same economic forces which determine individual prices at the level of the firm and industry.

The Quantity Theory and the Price Level

The simplest theory of the general price level is embodied in the classical quantity theory of money, which asserts that $P = f(M^o)$.[3] In classical thinking, in other words, inflation is essentially a matter of an excess quantity of money in circulation. The direct dependence of the price level on the money supply stems from the fact that output and the velocity of circulation are both assumed to be constant. Output is normally at the full-employment level. Given the classical view that money is important only as a medium of exchange, it follows that the general price level will vary directly with the amount of money in circulation.

The quantity theory is the basis for a very simple model showing the relationship between the money supply, output, and the general price level. While this model involves assumptions that are unrealistic, it nevertheless serves as an introduction to a more realistic and complex analysis that will illuminate the shortcomings of the classical analysis.

We begin with three assumptions:

1. All economic resources are in perfectly elastic supply at the going rate of remuneration as long as there is any unemployment in the economy.

2. All economic resources are homogeneous and perfectly divisible as well as being fully interchangeable in the productive process.

3. The only function of money of any importance is the medium-of-exchange function.

What is the significance of these assumptions? The third and last assumption guarantees that any increase (or decrease) in the money supply will result in an increase (or decrease) in effective demand in exactly the same proportion. The first two assumptions guarantee that the elasticity of the supply of output for the whole economy will be perfect as long as any unemployment exists anywhere in the economy.

Our three assumptions permit construction of a modified version of the quantity theory which links the money supply to the output level at less than full employment and to the price level once full employment is reached. If the conditions of the assumptions are present in the economy, it follows that an increase in the quantity of money will have no effect upon the price level as long as any resources are still unemployed. Perfect elasticity with respect to the supply of output means constant production costs, and thus prices will neither rise nor fall as output changes. Output will change in proportion to a change in effective demand, which, in turn, changes in proportion to the change in the money supply. Once the full-employment output level is reached, the elasticity of the output supply in response to change in the money supply (and effective demand) drops to zero; thus the effect of any further increases in money supply will be felt through price changes. At this point, of course, the traditional quantity

[3] Chapter 4, p. 100.

theory comes into its own and the price level changes in proportion to changes in the money supply.

The modified quantity theory provides us with a relatively simple framework for analysis of changes in the price level. If we assume that effective demand or spending increases (or decreases) in direct proportion to changes in the money supply, it follows that income and employment will change in proportion to changes in the money supply as long as there is unemployment. But when full employment is reached, it is the price level that will change in proportion to changes in the money supply.

The Modern Quantity Theory

Originated by Professor Milton Friedman of the University of Chicago, a modernized version of the quantity theory has evolved which, in some respects, brings it closer to the Keynesian analysis. The modern quantity theory, which Professor Friedman characterizes as a theory of the demand for money,[4] rather than a theory of the price level as in classical theory proper, has two major facets. The first places the modernized version squarely within the classical tradition, for it is maintained that the best documented empirical regularity among economic phenomena is the connection between substantial changes in the stock of money and the price level. Professor Friedman states that to the best of his knowledge there "is no instance in which a substantial change in the stock of money per unit of output has occurred without a substantial change in the level of prices in the same direction." [5]

The second facet of the modern quantity theory is more challenging because of the assertion that changes in the money supply are more closely related to changes in output and employment than are the changes in autonomous expenditure—that is, investment and government purchases of goods and services—which, in the Keynesian model, are the key to fluctuations in both output and employment. The modern classical theorists argue that this is the case because the velocity of money exhibits much greater stability than does the Keynesian multiplier relationship.[6] This view to the effect that the stock of money is more important than expenditures in explaining changes in the economic system has been vigorously criticized.[7]

[4] Milton Friedman, "The Quantity Theory of Money—A Restatement," in *Studies in the Quantity Theory of Money*, Milton Friedman, ed. (The University of Chicago Press, Chicago, Ill., 1956), pp. 3–21.

[5] Milton Friedman, "The Supply of Money and Changes in Prices and Output," in *The Controversy over the Quantity Theory of Money*, Edwin Dean, ed. (Boston, D. C. Heath and Company, 1965), p. 90.

[6] M. Friedman and D. Meiselman, "The Relative Stability of Monetary Velocity and the Investment Multiplier in the United States, 1897–1958," in *Stabilization Policies*, Commission on Money and Credit Series (Englewood Cliffs, N.J., Prentice-Hall, 1963).

[7] For an extensive criticism and defense of the modern classical position see the series of papers in the September, 1965, issue of *The American Economic Review*, pp. 693–792.

Most contemporary economists remain unconvinced that even a modernized version of the quantity theory provides a better framework for understanding changes in the general price level and in output and employment than does the Keynesian income-expenditure approach.

Income Theory and the Price Level

As a consequence of the development since 1936 of the analytical apparatus of income and employment theory, most economists recognize that the relationships between changes in the money supply, aggregate demand, and the general price level are more subtle and complex than the classical quantity theory suggests. Modern income and employment theory challenges quantity theory analysis in two essential ways. First, it is argued that the relationship between changes in the money supply and aggregate demand is not necessarily direct and proportional. Development of the concept of the demand for money as an asset means that increases in the money supply will not always result in increases in spending. Second, modern analysis rejects the notion that the general price level is unaffected by changes in aggregate demand until such time as the economy reaches full employment. Rather, the view is taken that even though unemployed resources are present, the general price level may rise prior to the point at which the economy's resources are fully employed. Modern analysis suggests the relationship between prices and output takes the form of a curve of the kind shown in Figure 13–3. As output rises toward full employment (Y_f) increases in the price level become more and more pronounced until eventually the curve depicting the relationship of the general price level to income becomes vertical. This happens at Y_f and signifies that at this point any further increase in aggregate demand will not lead to additional output, but simply to an increase in the price level. This is what Keynes designated as "true inflation."

In order to understand why the general price level may vary in the manner shown in Figure 13–3, we need to analyze the forces that determine prices at the level of the firm and the industry. The behavior of the general price level in response to changing levels of aggregate demand depends upon how *individual* prices respond to output changes that are brought about by changes in demand. Therefore we can employ the same key analytical concepts of demand and supply that we use to explain the process of individual price determination to explain the process through which the general price level is determined.

Traditionally, the body of economic analysis called "price" or "value" theory teaches that prices are governed by demand and supply conditions. In our analysis we have been concerned primarily with demand for the *whole* output of the economy. In a conceptual sense aggregate demand represents the sum of all the individual industry (or product) demand sched-

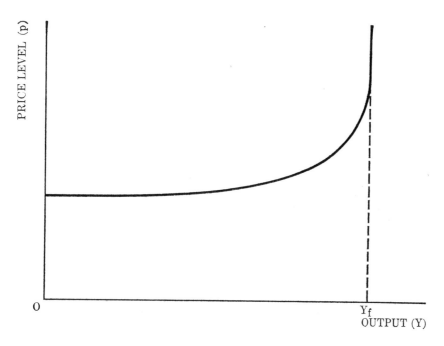

Figure 13–3. The Price-Output Relationship

ules that exist in the economy at any given moment. There is associated, in other words, with any given level of aggregate demand an underlying structure of demand schedules for all the different industries that make up the economy. It logically follows that some or all of the individual demand curves will shift when there is a change in aggregate demand, although the individual schedules will not necessarily shift to the same degree as the total demand.[8] If we thus assume some change in an industry demand schedule consequent upon a shift in aggregate demand, our problem reduces itself to one of explaining how output and price will respond at the industry level to such a change.

In Figure 13–4 we present a typical demand and supply diagram showing how market price is determined for some given commodity. Let us call this commodity A. Given the existence of the industry supply curve SS and the industry demand curve DD, the equilibrium price is P_1 and the equilibrium output is A_1. Since we are interested in the impact of a change

[8] The extent to which the demand for a particular commodity shifts as a result of a change in the aggregate demand function is primarily a matter of the income elasticity of demand, assuming that any increase in aggregate demand is accompanied by an increase in real income. For a discussion of the concept of income elasticity see John F. Due and Robert W. Clower, *Intermediate Economic Analysis,* fourth ed. (Homewood, Ill., Irwin, 1961), pp. 94, 95.

in demand on both price and output, let us see what happens if we shift the demand curve to the right, from *DD* to *D'D'*. The result of this shift is an increase in output to the level of A_2, and also an increase in price to the level of P_2. There has been both an output and a price response to the change in demand.

Why has this increase in price accompanied the higher level of output?

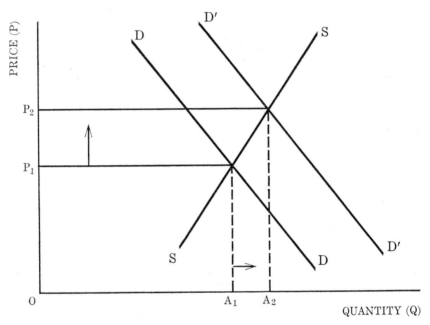

Figure 13–4. Determination of Market Price

If we are going to explain the price change depicted in Figure 13–4, it is necessary to "go behind" the schedules, so to speak, and analyze the factors that underlie supply. With an assumed shift in demand, the manner in which both price and output will change depends primarily upon supply considerations.

The position and shape of a typical supply schedule, such as *SS* in Figure 13–4, reflect the behavior of costs as output changes. From the standpoint of the individual business firm costs are the key determinant of the supply function. The most important cost element in the short run is *marginal cost*, defined as the cost of producing an additional unit of output. Since marginal cost represents costs associated with changes in output, it is apparent that the behavior of marginal costs is crucial to an understanding of the behavior of prices in response to changes in output. In the short run, with fixed plant capacity, marginal cost is the same thing as a change in variable costs, which are costs that vary directly with changes in output.

The most important variable costs are the wages of labor and the cost of materials.

Modern economic analysis asserts that, typically, the costs of the business firm are not constant as output expands toward the capacity level; rather, the presumption is that increases in output eventually lead to increases in variable costs per unit of output—and hence marginal costs—and that this will occur prior to the point at which the absolute upper limit of the firm's productive capacity is reached. The short run is characterized, in other words, by a rising level of both variable and marginal costs. Figure 13–5 depicts the shape of the variable and marginal cost curves for the typical business firm in the short run.

There are three reasons why variable costs may rise prior to the point

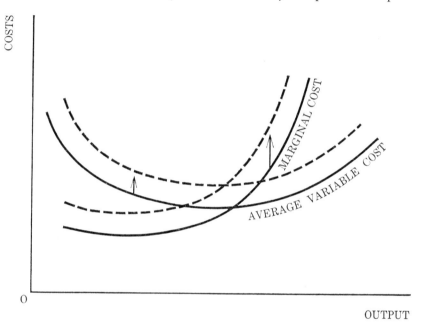

Figure 13–5. The Costs of the Business Firm

of maximum capacity. The *first* of these involves the classic principle of diminishing returns. Even if we assume all resources are homogeneous, additional inputs of a variable resource such as labor eventually lead to a less than proportionate increase in output as long as productive capacity remains fixed. This is the essence of the principle of diminishing returns. If the price of our variable resource, labor, is fixed—that is, money wages are constant—a decline in physical productivity is tantamount to a rise in variable costs per unit produced. Thus diminishing productivity means that ultimately the firm will be faced with rising labor costs per unit of output.

A *second* major reason for the increase of variable and marginal costs as output expands is the nonhomogeneity of resources that are variable in the short run. This is strongly stressed by Keynes.[9] In reality, labor and other resources are neither homogeneous nor fully interchangeable in the productive process. An expansion of output within the limits of ultimate productive capacity may require the use of labor units that are less and less efficient in relation to the going wage rate. This will cause an increase in the labor cost per unit of output even though the firm's capital equipment is not fully utilized. Rising labor costs may result in spite of the fact that suitable equipment is available for use in conjunction with added labor—if the labor units are not of the same degree of efficiency.

The *third* explanation for rising costs—and prices—as output expands is simply that the prices the firm must pay for its variable resources are unlikely to remain constant as output expands. If an expansion of output is general in the economy, it is most likely that the prices that firms must pay for labor and other resources will rise prior to attainment of the full-employment level. There are two reasons for this. First, the elasticity of supply of all commodities and services is not the same; thus for some resources supply may become perfectly inelastic before output as a whole has become perfectly inelastic, that is, before the full-employment level for the economy as a whole is reached. The emergence of "bottlenecks" in particular industries and for particular goods and services will cause the price of various *intermediate goods and services* to rise, and will thus ultimately affect the price of final goods and services. Second, a period of expanding demand and output will lead to increased pressure by organized labor for wage increases. If the economic outlook is generally favorable, business firms are not likely to resist these demands very strenuously. Changes in the prices that the business firm must pay for its variable resources will cause a change in its unit costs over the entire range of output possible within the limits of the firm's capacity. Thus changes of the type we have just been describing are subsumed in *shifts* in the position of both the variable and marginal cost curves of the firm, such as those depicted by the dotted lines in Figure 13–5.

Non-reversibility of the Price-Output Relationship

It is desirable to stress a phenomenon much noticed by economists during the postwar period: the *non-reversible* character of the relationship between prices and output. The schedule shown in Figure 13–3 is one depicting the relationship between output and the general price level during a period when aggregate demand is *rising*. But this curve is not an accurate picture of the relationship between output and the general price level during a downswing in economic activity. When aggregate demand and the level of economic activity decline, the general price level does not move

[9] John Maynard Keynes, *The General Theory of Employment, Interest and Money* (New York, Harcourt, Brace, 1936), pp. 42, 299–300.

downward as sharply as it moves upward. This is what is meant by the statement that the relationship between output and the price level is non-reversible. In general, prices and costs are much more sensitive to increases in demand than to decreases. This is strongly evidenced by the behavior of prices during three postwar recessions. In 1949, 1954, and 1958 *real* GNP declined, yet in each of these years both consumer and wholesale price indexes either declined hardly at all or rose.[10]

The non-reversible character of the price-output relationship for the economy as a whole is shown in diagrammatic form in Figure 13–6. The

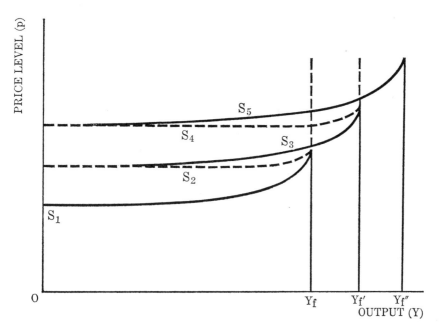

Figure 13–6. The Non-reversible Character of the
Price-Output Relationship

S_1 curve describes the behavior of prices as output rises initially toward the full-employment level, Y_f, which is determined by existing productive capacity in the first income period. The figure is constructed on the assumption that the boom comes to an end soon after the economy reaches the full-employment level. When this happens, aggregate demand and output fall off. But prices do not fall off to the same degree. In the diagram the downward path of the general price level is no longer along S_1; instead, because both prices and costs are strongly resistant to downward declines in demand, the general price level moves along the dotted line S_2. Thus the economy may fall back to a lower level of real income, but the general

[10] *1962 Supplement to Economic Indicators*, pp. 88, 92.

level of prices and costs is higher than it was at an earlier period when the same real income level prevailed.

During the next boom this same process will repeat itself. As recovery gets under way and the economy moves once again toward a new and higher full-employment output level, Y_f', the general price level will move along the S_3 curve. The full-employment output level moves further to the right along the horizontal axis because investment and expansion of population and the labor force during the preceding boom will have expanded the economy's productive capacity. But once again the same kind of "ratchet" effect with respect to the movement of the general price level can be observed. When the economy attains full employment at the peak of a new boom, prices once again will have risen to a new peak. When the boom collapses, prices will decline somewhat, but by not nearly so much as they rose during the preceding boom. Thus they move downward along the dotted line S_4. The same process repeats itself as the economy recovers and begins to move toward a new and still higher full-employment income level Y_f''. Thus over the longer run there may be a gradual but pronounced upward trend in the general price level.[11]

The rigidity of prices in the face of declining demand can be accounted for in several ways. In the first place, many markets—particularly those in manufacturing—are oligopolistic in structure; they are dominated by a relatively few, large business firms.[12] Prices in such markets are frequently *administered*, which means they are set by the seller and normally held constant for a period of time. Since firms in an oligopolistic industry usually operate in an atmosphere of uncertainty with respect to the reaction of their rivals to a shift in prices, they are extremely reluctant to reduce prices when demand falls off. Instead, oligopolistic firms prefer to adjust to shifting demand conditions through output and employment changes.

Many prices also remain stable in the face of a declining demand because wages tend not to yield to the slump in economic activity. Since money wages are a major element in the cost structure of the business firm, it logically follows that rigidities of wage rates will exert an important effect on the behavior of the price level. The chief reason for the rigidity of wages appears to lie in the strong determination of all workers—the unorganized as well as the organized—to resist cuts in money wages, even if such resistance comes at the expense of some employment. A recent study, for example, found that between 1900 and 1960 there were only five years in which average money wages in manufacturing industry declined below the average of the preceding year. In all other years the average rose over

---

[11] This is the "ratchet" effect at work. To date the available empirical evidence indicates that it is present only when recessions are relatively mild, as for example since World War II. A severe depression would no doubt bring drastic price decreases.

[12] J. S. Bain, *Industrial Organization* (New York, Wiley, 1959), p. 120.

that of the preceding year. Wages exhibited this strong resistance to any downward movement in spite of the fact that during approximately half the years of this period unemployment was four per cent or more of the labor force.[13]

A General Theoretical Framework

From the preceding discussion, it should be evident that the relationships between the money supply, aggregate demand, output, and the general price level are much more complex than envisaged in the simple classical quantity theory. Our discussion of the key factors which influence prices as output changes provides the foundation for developing a formal theoretical structure through which we can show how the relevant variables are related to one another.

The analysis at this point is based directly upon Keynes' effort to establish a theoretical system which relates the money supply to the general price level through concepts of supply and demand rather than through the quantity of money.[14] By means of this framework, it is possible to show, first, how the level of aggregate demand may be affected by changes in the money supply, and, second, how the price level is affected by changes in aggregate demand. The fundamental assumption underlying this analysis is that *neither* output nor the price level will change unless there is a change in aggregate demand. Increases (or decreases) in the money supply may cause increases (or decreases) in spending and thus shift upward (or downward) the aggregate demand function. It is equally true, however, that increases (or decreases) in spending may come about for reasons other than a change in the supply of money; thus, shifts in the aggregate demand function may be the cause of changes in the money supply rather than be caused by the latter. The theoretical framework developed in this section encompasses both possibilities, and provides the appropriate setting for discussing specific theories of inflation which have gained favor in recent years.

The basic analytical tool employed in the construction of our general theoretical frame of reference is the concept of elasticity. An *elasticity coefficient* is a ratio which measures the percentage change in one variable to the percentage change in another variable. In non-technical language such a coefficient provides an indication of how one variable in a theoretical system may respond to changes in another variable. The six variables employed in the construction of our general theoretical system are the money supply, M^o; the general price level, p; the aggregate demand function, DD;

---

[13] Charles L. Schultze, "Creeping Inflation: Causes and Consequences," *Business Horizons*, Summer, 1960, p. 68.

[14] The interested reader should read the much neglected Chapter 21 in the *General Theory* on "The Theory of Prices."

real income, Y; the level of employment, N; and the general level of money wages, w. The relationships between these variables are formulated in a series of elasticity coefficients.

Elasticity of Price

The first coefficient in our system is the *elasticity of price*, designated by the symbol e. This coefficient is at the apex of the system and shows the response of money prices to changes in the quantity of money. It may be defined as follows:

$$e = \frac{\% \Delta p}{\% \Delta M^o} \qquad (13\text{--}1)$$

This coefficient is nothing more than a statement of the quantity theory in a different form. The ratio expresses the relationship between changes in the general price level and changes in the quantity of money. In the classical scheme, the value of e would be zero prior to the full-employment level, and unity once the full-employment level is attained. When $e = 1$, the general price level increases in direct proportion to changes in the quantity of money, which is the essence of the classical version of the quantity theory. Implicit in the classical analysis is the assumption that aggregate demand will change in direct proportion to change in the quantity of money. This will lead either to a proportionate change in the output level if the economy has less than full employment, or if there is full employment, a proportionate change in the price level. But it is this assumption of a proportional relationship between the money supply and aggregate demand that modern income theory rejects. This being the case, the next step in construction of our theoretical framework is to consider the factors that actually determine the relationship between the money supply and aggregate demand.

Elasticity of Aggregate Demand

The second coefficient we shall consider is the *elasticity of aggregate demand*, designated by the symbol e_a. This coefficient measures the response of aggregate demand, DD, to a change in the money supply, M^o. The elasticity of aggregate demand may be defined as:

$$e_a = \frac{\% \Delta DD}{\% \Delta M^o} \qquad (13\text{--}2)$$

What determines the response of aggregate demand to changes in the money supply? The classical economist answers that aggregate demand must change in the same proportion as the money supply because the only meaningful function of money is as a medium of exchange. Thus, the coefficient of the elasticity of aggregate demand would have a value of unity. In contrast, the view of Keynes is that the response of aggregate demand to changes in the money supply is extremely complex, involving all the variables and functional relationships that enter into the determination of the income level itself.

The most important reason for rejecting the classical assumption of proportionality between changes in the money supply and changes in aggregate demand stems from the fact that the medium-of-exchange role is no longer regarded as the only important function of money. Modern theory places great stress on the store-of-value function. This means that if we want to understand the manner in which a change in the money supply affects the aggregate demand function it is necessary to begin with the asset demand schedule, the chief link between the money supply and the level of aggregate demand. According to current income theory, a change in the money supply affects first the rate of interest. The extent to which the rate of interest undergoes change as a result of changes in the money supply depends both upon the prevailing level of interest rates as well as the assumed shape of the schedules representing the asset demand for money. If interest rates are already quite low—that is, at or near the level represented by the "liquidity trap"—it is unlikely that they will be much affected by any change in the money supply. On the other hand, if they are relatively high, then small changes in the money supply may significantly affect their level. In income theory, changes in the rate of interest are of chief importance because they affect investment, a basic determinant of aggregate demand.

If the asset demand function for money is such that a change in the money supply significantly affects the rate of interest, and if, too, the investment demand schedule is relatively interest-elastic, then the elasticity of aggregate demand coefficient will be relatively high. The significance of this is that the level of aggregate demand may be influenced in a significant manner by changes in the money supply. On the other hand, if the rate of interest is little affected by changes in the money supply and, further, the investment demand schedule is relatively interest-inelastic, then the coefficient for the elasticity of aggregate demand will have a low value. Under these circumstances aggregate demand will be relatively independent of changes in the money supply.

Changes in the rate of interest may affect the aggregate demand schedule via the consumption component as well as the investment component. Interest rates possibly exert an influence on the amounts that people save out of current income either because they save more when interest conditions are favorable or because changes in interest rates affect asset values. Economists, though, are by no means in agreement on the precise effects that the rate of interest may have on consumer spending.

Once we have established the relationship between a change in the money supply and a change in aggregate demand, the next problem is to determine the response of the economy to a change in aggregate demand. In our earlier analysis we assumed a constant price level which meant that the only possible response to a change in aggregate demand was a change in output. Since we have dropped the assumption of a constant price level, a change in aggregate demand may lead to a change in both output and the general price level. This is what is implied in the aggregate supply curve shown in Figure 13–3. We shall, therefore, proceed to analyze the response of both output and the price level to a change in aggregate demand by appropriate elasticity coefficients.

Elasticity of Output

The third elasticity coefficient in our analytical framework is the *elasticity of output*. This coefficient we shall designate by the symbol e_y. It measures the response of real income, Y, to a change in aggregate demand, and it is defined as:

$$e_y = \frac{\% \Delta Y}{\% \Delta DD} \qquad (13\text{–}3)$$

Since we are concerned primarily with a short-run situation in which productive capacity is relatively fixed, the response of output to changes in aggregate demand is largely governed by the underlying physical conditions that determine the rapidity with which decreasing returns come into play as output is expanded.

Elasticity of Returns

From the point of view of the whole economy, what lies behind the coefficient for the elasticity of output is the response of output to an increase in employment. For the economy as a whole, labor is the major variable resource in the short run, and consequently, we can express the principle of returns also in the form of a coefficient. The "law" of returns concerns the relationship between the use of added units of a variable resource (all other resources presumed to be fixed in supply) and the added returns (i.e., product) that result. This principle can be stated as a coefficient which measures the ratio of a percentage change in output, Y, to a percentage change in labor inputs, N. Let us designate the coefficient of the *elasticity of returns* with the symbol e_r. We then have:

$$e_r = \frac{\% \Delta Y}{\% \Delta N} \qquad (13\text{–}4)$$

The purpose of this ratio is to express the response of output to an increase in employment. If e_r has a value of unity, it implies constant returns

and hence constant unit labor costs, assuming that money wages are constant. Under such circumstances the value of e_y would also be unity, which
means that any increase in aggregate demand would result solely in an
increase in output. If, however, e_r has a value of less than unity, it means
that the economy is operating in the range of diminishing returns and,
consequently, unit labor costs will rise as output expands. This is true even
though money wages may remain constant. Under these circumstances e_y
necessarily has a value of less than one. If the latter is the case, it signifies
that any increase in aggregate demand will lead partly to an increase in
output and partly to an increase in prices. The latter results directly from
rising costs associated with diminishing physical productivity.

Elasticity of the Price Level

The next coefficient we shall consider is that of the *elasticity of the
price level*, which we shall designate with the symbol e_p. This coefficient
measures the response of the price level to a change in aggregate demand.
The reader must be careful not to confuse the elasticity of the price level
with the coefficient for the elasticity of price, e. The coefficient for the
elasticity of the price level is:

$$e_p = \frac{\% \Delta p}{\% \Delta DD} \qquad (13\text{--}5)$$

This coefficient has a kinship with the elasticity of output coefficient in
that it represents a response of the system to a change in aggregate demand. But it is concerned with the response of the price level rather than
the output level. Since we cannot separate the price level from the behavior of costs—which is to say from the principle of diminishing returns
—it follows that the elasticity of returns coefficient, e_r, is a key factor in
any explanation of the response of the general price level to a change in
aggregate demand. To illustrate, an assumed value of unity for e_r means
constant returns to scale, and thus the value of e_p would necessarily be
zero, assuming constant money wage rates. Under such circumstances there
would be no price level response at all to a change in aggregate demand.
However, if e_r has a value less than unity, then returns are no longer constant, and there will be a price level response to a change in aggregate
demand. The coefficient e_p would then have a value greater than zero.

Elasticity of Money Wages

Diminishing returns and the corollary of rising unit labor costs are not,
however, the only factors that account for an upward movement of the
price level in response to an increase in aggregate demand. Increasing output may lead to upward pressure on the level of money wage rates as
well as on the prices of other resources that enter into marginal (variable)

costs in the short run. Thus behind the elasticity of the price level coefficient there lies yet another coefficient. This final coefficient in our
theoretical structure is the coefficient for the *elasticity of money wages,*
designated by the symbol e_w. It represents the response of money wages
and the price of other factors that are a part of marginal costs to an increase
in aggregate demand. We have:

$$e_w = \frac{\% \Delta w}{\% \Delta DD} \qquad (13\text{--}6)$$

A value of zero for this coefficient means that neither wage rates nor
other factor costs rise in response to an increase in aggregate demand.
Obviously this would not preclude price level changes as a result of any
increment of spending, but it would mean that such increases would be
less pronounced than otherwise would be the case. If the coefficient for
the elasticity of money wages were zero—a condition that is most unlikely
in reality—the response of the price level to changes in aggregate demand,
and hence the value of the coefficient e_p, would depend entirely on the
physical factors that enter into determination of the rate of diminishing
returns. On the other hand, a value greater than zero for the coefficient e_w
means that the price level will rise in response to an increase in aggregate
demand not only because of diminishing returns, but also because cost
curves will shift upward over the entire range of output possibilities due
to higher levels for money wages and other factor costs. The greater the
value of e_w, the less will be the response of output to any increase in aggregate demand.

The Phillips Curve

The effect of changes in aggregate demand upon money wage rates is
illustrated in somewhat different form by an analytical technique called
a "Phillips curve," so named because the British economist A. W. Phillips
first set forth the relationships involved in an article published in 1958.[15]
A Phillips curve is shown in Figure 13–7.

In the diagram the rate of change in money wages is shown on the vertical axis and the unemployment rate on the horizontal axis. The significance of this curve lies in the fact that the unemployment rate can be
expected to decline as aggregate demand increases, but a fall in the unemployment rate will be accompanied by a higher *rate* of increase in money
wages.

In the diagram the solid curve is drawn with a slope such that the rate
of increase in money wages is 3 per cent when unemployment reaches

[15] A. W. Phillips, "The Relation Between Unemployment and the Rate of Change of
Money Wages in the United Kingdom, 1861–1957, *Economica*, November, 1958.
pp. 283–299.

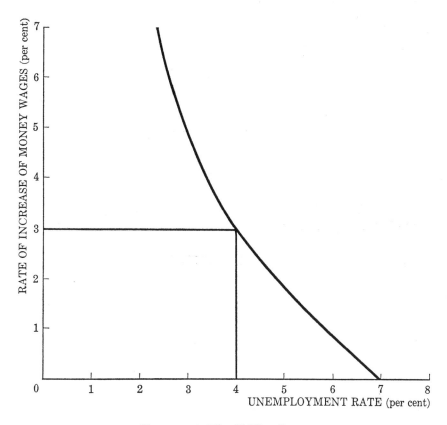

Figure 13–7. The Phillips Curve

a level of 4 per cent of the labor force. If the unemployment rate were reduced to 3 per cent through an increase in aggregate demand, the rate of increase in money wages rises to about 4 per cent. The extent to which any *particular* rate of increase in money wages would tend to cause increases in the price level depends upon the annual rate at which the average productivity of labor is increasing. If, for example, this rate were also 3 per cent, then it would be theoretically possible for the economy to attain an unemployment rate of 4 per cent of its labor force and have money wages increase at an annual average rate of 3 per cent without any increase in the general price level. Any reduction of the unemployment rate below the 4 per cent level would generate upward pressure on prices. A recent empirical study of the American economy suggest that if the annual average rate of increase in productivity is no greater than 2.5 per cent, price level stability may require an unemployment rate of between 5 and 6 per cent of the civilian labor force. On the other hand, this same study indicated that reduction of the unemployment rate to 3 per cent might entail an increase in the general price level by as much as 3 to 4 per cent per year.[16]

A word of caution is in order. The Phillips curve is a useful analytical device to demonstrate the "tradeoff" the economy may have to make between unemployment and price level stability, but we do not as yet have sufficient empirical information about the economy's performance to specify the precise rate of unemployment—or level of aggregate demand—at which increases in money wages become inflationary.

Interrelationships of the Coefficients

Now that we have explored the meaning of each of the six coefficients of elasticity, we can bring them all together in a formal theoretical framework. This is done in graphic form in Figure 13–8. The purpose of this figure is not only to show the interrelationships between these six coeffi-

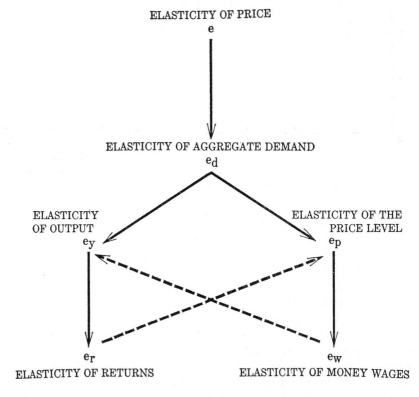

Figure 13–8. Elasticity Coefficients and the Price Level

[16] Paul A. Samuelson and Robert M. Solow, "Analytical Aspects of Anti-Inflation Policy," *The American Economic Review*, May, 1960, pp. 177–194.

cients, but also to provide a basis for exploring the various possible causes of inflation.

At the peak of the theoretical structure is the *elasticity of price* coefficient, *e*. The fact that we place this elasticity coefficient at the apex of our theoretical structure should not be interpreted to mean that money is regarded as the basic causal factor in the inflationary process. The response of prices to a change in the money supply depends, as we have seen, on a host of other variables. Thus, behind the coefficient for the elasticity of price lies another coefficient, that of the *elasticity of aggregate demand*, e_d, which embraces the major functions that enter into the determination of the income level: the liquidity-preference function, the investment demand function, and, to the extent that the level of the consumption function might be influenced by the interest rate, the consumption function.

Once the value of e_d is established, the next step is to determine the response of the economic system to a given change in the aggregate demand function. This involves us directly with the two additional elasticity coefficients that relate to the output level: the *elasticity of output* coefficient, e_y, and the *elasticity of returns* coefficient, e_r. The response of the price level to a change in aggregate demand is summed up in the *elasticity of the price level* coefficient, e_p. A major factor which influences the value of this coefficient is the response of money wage rates and other factor prices to a change in aggregate demand. The *elasticity of money wages* coefficient, e_w, therefore, is shown as a key factor in the determination of the response of prices to changes in aggregate demand. The price level is also influenced by the scale of output and diminishing returns; this explains the dotted line drawn from the coefficient e_r to the coefficient e_p in Figure 13–8. In like fashion, the indirect influence that changes in money wages and other factor costs exercise on the elasticity of output is represented in the diagram by the dotted line drawn from the coefficient e_w to the coefficient e_y.

The classical quantity theory assumes a direct relationship between the money supply and the price level. Thus in the most orthodox interpretation of the quantity theory the coefficient for the elasticity of price would have a value of unity. The price level would change in proportion to a change in the money supply. The explanation for this lies with the other elasticities that make up our theoretical structure. First, the elasticity of aggregate demand coefficient is also assumed to have a value of unity. This follows from the classical view that money is primarily a medium of exchange; if this is true, then aggregate demand must change in the same proportion as changes in the money supply. Second, the coefficient for the elasticity of output has a value of zero. This follows from the classical assumption that full employment is the normal state of affairs in the economy. Third, and on the basis of the foregoing assumption, the coefficient representing the response of wages and other factor costs to a change in aggregate demand must necessarily have a value of unity. If full employment prevails, then all resources will be in perfectly inelastic supply. A value of zero for e_y, and a value of unity for e_w means that e_p must also have a value of unity. Consequently, the whole of any increase in aggregate demand will expend itself in price level changes. This is the essence of the quantity theory.

The Causes of Inflation

In this chapter we are using the word *inflation* in the broadest possible sense to refer to any increase in the general price level which is sustained and non-seasonal in character. Before we discuss various causes of inflation, it is desirable that we distinguish carefully between various types of inflation.

Types of Inflation

Keynes defined "true" inflation as a condition in which any additional increase in aggregate demand produces no further increase in output. When the economy reaches this point any increase in aggregate demand expends itself wholly in price increases.[17] Inflation such as this is the kind envisaged by the quantity theorists, although it should be noted that this definition does not preclude some price increases prior to the point at which the economy has reached the absolute upper limit of its output potential. In speaking of "true" inflation Keynes meant to emphasize only that there is some point in the short run when the elasticity of output with respect to changes in aggregate demand falls to zero, and it is at this point that it is proper to talk of a "true" inflationary condition.

Our subsequent analysis will deal principally with a second type of inflation, variously described as "gradual" or "creeping," which is of more immediate concern to the world today. In creeping inflation, a slow but persistent upward movement of the general price level continues even when aggregate demand is not shifting upward at a particularly rapid rate, and often during periods of relatively slack demand. This has been the kind of inflation experienced by the American economy throughout most of the period since World War II. Consumer prices in the United States, for example, rose approximately 41 per cent between 1947 and 1965, an annual average increase of slightly more than 2 per cent.[18]

A third type of inflation is sometimes described as "suppressed." There is no inflation in the technical sense of the word here, because prices do not rise. Suppressed inflation is a situation in which by one means or an-

[17] Keynes, *op. cit.*, p. 303.
[18] *1962 Supplement to Economic Indicators*, p. 88; *Economic Indicators*, June, 1966, p. 26.

other the general price level is held down, but at the cost of a build-up of forces that may make for an explosive surge upward in prices at some later date. Suppressed inflation is most common during wartime when controls and rationing limit spending and prevent price increases but do not prevent the public from accumulating large amounts of liquid assets that can be readily turned into purchasing power at some future date.

Finally, there is hyper-inflation, which is best described as a situation in which the value of the monetary unit may be totally destroyed. Under conditions of hyper-inflation, prices may rise to astronomical heights, and the velocity of circulation of money becomes almost infinitely great. Money ceases to serve as a store of value and is used only as a medium of exchange. Money that has become almost worthless is still somewhat more efficient than barter. If the hyper-inflation goes far enough, there may be a complete collapse of the monetary system and people will have to resort to barter. Hyper-inflation is almost always associated with defeat in war, the revolutionary destruction of an existing government, or some other equally catastrophic event that brings normal productive processes to a halt and forces a government to resort to uncontrolled use of the printing press to finance its needs.

Theories of Inflation

Since the end of World War II there has been much discussion concerning the cause and cure of the gradual but persistent inflationary trend that has characterized the economies of most nations. As a consequence of such discussions, as well as extensive theoretical analysis and empirical research, three major theoretical explanations for the phenomenon of inflation have emerged. These may be described as the *demand-pull* hypothesis, the *cost-push* hypothesis, and the *structural* hypothesis. We shall examine each of these in turn, but the reader is cautioned at the outset that postulation of three theories of the inflationary process does not mean that they are mutually exclusive or that any one of them will suffice to explain the inflationary process. The slow but persistent upward trend of the general price level that appears to be an important characteristic of most modern economies is neither wholly understood nor readily controlled.

The Demand-Pull Hypothesis

The demand-pull hypothesis relates to what may be called the traditional theory of inflation. The theory holds that inflation is caused by an excess of demand (spending) relative to the available supply of goods and services at existing prices. In the classical view, the factor of key significance is the money supply, because in accordance with the quantity theory of money only an increase in the money supply is capable of driving the general price level upward. In modern income theory, demand-pull is interpreted to mean an excess of aggregate money demand relative to the economy's full-employment output level. This is similar, the reader will note, to the Keynesian definition of true inflation, although the demand-pull hypothesis should not be interpreted to mean that no upward movement in the general level of prices is possible prior to the point of full employment. The basic idea is that whatever upward pressure may exist on the price level emanates from demand. The theory further presumes that prices for goods and services as well as for economic resources are responsive to supply and demand forces, and will thus move readily upward under the pressure of a high level of aggregate demand.

The presumed cure for inflation in the demand-pull category is quite obvious; if there is an excess of spending, it must be cured by the vigorous pursuit of monetary and fiscal policies that will reduce total spending and thus lessen the upward pressure on the price level. The demand-pull thesis presumes, too, that prices and other costs are flexible downward as well as upward, and therefore that policy measures necessary to reduce total spending will not adversely affect employment levels. However, if money wages and prices are not flexible downward, serious doubts are raised concerning the possibility of controlling excess spending without significant reductions in employment. Our earlier discussion of the Phillips curve underscores this problem.

The Cost-Push Hypothesis

The cost-push explanation of the source of inflation has particularly come into favor since World War II.[19] This theory finds the basic explanation for inflation in the fact that some producers, groups of workers, or both, succeed in raising the prices for either their products or services above the levels that would prevail under more competitive conditions. Inflationary pressure originates, in other words, with supply rather than demand, and spreads throughout the economy. An inflation of this type is possible in theory because in the aggregate prices and wages are not only costs as seen from the standpoint of buyers, but also income when viewed from the standpoint of sellers of goods and labor. For any single commodity or factor service an increase in its price will reduce the quantity of the good or services demanded, but this is not necessarily true for the whole economy.

Inflation of the cost-push variety is most likely to originate in industries which are relatively concentrated, and in which sellers can exercise considerable discretion in the formulation of both prices and wages. Competitive conditions must be such that either business firms or trade unions have some control over the prices of their products or services. Cost-push inflation would not be possible in an economy characterized by pure competition. If recent inflationary pressures in the United States and other econ-

[19] This type of inflation is also described as "market power" inflation, "income share" inflation, and "administrative" inflation.

omies can really be attributed to cost-push factors, serious and difficult problems of policy are raised. An inflation caused by cost-push is not susceptible to control by traditional monetary and fiscal measures directed at the level of aggregate demand and spending because administered prices and wages by their very nature are insensitive to changes in demand. Thus measures that reduce over-all demand may not affect prices, but can affect quite adversely the economy's real output and employment level. On the other hand, any policy measures that involve direct controls over either wages or prices would, no doubt, be strongly resisted by both organized labor and the business community under peacetime conditions, so this approach to the control of cost-push forces is not especially satisfactory.

The Structural Hypothesis

The structural thesis was developed by Professor Charles Schultze to explain the inflation experienced by the American economy in the late 1950's. [20] It shows that inflation may be the consequence of internal changes in the structure of demand, even though over-all demand may not be excessive and there are no undue concentrations of economic power within the economy. This particular theory of inflation has its origin in the fact that in many areas of the economy wages and prices are flexible upward in response to increases in demand, but not flexible downward when demand declines. If this is the situation, it follows that inflationary pressure can be generated by internal changes in the composition of demand alone. In a dynamic economy such changes are an inherent part of the economic process, consequent upon continuous changes in the structure of consumer tastes and desires. The mechanism by which such changes can generate inflationary pressure in the absence of any marked excess of aggregate demand or aggressive exploitation of positions of market power is relatively clear-cut. The expansion of demand for the output of particular industries or sectors will lead to wage and price increases in these areas because wages and prices have an upward sensitivity when demand is rising. But the contraction of demand in other sectors will not lead to any corresponding downward movement of prices. Thus, over-all, the average level of prices will necessarily rise. The structural thesis makes price inflation inherent in the process of resource allocation, *if* wages and prices are flexible upward but not downward.

The Inflationary Process

No single explanation will suffice when we deal with a phenomenon as complex as inflation in the modern economy. The theories just described

---

[20] Charles L. Schultze, *Recent Inflation in the United States*, Study Paper No. 1, Joint Economic Committee, Study of Employment, Growth, and Price Levels, Washington, D.C., 1959.

should not be construed as alternatives in any absolute sense, but rather as approaches that lay stress on one factor relatively more than another. In the inflation characteristic of the contemporary American economy, elements present in each of the theories have been at work. Thus, it is not so much the question of one theory being "better" or more valid than another, as it is of the emphasis that should be placed on demand, cost, or structural factors.

Modern economic analysis no longer sees the problem of inflation as basically a matter of too much money in circulation. But this does not mean that the money supply is no longer in the picture. Barring unprecedented shifts in the velocity of circulation, all the theories of the inflationary process that we have discussed predicate increases in the money supply if the inflation is to continue. Modern analysis sees these increases in money as a secondary consequence of other changes that in themselves are primarily responsible for the increases in prices, while the older, classical approach sees the changes in the money supply itself as the basic "cause" of inflation.

Crucial to any understanding of the nature of the inflationary process, as well as the causes of inflation, is a knowledge of the sensitivity of prices and wages to changes in demand. Two possibilities are present: wages and prices may be "flexible" or "inflexible." By "flexible" we mean that both wages and prices respond readily and quickly to changes in demand. Wages and prices that are "inflexible," on the other hand, are sometimes said to be *cost-determined*,[21] that is, they do not respond to changes in demand. Wages are cost-determined in the sense that they are fixed in relation to some index of living costs, such as the consumer price index, and change only as the latter changes. Prices are cost-determined in the sense that they are determined on the basis of cost considerations and remain relatively fixed irrespective of demand conditions as long as costs do not change.

Demand-Pull Inflation

Let us begin our analysis of the inflationary process with the assumption that inflation gets under way with an excess of aggregate demand over *current supply at existing prices*. Given the slope of the aggregate supply schedule described in Figure 13–3, the excess of aggregate demand will drive the price level up, even if the economy is not initially at the full-employment level. The price level rises because the elasticity of output, e_y, has a value of less than unity, and the elasticity of the price level e_p has a value greater than zero. This initial increase in prices and costs does not mean that all prices and wages are affected equally. There will be some groups that register a net gain from the initial inflationary spurt in the economy because their money incomes have increased more than the prices of things they buy. Other groups find their real position unchanged; their

[21] *Ibid.*, p. 5.

money incomes and the prices of the things they buy have changed in the same proportion. Still others are net losers because prices increase more swiftly than their money incomes.

The extent to which an upward movement in the price level generated initially by aggregate demand *continues* depends basically upon whether or not all groups in the economy attempt to maintain their *real* income and expenditure positions. If all groups, in the face of inflation, try to maintain real expenditure positions, real aggregate demand is unaffected by changes in the price level. But real expenditure positions can be maintained only if aggregate money demand—that is, expenditure—continues to rise at the same rate as the general price level. For example, if the groups that initially saw their real economic position adversely affected by the original inflationary spurt succeed in raising either the prices of the things they sell or their money wages, their real income and expenditure position remains intact. But this, of course, will boost prices to still higher levels, and thus require additional upward adjustments in money income and expenditure on the part of still other groups that now seek to maintain intact *their* real expenditure positions. From the viewpoint of the whole economy, an added increase in the level of aggregate money expenditure is inevitable if the level of real aggregate demand is to remain constant.[22]

The reader should not forget that the level of aggregate demand in real terms—that is, constant prices—is of significance with respect to the employment level. The key to an understanding of the inflationary process lies in the impact that a rising price level has on real aggregate demand. An upward movement of the general price level can continue, irrespective of whether the initial inflationary impulse came from demand-pull, cost-push, or structural factors, only if aggregate real demand remains unchanged, which is to say only if aggregate money expenditures rise at the same rate as the general price level.

Some studies indicate that there are a number of possible ways in which a rising price level may have a dampening effect upon aggregate real demand.[23] For example, a progressive tax system may lead to a reduction in real consumption because money income in the hands of economy's spending units will not rise in proportion to a change in prices. It is possible, too, that a rising price level will reduce the real value of liquid assets held by consumers, and thus lead to a slackening of real consumer demand as households attempt to bring their asset holdings back to what they consider a desirable level. This is the so-called Pigou effect at work in reverse.

[22] In a dynamic setting in which output is rising, aggregate real demand must rise, not remain constant. See Schultze, *op. cit.*, p. 26. The student should note most carefully at this point that the analysis is attempting to spell out the circumstances under which the price level will continue to rise, given an *initial* excess of aggregate demand over supply at current prices. A *continued* expansion of demand is much the simpler case.

[23] *Ibid.*, pp. 21–26.

If, in addition, it is assumed that the money supply is fixed, an increase in the price level may have a depressing effect upon real investment outlays because under these circumstances the rate of interest will rise.

Granted that the possibility exists that aggregate real demand may decline—or, alternatively, that aggregate money demand may not rise in proportion to the change in the price level—the significance of this for a continuation of the inflationary process depends upon the sensitivity of prices and money wages to changes in demand. If we assume, first, that a rising general price level tends to depress the level of real demand, and second, that both money wages and prices are flexible, then the economy contains a kind of built-in corrective factor that makes a continued upward movement of the general price level difficult to sustain. More particularly, a cost-push type of inflation is practically impossible under these conditions, because the decline in the level of aggregate real demand means both a decline in the demand for the different categories of output and for the services of different economic resources, particularly labor. In the short run this will lead to growing unemployment of labor and excess plant capacity. But if prices and wages are sensitive to the state of demand, it will be impossible for any upward movement of either to continue. As long as wage and price sensitivity exists, the inflationary process will come to a halt unless there is a constant renewal of excess aggregate money demand. This is not likely as long as restraint is exercised by the government in the face of the downward pressure of the price level that will develop once the force of the initial volume of excess expenditure exhausts itself. Although a demand-pull type of inflation is possible under these circumstances, it cannot be sustained if prices and wages are flexible and if no new factor is introduced to push the level of aggregate monetary demand still higher. The initially high value for the elasticity of the price level coefficient characteristic of demand-pull inflation must decline since no mechanism exists to generate the necessary further increases in aggregate money demand to keep the process going.

Cost-Push Inflation

The result will be different if money wages and prices are not particularly sensitive to a change in demand, even though aggregate real demand is adversely affected by a general upward movement of the price level. Under these conditions the economy no longer contains any kind of internal corrective factor to limit the extent to which an initial excess of aggregate demand may push the price level. A reduction in real aggregate demand, given inflexible wages and prices, leads chiefly to a reduction in employment and to excess capacity. Prices and wages will not decline, and thus the inflation *may* continue. If unemployment and idle capacity lead to demands from organized labor and business that the government adopt monetary and fiscal policies which will increase aggregate money demand sufficiently to restore real aggregate demand to its prior level, a cost-push type of inflationary process is clearly possible. This situation sets the stage for a continuous upward movement of the general price level, particularly because all groups do not share equally in the initial round of price increases. When the price level first begins to rise, aggregate real demand may fall. But this does not bring prices down. As a consequence, groups which did not gain from the initial price rise now seek to boost their money incomes so as to maintain real expenditure positions. This creates more upward pressure on the price level and, indirectly, more pressure on government to take the necessary steps to sustain aggregate real demand and prevent unemployment. Unemployment presumably will be the more pronounced, the more inflexible are both money wages and prices. In this situation both the elasticity of the price level, e_p, and the elasticity of money wages, e_w, have values that are high with respect to any increase in aggregate money demand, but low with respect to a decrease in aggregate real demand. Beyond this, the mechanism presumably exists through which pressure can be generated to raise the level of aggregate money demand and thus prevent unemployment and idle capacity from developing.

If we drop the assumption that a rise in the general price level tends to reduce real aggregate demand, then there is less reason to assert that any kind of a built-in corrective factor is present in the economy. Under the assumption that aggregate real demand is not adversely affected by a rise in the general price level, no downward pressure on either prices or wages will develop in the event of an initial rise, irrespective of whether the *first* impulse toward higher prices resulted from demand-pull or cost-push forces. However, a cost-push type of inflation is much easier to sustain if a rising price level does not depress aggregate real demand. Then, no downward pressure on either prices and wages or employment levels will develop as various groups push prices and costs upward in an effort to sustain real expenditure levels. From the point of view of the whole economy, rising costs (and prices) can generate an equal increase in aggregate monetary demand as long as we assume that aggregate real demand is unaffected by a rise in the general price level. Thus a cost-push inflationary process can, in theory, continue indefinitely without any necessarily adverse effects on the employment level. Under the foregoing circumstances, the degree of flexibility or inflexibility of both wages and prices loses much of its significance, for this is a matter of importance chiefly when we assume that a rise in the price level will depress aggregate real demand.

The phenomenon of inflation in the modern economy cannot be fully explained in terms of either the demand-pull or the cost-push theories. As concluded in a recent comprehensive and penetrating report on inflation in the American economy,[24] the major distinction between these two theories of the inflationary process centers on the sensitivity of both money

---

[24] Schultze, *op. cit.,* p. 39.

wages and prices to changes in demand. Those who believe that significant price and wage flexibility exists in the economy would generally argue in favor of the demand-pull thesis as the basic cause of inflation because such flexibility makes it virtually impossible for any cost-induced inflationary trend to sustain itself if the level of aggregate real demand is sensitive to a rising price level. On the other hand, economists who are skeptical concerning the extent of wage and price flexibility in the economy are inclined to place more emphasis upon the cost-push theory as basic to an explanation and understanding of inflation. Such theorists do not deny the importance of demand factors, but they take the view that the basic insensitivity of wages and prices to demand conditions means that a substantial—and probably intolerable—level of unemployment and idle capacity would be required before the general price level was stabilized. Neither approach should be considered by itself as a completely satisfactory explanation of the cause and nature of inflation, although both approaches represent worthwhile contributions.

Structural Inflation

The most recent theoretical explanation offered for the inflation present in the American economy was described earlier as the "structural" thesis. As noted, it differs from both the demand-pull and cost-push analyses primarily in that it stresses changes in the composition of demand.

In this analysis the starting point for inflation is a change in the structure of demand which leads to an increase in the demand for the products of particular industries. There is nothing unusual in this, for in a dynamic economy it is presumed that a process of changing demand and resource reallocation is continuously under way. What is significant, though, is that both money wages and prices in the modern American economy are flexible upward in response to shifts in demand, but rigid downward. Prices will therefore move upward in those industries which experience an increase in the demand for their output, but prices will not fall in those industries where there is either an absolute or relative fall in demand. Not only will prices fail to fall in the industries where demand declines; they may actually rise. The increase in wages and other prices in the industries with an expanding demand will force the demand-deficient industries to pay higher wages for labor and higher prices for other materials in order to get the economic resources they need to continue in production, even though these industries are confronted with a decline in the demand for their output. Wage and price rigidity downward is basically the cause for this type of behavior, for it would not be possible for prices to move significantly upward in the industries which have an increase in demand if wages and prices elsewhere would move downward in response to a declining demand situation. Consequently, wage and price increases in particular sectors gradually spread out and permeate the whole economy.

The most important single implication of the structural explanation of the inflationary process is that monetary and fiscal measures of a general character are not capable of coping with this type of an inflationary situation. General monetary and fiscal measures aim basically at the control of aggregate demand, but this is much too blunt an approach for an inflation that has its origin in changes in the composition of demand. Restrictive measures designed to reduce the over-all level of demand may simply lead to unemployment of labor and idle plant capacity without any significant impact on the price level. Perhaps selective monetary and fiscal controls are needed, although Professor Schultze contends that an inflation which results from changes in the composition of demand is generally mild, and is a means by which an economy characterized by downward rigidities in its cost-price structure brings about the necessary re-allocation of resources in response to changing conditions of demand. In the development of any policy measures designed to cope with this type of inflation, care would have to be exercised not to control prices at the cost of blunting the process of resource allocation.

Wage Cuts, Employment, and the Price Level

The final problem we shall consider in this chapter is the relationship between the general price level and the economy's employment level. We have been concerned primarily with the manner in which the price level changes in response to a change in output and employment. More specifically, we sought to show, first, that a rising general level of prices is likely before the economy reaches the full-employment output level; second, that there are good reasons for believing that this relationship is non-reversible; and third, that under certain circumstances a rise in the general price level will lead to a fall in aggregate *real* demand. It is now our objective to reverse the analysis and inquire into the effects that a decline in the general price level may have upon both income and employment.

For practical purposes we are faced with the problem of the relationship between money wages and the output and employment level, because for the economy as a whole labor is the chief variable resource in the short run. Changes in money wages will shift the position of the cost curves of the individual firms and thereby the supply functions for the different industries of the economy. The general price level will change in response to these shifts. Thus the problem of analyzing the impact of a decline in the general price level on both output and employment can be reduced to the question of whether a cut in money-wage rates will favorably affect the economy's over-all employment level.

The Classical View of Wages and Employment

The classical view of the efficacy of money-wage cuts as a stimulus to employment is conditioned primarily by the classical conception of the nature of the demand curve for labor. The classical school held that the demand for labor was an inverse function of the real wage, that a higher level of employment will result if there is a reduction in the real wage.[25] The classical view applies not only to the demand for labor by an individual firm or industry, but to the whole economy, which is to say that the classical aggregate demand function for labor is essentially the summation of a series of individual demand curves.

The classical theorists further assumed that aggregate money demand was unaffected by a change in money wages. In doing so, they transferred an analysis that is valid at the level of the firm or industry to the economy as a whole. For the individual firm and industry a change in money wages is possible without affecting the level of demand for the output of that industry. But classical economists assumed this was true for *all* industries as well as any single industry.

Finally, the classical school assumed there was no direct link between money wages and prices. The general price level was considered to be dependent on the supply of money, and not on the basic supply and demand concepts employed to analyze price and cost phenomena for the firm and industry. It is this curious dichotomy in classical thinking that allows the general price level to be independent of movements in money-wage rates.

Given the foregoing assumptions and the classical conception of the aggregate demand function for labor, the essence of the classical point of view is readily stated: A fall in money wages will favorably affect the economy's level of employment because such a fall, under the conditions stipulated above, will lead to a reduction in the real wage, and thus entrepreneurs in the aggregate will find it profitable to employ more labor. To put the matter slightly differently, a decline in the general level of money wages will shift downward the variable and marginal cost curves for all firms in the economy. This decline in costs relative to prices disturbs an existing equilibrium, and as firms once again seek to return to the point at which profit is maximized, output and employment will necessarily expand. If the individual firm operated in a purely competitive market situation, an upward adjustment in output (and employment) would be possible without any change in price. But this is not necessarily the case for an entire industry. Within the context of industry supply and demand curves, a decrease in the general level of money wages has the effect of shifting the industry supply curve downward, as shown in Figure 13–9. This will affect price if it is presumed that the industry demand curve has a normal negative slope. This does not, however, invalidate the classical thesis so long as it is assumed that the position of the industry demand curve (*DD* in Figure 13–9) is unaffected by the change in the money wages. The lower price means a larger output, and this will entail more employment.

[25] Chapter 4, pp. 87–91.

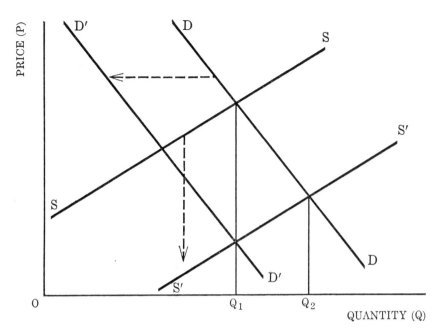

Figure 13–9. Cost and Demand Interdependence

The classical analysis breaks down when the explanations for the behavior of the individual firm or an entire industry are applied to the economy as a whole. Aggregate money wages are double edged; they are not
only a key factor in the level of costs and prices, but also a major source of
income for the greatest number of the economy's income recipients. It is
therefore logically impossible to maintain that the level of money wages
will have no effect upon the level of aggregate money demand. If we adhere to our basic assumption that in the short run labor is the major variable resource, the double-edged character of the money wage accounts for
the fact that aggregate money demand may fall more or less in proportion
to a decline in money wages. If this happens, it may mean that the general
price level will fall to about the same degree as wage costs, and thus the
real wage will not change. But if the real wage does not decline, then it is
not possible for the employment level to rise. In Figure 13–9 an outcome
along these lines is depicted by a shift to the left (to $D'D'$) of the industry
demand schedule consequent upon the downward shift of the supply
curve following the decline in money wages. The downward movement
of the industry demand schedule is due to the fall in aggregate money
demand.

A more refined and complex version of the classical analysis recognizes that a decline in money wages will lead to a fall both in aggre-

gate money demand and the general price level. But this does not necessarily mean that the money incomes of *non-wage* recipients must fall. If the money income of these groups does not decline, their real incomes will rise because of the fall in the general level of prices. This involves fundamentally a redistribution of real income from wage to non-wage groups. If non-wage groups increase their money expenditures because of the improvement in their real income position, then aggregate money demand will not decline in the same proportion as the reduction in money wages. This is the same as saying that there has been an increase in aggregate real demand, and consequently the employment and output level will rise. Or to put the matter in still another way, the general price level will probably not decline in the same proportion as money wages if aggregate money demand falls less than in proportion to the change in money wages. This would again mean a fall in real wages and consequently a higher level of employment.

This modified version of the classical approach is subject to a number of criticisms. In the first place, the assumption that the money incomes of non-wage recipients will be maintained in the face of a downward movement in the general level of wages is questionable, because any reduction in labor costs could conceivably lead to a substitution of labor for other resources and thereby depress the prices of the other resources. If this happened, non-wage incomes might fall at the same rate as wage incomes. The assumption is questionable, too, because it overlooks the fact that non-wage incomes may be dependent upon the level of aggregate demand just as much as wage incomes. Thus a decline in aggregate money demand brought about by a fall in money wages may cause non-wage incomes to fall as well. Only if the money incomes of non-wage groups are unaffected by a decline in money wages is it possible for employment to increase, either because of the substitution effect or because of a redistribution of real income to the non-wage groups. The analysis overlooks the fact that a redistribution of real income from wage to non-wage groups may have the effect of lowering aggregate money demand because the propensity to save of non-wage groups is, on the average, higher than that of wage earners. This, at least, was the view of Keynes.[26]

The Modern View of Wages and Employment

The position of modern theory is that wage cuts will have a favorable effect on employment only if they lead to an increase in aggregate real demand. This requires that both the price level and aggregate money demand decline less than in proportion to any fall in money wages. To determine the extent to which aggregate real demand rises, if at all, we must analyze the possible impact of a cut in money wages on the investment and consumption components of the economy's aggregate demand function.

[26] Keynes, *op. cit.*, p. 262.

The effect of a cut in money wages upon investment expenditure depends, in the first instance, on the impact that such a cut has on the marginal efficiency of capital. A cut in money wages which leads to a proportional decline in the general level of prices will leave the position of the schedule of the marginal efficiency of capital unchanged. If the downward movement in money wages is to have any effect on the investment component of the aggregate demand function, it must result either in an upward shift in the entire marginal efficiency schedule or, through a reduction in the interest rates, bring about a higher level of investment outlays without a shift in the position of the schedule. It is conceivable that a cut in the general level of money wages would have favorable repercussions on the state of business confidence. Keynes, for example, thought it possible that any wage reduction which was believed to be a reduction *relative* to future wages levels would have a favorable effect on the marginal efficiency of capital, although he did not believe that as a practical matter that kind of a "once-and-for-all" cut in money wages could be brought about.[27]

A second way in which a cut in money wages might influence the marginal efficiency of capital is through the impact of such a cut on the foreign balance. In an open economy a reduction in money wages relative to wages abroad may be expected to increase foreign demand for the nation's exports, and thereby improve the current account balance. Any general improvement in the current account balance would, via the multiplier, stimulate domestic output. This could have favorable repercussions on the marginal efficiency of capital in the domestic economy. Of course any retaliation by foreign nations would nullify the favorable effects.

Finally there is the possibility that a reduction in money wages will reduce the rate of interest and thus bring about an increase in investment outlays. With an *unchanged* money supply, a reduction in money wages increases the quantity of money available to hold as an asset since less money is needed to satisfy the transactions motive. As a consequence, the rate of interest will decline, and this should lead to an increase in the rate of investment expenditure. To be at all significant, money-wage rates would have to be reduced at a time when the demand for asset money was less than perfectly elastic with respect to the rate of interest, or otherwise the funds released from the transactions sphere would simply spill over into the liquidity trap. In addition, it must be presumed that the investment demand schedule is relatively interest-elastic, or else the response of investment expenditure to a downward movement of interest rates would not be large. It is presumed that the investment demand schedule itself will not shift downward as a result of any decline in aggregate money demand touched off by falling money wages. It is difficult to imagine, particularly during a period when the economy is in or tending toward a recession, that any of the foregoing conditions would be present.

If it is unlikely that investment expenditure will be stimulated to any

---

[27] *Ibid.*, p. 263.

great degree—if at all—by money-wage cuts, what are the possibilities with respect to the other major component of aggregate demand, namely consumption? [28] A reduction in money wages tends to alter the distribution of real income in favor of non-wage groups, but there is no assurance that a change along these lines would raise the level of the consumption function. It might, on the contrary, lower it because of the presumed higher, on the average, saving propensities of recipients of non-wage income. It is also possible that the decline in the general price level induced by a general cut in money wages would lead to an increase in the propensity to consume if consumers hold inelastic price expectations, which is to say if they believe current prices are below "normal" levels expected to prevail in the future.[29] There is no doubt that a possibility of this sort exists, but it is problematical whether it is a factor of real significance.

The basic case for the view that real consumption outlays will be stimulated by a fall in the level of money wages rests on the Pigou effect. It will be recalled that the Pigou effect holds that a decline in the price level will tend to shift the consumption function upward because any such decline will have a favorable impact on the real value of the stock of liquid assets held by consumers. Thus if a fall in the level of money wages leads also to a fall in the general level of prices, this should raise the level of real consumption by reducing the propensity to save. In this way employment will be stimulated. It is difficult, though, to argue that this "effect" has much practical significance, particularly since economists do not really know how holdings of assets in any form affect consumption decisions, let alone the impact of changes in the real value of such holdings.

To sum up our discussion, it is fair to state that modern income and employment theory takes a generally hostile view toward the efficacy of a policy of wage cutting to raise the employment level. As we have seen, modern analysis is skeptical of classical thinking in this area and finds no compelling reason to believe that cuts in money wages will lead to any significant increase in real aggregate demand as a result of either higher consumption expenditures or higher investment outlays. Moreover, since an increasing number of economists believe that wages and prices are insensitive in a downward direction, any policy that looks toward a reduction in money wages as a realistic solution to a problem of unemployment is largely academic. It may be correct, as Keynes apparently believed, that a reduction in real wages is still necessary in order to get an increase in employment, but even if this is a sound notion the desired result could be achieved much more readily through the fiscal and monetary measures than by attempting to reduce money wages.

[28] Government is omitted in this discussion simply because there is no logical reason to relate the level of government expenditures in any direct way to a cut in money wages.

[29] James Tobin, "Money Wage Rates and Employment" in Seymour Harris, ed., *The New Economics* (New York, Knopf, 1947), p. 584.

PART III

The Theory of Economic Growth

14 | The Nature and Problem of Economic Growth

We now turn our attention to the theory and problems of a growing economy. This is to be contrasted with Part II, where our concern was the determination of income, employment, and the general price level under conditions of relatively fixed productive capacity. The assumption of fixed productive capacity meant that the analysis was essentially static. Once we introduce growth into the analysis, we are no longer in a static realm in which productive capacity is a fixed magnitude. On the contrary, we must be prepared to take into account not only the question of growth in the economy's productive capacity, but the equally vital problem of the continuing upward adjustment of aggregate demand necessary to the utilization of an expanded productive capacity.

The Nature of Economic Growth

Economic growth can be defined most simply and directly as "the expansion of a nation's capability to produce the goods and services its people want." [1] Since the productive capacity of an economy depends basically on the quantity and quality of its resources as well as on its level of technological attainment, economic growth involves the process of expanding and improving these determinants of productive capacity.

Although the most fundamental definition of economic growth must be in terms of the economy's *potential* for the production of goods and services, this is not a sufficient definition. Productive capacity is obviously

[1] Joint Economic Committee, Congress of the United States, *Staff Report on Employment, Growth, and Price Levels*, Washington, 1960, p. 1. This document is cited hereafter as *Staff Report*.

crucially important to the concept of economic growth, but actual growth depends not only upon changes in the economy's potential for production, but also upon the extent to which that capacity is utilized. Economic growth involves, in other words, an increase over time in the actual output of goods and services as well as an increase in the economy's capability to produce goods and services.

Interest in the phenomenon of economic growth stems in large part from our concern with human welfare. There is, of course, no acceptable set of criteria for measurement of such a subjective matter as "welfare," but there is general agreement that material welfare (or well-being) is, in the last analysis, a matter of the availability of goods and services. A rising level of economic well-being for any society requires an expansion in its output of goods and services.

If we are interested in economic growth because of its significance for our material well-being, then what counts is not just an increase in capacity and output per se, but output per capita. What is important from a welfare standpoint is the availability of goods and services per person; it is reasonable to talk of an improvement in the material well-being of a people only if, over time, each person has a growing volume of goods and services at his disposal. Thus, the measure of economic growth that is most meaningful is the level of real output per capita. Analysis of economic growth on a per person basis requires that we take into account not only changes in a nation's productive potential and its use of that potential, but also changes in its population. If population grows at a faster rate than either output or capacity, no improvement in the average standard of material well-being on a per capita basis is possible.

Although most economists and statisticians measure economic growth by comparing data pertaining to real gross national product per capita or national income per capita over a given period of time, a more meaningful evaluation of material welfare or the standard of living could be made from consumption per capita. Increases in a nation's total output of goods and services do not necessarily imply that the individual's standard of living has improved; an expansion of total output may involve investment goods and public goods that do not contribute directly to the material well-being of the individual—for example, military "hardware" in the form of tanks, rockets, or planes. On the other hand, consumption expenditures per capita for privately produced consumer goods and services are not wholly adequate as a measure of material welfare on an individual basis because many of the goods and services supplied by governmental units—schools, recreational facilities, and roadways, to name a few—contribute to the welfare of the individual. Real consumption outlays per person would be a better measure of growth from a material welfare standpoint if such a measure were statistically feasible. But difficulties with respect to what should be properly included in "real consumption" makes this impractical. We are therefore thrown back upon some measure of real output or income per capita as the most reliable standard of economic growth.

The Importance of Economic Growth

What is the significance of economic growth for the American economy? The answer to this question largely depends upon the nature of the tasks that confront our economy. Economic growth in the sense of an expanding output of material goods and services is not an end in itself, but only a means to more basic ends. A recent comprehensive study of the American economy asserts that the fundamental purpose of economic growth is to increase the welfare of the nation's people.[2] An increasing potential for production serves this purpose in two principal ways: It leads to growth in the amount of goods and services available to the consumer for private use, and it provides the necessary resources to permit government at all levels to discharge its ever-increasing responsibilities without adversely affecting private consumption standards. Let us explore these facets of economic growth in more detail.

Although the material standard of living of the American people is without doubt the highest in the world, we have come to expect continued upward movement in our standard of living. For this to be realized, economic growth is an absolute necessity. Economic growth is all the more urgent in view of the increasing number of tasks imposed on government in our society. Ever since the end of World War II, the area of public responsibility has been growing in scope and importance. Without expansion of our productive capacities, it would be impossible for our society to meet a variety of critical challenges, all of which require more resources for public as distinct from private use. Let us summarize briefly the most important of these challenges.

Military Security

We live in a world in which war and the threat of war are day-to-day realities. We are confronted by the continuous "cold war" challenge of the Soviet Union and Communist China, societies whose long-term objectives are hostile to the Western world, and which furthermore possess a formidable military establishment and a first-class military technology. Our security and the security of all other Western nations depend upon the maintenance of military forces with sufficient strength to deter aggression and prevent a major war. No one really knows, of course, how successful military preparedness can be as a long-range deterrent to war, but at this stage in the development of international relations we as a people are not yet ready to rely wholeheartedly on other means for our security and the safeguard-

[2] *Ibid.*, p. 2.

under Summary

ing of the world's peace. The present defense requirements of our society demand that we devote an enormous amount of human and material resources toward military ends; without continued growth in both our productive capacity and actual output, the burden of defense for ourselves and our allies would become more and more difficult to sustain.[3]

Economic Aid to Underdeveloped Nations

Another area in which significant demands are made on the public sector of our society is assistance to the economically underdeveloped nations of the world. Since the end of World War II, great and profound changes have swept over most parts of Asia, the Near East, South America, and Africa. The peoples of these regions, who constitute roughly two-thirds of the world's population, are demanding changes in their societies and their economies that will bring them a better standard of material well-being. Since 1945, the demand for economic development—rapid economic development—has become a world-wide phenomenon. The United States, as the richest nation in the world, has assumed responsibility for providing economic aid to accelerate the economic progress of these areas. We have a vital stake in the economic, political, and cultural development of the underdeveloped areas because the challenge of the Soviet Union and Communist China is as critical and far-reaching in this area as it is in the realm of military strength and supremacy. It would be a well-nigh mortal blow to the future development of Western society if the peoples of the economically underdeveloped areas came to believe that communism offered the only hope and possibility for rapid and sustained improvement in their living standards. It will be practically impossible to meet this challenge without economic growth.

Public Responsibilities in the Domestic Economy

Finally, we can point to a number of areas within our domestic economy which in the coming years will require more and more resources. For example, we are confronted with continually increasing demand for resources for education as a result of a rapidly growing school population. Scientific research is another area of our society which will require increased public outlays. In the past, governments have been the chief suppliers of resources and funds for research, and, in view of the increasing demands being placed upon basic scientific research, the need for resources to carry out scientific programs will be even greater in the future. Other areas of public responsibility which will require more resources in the future involve the continued improvement in both the quantity and quality of health services, including medical research; the reconstruction and mod-

[3] In the second quarter of 1966, Federal government expenditures for national defense were at an annual rate of $57 billion. Because of the war in Viet Nam, these expenditures were up by nearly $7 billion over the 1965 rate. See *Economic Indicators*, July, 1966, p. 2.

ernization of the central portions of many of our cities, areas which have experienced serious physical deterioration over the last several decades; and the construction of an adequate system of superhighways for the whole nation, as well as continued improvement and development of outdoor recreational areas for a population with increasing amounts of leisure.[4] These are but a few of the tasks which governments at all levels in our society face and which demand continued economic growth if they are to be resolved without serious internal conflict and strife.

The Growth Record of the American Economy

A brief review of the long-term growth record of the American economy will yield us some insight into probable future development. The over-all record of growth of the American economy from 1839 to 1959 is summarized in Table 14-1. These data are taken from an analysis of the

TABLE 14-1.

Growth Trends in the American Economy, 1839–1959
(percentage increase per year)

	Entire period 1839–1959	40-year subperiods		
		1839–1879	1879–1919	1919–1959
Price level	1.15	−0.16	1.91	1.40
GNP in constant prices	3.66	4.31	3.72	2.97
Population	1.97	2.71	1.91	1.30
Per capita GNP in constant prices	1.64	1.55	1.76	1.64

SOURCE: Joint Economic Committee, Congress of the United States, *Staff Report on Employment, Growth, and Price Levels*, p. 34.

American economy undertaken on behalf of the Joint Economic Committee of the Congress of the United States. The data in the table are broken down into three subperiods, each of forty years' length. The average annual rate of growth for the real gross national product of the American economy over the entire 120-year period was 3.66 per cent, a record that is unmatched by any other economy over so long a period.[5] These data also show that there has been some slowing down in the rate of growth of total real output, although when the data are reduced to a per capita basis there does not appear to be any significant change in the long-term trends. Real GNP rose at an annual average rate of 4.31 per cent during

[4] For further details see *Staff Report*, pp. 4, 5, 6. The January 1965 *Economic Report of the President* discusses some of these problems in greater detail, especially those related to urban areas.

[5] *Ibid.*, p. 34.

the first forty-year period (1839–1879). In the period 1879 to 1919 the growth rate fell to 3.72 per cent per year, and then for the next forty years (1919–1959) declined further to an annual average rate of 2.97 per cent. The per capita data do not show the same long-term decline. During the first forty-year period GNP per capita in constant prices increased at an annual average rate of 1.55 per cent. This period, though, was the one in which population increased most rapidly; population grew at an annual average rate of 2.71 per cent, as compared to 1.91 per cent in the second forty-year period, and 1.30 per cent in the third forty-year period. The slower rate of population growth is reflected in the fact that real GNP per capita in constant prices actually increased at a more rapid rate in the second and third forty-year periods, even though this was not true for the aggregate GNP. In the period 1879–1919 real GNP per capita rose at an annual average rate of 1.76 per cent. During the next forty-year period (1919–1959) the rate declined to an annual average of 1.64 per cent, although this figure is still above the average of 1.55 per cent per year for the first one-third of the whole 120-year period.

Concern has been expressed that in the late 1950's the American economy grew at a rate that not only was below the long-term record of the economy, but was substantially lower than its potential growth rate. In the 1960's, however, the growth rate rose.[6] For the period 1960–1965 *real* GNP rose at an annual average rate of 4.4 per cent. There can be no doubt that the long-run performance of the American economy has been impressive, but the serious challenges mentioned demand an even better performance from our economic system. According to the Joint Economic Committee, the American economy can grow at an annual average rate of 4.5 per cent without any fundamental changes in the system, and even higher rates of growth are not impossible if necessary.[7]

Recent Interest in the Problem of Economic Growth

During recent decades there has been a sharp revival of interest by economists in the subject of economic growth. Adam Smith and the early classical economists were absorbed by the problem of economic growth, but by the middle of the nineteenth century questions of resource allocation and income distribution became the economists' dominant concern. In the 1930's the problem of the employment level and its determination came to the fore, and only recently have economists directed their attention once again to economic growth. There are several reasons for this.

In the first place, the emergence of modern income and employment theory could not help but lead to consideration of the problems of eco-

[6] The policy measures taken to stimulate the economy's growth in the early 1960's are discussed in Chapter 16.

[7] *Employment, Growth, and Price Levels, Report of the Joint Economic Committee, Congress of the United States*, Washington, 1960, p. 16.

nomic growth. Income and employment theory, it is true, was born during the Great Depression of the 1930's, and its major focus was on the forces that determine the level of employment in an advanced economy on the assumption that productive capacity was a fixed magnitude. But within the Keynesian analytical framework, investment expenditure occupies a key position, and the economists' concern with the phenomenon of investment has inevitably led into the broad area of growth analysis. By definition, net investment is a dynamic phenomenon since it is the same as an addition to the economy's stock of real capital assets. Once we admit of changes in capital stock we are no longer dealing with a situation in which productive capacity is fixed, and our analysis loses its static character.

A second major reason for the renewed interest in economic growth stems from the desire and pressure for rapid economic progress that emanates from the economically underdeveloped nations of the world. These newly-emerged states are faced with an almost irresistible demand from their people for rapid economic development. As Gunnar Myrdal has pointed out, these new nations, created mostly out of what were the colonial empires of the European power prior to World War II, have been touched by a "Great Awakening" and crave both national independence and economic development.[8]

A third source of interest in economic growth has to do with the experience of the Soviet Union. As Professor Simon Kuznets has pointed out, the Soviet Union contends that its peculiar and authoritarian form of social and economic organization is a particularly efficient instrument for dealing with the long-term problem of economic development.[9] The claim of the Soviet Union that organization of society along Marxist lines is the most effective means of bringing about the rapid development of an economically backward nation rests upon Soviet success in the transformation of Russia from a relatively backward peasant economy under the Czar to the world's second most powerful industrial economy in the space of less than half a century. Although it has been conclusively demonstrated that the Soviet Union did not begin its Marxist experiment in a society nearly so backward economically as it would like the rest of the world to believe,[10] the Soviet record of economic growth has been impressive nevertheless.

The Process of Economic Growth

The process of economic growth has to do with the means by which a nation expands its productive capacity. In any society four factors are of

[8] Gunnar Myrdal, *Rich Lands and Poor* (New York, Harper, 1957), p. 7.
[9] Simon Kuznets, "Toward a Theory of Economic Growth," in *Economic Growth and Structure* (New York, Norton, 1965).
[10] W. W. Rostow, *The Stages of Economic Growth* (Cambridge, England, Cambridge University Press, 1960), p. 66.

fundamental importance in the growth process. These are (1) the quantity and quality of the labor force; (2) the quantity and quality of natural resources; (3) the quantity and quality of real capital; and (4) the level of technological attainment of the society. These are the "fundamental" determinants of economic growth. They define in a fundamental sense the potential for production of any economy. As used in our analysis, technology is a broad term which refers to the effectiveness with which economic resources in the form of labor, natural resources, and capital are combined in the productive process. As a practical matter, it is difficult to separate technology from the resources themselves, for the quality of the latter is a reflection of a society's level of technological attainment.

In addition to the four "fundamental" determinants of the economy's productive capacity, we must recognize at least three other kinds of determinants that enter either directly or indirectly into the growth process. *First,* there are variables of an even more basic character that lie behind the fundamental determinants: the vast array of factors, economic and non-economic, that in some sense account for changes in the supply of labor, the level of technology, and the stock of capital. *Second,* there exist other variables that constitute the socio-economic structure of a society, within which the fundamental determinants must function. Among these variables are the underlying competitive nature of an economy, the distribution of income and wealth, the pattern of consumer tastes, dominant forms of business organization, and other factors of an essentially institutional character. *Finally,* there are all the crucially important variables that enter into the determination of the level of aggregate demand; these may be defined as "intermediate" determinants. They form an important part of the growth process, because economic growth is not merely a matter of a changing productive capacity, but involves, as well, the utilization of that capacity. Thus the variables that we studied earlier in our analysis of the determinants of aggregate demand are equally important to our understanding of the process of economic growth.

Economic Theory and Economic Growth

Economic theory seeks to understand and explain the process by which growth takes place in a society, first, by identifying the variables which are believed to be strategically significant as determinants of economic growth and, second, by attempting to ascertain the manner in which these variables are related in a functional sense both to one another and to other variables.

Theories that have to do with the process of economic growth are by no means new. Adam Smith and the early classical economists concerned themselves with the probable long-term development of a capitalistic system and Karl Marx was deeply interested in the same problem. What is relatively new, though, is the very rapid development since the end of World War II of a large volume of literature concerned with the theory and the problems of a developing economy. Modern growth theory has emerged almost entirely since 1945.

Modern growth theory has developed in two distinct directions. One group of theories is oriented primarily toward the problems of growth in the economically underdeveloped nations and seeks to build a comprehensive theory that will account for all the important variables, economic and non-economic, that enter into the process of economic growth. These theories dig deep into the underlying social and cultural structure of a society to identify and explain the forces that in some sense are determinants of the so-called fundamental determinants. The central problem of the economically underdeveloped nations is a severe shortage of productive capacity; a theory of growth that would be adequate to cope with the real problems of such societies must be broad in scope and extend beyond the usual boundaries of economics. Underdeveloped nations usually cannot increase their productive capacity without far-reaching changes in their economic, political, and cultural institutions and behavior patterns. While assessing such strictly economic variables as the supply of labor, the stock of capital, or the quantity of natural resources, growth theory must take into account the need for social reorganization, often on a grand scale.

A recent study by Professor W. W. Rostow gives an excellent illustration of growth analysis in its broadest possible sense.[11] Rostow attempts to analyze the process of growth in terms of a series of five stages through which all developing nations sooner or later pass, irrespective of their political, economic, and social systems. His aim is to develop a theory broad enough to encompass and explain the process of growth and development in such diverse societies as twentieth-century America, the Soviet Union, nineteenth-century feudal Japan, nineteenth-century imperialistic Germany, modern India, and Communist China.

The other group of modern growth theories centers primarily on the problem of growth and change in developed economies, such as those of contemporary Western Europe or the United States and Canada. These theories are often labeled "post-Keynesian" partly because they have been worked out entirely within the framework of modern income and employment analysis, and partly because their primary objective is to discover and understand the conditions under which sustained growth is possible in an advanced economy. The critical problem in an advanced economy is not that of productive capacity; more often the important problem is to insure a sufficiently high level of aggregate demand so that the existing productive potential is fully utilized. In advanced economies, however, the productive potential will not remain constant. Growth is inherent in the highly dynamic character of most advanced economies, and thus when we move

[11] Rostow, *op. cit.*

out of a relatively short-term setting we are confronted with the peculiar type of growth problem faced by the advanced nation.

The post-Keynesian type of growth theory does not attempt to explain change in any of the "fundamental" determinants of productive capacity. It assumes instead that one or more of these variables is undergoing change at a steady rate over time. The theories study the effect of a continuous change of this kind on the economy's productive capacity and seek to explain how the level of aggregate demand may be adjusted over time to the resulting changes in productive capacity. Such theories can yield valuable insights into the problems of growth in an advanced economy, even though they may not be able to provide a basic explanation for the phenomenon of growth itself. We will deal in the next two chapters with some post-Keynesian theories and see what light they throw on the problems of employment, output, and growth in an advanced economy.

15 | Post-Keynesian Theories of Economic Growth

In this chapter we shall analyze the contributions of two contemporary economists to the growing volume of economic literature devoted to the problem of economic growth. The economists are Evsey D. Domar, an American, and Roy F. Harrod, an Englishman. They are the best-known post-Keynesian growth theorists, and their analyses focus in common upon the conditions under which advanced economies, such as those of the United States or the United Kingdom, can achieve and maintain full employment and a rising level of real income over time.

Professor Harrod first broached the question of the conditions under which sustained economic growth is possible in a developed economy in a now famous article, "An Essay in Dynamic Theory," which appeared in 1939 in *The Economic Journal*, the official journal of the British Royal Economic Society. Curiously enough, Harrod's article attracted little attention until after World War II when, in February 1947, he returned again to the theme of sustained growth in a series of lectures delivered at the University of London. Meanwhile Professor Domar, in March, 1947, published his own analysis of the conditions under which both growth and continued full employment are possible in a developed society. His article, "Expansion and Employment," appeared in *The American Economic Review* and has become equally renowned as Harrod's 1939 article and 1947 lectures.[1]

[1] For Harrod's analysis see particularly "An Essay in Dynamic Theory," *The Economic Journal*, March, 1939, pp. 14–33, and *Toward a Dynamic Economics* (London, Macmillan, 1948), esp. Lecture Three, pp. 63–100. For Domar's analysis see "Expansion and Employment," *The American Economic Review*, March, 1947, pp. 34–55.

Review of the Keynesian Equilibrium

The appropriate point of departure for a discussion of growth theories applicable to the economy of an advanced nation is the condition of full-employment equilibrium in a short-run setting. A full-employment equilibrium is described as "Keynesian" because it refers to an equilibrium brought about within the framework of aggregate supply and aggregate demand. This, as we have seen, is the basic analytical framework developed by Keynes in the *General Theory*.

Before we review the full-employment equilibrium within this framework, it is important to remember that Keynes' analysis is static because it is not concerned with the problem of a continuing change over time in the fundamental determinants of the economy's productive potential. In his own words, the analysis takes as given "the existing skill and quantity of available labour, the existing quality and quantity of available equipment, the existing technique, the degree of competition, the tastes and habits of the consumer." [2] With capacity known and fixed, the central problem is the determination of the level of aggregate demand; in static analysis the level of aggregate demand determines the output and employment level, and shifts in the aggregate demand schedule bring about shifts in both output and employment.

In the simplest version of the Keynesian system aggregate demand consists of consumption and investment expenditure. The basic condition for equilibrium at *any* level of income and employment is that investment expenditure be sufficiently large to absorb the saving forthcoming at the income level in question. Consequently, the necessary condition for a full-employment equilibrium income level is that investment expenditure be sufficient to absorb the saving made at the full-employment income.

Full-employment equilibrium in the Keynesian framework is depicted in Figure 15–1. Output (real income) is measured on both axes, but it is convenient to view income on the vertical axis as a flow of expenditure, while income on the horizontal axis can be viewed as a flow of output. The aggregate supply function is shown by the 45° line OZ, while OC is the secular consumption function. If we know the average productivity of labor and the size of the labor force, it is relatively easy to determine the full-employment income level. Let us assume that full-employment income equals Y_1. On the aggregate supply schedule this level of income is represented at the point Z_1. If full-employment income is equal to the distance OY_1 (or Y_1Z_1), and the consumption function is given by the curve OC, the amount of saving forthcoming at full employment equals the distance Z_1C_1. Thus, for this full-employment level to be achieved and maintained,

[2] John Maynard Keynes, *The General Theory of Employment, Interest and Money* (New York, Harcourt, Brace, 1936), p. 245.

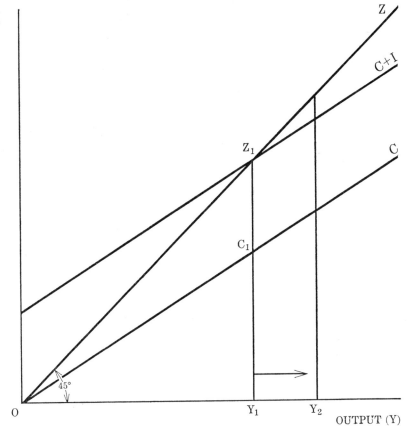

Figure 15–1. The Full-Employment Equilibrium

investment expenditure must also equal Z_1C_1. Then the aggregate demand schedule, $C + I$, will intersect the aggregate supply schedule OZ at the point Z_1.

There is nothing wrong with this analysis since it expresses an idea fundamental to all modern income and employment theory: namely, income paid out or created during the productive process must be returned in one form or another to the income stream if the expectations of producers are to be satisfied and equilibrium maintained. But, as Domar and Harrod have observed, the equilibrium so obtained his meaning only for a relatively short period of time because the *capacity-creating* effects of investment expenditure will cause the income level that is appropriate to the full employment of both labor and other resources to *rise* over time.

To facilitate our understanding of why a level of income sufficient to achieve full employment of all resources today may not be sufficient to achieve full employment of all resources tomorrow, let us assume that income, investment, and saving are defined in Figure 15–1 in the *net* sense, that is, after proper allowance has been made for the replacement of capital goods used up in the current production process. The output measured on both axes of the diagram would be the equivalent of the net national product in the terminology of national income accounting.

If our analytical framework is cast in net rather than gross terms, it does not change the underlying principle; the full-employment equilibrium requires that investment expenditure be equal to full-employment saving. The only difference is that now the basic statement describing the necessary condition for achievement and maintenance of a full-employment income level needs to be modified to read that *ex ante* net investment must be equal to *ex ante* net saving at full employment.

Once we put the analysis in net terms and define full-employment equilibrium in terms of an equality between net saving and investment, we are faced with a serious dilemma because the analytical system no longer retains its static character. Net saving is a dynamic concept, for if a society steadily saves some portion of its net income and just as steadily invests the income saved in productive capital, it follows that the stock of productive capital equipment, one of the basic determinants of both capacity and output, will change. Static analysis does not concern itself with a situation in which a basic determinant of productive capacity such as the capital stock changes. The paradox of the situation arises from the fact that net investment is by definition an addition to the economy's stock of wealth in the form of productive capital, and thus net investment must logically increase the economy's productive capacity. But if productive capacity is increasing, the analysis can no longer be static.

This paradoxical situation can be illustrated by referring once more to Figure 15–1. Full-employment income in the current income period is equal to Y_1. This income level can be defined and measured only on the assumption that capacity is fixed. Net investment in the current income period proceeds at the rate $Z_1 C_1$, which makes possible full-employment income during this period. But since this amount of net investment necessarily increases the economy's productive capacity by adding to the stock of capital, the income level Y_1 will not suffice to provide full employment of all resources in the next and subsequent income periods. The capacity-creating effect of net investment expenditure during the current income period is depicted by shifting the full-employment income level from Y_1 to Y_2. It is because of the capacity-creating effects of net investment that the level of output must grow over time if full utilization of the economy's productive capacity is to be continuously achieved.

The Domar Analysis of Economic Growth

The paradox that net investment is, on the one hand, a necessary offset to net saving if full employment is to be maintained and, on the other, an addition to the economy's stock of capital provides a setting for Domar's analysis of the problem of growth in an advanced economy. The dominant theme in his theoretical treatment of economic growth is that *net* investment raises productive capacity and thus causes the economy to grow. Given the *capacity-creating* impact of net investment, Domar attempts to determine the *rate* at which income must grow if full employment is to be maintained over time.[3]

To explore this problem, Domar develops an analytical model which seeks to show how growth in capacity over time can be linked to growth in aggregate demand, output, and employment. Domar's analytical framework is essentially Keynesian, although it is placed in a long-run setting and includes some new elements.

Before we examine Domar's analysis of the growth process, we must define the concepts he employs and state the assumptions underlying the analysis. The key concepts and assumptions are as follows:

1. *The propensity to save.* This is the ratio of saving to income at any given level of income. Domar assumes that S/Y is constant, which means he is working with a long-run or secular saving function. Also, the marginal propensity to save, $\Delta S/\Delta Y$, is equal to the average propensity to save, since mathematically the average propensity to save could not be a constant unless it was equal to the marginal propensity to save. In the analysis both the marginal and the average propensity to save are designated by α. In Domar's analytical system, as in Keynesian economics proper, the significance of the average propensity to save is that it determines the amount of saving that will have to be absorbed by investment for the achievement of a full-employment income level, while the significance of the marginal propensity to save is that it is the key to the value of the multiplier.

2. *The capital-output ratio.* This magnitude, which is sometimes called the capital coefficient, is the ratio of the capital stock of the economy, K, to full capacity output, Y. Basically, K/Y is a way of defining the economy's capacity in terms of its capital stock; given an existing level of technology, there will be, on the average, a certain physical quantity of capital required to obtain a given quantity of output. Since both capital (a stock phenomenon) and output (a flow phenomenon) must be measured in terms of their monetary values, the capital-output ratio becomes, as a practical matter, the number of dollars' worth of capital required on the average to get a dollar's worth of output. Domar bases his analysis on the average capital-output ratio for the whole economy, although the actual capital-output ratio may vary widely from industry to industry.

3. *The marginal capital-output ratio.* This ratio represents the relationship between changes in the capital stock, ΔK, and changes in the output level, ΔY. Since a change in the capital stock is the same thing as net investment, $\Delta K/\Delta Y$ tells us how much added capital or investment is needed to

[3] E. D. Domar, "Expansion and Employment," *op. cit.*, p. 38.

get an additional unit of output. The marginal capital-output ratio or capital coefficient may or may not be equal to the average capital-output ratio, but if the marginal ratio is constant and equal to the average ratio, technological change is said to be "neutral." [4] Technological change that is not neutral alters both the average and marginal capital-output ratios, but especially the latter, because new developments make themselves felt primarily at the time when additions to the capital stock are being made.

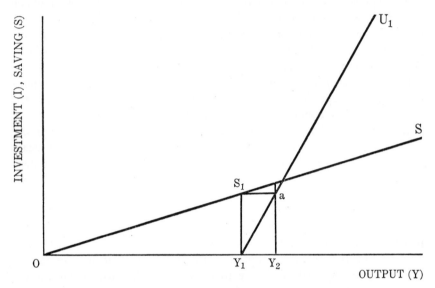

Figure 15–2. The Marginal Capital-Output Ratio

Technological change may, moreover, lower or raise these ratios by reducing or increasing the amount of capital required to obtain a unit of output. If the capital requirement has been reduced, "capital-saving" is said to have taken place; if it has been increased, the result has been "capital-deepening."

The nature of the marginal capital-output ratio can be shown by means of a diagram. In Figure 15–2, with output and capacity on the horizontal axis and net savings and investment on the vertical axis, OS represents the long-run saving function, the slope of which is such that the average and marginal propensities to save are equal.[5] If Y_1 is the full-employment income, then the full-employment requirement is that net investment be equal to saving at this income level. This is the distance Y_1S_1. The marginal capital coefficient is represented by the Y_1U_1, the slope of which is equal

---

[4] "Neutral" technological change leaves the capital-output ratio unchanged. See Harrod, *Toward Dynamic Economics, op. cit.*, p. 83.

[5] This diagram was developed by Harold Pilvin. See "A Geometric Analysis of Recent Growth Models," *The American Economic Review*, September, 1952, pp. 594–599.

to the ratio of an increment of capital to an increment of output. Thus, if investment in the income period proceeds at the rate Y_1S_1, the impact on the economy's productive capacity is shown by projecting a horizontal line from S_1 to the point at which it intersects the Y_1U_1 line (point a in the diagram), and then dropping a vertical line from this point to the horizontal axis. The distance Y_1Y_2 represents the increase in capacity that has resulted from net investment in the amount Y_1S_1 in the present income period.

4. *The productivity of capital coefficient.* In Domar's analysis, and in growth economics generally, the ratio Y/K (the reciprocal of the capital-output ratio) is a measure of the average productivity of capital in the same sense that a full-employment output, Y, divided by the labor force, N', is a measure of the average productivity of labor. The ratio Y/N', which may be called the *average productivity of labor,* has frequently been used to determine the economy's potential for production, as it is only necessary to multiply the average productivity of labor by the assumed labor force to get a measure of potential output. The ratio Y/K shifts the emphasis from labor productivity to capital productivity in the determination of capacity.

In Domar's analysis the ratio of an increment of output, ΔY, to an increment in the capital stock, ΔK, is designated by s. If the average and marginal ratios are assumed equal, s is both a measure of the average productivity of capital *ex post* and a measure of the amount by which each dollar's worth of newly created capital, taken by itself, will add to the poductive capacity of the economy. Viewed in the latter sense Domar's s is simply the reciprocal of the marginal capital-output ratio, because if on the average 3 dollars' worth of capital equipment is required to produce 1 dollar's worth of additional output, s will have a value of 0.33. In other words, the average productivity of capital will be 0.33, because each dollar's worth of new capital will increase capacity by this amount.

Although Domar employs the symbol s to describe the immediate and direct effect on capacity that results from added capital, this particular ratio is not the appropriate ratio for the whole economy, because, he asserts, normally some newly created capital goods will be brought into use at the expense of existing capital. Thus the amount by which over-all capacity is increased for each new dollar's worth of capital equipment will be less than s. To designate the amount by which productive capacity for *the whole economy* is increased for each dollar's worth of new capital Domar employs σ, which he calls the *potential social average productivity of investment.* Normally σ is smaller than s. As we shall see shortly, σ is the most important single concept employed by Domar in his analysis of the growth process.

5. *Some simplifying assumptions.* The concepts discussed in the foregoing paragraphs constitute the key ideas Domar employs in the construc-

tion of his growth theory, but there are some simplifying assumptions that should be made clear before we turn to discussion of the theory itself. In the first place, he assumes an economy in which there is neither government nor international economic transactions. This does not imply that public activity and international transactions have no role to play in the growth process, but simply reflects Domar's desire to concentrate the whole of his analysis on the growth potential embodied in the capacity-creating effect of net investment in the private sector. Second, the analysis assumes there are no lags in adjustment, which is to say that output is assumed to respond immediately to changes in expenditure and expenditure is assumed to respond immediately to changes in income. The absence of lags permits us to see as clearly as possible the key relationships involved in the growth process. Finally, the analysis starts with the assumption that a full-employment income level has been attained.

The Capacity-Creating Process

Having discussed Domar's key concepts, we can now examine the way in which he describes the capacity-creating process associated with a given amount of net investment. In Figure 15–1 the full-employment income level is assumed to be Y_1, and the amount of net investment required at this income level is given by the distance Z_1C_1. If investment expenditure proceeds during the income period at this rate, we can use σ to determine the effect of this amount of investment on productive capacity. Specifically, if net investment in the income period is equal to I dollars, the subsequent increase in the productive capacity of the whole economy is

$$\Delta Y_Q = I\sigma \qquad (15\text{--}1)$$

ΔY_Q represents the increase in the *productive potential* of the economy; it does not represent any actual increase in output. The expression $I\sigma$ reflects the *supply side* of the economic system, for it describes the extent to which productive capacity has been increased as a consequence of a specific amount of net investment. In terms of the Keynesian diagrammatic analysis this means that the full capacity output level has been pushed farther to the right along the horizontal axis. If, to refer back to Figure 15–1, Y_1 represented a full-employment income level at the beginning of the current income period, it no longer represents the full-employment income level at the end of this period.

The nature of the capacity-creating process of net investment can be clearly illustrated by a simple numerical example. Let us assume, first, that σ has a value of 0.3 and, second, that the average (and marginal) propensity to save out of net income is 0.10. Let us assume further that the full-employment income in the present period (the Y_1 of Figure 15–1) is $700 billion. Then, for full employment, investment expenditure must equal $70 billion (or 10 per cent of $700 billion). If the net investment of the economy is at the rate of $70 billion during the current income period, what effect does this have on productive capacity? The potential social average productivity of investment coefficient, σ, supplies the answer; if, on the average, every dollar's worth of new capital increases productive capacity by $0.30, then $70 billion of new capital will increase the over-all productive capacity of the economy by $21 billion ($70 billion $\times$ 0.3 = $21 billion).

What are the consequences of the above process? Although $700 billion represented the full-employment output level at the start of the income period, this is no longer the case. Capacity has grown and with it the full-employment output level. This fact underscores the fundamental necessity for output to grow if full employment is to be maintained over time in an economy in which there is positive net saving and positive net investment. What would happen if, in the next income period, income remained at $700 billion? As Domar points out, the creation of new capital will result in one of three possible effects, assuming the level of income remains unchanged: [6] (1) the new capital remains unused, in which case it should not have been produced in the first place; (2) the new capital is used at the expense of previously constructed capital, which also may represent a waste of resources if net investment is large; and (3) the new capital may be substituted for labor, which may lead to a substantial amount of involuntary unemployment if the introduction of the new equipment is not accompanied by a voluntary reduction in either the size of the labor force or the length of the workweek. If income remains at the same level in the next period, even though there has been net investment in the present period, the result will be either unemployed labor, unemployed capital, or both.

The Demand Requirement

The key point of the foregoing analysis is that if *net* investment increases the economy's productive capacity, it is essential that output grow through time to insure that the added capacity created by the investment process is continually absorbed into use. The problem is therefore to determine, first, how output can be made to expand so as to bring into use the added capacity and, second, the necessary rate at which output must expand to achieve the continued full utilization of additional capacity.

Domar's analysis of the growth process is carried out within the Keynesian framework of aggregate demand and aggregate supply, where the most important role played by aggregate demand is to bring capacity into use. Both output and employment result from the use of capacity, and

---

[6] Domar, *op cit.*, p. 37.

it is the expectation of demand that leads the entrepreneur to make use of the productive capacity at his disposal. It follows that *it is necessary for aggregate demand to rise if added productive capacity is to be brought into use.*

Since we have eliminated government expenditures and international transactions from the analysis, and since consumption is a dependent variable (in that it is a function of income), investment is the key determinant of the level of aggregate demand. Thus investment will have to increase if there is to be an upward shift in the aggregate demand function; the shift must be great enough to bring about an over-all increase in aggregate expenditure sufficient to utilize—and thus justify—the added productive capacity. This aspect of the problem is easy to understand, for the reader need only recall the multiplier analysis to realize that any given total increase in aggregate expenditure depends upon the amount by which investment itself has risen as well as upon the value of the multiplier. The latter, of course, is dependent upon the marginal propensity to save.

If the utilization of additional capacity requires an increase in aggregate expenditure equal to the amount by which capacity has increased, and if changes in investment expenditure are the ultimate source of changes in effective demand, we can express the required increase in effective demand in equation form as

$$\Delta Y_D = \Delta I \times \frac{1}{\alpha} \qquad\qquad (15\text{--}2)$$

This equation is simply the multiplier formula applied to an increase in investment expenditure. ΔY_D represents the over-all increase in effective demand or total expenditure brought about by the given increment in investment expenditure. $1/\alpha$ is the simple investment multiplier, since α represents the marginal propensity to save.

In conjunction with the equation depicting the demand side of his system, Domar places great stress on what he terms the *dual nature of the investment process.* By this he means that the capacity-creating effects and the demand-creating effects of investment expenditure are dissimilar, because *all* net investment expenditure adds to the economy's capital stock and thus increases the economy's productive capacity, but only increments to investment expenditure, operating through the multiplier effect, raise the level of effective demand. This, in short, is the real paradox of investment; if net investment expenditure simply remains constant through time, the income level will not change—that is, equilibrium will be maintained—but the result will be idle capacity and a growing volume of unemployed labor. Investment and income must grow in each succeeding income period if net investment expenditures in any specific income period are to justify themselves.

The Required Rate of Income Growth

If the maintenance of full employment over time for both the economy's labor force and stock of productive capital requires that output grow at the same rate at which productive capacity is increasing because of net investment, we can bring together the equations discussed above and compute the *necessary* rate at which output must grow. The basic condition is that, over time, increments of effective demand must equal increments of capacity. Symbolically, this can be stated as:

$$\Delta Y_Q = \Delta Y_D \qquad (15\text{--}3)$$

In the above definitional equation we can substitute the earlier values for ΔY_Q and ΔY_D. Thus:

$$I\sigma = \Delta I \times \frac{1}{\alpha} \qquad (15\text{--}4)$$

$I\sigma$ represents the supply side of the system, for it shows the potential increase in supply that results from current investment, while $\Delta I \times \frac{1}{\alpha}$ represents the demand side, since it depicts the amount by which aggregate effective demand must rise if the added capacity is to be utilized.

Domar "solves" the above fundamental equation by multiplying both sides by α and then dividing both sides by I. The result of this is the following *growth* equation:

$$\frac{\Delta I}{I} = \sigma\alpha \qquad (15\text{--}5)$$

The left side of this equation shows the absolute increment in investment expenditure divided by the total volume of investment expenditure. It is expressive of the percentage rate of growth of investment. Thus, Equation (15–5) means basically that *investment expenditure must grow at an annual rate equal to the product of the marginal propensity to save, α, and the potential social average productivity of investment, σ*, if a state of continuous full employment is to be maintained. Since Domar assumes that the average and marginal propensities to save are equal and that the average and marginal values of σ are equal, it is easy to demonstrate algebraically that income as well as investment must grow at a constant annual percentage rate equal to the product of α and σ.[7] Thus:

[7] This can be shown algebraically as follows:
(1) $I = \alpha Y$ [This assumes that the saving of the period is invested.]
(2) $\Delta Y_Q = \sigma\alpha Y$ [This is from Equation (15–1).]
(3) $\Delta Y_D = \sigma\alpha Y$ [This on the assumption that the change in aggregate effective demand must equal the change in capacity.]

$$\frac{\Delta Y}{Y} = \sigma\alpha \qquad (15\text{-}6)$$

The above equation, like Equation (15-5), indicates in a simple and direct way the necessary condition for the maintenance of full-employment output over time. It shows, to quote Domar, "that it is not sufficient, in Keynesian terms, that savings of yesterday be invested today, or, as it is so often expressed, that investment offset saving. Investment of today must always exceed savings of yesterday. . . . The economy must continuously expand." [8]

A Numerical Representation of the Growth Process

The nature of this growth process may be illustrated by numerical example. Tables 15-1 and 15-2 contain hypothetical data pertaining to the growth of net national output, consumption, and investment over a five-year period, assuming different sets of values for both α and σ. In Table 15-1, the propensity to save, α, has a value of 0.10, while the value of the

TABLE 15-1.

The Required Growth of Income: I
(in billions of dollars)

$\alpha = 0.10$
$\sigma = 0.30$
$\sigma\alpha = 0.03/\text{yr}.$

(1)	(2)	(3)	(4)	(5)
				Increase in
Year	Income	Consumption	Investment	Capacity
	(Y)	(C)	(I)	$(I\sigma)$
1	$700.0	$630.0	$70.0	$21.0
2	721.0	648.9	72.1	21.6
3	742.6	668.3	74.3	22.3
4	764.9	688.4	76.5	22.9
5	787.8	709.0	78.8	23.6

productivity of capital coefficient, σ, is 0.30. The "required" rate of growth is thus 3 per cent per year, since $\alpha \times \sigma = 0.03$. If the net national income of the economy is $700 billion in the first year, a 3 per cent annual rate of growth will raise income to the level of $787.8 billion at the end of five years. The effect of investment upon capacity in each income period is shown in Column (5). The figures in this column are the product of $I\sigma$, for we assume that the net saving of each income period is invested. The

---

(4) $\frac{\Delta Y}{Y} = \sigma\alpha$ [This follows algebraically from above.]

[8] Domar, *op. cit.*, p. 42.

amount of such saving is determined by the average propensity to consume. Investment (and saving) remain a constant proportion of income, but the absolute amount of investment is greater in each subsequent income period. This is a clear example of what Domar means when he states, as quoted above, that the investment of today must always exceed savings of yesterday. This simple example offers considerable insight into the difficulties inherent in maintaining full employment over time in an advanced economy; the economy must not only expand continuously in order to avoid unemployment, but in order to do this it must constantly find outlets in investment expenditure for a rising *absolute* amount of saving. Past experience as well as theoretical analysis suggest that this is something quite difficult to achieve for any sustained period of time.

Table 15–2 contains similar hypothetical data, except in this instance we

TABLE 15–2.

The Required Growth of Income: II
(in billions of dollars)

$\alpha = 0.12$
$\sigma = 0.40$
$\sigma\alpha = 0.48/\text{yr.}$

(1)	(2)	(3)	(4)	(5)
				Increase in
Year	Income (Y)	Consumption (C)	Investment (I)	Capacity $(I\sigma)$
1	$700.0	$616.0	$ 84.0	$33.6
2	733.6	645.6	88.0	35.2
3	768.8	676.5	92.3	36.9
4	805.7	709.1	96.9	38.7
5	844.4	743.1	101.3	40.5

are assuming higher values for both the propensity to save and the productivity of capital coefficient. Specifically, α is assumed to have a value of 0.12, and σ a value of 0.40. This means, first, that this hypothetical economy saves, on the average, a higher proportion of its net income and, second, that the productivity of capital is, also on the average, higher. As a consequence, investment expenditure equal to the saving at any particular income level will have a greater impact on the economy's productive capacity than was the case in the prior example. This is not only because the absolute amount of saving will be greater at each and every income level, but also because the higher value for the productivity of capital coefficient means, in effect, that every dollar of investment expenditure increases productive capacity by a greater amount. Thus, the over-all effect of higher values for both the propensity to save and the productivity of capital coefficient is to increase the necessary growth rate for our hypothetical economy. With the above assumed values for these coefficients, the "necessary" growth rate for maintenance of a full-employment output level over time becomes 4.8 per cent. The data of Table 15–2 show that such a growth rate, if sustained for a five-year period, would raise the output level from $700 billion in the first year to $844.4 billion in the fifth year. The reader should compare the impact of investment on productive capacity in each period, Column (5) in Table 15–2, with the same data in Table 15–1. In each period $I\sigma$ is greater.

A Diagrammatic Representation of the Growth Process

The growth process envisaged by Domar can also be illustrated by means of a diagram. Figure 15–3 is similar to Figure 15–2; the line OS represents the long-run saving function, and its slope is such that the average and marginal propensities to save are equal.

Let us assume initially that the full-employment income level is equal to

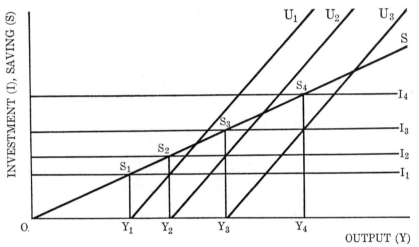

Figure 15–3. Net Investment and the Growth Process

Y_1, and investment expenditure is such as to absorb the saving at this income level. Investment is thus equal to Y_1S_1. Since investment is autonomous with respect to income, the investment function is represented by the schedule labeled I_1. The impact of this amount of investment on the economy's productive capacity is depicted by the line Y_1U_1, the slope of which is equal to the marginal capital-output ratio. Since the marginal capital-output ratio is the ratio of a change in the capital stock (after account has been taken of the displacement of some existing capital by new capital) to a change in the output level, the reciprocal of Y_1U_1 is the productivity of capital coefficient, σ.

If net investment proceeds in the first income period at a rate equal to Y_1S_1, productive capacity will be increased by an amount equal to the distance Y_1Y_2. This distance is determined, in Figure 15–2, by projecting a horizontal line from point S_1 to the point at which it intersects the Y_1U_1 line, and then dropping a vertical line from this point to the horizontal axis. Consequently, Y_2 now represents the economy's full-employment income level. But if this is the case, and given the saving function OS, the absolute amount of saving that will be forthcoming at the new full-employment income level has risen to the amount Y_2S_2. Since equilibrium in the Keynesian sense requires equality between saving and investment *ex ante*, investment expenditure must rise to the level depicted by the invstment schedule I_2 if the economy is to maintain full employment. This shift of the equilibrium income to the level represented by Y_2 requires, too, a shift in the curve representing the productivity of investment coefficient to the position Y_2U_2, because net investment in the amount Y_2S_2 will result in further additions to the economy's capital stock. Since σ remained constant during the time interval involved in raising income from Y_1 to Y_2, Y_2U_2 can be drawn parallel to Y_1C_1. Net investment in the second income period equal to Y_2S_2 will cause productive capacity to rise by an amount equal to the distance Y_2Y_3. Once again investment will have to increase if a full employment income level is to be maintained, because the saving at Y_3 is greater than the saving at Y_2. Investment must now rise to the level shown by the investment function I_3.

Inspection of this model reveals a number of important and interesting aspects of the growth process. If we assume fixed values for both the propensity to save and the productivity of investment coefficient, not only must investment expenditure rise continuously through time if full employment is to be maintained, but also the absolute increments of investment required in such subsequent income periods must become larger and larger. The logic of this is readily apparent, for if capacity increases through time by increasing absolute amounts, and if the investment multiplier is constant because of a constant marginal propensity to save, effective demand will increase through time in an amount equal to the increase in capacity only if the increments to investment expenditure become absolutely larger in each successive income period. Figure 15–3 clearly shows the formidable difficulties facing an advanced economy which habitually saves some significant portion of its net income. Such an economy must continuously find new outlets for not just a constant but a *growing* absolute volume of saving. For this reason, advanced economies have frequently found it exceedingly difficult to sustain a constant rate of growth over relatively long periods of time.

The above analysis may strike the reader as unduly restrictive because of the underlying assumption that both the propensity to save and the productivity of investment coefficient have constant values. Different results will ensue with different values of either α or σ, although an analysis of some of the possibilities in this respect does not reveal any situations in which the difficulties inherent in achieving a constant rate of

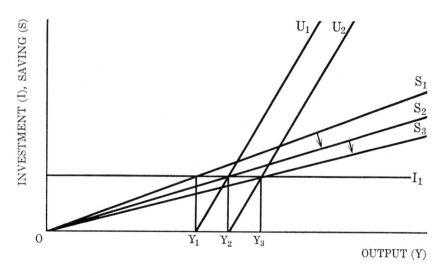

Figure 15–4. Downward Shift in the Saving Function

economic growth are less formidable. For example, the investment function would not have to shift upward continuously (as shown in Figure
15–3) if the long-term propensity to save were to undergo a decline. This
possibility is depicted in Figure 15–4, which shows the saving function OS
pivoting downward with each successive increase in capacity. This decline
in the value of the propensity to save does not eliminate the capacity-
creating effect of net investment, but means merely that the absolute
increases in capacity, ΔY_Q, in each income period would be constant because investment remains constant in each income period. It is scarcely
realistic, however, to assume that the secular saving function undergoes
a downward shift; this would mean that over time the economy saved a
smaller and smaller proportion of its net income, but empirical research
indicates that the proportion of net income saved remains constant over
the long run.[9]

A final possibility has to do with changes in the value of the productivity
of capital coefficient. A decline in the value of σ means that the impact on
capacity of any specific amount of investment is smaller, and, therefore,
the extent to which income would have to grow to absorb into use the
additions to capacity would also be lessened. A reduction in σ would, in
other words, make the problem of attaining a constantly rising volume of
investment expenditure less difficult, because with a slower rate of growth
of both capacity and income, the growth of saving in an absolute sense also
will be slower. A decline in σ is the same as a rise in the capital-output

[9] Simon Kuznets, *National Income: A Summary of Findings* (New York, National
Bureau of Economic Research, 1946), p. 53.

ratio, for if a given quantity of investment expenditure has a smaller effect on capacity than heretofore, more capital per unit of output is required. Unfortunately, it is quite unlikely that an advanced economy can easily resolve the problem of maintaining continuous full employment by a downward adjustment in the value σ. For one thing, the productivity of capital coefficient is basically a technological coefficient, and as such not easily adjusted to whatever value might be required for maintenance of a full-employment equilibrium. In addition, the long-term trend for the actual capital-output ratio in the United States appears to be downward.[10] If such a trend is characteristic of advanced economies in general, it means higher rather than lower values for the productivity of capital coefficient. Thus, the impact on capacity for any given amount of investment has tended to become greater rather than smaller.

Significance and Limitations of the Domar Analysis of Economic Growth

The analytical system that we have been discussing can be described as dynamic primarily because it goes beyond the assumption of a fixed productive capacity and examines the consequences of an increase in the quantity of a key economic resource, the economy's stock of real capital instruments. Domar's concern with the capacity-creating effect of net investment has a dual significance for economic analysis. First, the analysis concentrates on what is probably the single most important factor in economic growth, the process of capital accumulation. In this sense Domar's analysis follows an old tradition, for nearly all economists who have had something meaningful to say about economic development have accorded the accumulation of capital a priority role in this process.[11] Second, the analysis demonstrates that economic growth is not merely a desirable phenomenon for an advanced capitalistic economy, but an absolute necessity if the economy is to avoid a growing volume of unemployment of both labor and other economic resources. The analysis, moreover, shows that while the economy may grow at a satisfactory rate, there is no reason to expect it to do so automatically.

Our appraisal of Domar's analysis would not be complete if we did not point out some of its important limitations. For one thing, the derivation of a "required" rate obviously depends upon the existence of known and constant values for such crucial factors as the propensity to save and the productivity of capital coefficient. In reality, it is unlikely that either of these are constant all the time. But the difficulty of deriving a "required" rate does not in any way invalidate the basic theme of the analysis—that there exists *some* rate of growth that will insure a full-employment equi-

[10] William Fellner, *Monetary Policies and Full Employment* (Berkeley and Los Angeles, University of California Press, 1947), pp. 80, 81.

[11] See especially, Benjamin Higgins, *Economic Development: Principles, Problems, and Policies* (New York, Norton, 1959), p. 204.

librium over time.[12]

A second limitation is Domar's use of a productivity of investment coefficient that is an average for the whole economy. The meaningfulness of this procedure may be questioned, since σ is basically nothing more than the reciprocal of the marginal capital-output ratio. But the capital-output ratio, both on the average and at the margin, will vary widely from industry to industry because of variations in the capital requirements of different kinds of production. This means that it will be very difficult to determine the exact impact of a given volume of investment on capacity unless we know the composition in an industrial sense of the investment. For example, a given quantity of investment expenditure in an industry characterized by a high capital-output ratio will obviously have a smaller over-all impact on productive capacity than the same amount of investment expenditure in an industry with a lower capital-output ratio. Unless the exact effect of any given amount of investment on capacity can be determined, it is not possible to speak with accuracy of a "required" rate of growth.

One final limitation concerns the failure of Domar's analysis to distinguish between a rate of growth of income which will insure full employment of the labor force, and a rate of growth of income which will insure full utilization of the economy's stock of capital. This has been a matter of concern for some economists, who argue that the rate of growth sufficient to absorb additions to the economy's stock of capital will not necessarily provide full employment for a growing labor force.

In spite of the above limitations, our attention should not be detracted from the important and positive contribution that the Domar type of analysis has made to an understanding of the process of economic development in an advanced economy. Admittedly, Domar's system is overly simplified and, perhaps, overly rigid. But this is a criticism that could be justly leveled at most facets of contemporary economic theory. The real task of economic theory is to direct our attention to a few strategic relationships as a means of understanding somewhat better the vast complexities of the economy in the real world. It is doubtful that many would deny that an enlargement of the economy's productive potential is a factor of the utmost strategic significance in the process of economic growth.

The Harrod Analysis of Economic Growth

Since Harrod's analysis of the growth process in an advanced economy is in many respects similar to Domar's, it has become fashionable for econ-

[12] Domar has stressed in another place that growth models of the type he developed in his 1947 article cannot be used to determine the exact rate at which the economy should grow; rather, they are designed to show that the economy must grow, and that adverse consequences may result when it fails to grow. See E. D. Domar, *Essays in the Theory of Economic Growth* (New York, Oxford University Press, 1957), p. 8.

omists to speak of the "Domar-Harrod" theory when they are discussing recent developments which extend the basic concepts of Keynesian income and employment theory to the general area of economic growth. But there are also enough fundamental differences in their approaches to warrant separate discussion of the ideas of each.

Harrod, like Domar, is concerned with the necessary conditions under which the equality of *ex ante* saving and investment can be maintained over time, but he treats the central element in the growth process, investment expenditure, in a different manner. In Domar's schema we look to the effect that current investment expenditure has on future productive capacity, assuming that this investment expenditure is sufficient to offset the saving of the current income level. In a sense, Domar's analysis is "forward looking" because such a procedure requires us to determine how much both income and investment will have to grow in the *next* income period in order to absorb into use at that time the added capacity that is the consequence of investment in the present income period.

Harrod, on the other hand, constructs his analysis in terms of the response of current investment expenditure to a change in the economy's output or real income level. He seeks to determine whether the rate at which income has grown in the immediate past is high enough to induce an amount of investment expenditure sufficient to absorb the saving in the current income period.

The key analytical tool that Harrod employs in his analysis is the *accelerator*, which is defined symbolically as the ratio of a change in the capital stock, ΔK, to a change in the output level, ΔY. Since the change in the capital stock is the same as net investment, I_n, the ratio $\Delta K/\Delta Y$, or $I_n/\Delta Y$, when defined as the accelerator, represents a behavior coefficient in the sense that it seeks to express as a coefficient the investment response of entrepreneurs to a change in the output level. The acceleration approach makes current *net* investment a function of the rate of change in output. Fundamental to the notion of the acceleration coefficient, however, is the concept of the capital-output ratio conceived as a technical relationship, for if a relatively fixed relationship did not exist between output and the quantity of capital necessary for the production of that output, there would be no point in asserting that investment expenditure may be induced by changes in output.

Although the treatment of investment expenditure differs in the two analyses, both Domar and Harrod accord identical roles to the saving function. Both analyses are based on the long-run saving function, on an equality between the average and the marginal propensity to save. In both analyses saving *ex ante* and saving *ex post* are presumed to be equal, which means that saving "calls the tune." Other variables such as investment, the productivity of capital coefficient, and the accelerator must adjust to the rate of saving if full employment over time is to be maintained.

The basic procedure employed by Harrod is to postulate a series of "fundamental equations," each of which embodies a carefully defined rate of growth. By means of comparisons between these growth rates, it is possible to determine the conditions under which a steady rate of advance is possible for the economy.

The Warranted Rate of Growth

The most important growth rate developed by Harrod in his analysis is the *warranted rate of growth*, G_w, which he defines precisely as "that overall rate of advance which, if executed, will leave entrepreneurs in a state of mind in which they are prepared to carry on a similar advance." [13] In algebraic terms we have:

$$G_w = \frac{\Delta Y}{Y} \qquad (15\text{--}7)$$

More explicitly, the warranted rate of growth concept refers to a rate of advance for the economy as a whole that will leave entrepreneurs (in the aggregate or on the average) satisfied with the outcome of economic activity. Within the framework of Keynesian equilibrium analysis, a condition of "entrepreneurial satisfaction" is a situation in which investment and saving *ex ante* are in equilibrium. This is basically what Harrod means by the warranted rate of growth, except that he is talking of a developing rather than a static situation. The concept of a warranted rate of growth refers to a situation in which a growing absolute volume of *ex ante* investment is in equilibrium with a growing absolute volume of full-employment, *ex ante* saving.

To express the necessary condition for equilibrium in a steadily advancing economy, Harrod postulates the following equation, which, he says, describes the condition in which producers will be content with what they are doing: [14]

$$G_w \times C_r = s \qquad (15\text{--}8)$$

Before we examine the significance of this equation, it is necessary to explain the key concepts employed by Harrod in his analysis. We have already discussed G_w. The variable s represents the long-run propensity to save and is the same as α in Domar's analysis. Thus the average and the marginal propensities to save are identical. Harrod assumes that saving intentions are always realized; consequently saving *ex ante* and saving *ex post* are always equal. Algebraically:

---

[13] R. F. Harrod, *Towards a Dynamic Economics, op. cit.*, p. 82.
[14] *Ibid.*, p. 81.

$$s = \frac{S}{Y} = \frac{\Delta S}{\Delta Y} \tag{15-9}$$

The variable C_r in Equation (15-8) is somewhat more complex and requires a more detailed explanation. Harrod describes C_r as the symbol for the *capital requirement*, by which is meant "the requirement for new capital divided by the increment of output to sustain which the new capital is required." [15] Harrod conceives the capital-output ratio as a technical relationship, for, as he says, the above definition is "based upon the idea that existing output can be sustained by existing capital and that additional capital is only required to sustain additional output." [16] The capital-requirement concept must be interpreted with care, for if interpreted too literally it leads to the absurd conclusion that more capital is needed to increase output by the amount that output has just increased. Actually, since capacity is not a precise magnitude, the technical relationship embodied in the capital-output ratio means that at some point near the absolute upper limit of the individual firm's productive capacity, entrepreneurs will feel that more capacity will be required to provide additional output to meet a rising level of demand. Algebraically, we have:

$$C_r = \frac{\Delta K}{\Delta Y} = \frac{I_n}{\Delta Y} \tag{15-10}$$

Although C_r as defined above may be said to represent the capital requirement of the economy, the above ratio may also be defined as the accelerator. In this sense, C_r becomes an expression of entrepreneurial behavior, for it represents the coefficient which describes the amount of investment that will be induced by a change in the output level. Investment in the above equation is, in other words, *ex ante* or planned investment, the amount of which depends upon a prior change in output.

Which of these definitions of C_r is appropriate in the context of Equation (15-8), which purports to describe the condition under which equilibrium in a growing economy is possible? Basically, both are appropriate, for although the acceleration concept may be used to explain why investment has attained a particular level in the current income period, it can have no meaning unless an underlying technical relationship between capital and output is assumed.

To clarify this statement, let us make the following algebraic substitutions in Equation (15-8): $\Delta Y/Y$ for G_w; $I_n/\Delta Y$ for C_r; and S/Y for s. Then we have:

[15] *Ibid.*, p. 82.
[16] *Ibid.*

$$\frac{\Delta Y}{Y} \times \frac{I_n}{\Delta Y} = \frac{S}{Y} \qquad (15\text{--}11)$$

Since the ΔY's on the left-hand side of the equation will cancel out, we then have:

$$\frac{I_n}{Y} = \frac{S}{Y} \qquad (15\text{--}12)$$

The basic meaning, therefore, of Harrod's equation that expresses the equilibrium of a steady advance is that the rate of growth must be such that *ex ante* investment is equal to *ex ante* saving. Since, in accord with the accelerator concept, *ex ante* investment depends upon the rise in output, the necessary condition for equilibrium is that output (or income) rise sufficiently to induce enough investment to absorb the saving of the current income period. If this happens, then we can properly speak, as Harrod does, of the growth rate being a *warranted growth rate.*

The Actual Rate of Growth

The second crucial rate of growth in Harrod's analysis is the *actual rate of growth*, which represents the *ex post* percentage change in output between the present and the past income period. Algebraically, the actual rate of growth is:

$$G = \frac{\Delta Y}{Y} \qquad (15\text{--}13)$$

The actual rate of growth, G, to quote Harrod, is "the increment of total production in any unit period expressed as a fraction of total production." [17]

Harrod's fundamental equation pertaining to the actual or *ex post* performance of the economy is as follows:

$$G \times C = s \qquad (15\text{--}14)$$

G represents the actual rate of growth as defined above, while s is the actual saving ratio, which is assumed in Harrod's analysis to be the same always as the *ex ante* saving ratio. C may be defined as the actual (or *ex post*) as distinct from the intended (or *ex ante*) capital requirement (or accelerator). In other words, C is simply the ratio of the actual increase in the capital stock, ΔK or I_n', to the actual change in output, ΔY. If we substitute algebraically in Equation (15–14) in the same way as we did earlier in equation (15–8), we have:

[17] *Ibid.*, p. 77.

$$\frac{\Delta Y}{Y} \times \frac{I'_n}{\Delta Y} = \frac{S}{Y} \qquad (15\text{-}15)$$

Since once again the ΔY's on the left-hand side of the equation cancel out, we now have:

$$\frac{I'_n}{Y} = \frac{S}{Y} \qquad (15\text{-}16)$$

This equation simply means that investment *ex post* is equal to saving *ex post*. This is always true, irrespective of the income level. What Harrod has done is simply to place this truism in a growth context.

The Growth Process: The Actual and the Warranted Rates Compared

It should be apparent that, algebraically, the expression $G_w \times C_r$ equals the expression $G \times C$, since both are equal to s, the *ex ante* and *ex post* propensity to save. However, it does not follow that G_w necessarily equals G, or C_r equals C. There is no inherent reason, in other words, why the actual rate of growth experienced by the economy should correspond with the warranted rate. Nor need the actual change in the capital stock in an income period coincide with the intended change in capital stock in the same income period. Let us analyze what the results will be if G and G_w do not coincide.

We shall assume, first, that the actual rate of growth is greater than the warranted rate, that is, $G > G_w$. It then follows algebraically that C_r is greater than C. But if this is true it means that *ex ante* (planned) investment is greater than *ex post* (actual) investment in the current income period, because C_r conceived of as the accelerator shows the amount of intended investment induced by a given change in income. Thus if C_r is really greater than C, it has to mean that $C_r \times \Delta Y$ is greater than $C \times \Delta Y$, because ΔY is the same in both instances.

When investment *ex ante* is in excess of investment *ex post*, aggregate demand is greater than aggregate supply, a condition that, in Keynesian terms, will lead to an expansion in income and employment. To put the matter differently, we can say that when G is greater than G_w the economy is in a situation in which output has grown, but aggregate demand has grown even faster. In such circumstances the economy will experience a chronic shortage of capital, as investment *ex post* continuously falls short of investment *ex ante*. The outcome will be further pressure on planned or *ex ante* investment as entrepreneurs seek to make good the economy's capital shortage, but such a reaction only serves to drive the actual rate of growth further and further from the warranted rate. Thus, it is Harrod's contention that any movement away from the line of steady advance represented by his warranted rate of growth tends to be cumulative in its

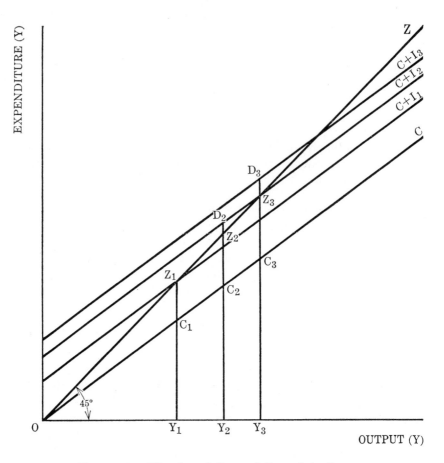

Figure 15-5. The Actual Rate of Growth in Excess
of the Warranted Rate of Growth

effect; departures of the actual growth rate from the warranted or equilibrium rate do not, in other words, set in motion forces tending toward a
restoration of equilibrium. Equilibrium once disturbed leads to a disequilibrium which becomes progressively worse.

The nature of the process of cumulative expansion envisaged by Harrod
when G is in excess of G_w can be demonstrated diagrammatically. For this
we can utilize the usual Keynesian type of income determination diagram,
as is done in Figure 15–5. Let us assume that the income level, which initially is at Y_1, moves to the level Y_2. The change in income is thus equal to
the distance $Y_1 Y_2$, while the actual rate of growth, G, is equal to the ratio
$Y_1 Y_2 / Y_1$. Since this growth rate is greater than the warranted rate, C_r is
greater than C. As a consequence, the amount of investment induced by

the change in income from Y_1 to Y_2 is seen to be equal to the distance C_2D_2. But since this amount of investment is greater than the amount prevailing at the prior income level, the aggregate demand schedule has, in effect, shifted from $C + I_1$ to $C + I_2$. Aggregate demand now exceeds aggregate supply at the income level Y_2, and this in turn tends to drive the economy toward the income level Y_3. Again the change in income from Y_2 to Y_3 induces an amount of investment expenditure, C_3D_3, that is greater than necessary to achieve equilibrium at the income level Y_3. Investment *ex ante*, in other words, once again exceeds investment *ex post*, and thus the income level will be driven still higher. The departure from the initial equilibrium, the income level Y_1, has not, as shown in the hypothetical model, brought a restoration of equilibrium; rather, forces have been set in motion that drive the economy further and further from the initial equilibrium position. In this situation, saving becomes a "virtue," in that a higher rate of saving means, algebraically, an increase in the warranted rate of growth, and thus restoration of equality between the actual rate and the warranted rate. More saving will permit a greater amount of actual investment in each income period, and this will tend to reduce the economy's capital shortage which, in turn, is the main reason why aggregate demand continuously runs ahead of aggregate supply.

The alternative to the situation just described is one in which the warranted rate of growth is greater than the actual rate of growth, that is, $G_w > G$. If this is the case, it must follow that C is greater than C_r; the ratio of actual investment to the change in income is greater than the ratio of intended (planned) investment to the change in income. Investment *ex ante* in the current period falls short of investment *ex post* and, consequently, excess capacity will appear, making it impossible for the economy to continue to advance at the same rate as in the past. In other words, a situation in which G_w is greater than G indicates a tendency in the economy toward stagnation and a chronic excess of productive capacity. In such circumstances it will be difficult enough to sustain any growth at all for a significant length of time, let alone at a rate that will justify itself only if net investment is continually increasing in absolute amount.

For a better understanding of what takes place when G_w is greater than G let us refer once again to an income determination diagram. In Figure 15–6 we will begin, as we have done previously, with an assumed full-employment equilibrium income level, Y_1. Now if income rises to the level Y_2, the actual rate of growth, G, again is equal to the ratio Y_1Y_2/Y_1. Since, however, the accelerator, C_r, is smaller than the actual capital coefficient, C, the amount of investment induced by the change in income falls short of the *ex post* investment at the higher income level.

Ex post investment at the income level Y_2 is represented by the distance C_2Z_2, which is also equal to both *ex post* and *ex ante* saving at this income level. The change in income from Y_1 to Y_2, however, induces an amount

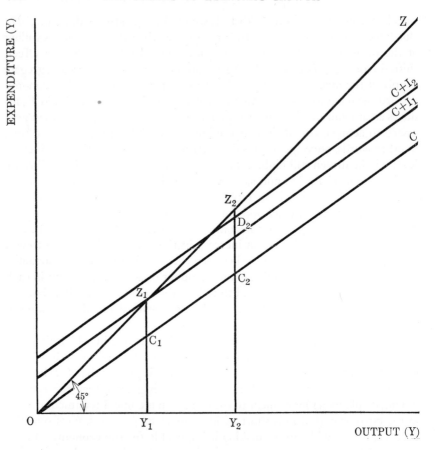

Figure 15–6. The Warranted Rate of Growth in Excess of
the Actual Rate of Growth

of investment equal to the distance C_2D_2, which falls short of actual investment at the Y_2 income level. Aggregate demand has shifted upward from $C + I_1$ to $C + I_2$, but the shift is not great enough to sustain the actual growth experienced by the economy when income moved from Y_1 to Y_2. At Y_2, aggregate demand now falls short of aggregate supply, so this income level cannot be sustained.

To summarize Harrod's analysis briefly at this point we can say that the necessary condition for an equilibrium rate of growth is that the actual rate be equal to the warranted rate. This means that in each income period planned investment, which is linked to the rate at which income has grown in the immediate past, will be equal to the planned saving of the income period. Furthermore, Harrod's analysis asserts that if G and G_w are not equal, which is a condition of disequilibrium, the result will not be a restoration of equilibrium, or a return to conditions in which G and G_w

are equal, but rather a greater and greater divergence between G and G_w. The growth process in Harrod's view is an inherently unstable phenomenon, as even the slightest departure from the exceedingly narrow path of an equilibrium rate of growth sets in motion forces making for either secular expansion and inflation or secular stagnation.

The Natural Rate of Growth

For a complete picture of the growth process as seen by Harrod it is necessary to introduce still another rate of growth. This is the *natural rate of growth*, which Harrod describes as "the rate of advance which the increase of population and technological improvements allow." [18] The use of the term "natural" is somewhat misleading. Harrod is not referring to any growth rate that comes about automatically as a consequence of the free play of market forces. It would be more accurate to describe this particular growth rate as the potential or even *maximum feasible rate of growth*,[19] since Harrod is really talking about the rate of growth required for the full employment of a growing labor force. Such a rate of growth depends upon, first, the average annual rate of increase in the labor force, and, second, the average annual rate of increase in the productivity of labor. If, for example, population and the labor force are growing at an annual average rate of 1 per cent, while output per worker is increasing, on the average, at the rate of 2 per cent per year, the rate of growth necessary to maintain full employment of labor is 3 per cent per year.

Introduction of the concept of a natural or feasible rate of growth into his analysis better enables Harrod to describe the conditions under which the economy will tend toward a condition of either secular stagnation or secular exhilaration. This is possible because there is no inherent reason, in Harrod's view, for the natural growth rate, G_n, and the warranted growth rate, G_w, to coincide. These two rates may be equal, but the more normal situation, in Harrod's view, is one of divergence between the natural and the warranted rate of growth. For example, Harrod asserts that the economy will tend toward secular stagnation if G_w is greater than G_n. The logic of Harrod's position is that, other than for short intervals of time, G cannot exceed G_n. Because given the rate at which the productivity of labor is increasing, the available labor supply will set a ceiling on the rate at which output can actually grow. If this is true, and if G_w is greater than G_n, it follows that G_w will be greater than G. Most of the time, in other words, the actual rate of growth will be below the warranted rate of growth.

But the above condition is one in which investment *ex post* will run ahead of investment *ex ante*, and, consequently, excess capacity will ap-

---

[18] *Ibid.*, p. 87.
[19] This is the term preferred by Joan Robinson. See her *The Rate of Interest and Other Essays* (London, Macmillan, 1952), p. 160.

pear. Because the accelerator is weak, the increase in aggregate demand is not sufficient to absorb into use all additions to the economy's capital stock. Such additions, of course, are determined by net *ex post* investment in the income period. If this is the economy's situation, it means basically that over time the economy will tend toward chronic underemployment of all resources, that, is secular stagnation.

Another way in which we can describe this situation is to say that the rate of growth required for the full utilization of a growing capital stock is greater than the rate of growth required for the full employment of a growing labor force. This will foster excess capacity and with it the impossibility of sustaining the existing growth rate, even though this rate is below the warranted rate.

The warranted rate of growth is interpreted as a full-capacity (as distinct from a full employment of labor) rate of growth. In what sense is this true? The concept of the warranted rate of growth is concerned with the amount of added capital needed to sustain added output. Therefore, the warranted (or justifiable) rate of growth is one that induces just enough of an upward shift in the schedule of aggregate demand (see Figure 15-5) so that the added capacity represented by net *ex post* investment at each successive higher level of income will be utilized. But the rate of growth that will induce a sufficient shift upward in the aggregate demand schedule to absorb into use a growing productive capacity does not necessarily have to be equal to a rate of growth that will give full employment to a growing labor force. This is basically what Harrod is attempting to demonstrate by asserting that the natural rate of growth does not necessarily have to equal the warranted rate.

The alternative situation suggested by Harrod is one in which the natural rate is greater than the warranted rate. In this instance, Harrod reasons that the actual rate of growth will stay above the warranted rate most of the time. As described earlier, *ex post* investment will continuously fall short of *ex ante investment*, with a consequent chronic shortage of real capital. Aggregate demand will run ahead of aggregate supply, the inducement to invest will remain high, and thus the economy will find itself in a state of secular exhilaration.

Concluding Observations on the Domar-Harrod Analysis of Economic Growth

Both the Domar and Harrod approaches to the broad problem of economic growth in an advanced economy accord investment the central role in the growth process. Furthermore, both Domar and Harrod undertake their analyses of the process of growth within an analytical, Keynesian framework. They agree that the central problem in the growth process in an advanced economy is that of the conditions under which planned investment will be continuously equated with a growing absolute volume of planned saving. Domar and Harrod are also in agreement with respect to the key role of saving, since their analyses are based on the assumption of a constant average and marginal propensity to save, and on the further assumption that actual and planned saving are always equal.

The two analyses differ mainly in the way in which they look at the investment process. Domar's analysis looks ahead in the sense that he stresses the effect of today's net investment on tomorrow's capacity or productive potential, and thus seeks to determine the rate at which the economy *must* grow if this productive capacity is to be absorbed into use in the future. He is concerned primarily with the essentially technical question of the effect of present investment on future capacity. Harrod's analysis, on the other hand, tends to look backward in the sense that he is seeking to determine if output has actually grown enough between yesterday and today so as to induce an amount of net investment sufficient to absorb today's full employment saving. Although his analysis rests in a fundamental sense on a technological relationship between output and capital, Harrod's key analytical tool is the concept of the accelerator, since this is the coefficient that links current investment to changes in the output level. Harrod's analysis centers primarily on the reaction of entrepreneurs to   past changes in the income level, and assumes that if entrepreneurs in the aggregate are satisfied with the past rate of growth, they will act in such a way as to promote future growth in the economy at the same rate.

Both the Domar and the Harrod analysis of the growth process are subject to the same general criticism of being perhaps excessively abstract and too dependent (insofar as their conclusions with respect to the economy's ability to achieve a satisfactory rate of growth are concerned) on some rather rigid assumptions concerning the values and fixity of such critical determinants as the propensity to save and the capital coefficient. Harrod, in particular, can be criticized for placing too much stress on the phenomenon of induced investment as the crucial factor in the growth process. As a consequence, there emerges a picture of the economy tied tightly to a very narrow path of growth—with the twin disasters of either secular exhilaration and inflation or secular stagnation threatening in the event of the slightest divergence from the precisely determined path of advance.[20]

[20] Harrod's analysis appears unnecessarily rigid because it is built almost entirely around the concept of induced investment. He does recognize, however, that some investment is autonomous in that it is not directly linked to immediate output requirements. The existence of such investment obviously reduces the amount of current saving that must be absorbed into investment as a consequence of past changes in the income level. The same is also true for net foreign investment, as the excess of exports over imports may also provide an outlet for current saving through foreign lending. The introduction of autonomous investment and the foreign balance makes the economy's growth path somewhat less precarious than originally suggested by Harrod.

Despite the shortcomings we have noted, the analyses of Domar and Harrod, by directing our attention to such strategically important ideas as the capacity-creating effects of net investment and the phenomenon of accelerator-induced investment, do succeed in providing important insights into the operation of the real-world economy. More specifically, their theories enable us to understand, first, why the economy must grow if full employment is to be maintained, and, second, why the economy cannot be expected to grow automatically at a rate that will insure full employment.

16 Economic Growth and Public Policy

The purpose of this chapter is to broaden our discussion of economic growth and take into account the role of government in the growth process, particularly with respect to the impact of government on the rate of economic growth and the economy's productive capacity. We shall follow this with a discussion of the measures actually taken to stimulate growth in the U.S. economy during the early 1960's.

The Role of Government in Economic Growth

There are two aspects to the role of the public sector in the process of growth. The first involves the relationship between government and the level of aggregate demand. The growth models developed in Chapter 15 indicate that economic expansion requires aggregate demand to be adjusted upward over time to insure full utilization of the economy's growing productive capacity. The government may enter at this point as an important determining force through the development of appropriate policies that insure a level of aggregate demand adequate to absorb into use whatever productive capacity exists in the economy. Fiscal measures are of greatest significance in this connection.

Second, government not only critically affects the level of aggregate demand, but also serves as a powerful force in the determination of productive capacity. We shall examine the direct and indirect effect of public activity on the economy's productive capacity after we have considered the use of fiscal measures to insure a level of aggregate demand sufficient to meet the needs of a developing economy.

Fiscal Policy and Economic Growth

The most direct and meaningful way in which we can demonstrate how fiscal policy measures may be linked to the phenomenon of economic growth is to review briefly the essential elements embodied in the simplified models developed in Chapter 15, and then enlarge these models to take into account the fiscal policy measures.[1] Harrod's analysis serves this purpose admirably, particularly because of the assumption implicit in his analysis that the saving ratio is a constant. In Harrod's growth model the key concept is that of the *warranted rate of growth*, which, it will be recalled, is defined as a rate of growth which leaves entrepreneurs in the aggregate satisfied with the outcome of economic activity.[2] It represents a rate of growth which utilizes fully the economy's productive capacity insofar as the latter is reflected in the stock of productive capital instruments. From the point of view of the entrepreneurs, a satisfactory condition of growth exists in the economy when the new capital brought into existence through operation of the acceleration principle is continuously utilized. In algebraic terms, Harrod's warranted rate of growth is equal to

$$G_w = \frac{s}{C_r} = \frac{\Delta Y}{Y} \tag{16-1}$$

G_w is the warranted rate of growth, s is the average and the marginal propensity to save, and C_r, the capital requirement or marginal capital-output ratio, which is equal to $\Delta K / \Delta Y$, or $I_n / \Delta Y$.

As stated in Equation (16–1), Harrod's fundamental growth equation pertains wholly to the private or market sector of the economy. C_r refers to private capital formation; s concerns private saving. In order to demonstrate the impact of government on the growth process, it is necessary to introduce variables representing fiscal policy parameters into Harrod's basic growth equation. To do this we shall, first, refer back to the basic equation which defines the essential condition of income equilibrium in an economy with government expenditures for goods and services, transfer expenditures, and taxes. This equation is

$$S + TX - TR = I + G \tag{16-2}$$

From which we have

$$S + TX - TR - G = I \tag{16-3}$$

---

[1] The discussion that follows is largely based upon the analysis by Kenneth K. Kurihara, "Growth Models and Fiscal-Policy Parameters," *Public Finance*, No. 2, 1956, pp. 148–160.

[2] Chapter 15, p. 430.

The values of the variables on the left-hand side of Equation (16–3) depend upon the appropriate propensities. The values stated are presumed to be net values. If we assume, as Harrod did for the propensity to save, that average and marginal propensities are equal for all variables that pertain to the government sector, we can then designate the propensity of the government to spend for goods and services, G/Y, by the symbol g; the propensity of the government to tax, TX/Y, by the symbol t_x; and, finally, the propensity of the government to transfer incomes, TR/Y, by the symbol t_r.[3] From this it follows that:

1. The level of saving, S, is equal to sY.
2. The level of taxes, TX, is equal to t_xY.
3. The level of transfers, TR, is equal to t_rY.
4. The level of government expenditures for goods and services, G, is equal to gY.

From Harrod's analysis and the definition of the capital requirement coefficient, it follows that net investment is equal to $C_r \times \Delta Y$, because $C_r = I_n/\Delta Y$. If we substitute the above expressions for saving, taxes, transfers, government expenditures, and investment in Equation (16–3), we then have the following statement of the basic condition essential for income equilibrium:

$$sY + t_xY - t_rY - gY = C_r \times \Delta Y \tag{16-4}$$

This equation may be manipulated algebraically to

$$Y(s + t_x - t_r - g) = C_r \times \Delta Y \tag{16-5}$$

And further:

$$\frac{\Delta Y}{Y} = \frac{s + t_x - t_r - g}{C_r} = G_w \tag{16-6}$$

Equation (16–6) constitutes a modification of Professor Harrod's concept of the warranted rate of growth that brings the fiscal operations of the government into the analysis as additions to the purely market-determined variables. As a result of this basic modification, we are able to analyze the potential impact of fiscal policy measures on the over-all rate of growth of the economy.

In Harrod's analysis the basic condition for equilibrium over time in the economy is one in which the warranted rate of growth, G_w, is equal to the natural rate of growth, G_n. Since G_w is interpreted as the full-capacity

---

[3] Y in this context may be thought of as the net national product.

rate of growth, a condition in which $G_w = G_n$ is an equilibrium condition in the sense that the rate of growth which insures the full utilization of a growing capacity is also the rate of growth which insures the full employment of a growing labor force.

To understand the manner in which fiscal measures may be employed to adjust the economy's over-all rate of growth to the foregoing equilibrium condition, it is necessary, first, to review the consequences of an imbalance between the warranted rate of growth and the natural rate of growth, and then see how fiscal measures may be employed to deal with such developments. Let us assume a situation in which the natural rate of growth tends to run ahead of the warranted rate of growth. According to Harrod, such a situation is one in which investment *ex post* will continuously fall short of investment *ex ante*, with a consequent shortage of real capital. Aggregate demand, in other words, will run ahead of aggregate supply and the result will be a persistent upward pressure on the general price level. In Harrod's analysis a situation of this type can most readily be corrected by an increase in the saving ratio, if it is assumed that the capital requirement is determined primarily by technological considerations, and thus not readily changed under short-term circumstances. A rise in the saving ratio increases the warranted rate of growth, thus bringing this rate into line with the natural rate. (See Equation 16–1.)

Our concern, however, is with a situation in which it is not possible to change the private saving ratio. Under such circumstances, fiscal measures must be employed to effect the necessary change in the warranted rate of growth. If private saving is inadequate, then this condition must be met by an increase in public (or government) saving, again on the assumption that the capital requirement is fixed in the short run.

Government saving exists when the sum of taxes less transfers (that is, net taxes) is greater than government purchases of goods and services. This is tantamount to a budgetary surplus position on the part of the public sector. The three possible budgetary positions of the public sector may be defined in terms of the fiscal policy variables incorporated into Equation (16–6) as follows:

1. $t_x - t_r = g =$ a balanced budget (no government saving or dissaving).
2. $t_x - t_r > g =$ a budgetary surplus (government saving).
3. $t_x - t_r < g =$ a budgetary deficit (government dissaving).

If an increase in government saving is needed in order to bring the warranted rate of growth into line with the natural rate of growth, the appropriate fiscal policy measure would be the creation of or an increase in the budgetary surplus of the public sector. In terms of the variables embodied in Equation (16–6) this will require an increase in t_x, a decrease in t_r, or a reduction in g. In actuality one or possibly all three of the fiscal policy parameters might be modified in an effort to achieve the necessary budgetary surplus.

In a situation where the warranted rate of growth is in excess of the natural rate and excess capacity results from the tendency for investment *ex post* to run ahead of investment *ex ante*, the economy will tend toward chronic unemployment and secular stagnation. In a broad sense the problem now is an excess rather than a deficiency of saving in the private sector, assuming once again that the capital requirement is not readily changed. From a fiscal policy point of view, the appropriate action is government dissaving to counteract the excess of saving in the private sector. The warranted rate of growth and the danger of stagnation can, consequently, be lowered by either a reduction in t_x, an increase in t_r, an increase in g, or some combination of all three of these measures.

The preceding discussion is framed in terms of *deliberate* changes by the government in the value of one or more of the fiscal policy parameters with the objective of creating—or increasing—the deficit or surplus on the income and product account of the public sector. The existence of a deficit or surplus in the public sector, however, given values for the fiscal policy parameters, will depend upon the level of national output. With a given tax and transfer structure and with a fixed level of government expenditures, a deficit will decrease and a surplus will increase as growth takes place in the output level. As the Council of Economic Advisors has pointed out, there is a whole range of possible surpluses and deficits associated with a given budget program; the actual surplus or deficit will depend upon the level of economic activity.[4]

This analysis of the role that fiscal policy may play in the achievement of a satisfactory equilibrium rate of growth for the economy is oversimplified and does not take into account the type of government expenditures, transfers, and taxes that ought to be either increased or decreased when such action becomes necessary. In any realistic appraisal of the role that fiscal measures may play in the achievement and maintenance of a satisfactory rate of growth these are considerations that should not be ignored. Although our analysis of the relationship between fiscal measures and Harrod's warranted growth rate yields a useful insight into the manner in which the fiscal powers of the central government can be employed to insure an adequate level of aggregate demand in an economy characterized by a growing productive capacity, we should be on guard against the temptation to apply the analysis in simple, mechanical fashion. Many complex problems which involve basic values and priorities lie behind the

---

[4] *Economic Report of the President*, Washington, 1962, p. 79. The only exception would be a situation in which the level of taxes was *wholly* independent of income. This is so unlikely that it need not be seriously considered.

aggregates of our analysis, and these must receive the fullest consideration and attention from the policy-maker.

Government and Productive Capacity

Fiscal policy measures, as we have just seen, are largely directed toward influencing the level of aggregate demand so as to bring it into line with the economy's changing productive capacity. Government expenditures, transfers, and taxes also can operate, so to speak, on the "supply side" of the picture and, thus, exercise an influence on productive capacity. For example, it is quite conceivable that fiscal measures will affect one or more of the variables which enter into Harrod's natural rate of growth. Such determinants as the long-term propensity to save, the growth of population and the labor force, and the pace of technological change are not "natural" in the sense that they are not subject to deliberate change through human action. They can and will be changed as either a primary or secondary consequence of fiscal policy measures, and when this happens the basic forces which determine the rate at which an economy's productive capacity changes are altered. It would be futile to argue that in the long run fiscal measures that impinge, say, on the distribution of income will not affect the propensity to save, which in turn has a bearing upon the economy's rate of capital formation.

The problem of determining the way in which the activities of the public sector affect the economy's productive capacity is extremely complex, particularly because economic analysis is just beginning to be concerned with the qualitative aspects of the public sector. The bulk of existing economic theory dealing with public activity centers primarily on the way in which such aggregates as government purchases of goods and services, government transfer expenditures, and taxes affect the level of aggregate demand. In Chapter 8 it was pointed out that economists are increasingly interested in the problem of the "proper" allocation of resources between private and public use. The effect that public activity has on the economy's productive capacity is basically an aspect of this larger problem; once again we find ourselves on a frontier of contemporary economic analysis and theorizing where no wholly adequate and satisfactory theoretical structure yet has been developed. There are, nevertheless, sound useful studies in this area.

Domar lists the following eight factors as the chief determinants of an increase in the productive capacity of the economy: [5]

1. An increase in the labor force, that is, an increase in man hours available.

[5] Evsey D. Domar, "Contribution of Federal Expenditures to Economic Growth and Stability," in *Federal Expenditure Policy for Economic Growth and Stability*, Joint Economic Committee, Washington, D.C., 1957, p. 269. See also Chapter 2 in the 1962 *Annual Report of the Council of Economic Advisors, Economic Report of the President*, Washington, D.C., 1962, pp. 108–143.

2. An improvement in the health, education, and training of the labor force.
3. Development of knowledge, including technical knowledge and its application.
4. Improved management and administration.
5. Accumulation of capital and improvement in its quality.
6. Changes in other economic factors, such as the composition of output, industrial structure, and competition.
7. More efficient utilization and discovery of new resources.
8. Changes in general factors such as attitudes toward work, effort, thrift, and risk.

All of the above factors enter in some way into the complex phenomenon of economic growth, but it should be apparent that it is exceedingly difficult to measure statistically the impact of changes in one or more of these basic determinants upon productive capacity. Moreover, as Domar points out, there is no simple formula that tells which of these factors ought to be the concern of government, and which ought to be left to the workings of market forces in the private sector.[6] It is Domar's judgment that in the United States the areas in which Federal expenditures can fruitfully contribute to growth in the economy's productive capacity are: (1) education and training; (2) development of knowledge, that is, research; (3) public health; and (4) natural resources. For other societies the extent to which government may seek to exercise a direct influence over these variables will obviously depend upon the circumstances peculiar to the society in question. For example, in many of the underdeveloped areas of the world, the government must participate directly in the formation of capital because these countries lack an effective market system and a class of venturesome entrepreneurs. In any event, it is largely a matter of qualitative judgment as to which of the factors are best managed through public rather than private action.

A potentially fruitful approach to the analysis of the role that the public sector may play in the determination of the economy's productive capacity involves a suggestion that the kinds of expenditures which enter into the aggregate demand function be reclassified. Typically, in modern income analysis, expenditures in the private sector of the economy are classified as either expenditures for consumption purposes, C, or for investment, I. In a net sense investment expenditures are, of course, capacity creating. In place of what has now become the traditional breakdown of the expenditure total, Professor Daniel C. Vandermeulen suggests that this breakdown be reorganized to include a third category of "productivity-increasing" expenditures.[7] Thus the expenditure total would be

---

[6] *Ibid.*

[7] Daniel C. Vandermeulen, "Federal Expenditures and Economic Growth: Analysis and Policy," in *Federal Expenditure Policy for Economic Growth and Stability* (*op. cit.*), pp. 308–318.

equal to $C + I + P$. He defines productivity-increasing expenditures as those "that tend to augment the quantity and quality of natural resources, the education and skill of labor, and the stock of pure and applied scientific and technological knowledge." Capacity-increasing expenditures, I, are, on the other hand, those "that utilize *given* resources, skills, and knowledge to augment productive capacity." [8] If Vandermeulen's classification came to be utilized, it would mean, for example, that private expenditures for education would no longer be considered simply as a form of private consumption comparable to all other types of consumption expenditures; rather, they would be viewed in the context of their probable impact upon the productivity of labor. Similarly, a new view would be taken of research expenditures by business firms, which, under present national income accounting procedures, do not fall within the category of investment outlays, yet clearly have an impact upon productive capacity. We should not forget that an increase in the efficiency with which existing resources are used is just as much an increase in the economy's productive potential as is an increase in the quantity of resources available.

Professor Vandermeulen's suggested new classification for the expenditure totals can just as readily be applied to the public as the private sector of the economy. These categories, like most categories in economic analysis, are not clear-cut and free of ambiguities, but they do serve the important function of stressing that expenditures can have vastly different effects upon the future potential of the economy for the production of goods and services. At present it is the practice of national income and social accounting to treat all government purchases of goods and services as current without regard to their impact upon capacity. The same is true of transfers, whether or not such expenditures simply serve to finance current consumption or have an impact upon the future productivity of economic resources. In the abstract, we can make the distinction between government expenditures and transfers that are (1) of a current character, (2) that add to productive capacity, or (3) that increase productivity. It must be recognized that formidable statistical and measurement problems confront any serious effort to deal with the expenditure totals of the public sector in accordance with the foregoing suggested framework, but it is equally important to realize that in an era in which questions relating to the economy's productive capacity and rate of economic growth are among the most crucial national problems it is essential that our analyses be flexible and adaptable to new approaches.

U.S. Economic Policy in the 1960's

When the Kennedy administration came to power in January, 1961, one of the first problems which confronted the Council of Economic Ad-

[8] *Ibid.*, p. 311.

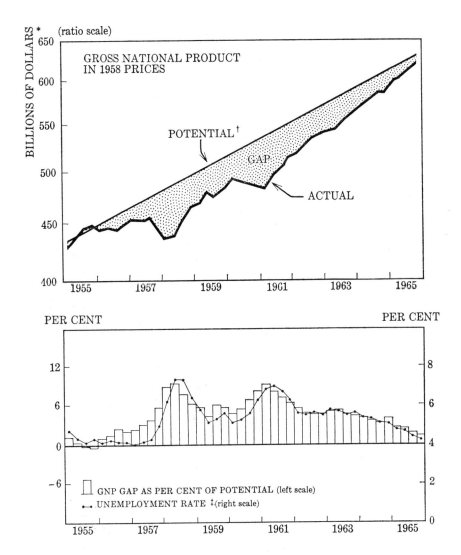

* Seasonally adjusted annual rates

† Trend line of 3½ per cent through middle of 1955 to 1962 IV; trend line of 3¼ per cent thereafter

‡ Unemployment as per cent of civilian labor force, seasonally adjusted

Source: Council of Economic Advisers

Figure 16–1. Gross National Product (Actual
and Potential) and Unemployment Rate

visors [9] was the economy's lagging rate of economic growth, a development accompanied by unemployment rates persistently in excess of the 4 per cent minimum which the council has regarded a desirable objective of stabilization policy. A year later, the CEA found in its first full report to the President that since mid-1955, when the unemployment rate last had been down at the 4 per cent level, the rate of growth of actual output was significantly below the economy's potential. The consequence of this lag in economic growth below the potential was a "gap" of $40 billion between the actual output in 1961 and the value of the goods and services that would have been produced if the economy had had full employment in 1961.[10] In subsequent years that gap has narrowed; Figure 16–1 shows *actual* and *potential* GNP and unemployment rates (as a percent of the civilian labor force) for 1955 through 1965. For the entire period the performance gap between actual and potential output was equal to $260 billion (in 1958 prices) in goods and services forgone because of the underutilization of the economy's productive resources.[11]

The CEA obtained its measure of potential output by the simple technique of projecting a trend for the actual GNP in mid-1955 forward at an annual average rate of growth of 3½ per cent. This trend rate of growth of potential output was used through 1962; beginning in 1963, the CEA raised the trend rate to 3¾ per cent. Mid-1955 was used as the base year for these calculations because, with unemployment down to 4 per cent of the labor force, actual output was equal to potential output. In determining the growth rate to be used to measure the trend of potential output, the CEA took into account the rate of growth of the potential labor force (from mid-1955 onwards), the annual average rate of labor productivity for the entire labor force, and the downward trend in hours worked per year.[12]

This concept of an output or performance "gap" emerged in the early 1960's as one of the key tools used by the CEA in its analysis of the economy's performance in this period. The concept of the gap, its statistical magnitude, and progress made toward reducing it, are discussed in detail in each of the *Annual Reports* of the CEA for the period 1962 through 1966. Of key importance is the ability of the CEA to measure satisfactorily the economy's potential output. Without an accurate measure of the economy's potential, no statistical measure of the amount by which its actual performance compares to that potential is possible. Although the CEA's technique for determining potential output has been criticized,[13] the coun-

[9] Members of the council were Professor Walter W. Heller, Chairman; Professor Kermit Gordon; and Professor James Tobin.

[10] *Economic Report of the President*, Washington, D.C., 1962, p. 51.

[11] *Economic Report of the President*, Washington, D.C., 1966, p. 40.

[12] *Ibid.*

[13] See especially the critique by Professor Arthur F. Burns, a former chairman of the Council of Economic Advisors, in *The Morgan Guaranty Survey*, May, 1961. The

cil asserted in its 1966 *Annual Report* that its estimates of the potential GNP associated with a 4 per cent unemployment rate were exceedingly accurate. In fact, the council stated that the concept of potential output proved "to be quantifiable within a sufficiently narrow range to justify its use as a key concept in the analysis of stabilization problems and policies." [14]

The Theory of Fiscal Stagnation

In explanation of the serious performance gap which characterized the American economy from mid-1955 onwards, the CEA developed what some observers have called the "theory of fiscal stagnation." [15] The council argued that the failure of the economy to expand at a rate sufficient to provide full employment was not due *primarily* to a deficiency of either private consumption or investment demand, but to the restrictive impact of the Federal budget on the over-all level of demand. President John F. Kennedy in his "Special Message to the Congress on Tax Reduction and Reform" on January 24, 1963, stated the essence of the theory as follows: [16]

The most urgent task facing our Nation at home today is to end the tragic waste of unemployment and unused resources—to step up the growth and vigor of our national economy—to increase job and investment opportunities—to improve our productivity—and thereby to strengthen our nation's ability to meet its world-wide commitments for the defense and growth of freedom. The revision of our Federal tax system on an equitable basis is crucial to the achievement of these goals.

Originally designed to hold back war and postwar inflation, our present income tax rate structure now holds back consumer demand, initiative, and investment. After the war and during the Korean conflict, the outburst of civilian demand and inflation justified this level and structure of rates. But it is becoming increasingly clear—particularly in the last five years—that the largest single barrier to full employment of our manpower and resources and to a higher rate of economic growth is the unrealistically heavy drag of Federal income taxes

August, 1961, issue of *The Morgan Guaranty Survey* contains a response by the CEA to this critique, as well as further comment by Professor Burns. For a detailed statement of the complex technical problems involved in the measurement of potential GNP, see the study by James W. Knowles, *The Potential Economic Growth in the United States*, Study Paper No. 20, Joint Economic Committee, Congress of the United States, Washington, D.C., 1960. A comparison of various techniques for estimating potential GNP is found in a study by Michael Levy, *Fiscal Policy, Cycles and Growth*, The Conference Board, New York, 1963, Chapter 5.

[14] *Economic Report of the President*, Washington, D.C., 1966, p. 42.

[15] It should be noted that the term "fiscal stagnation" has not been used by the CEA as a label for the basic explanation of the economy's slowdown. The CEA has preferred to speak more cautiously about the restrictive or expansionary effect of a given budget program on the level of demand. Professor Burns, however, spoke of the stagnation theory of the council. See Burns, *op. cit.*

[16] John F. Kennedy, "Special Message to the Congress on Tax Reduction and Reform," January 24, 1963, *Public Papers of the Presidents of the United States, John F. Kennedy, 1963*, United States Government Printing Office, Washington, D.C., 1964, p. 73.

on private purchasing power, initiative, and incentive. Our economy is check-reined today by a war-born tax system at a time when it is far more in need of the spur than the bit.

The key analytical tool utilized by the Council of Economic Advisors to demonstrate the restrictive effect of the Federal budget upon the economy has been the concept of "the full employment surplus." This may be defined as the budgetary surplus of the Federal government *on a national income accounts basis* that would be generated by a given budget program under conditions of full employment (a 4 per cent unemployment rate).

Figure 16–2 illustrates this concept. In the diagram the ratio of actual GNP to potential GNP is shown on the horizontal axis. This axis is labeled the "Utilization Rate"; the 100 per cent point represents full employment. It will be recalled that potential GNP is based on projecting a trend which

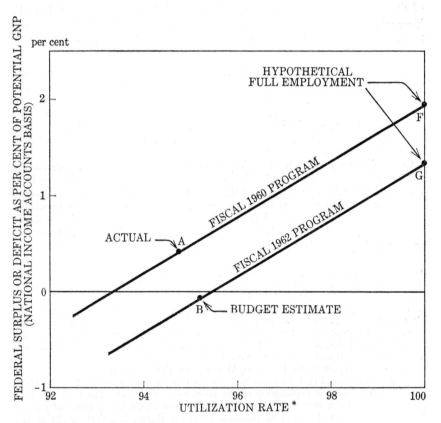

* Actual GNP as per cent of potential GNP
Source: Council of Economic Advisers

Figure 16–2. Effect of Level of Economic Activity
on Federal Surplus or Deficit

embodies a 4 per cent unemployment rate. Thus, when the ratio of *actual* to *potential* GNP equals 100, the economy must be operating at full employment. On the vertical axis, the Federal surplus or deficit is measured as a per cent of the potential GNP.

Two schedules are shown in the diagram, one of which reflects the tax and expenditure program of the Federal government for the fiscal year 1960 and the other for the fiscal year 1962. Both of these schedules slope upward to the right, which indicates that the surplus or deficit associated with any given budget program will depend upon the level of economic activity prevailing in the economy. By a "given budget program" is meant a particular pattern and level of expenditures combined with a particular structure of tax rates. With fixed expenditures and a given rate structure for the tax system, a deficit will decline or a surplus will increase as the economy's utilization rate increases—or as the economy approaches full employment. The height and steepness of the schedule depends upon the character of the budget program which exists at any given time—namely, the level of expenditures, tax rates, and the degree of progression present in the system.

Discretionary fiscal policy—action which deliberately changes the level of government expenditures or tax rates—will have the effect of shifting the schedule up or down. For example, a reduction in tax rates would lower the schedule, thus either increasing a deficit or reducing the surplus associated with a specific level of economic activity—the utilization rate shown on the horizontal axis. The effects of "built-in stabilizers," on the other hand, are reflected in a movement along the schedule as the level of economic activity changes. A rise in the income level will automatically generate a surplus sooner or later, as long as there is no change in expenditures. It should be noted, too, that *if* tax rates and expenditure programs remain constant, the full employment surplus will rise over time. The reason for this is that over time the full employment potential GNP grows, simply because a growing labor force which is fully employed and whose productivity is improving inevitably means a larger output. As long as tax rates are unchanged, the absolute volume of tax revenues yielded by a full-employment economy must increase over time. This being the case and with expenditures unchanged, the budgetary surplus has to grow. In its 1962 *Annual Report*, the Council of Economic Advisors estimated that with the tax rates in effect *at that time* and with *unchanged* expenditures, the full employment surplus would grow by about $6 billion per year. Viewed in another light, this means a schedule based upon the tax rates and expenditure level existing at that time would shift upward annually by about 1 per cent of the potential GNP.[17]

The fact that the full employment surplus must inevitably rise as potential full employment GNP increases is the basis for the view that the

[17] *Economic Report of the President*, Washington, D.C., 1962, p. 80.

economy may not only suffer on occasion from a "fiscal drag," but may also equally be in a position to enjoy a "fiscal dividend." By the latter is meant tax cuts which may have to be made periodically to hold down the size of the full-employment surplus or reduce tax revenues to equality with a relatively constant level of government expenditures. The first such tax cut was approved by the Congress in 1964. By late 1966, of course, any discussion of tax cutting and fiscal dividends was academic, primarily because of inflationary pressures induced by higher expenditures brought on by the war in Vietnam. But as Professor Walter Heller recently pointed out in a discussion of some of the problems involved in adjusting policy to the demands of high pressure prosperity, "The welcome mat is out for surpluses and debt retirement. But after Vietnam, we will again happily live with the threat of an unwanted fiscal drag to be removed by timely fiscal dividends. A central part of the job of fiscal policy is this delicate one of declaring fiscal dividends of the right size and timing, without inviting inflation." [18]

The true economic significance of the full-employment budgetary surplus lies in the fact that the actual achievement of full employment requires that gross investment expenditures (including net foreign investment in an open economy) must be large enough to offset the total private saving plus the net surplus of the public sector which the economic system generates at full employment. In equation form $I = S + (T - G)$, in which the variables represent full-employment, *ex ante* (or planned) values. The actual situation since 1955, according to estimates by the Council of Economic Advisors, has been a pronounced tendency toward full-employment saving (including government saving or the full-employment surplus) to run ahead of gross investment, including net foreign investment. In symbolic terms, $S + (T - G) > I$. Within the framework of Harrod's model expanded to include government (Equation 16–6), we can say that this situation has been one in which $(t_x - t_r) > g$. Figure 16–3 shows a comparison made by the CEA between *estimated* total full-employment saving and *actual* investment for the period 1956 to 1965. As the figure indicates, it was not until late 1965 that equality between investment and full-employment saving was achieved.

The Remedy for Fiscal Stagnation

The fundamental approach taken by the Kennedy-Johnson administrations to the problem of fiscal drag was a massive reduction in both personal and corporate income taxes. President Kennedy in his previously cited special message on tax reform, requested that the rates on personal income taxes be reduced from their 1963 range of 20 to 91 per cent to a range of

---

[18] Walter W. Heller, "Adjusting the 'New Economics' to High-Pressure Prosperity," in *Managing a Full Employment Economy*, The Committee for Economic Development, New York, 1966, p. 14.

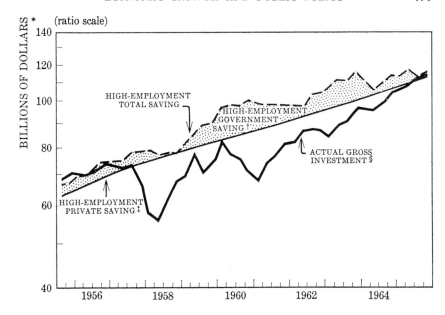

* Seasonally adjusted annual rates
† Federal high-employment surplus plus state and local actual surplus
‡ 15¼ per cent of trend GNP in current prices
§ Gross private domestic investment plus net foreign investment
Source: Council of Economic Advisers

Figure 16–3. Investment and High-Employment Savings

14 to 65 per cent, and that the rate on corporate income be reduced from 52 to 47 per cent. The Congress did not act on President Kennedy's request, but following his tragic assassination, essentially the same proposals were presented to the Congress in January, 1964. Speedy action was forthcoming and the Revenue Act of 1964 was signed into law on February 26, 1964. In its 1965 *Annual Report* the CEA estimated that the total of tax reductions taking effect in 1964 and 1965 would be $11 billion for individuals and $3 billion for corporations.[19]

It was expected that the tax cuts would operate to stimulate both consumption and investment spending, thus bringing output closer to the full-employment potential. The reduction in the personal income tax would add directly to the personal disposable income of consumers and since most of this added income would be spent, the multiplier would come into play and generate a cumulative expansion in consumption. Investment spending would rise both because the after-tax profit on new facilities would be increased and because more internal funds would be available to firms for investment purposes.[20]

[19] *Economic Report of the President*, Washington, D.C., 1965, p. 65. The Excise Tax Reduction Act of 1965 called for a reduction in excise taxes totaling $4.6 billion over several stages through 1969.

[20] *Economic Report of the President*, Washington, D.C., 1963, pp. 45–51.

In its 1963 *Annual Report,* the CEA presented a textbooklike explanation of the multiplier effects which could be expected to flow from the reduction in rates on the personal income tax. After taking into account all the various "leakages" at work in the economic system, the council concluded that each additional dollar of GNP generated initially by the tax cut would generate an additional $0.50 of consumption expenditures. In other words, the marginal propensity to consume out of the GNP is 0.50, which yields a multiplier of 2 to be applied against the initial increase in consumption spending stimulated by the increase in disposable income.[21] The ultimate expansionary effect was expected to be even greater because of the stimulus to investment resulting both from the initial reduction in the corporate rate, and also from the expansion in consumption generated by the cut in personal income tax rates.

The Effectiveness of the 1964 Tax Cut

While there are no absolutely conclusive tests that can be employed to determine the effectiveness of the 1964 tax cut, the available evidence is strong that the tax cuts did, in fact, achieve the results expected. In the first place, the "gap" between actual and potential output, which reached a peak of $50 billion at an annual rate in the first quarter of 1961, was reduced to an annual rate of $10 billion in the last quarter of 1965. The unemployment rate declined to 4.1 per cent by the end of 1965; in September, 1966, the rate stood at 3.8 per cent of the civilian labor force.

Additional evidence for the effectiveness of the tax cut is to be found in the performance of GNP. In 1964, GNP (in current prices) increased by $41.2 billion, in contrast to an increase of $30.2 billion (in current prices) in 1963. The CEA stated in its 1966 *Annual Report* that statistical analysis of the impact of the tax cut indicates that it was responsible for nearly $10 billion of the gain in the annual increase of the GNP. The increase continued in 1965, for during the second quarter, GNP was at an annual rate of $672.9 billion, which was $41.2 billion higher than the 1964 figure.[22] The second quarter rate of GNP is significant in this respect, because in the latter half of 1965, increased government expenditures resulting from the war in Vietnam began to exert a decisive expansionary effect upon the level of GNP. In current prices, the 1965 GNP totaled $681.2 billion, although in the final quarter of 1965, production was at an annual rate of $704.4 billion.[23] With respect to the entire expansion, the CEA estimated that by the end of 1965, the contribution of the tax cut had reached $30 billion.[24]

The third piece of evidence that can be cited in support of the effectiveness of the tax cut is the fact that from the close of 1963 to the close of

[21] *Ibid.*
[22] *Economic Indicators,* October, 1966, p. 2.
[23] *Ibid.*
[24] *Economic Report of the President,* Washington, D.C., 1966, p. 34.

1964, Federal revenues increased by $10.4 billion, in spite of the fact that in this same period tax *reductions* effected by both the Revenue Act of 1964 and the Excise Tax Reduction Act of 1965 totaled about $16 billion.[25] This experience bears out the claim of the CEA that a tax reduction, if it succeeded in stimulating economic growth, would lead to an *increase* rather than a decline in revenues. Thus, it is apparent that *if* the level of government expenditures had remained constant during this period, the Federal government would have experienced a substantial surplus by the end of 1965. Actually, total expenditures (including transfers) of the Federal government rose from $113.9 billion in 1964 (on a national income accounts basis) to $123.4 billion in 1965, an increase of $9.5 billion, a figure slightly less than the increase in revenues in the same period. Thus, the Federal government attained a small surplus of $1.5 billion in 1965. During the second quarter of 1966, the surplus, computed at an annual rate, rose to $3.8 billion, on a national income accounts basis.[26] In both the first and second quarters of 1966, Federal government receipts rose faster (on an annual basis) than did government expenditures for goods and services and transfers.

Looking Ahead

By late 1966, the American economy had moved into a phase of "high pressure prosperity," wherein once again the crucial domestic issue became what *Fortune* magazine recently termed "the greatest problem of industrial civilization" [27]—how a free nation can simultaneously achieve reasonably full employment and reasonably stable prices. By mid-1966, as pointed out earlier, the unemployment rate had dropped below 4 per cent for the first time since 1948; thus, the full-employment goal was substantially achieved. In moving toward the CEA target of an unemployment rate of 4 per cent or better, the economy achieved a remarkable degree of price stability. Between 1960 and 1965, the consumer price index rose at an annual average rate of only 1.3 per cent, a record, as Walter Heller has pointed out, unmatched by any major industrial nation.[28] If some allowance is made for qualitative increases in the nation's output during this period, a good case can be made for asserting that price changes in this period were, in fact, negligible. In spite of this impressive record, it is equally true that strong inflationary pressures made themselves felt during 1966. From December, 1965, through September, 1966, the consumer price index rose by 3.1 percentage points (from 111 to 114.1), a percentage increase of 2.7. Wholesale prices rose less sharply, although for the same period they recorded a gain

[25] *Ibid.*, and *Economic Indicators*, October, 1966, p. 37.

[26] *Economic Indicators*, October, 1966, p. 37.

[27] Gilbert Burck, "Must Full Employment Mean Inflation?" *Fortune*, October, 1966, p. 121.

[28] Walter W. Heller, "Using Fiscal and Monetary Policies to Further Employment Act Objectives," *Twentieth Anniversary of the Employment Act of 1946, An Economic Symposium*, Joint Economic Committee, Washington, D.C., 1966, p. 38.

of 2.2 percentage points.[29]

The economic situation as it actually unfolded during 1966 suggests primarily that the problem of applying both fiscal and monetary measures [30] to dampen down inflationary pressures, without at the same time bringing about an unacceptable level of unemployment, is much more difficult and delicate than the problem of insufficient demand and the full-employment surplus confronting the CEA in 1962. Throughout the first three quarters of 1966, the fiscal policy of the Johnson administration was to remain with a foot off the accelerator and poised over the brake, to paraphrase Professor Heller's description of the situation at the beginning of the year.[31] Aside from action taken in September to suspend temporarily the investment tax credit on machinery and equipment,[32] the administration did not ask the Congress during 1966 for new taxes nor propose any large-scale cuts in government expenditures. In spite of the real or alleged political risks which would confront *any* administration seeking a tax increase in an election year, the absence of decisive fiscal action during this period appears to have been the result of a high degree of uncertainty as to whether or not the added costs associated with the expanded war in Vietnam had, in the autumn of the year, reached a plateau that would permit the economy to "ride-out" the present pressures without development of a serious inflationary spiral.

One clear lesson which emerges from the experience of the recent past is the need for greater speed and flexibility in the administration of fiscal policy. In a "high pressure" economy, as Professor Heller has pointed out, the ideal policy is one that transfers demand to a later, lower-pressure economy.[33] The best way to achieve this is to devise new techniques which permit *temporary* tax adjustments. This means that new ways will have to be devised to reduce the amount of time required to get legislation involving changes in tax rates through the Congress. Eventually, perhaps, the Congress may delegate some of its power over tax rates to a fiscal authority within the administration that would be permitted to vary tax rates within broad limits in a manner similar to the authority that the Board of Governors of the Federal Reserve System has over the rediscount rate. Such an innovation would do much to impart the necessary speed and flexibility to the administration of fiscal policy. This development does not appear to be on the immediate horizon, but it is a safe assumption much future discussion on the efficacy of fiscal policy will necessarily focus on this problem.

[29] *Economic Indicators*, October, 1966, pp. 26, 27. (1957–1959 = 100 for both the consumer price and the wholesale price index.)

[30] The Federal Reserve acted in December, 1965, to tighten the money supply by raising the rediscount rate.

[31] Heller, *op. cit.*, p. 42.

[32] This tax credit for investment was put into effect in 1962. President Johnson, in his "State of the Union" address, January, 1967, asked for a 6 per cent surtax to the income tax to combat inflation and to finance the war in Viet Nam.

[33] Heller, *op. cit.*, p. 45.

PART **IV** | The Distribution
of Income

17 ‖ Theories of Aggregate Income Distribution

In this final chapter we turn to the theory of income distribution, a relatively unexplored aspect of modern income and employment theory. Our approach is from the point of view of the economy as a whole; we are concerned with the distribution of the national income on the basis of ownership of economic resources or "factors of production."

The purpose of an analysis of income distribution from the aggregate point of view is not only to determine what role the level of aggregate income plays in the distribution of the national income to the factors of production, but also to study the influence of the distribution of income on the income and employment level. We therefore have two objectives in this chapter: (1) to determine if there is any discernible way in which the pattern of income distribution to the factors of production changes with change in the output level, and (2) to find out if there is a functional relationship between the distribution of income and the level of aggregate demand, which, in the short run, is the prime determinant of the income level.

This is an area of economic analysis in which there does not exist any well-established and universally accepted body of economic analysis. David Ricardo, a founder of classical economics, thought that analysis of the principles that determine the distribution of the national output among different classes of claimants ought to be the major objective of economic analysis. However, throughout most of the nineteenth and early twentieth centuries economists were more concerned with the broad problem of resource allocation and the composition of the national output than they were with income distribution. After the appearance of Keynes' analysis in the mid-1930's, interest shifted almost exclusively to the problem of determination of the income and employment level in the short run. Since World War II there has been a renewed and intensive interest in the phenomenon of economic growth and with questions having to do with the distribution of the national income.

The Meaning of Income Distribution

Before we give our attention to various attempts to develop a theory of aggregate income distribution, it will be worthwhile to preface the analysis with a more thorough discussion of the meaning of income distribution. We are interested in *functional* or *factoral* income distribution, the claims on the national output that arise out of the ownership of economic resources. The productive process requires the services of economic resources, and payment must be made to the owners of the resources in order to secure these services. This gives rise to a claim by resource owners to a share of the national output. The broadest possible allocation of the national income is a twofold division with wage and salary income on one side and the various forms of property income on the other. Property income consists of income derived from ownership of economic resources in the form of either capital equipment or natural resources. In national income accounting, property incomes take the form of rents, interest, and profits. Beyond this fundamental division between labor and non-labor income, the functional distribution concept has to do with the relative share of the income total that accrues to the different types of non-human economic resources, that is, the relative share in the income total of different types of property income.

The functional distribution of income is to be distinguished both in theory and empirically from the *personal distribution of income*. Personal distribution involves the distribution of money income among different income classes. Personal income distribution depends upon a prior factoral or functional income distribution, because in modern society the major determinant of the personal money income of each individual is the quantity of economic resources that he owns and the price he obtains for each unit of such resources supplied to the productive process. But this is not the whole story, for the personal income of some individuals may be augmented by transfer payments, while the income claims of others based upon ownership of economic resources may be reduced either by taxation or the fact that all income earned in the productive process is not necessarily paid out to individuals.[1]

If, for the sake of analytical simplicity, we disregard transfer payments and the withholding from personal income of some portion of earned income, the income of an individual during a period of time depends upon the following:

[1] Chapter 3, p. 62.

1. The quantity of economic resources owned by the individual. Human labor is an economic resource, and, except in slave societies, such labor cannot be "owned" by anyone other than the individual who is the basic source of a particular kind and amount of labor power.

2. The extent to which the services of the fundamental kinds of economic resources (that is, labor, capital, and land) are being utilized. With respect to labor it is a matter of the employment level, and with respect to capital and land it is a matter of the degree of utilization of the existing stock of these resources.

3. The price that is paid for each unit of the economic resource utilized in the current productive process.

Thus, if an individual "owns" only his own labor power as an economic resource, and if his skill is such that his labor power can command a return of $3.00 per hour and, finally, if he is employed on the average a total of 2,000 hours per year (40 hours per week for 50 weeks per year), his income will be $6,000 per year.

Because the personal income of an individual depends upon the three elements discussed above, the problem of the distribution of income has usually been regarded as a *microeconomic* problem that must be treated at the level of the firm and the household.[2] This is so because, given the distribution of ownership of nonhuman resources as determined by the society's structure of property rights, the extent to which resources are actually utilized can be seen as an aspect of the theory of the firm, and the problem of the price paid for each unit of a resource utilized is handled simply as a special facet of the theory of individual prices.

Most contemporary textbooks treat income distribution basically as a problem in the pricing of factors of production.[3] These prices are determined presumably by the same basic forces that determine the prices of individual commodities and services, namely the interaction of demand and supply. The demand for an economic resource depends on its physical productivity and on the demand for the good or service whose production requires the use of the resource. The supply of the resource in question depends primarily on the quantity of the resource in existence at any particular time as well as the willingness of the resource owner to allow it to be used in the productive process.[4] The theory of resource pricing is thus not so much a theory of the distribution of the national income as it is a theory that explains both the nature of the business firm's demand for the services of economic resources and the process of relative price determination for economic resources. It does not provide us with an answer to the vital question of how the distribution of the national income into labor income

[2] Kenneth E. Boulding, *A Reconstruction of Economics* (New York, Wiley, 1950), p. 244.

[3] John F. Due and Robert W. Clower, *Intermediate Economic Analysis*, fifth ed. (Homewood, Ill., Irwin, 1966), p. 261.

[4] *Ibid.*

—that is, wages and salaries—and non-labor (or property) income is determined.[5] This remains an important theoretical problem.

Interest in the general problem of distribution of the national income along functional lines stems in part from the view of many economists that the relative share of labor and non-labor (or property) income in the national income is remarkably constant. For example, Keynes wrote in 1939:

> the stability of the proportion of the national dividend accruing to labour, irrespective apparently of the level of output as a whole and of the phase of the trade cycle . . . is one of the most surprising, yet best established facts in the whole range of economic statistics, both for Great Britain and for the United States. . . . It is the stability of the ratio for each country which is chiefly remarkable, and this appears to be a long-run, and not merely a short-period, phenomenon.[6]

More recently there have appeared a number of empirical studies which tend either to support or disprove the thesis that the relative share of labor and non-labor income in the national income has remained more or less constant over the very long run. For example, a statistical study published in 1954 by Professor D. Gale Johnson of the University of Chicago, dealing with the functional distribution of income in the United States for the period 1850 through 1952, concluded that although there had been some increase in the relative share of labor income in the national income total over this long period, the amount of the increase was relatively moderate and not inconsistent with the basic thesis of long-term stability in labor's share in the income total.[7] Even more recently Professor Sidney Weintraub has argued that the national income data for the period 1929 through 1957 show that the proportion of the gross business product—that is, that part of GNP originating in the business sector—which consists of employee compensation has been, for all practical purposes, a constant.[8]

Among the recent challenges to the thesis of the historical constancy of the share of labor income in the national income is the argument of Professor Irving B. Kravis who, using much the same data as Johnson, has asserted that there has been a decided shift in the distribution of the national income from property to labor income.[9] Skepticism concerning the

---

[5] Boulding, *op. cit.*, p. 246. The distribution of non-labor income between contractual income in the form of interest and rents and residual income in the form of profit is determined basically by the nature and extent of contractual obligations existing in a society.

[6] J. M. Keynes, "Relative Movements of Real Wages and Output," *The Economic Journal*, March, 1939, p. 48.

[7] D. Gale Johnson, "The Functional Distribution of Income in the United States, 1850–1952," *The Review of Economics and Statistics*, May, 1954, p. 182.

[8] Sidney Weintraub, *A General Theory of the Price Level, Output, Income Distribution, and Economic Growth* (Philadelphia, Chilton, 1959), pp. 14, 15.

[9] I. B. Kravis, "Relative Income Shares in Fact and Theory," *The American Economic Review*, December, 1959, p. 917.

constant relative share of labor in the national income has also been expressed by Professor Robert M. Solow.[10]

These studies and others attest to the continuing interest of economists in the broad problem of the functional distribution of the national income, even though there is neither agreement among them on the extent to which empirical data do or do not support the constancy of relative shares thesis, nor a generally accepted body of theoretical principles which explains the functional distribution of income, irrespective of whether relative shares are in fact constant. This is clearly one of the significant "frontier" areas of contemporary economic analysis which has yet to be provided with a clearly defined and generally agreed upon body of economic principles.

The Classical Theories of Income Distribution

The two most important figures in the classical approach to the distribution of the income of society are David Ricardo and Karl Marx.[11] Both Ricardo and Marx were interested in the long-term evolution of a capitalistic system of production, and as a consequence they developed definite notions on the manner in which this evolution would affect the distribution of income among the major economic classes. We shall first examine Ricardo's effort to develop a theory of relative shares, and then turn our attention to the Marxian theory, which stems directly from the theory developed by Ricardo.

Ricardo's Theory of Income Distribution

David Ricardo thought that discovery of the "laws" which regulate the distribution of the national output among the chief economic classes of society should be the principal problem in economic analysis. In a famous letter to his contemporary, Thomas Malthus, Ricardo put the matter in these terms:

Political Economy you think is an enquiry into the natures and causes of wealth—I think it should rather be called an enquiry into the laws which determine the division of the produce of industry amongst the classes who concur in its formation. No law can be laid down respecting quantity, but a tolerably correct one can be laid down respecting proportions. Every day I am more satisfied that the former enquiry is vain and delusive and the latter only the true object of the science.[12]

Ricardo's concern with the problem of income distribution arose not only from an interest in the question of relative shares per se, but also be-

---

[10] Robert M. Solow, "The Constancy of Relative Shares," *The American Economic Review*, September, 1958, p. 618.

[11] Marx is regarded as a classical economist because his analysis is in the classical deductive tradition, and because his fundamental notions are drawn directly from Ricardian theory.

[12] *Works and Correspondence of David Ricardo*, Sraffa edition (Cambridge, England, Cambridge University Press, 1952), Vol. 8, pp. 278–79.

cause he believed that the theory of income distribution held the key to an understanding of the whole mechanism of the economic system, especially the forces which govern the progress of the economy. Thus Ricardo's theory of relative shares yield a simplified macroeconomic model which shows the inevitable progression of the economy and society toward a "stationary" state in which all further capital accumulation and technical progress ceases.[13]

In Ricardo's theory the economy is divided into two broad sectors, industry and agriculture, but it is what happens in agriculture that is of crucial importance for the over-all development of the economy. Ricardian analysis rests upon three major assumptions. The first is that agriculture is characterized by diminishing returns if and when additional labor is applied to the production of foodstuffs, because agricultural land is not unlimited in quantity and is not of a uniform quality. Secondly, Ricardo accepts the Malthusian "law" of population, which asserts that the population tends to increase very rapidly whenever wages rise above the "subsistence" level,[14] and to decrease when wages fall below this level. Finally, the Ricardian analysis assumes that profit is the essential spur to capital accumulation, which is the key to economic progress.

In Ricardo's theory the output of the economy is allocated among the three major shares of rents, wages, and profits. Rent is the return on land, and it exists by virtue of the principle of diminishing returns. In a technical sense, rent is the difference between the product of labor on "marginal" land—land that yields just sufficient product to cover production costs—and the product of labor on land that yields more than enough product to cover production costs. Rent is thus a surplus based upon differences in the quality of land. On any given unit of land, rent is the difference between the average and the marginal productivity of successive units of labor.[15]

Wages are defined as the return to labor. In Ricardo's system it is essential to distinguish between the "natural" price (that is, wage) for labor, and the "market" price. The natural wage or price of labor is the level of wages toward which the actual or market wage will tend in the long run. It is basically a subsistence level of wages, a level of wages just sufficient to maintain the working population intact at a bare minimum of subsistence. In the earliest formulation of classical wage theory, the subsistence level was interpreted to mean a physical or biological level of wages just sufficient to permit the labor force to survive and raise enough children so that, over-all, the size of the labor force would neither increase nor decrease. In Ricardo's analysis, however, the idea of a subsistence level for wages is less a biologically determined minimum and more in the nature of a minimum

[13] Nicholas Kaldor, "Alternative Theories of Distribution," *The Review of Economic Studies,* Vol. XXIII, 1955–56, p. 84.
[14] The meaning of 'subsistence" is defined below.
[15] Kaldor, *loc. cit.*

standard shaped by cultural and social as well as physical forces.[16] Yet Ricardo retains the concept of a natural rate toward which the actual rates tend, and which is such as to just maintain intact the size of the labor force. In contrast to the natural price of labor there is the market wage, by which is meant the level actually prevailing in the market and which is determined by the forces of supply and demand. In Ricardo's analysis the demand for labor is dependent primarily on the rate of capital formation or accumulation, which in turn is a function of the rate of profit. A high level of capital accumulation would cause employers to compete vigorously for labor, thus forcing the market price of labor above the natural price.

The third and final share in the income total is that of profit. In the Ricardian scheme profit is treated as a residual. It is the amount left over after wage payments and rents have been subtracted from the income total. Profits, though, have an extremely important role to play because they determine the rate of net investment or capital accumulation which, in the classical system, is the chief source of economic progress. Moreover, profits are crucial, too, because they are the source of the saving that makes possible capital accumulation.

THE WORKING OF THE RICARDIAN SYSTEM

The basic objective of Ricardo's theory was to demonstrate what happens to the relative distribution of output as it expands. In seeking to explain the behavior of relative shares, Ricardo also provided economics with a very long-run theory on the course of development of a capitalistic economy.

Ricardo's theory of income distribution is based on the operation of two separate principles. Professor Nicholas Kaldor calls these the "marginal principle" and the "surplus principle." The marginal principle is employed to explain the division of national output between rent and the other two shares (wages and profits), and the surplus principle is called upon to explain the division of the national product *less rent* between wages and profit. The operation of these two principles and the resulting impact on the distribution of income into relative shares can be best explained with the use of a simple diagram.[17] This diagram is shown as Figure 17–1 and represents the forces operating in the agricultural sector of the economy.

Agricultural output or the basic "means of subsistence" is measured on the vertical axis, and the labor force in the sense of the number of workers employed in agriculture is shown on the horizontal axis. The curve AP depicts the average product of labor, and the curve MP represents the marginal product of labor. The AP and MP curves are both separate and downward-sloping because of the operation of the principle of diminishing re-

---

[16] *Ibid.*, p. 85.
[17] This diagram is derived from Kaldor's discussion of alternative theories of income distribution.

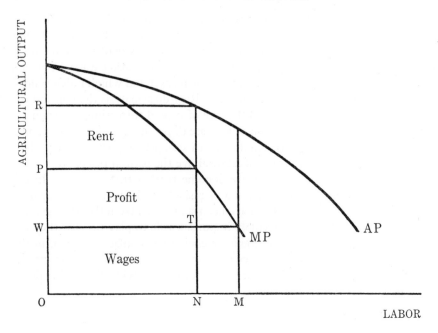

Figure 17-1. The Ricardian Theory of Income Distribution

turns. The one factor that differentiates this presentation from the more customary graphic analysis of the marginal productivity theory of wages [18] is that in Ricardo's analysis the marginal product is assumed to be equal to the sum of wages and profits. This is so because in the long run the level of wages is determined not by the marginal productivity of labor in the modern meaning of the term, but by the natural or subsistence price for labor. In Figure 17-1, therefore, the distance OW is equal to the "natural" or subsistence wage. This wage rate represents in real terms—that is, in terms of agricultural output—a level just sufficient to maintain intact the existing labor force at a subsistence (or culturally determined minimum) standard of living. If the marginal product is thus the sum of wages and profits in the Ricardian scheme, then the distance WP represents profit per unit of output, on the assumption that the employment level is equal to ON. Rent is equal to the distance PR, since we have already defined this share as equal to the difference between the average and the marginal product of labor. The actual level of employment—ON in Figure 17-1—is determined by the rate of capital accumulation because net investment serves to increase output, which in turn increases the demand for labor.

The fundamental character of Ricardo's theory of relative shares can

[18] Allan M. Cartter, *Theory of Wages and Employment* (Homewood, Ill., Irwin, 1959), p. 17.

be seen by analysis of what takes place as output expands in the economy's agricultural sector. In essence, the Ricardian schema postulates a sequence of events as follows: expansion of total production is the consequence of a high rate of capital accumulation (that is, net investment), which in turn results from the lure of high profits. Expansion leads to a high level of demand for labor, which has the effect of raising the market wage above the natural wage. Population will then rise, and there will be an increased demand for agricultural commodities, leading to an expansion of agricultural output. Since the total supply of agricultural land is fixed, the effort to expand the output of agricultural commodities by the employment of more labor (as shown on the horizontal axis of Figure 17–1) will sooner or later encounter diminishing returns, which will ultimately cause a reduction in both the average and the marginal product of labor. The latter effect is illustrated in the figure by the downward slope of both the *AP* and the *MP* curves.

As the attempt is made to expand agricultural output through the employment of more labor, the cost of production and thereby the price of agricultural commodities will rise. This is a consequence of diminishing returns or the decline in the average and marginal product of labor in the agricultural sector. When this happens, rents will necessarily increase, because rent is the difference between the product of labor on marginal land (land that yields just enough product to cover costs of production) and the product of labor on intra-marginal or average land. In Figure 17–1 this development will be reflected in a growing value for rent per unit of output (the distance *PR* with the employment level *ON*) as the volume of employment is expanded. At the same time the rising cost of production of agricultural output means that current money wages will have to rise in order to permit workers to maintain the subsistence standard of living for the labor force. The natural wage in real terms (the distance *OW*) will not change, but the share of the total output that is absorbed by wages will have to increase. This is shown by an increase in the size of the rectangle which represents the wage share of the total output. Initially this was the area *ONTW* at the employment level *ON*. This area will be elongated as employment expands toward the ultimate upper limit represented by the distance *OM*. What happens to profit in the process is readily apparent: as output expands, profit per unit of output (the distance *WP* at the employment level *ON*) continuously shrinks until finally at the employment level *OM* (at which point *MP* has fallen to a level just equal to the natural price of labor) it disappears completely.

The continuous fall in profit per unit of output depicted in Figure 17–1 takes place in the agricultural sector because of diminishing returns on land, but the same tendency toward a declining rate of profit will be at work in the manufacturing sector of the economy, even though the latter may not be subject to diminishing returns. The increase in the price of agricultural commodities with the resultant rise in the money cost of the subsistence standard of living will force manufacturers to pay higher wages. Profits will thus decline in the manufacturing sector. Moreover, as long as mobility of capital is assumed, profit will have to be the same in both agriculture and industry, or else capital will shift from one sector to the other.

We can summarize Ricardo's theory of income distribution by stating that, given the assumption of a constant technology and a constant natural wage in real terms, the relative share of wages in the output total will increase with a rising level of output and employment. The relative share of profit will decline and ultimately fall to zero. This is the point at which the economy reaches the "stationary" state of classical theory, a situation in which all accumulation, population growth, and technical progress cease. The basic causal force in this schema is the fact of diminishing returns in agriculture, a grim tendency which can only be postponed temporarily by technical progress. Technical progress cannot, in other words, prevent the ultimate disappearance of profit and the onset of the stationary state.

Although Ricardo saw clearly that his system would lead to an increase in the relative share of wages in the total output and that this would come at the expense of profit, he was less certain as to what would happen to the relative share of rent.[19] However, if the economic system reacts to increasing employment as depicted in Figure 17–1, the relative share of rent in the output total will rise along with the rise in the relative share of wages; the rent share depends upon the amount of rent per unit of output, which rises with successive increases in the employment level.

The Marxian Theory of Income Distribution

Karl Marx's theory of income distribution in an advancing capitalistic economy rests basically upon an adaptation of Ricardian ideas, even though his analysis reaches very different conclusions concerning the behavior of relative income shares as the level of income and employment changes. Marx's theory of income distribution is an essential aspect of his general and sweeping theory of capitalistic development because it is his contention that the economic development of capitalism is tied to the distribution of the output among the different economic classes.

The entire Marxian structure rests on the concept of the "labor theory of value" which, in essence, asserts that the value of a commodity or service is determined by the labor time necessary for its production. Thus labor power is the ultimate source of economic value. The reader should note that we are concerned, first, with the determination of exchange value rather than value in a broader, philosophical sense and, second, that Marx's

---

[19] Paul Davidson, *Theories of Aggregate Income Distribution* (New Brunswick, N.J., Rutgers University Press, 1960), p. 7.

labor theory of value is basically a cost of production theory because it makes exchange value dependent wholly on factors present on the supply side of the picture, specifically, the amount of labor power necessary to produce a commodity or service. For this reason, Marx's theory is sometimes said to be an "objective" theory of value in contrast to modern value theory which is in part "subjective" since it holds that value depends upon the usefulness (or utility) of the good or service to the ultimate purchaser as well as upon the cost conditions under which the commodity or service in question was produced.

What is unique in the Marxian analysis is not so much the labor theory of value—Marx derived this idea from Adam Smith and Ricardo—but the application of the theory to the value of labor power itself, which is to say, the wage of labor. According to Marx, the supply price for labor is determined by the amount of labor power required to produce the commodities and services that make up the minimum level of subsistence necessary to maintain the labor force intact. In the Marxian system, as in the Ricardian analysis, there exists a natural price for labor, a level of real wages which will just permit the labor force to survive and reproduce itself. In Marx's theory the value of the real wage corresponding to this minimum level of subsistence is determined by the amount of labor power necessary to produce the commodities that enter into the subsistence standard of living.

Marx's application of the labor theory of value to the determination of the value of labor itself is crucial because it forms the basis for his theory of "surplus" value, or theory of the exploitation of labor, which in turn provides the fundamental key to an understanding of the process of income distribution in a capitalistic society. Surplus value exists, according to Marx, because labor power in a given period of time will produce more economic value than the cost of labor itself as measured by the supply price of labor or the minimum real wage that will maintain intact the labor force. Because labor power is the source of all economic or exchange value, exploitation exists whenever the worker fails to receive the whole of the value of the output. The difference between the value of the total output and the supply price of labor represents surplus value which is expropriated by the capitalists, who, in the Marxian schema, are owners of the non-human instruments of production—capital equipment and land. It is through their ownership of the physical means of production that the capitalists exploit the working class and extract surplus value from it. This is the essence of the Marxian theory of exploitation, and its validity is no greater than the validity of its basic cornerstone, the labor theory of value. Most non-Marxist economists today would question the correctness of the labor theory as a satisfactory explanation of the phenomenon of exchange value.

Nevertheless, the notion of surplus value is crucial to the Marxian theory of income distribution; surplus value is the source of all profit, and thus the amount of surplus value that can be expropriated by the capitalistic class will determine the relative share of profit in the income total. Marx, it should be noted, was concerned primarily with the distribution of output between wages (or labor income) and profit (or non-wage income). He was not particularly interested in the allocation of the non-wage share among the various forms of property income. Unlike Ricardo, he did not believe in the principle of diminishing returns, and thus he did not distinguish in his analysis between rents and profit.[20]

In Marx's analysis of the productive process the value of a final good or service can be broken down into three component parts. These are: c, which represents raw materials and capital consumption;[21] v, which Marx defined as *variable capital* and which represents the value of the labor power entering into current production (that is, the wage bill in terms of the subsistence wage); and s, which is surplus value or profit. Thus, the value of any single final good or service is equal to $c + v + s$. For the economy as a whole, the value of the gross output may be defined as $C + V + S$, where C is equal to capital consumption alone (since at the level of the whole economy raw materials are intermediate products, and thus their value is included in the value of the final output). V is equal to Σv, and S is equal to Σs. The net output will, therefore, be equal to $V + S$, as it is derived by subtracting C from the gross output. Net output can thus be seen to consist of two basic shares, the wage share, V, and the profit share, S.

The ratio of the profit share to the wage share is of key importance in Marx's analysis, because this ratio, S/V, is more than a measure of the rate of exploitation; a change in S/V means that a change has taken place in the relative share of wage and non-wage (that is, profit) income in the output total. Consequently, if we understand how Marx thought that this ratio would change in response to the basic forces at work in the capitalistic system, we grasp the essence of the Marxian theory of income distribution. A rise in this ratio represents an increase in the rate of exploitation and, consequently, an increase in the share of profit relative to wages in the income total. A decline in the ratio represents the reverse.

According to Marx, the most important single force at work in the economy centers around the effort of the capitalists to increase the rate of exploitation of labor, that is, to increase the ratio S/V. At the core of Marx's theory of the long-term development of a capitalistic economy is the contention that the basic forces at work in such a system tend to bring about exactly this result. Let us examine the reasons postulated by Marx to explain this tendency. For one thing, Marx believed, as did Ricardo, that the

---

[20] Kaldor, *op. cit.*, p. 87.

[21] Capital and raw materials present a difficult problem in terms of the labor theory of value, because they contribute to current output, but are clearly not labor. Marx resolved this problem by regarding capital and raw materials currently utilized in the productive process as stored-up labor power from past periods.

market wage tended to fall toward a real wage equal to the minimum subsistence standard of living. In Marx's analysis this was not caused by population pressure, as was the case in the Ricardian system, but by a continuous excess of labor supply over demand, which Marx saw as the normal condition of a capitalistic economy. The continuous presence of what he termed a vast industrial "reserve army" of unemployed workers prevents the market wage from rising (for other than very short periods of time) above the minimum wage level necessary to maintain the labor force intact.

The excess supply of labor and the industrial reserve army of the unemployed are the inevitable products of certain forces at work in the economic system. One of the most important of these is competition. In Marxian theory competition takes the form of a struggle among the owners of the material instruments of production to increase the rate of exploitation or, and this comes to the same thing, the non-wage share in the income total. This might be done by lengthening the working day, thereby increasing the amount of surplus value expropriated from the labor force. Much the same result could be achieved by an increase in the intensity of labor. There are limits, though, to the extent that the rate of exploitation can be increased by either of these means. Technical progress—or a change in the physical productivity of the labor force—would achieve this result because with a constant length for the working day and no change in the real subsistence wage, the total product will expand with technical progress and thus there is necessarily an increase in surplus value or the rate of exploitation. This is true as long as the market wage does not depart significantly from the subsistence wage. Marx termed the increase in the rate of exploitation from this source an increase in "relative surplus value," and asserted that the latter would vary directly with the productivity of labor.[22]

Technical progress is primarily the result of the accumulation of capital. Consequently the struggle among the capitalists to increase the rate of exploitation forces them to accumulate capital—that is, to invest. In the Marxian system capital accumulation or investment is an activity that is not to be explained primarily in terms of the lure of profit, but as a necessary structural feature of the economic system which results from the intensity of competition among capitalists seeking to increase the rate of exploitation.[23] In any event, the combination of capital accumulation and technical progress provides the basis for Marx's fundamental proposition concerning the distribution of income in a capitalistic society: the "law of the increasing misery of the working class." According to this "law," capital accumulation and a growing level of real output must lead to a decline in the relative share of wages in the output total and a corresponding in-

[22] Davidson, *op. cit.*, p. 15.
[23] Kaldor, *op. cit.*, p. 88.

crease in the relative share of profit. This is a conclusion on relative shares diametrically the opposite of that reached by Ricardo. The fundamental cause of decline in the relative share of wages is technical progress, the fruits of which go entirely to the owners of the physical instruments of production. The alleged increasing misery of the working class does not come from any decline in the level of real wages, since their "misery" does not increase in any absolute sense; it is the result instead of the failure of real wages to advance along with gains in productivity. This is the heart of Marx's theory of distribution.

Although the logic of his own theories pertaining to surplus value and the role of competition led Marx to assume that the relative share of wages in the output total would decline as productivity and the income level rose, he also took over from earlier classical theories the view that capital accumulation would be accompanied by a falling rate of profit. Unlike Ricardo and other classical economists, Marx did not attribute this to the operation of the principle of diminishing returns, but to an increase in what he termed the "organic composition of capital," by which he meant, to employ more modern terminology, an increase in the capital-output ratio,[24] or a more capital-intensive productive process. Although there is no compelling reason why a more capital-intensive operation would lead to a decline in profit as long as wage rates remain unchanged at the subsistence level,[25] Marx's "law" of the falling rate of profits is nevertheless necessary to complete his analysis of the course of development of the capitalistic system. The process of capital accumulation and growth leads inevitably to a severe economic crisis. This crisis is the result of both the "falling rate of profit," which must sooner or later adversely affect capital accumulation itself and, second, overproduction because of an insufficiency of aggregate demand. The latter stems from the progressive decline in the relative share of wage income in the output total. Marx thought the capitalistic system would be increasingly wracked by crises of greater and greater severity until finally it would collapse amid an uprising of the working class that would usher in the era of communism. Marx proved to be a poor prophet concerning not only the behavior of the wage share in the national income, but also the long-term development of capitalism.

A Concluding Comment on Marx and Ricardo

The theoretical systems of Ricardo and Marx have in common the fact that they both represent an analysis of the economy on a grand scale. Both men were concerned with the fundamental economic forces which shape the nature of the economy over the course of decades, or even centuries. Beyond this, however, they failed to agree upon the impact that the long-term development of the economic system would have on the distribution

---

[24] Chapter 7, p. 217.
[25] Kaldor, *op. cit.*, p. 86.

of income. Ricardo, whose thinking was haunted by the specter of diminishing returns, believed that the relative share of labor in the total output would rise, and this would come at the expense of profit—that is, the non-wage share—as the economy moved inexorably toward the stationary state. Marx, on the other hand, thought that the fierce competition among capitalists to increase surplus value would lead to a smaller and smaller relative share for wages in the total output, and the economy would move inevitably not in the direction of the stationary state, but toward collapse, revolution, and, ultimately, a communist society. Neither Ricardo nor Marx provides the modern economy with a satisfactory theory of income distribution in a dynamic setting. Ricardo's analysis is unsatisfactory because it is tied too closely to the notion of diminishing returns, while Marx's system is rooted in what most economists would regard as an obsolete theory of value. Events have not vindicated either theoretical system, but in spite of this both represent bold and imaginative attempts to deal with the crucial problem of the distribution of the economy's output along functional lines.

Recent Theoretical Developments

The development of marginal utility and marginal productivity analysis in the latter part of the nineteenth century [26] had the effect of shifting attention from the macroeconomic or aggregate problem of the distribution of the national income into functional shares to the primarily microeconomic problem of the determination of the prices of the factors of production. Thus, for almost a century income distribution theory has come to mean the process by which factor prices are determined through the interplay of the firm's demand for the services of economic resources and the conditions under which varying amounts of the resource will be supplied. Analysis of the fundamental forces determining the distribution of income in the sense in which Ricardo saw the problem practically vanished from the literature of the science. More recently, though, there has been a revival of interest in the macroeconomic aspects of income distribution. The recent analyses have emerged primarily out of the framework of modern income and employment theory and must be regarded as probing efforts that seek development of a body of theory in this area rather than as a completed and fully acceptable set of conclusions concerning the forces that determine the functional distribution of income. We cannot touch upon all recent theoretical developments pertaining to the distribution of income in an aggregate sense, but we shall deal with the ideas of several individuals whose thinking seems most representative of

[26] Edmund Whittaker, *Schools and Streams of Economic Thought* (Chicago, Rand McNally, 1960), pp. 261–281.

recent tendencies. Specifically, we shall analyze the theories of Professors Allan M. Cartter, Nicholas Kaldor, and Sidney Weintraub.

A Simplified Keynesian Model

In his *Theory of Wages and Employment*, Professor Cartter has attempted to develop a relatively simple model which links the problem of distribution to the determination of the income level for the economy as a whole.[27] His analysis is considered "Keynesian" because it ties the distribution of income in a functional sense to the fundamental Keynesian conditon of income equilibrium, namely that saving and investment *ex ante* must be equal. The equilibrium income level is Cartter's point of departure. His major purpose is to show how an alteration in the functional distribution of income between a wage share and a non-wage share may affect the equilibrium income position. His analysis does not, however, come to grips with the problem of the relationship between changes in the income and employment level and changes in the functional pattern of income distribution. For this reason, his model lacks the generality that a true theory of aggregate income distribution ought to possess; it represents, nevertheless, an interesting and worthwhile effort to relate income distribution to some important macroeconomic variables.

Cartter's "model" rests on four basic propositions that may be summarized as follows: [28]

1. The initial assumption is that equilibrium in the income level depends upon the equality between saving, S, and investment, I, in an *ex ante*, or intended, sense. Thus, our first equation is

$$I = S \tag{17-1}$$

2. The rate of *ex ante* investment is assumed to be a linear function of profit, P. This gives us

$$I = \pi(P) \tag{17-2}$$

In the above equation, π is a constant defined as the investment-profit coefficient. It is equal to the ratio I/P. It is further assumed that the value of π is normally positive but less than one. The relationship between I and P is shown graphically in Figure 17–2. The value of π is represented by the slope of the curve. An upward or counterclockwise movement of the curve depicts a rise in the value of the investment-profit coefficient. The practical meaning of this is that a given amount of profit will generate (or induce) a greater amount of investment than heretofore.

---

[27] Allan Cartter, *op. cit.*, p. 155.
[28] The model is applicable to a simplified economy with no government and no foreign Balance. See Cartter, *op. cit.*, p. 155.

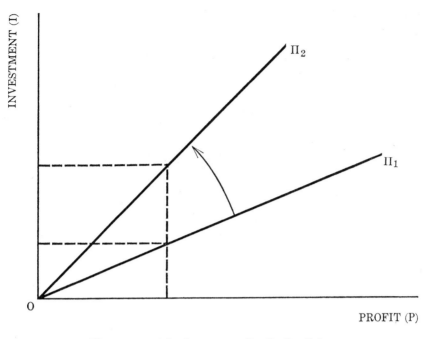

Figure 17-2. The Investment-Profit Coefficient

3. Income is assumed to be allocated between two factors, "laborers" and "capitalists," the latter being the owners of all non-human economic resources. Thus the two functional shares of the national income are wages and profits. Cartter designates the proportion of the total income, Y, which goes to labor in the form of wages by the symbol λ. The share of the income total going to capitalists in the form of profits is thus $1 - \lambda$. This gives us the following two definitional equations for the total of wages and the total of profits:

$$W = \lambda Y \tag{17-3}$$
$$P = (1 - \lambda)Y \tag{17-4}$$

From Equation (17-4) and from Equation (17-2) it follows that investment can be further defined as

$$I = \pi(1 - \lambda)Y \tag{17-5}$$

4. The fourth proposition that enters into Cartter's model is that the level of saving in the economy depends upon the marginal (and average) propensities to save of the major groups in the economy; the division of income between these groups; and, finally, the extent to which profits are retained by business firms or distributed to the owners (that is, the share-

holders). The foregoing factors are defined symbolically by Cartter as follows:

$a =$ The propensity (marginal and average) to save out of wage income.

$b =$ The propensity to save out of shareholder's income.

$v =$ The share of profit income that is distributed to shareholders or the owners of business firms. This is distributed profit.

$1 - v =$ The share of total profits retained in business firms. This follows from the definition of v.

On the basis of the foregoing, Cartter finds it possible to rewrite the fundamental equation defining the necessary condition for income equilibrium (equality between *ex ante* saving and investment) as follows: [29]

$$\pi(1 - \lambda) = \lambda a + (1 - \lambda)[vb + (1 - v)] \qquad (17\text{--}6)$$

This equation expresses the saving-investment identity in a form which will show the possible impact on the equilibrium income level of a change in the functional distribution of income between wage and the non-wage (that is, profit) share. Let us examine some of its significant implications.

In the first place, an increase in the relative share of wages in the income total will reduce profits and thereby bring about a decline in investment expenditure.[30] As a consequence the equilibrium income level will decline. The fall in investment might be offset by an equal downward shift in the saving function, but this would depend upon the marginal and average propensities to save of the two income groups as well as the possible effect of a change in the distribution of income on the share of profit income distributed to shareholders (the value of v). It is Cartter's view that an increase in labor's share will reduce investment by more than it reduces saving. This implies that there is not enough of a difference between the saving propensities of the two groups to cause a significant decline in the saving function for the whole economy in the event of an increase in the relative share of wages in the income total. Wage earners would have to have a significantly lower propensity to save (marginal and average) than non-wage groups for such a shift to come about.

A decline in investment brought about by an increase in the relative share of labor income can be offset by an increase in either the investment-profit coefficient, π, or by an increase in v, the proportion of profit income distributed to shareholders. An increase in π implies that a given amount of profit will induce more investment expenditure than heretofore, a condition that will be realized only if expectations of future profits are highly

---

[29] The algebraic derivation of this equation is shown in the appendix to this chapter.
[30] Cartter, *op. cit.*, p. 158.

favorable or improving. In the event of a shift in the distribution of income in favor of wage earners and a consequent decline in the relative share of profit, a higher level of investment is likely only if the change in income distribution brings a sufficient increase in consumption expenditure to justify more favorable expectations with respect to future income. This, though, implies that the saving function will fall by more than the investment function in the event of an increase in labor's share.

An increase in the value of v would also tend to offset the decline in investment brought about by the reduction in the relative share of profit in the income total. An increase in v at any income level presumably means a decline in the proportion of income saved, because normally the marginal (and average) propensity to save of profit recipients is less than unity. Thus, an increase in the value of v is tantamount to a downward shift in the saving function. If this shift is large enough, the equilibrium income level will be unaffected.

A second set of possibilities centers around the effect of a decline in the relative share of wages in the income total. Within the strict algebraic framework of Cartter's model, such a decline will automatically increase the profit share and thereby cause investment expenditure to rise. If it is assumed that saving increases less than in proportion to the upward shift in investment spending, then the equilibrium income level will rise in the unlikely case that there is no change in any of the other variables that are a part of the analysis. The assumption that the saving function will shift upward, although to a lesser degree than the shift in the investment function, necessarily implies a fall in current consumption. It is difficult to see how such a change can leave the investment-profit coefficient unaffected. The larger level of profit which results from the initial decline in the relative share of wages in the income total will result in a greater investment expenditure only if we totally ignore the unfavorable effects on expectations with respect to future profit possibilities of an absolute decline in the volume of consumer spending. It seems likely, in other words, that a change in the distribution of income in favor of profit and at the expense of wage income will lead, sooner or later, to a decline in the value of the investment-profit coefficient. If this happens, it means that a given amount of profit will induce less investment expenditure than heretofore, and thus the absolute amount of investment may not increase, even though the relative share of profit in the current income total has risen. Less certain is the impact of a decline in labor's share on the value of v. There seems to be no *a priori* reason for the value of v to change one way or another with an initial alteration in the functional distribution of income in favor of the non-wage share. However, if the absolute decline in consumption outlays caused the investment-profit coefficient to fall so drastically that the equilibrium income level fell rather than rose, pressure might be exerted by shareholders to increase the proportion of total profit actually distributed so that the shareholders would be able to maintain customary standards of living. Beyond this, though, no generalization seems possible with respect to changes in the value of v as a result of changes in the distribution of income.[31]

Cartter's analysis represents a thoughtful attempt to bring distributional problems into the framework of modern income and employment theory. His reformulation of the basic investment-saving equilibrium equation, Equation (17–6), is useful because it offers insight into the way in which a shift in the functional distribution of income *may* affect the income equilibrium itself. The weak link, perhaps, in his analysis is the assumption that investment is a direct function of profit, and the further implicit assumption that the absolute amount of consumer spending will not have any direct impact upon either profit or profit expectations. Beyond this, though, the analysis does not offer an explanation of the behavior of relative shares as the income and employment level changes.

Kaldor's Theory of Income Distribution

Kaldor's analysis is similar to that of Cartter's in that his point of departure is the fundamental condition for an income equilibrium; saving and investment *ex ante* are equal. But the similarity ends at this point because Kaldor attempts to demonstrate how changes in the ratio of investment to income will cause a change in the relative share of profits and wages in the income total, whereas Cartter's analysis concerns itself with the impact of changes in the distribution of income on the absolute amount of investment. The key characteristics of the Kaldorian theory can be summed up algebraically in a series of equations: [32]

$$Y = W + P \qquad (17-7)$$

The above equation is simply an identity which asserts that the national income, Y, consists of the sum of wage payments, W, and profits, P. This is identical with Cartter's proposition that the income of society is allocated between two factors, "laborers" and "capitalists."

$$I = S \qquad (17-8)$$

This is the basic condition for income equilibrium. I and S are intended or *ex ante* values.

$$S = S_w + S_p \qquad (17-9)$$

---

[31] As defined by Cartter, v is the share of *gross* profit that is distributed to shareholders. Replacement investment will limit the extent to which the value of v can be increased.

[32] Kaldor, *op. cit.*, p. 95.

This identity asserts that total saving (*ex ante*) for the economy is equal to the sum of saving out of wage income, S_w, and saving out of profit income, S_p. The amount of saving in equilibrium thus depends upon the average propensity to save of each of the two income classes present in the Kaldorian system. If we label the average propensity to save of wage earners as s_w and the average propensity to save of profit recipients as s_p, we then have

$$S_w = s_w \times W \qquad (17\text{--}10)$$
$$S_p = s_p \times P \qquad (17\text{--}11)$$

Equation (17–10) gives us the absolute amount of saving out of wage income; Equation (17–11), the absolute amount of saving out of profit income. The sum of the two yield the total of saving.

By the process of substitution and algebraic manipulation, Kaldor derives an equation which describes in symbolic form the essential features of his theory of income distribution: [33]

$$\frac{I}{Y} = (s_p - s_w)\frac{P}{Y} + s_w \qquad (17\text{--}12)$$

Before we discuss the theoretical meaning of the foregoing equation it is essential to make clear the underlying assumptions of the Kaldorian theory. First, he assumes that full-employment conditions prevail in the economy and, second, that the saving propensities for both the wage and the non-wage groups are constant. There are some added assumptions which we shall bring out as we discuss the model.

Given these two assumptions, Kaldor's thesis is that the share of profit in the income total is a function of the ratio of investment to income (or output). This thesis can be expressed in algebraic form by re-arrangement of Equation (17–12).

$$\frac{P}{Y} = \frac{1}{(s_p - s_w)} \times \frac{I}{Y} - \frac{s_w}{(s_p - s_w)} \qquad (17\text{--}13)$$

In algebraic terms it can easily be seen that an increase in the investment-output ratio, I/Y, will result in an increase in the share of profit in income, P/Y, as long as it is assumed that both s_w and s_p are constants and, further, that $s_p > s_w$.

Of greater importance to us is the underlying economic rationale for Kaldor's theorem that the share of profit in the income total is a function of the investment-output ratio. Under full employment conditions an increase in investment expenditure must, in real terms, bring about an

---

[33] The algebraic derivation of this equation is shown in the appendix to this chapter.

increase in both the ratio of investment to output, I/Y, and also an increase in the saving-output ratio, S/Y. This is necessary if equilibrium at a higher level of real investment is to be obtained. If the saving-output ratio did not rise, the result would be a continuous upward movement of the general level of prices. The heart of Kaldor's theory lies in his demonstration that a shift in the distribution of income is essential to bring about the higher saving-output ratio which is the necessary condition for a continued full-employment equilibrium with a higher absolute level of investment in real terms.

This brings us to another key assumption in his analysis: propensities to save for the two income classes differ. The propensity to save out of profit income is greater than the propensity to save out of wage income. This assumption, according to Kaldor, is a necessary condition for both stability in the entire system and an increase in the share of profit in income when the investment-output ratio increases.[34] The underlying rationale is that with a fixed level of real income (the full-employment assumption) the only way in which an increase in the saving-output ratio for the whole economy can be brought about is either through a change in the propensity to save itself, which Kaldor rules out by his assumption that both s_w and s_p are constant, or by a shift in the distribution of real income from the income class with the lower propensity to save to the income class with the higher propensity to save.

The mechanism which brings about the redistribution of income in favor of the profit share whenever there is a rise in the investment-output ratio is essentially that of the price level. The increase in investment expenditure under full-employment conditions leads initially to a general rise in prices. Since, according to Kaldor, no mechanism exists to insure that money wages rise at the same rate as prices, there presumably will be an increase in profit margins relative to wages. The failure of money wages to keep pace with the rise in the general price level will thus reduce the real income of wage earners, while the increased profit margins increase the real income of non-wage income recipients. Since the propensity to save of the latter group is, on the average, higher than that of wage earners, the inflation-induced shift in the distribution of real income in favor of profits will raise the over-all level of real saving in the economy. This process will continue until the saving-output ratio is once again in equilibrium with the investment-output ratio. The reader should understand, though, the key importance to the Kaldorian system of the assumption that the propensity to save of profit recipients is greater than that of wage earners. Without this assumption, the real saving-output ratio would not rise, irrespective of any alteration in the distribution of income, and thus the system would be unstable.

Since Kaldor seeks to relate the functional distribution of income di-

[34] Kaldor, *op. cit.*, p. 95.

rectly to variables that are of crucial importance in the determination of the level of income and employment, his analysis is appropriately described as an aggregate or macroeconomic theory of income distribution. But it must be recognized that Kaldor's analysis is severely restricted by its underlying assumptions. The theory does not tell us how the distribution of income in a functional sense will be affected by changes in real income (or output) below the full-employment level, although it does suggest that any attempt to increase capacity once full employment is reached will bring about a relative increase in the non-wage share in the income total. In this sense Kaldor's analysis has a distinct classical flavor, even though his framework is that of modern employment theory.

Weintraub's Theory of Income Distribution

The most recent and, perhaps, the most ambitious effort to date to construct an aggregate theory of income distribution is that of Professor Sidney Weintraub. In *An Approach to the Theory of Income Distribution*,[35] he attempts to analyze the functional distribution of income through the device of the aggregate supply function, a concept of key importance in modern income and employment theory. Weintraub believes that an aggregate supply function constructed in terms of current rather than constant prices provides the necessary bridge between income and employment theory and a theory of aggregate income distribution. Weintraub employs the aggregate supply schedule to show how the functional distribution of income will change as the level of employment (and output) changes. In addition, he seeks to make his theory complete by relating the level of the aggregate demand function to the functional distribution of income. Thus, Weintraub's analysis has a more ambitious objective than any of the theories we have surveyed to this point.

THE AGGREGATE SUPPLY FUNCTION AND THE
THEORY OF RELATIVE SHARES

The point of departure for Weintraub's theory of income distribution is the aggregate supply function. He designates this function with the capital letter Z. In concept, Weintraub's Z is identical with the so-called "Keynesian" aggregate supply function that we discussed earlier.[36] It is a schedule which relates money proceeds to the employment level. In the Weintraubian system money proceeds are measured in current rather than constant prices. As is true of any aggregate supply function, there will be a unique level of employment associated with each level of money proceeds, and because of the static character of the analysis each level of employment will be uniquely associated with a particular level of output

[35] Sidney Weintraub, *An Approach to the Theory of Income Distribution* (Philadelphia, Chilton, 1958).
[36] Chapter 5, pp. 112–114.

(that is, real income). An aggregate supply schedule of this kind is shown in Figure 17–3.

The money proceeds associated with each and every possible employment level must be allocated in accordance with the following equation:

$$Z = wN + F + R \tag{17-14}$$

In the above equation the symbols have the following meanings:

$w =$ the money wage rate
$N =$ the employment level
$F =$ fixed or contractual incomes or payments
    (rents, interest, contractual salaries)
$R =$ the residual or profit

The wage bill in total is thus equal to wN. Weintraub uses the symbol W to designate the total wage bill, as distinct from the level of money wages, w. Therefore, $W = wN$. These three component parts of aggregate supply measured in terms of money proceeds correspond to the three allocative shares of the national income: wages, rentier or fixed incomes, and profits.

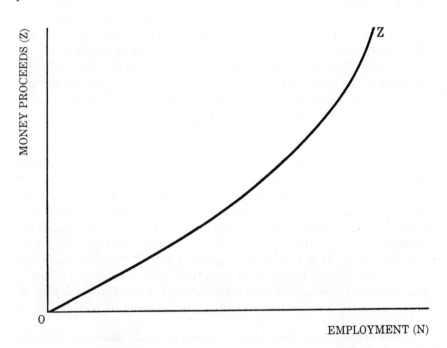

Figure 17–3. Weintraub's Aggregate Supply Function

The relationship between the three types of incomes which make up the economy's aggregate supply function is depicted in Figure 17–4.[37] The aggregate supply function is represented by the curve OZ. The line OW represents the total wage bill W on the assumption that money wages are constant. The dotted line FF' represents fixed (or contractual) pay-

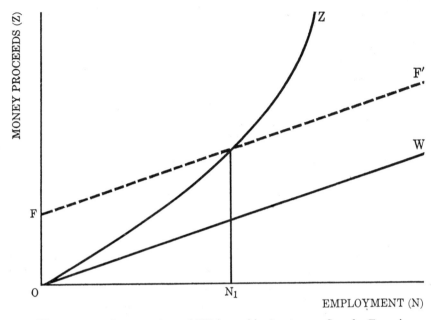

Figure 17–4. Construction of Weintraub's Aggregate Supply Function

ments, and it is drawn to exceed W by the absolute amount of these payments. The residual (or profit) is equal to the difference between the schedule OZ and the FF' curve. Thus $R = OZ - FF'$. It may be noted that proceeds fall short of factor costs up to the employment level ON_1, which means that profits are negative until the economy reaches this level of employment. It follows that the economy cannot remain indefinitely at an employment level below ON_1 as this implies that firms, on the average, are experiencing losses.

It is Weintraub's contention that the aggregate supply function, Z, is non-linear. He employs the concept of the elasticity of aggregate supply as a measure of the shape of the function Z. The elasticity of aggregate supply, which Weintraub designates as E_z, shows the relationship between a change in money proceeds and a change in employment. In equation form we have [38]

[37] Weintraub, *op. cit.*, p. 29.
[38] Technically, the elasticity of aggregate supply is the ratio of a percentage change in employment, $\Delta N/N$, to a percentage change in proceeds, $\Delta Z/Z$.

$$E_z = \frac{\Delta N}{\Delta Z} \times \frac{Z}{N} \qquad (17\text{--}15)$$

If the coefficient E_z has a value greater than one, $E_z > 1$, it means that a 1 per cent increase in proceeds would lead to a more than 1 per cent increase in employment. This would be true under conditions of increasing returns. On the other hand, a value for the elasticity of aggregate supply coefficient of less than one, $E_z < 1$, means that a 1 per cent increase in proceeds leads to a less than 1 per cent increase in employment. This is the usual situation under conditions of decreasing returns. The static character of Weintraub's analysis means that the normal situation is one of diminishing returns to additional labor and, therefore, the coefficient E_z will have a value of less than unity. If this is correct, and if it is further assumed that the money wage is a constant, it follows that OZ will curve upward and to the left in the fashion depicted in Figure 17–4, because the combination of diminishing returns to labor and fixed money wages means that labor costs per unit of output will rise as more employment is offered. As a consequence, the general price level will rise with a growing volume of employment, and the aggregate demand function will have to reflect this fact. A straight-line function would be possible only on the assumption of constant prices.

The foregoing discussion sets the stage for consideration of the essentials of Weintraub's theory of relative shares. The key to what happens to the relative importance of the three types of income as changes take place in the income total depends upon what assumptions are made concerning the shape of the OZ, the FF', and the OW curves. Let us consider each income category in turn, beginning with the share going to fixed income groups. We shall assume we are dealing with a situation in which employment (and output) expands.

If OZ has, in reality, the shape shown in Figure 17–4, the relative position of the rentier or fixed income group must worsen, because its absolute money income does not change. Therefore its relative position would worsen even if prices remained constant. Prices are not constant when the aggregate supply function assumes the shape of the schedule shown in Figure 17–4. The necessary condition for an improvement in the relative income position of the rentier group is a fall in the general price level as output and employment expand, but this possibility is ruled out by the assumption of a constant money wage and decreasing returns.

Figure 17–4 also depicts a situation in which the share of wages in the output total, wN/Z, will decline as the output level advances. Actually, the behavior of the wage share as the output and employment level changes depends upon the value assumed for the coefficient E_z. If $E > 1$ this means increasing returns or a rising marginal product. Under such circumstances the wage share in the income total would rise, because a rising marginal product when combined with a constant money wage implies a falling price level, and the gap between the OW curve and the OZ curve would narrow. Such would be the graphical representation of an increase in the relative share of wages in the income total. On the other hand, the assumption that $E_z < 1$ implies decreasing returns or a declining marginal product for labor. The consequence would be a decline in the relative share of labor in the income total because the gap between the OW and the OZ curves becomes larger and larger. This is the kind of situation depicted in Figure 17–4. If we assume diminishing returns to labor, an assumption that is not wholly unrealistic in the short run, the tendency will be for the relative share of wages in the income total to decline with advancing employment and output. This is the basic conclusion reached by Weintraub and rests essentially on the application of the principle of diminishing returns or productivity to the problem of relative shares.

Since profit is a residual, its relative share in the income total is determined primarily by what happens to the other two income categories. The general presumption, though, is that the residual share will increase relatively as employment and output expand. This is true irrespective of the behavior of the wage share because the entrepreneurial groups or profit recipients are the chief beneficiaries of the relative decline in the income position of the rentier class as output expands.[39] If the wage share also declines because of diminishing returns, the gain in the relative importance of the residual share will be all the greater.

In essence, Weintraub's theory of relative shares presumes that, in the short run and under the usual conditions of static analysis, a rise in the income and employment level will bring about a redistribution of income which tends to favor the recipients of income in the form of profits at the definite expense of persons or groups whose incomes are fixed in money terms, and at the probable expense of wage earners—as long as the principle of diminishing returns is assumed operative and money wage rates remain constant. In *An Approach to the Theory of Income Distribution*, Weintraub expands this basic framework to take into account the effect of other influences upon the division of the economy's output into relative income shares. For example, he argues that the general effect of monopoly is to lower the relative share of wages in the income total, while an increase in money wages may or may not favorably affect the wage share. Changes in the physical stock of capital *may* have a favorable impact on the wage share if such changes increase the marginal productivity of labor, although a definite conclusion to this effect is not always warranted. With respect to labor's productivity, Weintraub demonstrates that a change in the relative share of labor is dependent not upon changes in marginal productivity alone but upon the ratio of the marginal to the average product of labor. Therefore, an increase in the marginal product of labor will not

---

[39] Weintraub, *op. cit.*, p. 47.

lead to an increase in the relative share of wages if the average product of labor rises in the same proportion.[40] Changes in the capital stock as well as technological improvements may have this effect.

INCOME DISTRIBUTION AND THE AGGREGATE DEMAND FUNCTION

Weintraub's analysis does not end with his theory of relative shares. He has constructed an aggregate demand function, D, which links the spending decisions of the economic system to the distribution of income. In this way he attempts to show not only how the income and employment level will affect the functional distribution of income but, further, how the income level itself is related to income distribution through the impact of distribution on the position of the aggregate demand function. As is the case with his aggregate supply function, the aggregate demand schedule worked out by Weintraub is in current rather than constant prices.

For the purposes of simplicity we shall limit our examination of Weintraub's aggregate demand analysis to two categories of expenditure: consumption and investment. We shall assume that investment expenditures are a constant (in real terms), that is, they are autonomous with respect to the income level. Since our analysis is cast in terms of current prices, the current money value of investment outlays will increase as the price level rises.

The crucial consideration, then, in Weintraub's concept of aggregate demand is the level of consumption spending. Weintraub postulates an essentially Keynesian consumption function, except that he introduces asset holdings in addition to current disposable income into his analysis as a factor determining current outlays for consumption purposes. In equation form,

$$C = cY_d + \lambda A \qquad (17\text{--}16)$$

In this equation, c represents the average propensity to consume; λ represents the possible dissavings out of asset holdings, A.

For our purposes the most significant variable in Equation (17–16) is disposable income, Y_d, as this provides the necessary link to the distribution of income. Y_d may be defined in equation form as follows:

$$Y_d = wN + F + kR \qquad (17\text{--}17)$$

All the variables in this equation have the same meaning as heretofore, except that a new variable, k, is introduced. Weintraub defines this as the fraction of profits, R, that is actually distributed to individuals. (The reader should be careful not to confuse Weintraub's k with the k of the multiplier theory.)

[40] *Ibid.*, p. 51.

Since the consumption function for the economy as a whole is constructed from the consumption spending patterns characteristic of the three major classes of income recipients (rentiers, wage earners, and profit recipients), we must examine the probable behavior of each of these classes as the level of employment and income rises. In our discussion of the aggregate supply function we saw that the relative income position of the rentier groups would worsen with a rise in the income level. Under such circumstances their current expenditures for consumption purposes would have to increase if such groups attempted to maintain intact their real consumption position. This follows from the assumption built into the aggregate supply function that the general price level will rise as employment and output expand. Thus, the consumption expenditures curve for these groups will slope upward toward an absolute maximum represented by the total of their fixed money receipts. The average propensity to consume will steadily increase, finally reaching 100 per cent at that point at which the general price level has risen sufficiently to require the rentier groups to spend the whole of their current money income in order to maintain real consumption unchanged.

The money incomes of wage earners are represented by the OW curve in Figure 17–4. This assumes that money wages are a constant. The consumption expenditure pattern of wage earners will move along a curve that is roughly similar to the curve depicting the total wage bill, OW, although the slope of the wage earners' expenditure curve is likely to be less than that of the wage-bill curve, if it is assumed that wage earners save greater absolute amounts as their money income grows. The rise in the price level may prevent wage earners from enlarging the proportion of real income saved as the income level rises, but it does not preclude them from increasing money expenditures at a rate sufficient to maintain real consumption. There will be a limit, though, to the extent to which this can be done without ultimately bringing about a decline in the proportion of real income saved if, as was assumed earlier, the relative share of wages in the income total declines with advances in income and employment. In any event, the consumption function of the wage-earner class will most likely slope upward to the right at a rate that is slightly lower than that of the schedule representing the total wage bill.

Consumption expenditures for profit recipients depend, first of all, on the proportion of total profit that is distributed to shareholders in the form of dividends. If this is presumed to be a constant after the economy has reached that level of employment and output at which profits are positive (the employment level ON_1 in Figure 17–4), the consumption pattern of the entrepreneur class is determined largely by what happens to profits with further increases in the income level. In view of our earlier assumptions about constant money wages and fixed money incomes for the rentier class, profit income will rise at a rate in excess of the rise in the price level. If this happens, Weintraub contends that the entrepreneurial class can readily sustain its real consumption position by increasing consumption outlays out of distributed profits at about the same pace at which the general price level is increasing. Thus, he concludes that the consumption expenditure by this group is likely to move upward along a path that is roughly parallel to OZ in Figure 17–4.

When we combine the consumption behavior patterns for the three major groups of income recipients into a single consumption function for the whole economy, the result is a schedule which slopes upward to the right, but at a slower rate than the aggregate supply function. This is explained primarily by the inability of the rentier group to sustain their real consumption position in the face of rising prices and the personal saving of both the entrepreneurial and the wage-earner groups. Even if wage earners succeed in preventing a decline in the proportion of their real income saved as income rises, the rate of increase in consumption outlays will still be less than the rate reflected in the aggregate supply function. Consequently, the over-all slope of the consumption function will be less than that of the aggregate supply schedule.

The construction of the aggregate demand schedule is completed by adding an amount equal to autonomous investment expenditure to the consumption function. That has been done in the D schedule of Figure 17–5. If real investment is assumed to be a constant, then current monetary

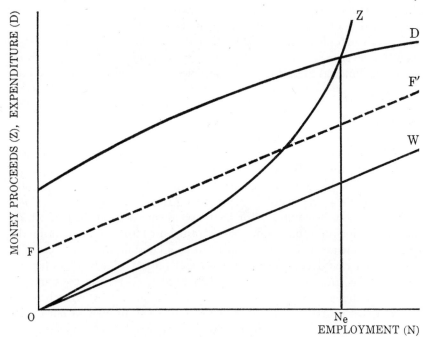

Figure 17–5. Weintraub's Aggregate Demand and Aggregate Supply

outlays for investment will rise along with the rise in income and the general price level. The addition of investment expenditure to the consumption function provides us with the aggregate demand which embodies the same price phenomena that are built into Weintraub's aggregate supply function. The equilibrium level of employment and income is determined by the intersection of the D and OZ schedules. It is at this point and only at this point that there is an employment (and income) volume at which the expected sales proceeds will be exactly equal to expenditures forthcoming from the consuming and investing groups.[41]

A Concluding Note on Distribution Theory

In this chapter we have sought to survey and analyze some of the major contributions that have been made toward the development of an aggregate theory of income distribution. Our discussion has ranged over more than one hundred years of economic thought, for the problem of the functional distribution of the national income is one that has excited the interest and attention of classical as well as modern economic theorists. We conclude as we began by observing that there is no general agreement among economists, classical or modern, on the nature and significance of the forces that determine the distribution of the national output into relative shares. Ricardo and Marx, both members of the classical "school," reached diametrically opposite conclusions about the impact of a change in output on the distribution of income. Modern theorists have not succeeded in developing a wholly accepted body of theory in this area. But there is one element common to all their endeavors. The modern effort to develop an aggregate theory of income distribution takes as its point of departure the now generally accepted theoretical framework that we define as modern income and employment analysis. It is reasonably safe to predict that whenever an adequate theory of the functional distribution of the national income is developed, it will be done within this framework. At the present, though, such a theory is still in an emerging state, and the ideas, concepts, and theoretical schema that we have surveyed in the chapter must be regarded as pioneering efforts directed toward this still unrealized goal.

APPENDIX

Algebraic Derivation of Equation (17–6)

(1) $I = S =$ the basic equilibrium condition
(2) $I = \pi(P)$ [Equation (17–2).]
(3) $P = (1 - \lambda) Y$ [Equation (17–4).]

[41] *Ibid.*, p. 44.

(4) $I = \pi(1 - \lambda) Y$ [Equation (17–5). This is derived from the two preceding definitional equations.]

(5) $a \times \lambda Y =$ saving by wage earners [a is the propensity (marginal and average) to save out of wage income. It is a constant, $0 < a < 1$.]

(6) Non-wage saving is derived as follows:

    (a) $bvP + (1 - v) P$ [bvP is saving out of distributed profit; and $(1 - v) P$ is nondistributed profit. The latter is by definition saving; b is the propensity (marginal and average) to save out of shareholder's income. It is a constant, $0 < b < 1$.]

    (b) $P = (1 - \lambda) Y$ [From Equation (3) above.]

    (c) Therefore, non-wage saving equals:

        (1) $bv (1 - \lambda) Y + (1 - v) (1 - \lambda) Y$

        (2) $(1 - \lambda) Y \times [bv + (1 - v)]$ [This is derived by substitution of $(1 - \lambda) Y$ for P in Equation (6a) above.]

(7) Total saving is therefore equal to:

    (a) $S = (a \times \lambda Y) + [Y (1 - \lambda) (bv + (1 - v)]$

    (b) $S = Y [a\lambda + (1 - \lambda) (vb + (1 - v)]$

(8) Since $I = S$ (in equilibrium) it follows:

    (a) $\pi (1 - \lambda) Y = Y [a\lambda + (1 - \lambda) (vb + 1 - v)]$

    (b) Divide both sides of the above by Y and we have Equation (17–6):

        $\pi (1 - \lambda) = a\lambda + (1 - \lambda) [vb + (1 - v)]$

Algebraic Derivation of Equation (17–12)

(1) $I = S =$ the basic equilibrium condition

(2) $Y = W + P$ [Equation (17–7).]

(3) $I = s_p P + s_w W$ [Saving equals the sum of saving out of profit income, $s_p P$, and saving out of wage income, $s_w W$.]

(4) $I = s_p P + s_w (Y - P)$ [This is from Equation (2) above. $W = (Y - P)$.]

(5) $I = s_p P + s_w Y - s_w P$ [From Equation (4) above.]

(6) $I = P (s_p - s_w) + s_w Y$ [From Equation (5) above.]

(7) $\dfrac{I}{Y} = (s_p - s_w) \dfrac{P}{Y} + s_w$ [Divide both sides of Equation (6) above by Y. This gives Equation (17–12).]

Index

Abstraction in economic analysis, 12–13
Acceleration principle (accelerator)
  criticisms of, 208–10
  fluctuation of output of capital goods
    and, 205
  formulation of, 203–5
  in Harrod's analysis, 208–10
  multiplier and, 207–8
Administered prices, 374
Aggregate demand, *see* Demand
Aggregate supply, *see* Supply
Agriculture in Ricardian analysis, 465–
  68
Allen, R. G. D., 141
Allocation of resources
  through mechanism of market, 243–44
  optimum allocation, 241–43
  through political process, 244–46
  structural inflation and, 387
  See also Social goods
Allocations, 59–63
Asset, defined, 178
Asset demand, *see* Money—demand for
Asset holdings
  consumer spending and, 161–64
  in Weintraub's analysis, 488
  See also Money
Assumptions
  in deductive method, 16–18
  economic analysis based on, 4
  realism in, 7–8

Bain, J. S., 374n
Balance of payments
  autonomous vs. induced charges in,
    283

capital account, 281–82
current account, 280–81
equilibrium in foreign balance, 282–83,
  290–91
function of, 50, 278–80
gold account, 281
income changes and, 298–301
"residents" in, 279n
See also Foreign trade
Bator, Francis M., on growth of government expenditures, 233
Bills, defined, 306
Black, Max, on scientific method, 19
Bonds
  defined, 306–7
  expectations and, 327–30
  government, 358
  in liquidity-preference theory, 325–30
  rate of interest and prices of, 320–21
Borrowing, *see* Consumer credit; Install-
  ment purchasing; Interest
Bottlenecks, 372
Boulding, Kenneth E., 463n, 464n
Bowen, Howard R., 229n
  on technological change, 217–18
Bronowski, Jacob, on classification in
  science, 5
Brozen, Yale, 216n
Brown, A. J., 181n
Buchanan, James M., 227n, 231n, 240n
Budgets, *see* Government—budgets of
Built-in stabilizers, 271–75
Burck, Gilbert, 457n
Burns, Arthur F., 450n
Business cycles
  acceleration principle and, 207–8

Business cycles (*cont.*)
  built-in stabilizers and, 271–75
  money, debts, and equities during, 334–37
  nonreversibility of price-output relationship in, 373–75
  See also Depressions; Inflation

Cambridge version of quantity theory, 310–13
Capacity, *see* Productive capacity
Capital
  capital consumption
    capital consumption allowances, 59–60
    in Marxian analysis, 472
  capital goods
    effectiveness of, 180–81
    output of, fluctuates violently, 206
    rate of return over cost of, 184
    as stream of expected income, 181–82
    symbol for, 82
    technological change and, 217–18
  capital-output ratio
    in Domar's analysis, 415–17
    in Harrod's analysis, 431
    Marx's "organic composition of capital," 474
    symbol for, 204
    see also Acceleration principle
  capital stock
    of current period, 205
    increase in (Harrod's analysis), 432–33
    symbol for, 82
  demand for, 187–88
    demand schedule, 189–98
    interest rate and, 188–89
    human, 35
    marginal efficiency of, 184–87
    based on expectations, 211
    investment demand schedule and, 197–98
    symbol for, 186
  productivity of capital coefficient, defined, 417
  supply price of, 182–83, 189
  symbol for, 187
  variable, 472
  See also Economic growth; Investment
Cartter, Allan, theory of income distribution of, 476–80
Cause, functional relationships and, 13–15
Ceteris paribus, defined, 15
Chandler, Lester V., 307n
Charges, *see* Gross national product
Clark, Colin
  on induction, 18–19
  on upper limit of taxation, 240

Clark, John Maurice, formulates acceleration principle, 203–4
Classes, economic, consumer spending and, 164–67
Classical economics
  diagrammatic summary of, 102–4
  major assumptions of, 86
  objectives of, 85–86
  policy implications of, 104–5
  price and distribution theory in, 108
  See also Employment—classical theory of; Keynes, John Maynard; Money
Clower, Robert W., 369n
Commerce, Department of, 69
  National Income Division, 27–28, 74
Committee of Economic Development, 356n
Compensation of employees, defined, 57–58
  See also Wages
Competition (pure competition)
  allocation of resources under, 243–46
  in classical economics, 104–5
  cost-push inflation impossible under pure competition, 386–87
  investment and, 218–20
  in Marxian analysis, 473
Conant, James B., 106
Construction, in Department of Commerce classification, 43–44
Consumer credit, 160
  consumption expenditures and, 169–70
Consumer expectations, 168–69
Consumption
  as component of aggregate demand, 121
  defined, 35–36
  as "cmulative," 166
  income and, 37–38, 122
    disposable income, 132–42
    income as prime determinant of consumption, 131–33
    in the long run, 170–75
    See also Consumption function; Income—level of
  induced consumption expenditure, *see* Multiplier
  influences (other than income) on
    consumer credit, 169–70
    distribution of income, 164–67
    liquid assets, 161–62, 164–67
    prices and shifts in expectations, 168–69
    rate of interest, 167–68
    standard of living, 163–64
    stocks of durable goods, 162–63
    thrift, 159–60
  nonconsumption, *see* Saving
  progressive taxes may reduce real consumption, 389

Consumption (*cont.*)
symbols for, 37, 45, 137
tax cuts and, 455–56
in traditional economic view of man, 3–4
See also Demand; Propensity to consume
Consumption function, 133–38
algebraic expression of, 137
distribution of income and, 164–67
empirical data and, 139–42
fall in prices and, *see* Pigou effect
not necessarily linear, 136n
parameters and, 159
saving function and, 138–39
secular, 171
Dusenberry's hypothesis, 171–74
Modigliani's hypothesis, 174–75
symbol for, 172
upward drift of, 142–43, 171
stability of, depends on normal conditions, 141
technical attributes of, 134–38
See also Income determination
Controlled experiments, 17–18
Corporate profits tax liability, 58
Cost-push hypothesis of inflation, 386–87, 390–92
Costs
factor, 57–60
financial, 183
marginal, 370–72
social, 67, 243
Council of Economic Advisors, 171n, 228, 330
fiscal policy and, 357, 445, 449–58
on taxation and investment, 222
on unemployment rate, 81

Davidson, Paul, 470n, 473n
Debt instruments, 306–7, 318
relationship between money, equities, and, 334–37
See also Bonds
Deductive method, 16–18
used by Keynes, 109
Defense expenditures, growth of, 238–39, 403–4
Demand
added capacity and, 419–20
for capital, *see* Capital—demand for
demand function
in determination of market price, 369–70
in equilibrium level of income, 122–30
for investment, *see* Investment—demand schedule
for labor, 87–91, 93–94

in modern theory, 119–22
for saving, 97–98
in Weintraub's analysis, 488–90
See also Income determination
elasticity of aggregate demand, 376–78, 380–82, 383
expectation of, *see* Expectations
income elasticity of, 369n
"law" of, as equation, 134
monetary and fiscal policy and, 354–58
for money, *see* Money—demand for
price level and
in cost-push inflation, 391–92
in demand-pull inflation, 390
in structural inflation, 392
See also Price—price level
supply and
demand created by supply, 95–97
See also Supply
wage cuts and, 393–98
See also Consumption; Foreign trade; Income; Multiplier
Demand-pull hypothesis of inflation, 385–86, 388–90
Democracy, social goods in, 244, 249
Depreciation
capital consumption allowances and, 59–60
investment funds and, 223
See also Investment—replacement
Depressions (recessions)
money, debts, and interest in recovery from, 335–36
"ratchet" effect in, 374n
redistribution of income in, 174–75
See also Business cycles; Great Depression
Dillard, Dudley, 334n
Diminishing returns
of agriculture, in Ricardian analysis, 466, 469
principle of, 89, 371–72
Discount formula for finding present value of future income, 185–87
Disinvestment
inventories and, 39–40
unintended (unplanned), 124–25
Displacement effect, 240
Disposable income, *see* Income—disposable
Dissaving, 40
Distribution theory, *see* Income distribution
Disutility, 4
Dividends, defined, 58
Domar, Evsey D.
on factors determining increase in capacity, 446–47
on investment and monopoly, 219

Domar, Evsey D. (*cont.*)
  theory of economic growth of, 411,
    414–28
    critique of, 427–28, 438–40
    his σ, 417, 421–22, 428
Downs, Anthony, on social goods, 248–49
Due, John F., 369n, 463n
Duesenberry, James S., 166n
  on secular consumption function, 171–
    74
Durable goods
  defined for national income account-
    ing, 37–38
  as influences on consumption, 162–63
Dynamic economy, defined, 82
  See also Economic growth

Economic analysis
  abstraction in, 12–13
  based on assumptions, 4
  branches of, 2
  economic policy and, 19–22
  functional relationships in, 13–15
  methods of, 15–19
  use of mathematics in, 15
  See also Classical economics
Economic costs vs. social costs, 67
Economic growth
  defined, 401–3
  fundamental factors in, 407–8
  government's role in
    fiscal policy, 442–46
    Kennedy-Johnson policies, 451–58
    measures affecting capacity, 446–48
  Harrod's rates of, 454
    actual rate, 432–33
    natural rate, 437–38
    warranted rate, 430–32, 442–44
    warranted and actual rates com-
      pared, 433–37
  historical statistics on (1839–1965),
    405–6
  Keynesian, 412–14
  maximum feasible rate of, 437
  measurement of, 402–3
  potential U.S., 450–54, 456
    concept of performance "gap," 450–
      51
    under present system, 406
  recent interest in problem of, 406–7
  required rate of (Domar), 421–22
  secular stagnation vs. secular exhilara-
    tion, 438, 439
  theories of, 408–10; *See also* Domar;
    Harrod
  unemployment and, 381
Economic policy
  economic analysis and, 19–22

fiscal policy, *see* Government—fiscal
  policy of
implications from classical theory, 104–
  5
monetary policy, *see* Government—
  monetary policy
principles of, 353–54
Economic production, defined, 56–57
Economic resources, *see* Allocation of
  resources
Economic stabilization, built-in, 271–74
Economic system, model of, *see* Equilibrium
Economic values vs. social values, 68–69
Economics
  defined, 1–4
  "positive," 20–21
  scientific character of, 11–15
  value judgments in, 20–22
  See also Economic analysis
Eilbott, Peter, 275n
Eisner, Robert, 218n
Elasticity
  of aggregate supply, 485–86
  coefficients of, 375
    aggregate demand, 376–78, 380–82
    interrelationships of, 382–84
    money wages, 379–82
    output, 378
    price, 376
    price level, 379
    returns, 378–79
  income elasticity, 369n
  symbols for, 196, 376, 378, 379, 380
  See also Interest-elasticity
Employment
  classical theory of
    arguments against, 105–9, 395–96
    basis of, 86–87
    demand for labor in, 87–91
    diagrammatic summary of, 102–4
    equilibrium level of employment in,
      93–95
    supply of labor in, 91–93
    wages in, 393–96
  elasticity of returns and, 378–79
  level of
    equilibrium, 93–95, 122–30; *See also*
      Income determination
    function of real wages and, 87–88
    wage cuts and, 393–98
    when *ex ante* and *ex post* values do
      not coincide, 128–30
  modern theory of, 110–30
  "overly-full" employment, 128
  See also Full employment; Labor; Un-
    employment
Employment Act of 1946, 28, 79–80, 353
Equations, identity vs. behavior, 45

Equilibrium
  of balance of payments, 282–83
  full-employment, 412–14
  general, 348–52
    algebraic presentation, 361–62
  in goods sphere, 345–48
  of income and employment, 122–30;
    See also Income—equilibrium
  in monetary sphere, 341–45
Equity instruments, 307, 318
  money, debts, and, 334–37
Ex ante and *ex post,* and identity of saving and investment, 145–46
Excise Tax Reduction Act of 1965, 455n, 457
Exhaustive expenditures, 228–29
Expectations
  consumer, 168–69
  investment and, 181–83, 211–15
  in liquidity-preference theory, 327–34
  utilization of capacity and, 110–11
Experimentation, *see* Science
Exports
  as counterpart of investment, 44
  defined, 43
  equilibrium income level and, 286–90
  export function, 284
  in foreign transactions account, 72, 74
  multiplier and, 290–93
  symbols for, 43, 45
  See also Balance of payments; Foreign trade

Fabricant, Solomon, 239n
Factor costs in measurement of GNP, 57–59
Federal Reserve System, 354, 458
  flow-of-funds accounting by, 50
  public debt management by, 358
Fellner, William, 427n
Final goods and services, 54–56
Finance
  functional, 355–56
  role of, 222–25
Financial costs, 183
Firms
  administered prices of, 374
  in classical theory, 89–90
  marginal and variable costs of, 371–73
  See also Capital
Fiscal policy, *see* Government—fiscal policy of
Fiscal stagnation, 451–54
Fisher, Irving, money illusion of, 91–92
Flow-of-funds accounting, 49–50
Forecasting and prediction distinguished, 9–10
Foreign trade
  foreign-repercussion effect, 295–98

multiplier and, 290–93
net foreign investment, 43–44
See also Balance of payments; Exports; Imports
Foreign transactions account, 72, 74
Free will, 11
Frictional unemployment, 80–81
Friedman, Milton
  on experience as evidence, 18
  modernized quantity theory of, 367
  "permanent-income" hypothesis of, 175
  on positive economics, 20–21
Full employment
  defined, 79–81, 452–53
  Depression destroys assumption of, 106
  in Domar's analysis, 419–22
  Employment Act of 1946 and, 28, 79–81
  investment required for, 454
  in Kaldor's analysis, 481–82
  Keynesian equilibrium and, 412–14
  not automatically income equilibrium level, 127
  "overly-full" employment, 128
  price-output relationship and, 372–75
  restrictive impact of budget on, 451–54
  symbol for, 373
Full employment surplus, 452–54
Functional relationships
  in economic analysis, 13–15
  symbol for, 13, 83
"Fundamental psychological law" (Keynes), 133, 136–37

Galbraith, J. K., 3n, 105
  on social imbalance, 247–49
Gee, Wilson, 18n
General model of economic system, *see* Equilibrium
Generalization
  in economics, 12–15
  in science in general, 6–7
GNP, *see* Gross national product
Goods and services
  intermediate
    defined, 54–56
    rising costs and, 372
  propensity of government to spend for, 443
  qualitative changes in, 68
  social, *see* Social goods
  See also Consumption
Goods sphere
  defined, 345
  equilibrium in, 345
Gordon, Kermit, 450n
Government
  budgets of, 356
    balanced budget thesis, 275–76

Government (*cont.*)
    full employment and, 451–57
    possible budgetary positions, 444–45
economic activities of, 227–31; *See also*
    Welfare
enterprises of
    "current surplus," 60
    in national income and social ac-
        counting, 72
expenditures of
    as basic component of national in-
        come, 41–43
    exhaustive, 228–29
    income level and, 251–55
    multiplier and, 256–59
    1929–1960, 234–36
    non-exhaustive, 229–30
    symbol for, 43, 45
fiscal policy of
    aggregate demand and, 355–358
    defined, 230
    economic growth and, 442–46
    general equilibrium model and, 358–
        61
    under Kennedy and Johnson, 357,
        451–58
    need for speed and flexibility, 458
    public debt management, 358
    See also Taxes
growth of economic influence of, 231–
    41
    causes, 238–41, 403–5
    criteria for measurement, 231–32
    1929–1964, 28
    See also Economic growth
investment and, 220–22
monetary policy of
    aggregate demand and, 354–55
    defined, 231
    general equilibrium model and, 358–
        61
    liquidity trap and, 329
    money supply and, 308–9
output of, 41–42
subsidies by, 230
transfer expenditures of, *see* Transfer
    payments
See also Allocation of resources; Social
    goods
Government receipts and expenditures
    account, 71–74
Gower, Robert W., 463n
Great Depression
    collapse of classical theory in, 106
    interest rates in, 329n
    unemployment in, 81
Gross national product (GNP)
    aggregate supply schedule constructed
        from data of, 117

charges against, 57–60
defined, 53–54
final vs. intermediate goods and ser-
    vices in, 54–56
marginal propensity to consume out of,
    456
measurement of, 56–60
net national product and, 61
1839–1959, 405–6
1929–1965, 55, 63, 66
1960–1965, 406
1964 tax cut and, 456
potential, 450–54, 456
price level and (1947–1965), 363n, 364
relatively slow growth of, 406–7
Growth, *see* Economic growth

Hamburg, D., 180n
Hansen, Alvin H.
    on autonomous investment, 180
    on categories of money, 309
    on changing expectations, 335–37
    on fiscal policy, 357
    on investment demand schedule, 214
    on technological change, 217
    on transactions demand, 317
Harrod, Roy F.
    theory of economic growth of, 411,
        428–38
        critique of, 438–40
        full employment and, 454
Heller, Walter, 180n, 222, 223n, 357, 450n,
    457, 458
    on fiscal policy, 454
Hennipman, P., 220n
Hicks, J. R., 340n
Higgins, Benjamin, 427n
Hoover, Edgar M., 223n
Human capital, 35
Human nature
    in classical economics, 3–4, 86
    thrift and, 159–60

Imports
    equilibrium income level and, 286–90
    exports and, 43–44
    in foreign transactions account, 72, 74
    import function, 285–86
    multiplier and, 290–93
    propensity to import, 285–86
    symbol for, 45, 285
    See also Balance of payments; Foreign
        trade
Imputations, 57
Income
    consumption and, *see* Consumption—
        income and

Income (*cont.*)
  disposable
    consumption function and, 132–42
    defined, 62
    marginal propensity to consume out of, 274, 275–76, 278
    1929–1965, 63, 139–42
    symbols for, 132, 259–60, 488
    transfer expenditures and, 259–65
  distribution of, *see* Income distribution
  equilibrium, 122–30
    algebraic determination of, 177, 226, 278
    in Cartter's analysis, 478–80
    changes in, 350
    Keynesian full-employment equilibrium, 412–14
    marginal propensity to invest and, 200–2
    savings and taxes in, 254–56
    See also Income determination
  as flow phenomenon, 29
  future, discount formula for, 185–87
  investment and, *see* Investment—income and
  labor vs. non-labor (property), 462
    historical trend, 464
    See also Income distribution—theories of
  leakages from income stream, 158, 255, 259
  level of
    balance of payments and, 298–301
    changes in, 128–30; *See also* Multiplier
    government purchases and, 251–59
    rate of interest and, 341–45
    taxes and, 265–68
    transfer expenditures and, 259–65
  modern theory of
    central problems in, 110–11
    summary, 130
    See also Employment—modern theory of; Income determination
  non-wage recipients and wage cuts, 396, 398
  personal
    defined, 61–62, 462
    1929–1965, 63
    "permanent" vs. "transitory" components of, 175
    personal income and outlay account, 70–72
  proprietors', defined, 58
  redistribution of
    in downward phase of cycle, 174–75
    as policy to raise consumption function, 166–67
    through transfer payments, 229–30

  See also Income distribution
  saving and, *see* Income—saving and
  wealth and, 32–33, 35–37
  See also National income
Income and product
  aggregate measures of, 53
    limitations of, 66–69
  surplus or deficit on income and product determination, 73
Income determination
  in Harrod's analysis, 433–37
  process of, 143–45
    with government expenditures, 252–55
    in open economy, 286–90
  See also Income—level of
Income distribution
  consumer spending and, 164–67
  labor vs. non-labor (property), 462
    historical trend, 464
  theories of
    Cartter's, 476–80
    Kaldor's, 480–83
    Marxian, 470–75
    Ricardian, 465–70, 474–75
    Weintraub's, 483–90
  See also Income—redistribution of
Income tax, reductions in, 454–56
Inductive method, 18–19
Inflation
  "administrative," 386n
  cost-push hypothesis, 386–87, 390–92
  demand-pull hypothesis, 385–86, 388–90
  high taxation and, 240
  "income share," 386n
  "market power," 386n
  1966, 457–58
  structural hypothesis, 387, 392–93
  types of
    "creeping," 384
    hyper-inflation," 385
    "suppressed," 384–85
    "true," 368, 384
  See also Price—price level
Innovation, 216–17
Input-output tables, function of, 50
Installment purchasing, 160; *See also* Consumer credit
Interest
  classical theory of, 97–100
    Keynes' criticism of, 108
  liquidity-preference theory of, 304n
    basic mechanism of, 322–25
    bond market in, 325–30
    changes in rate of interest, 330–34
    critique of, 334
    liquidity trap, 329
    terminology, 319

Interest (*cont.*)
  Tobin's formulation, 329–30
  loanable-funds theory of, 304*n*, 337–39
  net, 59
  on public debt, 230
  rate of
    bond prices and, 320–21
    changes in, 330–32
    changes in equilibrium values of, 350
    in decisions to invest, 182–87
    demand for capital and, 188–89
    as determinant of consumption and
      saving, 167–68
    elasticity of aggregate demand and,
      376–78
    income level and, 341–45
    monetary and goods spheres linked
      together by, 348–50
    no "one" rate, 304*n*
    symbol for, 186
    total demand for money and, 332–34
  See also Investment
Interest-elasticity in classical theory, 99–
  100
Intermediate products, 54–56
Inventories, investment and disinvest-
    ment in, 38–40
  unintended (unplanned), 124–25
Investment
  autonomous
    defined, 180
    symbol for, 202
  capacity-creating effects of, *see* Pro-
      ductive capacity
  in Cartter's analysis, 478–80
  decisions to invest, 181–83
    "residual-funds" theory, 225
    See also Capital—marginal efficiency
      of; Finance
  demand schedule, 189–94
    elasticity of, 195–97
    ephemeral character, 194–95
    in general model of economic sys-
      tem, 346–50
    induced investment in, 201
    instability of, 214
    Keynesian formulation, 192, 197
    marginal efficiency of capital, 197–
      98
  disinvestment
    inventories and, 39–40
    unintended (unplanned), 124–25
  economic growth and, *see* Economic
    growth
  expectations and, *see* Expectations
  exports as counterpart of, 44
  foreign
    symbol for, 43
    See also Foreign trade

full employment and, 454
government and, 220–22
gross saving and investment account,
  72, 75
gross vs. net, 40, 179
income and, 198–210
  in general model of economic sys-
    tem, 345–50
  investment as basic component of
    national income, 38–40
  in Kaldor's theory, 480–83
  marginal propensity to invest, 199–203
  in process of income determination,
    143–45
induced
  aggregate demand and, 201–2
  in algebraic determination of equi-
    librium, 226
  defined, 180
  as function of rate of change of out-
    put, 203–5
  in Harrod's analysis, 439
  multiplier and, 202–3
  symbol for, 199, 202
  See also Acceleration principle
innovation and, 216–17
interest-elasticity of, 195–96
investment-profit coefficient, 476
marginal propensity to invest, 199–203,
  275–76
replacement
  acceleration effect and, 205–7
  defined, 40, 179
  in Ricardian analysis, 467
  as saving, 37, 145–49
  significant role of, 178–79
  symbols for, 38, 45, 192, 199
  taxes and, 221–22
    1964 tax cuts, 222, 454–57
  technological change and, 215–18
  unintended (unplanned), 124–25, 147*n*
  wage cuts and, 397
  See also Capital; Interest; Multiplier;
    Profit
"Invisible hand," 86

Johnson, D. Gale, on functional distribu-
    tion of income, 464
Johnson, Lyndon B., 454, 458
Joint Economic Committee, 406

Kaldor, Nicholas, 466*n*, 467, 473*n*
  theory of income distribution of, 480–
    83
Katona, George, 161*n*, 169*n*
Keezer, Dexter M., on stability in invest-
    ment, 214
Keirstead, B. S., on expectations, 211

Kennedy, John F., 222
on economic policy, 1
economic policy under, 448–55
Keynes, John Maynard
aggregate supply function in, 112–14
on classical economics
economic theory, 87, 91, 95, 106–9, 127
General Theory refutes classical economics, 87, 106
his use of term, 85
interest theory, 99, 108
summary of his criticism, 106–9
on consumption, 133–37, 141
consumer expectations, 169
determination of income and employment in, 122
full-employment equilibrium in, 412–14
General Theory, central theme of, 111
on income distribution, 464
on investment
critique of his theory, 198–99, 334
on expectations, 211, 212–13
investment decisions, 181, 182
investment demand schedule, 192, 197
marginal efficiency of capital, 184–87
monetary theory of, 303–4, 313–15, 367–68; *See also* Interest—liquidity-preference theory of
on price level, 363, 365, 372, 375
"true inflation," 368, 384
on thrift, 160
uses deductive analysis, 109
on wage cuts, 397, 398
See also Multiplier
Keynes, John Neville, on positive science, 20
Keynes effect, 352n
Kindleberger, Charles P., 215n, 280n, 299n
on equilibrium of foreign balance, 282
King, W. I., 27
Klein, Lawrence, 162, 167n
Knowles, James W., 451n
Knox, A. D., 210n
Korean War, *see* Postwar period
Kravis, Irving B., on income distribution, 464
Kuh, Edwin, 209n, 219n
Kurihara, Kenneth K., 210n
Kuznets, Simon, 171n, 426n
on Soviet Union, 407

Labor
cost of, in economics of firm, 372
demand for, in classical theory, 87–91, 93–94
in Domar's analysis, 428
exploitation of (Marx), 471–72

income of, vs. property income, 462, 464
productivity of
average, 417
symbol for, 83
supply of
in classical theory, 91–93, 107
symbol for, 91
See also Employment
Labor force, symbol for, 83
See also Unemployment
Labor theory of value, 470–71, 472n
Laissez faire, 104–5
Leakages from income stream, 158, 255, 259
in open system, 293
Leisure, 67
Lerner, Abba P., 242n, 355n
Lewis, John P., on consumption and standard of living, 163–64
Levy, Michael, 451n
Liquidity, 161–62
defined, 305
See also Money
Liquidity-preference theory, *see* Interest—liquidity-preference theory of
Liquidity trap, defined, 329
LM schedule, 343–45
in general equilibrium, 348–52
Lubell, Harold, 165n

Macroeconomics, defined, 2
Malthus, Thomas, 466
Marginal capital-output ratio, 415–16
Marginal costs, 370–72
Marginal efficiency of capital, *see* Capital—marginal efficiency of
Marginal propensity to consume, *see* Propensity to consume—marginal
Marginal propensity to import, 285–86
Marginal propensity to invest, *see* Propensity to invest
Marginal propensity to spend, 201–2
Marginal propensity to tax, 270–71, 275–76
Marginal social benefit, 243
Market
allocation of resources through, 243–44
determination of market price, 369–70
expectations in a market economy, 213–14
investment and structure of, 218–21
for money, 341
See also Business cycles; Competition; Say's Laws of Markets
Market structures, defined, 218
Marshall, Alfred, 85
Cambridge version of quantity theory, 310–13

Marshall, Alfred (*cont.*)
  on *ceteris paribus*, 15
  on saving, 97
Marx, Karl, 85*n*
  theory of income distribution of, 470–75
Massell, Benton F., on technological change, 218
Mathematics in economic analysis, 15
Meiselman, D., 367*n*
Meyer, John R., 209*n*, 219*n*, 225*n*
Microeconomics, defined, 2
Military expenditures, growth of, 238–39, 403–4
Mill, John Stuart, 85
  on deductive method, 16, 17
  on deficiency of demand, 96–97
Modigliani, Franco, on secular consumption function, 174–75
Monetary policy, *see* Government—monetary policy of
Money
  demand for
    asset demand, 318–20, 325–30
    in general equilibrium, 348–50
    in monetary equilibrium, 341–45
    rate of interest and, 332–34
    symbols for, 311, 316, 319, 321
    total demand, 321–22
    transactions demand, 315–18
  deposit vs. reserve, 308–9
  functions of, 305–6
  as measuring device
    of GNP, 56–57
    of income and output, 30–31
  monetary equilibrium
    defined, 309
    in general model of economic system, 341–45
  monetary sphere, 341–43
  money illusion, 91–92
  more than medium of exchange, 303
  motives for holding, 313–15, 330
  quantity theory of, 100–2, 309–13
    Cambridge version, 310–13
    coefficient in, 310
    elasticity and, 376, 383–84
    modern, 367–68
    price level and, 366–67
  relationships between debts, equities, and, 334–37
  supply of, defined, 307
  See also Interest; Wages
Monopoly, investment and, 219–20
  See also Interest; Wages
Multiplier, 149–59
  acceleration principle and, 207–8
  algebraic proofs of, 176
  algebraic statement of, 157–58
  balanced budget thesis and, 275–76

defined, 150
effective
  algebraic determination of equilibrium level using, 278
  defined, 203, 270
  foreign trade and, 290–93
  government expenditures and, 256–59
  induced investment expenditure and, 202–3
  not limited to investment expenditures, 151
  in open system, 293–95
  process described, 149–55
  summary remarks on, 158–59
  symbols for, 150, 202–3, 258, 270–71, 293
  taxes and, 269–71, 276–77
    in 1964 tax cut, 455–56
  transfer expenditures and, 263–65, 269–71, 276–77
Musgrave, Richard A., 245
  on government activities, 227–28, 353
Myrdal, Gunnar, 407
  on welfare state, 238

National balance sheet accounting, as expected development, 51
National Bureau of Economic Research, 27, 28, 74
National income
  basic components of, 37–44
    fundamental identities, 45–48
    See also Consumption; Foreign Trade; Government; Investment
  defined by Dept. of Commerce, 61
  as flow phenomenon, 29–32
  gross, 53
  not same as aggregate of personal incomes, 30
  symbol for, 45
  See also Income and product; National output; United States
National income and product accounting
  five-account system for, 69
  open-economy identity equations and, 51–52
  purpose and structure of, 28–29, 69–75
    foreign transactions account, 72, 74
    government receipts and expenditures account, 71–74
    gross savings and investment account, 72, 75
    national income and product account, 70
    personal income and outlay account, 70–71
National income and social accounting
  nature of, 26–28

National income and social accounting (*cont.*)
types of statistical data in, 49–51
use of, 28–29
National Income Division, Dept. of Commerce, 27–28, 74
National output
circular flow of, 31–32
distribution of, 69; *See also* Income distribution
measured by money value, 30–31
potential, 450
qualitative changes in, 68
statistics on growth of, *see* United States
symbol for, 45
See also Gross national product; National income
Natural resources, symbol for, 82
Net foreign investment, 43–44
Net national product
defined, 61
disposable income and, 143n, 199n
marginal propensity to consume out of, 270–71
symbol for, 143n, 150, 155, 157, 258–59, 283
Nonconsumption, 37; *See also* Saving
Nourse, Edwin G., 353
on economic policy, 20

Oligopoly, administered prices in, 374
See also Monopoly
Open economy
current data and identity equations in, 51–52
defined, 283
income equilibrium in, 286–90
algebraic determination of, 301–2
See also Foreign trade
Organization for European Economic Cooperation (OEEC), 73
Output
determined by labor input, 83–84
elasticity of, 378, 383
in Marxian analysis, 472
in Ricardian analysis, 466
wealth and, 36
See also Capital—capital-output ratio; Income; National output; Price; Production—production function
Overproduction, impossible in classical theory, 96–97

Parameters
defined, 159n
"shift," 83, 210
Peacock, Alan T., on growth of government, 240
"Permanent-income" hypothesis, 175

Personal income, *see* Income
Personal income and outlay account, 70–71
Phillips, A. W., 380
Phillips curve, 380–82
Pigou, A. C., 85, 162
Pigou effect, 162, 353n
in reverse, 389
Pilvin, Harold, 416n
"Pleasure-pain" calculus, 86
Policy, *see* Economic policy; Government—fiscal policy; Government—monetary policy
Population
economic growth and, 405–6
government expenditures and, 236
Malthusian "law" of, 466
Postwar period (1945–1965)
built-in stabilizers during, 274
consumer credit in, 169–70
consumer expectations in, 168–69
consumption function in, 141
disposable income in, 139–41
GNP in, 363n, 364, 406, 450, 456
government expenditures in, 232–38
growth rate in, 450
prices and inflation in, 373, 384, 457
social imbalance in, 247
standard of living in, 163–64
taxes during, 221–22, 451–52, 454–57
unemployment in, 81, 450, 456, 457
Potential social average productivity of investment (σ), 417, 421–22, 428
Prediction and forecasting distinguished, 9–10
President's Council of Economic Advisors, *see* Council of Economic Advisors
Price
administered prices, 374
cost-determined prices, 388
elasticity of, 376, 383
market determined by supply and demand, 369–70
price indexes
in compiling GNP, 64–66
in postwar period, 373, 457
price level
consumer expectations and, 168–69
elasticity of, 379, 383
employment level and, 393–98
historical, 405–6
Pigou effect, 162, 353n, 389
quantity theory of money and, 100–2, 366–67
real GNP and, 363n, 364
stability (1960–1965), 457
symbols for, 89, 100
unemployment rate and, 382

Price (cont.)
    variable and marginal costs and, 371–72
    See also Inflation
    price-output relationship, 368–69
        nonreversibility of, 372–75
    supply price
        of capital goods, 182–83, 187
        defined, 112
Producer's plant and equipment, 38–39
Product
    circular flow of income and, 31–32
    final vs. intermediate, 54–56
    See also Gross national product; Income and product; Net national product
Production
    defined, 34, 56–57
    income distribution and factors of, 463
    overproduction impossible in classical theory, 96–97
    production function
        in classical theory, 87
        equations for, 83–84
        technological change as shift in, 216
    productive potential of economy, 418, 450
Productive capacity
    acceleration principle and, 208–10
    determinants of, 82–84
        in increase of capacity, 446–47
    expectation and, 110–11
    government influence on, 446–48
    investment and (Domar), 413–15, 418–19
    symbol for, 82
Productivity
    diminishing, 89
    of labor, see Labor—productivity of
    rate of increase of, and unemployment, 381
Productivity of capital coefficient, 417
Profit
    in Cartter's model, 477–80
    corporate, 58
    in Kaldor's theory, 480–83
    Marx's law of falling rate of, 474
    share of, see Income distribution
    symbols for, 476, 477, 480, 481, 488
    undistributed, 58
    See also Investment
Profit-maximization principle, 89–91
Propensity of government to spend for goods and services, 443
Propensity to consume
    average, 134–36
        price changes and consumer expectations, 168–69
        secular consumption function, 171–74

    Weintraub's symbol for, 488
    defined, 133
    empirical examination of (1929–1965), 139–42
    of high- and low-income groups, 165–66
    marginal, 136–38
        algebraic proof of, 176–77
        determines induced spending, 152–53
        in mathematical statement of multiplier, 157
        normal value of, 158–59
        out of disposable income, 274, 276–78, 278
        out of GNP, 456
Propensity of import, 285–86
Propensity to invest, marginal, 199–203, 275–76
    defined, 199
    equilibrium income and, 200–2
    out of retained corporate earnings, 274–75
Propensity to save, 138–39
    in Cartter's analysis, 478
    in Domar's analysis, 415, 421–22
    in Kaldor's analysis, 481–82
    marginal, multiplier equal to reciprocal of, 157
    symbols for, 188, 420, 430–31
Propensity to spend, marginal, 201–2
Propensity to tax, marginal, 270–71, 275–76
Proprietors' income, defined, 58
Public debt management, 358
Public sector, defined, 227
    See also Government
Purchasing power, sources of, 121
    See also Spending
Pure competition, see Competition

Quantity theory, see Money—quantity theory of

"Ratchet effect," 374n
Rate of return over cost, 184; See also Capital—marginal efficiency of
Recessions, see Depressions
Rejda, George E., 275n
Relative shares, see Income determination
Rent, in Ricardian analysis, 466, 469
Rental income of persons, 58
"Residual-funds" theory of investment, 225
Resource allocation, see Allocation of resources
Returns, elasticity of, 378–79, 383
Revenue Act of 1964, 455, 457

Ricardo, David, 85
 theory of income distribution of, 465–70, 474–75
Risk, defined, 212
Risk-lovers and risk-averters, 330
Robbins, Lionel, on assumptions, 16
Robinson, Joan, 437n
Robinson, Romney, 297n
Rostow, W. W., 407n
 on economic growth, 509

Samuelson, Paul A., on multiplier and acceleration, 207–8
Saving
 in Cartter's analysis, 477–80
 dissaving, 40
 full-employment, 454
 by government, 444–45
 gross saving and investment account, 72, 75
 imports as counterpart of, 44
 income and
  in general model of economic system, 345–53
  "institutionalization of saving," 160
  saving function, 138–39
  See also Income determination
 as investment, 37, 145–49
 liquid assets and, 161–62
 symbol for, 45
 transactions demand and, 316n
 unplanned, 147n
 See also Consumption; Interest; Investment; Propensity to save
Saving function, 138–39
Say's Law of Markets, 95–100
 Keynes' criticism of, 107–8, 127
Scatter diagram, 141
Schultz, Theodore W., 35
Schultze, Charles L., 375n, 389n, 391n
 structural hypothesis of, 387, 393
Schumpeter, Joseph A., on innovation, 215–16
Science
 economics as, 11–15
 experimentation in, 17–18
 methods of, 15–19
  deductive, see Deductive method
  inductive, 18–19
 nature of, 5–8
 "positive" vs. "normative," 20–21
 utility of, 8–11
 value judgments in, 20–23
Sector accounting, see National income and product accounting
Seligman, E. R. A., on science, 4–5
"Shift" parameter, 83, 210
Short run, defined, 84

Smith, Adam, 85n, 408
 "invisible hand" of, 86
Social costs, 67, 243
Social goods
 allocation of
  optimum, 241–43
  political process in, 244–46
  social imbalance in, 246–47
 characteristics of, 228–29
Solow, Robert M., 465
Soviet Union, economic growth of, 407
Spending
 induced, see Multiplier
 marginal propensity to spend, 201–2
 sources of, 119–22
 See also Consumption
Stabilizers, built-in, 271–75
Standard of living, consumption expenditures and, 163–64
"Stationary" state of economy, 466, 470
Strayer, Paul J., 169n
Structural change, see Economic growth
Structural hypothesis of inflation, 387, 392–93
Studenski, Paul, 27n
Subsidies less current surplus of government enterprises, 60
Subsidies to business, 230
Supply
 "creates own demand," 96–97
 elasticity of aggregate supply, 485–86
 supply function
  in equilibrium level, 122–30
  for labor, 91–104
  in modern theory, 112–19
  for saving, 98
  symbol for, 483–84
  in Weintraub's analysis, 490
 See also Demand
Supply price
 of capital goods, 182–83, 187
 defined, 115
Survey of Current Business, 28, 51
Survey Research Center, 169

Taxes
 as built-in stabilizers, 271–75
 corporate profits tax liability, 58
 income level and, 265–68
 indirect business, 59
 investment and, 221–22
  1964 tax cuts, 222, 454–57
 multiplier and, 269–71, 276–77, 455–56
 as "negative transfers," 43, 265
 net, defined, 267, 270
 possible upper limit of, 240
 progressive, may reduce real consumption, 389

Taxes (*cont.*)
  reduction in, and economic growth, 451–52, 454–57
  symbols for, 43, 45, 51, 267
  temporary adjustments in, 458
  as "voluntary" payments, 245
Technology
  level of
    constant, in Ricardian analysis, 470
    symbol for, 82
  in Marxian analysis, 473–74
  technological change
    capital-output ratio and, 416
    defined, 216
    investment and, 215–18
Theory, new needed to replace old, 106
  See also Generalization; Science
Thrift as influence on consumption, 159–60
Tobin, James, 398*n*, 450*n*
  on demand for money, 330
Transactions demand, *see* Money—demand for
Transfer payments (expenditures)
  as built-in stabilizers, 271, 274
  from business, 60
  to business, 230
  classification of, 230
  defined, 43, 229
  income level and, 259–65
  multiplier and, 263–65, 269–71, 276–77
  1929–1965, 233, 237
  symbols for, 43, 45, 51–52, 267
Treasury, public debt management by, 358

Uncertainty
  defined, 212
  in liquidity-preference theory, 323
  speculative motive and, 315
Underdeveloped nations, 407
  economic aid to, 404
Unemployment
  consumption and, 174
  in cost-push inflation, 390–91
  deficiency of demand and, 128
  frictional, 80–81
  in Great Depression, 81
  involuntary, 80, 95
  rate of
    money wages and, 381–82
    1955–1965, 450
    1964 tax cut and, 456, 457
    "reasonable," 81
  wages and, 374–75
    Phillips curve, 380–82

United States
  disposable income in (1929–1965), 69, 139–42
  economic growth rate of (1839–1965), 405–6
  functional distribution of income in (1850–1952), 464
  GNP in (1929–1965), 55, 63, 66
  government expenditures in (1929–1960), 232–38
  money wages in (1900–1960), 374–75
  national income and product accounts of (1965), 70–72
  national output of, historical growth, 26
  thrift in, 160
  See also Great Depression; Postwar period
USSR, economic growth of, 407
Utility, defined, 3–4

Value, labor theory of, 470–71, 472*n*
Value judgments in economics, 3, 20–22
Vandermeulen, Daniel C., on "productivity-increasing" expenditures, 447–48
Variables, functional relationship and, 13–15
Vietnam war, 454, 456, 458
Voluntary-exchange theory, 245
Von Mises, Ludwig, on assumptions, 16–18

Wages
  compensation of employees, defined, 57–58
  cost-determined, 388
  money wages
    aggregate demand and (Phillips curve), 380–82
    elasticity of, 379–82
    in Keynesian supply function, 112–14
    money illusion and, 91–92
    1900–1960, 375–76
    non-wage recipients and, 396, 398
    symbols for, 90–91, 376
  real wages
    in classical theory, 87–95, 107
    defined, 89
    symbol for, 87
  rigidities of, 374–75
  shares of, *see* Income determination
  "subsistence" level of
    in Marxian analysis, 471
    in Ricardian analysis, 466–68

Wages (cont.)
  wage cuts, 393–98
  See also Employment
Wagner's Law of the Increase in State
    Activities, 240–41
Wallich, Henry C., 355n
Wants, 2–4
Warranted rate of growth, 430–37, 442–
    44
Watson, Donald Stevenson, 354n
Wealth
  claims to, 33–34
  as human skills and knowledge, 35
  income and, 32–33, 35–37
  productive vs. nonproductive, 34

Weintraub, Sidney
  on employee compensation, 464
  theory of income distribution of, 483–
    90
Welfare
  criteria of measurement of, 402
  increasing acceptance of concept of,
    238
  as purpose of economic growth, 403
Whittaker, Edmund, 475n
Williams, John H., on economic theory,
    21
Wiseman, Jack, on growth of govern-
    ment, 240
Work as disutility, 3–4